BRAZIL

Equitable • Competitive • Sustainable

Contributions for Debate

160401

THE WORLD BANK
WASHINGTON, DC

The cover illustration is "Bichos" (1996) by Athos Bulcão, reproduced courtesy of the Athos Bulcão Foundation, Brasília, Brazil.

ISBN 0-8213-5547-3

Library of Congress Cataloging-in-Publication Data

Brazil : equitable, competitive, sustainable.
    p. cm.
  Includes bibliographical references.
  ISBN 0-8213-5547-3
    1. Brazil—Economic policy. 2. Brazil—Social policy.
  HC187.B8697 2003
  330.981—dc21

                                              2003053816

Contents

PART III
Chapter 8. Development and Conservation of Forests

Chapter 9. Rural Development and Natural Resources

Chapter 10. Municipal Urban Services, Housing, and Land Markets

Chapter 11. Water, Poverty Reduction, and Sustainable Development

PART IV
Chapter 12. Macroeconomic Stability

Preface

This volume presents a set of Policy Notes prepared by the World Bank's Brazil Team with partners during 2002 as a contribution for the debate of policies by the new federal and state governments elected in October 2002.

The objectives of making these Policy Notes available to a broader audience is two-fold. It could contribute to the discussion in Brazil and elsewhere about public policies to be formulated by the Brazilian governments for the period 2003–2006, and beyond. It could also serve as a vehicle to exchange lessons of experience from Brazil to the rest of the world and vice versa.

Since the Policy Notes were written for an incoming administration that would be well familiar with recent developments in Brazil, they do not attempt a comprehensive assessment of Brazil's impressive recent progress but rather focus on the challenges in areas where World Bank and related partner experience appears relevant.

The Policy Notes were prepared during 2002, a period during which economic uncertainties mounted ahead of the presidential elections of October 2002. They do not reflect information on the important policy discussions and developments after the elections.

These notes do not deal with all policy issues of relevance for Brazil. Even on those issues which are addressed, the assessment may be focused on specific aspects. The selection of topics and the emphasis in the Policy Notes are, thus, driven by policy priorities and their timeliness. The Policy Notes do not attempt to present a comprehensive policy agenda; rather, they are meant to constitute timely contributions for discussions.

The initial objective was to pull together findings of past World Bank Group studies, based on numerous other work by Brazilian and international authors, and experiences on Brazil, as well as relevant international experiences, and make them available to the new governments in a synthetic form.

The Policy Notes are motivated by a vision of an equitable, competitive, and sustainable Brazil. The work presented here is organized along five overarching themes: investing in people; improving productivity; managing natural resources; delivering government services to all; and stabilizing the economy. The main messages within each of these themes are captured in their respective thematic chapters, and summarized and woven together in an opening synthesis chapter. Part I brings contributions on education, health and social protection, discussing human and social capital challenges. Part II is focused on finance, infrastructure, private sector development, and innovation and technology issues, summing up the experience and views on physical capital and investment climate. Part III corresponds to natural capital and quality of life issues, bringing messages on forest use and conservation, rural development, natural resources, and urban and water services. Finally, Part IV addresses the prerequisite for the other themes, analyzing conditions for macroeconomic stability, fiscal sustainability, and good governance.

We believe Brazil's governments and its citizens share the vision of an equitable, competitive and sustainable Brazil. The World Bank continues to support Brazil in its effort to turn this vision into reality and is grateful for the privilege of being part of this quest.

David de Ferranti	Vinod Thomas	Joachim von Amsberg
Vice President	Country Director	Lead Economist
Latin America and the	Brazil	Poverty Reduction and
Caribbean Region		Economic Management

November 2002

Acknowledgments

The Policy Notes were prepared in a collaborative effort by the World Bank Brazil Team under the overall guidance of Vinod Thomas, Country Director. Joachim von Amsberg, Lead Economist, led this task with the assistance of Leila Ollaik.

The overview—a synthesis of the volume—was written primarily by Mark Roland Thomas; and the chapters' lead authors were Luiz Gabriel Azevedo, Jacques Cellier, Dean Cira, Luis Coirolo, Chris Diewald, Bill Dillinger, Jerry La Forgia, Jose Luis Guasch, Santiago Herrera, Robin Horn, Theresa Jones, Anjali Kumar, Yasuhiko Matsuda, Abel Mejia, and Bill Tyler. The main contributors of specific chapters were: Anabela Abreu, Alexandre Baltar, Fernando Blanco, Edward Bresnyan, Jayme Porto Carreiro, Martin Gambrill, Linn Hammergren, Jose Luis Irigoyen, Aymeric-Albin Meyer, Charles Mueller, Anna Roumani, Alvaro Soler, Rogerio Studart, Thelma Triche and Asta Zviniene.

Many people contributed to the production of this work with background papers, research, criticism, and peer review. Vicente Ferrer-Andreu presented the background paper on Capacity and Learning Enhancement and the Knowledge Economy. Clemente Luis Del Valle and Oliver Fratzscher presented the background paper on Domestic Debt Management. Useful comments were received from a large number of individuals at various stages of the process, specially from Eleoterio Codato, Angela Furtado, Daniel Gross, Chris Parel, Maria Madalena dos Santos, Mary Sheehan, Dorte Verner, and Zeze Weiss. There were many reviewers and contributors, we would like to thank them all specially Cecile Ramsay, Bernard Coutollenc, Vivien Foster, Maria Emilia Freire, Indermit Gill, Susan Goldmark, Lawrence Hannah, Uma Lele, Kathy Lindert, Antônio Rocha Magalhães, Sergio Margulis, Fernando Montes-Negret, Truman Packard, Jorge Rebelo, Mark Sundberg, and Augusto de la Torre. There were several enriching debates based on witty criticism, specially during a retreat held in Rio de Janeiro – RJ on March 18-19, 2002; and a workshop held in Washington, D.C., on July 1, 2002. We would like to thank all participants, including Wolfgang Bertelsmeier (IFC), Andreas Blom, Mauricio Carrizosa, Jose Augusto Carvalho, Patricio Duarte (IADB), Lauritz Holm-Nielsen, Suresh

Khosla, Josef Lloyd Leitmann, Graciela Lituma, Toshiya Masuoka (IFC), Bernard Pasquier (IFC), Ricardo Luis Santiago (IADB), Carlos Velez, Waldemar Wirsig (IADB), and Juan Yermo (OECD). The retreat and the workshop were facilitated by Maury Sterns and Jeannie Egan, and organized mainly by Patricia Bacelar, Daniela Campos, Julia Conter, Adriana Costa, Lygia Lobo, Cristina Perez, and Carolina Sanchez. Many people assisted in assembling and reviewing specific chapters, we would like to thank them all specially Andre Averbug, Mauro Azeredo, Ademildes Dantas, Fabiana Imperatriz, Adam Parsons, and Monica Singh.

The production team included Myrna Vallido, who dealt with the task budget; Meta de Coquereaumont and Bruce Ross-Larson from CDI, who edited the English version; Maria Helena Falcão, Lucinda Magalhães, and John Stephen Morris and his staff, who translated the original English version into Portuguese; Henry Curley who revised the English edition; Marcos Rebouças, Beatriz Machado, Eduardo Meneses, Fábio Brumana, Laura Tosta, Bruno Sattin and Tatiana Rodrigues from TDA Desenho & Arte, who created the graphic design and layout of the book; and Valéria Cabral and the Fundação Athos Bulcão who authorized the use of Athos Bulcão art on the cover of the book.

The general guidance provided by David de Ferranti (Vice-President for Latin America and the Caribbean Region), Guillermo Perry (Chief Economist), as well as Ana-Maria Arriagada, Danny Leipziger, Ernesto May, and John Redwood (Sector Directors) is much appreciated. Gobind T. Nankani provided valuable advice. Many of the studies from which this volume draws were prepared under his guidance as Country Director for Brazil until September 2001.

Most importantly, the text was built on, and would not have been possible without, the previous work and experience of many Brazilians and analysts of Brazil. The book has benefited from discussions with a large number of individuals in Brazil, including government officials, main economic advisors of the candidates who were running for office in 2002, researchers and analysts. All these discussions have been critical for the preparation of the Notes and are gratefully acknowledged.

Acronyms

ANA	Agência Nacional de Águas
ANAC	Agência Nacional de Aviação Civil
ADN	Agência para o Desenvolvimento do Nordeste
ANEEL	Agência Nacional de Energia Elétrica
ANATEL	Agência Nacional de Telecomunicações
ANP	Agência Nacional do Petróleo
ANT	Agência Nacional de Transportes
ANTAQ	Agência Nacional de Transportes Aquaviários
ANTT	Agência Nacional de Transportes Terrestres
ANVISA	Agência Nacional de Vigilância Sanitária
APEX	Agência de Promoção de Exportações
ARPA	Amazon Region Protected Areas Program
BCB	Banco Central do Brasil
BMF	Bolsa de Mercadorias e Futuros
BNB	Banco do Nordeste Brasileiro
BNDES	Banco Nacional de Desenvolvimento Econômico e Social
BNDESPar	BNDES Participações S.A
BOVESPA	Bolsa de Valores de São Paulo
CACEX	Carteira de Comércio Exterior
CADE	Conselho Administrativo de Defesa Econômico
CBLC	Companhia Brasileira de Liquidação e Custódia
CENATECS	Centros Nacionais de Tecnologia
CLT	Consolidação das Leis do Trabalho
CNPq	Conselho Nacional de Desenvolvimento Científico e Tecnológico
CODEVASFP	Companhia de Desenvolvimento dos vales do São Francisco e do Parnaíba
COFINS	Contribuição para o Financiamento da Seguridade Social
CONAMA	Conselho Nacional de Meio Ambiente
CONFAZ	Conselho de Política Fazendária
CONTAG	Confederação Nacional dos Trabalhadores na Agricultura
CPMF	Contribuição Provisória sobre Movimentação ou transmissão de valores e de créditos e direitos de natureza Financeira
CREMA	Contrato de Restauração e Manutenção
CRSFN	Conselho de Recursos do Sistema Financeiro Nacional

CSLL	Contribuição sobre o Lucro Líquido
CVM	Comissão de Valores Mobiliários
DNER	Departamento Nacional de Estradas de Rodagem
DNIT	Departamento Nacional de Infra-estrutura de Transportes
DRU	Desvinculação de Receitas da União
EMBRAPA	Empresa Brasileira de Pesquisa Agropecuária
EU	European Union
FAPESP	Fundação de Amparo à Pesquisa do Estado de São Paulo
FAT	Fundo de Amparo ao Trabalhador
FCVS	Fundo de Compensação de Variacões Salariais
FDA	Fundo de Desenvolvimento da Amazônia
FDI	Foreign Direct Investment
FDN	Fundo de Desenvolvimento do Nordeste
FEBEM	Fundação Estadual para o Bem-estar do Menor
FETAG	Federação dos Trabalhadores na Agricultura (Estaduais)
FGTS	Fundo de Garantia por Tempo de Serviço
FINAME	Financiamento, sem Limites de Valor para Aquisição Isolada de Máquinas e Equipamentos Novos de Fabricação Nacional
FINOR	Fundo de Investimentos do Nordeste
FLONA	Floresta Nacional
FNDCT	Fundo Nacional para o Desenvolvimento da Ciência e da Tecnologia
FNE	Fundo Constitucional de Financiamento do Nordeste
FNO	Fundo Constitucional do Norte
FPE	Fundo de Participação dos Estados
FPM	Fundo de Participação dos Municípios
FTAA	Free Trade Association for the Americas
FUMAC	Fundo Municipal de Apoio às Comunidades
FUNCAFÉ	Fundo de Defesa da Economia Cafeeira
FUNDEF	Fundo de Manutenção e Desenvolvimento do Ensino Fundamental e de Valorização do Magistério
FUNDESCOLA	Fundo de Fortalecimento da Escola
GDP	Gross Domestic Product
GEF	Global Environment Facility
IBAMA	Instituto Brasileiro do Meio Ambiente e dos Recursos Naturais Renováveis
ICMS	Imposto sobre Circulação de Mercadorias
INCRA	Instituto Nacional de Colonização e Reforma Agrária

INPI	Instituto Nacional de Propriedade Industrial
INSS	Instituto Nacional de Seguro Social
IPEA	Instituto de Pesquisa Econômica Apliacada
IPI	Imposto sobre Produtos Industrializados
IPTU	Imposto Predial Territorial Urbano
IRPF	Imposto de Renda de Pessoas Físicas
IRPJ	Imposto de Renda de Pessoas Jurídicas
ISS	Imposto sobre Serviços
ITR	Imposto sobre Território Rural
LAC	Latin America and the Caribbean
LOAS	Lei Orgânica da Assistência
LRF	Lei de Responsibilidade Fiscal
MERCOSUL	Southern Cone Common Market (Argentina, Brazil, Paraguay, and Uruguay, with Bolivia and Chile as associate members)
MPAS	Ministério da Previdência e Assistência Social
MP	Ministério de Planejamento, Orçamento e Gestão
OECD	Organization for Economic Cooperation and Development
ONS	Operador Nacional do Sistema
OTM	Operador de Transporte Multimodal
PADCT	Programa de Apoio ao Desenvolvimento Científico e Tecnológico
PETI	Programa de Erradicação do Trabalho Infantil
PIS/PASEP	Programa de Integração Social / Programa de Formação do Patrimônio do Servidor Público
PISA	Programa Internacional de Avaliação de Alunos
PMAT	Programa de Modernização das Administrações Tributárias Municipais
PNAD	Pesquisa Nacional por Amostra de Domicílios
PNFAM	Programa Nacional de Apoio à Administração para os Municípios
POEMA	"Programa Pobreza e Meio Ambiente na Amazônia" da Universidade do Pará
PPA	Plano Plurianual
PPG7	Programa Piloto para a Proteção das Florestas Tropicais do Brasil
PROAMBIENTE	Programa de Desenvolvimento Sócio-ambiental da Produção Familiar Rural da Amazônia
PRODEAGRO	Programa de Desenvolvimento Agro-ambiental do Mato Grosso
PRONAF	Programa Nacional de Fortalecimento da Agricultura Familiar
R&D	Research and Development
REFORSUS	Reforço à Reorganização do Sistema Único de Saúde

RGPS	Regime Geral da Previdência Social
RJU	Regime Jurídico Único
RPPN	Reserva Particular de Patrimônio Natural
RPPS	Regimes Próprios da Previdência Social
SAEB	Sistema Nacional de Avaliação da Educação Básica
SBPE	Sistema Brasileiro de Poupança e Empréstimo
SDE	Secretaria de Direito Econômico
SEAE	Secretaria Especial de Acompanhamento Econômico
SEBRAE	Serviço do Apoio às Micro e Pequenas Empresas
SEDU	Secretaria de Estado de Desenvolvimento Urbano
SELIC	Sistema Especial de Liquidação e de Custódia
SERASA	Centralização de Serviços dos Bancos S/A
SISCOMEX	Sistema Integrado de Comércio Exterior
SNV	Sistema Nacional de Viação
SRF	Secretaria da Receita Federal
STI	Secretaria de Tecnologia Industrial
STN	Secretaria do Tesouro Nacional
SUDAM	Superintendência de Desenvolvimento da Amazônia
SUDENE	Superintendência de Desenvolvimento do Nordeste
SUS	Sistema Único de Saúde
TJLP	Taxa de Juros de Longo Prazo
USPTO	United States Patent and Trademark Office
VAT	Value Added Tax
WIPO	World Intellectual Property Organization
WTO	World Trade Organization
ZEE	Zoneamento Econômico e Ecológico

Overview

Overview

A vision of Brazil's future – three goals

Brazil ranks among the largest countries in the world, in terms of its people, its landmass, and its economy. It is endowed with a highly entrepreneurial people, rich cultural heritage, precious natural resources, well-developed socio-political institutions and a sophisticated economy. Over the last decades, Brazil has made vast progress, in particular in its social indicators and its economic institutions. Based on these advances, Brazil seems poised for a decade of far-reaching improvements in people's welfare.

This overview synthesizes options and suggestions for Brazil's new administration to advance further toward realizing the country's potential and its vision of an equitable, sustainable and competitive country. It does not attempt a comprehensive assessment of Brazil's substantial development progress but rather focuses on key priorities and challenges.

Brazil's vision that drives these considerations for the new administration is a more equitable, sustainable and competitive country. These goals are based on the country's vast progress and promise. They suggest giving priority to a further big push on primary and in particular secondary education, on the system of social transfers to reduce inequality, and on higher productivity growth through fiscal balance, less red tape, and more foreign trade. These priorities imply choices: to empower people rather than an approach of government favors, to channel social spending to the poorest rather than the most vocal, to generate growth through private sector productivity rather than public sector spending, and to use natural resources in a sustainable way. All require government resolve, communication, and consultation.

This vision is the product not only of World Bank experience in Brazil and elsewhere, but also of close consultations within and outside Brazil: with Brazilian civil society and policymakers, international organizations such as the International Monetary Fund and the Inter-American Development Bank, and academic specialists and many others. The

---

A draft of this chapter was written by Mark Thomas in November 2002. The analyses and suggestions presented here are based on the 14 chapters presented in this book as a contribution to the debate and formulation of public policies.

vision emphasizes that Brazil has made striking progress, particularly in social sectors such as health and education, and uses this important progress as the basis for ambitious recommendations.

Ambition dictates urgency. Concern among the holders of Brazilian debt about macroeconomic policy after the election drove secondary-market spreads on this debt above 20 percent (over US Treasury bonds) and the exchange rate to levels of around 4 Reals to the dollar in September 2002. Careful economic management has been a hallmark of recent Brazilian policy. Restoring and maintaining confidence remains a top priority. Swift actions signal unwavering economic management.

Many of the actions required are structural and seemingly long term in nature—reforms in public spending, taxation, and social security—but their signaling value is immediate, and thus their urgency. Short-term credibility and longer term social goals are mutually dependent. While the focus of the proposals presented here is on medium-term structural reforms, many are integral to maintaining more immediate stability.

- In a more equitable Brazil, opportunities would be more equally spread, and therefore so would be wealth, health, and welfare. In spite of considerable efforts Brazil is one of today's more unequal societies: before transfers, the richest 1 percent of the population receives the same 10 percent share of total income as the poorest 50 percent. Poverty rates in the Northeast region are nearly twice the Brazilian average.
  - Social security reforms—eliminating subsidies to relatively better-income public sector retirees—and changes to the indirect tax system could cut this inequity significantly.
  - Equity is also undermined by high crime, which affects the poor more deeply. Restoring the credibility of the police and judiciary through institutional reforms could lead to lower crime rates.
  - Public services, public employment, infrastructure, and social assistance would be allocated transparently to serve their aim rather than granted as favors to people or special interests.
  - Finally, the long-term key to reducing inequity in Brazil is the secondary education system: a recent World Bank regional study estimated that Brazil's secondary enrollment in 1998 trailed the average for its income level by 36 percent.

- A SUSTAINABLE Brazil would build on the sustainable use of its tremendous wealth of natural resources, but combine these with higher levels of human capital, trade, and innovation to build a knowledge- and natural-resource-based economy. Higher growth would be sustained by productivity enhancements rather than costly resource depletion.

  - Scarce water in the Northeast could be managed sustainably at the level of the water basin.
  - High-productivity agriculture would coexist with the protection of precious ecological reserves in the Amazon, Caatinga, Cerrado and Mata Atlântica.
  - Sustainability of welfare, more broadly defined, implies balance in public finances and better quality of government spending, which would make room for investment and the maintenance of infrastructure.

- A COMPETITIVE Brazil would cut the government's financing costs by putting the public debt ratio on a downward path. A measurable objective, realistic even in the medium term, would be for Brazilian government bonds to achieve investment-grade rating on international markets.

  - Investor confidence—built by consistently meeting fiscal and inflation targets—would allow Brazil to reduce interest rates and multiply long-term private sector credit.
  - Actions to recognize and reduce public sector pension liabilities could shore up the credibility gained in other areas, such as the Fiscal Responsibility Law.
  - Fiscal and productivity-related reforms would help to reduce Brazil's external finance needs: export growth is likely to be more sustainable through productivity gains than through targeted assistance.

A diagnosis of the present – five ways forward

Central to the diagnosis is Brazil's level of education, which lags behind Latin America and the world. Recent progress on education has been remarkable, yet Brazil started out with a lot of catching up to do. Today, the low secondary enrollment level is Brazil's most obvious shortcoming by international comparison, damaging both equity and productivity. Policies need to focus not only on the secondary system, but also on the quality of primary education, since primary completion (or time to graduation) is part of the problem.

Brazilian private sector productivity picked up in the mid-1990s[1] but remains low for Brazil's income level. Yet Brazil spends more per capita on R&D and higher education than most Latin American countries. What explains this paradox? First, the public sector dominates R&D: research links between universities and the private sector are weak. Second, the private sector operates in a rather bureaucratic environment, which militates against newer, smaller firms and innovation. Third, Brazilian companies' exposure to frontier technology and management through trade (and export-oriented foreign investment) is relatively low. Fourth, higher education spending benefits a privileged few and could be rationalized to target the poor and upgrade research facilities. Addressing these factors can improve economic growth. Also, Brazil possesses extraordinary natural resources, which represent an opportunity for knowledge-based growth but also a responsibility for sustainable management.

---

[1] The Global Development Network's growth study for Brazil estimates annual growth of total factor productivity for 1994–2000 at about 2 percent, compared to about zero for 1980–1993.

The sector notes

A series of 15 Policy Notes (including this overview) aims to summarize the World Bank's and related international experience, as well as the understandings of the successes and challenges facing Brazil. By their nature, they focus more on challenges than successes. The notes do not constitute a policy program: there are many government decisions on which the Bank has insufficient experience to offer advice. And options are presented with the modesty that incomplete knowledge dictates. They are offered in the hope of supporting policymakers.

The Overview is based on the following 14 Sector Notes prepared by World Bank specialists with extensive experience in their respective areas:

(1) Education

(2) Health

(3) Social Protection

(4) The Financial Sector

(5) Infrastructure Provision and Regulation

(6) Private Sector Development

(7) Innovation and Knowledge

(8) Forest Development and Conservation

(9) Rural Development and Natural Resources

(10) Municipal and Urban Management and Housing

(11) Water Agenda

(12) Macroeconomic Stability

(13) Fiscal Sustainability

(14) Governance and the Public Sector.

None of these topics should be viewed in isolation, since the dynamics of each is a function of others. Water and sanitation is a primary determinant of health outcomes, for example, and innovation in the knowledge economy depends on secondary and higher education. All sectors exert demands on a tight budget. While many of these links are accentuated in the sector notes, the Overview aims to provide an integrated account suggesting synergies, tradeoffs, and priorities.

Brazilian social exclusion also curbs economic growth (the link between inequality and growth is clear in international data). Low growth puts pressure on public finances and makes redistribution harder, but Brazil has nonetheless developed excellent models of income transfer such as Bolsa Escola, the program to eradicate child labor (PETI), and the rural pension. These programs deserve integration and expansion. Poverty fell in Brazil in the mid-1990s (figure 1), but today about a third of the population still lives below the poverty line defined by the Institute for Applied Economic Research (IPEA). Yet Brazil is not a poor country: the poverty gap is equivalent to only 1.6 percent of national income.[2] Brazil spends more than 10 times this amount on various forms of social spending: this spending could clearly be better targeted.

With progress on education, faster productivity growth, improved natural resource management, and income redistribution, Brazil needs to address its twin vulnerabilities of high domestic and external debt in order to further avoid episodes of economic turbulence, and therefore low economic growth. Domestic debt imposes a large fiscal burden, making it hard to finance important public investments. External debt makes Brazil vulnerable to events outside its control and cycles of investor confidence, which manifest themselves in a vicious circle of exchange rate weakness and increasing debt burden.

Based on this diagnosis, the positive vision outlined here is organized around five principles, through which the goals of greater equity, sustainability and competitiveness may be reached:

- Investing in people
- Growing through productivity
- Stabilizing the economy
- Delivering government services to all
- Managing the natural inheritance.

---

[2] The poverty gap mentioned does not use the IPEA poverty line (which gives 33.9 percent of the population below the poverty line in 1999) but a lower food-based poverty line of R$ 65 in 1996 Reals (see World Bank report no. 20475-BR, "Attacking Brazil's Poverty"). The poverty gap using the IPEA poverty line would therefore be higher.

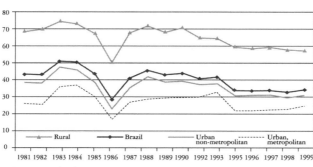

Figure 1. Poverty rate, 1981–99 (percent)

Source: IPEA based on PNAD / IBGE

Messages toward the vision of an Equitable, Sustainable, and Competitive Brazil

Rapid welfare improvements will require efficient public expenditure, while economic stability will be vital to underpin social progress. Investing in people, improving productivity, stabilizing the economy, expanding government services for all, and sustaining natural capital are the means to improve Brazilian living standards.

1. INVESTING IN PEOPLE entails expanding secondary education and improving quality at the primary level, focusing on under-achieving schools. Effective transfers such as Bolsa Escola deserve expansion, but Brazil's many transfers would benefit from integration across ministries and monitoring at the household level. To improve quality and equity in healthcare, capitation payments could adjust for social and epidemiological need. And more flexible public spending would improve the impact of social expenditure. In the absence of such reforms, social indicators may stagnate, since the money available is small in relation to the needs.

2. IMPROVING PRODUCTIVITY would raise growth and exports and reduce Brazil's dependence on external finance. Horizontal reforms can improve productivity: instituting a broad-based federal value-added tax and eliminating price-distorting payroll and sales taxes, cutting the bureaucratic red tape faced by firms, reducing the mandated costs in the formal labor market, increasing trade openness, and

deepening financial markets. Together with a focus on productivity and deep reforms to the investment climate, Brazil's disappointing recent growth rates can be reversed.

3.   Stabilizing the economy, pursuing an adequate primary surplus, would reduce the chance of economic shocks undermining debt sustainability. A strong primary surplus is necessary for cutting interest rates and would also reduce external vulnerability by raising national savings. A desirable way to raise the primary surplus and avoid damaging cuts to basic investments and services is deep structural reform of public spending, probably undertaken within the context of multi-year planning (PPA). Social development will be promoted if debt sustainability is emphatically ensured: control over public debt and avoiding high inflation would vastly help the foundations of growth and poverty reduction.

4.   Delivering government services to all—based on an accessible, efficient, and accountable public sector—will build social inclusion. More inclusive government would contribute to all three goals of a more equitable, sustainable, competitive Brazil. Empowering people to participate in public decisions results in decisions that better reflect their needs and builds consensus for policies. Brazil can further accelerate reforms relating to improved governance.

5.   Managing natural resources requires stronger institutions. Brazil could protect in some form a large share of the existing Amazon Forest, while still ensuring the living standards of the local population. The zoning of activities in the Cerrado and Caatinga is also needed, owing to intense environmental pressure from new agricultural land use. Speed is of the essence: many of Brazil's natural assets, including biodiversity, are being irreversibly eroded through lack of planning, oversight, and enforcement.

Investing in people

Low worker productivity and inequality both follow from Brazil's education system, which remains behind other countries' despite rapid advances (figures 2 and 3). Investing in people means improving the quality of education and the design and delivery of public services and transfers.

- Municipalities need to be able to strengthen weaker schools. Measuring school quality against set standards would help monitor and improve equity across schools, directing capital spending and teacher training to struggling schools.
- A related option would be federal incentives for municipalities to expand subsidized preschool programs for the poor. All but the poorest of families are willing to pay preschool fees, so preschool investments could be targeted to currently excluded poor areas.
- Greater educational access is still needed for poor rural students, and for grades 9 through 11 in urban areas. Mechanisms to achieve this expansion in coverage and quality could include improving night-time secondary schooling, distance learning, and collaboration with private schools. An option would be to reassess policies that discourage schooling provision in rural areas (incentives against small schools).

Figure 2. Percentage of children 7–14 out of school

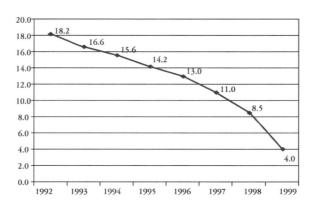

Source: PNAD / IBGE

Figure 3. Brazil's net secondary enrollment lag

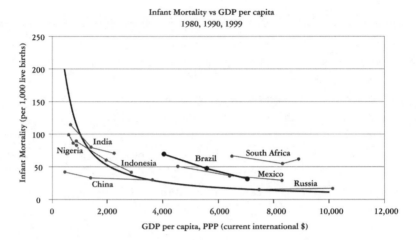

Infant Mortality vs GDP per capita
1980, 1990, 1999

Source: Woirld Bank Analysis

- Many transfer programs could be integrated into one system of social protection, and modern systems of program evaluation and means testing could be developed. Brazil's poverty gap has been estimated at R$20 billion: transparency and public participation could improve targeting of the R$240 billion (20 percent of national income) that Brazil spends annually on social sectors, to halve this poverty gap in perhaps the next 10 years (figure 4). One option would be to move from a sector-based approach (transfer programs located within education, health, social assistance, and other ministries) to a household-based approach that organizes services to ease access to available programs.

- Strengthening state and municipal management capacity is a key to improving social outcomes. One option for health would be to expand capitation payments to include more types of care, and to adjust capitation rates according to costs and to indicators of need (epidemiological, demographic, or socioeconomic).

Figure 4. Brazil's rapid progress on infant mortality

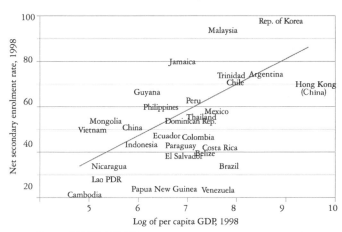

Source: PNAD / IBGE

Growing through productivity

To raise productivity across the board, a series of measures could improve the environment for private sector-led growth. With improved productivity, Brazil's economic growth is likely to improve, creating more room for social spending or infrastructure investment.

- Private investment in infrastructure will increase under strengthened regulatory institutions. One option is a deregulation review. A high-level concerted effort could be directed at reassessing regulations and eliminating those that are unnecessary or detrimental to the public interest. This would involve impact studies of current (and future proposed) regulations—to assess social benefits and costs.

- Deeper and better distributed financial intermediation will follow from the reduction of directed credit, which currently crowds out private credit, raises borrowing costs, and reduces financial depth. Focusing subsidies on appropriately qualified end users rather than on broadly defined sectors or intermediary institutions could reduce directed credit while improving efficiency.

- Measures to expand trade, such as a more efficient tax structure that does not penalize exporters and labor-intensive companies, could increase productivity. One option would be to replace the Social Contributions Tax (COFINS) and the

Social Integration Program/Program of Assistance to Civil Servants (PIS/PASEP) taxes with a federal value-added tax (VAT). Alternatively, turnover taxes could be replaced by a broadened federal income tax.

- Measures to decrease administrative barriers to enterprise creation and innovation would also increase productivity. One option would be to permit greater freedom in contracts. The number of documents required for business registration could be reduced and a centralized system introduced, most likely at the state level, with one identification number for the company nationwide.

Actions to generate employment within fiscal constraints

- The most important contribution that the public sector can make to a lasting reduction in unemployment is stabilizing the public debt. Sound fiscal policy reduces interest rates and increases investment and employment.
- Labor demand could be strengthened (and informality discouraged) by reducing the burden of payroll taxes.
- Labor turnover would fall and employment would increase if the Severance Fund (FGTS) were reformed to eliminate incentives to seek dismissal in order to access funds.
- Workers' incentives to force dismissals could also be offset by financing unemployment insurance through a dismissal fine rather than PIS/PASEP taxes.
- Deductions on personal income tax (IRPF)—0.3% of GDP, benefiting the middle class—could be replaced with deductions on corporate income tax (IRPJ) to increase demand for labor.
- Measures to improve the investment climate, such as reducing bureaucratic red tape and impediments to foreign technology, would increase labor demand.
- Cutting financial intermediation costs by reducing financial market concentration, directed credit, and reserve requirements would also increase labor demand.

Stabilizing the economy

Economic stability is an urgent objective that is widely recognized. Brazil's progress in building modern institutions of economic management is striking, yet, some of its debt is a structural legacy of much earlier policies (figure 5). Economic growth will undoubtedly help. But growth other than from rising productivity may increase external vulnerability: other steps are urgent.

Figure 5. Federal bonded debt, 1994–2000
(percent of GDP)

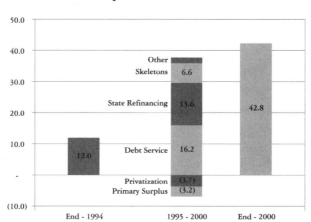

Note: For the same period, increases in state and municipal net debt have been approximately offset by reductions in the debt of state owned enterprises.

Source: A.S. Bevilaqua and M.G.P. Garcia, 2002, "Debt Management in Brazil: Evaluation of the Real Plan and Challenges Ahead," International Journal of Finance and Economics 7 (1).

The economic challenges are many, but complexity does not obscure the primacy of debt stabilization as needed for lasting progress on any of the other fronts discussed here. Despite marked progress in the social sectors, the Brazilian economy has now spent two decades in stop-and-go stagnation for one essential reason: the long-term difficulty of keeping expenditures in line with revenues in the consolidated public sector.

- Pension reform, it is recognized, is central in the platform of fiscal credibility for building growth. The efficient, equitable way forward is to cut the overgenerous pension benefits to civil service retirees through a forward-looking transition rule. This could increase national saving by up to 2 percent of GDP, raising investment and reducing external financing needs. Several options, that are being considered could move in this direction: levying a contribution rate on retirees' benefits; raising the contribution rate for current federal civil servants; increasing the retirement age and equalizing it for men and women; indexing pensions to inflation rather than wages; increasing to a worker's entire career the reference period for calculating the retirement benefit; changing the retirement benefit formula to include the same fator previdenciário that has linked benefits to workers' contributions in the general Social Security System (RGPS) since reforms in 1998; and instead of protecting all current civil servants and applying 1998 reforms only to new hires, reforms of the RJU employment regime could be applied to, for example, anyone who is more than five years from retirement, or applied in inverse proportion to years of service.

- An adequately high primary fiscal surplus and a more flexible public spending structure might create fiscal room by lowering borrowing costs. Past primary surpluses have come more from increased taxation than from decreased spending (figure 6). Reduced earmarking would increase flexibility. An alternative would make more use of ordinary laws with sunset clauses rather than constitutional amendments.

Figure 6. Tax revenue and primary expenditure
(percent of GDP)

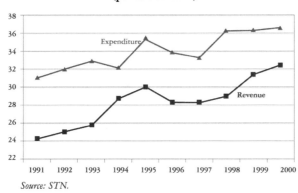

Source: STN.

• Moving to central bank autonomy would increase the effectiveness of monetary policy. Legal protection for supervisors of the Central Bank could also improve independence from political intervention.

• As conditions allow, it may be worth considering paying the price to reduce the risk inherent in the high proportion of government bonds indexed to the exchange rate and short-term interest rates.

Delivering government services to all

Expanding government services for all would contribute to equity, sustainability, and competitiveness. Empowering people, especially the poor, to participate in public decisions makes these decisions better reflect communities' needs and builds consensus for public policies. This may mean removing political discretion in government decisions, from who receives Bolsa Escola benefits to the location of public construction projects. Expanding access to government services builds social capital, which can improve public investment outcomes, productive activities, and ultimately Brazil's socio-economic performance.

Excellent models already exist in Brazil:

- Community associations identify investments in rural poverty reduction in the nine Northeastern states. These activities could be scaled up to other sectors and to urban areas.
- During the building of the São Paulo Belt Highway (Rodoanel), families displaced by the construction organized associations to manage site selection and development of new housing projects, with results that are likely to be better and less costly than traditional models.
- Some local governments have set up one-stop shops, grouping public services in a single place.
- Systematic program evaluation is still not widespread in Brazil and could be made an integral part of the multi-annual planning process (PPA). Regular public expenditure reviews would then channel spending away from ineffective or inefficient uses toward proven successes, improving the overall quality of spending.

The challenge is to spread models with proven effectiveness to the whole country. Brazil is a modernizing state, moving from less transparent modes of public decision making to performance-driven institutions. Problems of social and economic exclusion, and ultimately high levels of crime and violence, require further progress down this road.

Managing natural resources

Managing natural resources is crucial for a country of Brazil's wonderful natural wealth. In many parts of Brazil, particularly the North and parts of the Northeast, natural resources constitute a much higher proportion of the assets of the poor than of the rich. Ensuring their preservation and controlled use is thus a condition of equity as well as of sustainability. Environmental protection is not a decision that can simply be delayed, since much damage is irreversible (as illustrated by the near disappearance of Brazil's unique Mata Atlântica). Urban degradation also affects the poor disproportionately: inadequate water and sewerage, in particular, have a significant health impact on the poor.

- Land tenure is fundamental, particularly in the precarious agricultural economy of the Northeast. Viable models—Crédito Fundiário, for example—have been developed and could be expanded, although further impact assessment is needed.

- Successful models of community-driven micro-catchment water basin management, such as those developed in Paraná and Santa Catarina, may be replicated or adapted elsewhere, particularly in the Northeast.

- In the Amazon, limiting open access in the interior, while promoting the sustainable use of forested areas, is the key to avoiding as yet poorly understood (and possibly irreversible) damage that would foreclose future options. One possible scenario foresees half of the Amazon Forest effectively protected in some form.

- Other ecological systems are equally important to Brazil's poor, notably the Caatinga and Cerrado biomes, the protection of which will require ecological zoning, including increased reserves.

- The "brown agenda" is pressing in almost all urban areas. Priorities are to relax unrealistic technical standards (which block provision of water and sanitation services to the poor) and concentrate water subsidies on the poor, to integrate urban planning and slum upgrading, and to work with municipalities to expand successful solid waste management initiatives (such as the *Lixo que não é lixo* program in Curitiba).

The Northeast and the North: a regional focus versus regional policy

Poverty and inequality have a regional dimension in Brazil. Poverty is three-quarters higher than the national average in the Northeast and a third higher in the North. But regional policies—directed subsidized lending, tax incentives, federal investments, and regional development institutions—have not induced convergence in average regional incomes. Nor have they reduced inequality overall. One reason is that inequality is just as great within the poorest states as it is between states.

Alternatively, a regional focus could pursue the same five means sought for Brazil as a whole, with even greater emphasis for the poorer regions:

- Investing in people: quality in primary education and access to secondary education in rural areas become even more crucial.
- Improving productivity: infrastructure, particularly transport, is even more lacking, lending impact to the design of private sector contracts and to avoiding corruption.
- Stabilizing the economy: federal social security reforms will create greater flexibility in the states' budgets and therefore help the poorest states to invest.
- Delivering government services to all: weak governance and the associated social exclusion, as well as vested interests have interfered in public investment decisions, increasing the potential gains from more participatory government.
- Managing natural resources: the economies of the North and Northeast are especially reliant on natural resources, with water in the Northeast an obvious development bottleneck.

Policies for the North and Northeast are therefore not qualitatively distinct from those for Brazil as a whole. Emphasis is merited on governance capacity and greater coordination and integration than in the past between regional initiatives (such as CODEVASFP or ADENE) and state governments.

1. Investing in people

Table 1. Introduction for investing in people

Indicator	Brazil	Comparison		2010 target
		Latin America	OECD/Other	
Net Secondary Enrollment[a] (%)	33	58 (Mexico) 70 (Chile)	98 (Rep. of Korea)	60?
Illiteracy rate - 15 and older (%)	14.4	4.1 (Chile) 8.3 (Mexico)	0	10?
Infant mortality per 1,000 live births	30	10 (Chile) 29 (Mexico)	7 (United States)	15?
Life expectancy (years)	68.1	75.7 (Chile) 73.0 (Mexico)	77.1 (United States)	70?
Homicides per 100,000 people	26.2	17.1 (Mexico)	14.7 (United States)	20?

a. World Bank-adjusted numbers. Source: World Bank SIMA Database.

Human capital—investments in people—may be thought of as personal stocks of privately embodied assets that reflect people's ability to produce well-being for themselves and their families. These assets include health, education, training, experience, and natural ability. Human capital assets may be depleted if a person or household is subject to excessive economic risk: households with more variable income may withdraw their children from school; uninsured workers may endure greater damage to their health before seeking medical attention. Human capital is also wasted when otherwise qualified people are rejected for employment or advancement because of their skin color. Investments in people also include social capital, or the ability of societies to come together to complete undertakings, controlling for other assets. An erosion of social capital may be reflected in high levels of crime, for example.

Education: increasing equity and completion rates

Education creates both human and social capital. Investments in education may transmit cultural messages and build social cohesion, but they also raise the earning potential of individuals and the productivity of the economy. Although the positive effects on economic growth of public investments in education seem to take some time to appear, the benefits to individuals are more immediate.

Strengthening municipal education functions would seem to imply renewing the Fundef Law, which expires in 2007. Brazil has made great strides in education since the early 1990s. Household surveys show that the percentage of children ages 7–14 attending school rose from 80.5 percent in 1991 to 96.5 percent in 2000. Rather than being a corollary of economic growth, which was weak during the period, these gains arose from changes in policy, in particular strong federal initiatives to boost enrollments and guarantee funding per child, such as Fundescola and Fundef, combined with effective decentralization to states and municipalities.

Brazil is cited internationally as an example of good practice in education reform, but its low starting point implies that its levels of education still lag behind those in the region and elsewhere. Today a young Brazilian enters the labor market with an average of about 6 years of schooling: considerably less than the 11 years in OECD countries and 8 years in East Asia. The most equitable way of increasing Brazilian educational attainment would be to focus investments at the fundamental cycle to help more of the poorest children complete 8th grade. But for the workforce to be globally competitive, Brazil needs more secondary school graduates.

Improving the quality of education in Brazil's decentralized system requires addressing the shortages in teacher skills and the lack of a formal division between state and municipal functions and removing political influence over staff appointments. Strengthening municipal education functions would seem to imply renewing the Fundef for states and municipalities, since the law expires in 2007. Moreover, state and municipal governments have not managed to guarantee that all their schools meet minimum quality standards for teaching, materials, furniture, infrastructure, and instructional time. Because children attend schools that reflect residential income patterns, substandard schools are generally attended by poor children, continuing the cycle of inequality.

There is a strong case to be made for channeling additional resources to under-perform-ing schools.

Despite national curriculum parameters and assessment and the guaranteed provision of textbooks, improvements in classroom teaching remain the major challenge. Results on the National Basic Education Evaluation System (SAEB) tests have shown that Brazilian children are learning less than expected, and repeated "bottom-up" attempts to ameliorate matters have had limited impact. Two models of pedagogical reform are particularly rele-vant for Brazil: the school-based approaches favored by India, New Zealand, and the United Kingdom, or nationwide initiatives to upgrade teacher instructional skills through distance education, teacher colleges, networks, and qualification standards, such as have been applied in Chile, China, and France.

Another policy choice lies in the area of early childhood development. Educational research has repeatedly demon-strated the welfare significance of early childhood develop-ment. Programs in Brazil disproportionately serve children who are older, from richer, better-educated families, and live in urban areas. Returns to investments in this area are probably high enough to justify channeling public resources to it – possi-bly from areas of public subsidies such as higher education.

Early childhood development investments are worth channeling resources to.

Health: improving efficiency and access

Few concerns more readily dominate people's attention than illness. Employment, educa-tion, personal commitments, all come second if a serious health concern arises. Moreover, health services have complicated economic characteristics that make government finance and provision the most common mode of delivery in most countries. Even when services are private, norms and regulations are required to govern health insurance markets. Access to good health services—prevention and treatment—are one of the main demands on governments from people the world over.

Brazil has made marked progress in health indices in recent years. Infant mortality per thousand live births fell from nearly 48 in 1991 to less than 30 in 2000. Life expectancy at birth increased by two and a half years from 65.6 to 68.1. Few other countries equaled this progress during the period (Cuba and Malaysia, which are much smaller countries, and Ecuador, Egypt, and Peru, which all started from worse initial conditions). Moreover, as with education, the improvement in health indices was achieved despite weak economic growth in Brazil and is therefore explained primarily by changes in public policy. Most important have been the universalization of services (the Unified Health System, SUS), focused programs (such as the *Programa de Atendimento Básico* and those for AIDS and malaria), decentralization, and greater participation of communities (as in the introduction of community health agents).

Despite these improvements, disparities in health care funding across geographical units and in utilization rates among social groups remain large. Many poor households lack regular access to basic services while richer households enjoy access to costly, complex care at the expense of the public purse. This suggests introducing resource allocation and provider payment mechanisms to improve equity across states and municipalities.

Expanding the Family Health Program may necessitate channeling health investments to certain larger municipalities.

Similarly, expansion of the Family Health Program has been uneven and has lagged in large municipalities, suggesting the need for a sustainable extension of coverage and benefits. The Family Health Program covers about 10 percent of urban populations in municipalities larger than 100,000 and just 7 percent in the largest municipalities with populations greater than 500,000, compared with 50 percent in rural areas and 25 percent nationally. Some municipalities lack the installed capacity to provide the services mandated by law, and this may necessitate channeling health investments to these municipalities.

Further decentralization combined with performance-based management and financing could raise the efficiency of the SUS, whose financing is currently largely unrelated to results, which are in turn not sufficiently evaluated. Policy options include performance agreements and contracts between payers and providers, autonomous hospital management with greater community participation, and integrated delivery systems at the microregion level.

Many health costs could be avoided altogether through more effective prevention. Here, health promotion and social interventions can significantly reduce the burdens of noncommunicable diseases (especially cardiovascular disease) and injuries caused by industrial and vehicular accidents. This issue will become increasingly relevant as Brazil's demographic structure ages.

Finally, water pollution is also a major concern in Brazil and a further source of preventable disease, particularly diarrhea, a major killer of infants and children. Rapid urbanization and industry, agriculture, and mining have caused progressive worsening of water quality. Many urban and rural dwellers, particularly in informal settlements, are in direct contact with domestic wastewater because of inadequate collection. Wastewater discharges are rarely monitored, and untreated effluents are commonly released directly into rivers and lakes. Only 52 percent of urban sewerage is collected through sewer systems and 80 percent is released without any treatment. As a result, most rivers crossing urban areas are highly polluted, causing serious health problems for the poor; environmental damage, especially to sensitive areas such as wetlands; and higher costs for water treatment. Infant mortality is closely associated with waterborne diseases and has a greater impact on the poor. Infant mortality reaches rates of more than 60 deaths per thousand live births in poorer northeastern states.

There is complementarity between ensuring universality, one of the system's core values, and concentrating resources on poorer, sicker populations while improving quality. Poorer households have lower utilization rates than richer households, and the well-off receive implicit subsidies for high-cost procedures. The system provides few incentives to local and facility managers to use resources efficiently or to improve quality, leading to decreasing efficiency and quality of SUS-financed services.

Monitoring and treating more wastewater is one key to reducing infant mortality.

Solutions may mean reducing subsidies (but not access) to the well-to-do and redefining public and private roles. However, reallocating resources to poor and underserved populations will yield few results if the poor shun services because of low quality, long queues, stock-outs, incorrect referrals, and other inefficiencies. Efficiency and quality would thus be key components of the next reform phase.

Social insurance: safeguarding human capital investments

Brazil has a wide array of good social protection programs for a country of its income level, but from a technical point of view there are many ways in which the system as a whole could be improved. Many programs offer benefits to the middle class, while most that are aimed at the poor have limited coverage. Older segments of the population are relatively well protected, while the young receive few social protection resources. This message is amplified if social protection programs are viewed as an attempt to help citizens build their assets in the face of economic volatility. The young and the poor are the two groups whose human capital (accumulation) is most at risk through adverse shocks such as unemployment and illness in the family.

Under this view of social protection, three options for improving the system as a whole present themselves: reallocating away from programs favoring the middle-class and older age groups toward social assistance programs that favor the poor and the young, extending income security programs to cover informal sector workers, and reducing duplication in coverage and modernizing programs away from in-kind toward cash benefits and from sector-based toward household-based approaches. Helping provide people, especially the poor, with the means to invest their savings securely would also improve social protection.

Before discussing these areas of reform in social protection policies, it is important to acknowledge the primacy of employment (discussed below) as a means of risk reduction for Brazilians and to emphasize two facts about Brazilian labor markets that are relevant to human capital formation. First, turnover in Brazilian labor markets is high and has increased by 60 percent in the past decade, with one in three workers changing jobs within a year. High turnover reduces productivity because workers do not stay in one firm long enough to accumulate adequate training and experience, part of their human capital. Second, Brazilian labor markets are highly informal—and becoming more so. In 1980, 40 percent of the labor market was informal; by the late 1990s this proportion had risen to about 60 percent. Greater informality increases wage flexibility and reduces unemployment, but it also reduces the reach of many formal market-based social policies and increases the need for income security programs. Informal workers have more variable wages and more dependents on average, and income volatility in the informal sector is a significant threat to human-capital accumulation.

A human capital perspective therefore suggests two approaches to labor markets. First, the current subsidization of labor turnover could be replaced by changing the design of the Severance Fund (FGTS), since workers who have accumulated severance rights have an incentive to induce dismissals. Second, the cost to employers of creating secure jobs needs to be lower. Many employers rely on high worker turnover, interns, and indirect labor contracts to avoid the high costs of benefits and severance.

Labor turnover could be reduced by changing the design of the FGTS.

More competition in FGTS account management would ensure that workers are paid market rates of return, decrease the tax component in FGTS, and cut turnover. Alternatively, FGTS contributions could be capped, cutting the incentive to trigger a dismissal. A further option would be to, in effect, make the FGTS a "no-fault" insurance scheme. This would also reduce turnover and increase the investment in skills. Finally, FGTS accounts could be converted to retirement accounts. This would strengthen the social security system and ease other reforms, while eliminating duplication of formal sector unemployment insurance.

Policy could also aim to provide income security for informal workers in the short run while gradually increasing formality in the long run. Probably the best way to help the weakest segments of the population is to gradually introduce greater flexibility in some contracts. Reducing some of thes mandates would be a way to cut informality among the poor, and thus increase productivity, employment, and earnings security. Furthermore, eliminating overlaps in unemployment insurance and FGTS could create room to reduce payroll taxes and redirect unemployment insurance to informal workers.

What about reform to social protection itself (rather than labor markets): the three themes of reallocation, extension, and modernization listed above? For reallocation, by far the greatest source of potential gains is the system of social security. Social security accounts for fully half of all social spending in Brazil. The main dimension of social security reform is thus fiscal, and the constraints largely political (the problem is therefore discussed in section 4). From an income security standpoint, a sensible overall goal would be a system with a lower benefits package that permits a widening of the number of beneficiaries (to reach poorer segments of the population).

Bolsa Escola could be extended to secondary school, where enrollment gaps between rich and poor are high.

For extension of social protection to informal workers, the long-run aim may well be to extend formality to the whole workforce. In the short run, however, this is unrealistic, and there is an argument for expanding programs that can be better targeted to the poor. Brazil's initial experience implementing the Bolsa Escola, a means-tested program, has been encouraging and could be extended. Some states, such as Ceará, are experimenting with proxy means testing. In addition, the Bolsa Escola could be extended to secondary school, where enrollment gaps between lower and higher income groups are high.

Reform could include a move from in-kind benefits, such as food, to cash transfers. For greater impact, nutrition programs could be integrated with other services, such as primary health or, especially, early childhood education. The government could shift some programs from a sector-based approach to one that addresses the household as a unit. Services could be organized in ways that make it easier for households to know about and access the variety of interventions that are available.

There is recent evidence from São Paulo that assistance and insurance programs have measurable effects on social capital. An evaluation of four of the municipality's social programs *(Renda Mínima, Bolsa Trabalho, Operação Trabalho, and Começar de Novo)* compared changes in indices in the 13 districts reached by the social programs in 2001 with districts that were not reached. Of São Paulo's 20 most violent administrative districts, for example, the 7 that had benefited earliest in 2001 from social programs experienced a 10 percent decline in violent deaths, whereas the other 13 districts experienced a 1.5 percent increase.

Employment: creating jobs through better regulation and higher growth

Having a job is the main way in which people perceive themselves as participating in society. Citizens view employment generation as a primary responsibility of government, yet experience suggests that government attempts to create jobs by intervening in labor markets or creating jobs directly are unlikely to succeed. Urban unemployment has risen in recent years, more because people are out of work longer on average than because of increases in dismissals. This suggests that labor market regulation may do more to reduce unemployment than more explicit attempts by public institutions to create work. Some labor market institutions—FGTS, unemployment insurance, labor courts—set up to protect workers' legitimate interests, often do a poor job of protecting those interests while at the same time suppressing formal employment by making formal employees far more costly to employers. Reforms in this area could therefore be open-minded and pragmatic in pursuit of protecting vulnerable workers and increasing flexibility in the formal labor market.

The Brazilian labor market is characterized by low job creation, declining participation, rising unemployment, low productivity, frequent litigation, high informality, and inadequate income security. Labor market regulation consists mainly of a series of public interventions in the relationship between employer and employee. Some of these are funded through payroll taxes, which constitute an incentive for employers to substitute capital for labor and informal for formal labor. The degree of informality in the labor market, while creating flexibility in prices and employment that might otherwise be more rigid, contributes to social exclusion by robbing more than half the workforce of the rights of formal workers such as unemployment insurance, active labor market schemes such as job search assistance, and many training initiatives.

Access to financial services is also unevenly distributed away from the poorest, both geographically (with fewer services available in the poorer North and Northeast regions) and within regions. Small entrepreneurs suffer greater difficulties of access (Brazilian enterprises in general tend to rely heavily on retained earnings), and capital markets and other nonbank financial institutions have not been able to compensate for these difficulties. The expansion of financial services to small-scale entrepreneurs and those in remote regions would increase employment and economic inclusion and could be aided by new technologies. Although Brazil is advanced in Internet banking, there is scope for improving productivity for smaller and less well-off customers and for improving phone connectivity (the structure of telephone charges may play a role here). Expanding microfinance and nonbank financial services may also offer employment growth.

The primacy of employment underlines another link between policies to foster economic growth and stability on one hand and efforts to increase social inclusion on the other. The main generator of employment is economic growth, and this will not be attained without low inflation, falling interest rates, and greater investor confidence, to allow longer term planning in the private sector.

Links with productivity and innovation

Human capital, by raising the capacities of individuals, raises the productivity of the economy. Firms cite the education of the workforce, in particular, as an obstacle to investment in Brazil. Productivity gains from investments in education are slow to appear though, and the magnitude of the gains (measured by earnings returns to additional years of education) is greater at the secondary and tertiary levels. Finally, improvements in the schooling system raise the quality of the workforce one year at a time, as new young workers enter the labor market, but leave older workers unaffected directly. Economic studies of education in Brazil thus caution against expecting immediate education-led economic miracles.

People also add to their own human capital through on-the-job learning or learning by doing. Many people in Brazil learn to operate computers, prepare food, and other skills without formal instruction. There is nevertheless a digital divide in Brazil because many children in poor households cannot acquire computer literacy by using a computer at home the way many middle-class children do. The extent to which learning-by-doing occurs in an economy is conditioned by its level of technology and innovation and by the frequency with which workers change jobs. Frequent turnover reduces firm-specific human capital. Labor turnover has already been mentioned: important revisions are needed to the nexus of FGTS, the Workers Assistance Fund (FAT, financed from the PIS/PASEP tax), and unemployment insurance (see "The FAT–FGTS nexus" in section 3 for more detail).

Technology and innovation are sensitive to the environment for intellectual property and to the economy's interaction with the rest of the world. Brazil's relative economic isolation (at 20 percent of GDP, Brazil's trade share is one of the lowest in the world, even allowing for Brazil's large economy) can be seen as an opportunity for gains to its workers through increased trade, innovation, and productivity. Recent economic research at the World Bank suggests that despite the rising skills premia in Brazil (measured by differences between salaries of university graduates and workers with only secondary schooling, for example), skill-biased technological change has been slower than in Argentina, Colombia, or Mexico.

Crime and violence: investing in prevention

As in many other countries, among the factors that affect the life chances of poor people in Brazil is the lack of personal security: the high risk of fraud, robbery, injury, or death from criminal behavior. The poor are the greatest victims of crime, and the high prevalence of crime leads to lost opportunities (failure to attend school or fear of investment, for example) as well as the costs of investments in security. Crime rates have been rising since the 1980s. The number of homicides rose from 11.7 per 100 000 inhabitants in 1980 to 26.2 in 1999, and the rising trend continues.

Violence is highest in the Southeast region, particularly the states of Rio de Janeiro (with a homicide rate of 52.6 per 100 000 inhabitants in 1999) and São Paulo (44.0), and homicide rates are above 60 in the cities of Recife, Rio de Janeiro, São Paulo, and Vitória (ES). Minas Gerais and Piauí recorded falling crime in the 1990s. Certain types of crime victims are selected by social status: while the recent rise in kidnappings causes more unease among the middle and upper classes, domestic violence and victimization by the police are crimes suffered disproportionately by the poor. A recent Fundação Seade study in São Paulo found that residents of smaller peripheral favelas were exposed to the highest rates of homicide. Much of this crime is related to the drug trade, particularly in urban slums where the authorities have virtually relinquished control to highly organized gangs. Reportedly one of the problems facing Brazil is the diversion of international narcotics traffic through the favelas of the larger Brazilian cities, increasing the resources and the stakes associated with gang dominance.

It is commonplace to attribute crime and violence to deprivation and to the gap between rich and poor. Yet there is no evidence that the poor are more prone to commit crime. The deprivation hypothesis would also suggest that crime would rise during periods of high unemployment or depressed wages, but crime and violence have risen in Brazil during growth periods as well as recessions. Over the past decade, poverty has diminished and standards of living have risen, and yet so has crime. Crime in Brazil is not a simple matter of resorting to illegal means to redress the income gap.

Another theme has been impunity. Criminals have a low likelihood of being apprehended or convicted. Suspects who are apprehended are sometimes able to bargain or bribe their way out of jail. The courts are slow and can fail to convict known perpetrators. Yet it is hard to assess how much impunity contributes to actual criminal behavior and harder to imagine that it is an underlying cause of crime, except by assuming that people are deterred from criminal acts only by likely detection.

A third theme is the breakdown of social control. Brazilian society over the past half century has experienced massive migration and urbanization, changing from a predominantly agrarian to a predominantly urban society. The controls once exercised by families and local communities have weakened. Brazilians have compensated through a variety of channels: religious organizations, samba schools, organized football supporters, and even criminal gangs. Some, particularly young men, paradoxically may have turned to gangs in a quest to reestablish order and authority in their lives.

Finally, violence has engulfed large segments of the penal system. In São Paulo, Brazil's richest state, state penitentiaries and the youth corrections system (FEBEM) have become scenes of violence, including the notorious Carandiru prison massacre in which police, brought in to quell an uprising, killed 118 prisoners. In the past year, there have been coordinated uprisings in several penitentiaries, major jail breaks, and murderous rampages of prisoners against other prisoners.

Most of the public outcry against crime and violence has focused on reforming and strengthening the police, building more prisons, and repressing crime more effectively. But increased support for the police has not necessarily resulted in lower crime rates. Neither has police and judicial corruption received commensurate attention. Investments are called for, but before major outlays, the government could assess where the most effective interventions lie. A Seade survey found that 55 percent of robbery victims in São Paulo did not report the incident, and the Fundação Getúlio Vargas found that 60 percent of victims did not do so in Rio de Janeiro: the main reason given is distrust of the police. Public studies of crime and violence could provide needed information on the location, perpetrators, and victims of crime and violence. Data on the effectiveness of measures to combat crime—such as reorganizations of the police, prosecutors, and the courts—could also be made public.

Police reform would augment measures spanning reforms to legislation, courts, prosecution and defense, and prison modernization.

In recent cases, current or former members of police forces have engaged in extrajudicial killings and kidnapping for ransom, and on-duty police have been involved in shakedowns and extortion. In January 2002, a Brazilian weekly reported that in 2001 homicides by police totaled more than 400 in São Paulo compared with 8 in New York City. All this points to the importance of establishing the accountability of law enforcement. Analyzing successful reform campaigns could serve well. Public involvement and an informed constituency for police reform are the most basic conditions.

The experience of New York City brings out key elements of the successful reform of that city's police force: eliminating corrupt police by recruiting outsiders and punishing all police misdemeanors, establishing local goals and accountability for crime reduction, insisting on zero tolerance of crime (eliminating petty crime as a way of reducing serious crime), creating special funds to prosecute criminals and counteract the resources of organized crime, and instituting community policing. The division of Brazil's police forces into civil and military units, with separate but overlapping responsibilities, has been pointed out as a problem. Police training, equipment, and pay are also issues. Police reform would have to be accompanied by measures spanning legislation, court reforms, work with prosecution and defense, and prison modernization to avoid gridlock in the justice and prison systems as well as brutality and other abuses.

Judicial processes can be slow and court calendars are often clogged affecting the efficacy of the judicial process. Judicial costs are high, reflecting salaries and benefits set (by magistrates) much higher than in other public sector occupations. Better court administration, court schedules, and supervision of less experienced judges by more seasoned judges could help. In the long term, as with the police, a responsible press, legal scholars, law schools, and politicians could help raise public awareness and create a public constituency for judicial reform.

Another key ingredient would be penal reform. Most Brazilian prisons do not meet minimum international standards for safety and security. Investments will be necessary to raise both physical plant and prison programs to adequate standards. The experience from other countries in prison work programs, open jail programs for nonviolent prisoners, education programs, and drug and alcohol treatment programs is instructive.

Despite understandable public demands to curb crime and restore safety, increased suppression has done little to change criminal behavior in Brazil. There is widespread agreement that crime prevention requires reintegrating key segments of the population, particularly urban males between ages 15 and 24, into a system of social control. The premise of this epidemiological approach to crime and violence is that the enabling conditions for crime must be reduced by identifying people most at risk and helping them develop a sense of belonging to a social unit and having a purpose in life. Gang behavior in Brazil, as elsewhere, shows the enormous power of peer pressure and the need that young people have to feel that they belong to powerful institutions.

Dedicated NGOs could contribute a great deal to new models of crime prevention.

Brazil is rich in successful programs that work with youth at risk for criminal behavior or addiction. A good example is the Police and Community Cooperation for Reduction of Violence project in Diadema (SP), which is supported by the Fernand Braudel Institute. This initiative contributed to a 12 percent drop in homicides in 2001, the largest improvement among the 64 São Paulo municipalities with populations greater than 100,000. Yet such programs are underfunded and reach only a small percentage of youth at risk. Specialized NGOs could thus contribute a great deal to new models of crime prevention. The Brazilian AIDS prevention program has shown that exposure to HIV can be reduced by programs that work through neighborhood-based NGOs. It is plausible that a similar approach involving neighborhood organizations can also reduce crime.

Options for investing in people

Lack of access to opportunities in Brazil is most acutely related to investments in people. Two-thirds of the difference between (after-tax) income inequality in Brazil and in the United States is traceable to education alone. The link between parents' educational attainment (the highest grade reached before leaving education) and their children's is stronger in Brazil than in most countries. And even in cities with high proportions of people of Afro-Brazilian descent, university admissions are skewed toward lighter skinned Brazilians. Investing in people is fundamental to building a more equitable Brazil. Many of the investments needed to make Brazil more sustainable, socially and environmentally, are institutional, and institutions rely on the people who work for them. And human capital lies at the heart of long-run improvements in productivity and growth.

Brazil has indicated its intention to reduce poverty by half by 2015. Different combinations of economic growth and redistribution may achieve the same poverty reduction objective, with greater effort at redistribution required to meet this goal at lower levels of economic growth (figure 7). Extrapolations from educational improvements of the recent past suggest that annual economic growth of about 6 percent (optimistic given recent history but perhaps possible with a determined program of macroeconomic stability and reforms to trade and investment) would achieve the poverty reduction target without significant redistribution of income. However, a less optimistic growth assumption of 3.5 percent leaves a significant shortfall to be filled by improvements to Brazil's social protection system of transfers and insurance.

Figure 7. Meeting the 2015 poverty goal – alternative scenarios

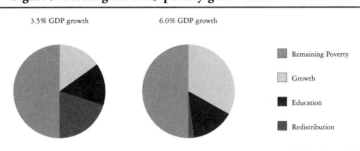

Source: World Bank analysis

Based on the discussion in this section, a short list of policy options to raise investment in the Brazilian people in the next few years would be the following:

- Mounting a campaign for universal secondary education, including
    - Targeting resources to primary and secondary schools based on low (and possibly on improving) SAEB scores
    - Targeting reduced repetition and faster completion by students of primary education
    - Where necessary, expanding the number of secondary school places.

- Integrating and properly evaluating the main transfer programs, leading to a significant expansion of overall transfers well-targeted to the poor.
- Replacing subsidies to labor turnover by reforms of unemployment insurance and FGTS.
- Cautiously transferring public resources to early childhood development from areas of ineffective subsidies.
- Reforming police, following (to the extent relevant) international best practice combined with intensive community-based initiatives to address violence among young males, particularly in the urban periphery.

2. Growing through productivity

Table 2. Indicators for growing through productivity

Indicator	Brazil	Comparison		2010 target
		Latin America	OECD	
GDP growth, 1990-2000[a] (%)	2.7	3.1 (Mexico) 6.8 (Chile)	3.4 (United States)	5.0?
Labor productivity, 2000 (value added per worker, US$)[b]	13,894	18,492 (Mexico) 27,765 (Chile)	54,879 (United States)	16,000?
Trade volume, 2000[a] (% GDP)	23	63 (Chile) 64 (Mexico)		40?
Days to start a business, 2001[c]	63	28 (Chile)	1-3 (Ireland)	20?
Private sector credit, 2001[a] (% GDP)	35	69 (Chile)	143 (United States)	50?

Source: World Bank – a SIMA database, b Brazil Jobs Report, c Foreign Investment Advisory Service.

Economic history and comparisons

Brazil has a history of high economic growth: in the last century, it was one of the three fastest growing economies in the world. Between 1901 and 2000, GDP per capita grew at an average annual rate of 4.4 percent. Few countries have done better. Argentina and Chile, for example, had growth rates of about 3.3 percent. Had per capita output in the three countries been the same in 1900, by 1999 the average Brazilian would have been three times as rich as a Chilean or an Argentine. But Brazil's growth during the last two decades has been less than stellar, and the contrast with the earlier periods has magnified the sense of disappointment.

Compounding this is the fact that even more recently, during the last decade, for example, many of Brazil's neighbors have done better. In the 1960s, economic growth in Brazil kept pace with that in Latin America and the world, but Brazilians remember better the miracle years of the 1970s, when Brazil grew twice as fast as other countries. Along with the rest of Latin America, Brazil's economy sputtered during the 1980s, but while growth in the region picked up in the 1990s, Brazil's has remained erratic.

While this is disappointing, such comparisons also indicate that at least in the matter of economic growth Brazil should not be regarded as unusual. Chile, for example, did poorly in the 1970s and early 1980s when most other countries in Latin America were doing well, and did well later when others stumbled. Such variations in growth are common. Steady sustained growth for more than a decade is more the exception than the rule—economic growth seems to occur in spurts.

Why isn't Brazil growing faster?

Trade-related improvements, higher education levels, and greater global integration leading to greater access to credit all presaged higher growth rates for Brazil in the 1990s than in the 1970s. What explains the divergence of growth rates from such hopeful forecasts?

Countering these positive changes were the effects of slower world economic growth in the 1990s, Brazil's own higher income (richer countries grow more slowly), and higher inflation until 1994. Since then, Brazil's debt, falling infrastructure investment (particularly in transport), exhaustion of the benefits of transformation to urban industrial status, and quality shortfalls in the work force (perhaps owing to skill-biased technical change) have all contributed. More analysis is still necessary to account for the 6 percentage point decline in Brazilian economic growth in the 1990s from the 1970s: cross-country comparisons leave two-thirds of this variation in economic growth unaccounted for.

Trade and macroeconomic policy improvements may have mitigated these effects, but cross-country analysis suggests that reforms have some way to go before the effects are fully felt. Regional trade integration cannot be expected to deliver spectacular results, since Brazil makes up more than two-thirds of the economic heft of its trading bloc, and Brazil's own openness must be viewed against the backdrop of similar reforms in developing countries and the continued protection by OECD countries in markets for Brazil's exports. Inflation eradication, while necessary, has not yet sufficiently reduced economic uncertainty, partly owing to Brazil's debt levels. And fiscal constraints in combination with regulatory obstacles continue to hamper infrastructure investments. The world has also changed in other ways. Technological innovation has increased. Knowledge flows have become faster and more global. International capital flows have grown exponentially.

Slower world economic growth is one reason why Brazil's recent growth has been lower than during the miracle years.

Accompanying these changes is the need for policy reform. This section examines factors assessed as central to the new growth agenda. This agenda focuses on Brazilian productivity as the engine of sustainable economic growth.

The investment climate: cutting red tape and increasing competition

Productivity improvements are often embodied in physical investments (and in technical managerial innovation), and it is worthwhile asking what prevents more dynamic private sector activity in Brazil. One factor is undoubtedly the scarcity of finance, related to macroeconomic conditions (in particular the public sector borrowing requirement) and financial sector characteristics (discussed in the next section). But businesses themselves cite many obstacles having to do with bureaucracy, regulation, and uncertainty over policy as equally significant.

Reducing constraints on market entry could increase investment, competition, and productivity. Administrative barriers render the establishment of new firms complex and time-consuming. Simplified administrative procedures for firm registration (commercial and tax), land acquisition, site development, and environmental approvals would all help. Related measures might be to liberalize the issuance of temporary work permits and visas for foreign employees and to facilitate firm entry and investment through greater use of private sector-operated industrial parks and export processing zones.

Reducing constraints on market entry could increase investment, competition, and productivity. In one international comparison of procedures required to establish a new business (cited in World Bank, Brazil – The New Growth Agenda), the average time required in Brazil was 82 days, three times as long as was needed in Chile. In particular, the number of separate official procedures, at 15, is high—Ireland has 3. As part of the registration process for a partnership (limitada) or corporation (sociedade anônima), the company must obtain licenses and permits from federal and state environmental, health, and labor authorities and register for taxes at three levels of government, presenting abundant documentation at every step, including membership in the relevant trade association.

For firms beginning operations in Brazil, there are other considerations: a fully owned Brazilian subsidiary is not permitted, but the company can be registered as a Brazilian corporation with one Brazil-resident director. Further steps include opening a bank account, legalizing firm documents, receiving approval by the patent office (INPI) of contracts involving technology transfer, registering the foreign investment at the Central Bank, transferring funds to Brazil, and getting approval of registration from the state commercial council (*junta comercial*). These processes take about 60 days in Brazil, compared with less than 30 in Chile, Hong Kong, Malaysia, and Singapore.

Several initiatives in Brazil attempt to simplify procedures at the interface between the private and public sectors (for instance, the *Sistema Fácil* in Sergipe and the Federal District and anticipated in other states). Recognizing these, it is still possible to outline short-run opportunities to spur growth. These include easing temporary work permits for foreigners, relieving the role of INPI in their approval, reducing the documents required for business registration, and instituting a centralized registration system (most likely at the state level, with one nationwide company identification number). Tax registration could be unified, with one identification number for all levels, and duplication of documents for different levels eliminated. Stronger capacity in the environmental regulatory institutions and clearer roles for federal, state, and municipal environmental authorities would also help. And support for municipal land use zoning, including the allocation of more land for industrial or commercial use, may ease delays. Processing land use approvals case by case increases the discretionary power of public employees. It may also be worthwhile to evaluate the present system for transferring and registering real estate.

Firms also cite uncertainty, legalism, and an approvals approach as problems of regulatory agencies and competition policies. Under Law 8,884 of June 1995, three government agencies enforce antitrust regulations: the Antitrust Agency (CADE), the Secretariat for Economic Monitoring (SEAE) in the Ministry of Finance (a unit that deals with effects on prices), and the Economic Law Office (SDE) in the Ministry of Justice. CADE has primary responsibility for protecting competition and consumers. Antitrust regulations consist of rulings on mergers and acquisitions and on complaints of anticompetitive behavior. In practice, many anticompetitive proceedings are shelved for lack of evidence, and CADE thus focuses mainly on mergers and acquisitions.

Linking SEAE and SDE functions with CADE could increase regulatory efficiency.

There is room for developing a consistent framework and program for antitrust and competition policies, leading to a consideration of the roles of CADE, SEAE, SDE, INPI, and the sector regulatory agencies, based on the public interest. For antitrust regulations, linking SEAE and SDE functions with CADE could increase regulatory efficiency.

The financial sector: lowering costs, increasing access

Fundamental reforms in Brazil's financial system in the 1990s have transformed its structure and increased its stability and transparency. Restructuring following the banking crisis of 1995–96 led to consolidation and reduction in the number of private domestic financial institutions and a decline in state-owned financial institutions. Private foreign banks have entered the sector. Yet structural impediments still hinder deep, efficient, and safe financial intermediation.

Brazil's financial system is large, yet government borrowing accounts for much of its size. Lower exposure of banks and institutional investors to government debt—linked to fiscal reform—would reduce Brazil's systemic risk. A lower share of government instruments, together with less directed credit and more efficient public banks would also reduce the high cost of financial intermediation (base rates and spreads) and the crowding out of private credit. Less financial sector taxation, including lower reserve requirements, would also reduce bank spreads. Improved resolution procedures for default and bankruptcy could further cut intermediation costs.

Less financial sector taxation and improved bankruptcy procedures would reduce bank spreads.

Much has been done to improve access to financial services, but they could be more evenly distributed geographically, with coverage especially increased in the North and Northeast. Small entrepreneurs rely heavily on retained earnings. Stronger capital markets and nonbank financial institutions could fill some of the financing gap. New technologies may expand services to small firms and firms in remote areas: although Internet banking is relatively advanced in Brazil, there is scope for improving connectivity and telephone charge structures. Expansion of microfinance could also improve financial access, as could attention to the infrastructure for financial services, especially creditor information systems and the framework for collateralized lending.

Strengthened by recent recapitalization, Brazil's federal banks nonetheless continue to face difficulties. How they evolve will critically affect their soundness and that of the rest of the financial system. Much vulnerability is related to directed credit, channeled largely through the federal bank system. Although sharply reduced in 2001, a large proportion of credit in the financial system (40 percent), especially for the housing and rural sectors, is subject to administered interest rates. In discharging their selective credit mandates, federal banks have accumulated problem portfolios. Much of this credit goes to clients who could borrow at market rates rather than to targeted clients. Focusing credit subsidies on appropriately qualified consumers rather than sectors could increase financial sector efficiency.

Is is recognized that public banks can improve efficiency with lower operating and overhead costs. Special programs provide low-cost funds for public banks through transfers from earmarked taxes, but direct transfers to these institutions to meet their government mandates would improve transparency. Solutions will differ for each institution, but defining a strategy and clear mandates for the federal banks will be important.

Brazil's capital markets have suffered a gradual decline over the last four to five years. Reducing transaction costs could help to bring back larger companies, which now seek financing abroad. Other options could be explored for smaller companies, which have been unable to tap into these markets. A reinvigorated securities market would enable Brazil's enormous pension funds to diversify their assets and reduce their problems of institutional risk, governance, and supervision.

Brazil has taken bold steps to strengthen the governance of listed companies and to extend the mandate of the securities commission (CVM). A larger budget and properly trained staff could help the CVM carry out its responsibilities. Its supervisory role could also be strengthened by greater information sharing with the Central Bank and by reform of appeals procedures that weaken its enforcement capacity. Updating minimum capital requirements for brokers and dealers and establishing criteria for greater transparency in order-flow and order-execution in secondary markets would also strengthen the regulatory and supervisory environment. Improving techniques of asset and risk man-

Focusing credit subsidies on qualified consumers rather than sectors could increase financial sector efficiency.

agement and reducing the concentration of government securities in the portfolios of institutional investors could improve the climate for capital markets. In addition, rules governing pension fund investment could be replaced by a "prudent professional" rule, and the institutional framework for pension fund regulation and supervision could be simplified, merging the multiple regulatory agencies and regimes for closed- and open-end funds.

The FAT–FGTS nexus: simplifying and weighing the interests of all

The historical complexity and the need for reform of Brazilian systems of tax, spending, and social policies is perhaps best exemplified by the intersection of policies governing labor markets, housing markets, directed credit, and social protection embodied in the PIS/PASEP (FAT)–FGTS system. This system forms an important part of both Brazilian government revenue and spending commitments. There is the undoubted value of many of the spending programs financed by the FAT and the FGTS. Yet, this nexus could benefit greatly from careful reform that weighs the interests of the many parts of Brazilian society touched by the FAT and the FGTS: all Brazilian formal sector workers, many of the unemployed, middle-class house buyers, recipients of subsidized lending from the National Bank for Economic and Social Development (BNDES), and many others.

Directed credit might be cut, but the role of BNDES could include co-financing, underwriting, bond purchases, and credit information.

FGTS, raised as a payroll tax, essentially requires workers in the formal sector to lend money to the government at an extremely low real interest rate (3 percent). Workers participating in the FGTS receive severance benefits in return, but the value of these benefits is less than the cost to them of their FGTS contributions. The FGTS is, in effect, a payroll tax that does not appear as government revenue. The proceeds are used as a source of funds to support the operations of Caixa Econômica Federal, the largest part of them being housing loans to middle-class families.

The FAT is financed from PIS/PASEP, cascading turnover taxes, 40 percent of which go directly to BNDES to subsidize various credit programs (such as the National Program to Strengthen Family Agriculture, PRONAF, and the Special Agency for Industrial Financing, FINAME). The remaining 60 percent is used to pay unemployment insurance benefits, *abono salarial*, and others such as PLANFOR and PROGER. The widely supported reform of PIS/PASEP into a less distorting tax (like a federal value-added tax) would address the cascading problem, but still leave the question of the optimal use of these resources.

For Caixa Econômica Federal, its past losses and its multiple and important roles mean that a decision regarding its new directions is crucial. A new housing finance strategy would be needed if Caixa were to change its involvement in housing loans. Caixa is already branching into new areas such as credit cards and ATMs, where it faces strong competition from other institutions. The final cost of its recent restructuring package could be among the world's largest, reflecting past credit decisions and loan non-recovery. As recognized, transforming Caixa into a successful bank requires deep reforms. Important steps have been taken during and after the 2001 restructuring. By successfully turning around its credit and collection practices through reforms, Caixa could avoid the consideration of other, more radical options, for example, to convert it into a more specialized bank, make it a government agency, or other options.

Net inflows from FAT/FGTS to BNDES are declining as employees who pay PIS/PASEP retire and become eligible for payouts. Hence, BNDES, the most successful and efficient of the public sector banks, might gradually start to rely more on market-based financing, which will mean higher lending rates. Today, a large part of BNDES low-cost funds are on-lent to other banks, including Banco do Brasil and private banks. BNDES has begun to transform itself from lender to cofinancier and is playing catalytic roles in project finance, underwriting, and (possibly in future) corporate bond markets. Such roles could help standardize private bond contracts and accelerate development of a secondary bond market. BNDES could also play a role in improving credit information by disseminating data on its own portfolio.

Regulation, infrastructure, and privatization

Regulatory agencies could incorporate clauses in concessions ensuring access for the poor to infrastructure services. Independent regulatory institutions should be capable of developing and enforcing effective regulations, monitoring industry structure and performance, resolving disputes, increasing transparency, and thus reducing investors' risks. Building on the successful experience of the telecommunications sector, regulatory agencies in energy, transport, and water could improve the designs of concessions, revising tariff structures and adjustment procedures, clarifying renegotiation rules, and incorporating clauses ensuring access and affordability for the poor. Long-distance training technologies also provide the opportunity to develop a corps of well-qualified and trained regulatory professionals.

Complementary policy options would be to improve the quality of public spending and promote private investment and finance in infrastructure. An effective strategy would strengthen the strategic planning process initiated with the Eixos study and the PPA, emphasizing spatial interactions, substitution effects, synergies, and efficiency and equity tradeoffs. It would also build up project finance capacities in sector ministries to support such a planning process and to develop pipelines of "bankable" projects that can be financed by capital markets with minimum public financial support. Such a strategy could pilot financial instruments such as guarantees, insurance, and incentives for pension funds, in order to attract or leverage private funding for infrastructure.

Efficient multimodal transport services would reduce firms' logistics costs, including inventory levels and related costs, and increase their productivity. Transport policies could focus on restoring federal and state highway networks to satisfactory condition through long-term, output-based contracts and, where feasible, concessions and decentralization. And the port reform could be completed by facilitating the retrenchment and redeployment of redundant personnel, delegating remaining federal ports to states and municipalities, promoting competition, and reforming customs clearance procedures. The recently established land and water transport regulatory agencies (ANTT and ANTAQ) can rapidly address a number of important regulatory issues. A pipeline of critical transport infrastructure projects could be developed, particularly for missing links and terminals to ensure intra- or inter-modal connectivity in major inter-regional corridors, with appropriate risk-mitigating instruments to promote private sector management and financing.

To avoid a new energy crisis and ultimately to provide universal access to fuels and reliable electricity service, public policies in energy could focus on several elements. The pricing system and contracting structure could be designed to restore incentives for reliable energy supply. Establishing efficient wholesale energy markets, improving governance of the system operator (ONS), and introducing effective competition in gas supply would also be important. An appeal mechanism for decisions would improve the regulatory agencies, which need to address market power arising from vertical integration. Successful energy conservation and demand management initiatives could be mainstreamed and a strategy for rural electrification and regulations could be developed to ensure affordable access for poor households.

Privatization of remaining public enterprises has slowed in Brazil, and support by the public is weak. Some tend to associate the tariff increases that result from the removal of subsidies with the privatization of state enterprises. Yet the two are conceptually distinct: subsidies may be provided to the private sector, and public firms may be run on a commercial basis. Privatization in telecommunications shows how competition, ensured by an appropriate regulatory environment, can bring great benefits to consumers. The main lesson here is that future privatizations entail first setting up the necessary regulatory institutions and ensuring that public sector monopolies do not retain either excess market power or undue political influence after privatization.

Taxation: reducing distortions to restore competitiveness

There is considerable agreement in Brazil about the urgency of tax reform, and there is the need for progress to achieve this. Part of the problem is clearly the large number of winners and losers from any meaningful reform. The system is complex—with revenue sharing among federal, state, and municipal governments; many earmarked taxes; and certain aspects enshrined in the constitution—that the feasibility and design of reform will always be highly political. An unwillingness to risk a decline in federal revenues during periods when the Brazilian economy was vulnerable to investor perceptions about fiscal sustainability also reduced reform momentum.

Nonetheless, there is broad agreement on some elements of desirable reform. Brazil will need to maintain high levels of taxation to generate the primary surpluses needed to reduce public debt. But the federal tax structure is dominated by two forms of distorting taxes that impose unnecessary costs on the economy, turnover taxes and payroll taxes. Turnover taxes account for roughly 30 percent of taxes (counting so-called contributions but excluding FGTS), including the PIS/PASEP and COFINS. The burden varies across and within sectors and across enterprises, depending on production structure and number of stages in the production process, distorting relative prices, input mixes, industrial concentration, and decisions on whether to outsource noncore business activities. Payroll taxes add to the cost of labor in the formal sector, creating an incentive to operate informally, with the losses of scale economies, access to credit markets, and other benefits that this implies. Payroll taxes, including social security contributions, the *salário educação*, and payroll training levies (the various "S" taxes), account for slightly over 25 percent of federal revenue.

The FGTS—although not considered a tax in federal accounting—also belongs in this group, since FGTS is a forced savings scheme. Although workers can withdraw their FGTS funds under certain conditions, FGTS accounts receive below market rates of return, so employees would be better off investing their FGTS contributions in private savings accounts. Because they cannot, the FGTS provides the same incentive to operate informally as the officially recognized payroll taxes.

One option considered would be to replace COFINS, PIS/PASEP, and perhaps the industrial products tax (IPI) with a federal valued-added tax (VAT). This would provide a broad-based source of indirect tax revenues, while eliminating the distortions caused by cascading taxes. Because the states already impose a VAT, there is some risk that a second, federal, VAT could raise the aggregate total VAT rate to excessive levels. This could be ameliorated by ensuring that the base of the federal VAT is as broad as possible and that it is supplemented by excise taxes on such products as tobacco and alcoholic beverages.

Alternatively, turnover taxes could be replaced by a broadened federal income tax. Personal and corporate income taxes account for only 25 percent of federal revenue. Despite administrative reforms in 1995–96, room remains to broaden the base of the tax. One option would be to lower the threshold for tax liability, now 1.3 times average income, excluding the vast majority of Brazilian wage earners. Deductions, many benefiting mostly higher income taxpayers, could also be reduced. Evasion could also be reduced. The income tax is largely raised through withholding. In 2001, individual filers accounted for less than 9 percent of personal income tax receipts. Recent Supreme Court decisions allow banking data generated by the tax on financial transactions (CPMF) to be used to track tax compliance. The federal government could increasingly exploit this opportunity.

Taxation at the state level is also a source of economic inefficiency. The ICMS, a VAT, accounts for 91 percent of state tax revenues. Brazil is unique in assigning a VAT to subnational governments. With 27 different VAT regimes, there are wide variations in rate structures, exemption policies, and administrative procedures, complicating compliance for firms with sales in more than one state. Perhaps the most pernicious effect of the ICMS system has been the fiscal wars between states, which have damaged the states' main source of revenue. The base of the tax has become concentrated on the relatively few goods and services for which administration is most straightforward, particularly fuel, power, and telecommunications. Since these are business inputs that many companies are unable to deduct fully from other tax liabilities, this reduces the competitiveness of Brazilian firms.

One option would be to federalize the ICMS and create uniform rates and exemptions throughout Brazil, reducing compliance costs. Proceeds could be distributed among the states on a basis other than origin, reducing interstate tax wars and tax exporting. Another option would be to leave tax administration at the state level but create uniform national rates and exemptions and a zero rate on interstate sales. In principle this would reduce interstate tax exporting, but in practice it could create a strong incentive for fraud. Proposals to address this issue through an interim federal tax on interstate sales may be difficult to implement.

One option would be to federalize the ICMS and create uniform rates and exemptions throughout Brazil.

Comprehensive ICMS reform is unlikely in the short term, due to the amount of revenue redistribution between states it would entail, so more modest reforms could be considered. A recently proposed constitutional amendment would have established nationally uniform rates for various classes of products (with only five rates), prohibited exemptions, and authorized a nationally uniform set of regulations. States could also reduce compliance costs by raising the threshold for ICMS tax liability. International experience shows that in most countries, 90 percent of VAT revenues are collected from the largest 10 percent of firms. This suggests that exempting small firms would not significantly reduce revenues. Critics have argued that exempting small firms would break the chain of tax credits and debits that is used to ensure compliance with the ICMS, but international evidence belies this claim. While the credit and debit system is a helpful adjunct to enforcement, experience suggests that it is not essential.

Boosting trade, foreign direct investment, and innovation

Some of the industrial sectors with the least foreign competition through import penetration have also experienced the lowest rates of productivity growth, as in other countries. And sectors with higher import penetration as a consequence of the tariff reductions
of the early 1990s have shown greater productivity gains (research has suggested that
1990s trade opening was responsible for a 6 percent increase in firms' total factor productivity). Brazil's trade opening has stalled in recent years as recessions have led Mercosul
members to negotiate a series of small tariff increases. There is little quantitative work on
nontariff barriers, but these too were significantly reduced in the early 1990s. Further tariff reductions everywhere will likely occur mainly in the context of multilateral negotiations. Any remaining nontariff barriers, meanwhile, such as customs inefficiency, may still
offer potential productivity gains.

Imports have two main effects on the economy. At the firm level, they subject Brazilian
industry to greater competition and provide cheaper or higher quality inputs to domestic
manufacturing, raising productivity (and consumer welfare). At the level of the economy,
they create short-term external financing needs. Their longer run microeconomic effect
works in the opposite direction, since raising productivity promotes exports. Yet the short-
run effect often dominates the discussion and justifies protectionist policies in many
countries, ignoring the long-run damage to productivity. In Brazil, this, together with
other factors, especially serious protectionism in countries to which Brazil exports, has
contributed to the low volume of trade (even considering Brazil's large size), the high elas-
ticity of the currency to the current account, and thus external vulnerability and low
growth.

Foreign direct investment (FDI) plays a similar microeconomic role, raising domestic
productivity by bringing more advanced technologies and managerial practices. Firm-level
studies of FDI emphasize the dynamic gains to the host country from parent companies'
continually upgrading technologies or production methods in their plants. But these gains
are much stronger when FDI is intended to develop exports and when frontier practices
are needed than when FDI is hoping to benefit from protected or monopolistic local markets. Many of the barriers to FDI in Brazil are related to the investment climate more generally. Removing restrictions on workers, technology transfer, foreign currency transactions, and ownership would help enable more export-oriented FDI.

Technology transfer to and from domestic companies is also important for Brazil's competitiveness but hindered by regulations originally intended to limit foreign exchange repatriations. Licensing, franchising, or leasing arrangements for technology must meet the approval of the patent office (INPI): without INPI's approval the Central Bank may not allow payment of royalties abroad. INPI may question the type and conditions of technology transfer, pricing arrangements and terms, royalty rates, and other details. There is also a 15 percent statutory rate of withholding tax on remittances of royalties on imported technology. Such restrictions are not necessary based on other country experiences, and Brazil could leave such agreements to the parties involved. Licensing or restrictions on payments would not be needed, nor would INPI need to enter the process.

Removing restrictions on workers, technology transfer, foreign currency transactions, and ownership would increase export-oriented FDI.

Foreign exchange transactions are regulated, as in many other countries. Exporters are not allowed to operate in foreign exchange. A foreign exchange contract with a Central Bank-approved bank must accompany export transactions, to prevent the exporter from having access to the foreign exchange proceeds of the sale. The move to a floating exchange rate has rendered many of these restrictions obsolete, and there may be gains from reevaluating restrictions limiting the freedom of Brazilian citizens and firms to deal in foreign exchange, while keeping in sight the macroeconomic benefits of limiting dollarization in the domestic financial system.

Finally, concern that Brazil's natural resource endowments may impede knowledge- and innovation-led productivity growth should be tempered by the experience of counter-examples such as Australia, Canada, Chile, Finland, and Sweden. Rather than hindering technological innovation, the combination of knowledge with natural resource endowments, human capital investment, and open trade policies is a potentially powerful engine of growth. Knowledge and natural resources are complements whose potential can best be unleashed through greater openness, continued negotiation to reduce barriers to exports, investment in human capital, and public-private R&D partnerships in natural resource-intensive sectors.

The link with macroeconomic stability

The effectiveness of the reforms outlined in this section will benefit heavily from continuing macroeconomic stability in the coming years, the topic of the next section. A healthy economy magnifies the effects of reforms on the investment climate.

Stability has been hard won in Brazil, and as discussed at the beginning of this section, its growth dividend has been perceived by many as disappointing. Yet if the main effect of stability is that it allows private sector agents to form reliable expectations, and ultimately to invest resources based on those expectations, some of the failure of Brazilian physical investment to respond to the new economic environment of the 1990s and 2000s is not so surprising. There are natural time lags before the private sector updates its assessment of economic uncertainty: investment will not resume the minute economic instability (inflation, for instance) is reduced. Stability has not yet adequately reduced investor uncertainty, as borne out by the devaluation in 1999 and the turbulence Brazil has experienced in 2002.

Meanwhile, strong dividends have come. Trade opening has increased Brazilian competitiveness: Brazilian productivity (measured as total factor productivity) during the late 1990s rose at rates comparable to those during the miracle years of the 1960s and 1970s. Private sector confidence in government management is also higher than ever before. Physical investment has yet to regain its past values as a proportion of GDP, however. For this, the reforms suggested in this section would need to be augmented by continued economic stability.

Options for spurring growth through productivity

Economic analysis is clear on the matter: productivity growth is the main long-run source of steady per capita income growth. Physical investment must be financed by savings (domestic or foreign), and in the absence of productivity growth a country's capital stock will not grow without bound. Similar reasoning applies to human capital. Only productivity growth—whether from technological progress or managerial improvements—allows sustained increases in living standards.

Raising the productivity of the poor is the most inclusive way to improve Brazil's income distribution. In urban and rural areas a common theme among those questioned by researchers is people's desire to raise themselves out of poverty through employment rather than assistance. Rural productivity growth also relieves the pressure to deplete natural resources for income and consumption. Finally, productivity growth is one of the keys to reestablishing economic stability. Rising productivity leads to growth that does not have to be financed from domestic or foreign savings and therefore does not threaten internal or external balance. Higher productivity typically leads to higher exports.

Based on the discussion in this section, a short list of policy options for pursuing sustainable economic growth in Brazil over the next few years would be the following:

- Continuing efforts to rein in the fiscal deficit through macroeconomic management, as discussed in the following section.
- Intensifying the campaign of "debureaucratization" of the business environment, with special focus on start-up firms and FDI.
- Reducing public sector directed credit in order to reduce banking spreads, increase financial sector competition, and expand competitively intermediated credit to the private sector.
- Eliminating or reducing turnover and payroll taxes, probably replacing them with a federal VAT.
- In the absence of root-and-branch tax reform, current proposals to reform PIS/PASEP are positive reforms.
- Pursuing bilateral, regional, and multilateral negotiations with the aim of lowering Brazil's as well as other countries' trade barriers and increasing trade and FDI flows with the rest of the world.

3. Stabilizing the economy

Table 3. Indicators for stabilizing the economy

Indicator	Brazil	Comparison		2010 target
		Latin America	Other	
Public debt to GDP, latest estimate[a] (%)	62	23 (Mexico, Chile)		50?
External debt to exports, 2000[b] (%)	344	78 (Mexico) 156 (Chile)		200?
Currency variation, minimum to maximum, April-Sept. 2002[c] (%)	57	15 (Chile) 9 (Mexico)		-
Share of foreign exchange-indexed long-term public debt, 2001[b] (%)	72		55 (Turkey)	Lower
Inflation, 2001[b] (CPI%)	6.9	3.6 (Chile) 6.4 (Mexico)		3.5

Sources: a BCB, b World Bank SIMA database, c Bloomberg.

Interwoven threads: fiscal and external sustainability

Brazil's ability to generate economic growth is conditioned by its level of public debt, which both limits the domestic financing available for private sector investment and exposes the economy to uncertainty about the government's ability to meet its financing needs, domestic and external. Domestic and external are related: nervousness at home over public debt sustainability widens spreads and affects foreign investors' perceptions of country risk and the exchange rate, which makes the (mainly private sector) external debt more expensive to finance.

Debt translates into what is often termed Brazil's vulnerability. Events outside the control of the government, such as world economic conditions or international investor perceptions, have a direct effect on Brazil's real economy through financing costs, exchange rates, domestic interest rates, and levels of (indexed) debt. The sensitivity of the economy to public management becomes amplified as, for example, a small deviation in public borrowing worsens public perceptions about debt sustainability, which raises borrowing costs and in turn makes it harder to control the debt, confirming market fears. In the extreme cases, the initial shock may simply come from worsening perceptions about Brazil, which then become self-fulfilling. Fluctuations in the exchange rate or the current account (and related market perceptions) behave in the same way. Much debate in Brazil has revolved around how to reduce this dual vulnerability of the fiscal and external accounts.

How might success in this pursuit of stability be defined? A useful indicator of success in reducing vulnerability would be investment grade status with the main credit rating agencies, a position recently achieved by Mexico. Such a rating would reduce Brazil's vulnerability to events outside its control to the level where joint debt and currency crises would be very unlikely.

A useful indicator of success in reducing vulnerability would be investment grade status with the main credit rating agencies.

Credibility: the importance of consistent signals

Brazil's economy has progressed vastly since the chaos of asset freezes and rampant inflation of the early 1990s. What has made the difference? Three sets of changes: trade opening, inflation reduction, and fiscal control.

First, the early 1990s saw trade opening through the steep reduction in tariffs and non-tariff barriers. Brazil's trade volumes increased, but the impact on the trade balance was not positive for a number of reasons. The exchange rate was maintained at overvalued rates in the mid-1990s as part of the strategy to eliminate inflation. Brazil's terms of trade worsened owing to commodity price movements throughout the 1990s. And the real economy still contained many impediments to improved export performance, mainly in the form of over-regulation and bottlenecks in finance and infrastructure. Exports grew at 5.8 percent a year from 1990 to 2000 (while GDP grew at 2.7 percent) after growing at 4.5 percent a year from 1980 to 1990 (with GDP growth of only 1.6 percent). Imports rose too. From 1993 to 1996 the current account moved from approximate balance to a deficit of about 4 percent of GDP, where it remained until recently (depreciation has caused it to fall). Consequently, although Brazil's trade flows with the rest of the world have increased relative to the size of its economy, other factors have prevented the reduction in external vulnerability that might otherwise have been expected from this openness.

It has also been suggested in Brazil that the nation's trade opening was disorderly in that certain industries suffered severe recessions as a consequence of sudden exposure to foreign competition. But industry-level data do not support this hypothesis very strongly. Recent World Bank research and much work in Brazil suggest that increased imports have had a significant positive impact on the competitiveness of the industries most exposed to foreign competition. Whatever the consensus on this question, however, the focus here is forward looking, and the question of the precise ordering of the 1990s reforms may not be central to today's macroeconomic concerns.

Second, the use of a nominal exchange rate anchor during the Real Plan succeeded in eliminating inflationary expectations from the Brazilian economy. The fact that expectations changed made the reduction of inflation itself in 1993–94 a sustainable reduction. There was a cost: high interest rates—and government borrowing to pay them—kept the nominal anchor in place until January 1999, when Brazil floated its currency. Partly as a consequence, the debt to GDP ratio rose from 25 percent in 1993 to 53 percent at the end of 2001, although fiscal skeletons (previously unaccounted-for government liabilities) and the refinancing of the states contributed to the increase.

Third, to reconcile the need for fiscal restraint with Brazil's historical lack of control over the states' finances, the Fiscal Responsibility Law of 2000 gave the federal government greater legal control over the nation's consolidated fiscal position. The law has been a great success and has underlined the central importance (given Brazil's vulnerability to perceptions of its likely future performance) of credibility.

In the short run, the primary surplus serves as the main variable to build credibility on debt sustainability.

Credibility may be broadly defined as the confidence of lenders in the authorities' willingness and ability to manage the economy successfully, here meaning the government's ability to repay the money paid by lenders for its bonds. Credibility or its absence then become manifest in interest rate spreads, exchange rates, inflation expectations, and ultimately economic growth rates.

Credibility in this sense is built through clear signals about future actions and their intended effects. Meeting inflation targets builds credibility, as did Brazil's well-managed response to the 2001 energy crisis. With respect to debt sustainability, the key variable that the government controls is the primary surplus, and thus the best way of building fiscal credibility is by focusing on this variable, adjusting the target when necessary in response to events and achieving it. A secondary source of credibility is transparency with

regard to previously unaccounted-for government liabilities, such as hidden pension liabilities in publicly owned companies or underperforming assets in public banks. Given
the sensitivity of debt sustainability calculations for Brazil, credibility of this kind is an
intangible asset with very tangible returns in the form of lower public sector financing
costs. The importance of several components of Brazilian macroeconomic policy: the
PPA, the Fiscal Responsibility Law, inflation targeting, and a healthy degree of central
bank independence, are all best understood in this light.

Social security and fiscal responsibility

It is recognized that the main source of fiscal risks resides in Brazil's social security system,
particularly that of its civil servants, which with its 100 percent replacement ratios and
early retirement options is more generous than the system in any OECD country and
imposes a cost of 4 percent of GDP on public finances on a cash basis.

For Brazil as a whole, payments to inactive (retired) staff made up a third of all personnel costs in 2000 and 2001. The problem is severest in several states of the South and Southeast, where retirees make 38 to 50 percent of the wage bill. The RJU employment regime for public sector workers, protected in the 1988 Constitution, makes it impossible for most states to contemplate salary increases for existing personnel without putting themselves on a collision course with the Fiscal Responsibility Law, since in a few years they would either fail to meet constitutionally obligatory pension payments (linked to the salaries of active personnel) or fail to observe the Fiscal Responsibility Law. Since the law itself is the cornerstone of Brazil's fiscal cred- ibility, a strong signal on the country's willingness to tackle the social security burden is the most logical next step in reinforcing credibility and reducing financing costs and vulnerability. Comprehensive social security reform will no doubt be a slow process of consensus building for Brazil, but signaling clear intentions to tackle the system's imbalances is a priority. The main gains would be domestic—most holders of Brazilian public debt instruments are domes- tic financial institutions—but there is no doubt that the benefits would be felt on the external side as well, not least through increased national saving and reduced external financing require- ments as public pension liabilities were reduced.

Signaling clear intentions to tackle the social security system's imbalances is a priority.

Chile's successful reform is similar in spirit to the social security predicament Brazil faces in the RJU, and provides an illustrative example. Chileans traded high and uncertain obligations for lower but serviceable ones.

Making government spending more flexible

Social security is not the only category of public spending that is rigidly set and constitutionally guaranteed. Under current arrangements, there is little additional scope for the government to cut public spending, should this become necessary from a macroeconomic point of view, without either changing the Constitution or decimating basic social services. The logical response would be to introduce more budget flexibility in areas where spending is less essential, while preserving essential spending, thereby increasing the overall quality of public spending.

To retain some flexibility in public expenditure, the extension of the Fiscal Stabilization Fund (DRU, which expires in 2003) is probably necessary. This constitutional amendment allows 20 percent of net tax revenues to be excluded from distribution to states and municipalities. With an increase of this proportion to, for instance, 30 percent, total government saving could rise by up to 1.4 percent of GDP.

The primary surplus: paying down debt and winning confidence

Redesigning the social security system and building more flexibility into other forms of public spending may take time. But Brazil's macroeconomic progress is an immediate priority. In the short run, therefore, the government can focus only on variables that it controls over the immediate horizon, the most important being the primary surplus. This would be complemented by policies with important, but indirect effects on fiscal sustainability, including policies to improve the quality of spending and taxes and the public sector balance sheet, policies to support growth of incomes and exports, and policies that would allow interest rates to fall over time.

Recent events have shown that especially under adverse conditions, adequately high primary surpluses are needed to stabilize Brazil's debt, given current growth rates, exchange rates, sovereign spreads, and debt level and composition. Part of the solution lies in increasing growth rates (primarily through increasing productivity, given the limited scope for increasing the quantity of investment), discussed in the previous section. But Brazil's structural growth rate (the rate consistent with sustainability in the external accounts) will change only slowly. For this reason, and acknowledging that the scope for revenue generation and spending cuts is narrow, the primary surplus could continue to be the key variable within the government's control.

The buyers of Brazil's sovereign bonds, whether in Brazil or abroad, understand this well, and hence the signaling role of the primary surplus. There is thus a long-run relationship in post-Plano Real Brazil between the primary balance, spreads, and the debt ratio (figure 8 shows that this relationship was one of the main distinguishing features between Argentina and Brazil). With debt held constant, an increase in spreads accompanies a decrease in the surplus. Using this relationship at current values suggests the continued importance of pursuing an adequately high primary surplus in order to achieve investment-grade spreads of, say, about 500 basis points over risk-free assets such as US Treasury Bonds.

Figure 8. Public debt ratios and primary balances in Argentina and Brazil

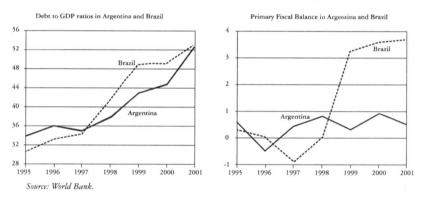

Source: World Bank.

A further worry is the world economic environment in the immediate future, which may not be favorable to Brazilian economic growth or external financing, with security concerns dominating the scene. Brazil's fiscal posture should be prudently defensive in this setting.

Brazil could seek savings in public pensions, subnational transfers, higher education, health insurance, and subsidized directed credit.

Where could further savings come from? A significantly higher aggregate tax burden is unlikely and would harm productivity unless raised extremely efficiently: Brazil's tax burden is already higher than those in most middle-income countries. And clearly Brazil does not have many options for cutting spending, and constitutional changes will be needed. The main areas where spending could be cut with strong political leadership are public pensions, subnational transfers (DRU), university education, health insurance, and the FAT–FGTS through a decline in the amount of subsidized directed credit through the public banking sector.

Reducing vulnerability through debt management

Brazilian public debt is mostly domestic (the ratio of domestic to external debt is 4:1), has short maturity and duration, and is biased toward indexed debt. Debt management in Brazil has successfully increased the maturity and duration of public debt significantly (figure 9). If external conditions permit, two further opportunities for improvement may arise. First is debt composition (duration and indexation); second is the link with financial structure.

Figure 9. Average maturity and duration of domestic public debt

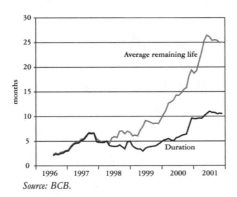

Source: BCB.

At present, there is no market for Real-denominated securities beyond a 24-month horizon. Lengthening debt maturity reduces rollover risk (the risk of going to the market to roll over a large debt volume when interest rates are high or the market is thin) and reduces exposure to short-term interest rate fluctuations (which also makes monetary policy more credible). Credibility about the stability of the economy influences rates on Brazilian long-term bonds relative to the typical term premia: this has made shorter maturities a cost-minimizing debt strategy. Brazil has been balancing these considerations in its debt management.

Indexation can help in a situation of incomplete credibility. Increased economic uncertainty in 2001 made lengthening Brazil's public debt profile harder, and longer term debt was increasingly linked to the dollar or the overnight interest rate. This holds the debt to GDP ratio hostage to the real interest rate and the real exchange rate. Ultimately, it may be worth paying the price of lengthening the maturity of public debt without indexation.

Diversifying public debt towards fixed coupons, reducing concentration in the banking sector, and reforming the role of public banks may combine to cut vulnerability.

One option, some suggest, is issuing longer term bonds with put options (allowing the creditor to redeem the bond before the maturity date). Borrowers who expect declining spreads use put options to lengthen debt without paying the market premium. Unlike floating instruments, the cost of bonds with a put option does not move with short-term interest rates. Such bonds do carry the risk that, if they expire during a crisis, the cost of debt service will increase. But they have been used recently by emerging markets in contexts similar to Brazil's. A second option, one that may increase credibility in the short term and has already been introduced by Brazil, is inflation-linked debt instruments.

Public debt relates to financial structure in two ways. First, Brazilian public debt is concentrated in just a few players (three banks and seven mutual funds hold well over 50 percent of government debt). This concentration raises issues about possible collusion over price setting, rollover risk (the buyers are subject to similar shocks), and moral hazard (bargaining power from the potential to transmit systemic shocks to the economy may lead buyers to assume greater risks knowing they can demand rescue).

Second, through the actions of public banks, the public sector absorbs the credit risk of private sector economic agents. This leads to higher public debt, whether through repeated capital injections or direct subsidies. Limiting the role of public banks and enhancing their risk-monitoring effectiveness will reduce public exposure to private sector risk and in turn reduce banking spreads.

These interactions increase the gains from acting on three fronts sequentially: diversifying debt issuance (when possible) toward fixed coupon instruments, reducing concentration in the banking sector, and reforming the role of public banks. First, fiscal surpluses and central bank autonomy signal credibility and reduce perceived default risk, term premia, and thus the cost of changing the debt composition. Next, the central bank may alter the debt composition toward longer maturities and away from indexation to short-term interest and exchange rates. Since monetary stabilization has now broken price-indexation habits, the issuance of inflation-indexed debt may further strengthen the credibility of inflation targeting by raising the costs to the sovereign of inflation. Nonetheless, the change in debt composition would probably raise financing costs initially. But in time the new debt composition would reduce risk in public sector finances and free monetary and exchange rate policy from fiscal dominance.

Inflation: the anti-poor tax

The alternative to more aggressive fiscal and debt management, in the absence of a sudden upturn in the external environment or in productivity, is higher inflation. Allowing inflation to rise again in Brazil would have many undesirable consequences. As is recognized, it would hurt the poor.

Recent work by various authors has shown quite clearly that the elimination of inflation in Brazil in the early part of the Real Plan led to a significant and sustained reduction in the number of people living below the poverty line. Poverty, measured using the annual household survey (PNAD) and the indigence line defined by the Brazilian Institute of Geography and Statistics (IBGE), fell by about 10 percentage points between 1993 and 1995, as inflation was cut and a consumption boom occurred. Further poverty cuts were not apparent after 1995, but the 1993–95 gains remained. This decline in poverty is not explained by the economic growth rates of the period, which while healthy were not extraordinary. There is some evidence that they were associated with a real increase in the minimum wage in May 1995. Whether the increase in the minimum wage was a driving factor, there is little question that this progress could not have been made (and consolidated) without the elimination of chronic inflation.

An external focus: export promotion and import substitution

Within Brazil there are differing views of the current macroeconomic challenge that have wide currency. One view emphasizes fiscal aggregates as the main target variable, implying attention to the signaling value of the primary surplus, recognition and reduction of public liabilities, and greater flexibility in public spending. This view acknowledges the problems of external vulnerability but stresses cutting the current account deficit essentially through the increase in public saving implied by the strong fiscal position.

Another view sees the external sector as the main constraint on growth. In this view, by explicitly pursuing exports, Brazil could raise the GDP growth rate without generating current account imbalances and then address fiscal imbalances with fewer difficult choices to make about cuts in public spending. Looking back, this view emphasizes the buildup of external liabilities (including those implicit in FDI) in the 1990s as today's primary weakness. Looking forward, it suggests policies focused on the current account, and more specifically the trade balance. Some go further and call for a more proactive industrial policy to target higher exports. The seeming attraction of this approach is that, conceptually at least, it solves Brazil's macro imbalances through a less austere fiscal policy than an immediate policy focus on the primary surplus.

There are two main qualifications, however. First, certain policies that target exports per se can be costly and ineffective. Second, as noted above, a shorter route to cutting the current account deficit associated with a given growth rate is to raise public saving, that is, cut the fiscal deficit. (The economy could also raise private saving, but there are few simple or advisable policy prescriptions that reliably achieve increases in private saving).

Export policies come in at least four forms. First, and perhaps most significant for Brazil, is the tax system. Brazil's tax system, discussed in the previous section but revisited here as it pertains to exports, certainly introduces an anti-export bias. Second comes the regime of tariffs and nontariff barriers. Brazil's import tariffs are lower than during the early 1990s but remain high by international standards, although tariffs probably do not affect exports directly through costs because drawback arrangements work well. But there may be harder to measure, longer run productivity effects. Third, Brazil, like most countries, has dedicated public institutions to promote exports: the Special Program for Exports (PEE) within the Chamber of Foreign Trade; the Foreign Trade Secretariat (SECEX) within the Ministry for Development, Industry, and Trade; and the Export Promotion Agency (APEX). Fourth, public and private sector institutions may offer a

variety of instruments for trade finance: in Brazil they mostly come from the public sector financial institutions (Banco do Brasil and BNDES).

Parts of Brazil's tax system function smoothly with respect to exports, causing little
or no distortion. Duty drawback arrangements work well to neutralize import tariff
costs (with the new electronic drawback increasing accessibility for small and medium-
size enterprises). The system of earning export credits against the industrial production
value-added tax (IPI) is also reported to operate smoothly without impeding exports.
Exporters do encounter problems with the state sales tax (ICMS) export credits, however. States tend to make the ICMS credit hard for firms to obtain because states face
fiscal constraints and do not benefit directly from raising foreign exchange through
exporting. Large exporters accumulate high, nontransferable ICMS credit balances with
certain states. And the cascading effect of the ICMS implies that in practice it finds its
way into the cost structure of many exports, despite the theoretical possibility of credits. The same is true for the federal financial transactions tax (CPMF), and the
COFINS and PIS/PASEP sales taxes, which are levied on firms. As the share of these
taxes in federal revenues has increased, so has the size of the anti-export bias, adding as
much as 7 percent to ex-factory costs in cases where intermediate product exemptions
are not obtained.

Brazil's three main public programs or agencies aiming to promote exports—PEE,
SECEX, and APEX– perform well by international standards. SECEX has developed an
Internet gateway for exporters, an export awareness program within *Avança Brasil,* and
information technology analytical tools. The PEE helps define government export policy
(including taxes, anti-dumping measures, customs policies, and international trade negotiation), follows up on implementation, and disseminates information. APEX pursues
active export support at the firm level and, despite its youth (founded 1998), reports success in generating first sales from trade fairs. Despite these achievements, experience suggests realism about the export stimulation through active public policy. Few trade promotion organizations have had significant impacts on national exports (Australia,
Finland, Ireland, New Zealand, and Singapore are often cited as the most successful), and
these organizations are no substitute for an appropriate macroeconomic and regulatory
framework.

Similar remarks apply for trade finance. The main program here, Banco do Brasil's
PROEX, reached 4 percent of active exporters in 2000 or about 15 percent of exports by
value. Although Banco do Brasil has increased the number of firms reached by trade

finance, broader financial constraints will limit its expansion and trade finance will remain a highly rationed form of credit for some time to come.

Exports are crucial. At the same time, relying on special export incentives is not a reliable remedy for closing Brazil's external and fiscal imbalances. Exports, much like economic growth, are not an aggregate variable directly controlled by the government. Even with international best practice, the effects on exports of tax reform, export promotion, and increased trade finance, while positive, will be uncertain, limited, and perhaps slow. This is in contrast with relying on fiscal arithmetic, which, while undoubtedly difficult politically, is composed of aggregate variables more closely under government control.

Special export incentives need to remain fiscally neutral and are not a reliable remedy for Brazil's external and fiscal imbalances.

If exports represent a difficult target for public policy, imports may seem a surer alternative, subject as they are to active policies of import substitution such as selective quotas and tariffs. Here too caution is warranted. Despite the lure of infant industry arguments for protective tariffs applied to specific industries, international experience is that these programs become subject to political capture by powerful industry lobbies (not necessarily those to whom the arguments for protection best apply). Their long-term effect often has been to create inefficient industries surviving by influence peddling behind state-erected protection. Recent farm and steel policy in the United States amply illustrates the problem. Long-run productivity is served by avoiding such traps.

A further argument against targeting imports is that this strategy could increase external vulnerability rather than reduce it, as intended. First, imports (particularly of capital goods) embody technological progress. Cutting them may therefore slow productivity growth directly. Second, imports represent competition for domestic industries. Cutting them may therefore slow productivity growth indirectly, by encouraging uncompetitive managerial practices. In the long run, these effects will combine to reduce productivity growth and thus, in particular, the level of growth compatible with a sustainable current account. Moreover, with lower overall trade flows, the sensitivity of the trade balance to the exchange rate will also likely be lower, and this increases the vulnerability of the economy to external shocks such as fluctuations in terms of trade or in world demand for Brazilian exports. An undue focus on imports may therefore turn out to be self-defeating.

This discussion highlights an approach for external vulnerability: the combination of domestic productivity growth with domestic saving. Productivity growth drives export growth and reduces the need for foreign currency, and it is best pursued through the horizontal policies outlined earlier. Domestic saving also reduces the need for foreign currency, and is, in turn, most sensitive to the government's fiscal position.

Options for ensuring economic stability

The value of macroeconomic stability is increasingly emphasized in Brazil, vulnerable as the economy is to interest rate and exchange rate shocks. Investment-grade rating has sometimes been used as shorthand for macroeconomic stability, a well-defined objective that Brazil could reach with deep reforms. But stability also serves equity and sustainability. In the long-run, an investment grade Brazil would have more resources to invest in its people. The inequitable inflation tax is one of the greatest risks inherent in unsustainable macroeconomics. Social sustainability—reductions in crime, for example—would also improve in an investment-grade Brazil. The capacity to invest in the public institutions that manage resources and protect the environment would be greater. As recognized, the prospects for social progress, redistribution, opportunities for the excluded, and employment would be greater with macroeconomic stability.

Based on the discussion in this section, a short list of policy options for maintaining long-term macroeconomic stability in Brazil would be the following:

- Legislating a forward-looking transition rule to reduce the government's liabilities in the social security system.
  - One long-run option would be to unify the general and the special regimes (RGPS of CLT and RPPS of RJU), and complement the unified public and mandatory pay-as-you-go system with private fully-funded systems.
- Achieving an adequately high primary fiscal surplus by building flexibility into public spending (extending the DRU and reducing earmarking and constitutionally guaranteed spending) and seeking possible spending reductions in subnational transfers, higher education, health insurance, and subsidized directed credit.
- Institutionalizing Central Bank autonomy to increase monetary policy effectiveness, and maintaining the commitment to inflation targets.
- Continuing efforts to reduce indexation to interest rates and exchange rates in the debt composition, and gradually lengthening maturities (recognizing that this would entail costs and that the Central Bank's ability to pursue the strategy would

be limited by market conditions). Inflation-linked bonds may enhance credibility.

• Promoting export policies that respect the basic test that they are fiscally neutral and productivity enhancing.

4. Delivering government services to all

Table 4. Indicators for the delivery of government services

Indicator	Brazil	Comparison		2010 target
		Latin America	OECD	
Government effectiveness indicator (rank), 2000/2001	-0.27 (89 of 159)	Chile: 1.13 (23) Mex.: 0.28 (59)	Spain: 1.57 (14) USA: 1.58 (12)	-
Control of corruption indicator (rank), 2000/2001	-0.02 (70 of 160)	Chile: 1.40 (17) Mex.: -0.28 (82)	Spain: 1.45 (16) USA: 1.45 (15)	-
Voice and accountability indicator (rank), 2000/2001	0.53 (57 of 173)	Chile: 0.63 (52) Mex.: 0.12 (73)	Spain: 1.15 (27) USA: 1.24 (23)	-

Sources: World Bank Institute Governance Unit. Rankings can range from –2.5 to +2.5, higher is better.

Reducing inequity and exclusion

Brazilian inequity is a legacy of its history and has roots such as the Northeastern sugar economy. Efforts to reduce inequity have increased in recent years, but progress has been mixed. On one hand, many social indicators have improved markedly since the early 1990s: illiteracy fell from 19.1 percent to 13.3 percent between 1991 and 2000, for instance. On the other hand, income inequality, as measured by annual household surveys and decadal census, has remained unchanged for at least 20 years.

Inequity goes hand in hand with social exclusion, a problem requiring deeper remedies than simply redistributing income or improving access to public services. The poor repeatedly cite their participation in decisions and empowerment over their own affairs as some of their most pressing concerns. The first step in reducing exclusion is to be aware of how it acts. Exclusion may be obvious, as in residential racial segregation (supported by discrimination in housing), or it may be more subtle, as in discrimination in job promotions. Even where there may be a completely objective test for access, such as in university entrance examinations, the accumulated burden of substandard schooling in poor neighborhoods and the high cost of college-preparatory courses effectively exclude many non-whites from higher education, for instance.

This broader vision of the reforms needed for social inclusion leads to consideration of public participation, transparency in public decisions, and consultation with civil society. All are ways in which government can enhance its delivery of health, education, transfers, infrastructure, and crime prevention and more profoundly increase the inclusion of the least privileged in society and their empowerment to improve their lives.

Race and exclusion

Brazil's racial heterogeneity, combined with diffuse boundaries between racial groups, have led many to label Brazil a racial democracy. Yet it is noted that race plays a significant role in determining opportunities in Brazil in employment, education, housing, and other areas, something increasingly recognized in public discourse. Controlling for education, race-related income differences are lower in Brazil than in the United States, as an example. But absolute differences in income between blacks and whites are large (mainly caused by education differentials). Furthermore, there is evidence that social mobility is lower, controlling for education and other characteristics, among blacks. This last observation suggests that unobserved ability may be less rewarded by markets in Brazil: racial discrimination is the most likely explanation.

Education and labor markets seem to be the major sources of racial exclusion.

Further work is needed to understand these phenomena and develop appropriate policy responses, but labor market discrimination and the causes of race-related differentials in educational achievement appear to be sensible places to begin. Brazil has already mandated racial quotas in hiring in some federal agencies, and there are proposals to use quotas in university admissions. However, quotas have at least two drawbacks: one is that they can produce backlash and polarization caused by reverse discrimination. Another is that a racial test is difficult to apply in Brazil since the society is not divided into conventional race-based social categories as in some other countries.

Other countries have been able to deal with racial inequality once they recognized that it exists. Countries like South Africa, the United States, and several Eastern European countries have begun the hard task of dismantling the discrimination that prevents some of their citizens from becoming fully productive members of society. Recent debates show that the existence of racial discrimination is increasingly being ackowledged in Brazil.

Public sector governance and transparency

When asked, poor people often complain that government institutions do not represent their interests or hear their concerns. Dwellers of Novo Horizonte, a favela in Itabuna (BA) reported to the authors of a recent World Bank study, Voices of the Poor, that institutions such as the police and municipal health services, while important, seemed discourteous and uninterested in solving their problems. A comparison of Brazil's public sector with that of countries at similar stages of development suggests that Brazil scores fairly well on measures of democracy such as "voice and accountability," on "political stability and political violence," but not so well on "government effectiveness," or on "rule of law" (or on "regulatory quality," discussed in section 3).

These rankings suggest that measures to enhance social inclusion could center around public service delivery (including the rule of law; protection from crime is discussed in section 2). An excellent measure taken by a few states (Bahia and Goiás, for example) has been to group many government services together in one-stop shops staffed by service-oriented staff. The quality of state and municipal services in Brazil could be improved by making institutions more results-oriented before undertaking major organizational restructuring. Organizational performance targets in the next PPA are one option, realigning the internal structures of ministries and agencies to fit their objectives and specifying clear performance standards. The debureaucratization program could be deepened, linking it to transparency measures and providing citizens with mechanisms for recommending improvements and seeking redress for improper treatment. There may be room for more systematic dissemination of innovative approaches to improving service delivery (such as the one-stop shops) to promote demonstration effects among states and municipalities. There may also be a greater role for federal certification (with technical assistance) of municipalities (as in the health sector).

Debureaucratization could be deepened and linked to transparency measures to provide citizens with mechanisms for recommending improvements.

One place where problems of access remain acute is the justice system. Further research is needed to understand the structure of judicial outcomes, but experience in more developed countries suggests that avenues to include greater automation (with training), enhanced performance monitoring and planning, demand management strategies (such as reducing multiple appeal opportunities), enhanced judicial enforcement powers, and reforms to administrative law defining the civil and administrative roles of government agencies.

Participation of stakeholders in public decisions is most important when the decisions are not wholly technocratic (central banks do not generally ask the views of the man or woman on the street when setting inflation targets), and when government information about stakeholders and their preferences is imperfect (typically the case in such instances as local infrastructure). Participation also increases the public's knowledge about government projects and the allocation of resources, reducing the scope for fraud and inefficiency.

Social assistance: efficient and impartial delivery

Social assistance programs may also be an instrument for increasing social inclusion, and in this area Brazil has been an innovator and world leader. Programs like Bolsa Escola (and Progresa in Mexico) have proved effective in increasing school attendance, notably in Brazil's case with a relatively small cost per child.

Recent analysis, modeling household educational decisions, has suggested ex ante that Bolsa Escola may have encouraged attendance by up to a third of children ages 10–15 who were outside of school. It will be interesting to see such ex ante modeling followed up with ex post program evaluation. A careful evaluation of Bolsa Escola and programs like it is vital: further analysis may suggest modifications, such as scaling payment with age, with higher payments for older children reflecting the higher opportunity cost of their time in labor markets.

A note of caution: while a R$15 transfer per child per month sounds small, the aggregate impact of the program on many poor rural communities has been quite large, particularly since many are small-scale agricultural economies where many transactions have been nonmonetary. (The same monetizing effect on rural communities has been noted with the *previdência rural*, the rural pension). The program places responsibility for identifying beneficiaries with the mayor, and this implies significant discretionary power. Anecdotal evidence suggests that in some places this power has been used to reinforce clientelistic politics. As the program gains maturity, and possibly is modified and broadened, evidence in this direction would suggest designing more objective ways of assigning beneficiaries. Such methods are widely applied in Colombian social programs, for example. Mexico's Progresa involves the federal government fielding surveys and identifying beneficiaries.

Valuing the assets of the poor: the urban space

The urban poor depend most on actions in the public sphere to protect their assets. Law and order, discussed earlier, is a fundamental public good of obvious relevance in urban areas. Many of the urban poor rely on public transportation to get to and from work and to visit family. Water and air pollution and their health consequences are predominantly urban problems, and they affect the poor most. And in peripheral urban areas many poor people do not have secure property rights to their land and housing, with consequences for their ability to participate in credit and even some labor markets.

Hernando de Soto has estimated that in many developing countries up to 80 percent of assets are in the form of land and buildings (even in the United States this percentage is estimated to be greater than 50). And land and housing is much more valuable to its owner when it is clearly registered and titled. Housing policy for the urban poor has thus become a priority in Brazil.

Urban housing and land markets are impeded from equitable functioning by the lack of vacant land suitable for development and of adequate infrastructure to serve vacant land. Urban plans are often restrictive, with excessive zoning and subdivision standards, and competition is limited in the housing industry for middle- and low-income markets. All of these problems lead to the continued growth of informal settlements.

Federal housing programs might become matching grant schemes for states and municipalities and include NGOs for urban upgrading.

Reforming local master planning, subdivision regulations, building codes, and zoning ordinances might improve land use and increase the supply of land for low-income housing to arrest the growth of informal settlements. Local upgrading programs could put more emphasis on tenure and registration. Federal housing programs might become matching grant schemes for states and municipalities and include NGOs for urban upgrading.

Public transport systems constitute a further asset that is important to the poor and that contributes to the value of land and housing assets when markets are functioning well. Here the needs of medium-size cities are particularly acute. Brazil has more than 30 cities (excluding state capitals) with populations between 250 000 and 1.5 million, represented by such places as Campinas and Santos (SP), Niterói and Campos (RJ), Juiz de Fora (MG), and Petrolina (PE), and their population growth rates are among the highest in Brazil. With growth comes demand for housing, water, sanitation, waste management, and urban transport. Timely investments can avoid more expensive retrofitting in future (see also "water" in section 6).

Curitiba, a medium-size city, is world-famous for its integrated approach to urban and transport planning. A 1992 study by the International Institute of Energy Conservation showed that Curitiba achieved a 28 percent shift from car use to bus use, and the city now has the cleanest air of all Brazilian cities. Despite the second highest rate of car ownership after Brasília, Curitiba has less congestion owing to a 75 percent public transport share (it is 57 percent in Rio de Janeiro and 45 percent in São Paulo). Curitiba experienced 4 percent annual growth in the 1970s and 1980s, one of the highest growth rates among Brazilian cities, but the city planned for future transport needs by acquiring rights of way. Curitiba's planning was pragmatic and incremental, and its regulatory framework insulated the process from political manipulation. Curitiba's poor spend about 10 percent of income on transport, which is half the national average. And Curitiba has shown the feasibility of public-private partnerships: Volvo invested in its bus service.

Valuing the assets of the poor: the rural space

The rural poor live from the land, or from services related to agriculture, and therefore land and natural resources play the most important role for them, in addition to their own human capital. The 1996 Agricultural Census shows 4.5 million rural households with insufficient land for subsistence; these households are likely to be home to almost all of the 16.5 million rural poor in Brazil. Research in the Northeast shows that family farms can be more efficient and labor-intensive than large farms: skewed landholding depresses agricultural productivity and employment. Economic distortions, which historically fostered land concentration (agricultural subsidies, inflation, tax incentives), were removed in the 1990s, reducing the financial attractiveness of holding land for nonproductive purposes. The supply of available land then increased and its price fell, especially in the Northeast.

Brazil has made progress in improving the distribution of land ownership and securing property rights for poor landowners. The federal government developed the *Cédula da Terra* project in five Northeastern states in response to a successful 1996 pilot in Ceará: *Cédula da Terra* will close at end-2002 with 17,000 families settled on 442,000 hectares at an average cost of R$4,900 per family (R$190 per hectare). The program has already been followed up with the 14-state *Crédito Fundiário*. Both programs target lands not subject to expropriation (thus working alongside traditional nonmarket approaches), and self-selection targets the poorest landless. Community associations identify suitable lands, negotiate their purchase with willing sellers, and receive a grant for on-farm investments: acquisition usually takes about 90 days. Most acquired properties have been small relative to traditional land reform, with group size in practice of 15–30 families, and communities have consistently bought good land more cheaply than under expropriation. Most subprojects promise financial viability: in more favorable regions returns are likely to exceed initial estimates, while in the Sertão returns depend on water access. Family incomes are expected to rise two- to four-fold from a typical income of R$1,400 per year within three to six years, net of loan repayment (which appears likely, though strong management information systems and continuous evaluation are critical).

Social inclusion through participation has increasingly helped federal initiatives to devolve responsibilities to local authorities throughout the 1990s, and there is now greater optimism about rural development programs. The challenge is to expand coverage and integrate commercial activities, land reform, natural resources management, and education. In the Northeast, Rural Poverty Alleviation projects (PCPR) have been successful in delivering funds to poor rural communities for infrastructure and services.

A challenge is to incorporate commercial activities into community-driven rural projects.

The core institutional feature of these projects is the Municipal Council (FUMAC), with 80 percent of members from the community and 20 percent from the municipal authorities. These councils establish priorities, approve community proposals, and monitor and supervise execution. A more decentralized variant (FUMAC-P) manages its own budget based on an approved annual operating plan. In 1993–2000, at a total cost of US$800 million, over 44,000 subprojects in more than 1,400 municipalities were completed, benefiting about 1.7 million families. Of an evaluation sample of 8,123 subprojects funded in 1995–98, 89 percent were fully operational. The investments resulted in almost

100,000 permanent jobs and increased cultivated land by 80,000 hectares, generating annual income of US$200 million. Community participation indices were developed for 225 communities to analyze changes in social capital. A composite index improved by 36 percent. Notably, social capital increased by 90 percent under the FUMAC-P approach and 64 percent under the FUMAC approach while remaining constant where there had been a direct relationship between communities and the Technical Unit but no FUMAC.

Delivering education to all: the link with social capital

Education is recognized by virtually all policymakers as central to almost every aspect of development, from economic growth to environmental protection. It also plays a key role in increasing social capital and fostering the inclusion of poor people in society.

Not surprisingly, educational exclusion increases at higher levels of the Brazilian education system. While many middle-class children continue to post-secondary education, the likelihood that a child from the lowest three income deciles completes primary education is only 15 percent. Only 4 percent from this background complete secondary school. And at the university level, the free, often high-quality, public universities attract many applicants, but only one in nine gains entry. Qualified but disadvantaged students are relegated to private fee-paying institutions.

Educational efficiency has unexpected links with efforts to build social inclusion. Student flow analysis suggests that repetition, not access, is the main impediment to the expansion of secondary education in Brazil. Moreover, international practice has established that children in early grades who have participated in developmental early childhood programs have a much better chance of making good progress in school. In Brazil preschool programs are largely limited to older children from wealthier families, although public crèches do reach the poorer income groups and could be a candidate for expansion. Consistent with these findings, recent analysis of inequity in Brazil has also found that the correlation of children's educational achievements with those of their parents is higher in Brazil than in other Latin American countries (although in Brazil this relationship has weakened in recent years, a welcome sign).

Thus efforts to improve equity in the education system are likely to pay dividends in social capital as well as in human capital. Fundef has been a turning point: poor municipalities have gained substantial educational resources. The Minimum Operational Standards for Schools policy within the federal Fundescola program has provided yardsticks—consisting of essential inputs, resources, and conditions—for evaluating and improving quality across schools within the same jurisdiction and has been adopted by several states, including Bahia and Ceará. Under this model investments are channeled to schools that need them most. Supply-side policies that use positive discrimination to raise standards in the lowest performing schools are not widely used by state or local government. They offer the potential for huge gains in the long-run fight against social inequity and exclusion.

Supply-side policies could channel resources to under-performing schools based on SAEB results.

Options for delivering government services to all

Improving the quality of public services will contribute to all three goals of a more equitable, sustainable, competitive Brazil. Empowering people, especially the poor, to participate in public decisions will result in decisions that better reflect their needs and build consensus for public policies. And greater social inclusion can improve public investment, which affects productive activities and thus Brazil's economic performance.

Based on the discussion in this section, a short list of policy options for delivering government services to all in Brazil over the next few years would be the following:

- Establishing performance targets and further debureaucratizing state and municipal public services.
- Reforming local master planning, subdivision regulations, building codes, and zoning ordinances to increase the supply of land for low-income housing, and improving tenure and registration.
- Engaging in more detailed evaluation linked to possible expansion of Crédito Fundiário and land reform.
- Incorporating commercial activities in rural poverty alleviation programs.
- Examining mechanisms to improve racial inclusion in the education system.

5. Managing Brazil's natural inheritance

Table 5. Indicators for managing natural inheritance

Indicator	Brazil	Comparison		2010 target
		Latin America	OECD	
Protected land, 2002 (%)	4.4	18.9 (Chile)	9.8 (Canada) 7.1 (Australia)	10?
Deforestation, 2002 (% per year)	0.42	0.13 (Chile)	0 (Canada)	0.10?
Forested area, 2002 (%)	63	29 (Mexico)	27 (Canada)	-
Urban access to sanitation, most recent estimate (%)	85	87 (Mexico) 98 (Chile)	100	95?
Rural access to sanitation, most recent estimate (%)	37	28 (Mexico) 93 (Chile)	100	60?

Source: World Bank SIMA database.

Brazil has a unique inheritance of precious natural wealth. Such resources are a blessing, but can become a curse. On the one hand, natural resources are assets and thus allow a higher per capita income for a given level of productivity. On the other hand, many natural resource-based economies have found themselves subject to volatile and perhaps declining terms of trade and production patterns that do not favor innovation and productivity growth. However, Australia, Canada, Chile, New Zealand, and Scandinavian countries all offer successful models of economies based on natural resources. Brazil can aim to add itself to this list by using renewable resources judiciously and getting ahead of the moving agricultural frontier in environmentally sensitive areas.

Making the best of natural resources

It is appropriate for a country to benefit from its natural resources, but to do this sustainably entails adjusting policies, strengthening public institutions, and educating private users to ensure their optimal use.

A good example in the case of Brazil is provided by water resources management. Two issues stand out for their social impact and the pressure they exert on government investment: droughts in the Northeast and water pollution near large cities. There are about 2 million households without adequate water supply in the Northeast, most in extreme poverty. Almost all rivers crossing urban areas in Brazil are highly polluted, causing serious health problems for poor populations, environmental damage, and water treatment costs for downstream users. The solutions to these problems lie in decentralized management and clearly defined roles of federal and state agencies, river basin authorities, and water user associations. With clearly defined and enforced water rights will come pressure for improved management, since those who hold the rights have a powerful interest in sustainability. And bulk water pricing promotes sustainable operation of infrastructure. Otherwise, the current situation, considered a deadlock, may persist, with inefficient water services causing user unwillingness to pay, in turn undermining the financial viability of water systems and frustrating reform efforts.

Bulk water pricing promotes sustainable use of infrastructure

A second example is making standing Amazon forest areas more valuable by promoting their sustainable use. Options include certified sustainable forest management, community forestry, agroforestry, nontimber forest products, fisheries, and ecotourism, all of which are also more labor intensive than ranching. The returns to sustainable timber management can be high, but illegal, unsustainable logging is often more profitable. Logs can be obtained cheaply from those clearing their land anyway, or by applying for a clear-cutting license instead of developing a costly and time-consuming forest management plan. Federal Land Reform Agency (INCRA) settlements have also been a common source of timber and enjoy local political support. Law enforcement against illegal loggers in the vast Amazon forest, with scarce human and technical resources,

Sustainable forestry produces more employment than either ranching or crop cultivation.

has become more effective but remains a daunting challenge, and certified exports of timber still represent but a small part of the market. Rural and indigenous communities lack the legal framework, technical assistance, and capital to exploit timber resources sustainably. One innovative program, in Oaxaca State in Mexico, helps indigenous communities exploit their timber resources rationally, providing a steady source of income and increasing the area of forest under sustainable management.

The logging frontier is moving rapidly from exhausted areas to new ones, such as along the Cuiabá–Santarém highway, where new sawmills are set up every month. New communities on the Amazon frontier choose between a quick-return logging boom, followed years later by a bust that destabilizes the community, and careful resource management that would allow the community to sustain employment over the long term, sacrificing initial higher returns. Ranching or crop cultivation often follow unsustainable logging, but sustainable forestry creates many times more employment. Poverty is hardly reduced in unstable communities, except perhaps for the short windfall made by pioneers.

The National Forest Program proposes to set aside 14 percent of the Amazon as designated National Forests, where logging companies would bid for concessions to produce under public supervision. Attracting companies to these areas and away from uncontrolled access will depend on the conditions of the concessions and on an effective clampdown on illegal logging, identifying the origin and legality of logs transported. Without such a strategy of stronger control over illegal logging and promotion of sustainable forest management, wildcat logging will continue to penetrate the frontier and operate in more remote areas, such as the floodplains of the Juruá River in Amazonas State, while the capacity of the Brazilian government to create and maintain strict conservation areas will remain limited.

It may be worthwhile to review the strategy of rural settlements in the Amazon. At least 60 percent by area of INCRA's settlements are in the Amazon region. Often unplanned, these settlements usually regularize prior invasions of "unproductive" forest areas, immediately clearing it. Invaders have reason to hope that clearing will encourage expropriation, and by similar logic owners have reason to fear expropriation if land is left forested. INCRA has traditionally tolerated slash-and-burn agriculture: many settlers abandon or sell their plots later and apply for other settlements. The overall impact of INCRA's resettlement policy has probably not improved land distribution in the Amazon, nor provided sustainable livelihoods to many settlers. Settlements could rely more on nonagricultural options that do not require forest clearing and on the use of degraded areas. Federal policies have moved in this direction, but practice in the states lags behind. It may be worthwhile to review the strategy of rural settlements in the Amazon. One option may be expansion of a model similar to the Crédito Fundiário program being implemented in the Northeast.

Alternative uses of standing forests, such as extractive activities and agroforestry, also require new knowledge, from research and from systematic analysis of pilot projects and learning by doing. Support of such research is still weak in comparison to that given to agriculture and ranching, and pilot projects have yet to prove themselves. Once reliable knowledge is available, it needs dissemination. Traditional agricultural extension services in the Amazon are in a precarious condition, ill equipped to deal with alternative production models. NGOs and research centers have been the main source of technical advice to experimenting farmers, but such sources have limited reach and innovative solutions are needed.

Protecting the environment

The value of many ecosystems is maximized by their conservation rather than conversion. Indeed, part of the strategy of protecting ecosystems consists of the range of actions outlined in the previous sections: maximizing the productive value of land already cultivated and of standing forest, in order to minimize the incentives for invasion of untouched areas by ecologically destructive activities. In addition, changes in land use that alter ecosystems have economic impacts on ecosystem goods, such as timber, forest products, fish, and fresh water, and environmental services, such as soil fertility, flood control, climate regulation, and natural pest control. Given the imperfect state of existing knowledge, it would be prudent for Brazil to stay clear of thresholds of irreversible environmental damage.

It would be prudent to stay clear of thresholds of irreversible environmental damage.

Clearly there are tradeoffs. Use of forest for ranching or crops contributes to economic growth and exports. Tangible, immediate benefits have to be compared with uncertain future benefits from letting the forest stand. Despite this uncertainty, however, studies worldwide indicate that standing forest may be far more valuable than cleared forest. It may therefore pay Brazil to keep options open.

Restricting access and enforcing roadside reserves would limit damage to the Amazon.

The Amazon region has become emblematic of the major choices facing Brazil in natural resource management. Although most of the Amazon rainforest is still standing, the rate of deforestation is relatively very high, and the potential effects on hydrology, biodiversity, and climate are largely unknown (figure 10 shows the rate of deforestation since 1989). If Brazil opts to keep most of the remaining Amazon rain forest, government must get ahead of the frontier of agricultural land use. First priority might be given to setting aside land as conservation units with varying restrictions of access. Despite skepticism about the viability of enforcing access control, public areas reserved for conservation, with a minimum of surveillance and enforcement, appear to be less prone to invasion and degradation than other areas. Incorporating 50 million hectares of primary Amazon forest into strictly protected and sustainable use reserves is the goal of the Amazon Protected Areas Project (ARPA). Taking together all current and planned lands under protection or restricted use, half the Amazon forest may fall under some form of conservation.

Figure 10. Annual deforestation in the Amazon, 1989–2001

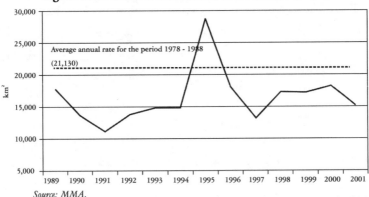

Source: MMA.

From the viewpoint of keeping primary forests in place, it is less important whether conservation areas are for strict protection or for sustainable use (sustainable use areas also being important as buffer zones). Building new primary roads into hitherto inaccessible interior forest regions has been firmly associated with deforestation and is incompatible with maintaining standing forests in such regions. Paving existing roads may have similar effects. The BR163 Cuiabá–Santarém is a case in point: forests are already being cleared along the highway in anticipation of paving. Restricting access and enforcing reserves alongside this road would limit damage.

The possibility of control of forest clearing through rural licensing and surveillance has been demonstrated by the government of Mato Grosso, by combining remote sensing technology with the political will to enforce legislation. Deforestation has dropped by a third there since 1998. Pará and Rondônia could follow this example, although they face additional difficulties stemming from land tenure. These efforts require political will and a clear definition of roles of federal and state authorities.

Given government's limited means of monitoring such vast forest regions, control should be targeted to areas under threat. With tracts set aside for conservation, zoning at a finer scale should be concerned with land use at the frontier, within occupied areas and along development axes. Clarifying property rights is also essential to create incentives for sustainable use.

Reform of the property registration system is essential for the government to get ahead of uncontrolled and illegal land appropriation, resource extraction, and forest conversion. Reducing open space and limiting access would raise land value and diminish areas open to predatory resource exploitation.

There are other, noncoercive means of influencing the land use decisions of private owners. Further modifications of the rural land tax (ITR), clear recognition of standing forests as a productive use of land, and changes to INCRA's settlement practices would give additional incentives not to clear land. Although legislation has changed over the last decade, landholders still feel safer

Ecological and economic zoning of the Cerrado and Caatinga are huge priorities.

from invasion and expropriation when they clear their land for (real or apparent) ranching. Tradable legal reserve obligations (or development rights) could also enhance the effectiveness of the legislation and promote the clustering of legal reserves to form larger contiguous habitats. And the "green" ICMS revenue allocation among municipalities, as already practiced in Paraná, Minas Gerais, and some other states, or a modified allocation of the Municipal Participation Fund (FPM), might increase the willingness of local governments to create reserves. A tax on deforestation could also be a disincentive. Economic instruments still require monitoring of land use but may have a better chance of influencing behavior than command and control.

Another example is the Cerrado, the nation's second largest ecosystem after the Amazon. Agricultural expansion in the Cerrado, strong since the 1970s, intensified in the 1990s, owing to a number of factors, including improved varieties of grain and soybean adapted to local climatic and soil conditions.

A Brazilian choice on use of the grass, shrub, and forest lands of the Cerrado, with the tradeoff between high biodiversity and agricultural potential, is of urgency: probably more than half the land has already been occupied by agriculture and ranching and further occupation is occurring fast. Apart from percentage rules for legal reserves, there is no policy on how much of this biome should be used for production and how much conserved. Protected areas amount to less than 1 percent, insufficient to conserve biodiversity. The consequences of degrading land use are already beginning to be felt, with soil erosion and changes in dry season stream flows. Some degradation can be corrected with appropriate agronomic technologies, but loss of biodiversity from land conversion is irreversible. Percentage rules alone are insufficient. More important is macro-zoning: the spatial differentiation of land uses within each biome. Differences arise in geological, soil, and climatic characteristics; biodiversity significance; distance from the frontier, urban centers, and transport axes; and finally current land tenure.

The Cerrado deserves a Brazilian vision of its long-term use and conservation. Zoning has already been undertaken in Tocantins and Mato Grosso. A 2000 workshop on Cerrado conservation priorities identified areas of priority, and these recommendations can now be put into practice, preferably through a biomewide project similar to the ARPA project for the Amazon. International support is likely. Control of land use through licensing, monitoring, and enforcement with the assistance of economic instruments could be employed in the Cerrado just as in the Amazon.

Other endangered biomes in Brazil include the Mata Atlântica, of which only an estimated 7 percent remains standing. The Mata Atlântica is important not only for its rich biodiversity but also because the watersheds supplying Curitiba, São Paulo, Rio de Janeiro, Belo Horizonte, Salvador, and Recife are all located there. Development along the coast continues with the tourism industry and other activities, and government has yet to find an effective formula for protecting this dwindling resource.

The Caatinga of the semi-arid Northeast is also seriously endangered. This rich biome has been fragmented by slash and burn agriculture, inappropriate expansion of grazing lands, and charcoal and firewood production. It is perhaps the poorest region of Brazil and continues to contribute thousands of migrants to other regions, particularly during drought years. Its destruction has reached a critical point in some areas, which are threatened with irreversible desertification. Appropriate policy instruments could reverse the destruction of this region and its natural resources.

Many benefits from forest conservation are global. While there is willingness from public and private sectors in other countries to contribute to specific incremental costs of conservation, there is no mechanism in sight that would provide for larger global transfers to Brazil in recognition of the global value of its forests. The emerging market in carbon offsets may one day provide such a mechanism, but it will not do so in the short term. Without prejudice to its sovereignty, Brazil has an interest in an international dialogue on the global environmental services that it provides and on compensation mechanisms.

Natural resources and the poor

The link between natural resource management and the poor lies in the observation that many natural resources are commonly shared assets, and since the poor have fewer of their own assets, natural assets make up a larger share of their total wealth than for the non-poor. Natural resources are a key part of the livelihood of many poor people.

Perhaps nowhere is the link between the environment and poverty closer than in poor urban areas. Water pollution from inadequate wastewater collection and transportation or lack of appropriate treatment undermines health and development in towns, with a disproportionate impact on the poor in the slums surrounding the largest cities. Studies by the Pan American Health Organization and the World Health Organization have shown that water supply and sanitation services reduce typhoid incidence by 80 percent, trachoma and schistosomiasis by up to 70 percent, and gastrointestinal infections and diarrhea by up to 50 percent. Similar statistics apply to the lack of solid waste collection and its appropriate disposal. Air pollution also tends to affect the urban poor more intensely, since they generally live in more polluted neighborhoods and have less access to protection and remedies.

In rural areas, most land under cultivation was cleared in the last 30 years, including significant areas of unsuitable land. Many areas have been abandoned altogether. Exposed to erosive rains, vulnerable areas continue to degrade and pollute rivers through silting. Brazil loses over a million hectares of topsoil to erosion each year, representing annual losses of about R$3.2 billion. Soil degradation produces its most destructive impact on small farmers and is at once a cause and consequence of rural impoverishment, leading to declining yields that in turn encourage expanded land clearing. Subsidies to technologically advanced producers reinforce these pressures on small semi-subsistence farmers, who would therefore benefit greatly from policies that encourage sustainable methods of soil use.

The states of Paraná and Santa Catarina offer a successful strategy to maximize soil cover, improve soil structure, minimize surface runoff, and control pollution. In selected "microcatchments," commissions were set up to run soil surveys and prepare management plans. Commission members received management training, while farmers received technical training on land management and technologies. The projects assisted about 2,100 microcatchments in Paraná and 530 in Santa Catarina, reaching about 300,000 families at a cost of about US$700 per family (US$80.00 per hectare). Soil loss was cut in half and runoff water in streams contained fewer suspended solids, bacteria, and pesticides, lowering silting and water treatment costs downstream and reducing water borne-diseases and pesticide poisoning. Maintenance costs for rural roads were reduced by up to 80 percent, while better all-weather access stimulated commercial and social activities. Crop yields improved, and groundwater levels rose. The new land management practices proved more profitable to farmers than the practices they replaced.

These projects incorporated features common to most successful community-based natural resource management experiences: initial social organization to catalyze collective action, flexibility (adaptation rather than adoption), early tangible benefits, and subsidized investments with mandatory contribution (in cash or in kind) by beneficiaries to increase commitment. Extension workers were responsible for mobilizing farmers and helping them identify problems and solutions. The participatory microcatchment strategy is already being replicated in Mato Grosso, Mato Grosso do Sul (Pantanal buffer areas), and São Paulo, and in a new generation of projects in Paraná and Santa Catarina. Unfortunately, however, intensive livestock operations (particularly hogs) in Southern Brazil and now in other regions, threaten to reverse gains made in the microcatchment projects. Governments, farmers, and the large livestock integrators must work together to reduce water pollution levels caused by the increasing concentration of livestock operations.

Improving water management and investment allocation

Water is one of Brazil's most important assets, so abundant in some areas and so scarce in others. This pattern makes water resource management something of a unique challenge for Brazil. Brazil's fresh water availability, 70 percent of it concentrated in the Amazon Basin, represents an estimated 10 percent of the world's total. The semi-arid Northeast region, with 28 percent of the population, has only 5 percent of the country's water resources. Water is also scarce in the humid but industrialized South and Southeast regions, with nearly 60 percent of the population.

Water is a key element of Brazil's strategy to promote sustainable growth and a more equitable and inclusive society. While Brazil's achievements over the past half century have been strongly tied to the development of its water resources, urgent new issues in water resource management and water supply and sanitation services present related challenges and poverty implications, although requiring different institutional models and funding mechanisms.

Water resource management in Brazil over the past two decades has suffered from a fragmented institutional approach, overattention to new investment relative to operation and maintenance of existing infrastructure, and a failure to integrate environmental considerations. Since the 1990s, Brazil has sought to overhaul its water management framework, with a focus on improved management and investment allocation. The implications of promising recent legal and institutional innovations in water resource management have not yet been fully assessed.

Water supply and sanitation services are unevenly distributed—the rate of service coverage in the North and Northeast is particularly low—and the poor are least likely to have access to adequate service. It is thus the poor who suffer most from poorly managed and inadequate water supply and the unhealthy environment that exists in the absence of adequate water, sewerage, and wastewater treatment. Good management of water resources and access to basic water services promote employment, health, and environmental quality. Progress will require reform and innovation on several fronts: legal, institutional, financial, and technical.

Prematurely stringent standards can lead to high investment costs in water supply and sanitation.

Although utility tariffs for water supply and sanitation services in Brazil are at a level that could cover operation and maintenance costs and leverage substantial investments, half of these utilities show operational deficits requiring fiscal support. Meeting these financial challenges will require carefully concentrating subsidies on the poor. If utility managers were given the incentives and autonomy to improve efficiency, the efficiency gains could be allocated to improve service coverage and quality for the poor. Services could also be improved with a clearer legal framework, financing incentives to improve efficiency, and tariff and bulk water pricing reforms to promote conservation and efficiency.

Moreover, prematurely stringent standards imply unnecessarily high investment costs that are not reflected in consumer tariffs for water supply and sanitation services. The federal government could help with more realistic programs and investment guarantees for innovative projects. More analysis of health and environmental benefits would help to prioritize investments and cost recovery objectives. But unattainable standards should not block provision of basic sanitation services to the poor. Cooperation among agencies could permit an integrated approach to slum upgrading, including regularizing land ownership to promote pollution control and increase willingness to pay for services.

Trade openness and comparative advantage in natural resources

There is a strand of development thinking that suggests that natural resource economies have tended to grow more slowly than others. The usual explanations given for this are declining commodity prices and higher rates of innovation in manufacturing than in resource-based activities such as agriculture or mining.

There is much recent evidence against this fear, however, and country experience suggests ways for Brazil to optimize the benefits from its natural resources. First, the trend of falling commodity prices seems not to have persisted later than the 1970s. Second, productivity growth from 1967 to 1992 in a large sample of countries was 50 percent higher in agriculture than in manufacturing. Brazil's successful experience in developing Cerrado agriculture through the technical leadership of Embrapa is telling in this regard. Third, the growth experiences of Australia, Canada, Finland, Sweden, and the United States provide compelling evidence that a strategy that builds on the natural resource base can lead to rapid productivity growth. Finally, with appropriate regulation, economic growth need not come at the expense of greater pollution.

Comparative advantage in natural resources therefore logically leads to an economic strategy emphasizing trade openness – including the need to maintain pressure for openness of markets in industrialized countries –, an educated and flexible workforce, a positive climate for innovation (including business-research links and possibly incentives for private sector research and development, particularly related to agriculture and natural resource management), and a good enabling environment for Internet and communications technology.

Options for promoting sustainable natural resource management

A natural resource-based economic strategy can lead to rapid productivity growth. Combined with these factors, the careful management and protection of natural resources becomes a key tool for economic growth and stability in addition to a goal in itself. Natural resources are the common patrimony of Brazilians, and their preservation and prudent use is therefore also a condition of equity in economic management.

They are particularly important in the lives of the rural poor, whose voices should be heard in the design of natural resource management policies.

Based on the discussion in this section, a short list of policy options to promote sustainable natural resource management in Brazil would be the following:

- Maintaining decentralized environmental management but increasing policy attention and investment for enforcement (including stronger control over illegal logging).
- Integrating environmental policies with planning policies (mainstreaming), making environmental measures proactive rather than remedial.
- Using economic incentives where possible (such as to promote sustainable forest management) and revising unrealistic, costly standards (such as for wastewater collection in urban areas).
- Combining ecological and economic zoning with institutional strengthening for its enforcement in the Cerrado and the Caatinga.
- Better integrating federal, state, and municipal agencies; a federal review could initially clarify overlapping responsibilities.

From consensus to choices: building a quantitative agenda

At a general level, a more equitable, sustainable and competitive Brazil is a vision that people are likely to agree on. At the next level, the five means to this end used to structure this report also probably represent, as descriptions, a general consensus. Yet each of the five represents choices, which may be a valid source of debate.

Investing in people entails expanding the secondary education system at a rapid pace, to catch up with other countries of Brazil's income level. Education spending could be focused on underachieving schools, and health spending could be focused on high-quality basic services by cutting the number of costly, complex operations provided free of charge. Dramatic victories against AIDS and in the universalization of primary education have shown that Brazil can mobilize social spending efficiently. A possible aim might be to reach a net secondary enrollment rate similar to that of Chile, about 70 percent, over the next five years, which would entail doubling Brazil's net secondary enrollment.

The inclusion of the excluded is the lifeblood of social development, but will require curtailing vested interests. Transparent decisions reduce local political discretion. Bringing informal workers into social safety nets requires reducing the mandated benefits conferred on formal workers. But even small reductions in inequality may have large effects on poverty in Brazil. By one measure, the public sector spends more than 10 times the poverty gap on the social sectors each year. Even modest improvements to Brazil's transfer programs, widening and increasing the well-targeted and efficient such as Bolsa Escola, can transform communities and raise many people out of the most extreme poverty. More broadly, Brazil's poor will benefit from getting even further away from clientelistic traditions of government toward transparent and accountable delivery of government services to all.

There is increasing consensus, in Brazil and in the wider development community, about the value of measurable targets to be used as progress benchmarks and to encourage transparent policymaking. Some have been discussed in Brazil while others have come out of high-level international agreements such as the recent Monterrey summit. Perhaps the most central of these is Brazil's commitment to cut extreme poverty in half by 2015. Most estimates suggest that to achieve this without significantly increased income redistribution, Brazil would have to record annual GDP growth of more than 5 percent between now and 2015. Even with optimistic forecasts of world economic conditions and Brazilian reforms, recent history suggests that this is unlikely as an average, at least in the next few years. Redistribution and the reduction of inequality will therefore be central to Brazil's pursuit of social progress from 2003 onwards. Halving poverty by 2015 remains a viable goal, and this would suggest aiming to cut measured poverty by perhaps 10–20 percent in the next five years.

Stronger management of natural resources may mean changes in many public sector institutions. Getting ahead of the frontier in the Amazon, Cerrado, and Caatinga will adversely affect some existing livelihoods from extractive activities. But it is reasonable for Brazil to strengthen its institutions and make arrangements to place, for example, half the existing Amazon under some form of protection. Formulating policy for the Cerrado and Caatinga is equally pressing, as these biomes are under intense pressure from agricultural users. For the Cerrado and Caatinga, many competing interests are at stake and consultation will be vital to set the appropriate targets.

Productivity-led growth means increasing competition, including that from abroad, against the lobbying of powerful industries. Cutting bureaucratic red tape may mean reducing the powers of some public sector institutions in some decisions. And cutting directed credit will mean reducing the influence of the public banks in some areas. Higher Brazilian productivity will take time to appear and will depend on improving macroeconomic conditions too, but a 4-5 percent growth target is attainable only with reductions in the administrative and financial burden on Brazil's private sector. Adhering to the fiscal arithmetic, while addressing the need for investing in key areas, is vital.

Progress in the 21st century can be far stronger than in the last two decades. Maintaining primary surpluses and reforming the financial sector can unleash the potential of Brazil's economy. Socio-environmental programs can support social inclusion and broad-based progress with social and environmental sustainability. Brazil's potential for improving the welfare of its people is vast. With broad-ranging and sustained actions, this vision could become a reality.

PART I

1

Education

1

Education

Introduction

In the last decade, Brazil's commitment to improving educational outcomes yielded dramatic gains at an almost unparalleled rate. Now, to consolidate those gains and create an education system that meets Brazil's needs, the key challenge for the Federal Government, as well as for state and municipal governments, is to intensify their efforts to improve Brazil's educational equity and efficiency while focusing on the improvement of student learning, institutional capacity, and accountability.

Brazil is close to achieving universal basic education. There has been a massive expansion in basic education enrollment, significant increases in school grade promotion rates, as well as substantial improvements in equity, all supported by a substantial rise in public expenditure in education at all levels of government. More specifically, the following trends are indicative of these gains:

- A dramatic rise in enrollments. During the five-year period from 1996 to 2001, Brazil enrolled an additional 2 million primary school-aged children, raising the net enrollment rate of 7 to 14 year old children to over 95 percent. Enrollment at other levels of schooling also increased: including from 382,000 to 1.1 million children in crèches (0-3 years), from 4.1 million to 4.8 million children in pre-school (4-6 years), and from 5.7 million to 8.5 million students in secondary education (grades 9-11).

- Widespread reductions in repetition. From 1996 to 2000, student grade promotion rates rose 8.8 percentage points in municipal systems and 5.2 points in state systems. Besides the obvious direct benefits to children and their families, every 1 percent reduction in students in grades 1-4 who are held back to repeat a grade implies a saving of US$240 million.

The draft of this chapter was completed by Robin Horn in November 2002. The analyses and suggestions contained in this chapter are based on the international technical experience of the World Bank and are presented as a contribution to the debate and formulation of public policies.

- Significant improvements in equity. Between 1996 and 2000, even as median spending per student increased, Brazil experienced substantial reductions in the variation of per-student spending across states and municipalities. For example, the difference in unit expenditures between the municipalities at the 95th percentile of the spending distribution and the 5th percentile decreased from 22 times higher spending to only 8 time higher spending.

Substantial Reforms in the Education Sector

Increased financing of education has played a major role in generating these impressive performance gains. Public spending in education steadily increased during the past eight years by about 30 percent, from 4.2 percent of GDP in 1995 to 5.5 percent in 2000. Municipalities alone spent nearly R$24 billion on education in 2000, nearly twice what they were spending, in real terms, in 1995. While the federal government has provided incentives for state and local governments to increase the performance of their education systems, and introduced far reaching education reforms, legions of municipal and dozens of state governments have complemented the federal reforms by unleashing their own creativity and resources to develop important reforms, initiatives and experiments of their own. This combination of actions has dramatically altered the educational landscape in Brazil. The key national reforms introduced during the last decade include the following:

In 1996, the approval of the National Education Law (LDB) provided a markedly improved delineation of the roles and responsibilities of the state and municipal governments with respect to the provision of education. This law also supports the establishment of minimum quality standards (including curriculum and teacher qualifications standards), and further decentralizes service provision to sub-national governments, reserving for the Federal government primarily normative, monitoring and financial roles.

The Fund for Development and Maintenance of Basic Education and Teacher Valorization (FUNDEF) which began operating in 1998, simplifies and makes more transparent and equitable the transfer of federal funds to finance basic education, and establishes clear cost-sharing obligations for sub-national governments. Resource allocation with states and across municipalities through FUNDEF is based on student enrollment in the respective jurisdictions, and has proven an important incentive for states and municipalities to increase service coverage.

The Ministry of Education's Fundescola Program provides technical assistance services and transfers of federal subsidies to help the poorest states and municipalities improve the quality of schooling in their jurisdictions. With this support, sub-national governments are encouraged to increase coordination, assure minimum quality standards for all of their the schools, and implement more efficient and effective school improvement programs.

School autonomy has become a major public education policy objective, which has been supported through the creation in 1995 of the "Money to the Schools"(Dinhero Direito na Escola) program, financed by the Ministry of Education's National Education Development Fund (FNDE), which in turn is funded through the federal share (quota federal) of the Education Salary Tax (Salário Educação). The FNDE transfers federal funds directly to the school bank accounts set up and managed by their school-parent councils, with the amounts based on school enrollment.

The creation of the Basic Education National Evaluation System (SAEB) and the annual School Census (Censo Escola) put in place essential instruments to improve the quality and equity in education. The SAEB evaluation and the School Census results are widely disseminated by the Ministry of Education (MEC), contributing to promote social mobilization in support of education reform, and to strengthen the efforts by schools and education authorities in improving service delivery. At the secondary level, graduates are tested on proficiency with respect to the national curriculum parameters by means of the recently created National Upper-Secondary Education Exam (Exame Nacional de Educacão Média -- ENEM). At the tertiary education level, quality assurance has also been introduced with the creation of National Exams (Provão). ENEM and Provão results are widely disseminated and have improved student choice and quality control on the part of schools and universities. Combined education and social assistance policy reforms have created strong incentives to attract children to schools, particularly through conditional cash transfer programs such as the national Bolsa Escola program. These efforts have paid out with impressive enrollment increases at the fundamental education level. At the upper-secondary level efforts are still timid and should be intensified as a key policy priority for the coming years.

Understanding the remaining problems of equity and performance

The unprecedented gains in performance listed above, supported by these policy reforms and programs, need to be followed up by increases in the efficiency and quality of schooling to improve Brazil's long-term growth prospects and young people's opportunities. The quality of schooling varies considerably across Brazil. Children attending some public schools in Brazil lack the basic educational opportunities that are available to children attending schools in other parts of the country or even in better endowed schools within the same jurisdictions. Furthermore, Brazilian schools are still not managing to educate most of their students. SAEB test performance appears to have reached a plateau at a relatively low level, with no significant gains since the 1995 test administration. For example, the 2001 SAEB results show that less than half of 4th grade students in Brazil perform at level 3 on a 10-level mathematics proficiency scale, and this percentage has not increased since SAEB was introduced in 1995.

What is behind the relatively poor performance? Much of the failure begins in the first grade, where poor instruction and inadequate monitoring in initial reading skills result in hundreds of thousands of children slowly moving through the school system with an increasingly insurmountable handicap. Most first grade children have never participated in preschool or early childhood development programs. Although the federal government has been promoting improved learning standards—for example, and as mentioned above, by introducing national curriculum parameters, national assessment, and guaranteed provision of textbooks—improvements in classroom teaching practice are slow to materialize. Research shows that in elementary schools, most teachers continue to rely on traditional "chalk and talk" instructional approaches at all grade levels of basic education—an approach that fails to engage or motivate students.

The widespread practice in Brazil of using of grade repetition as an instrument of quality control, while diminishing over time, remains a formidable challenge for education policymakers to overcome. Students are forced to repeat an entire school year if they fail to master what is expected of them in even one subject. The underlying problem is that state and municipal governments, schools, and teachers have few strategies for helping, with remedial or compensatory programs, failing students or students who start school ill prepared or with little support at home. While educators and policymakers throughout the country have come to recognize these problems, and individual municipalities or schools have achieved some limited success in improving educational outcomes, attempts to improve teaching and learning on a large scale have been frustrated. Efforts to encourage schools to innovate have yielded a few isolated success stories, but they are dispersed and sometimes short-lived because of their dependence on an exceptional school principal or a committed sponsoring organization. Mandates for change from federal or state levels have also proven largely ineffective, with some exceptions. The principal constraint to improving student outcomes is the inability of local governments to translate the objective of providing quality schooling to all children into a program of coherent, integrated, large-scale, and sustainable actions.

Effecting a substantial change in teaching and classroom pedagogy in a country the size of Brazil is an extremely difficult task. The federal government has little direct leverage because public schooling in Brazil's 184,000 public schools serving 44 million children is the responsibility of state and municipal governments. To effect change, the federal Ministry of Education needs to mobilize the 27 state governments and 5,561 municipal governments to undertake the desired reforms and investments. It also needs to mobilize the broader public as well: citizens have to know the failings of their schools and know how to demand a better quality education for their children.

Message 1. Prioritizing investments that increase educational equity and raise outcomes for the disadvantaged.
Public policy should actively ensure that all children, especially those coming from disadvantaged backgrounds, have both adequate educational opportunities as well as other compensatory support as needed to complete a basic education program of acceptable quality.

FUNDEF has contributed to increasing inter-regional and especially inter-state equity. Although more can and should be done to improve equity across the nation, states and municipalities also need strong policies and programs to reduce educational disparities in their own jurisdictions. Sub-national governments can define a set of quality standards for their schools and school staff, and then use these standards as a yardstick for reducing differences in the quality of service provision across their schools.

Efforts of sub-national governments to discourage the establishment of very small schools in rural areas may need to be reexamined in light of the negative consequences on the educational attainment of children living in these settings. To improve schooling outcomes in rural areas, the federal government should evaluate the numerous rural schooling interventions that are under implementation throughout Brazil, and disseminate best practice experiences.

Targeted and compensatory programs, including conditional cash subsidies and positive discrimination programs, could be developed or, where they exist, strengthened to provide assistance for disadvantaged children to enroll in school, attend regularly, learn at adequate levels, and persist through secondary education.

Context
The Brazilian constitution mandates that government provide all children with equal conditions of access and permanence in school, and guarantee standards of quality for these educational services. Nevertheless, millions of children in the North and Northeast, in the favelas of Rio de Janeiro, São Paulo, and the margins of numerous other cities, and in

poor villages throughout Brazil's rural areas have no choice but to attend schools that lack the basic learning resources available to children in other parts of Brazil or even in better endowed schools within their own cities and towns. In practice, this means their schools have teachers who are unqualified, inadequately trained, or have low morale and expectations; their classrooms have inadequate reading and reference books or other learning materials; and their school buildings are in unsafe environments or lack ventilation, adequate lighting, drinking water, or functioning toilets.

The most vulnerable children are served by the lowest quality schools. Children's access to public schooling tends to reflect residential patterns of economic differentiation, so that the worst schools are more often those located in the cities, towns or neighborhoods in which the poorest families live. These educational characteristics are even reflected in such broad geographic categories as region (Table 1). Moreover, poor children with additional disadvantages, such as those from racially discriminated minority groups or with physical or emotional handicaps, are especially at risk because their educational opportunities are simultaneously circumscribed by poverty and affliction as their parents have no means to locate or demand schools or services that can address their children's special needs. Consequently, it is in particular the poorest and most vulnerable children who suffer from the worst quality schooling services. Repeated deprivation of basic learning experiences compounds the deleterious effect of educational deficits over time, so that poor children grow to adulthood with almost no opportunity to escape the cycle of poverty.

Table 1: Distribution of quality characteristics by region, 1-4th grades.

Region	enrolled (2002)	postsecondary	Computer	Library	at least twice
North	2,111,735	6.64%	12.5%	30.79%	42.59%
Northeast	7,138,528	15.14%	11.1%	23.33%	40.91%
Southeast	6,902,921	43.99%	40.9%	60.68%	14.27%
South	2,272,831	45.51%	41.4%	75.24%	12.54%
Centerwest	1,296,676	41.02%	33.6%	48.88%	20.68%
TOTAL	19,722,691	29.51%	26.7%	44.91%	47.38%

From INEP School Census, 2002estimates

CHILDREN IN RURAL AREAS SUFFER ADDITIONAL DISADVANTAGES. The deficiencies of education provided to children living in rural settings are striking when compared with schooling provided to children living elsewhere. Rural children have the lowest education indicators in Brazil. They lower net enrollments (91 percent) than urban children (96 percent) and much lower average promotion rates (66 percent versus 82 percent). As measured by the SAEB assessment system, students in rural areas are considerably less likely to attain mastery of basic content areas in Portuguese language skills and mathematics than children in urban areas, and are considerably less likely to attain the 175-point SAEB threshold performance standard in 4th grade mathematics (39 percent versus 57 percent) or Portuguese (25 percent versus 43 percent). Teacher quality is also lower in rural areas: in 1998, 34 percent of the rural teaching force was extremely underqualified (less than a secondary education) compared with 2 percent of the urban teaching force.

Table 2: Distribution of quality characteristics by type of rural school, 1-4th grades.

Type of School	Number enrolled (2002)	Teachers with some postsecondary	School has Computer	School has Library	Students repeated at least twice
Single-grade rural			12.5%	30.79%	42.59%
school	2,635,218	4.6%	11.1%	23.33%	40.91%
Multi-grade rural			40.9%	60.68%	14.27%
school	2,165,579	10.8%	41.4%	75.24%	12.54%
Urban school,			33.6%	48.88%	20.68%
rural children	93,947	32.6%			47.38%
Urban-located school, rural children	14,827,947	36.4%			
TOTAL	**19,722,691**	23.5%			

From INEP School Census, 2002 estimates

Perhaps in recognizing the deficiencies of small and isolated schools staffed with less qualified teachers, and accepting their inability to raise the quality of these schools, some sub-national governments have undertaken policies to close such schools and reassign students to larger and ostensibly more efficient schools in less rural settings. More specifically, legislation stipulates that small schools should be established only where there is no other option. Unfortunately, one of the consequences of this action in many parts of rural Brazil is to require children to travel vast distances to attend school, adding further hardship to poor children's conditions and thus contributing to lower educational indicators for children from these areas. Furthermore, many municipal governments have difficulties financing reliable transportation for rural students who are forced to commute to school.

THE DISADVANTAGED HAVE LIMITED ACCESS TO SECONDARY AND HIGHER EDUCATION. Access to higher levels of education is particularly inequitable. Geographic, urban-rural, and socioeconomic disparities are prevalent in secondary education. The likelihood that a student from the lowest three income deciles will complete lower secondary education (8th grade) is 15 percent. The likelihood of completing upper secondary school (11th grade) is just 4 percent. There are also large differences in the educational attainment across racial groups. For instance, only one in four students attaining nine or more years of education is non-white. Differential access to upper grade levels begins in the early years, where children from disadvantaged groups repeat grades more frequently than their less disadvantaged counterparts. Figure 1 shows that nearly 6 times as many 7-14 year olds from the lowest 10 percent of the income distribution are enrolled in the 1st through 4th grades than in the 5th through 8th grades. Ideally the proportion enrolled in 1st through 4th grades would be about equal to 5th through 8th grades, which is nearly the case for children from the highest income levels. The graph also shows differences, although less extreme, for rural and black children.

Figure 1. Distribution of the Enrollment of 7-14 Years Old

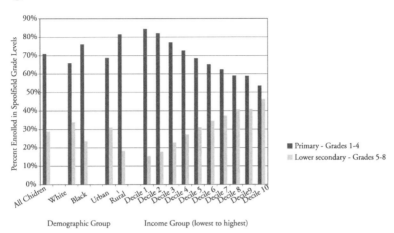

Source: 2001 PNAD microdata

Figure 2 shows the distribution of children from the 15 to 18 year age group, that is, the secondary school age group. This graph indicates the cumulative effect of repetition at the lower years disproportionately affects poor, minority, and rural children the most. If there were no repetition, nearly 100% of 15 to 18 year olds enrolled in school would be in upper secondary level. In fact, by for this age group, the vast majority of children from poorer or rurally-based families, or from minority groups, are still stuck in lower secondary (grades 5-8), or even in earlier grades. Few will complete upper secondary to progress to post secondary education.

In addition, the free, high-quality state-run higher education institutions attract so many qualified youth, given the high and rising private rates of return to higher education, that only one of nine applicants is accepted, further limiting the possibilities for disadvantaged families. Children from better-off families benefit from knowledgeable parental guidance in the admissions process and from a higher quality (private) secondary education. Qualified, but disadvantaged students, most often from lower-middle or poor backgrounds, without the same benefits, end up having to attend private fee-charging institutions, many of which are of poorer quality.

Figure 2. Distribution of the Enrollment of 15-18 Years Old

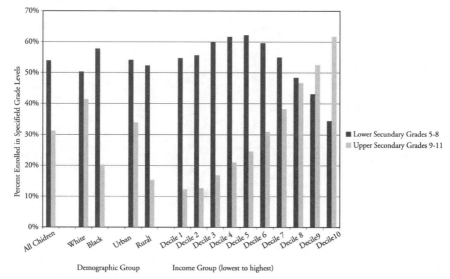

Source: 2001 PNAD microdata

WHY EDUCATIONAL INEQUALITIES PERSIST. There are several reasons for the prevalent and enduring inequality of educational opportunities and outcomes. First, until recently public policy has not focused on educational inequality, but rather on facilitating broad access to schooling, a policy that incidentally has proven largely successful, as reported above. Second, most state and municipal government do not have policies that prioritize investment and the delivery of support services to the worst schools in the worst neighborhoods, a practice that could assure a fairer distribution of quality in their jurisdictions. Finally, few sub-national governments have programs that explicitly target the most disadvantaged children with compensatory assistance to help them achieve at the same levels as those who are better off.

Considerations for Policy Formulation

Notwithstanding the substantial problems in equality of schooling and educational outcomes, Brazil has achieved some important gains in recent years. A key advance was the introduction of the FUNDEF constitutional amendment and law in 1996. This redistributive legislation has provided a financial basis for redressing imbalances in educational quality across jurisdictions in each of the 26 states of the republic. Poor municipalities have gained substantial amounts of funds because of the reduction of within-state varia-tion in resource availability, which has led to an overall improvement in the equity of edu-cational resources for municipal and state educational systems.

As important as FUNDEF has been for reducing disparities in financing across munic-ipalities and states, it just one step on the road to improving educational outcomes for the poor. Differences in the quality of schooling within jurisdictions, and for disadvantaged populations in general, remain a pertinacious challenge for sub-national governments. In addition, improving equity in the provision of quality basic education services, and in par-ticular, improving the equality of schooling outcomes, unfortunately involves tradeoffs. If a chief policy objective in a jurisdiction is to improve the equity of educational outcomes, then the government may need to direct marginal resources at schools or individuals most in need, and therefore may not be able to focus as well on raising the standards further in its top quality schools, or in financing the costs of higher education for its most talented students. Because state and municipal governments have to work within a constrained financing envelope for education, raising the quality of the weakest schools and financing compensatory programs to help children from the poorest families improve their school achievement and attainment means that some other potential investments may have to be postponed.

ESTABLISH A MINIMUM QUALITY STANDARDS POLICY AND INVEST NEW RESOURCES TO RAISE QUALITY FIRST IN SUBSTANDARD SCHOOLS. Governments can reduce educational dispari-ties by defining a set of quality standards for their schools and then using these standards to evaluate and improve learning conditions across the schools in their systems, giving attention first to schools furthest below the standard. The benchmark could consist of a set of acceptable professional qualifications and performance standards, essential teaching inputs, instructional conditions, and other basic resources needed for a school to provide adequate learning opportunities to all of its students. With such a model in place, munic-ipalities and states would be able to establish an investment program to prioritize addi-tional investments and technical assistance to schools that fall farthest from the minimum quality standard benchmark, thereby reducing disparities across their schools until they all meet the benchmark. Over time, with additional resources, governments can elevate the standard of all schools, while assuring that differences in quality remain a problem of the past. This two-step strategy is portrayed in Illustration 1.

Illustration 1. Raising school quality standarts

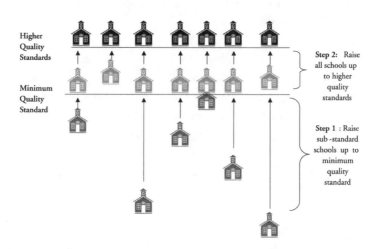

The Ministry of Education's Fundescola Program has developed such a program that has been subsequently expanded to and adapted by several state governments, including Acre, Bahia, Ceará, and Pernambuco, as well as numerous municipal governments.

POLICIES FOR RURAL EDUCATION. Efforts that discourage the establishment or continuation of small schools in rural areas should be reexamined in the light of the negative consequences for rural families and their children. Numerous rural education interventions are being supported and practiced throughout Brazil. These include the Escola Ativa model developed and financed by the Ministry of Education, and other programs supported by local governments and NGOs, including Rural Family Home (Casa Familiar Rural), Agriculture Family School (Escola Família Agrícola), Nucleus School Strategy (Nucleação), and the Itinerant School (Escola Itinerante) programs in the Landless Movement (MST) areas. The federal government has a responsibility to create systematic information about these initiatives, assess their penetration, evaluate their cost-effectiveness, and disseminate these findings in order to promote the implementation by state and municipal governments or other organizations of effective, viable, and replicable rural schooling programs.

CONDITIONAL TRANSFER PROGRAMS. There has also been some progress in the use of demand-side programs to help the poorest families overcome any economic hurdles they face to keep their children in school. The new national Bolsa Escola program and its variants recently implemented by some state and local governments are promising. A detailed discussion of this program, and the options for improving it, is presented in the section on "Conditional Transfer Programs" of the Policy Notes chapter entitled Social Protection.

POSITIVE DISCRIMINATION, AFFIRMATIVE ACTION, OR COMPENSATORY PROGRAMS. Brazil has little experience in the use of whole-school or targeted assistance programs for disadvantaged students. The central idea behind these kinds of programs is that public policy may need to include positive discrimination actions to assure that children with disadvantaged backgrounds receive additional opportunities and support to succeed in education to the same degree that non-disadvantaged children do. Many countries, including the United States (Title 1 under the Education and Secondary Education Act and the current No Child Left Behind program), England (Education Action Zones), Chile (900 Schools), and elsewhere in Europe, Asia, and Africa, have compensatory programs that allocate additional educational resources to disadvantaged students, such as children from poor families or minority population groups, or to schools with high proportions of these students. A great deal of research has shown that these programs have a significant and positive impact on the educational outcomes of poor and disadvantaged children. In addition to providing subsidies or in-kind support such as food, clothing, or school supplies, successful programs are effective because they involve parents and communities, promote processes in schools and jurisdictions based out outcome benchmarks, use data to guide decision-making, align goals for student performance with local and national standards, and evaluate results to fine-tune compensatory strategies.

USING FEDERAL FUNDING TO INDUCE EQUITY POLICIES IN LOCAL JURISDICTIONS. The Federal Government spends substantial resources on bringing materials and services to state and municipal schools, on the training of local administrative staff and teachers, and on a wide range of other specialized programs. But very few of these sub-national governments integrate these federal resources and program into their budgets and delivery plans for educational services. In particular, sub-national governments often fail to absorb successful practices from Federal education initiatives into their own systems or complement the federal funding for these initiatives with their own allocation of funds. Instead, many seem to prefer to ignore these programs, instead developing their own initiatives they believe would be more relevant to their own historical or cultural characteristics. The potential impact on improving equity in these jurisdictions can be very high if federal resources and support were to be made contingent on the adoption of pro-poor and pro-equity policy reforms by beneficiary municipal or state governments.

Message 2. Encouraging municipalities to increase their delivery of preschool services
Research in Brazil shows that early intervention in the development and schooling of four- to six-year-old children can substantially reduce repetition at primary school, improve their chances of attaining higher levels of education, and ultimately improve their employment prospects and incomes. Overall, rates of return to these investments are estimated to be well above returns for other levels of education.

Brazil's constitution recognizes the value of early childhood education, and includes a guarantee of free preschool for every child. Unfortunately, putting this guarantee into practice in the short- to medium-term may not be fiscally viable for most municipal governments, which are the authorities legally responsible for providing preschool. Therefore, municipal governments should be encouraged to prioritize their provision of free preschool education to poor families, with careful targeting to assure the best use of scarce resources. The Federal government can also provide financial incentives for municipal governments to expand preschool programs, especially for children from the poorest families. These incentives can stimulate increased investments in preschool provision, assure the conditions for quality and safety, and promote the engagement of non-government organizations in the provision of early childhood development services.

Context
One of the weakest links in Brazil's array of education services is early childhood education. There is now an enormous and incontrovertible body of evidence from Brazil as well as from around the world that shows the contribution of developmentally-sound early childhood programs or activities to the success of subsequent educational and economic outcomes.

THE ROLE OF EARLY CHILDHOOD DEVELOPMENT ON SUBSEQUENT COGNITIVE DEVELOPMENT. Over three decades of research has shown that the brain develops from early infancy. Recent findings confirm that environmental conditions during the preschool years substantially affect the growth of children's neural pathways and, therefore, how the brain's "circuitry" is wired. According to this research, the vast majority of a person's neural pathways are formed before he enters school. For this reason, the body of evidence linking the early childhood development programs to subsequent outcomes is so strong.

INTERNATIONAL EVIDENCE ON THE VALUE OF EARLY CHILDHOOD PROGRAMS. Studies of international experience, including a review of 19 Latin American early childhood development (ECD) programs, have found that young children exposed to ECD do better in school than do children not exposed to early intervention, show improved nutrition and health. ECD programs help to ensure that children receive health status, have higher intelligence scores, have higher rates of school enrollment, reduced repetition and dropout. This research, conducted over many years in countries as different as Argentina, Bolivia, Colombia, Guatemala, Uruguay, India, Jamaica, Mexico, and Turkey, provided strong support for the conclusion that a comprehensive national program of early childhood services is a strong weapon against poverty, a builder of human capital, and an excellent investment in a country's overall development.

RESEARCH IN BRAZIL SHOWS THE BENEFITS OF EARLY CHILDHOOD PROGRAMS. Recent research was carried out in Brazil examining the impact of pre-school enrollment on education outcomes, employment, and future earnings using data from the 1996 and 1997 living standards survey for the cohort between the ages of 25 and 64 (IBGE 1997). The analysis of the data finds that the number of years of attendance at preschool has a positive and statistically significant impact on ultimate school attainment. An additional year of preschool increases schooling attained by approximately 0.5 years. For families in which parents have had 4 years of schooling, children gain an additional 0.4 years of education due to attendance in preschool. For children of illiterate parents, the impact of preschool attendance on educational attainment is even higher. The analysis also shows that preschool attendance has a positive and statistically significant effect on the probability of being promoted to the subsequent grade level. The impact on repetition rates is also positive and significant. On average, the probability of repeating a grade is reduced by about 4 percentage points for each additional year of preschool, independent of the quality of the preschool program. The main impact of preschool seems to be one of better preparedness for further schooling. Therefore, investment in good-quality preschool is expected to improve the attainment and the efficiency levels of future schooling. Overall for children of poorly educated parents in particular, social rates-of-return for public investments in preschool education are estimated at above 12 percent (see figure 3) for uneducated parents.

Figure 3: Increase in future earnings associated with preschool attendance for children of illiterate parents.

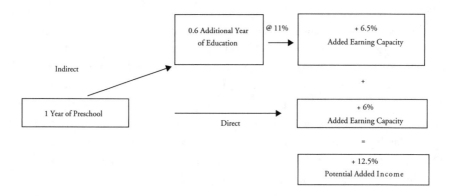

Brazil Early Child Development: A Focus on the Impact of Preschools, World Bank, 2001.

AVAILABILITY OF EARLY CHILDHOOD SERVICES IN BRAZIL. Middle- and upper-middle-class children, who already usually have the advantage of a more stimulating and supporting family background, also have access to private early childhood development programs to which poor children rarely have access in Brazil. Figure 4 shows that anywhere in Brazil, children from the poorest 40 percent of families consistently have less than half the access to preschool programs than those from wealthy families. In fact, preschool programs in Brazil disproportionately serve children who come from wealthier families, live in urban areas, and have better educated parents. Because poor households lack productive assets, market reforms will not necessarily help them. Conventional efforts are usually not supplemented with aggressive policies and programs to ensure that poor families can exploit new opportunities. The more unequal the society, the greater the logic for the state to provide incentives or subsidies to early child intervention programs, at least until there are sufficient resources to complete coverage for all children.

**Figure 4: Early education enrollments by
per capita income, for children age 0-6**

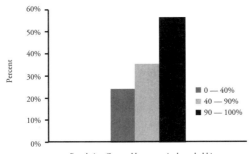

FINANCING OF PRESCHOOL IN BRAZIL. Although Brazil spent approximately US$1 billion in direct expenditures on early childhood education in 1995 (the most recent year in which data are available), per child spending ranged from a low of US$37 to US$55 in the North and Northeast regions to US$173 in the South, US$324 in the Midwest, and more than US$660 in the Southeast. The state of São Paulo alone accounted for 92 percent of spending in the Southeast region and for 75 percent of the nation's total spending on early childhood services. In other words, total public spending for preschool in Brazil primarily reflects the early education budget of a single wealthy state. With the exception of that one state, spending on preschool education is trivial. Moreover, in 1995, only 5 percent of public expenditures on early childhood services was spent in the Northeast, while about two-thirds of the country's poor lived in that region (IPEA 1999).[1]

INEQUALITIES IN THE FINANCING OF PRESCHOOL SERVICES. The data from the Brazilian Living Standards Measurement Survey indicate that children from all economic levels have approximately equal access to public preschools. In fact, in areas where the number of poor children in the population is large, even-handed participation in the public system reflects the failure to target scarce public services to those who need them most, rather than equity of access, as indicated by enrollment figures for children from different

---

[1] Municipal expenditures on preschool education increased following the introduction of FUNDEF. Only approximately 7 percent of municipalities reduced their expenditure on pre-school education in the period from 1997 to 2000, where as 55% increased their expenditure, and 36% had expenditures on pre-school education unchanged.

income groups in Figure 4. Although almost all (95 percent) of the 4-6 year olds in the wealthiest fifth of the metropolitan Northeast are enrolled in some form of preschool (81 percent in private programs, 14 percent in public), only a third (33 percent) of children in the poorest fifth go to preschool or day care (1 percent in private programs, 32 percent in public). Part of the problem stems from policymakers' effort to comply with the Constitutional guarantee to provide free preschool services for every Brazilian child. Accordingly, public preschools accounted for 76 percent of all free childcare in Brazil in 1997, and half of all urban 6-year-olds paid nothing to attend public preschool (Paci 1999). Because many of those enrolled are not poor, however, the provision of free public preschools for all constitutes a substantial subsidy to the non-poor.

Data from the earlier National Household Sample Survey (PNAD) (IBGE 1989) suggest that parents in Brazil, especially mothers, are willing to pay for childcare if the short-term benefits outweigh the costs. Working mothers who are richer and better educated, and therefore likely to earn more, are also more willing to pay for private preschool than are mothers who are less educated or not formally employed (Levison 1990). Although most funding for private preschools is derived from fees paid by parents, the federal government spent US$180 million in 1995 on subsidies to privately run preschools and day-care centers (creches conveniadas) which served approximately 1.4 million poor children (IPEA 1999). In addition to public subsidies, charitable organizations and other outside donors fund a number of preschools that provide childcare for low fees or free of charge. Yet, the PPV data (IBGE 1997c) also show that, in fiscal 1996, private, low-fee preschools catered mainly to the top two quintiles of the population based on household expenditure.

Considerations for Policy Formulation

The Constitution and national legislation stipulate that municipal governments, and not the federal or state governments, are responsible for providing early childhood education services. Moreover, while the Constitution guarantees free preschool for every child, municipalities are also required to give priority attention to primary education (fundamental level), and to spend at least two-thirds of their constitutionally-mandated 25% of total revenues on that level of education.

MUNICIPALITIES PRIORITIZING PRESCHOOL FINANCING FOR THE POOR. Given the tremendous value of early childhood development services, and the financing constraints faced by municipal governments, improving preschool access to the poorest Brazilian children should become a policy priority. The Constitution's guarantee of free preschool for every

Brazilian child is a commendable commitment that needs to be made more effective through targeting. Poverty mapping within states, especially in the poorest regions of the Northeast and North, is needed to identify gaps in access to preschool. The optimal method of delivery should then be determined, utilizing best international practice and tailoring it to local needs and conditions. Locations of preschool services should be prioritized in areas of high concentrations of the poor.

INTEGRATING PRESCHOOL WITH OTHER EARLY CHILDHOOD DEVELOPMENT SERVICES. Because children aged 0-3 are mostly cared for at home, interventions for this age group may be most beneficial in connection with primary health programs and dissemination of information to parents, especially mothers. Informing poor parents about the benefits of early childhood education is an important factor in increasing utilization of these services.

STRENGTHENING PRESCHOOL FINANCES TO INCREASE ENROLLMENTS AND EFFICIENCY. Research shows that there is an impressive willingness to pay for preschool services. The actual fees charged, however, undervalue the true demand. In the Northeast, for example, even middle income parents may be charged an annul fee equivalent to the price of one pair of jeans. A better fee structure, perhaps with an income-based sliding scale arrangement, would be an important measure for improving the financing of pre-school without resorting to additional budgetary outlays. Other measures could include exploring and expanding informal programs and NGO-managed services as low-cost alternatives to standard public services.

FEDERAL INCENTIVES TO MUNICIPALITIES. The federal government can create an incentive matching fund to leverage financing from municipalities as an incentive for them to set up integrated ECD programs according to a framework agreed with the Ministry of Education. The framework could include multiple dimensions of early childhood development, it could incorporate various types of providers, it could mandate safety factors for these providers, and it could set up established process and outcome targets that the federal government could monitor. The determination of the level of cost sharing needs to be carefully assessed to leverage the largest amount of municipal funds with the smallest possible matching subsidy.

Introduce a FUNDEF-type incentive to expand provision of preschool services. The demonstrated success of FUNDEF in raising the enrollment of students at the 1st through 8th grade levels suggests that a similar mechanism may be applied to preschool education where enrollment remains low, namely pre-school and secondary education. A formula funding mechanism based on the number of children enrolled in preschool programs would provide an incentive for municipalities to boost their own spending efforts to expand the provision of preschool services in their jurisdictions.

Message 3. Intensifying practices that enhance the quality and efficiency of schooling. The unprecedented increases in primary school coverage in recent years need to be complemented with improvements in the quality of schooling to boost Brazil's long-term growth prospects as well as young people's opportunities. Brazil scored last out of 38 countries on the Organization for Economic Cooperation and Development (OECD) Program for International Student Assessment (PISA 2000), and most students score below standard on Brazil's own national assessment in reading and math achievement.

Low efficiency in resource utilization is a critical bottleneck in efforts to improve educational quality. A high repetition rate, an indicator of low quality, is stubbornly persistent, with only two of three children completing the eighth grade, increasing the cost per graduate by up to 70 percent. Moreover, the wide variation in educational results across the 27 states and thousands of municipalities per dollar spent provides solid evidence that some sub-national governments succeed in making much more efficient use of their resources than others.

Efficient school systems and effective schooling practices are already under implementation in numerous states and municipalities throughout Brazil. These models are helping students of every background achieve better learning outcomes and progress efficiently through the school system to higher and higher levels of attainment. A combination of incentives, social pressure, and approaches based on "positive deviants" can encourage municipal and state governments to learn from successful practices and adapt effective models to their own conditions and needs. These models include: decentralizing resources and authority to schools, agreeing on performance targets with schools; publicizing information on standardized test scores and other performance measures to help the public hold schools accountable for results; having schools prepare development plans and receive incentives to align their programs on learning outcomes; and deploying empirically-validated instructional packages to their schools that integrate learning standards with periodic diagnostic testing, increased use of books and didactic materials, content and skill based professional development for principals and teachers, and greater parental engagement.

Context

LOW COMPLETION RATES CAPTURE THE INEFFICIENCIES IN BRAZILIAN EDUCATION. With the possible exception of children living in isolated rural communities or from certain disadvantaged groups, access to school, even up through the lower secondary level (grades 5 through 8), does not appear to be an intractable problem. Completion rates, however, tell a different story. Although a continual but gradual increase in investments in education since 1980, especially during the last eight years, has resulted in a mammoth 5-fold increase in proportion of students completing eighth grade (from 12 percent in 1980, to 37 percent in 1995, to nearly 50 percent in 2001 --see Figure 5), the proportion of entrants who survive in the system to the next grade level, and eventually graduate from the fundamental cycle or from secondary school is still very low. Completion rates are lowest for children attending school in certain regions of the country, especially in the States of the North and Northeast regions.

PRIMARY LEVEL REPETITION IMPEDES SECONDARY LEVEL EXPANSION. Furthermore, student flow analysis demonstrates that repetition, rather than access to school, is the principal impediment to the expansion of enrollment in secondary education. Repetition is the main reason why only two of three children entering first grade complete grade 8—and take 10 years to do so. (See Message 1, above.) Because of repetition, Brazil spends 35 percent more than is needed for students in first through fourth grades, 22 percent more per student in fifth thorough eighth grades, and 23 percent more per student in ninth through 11th grades. Worse, when dropouts are factored in, the corresponding inefficiencies are 45 percent, 70 percent, and 106 percent. For purposes of comparison, Brazil spends nearly as much per eighth grade graduate as countries like Hungary and Malaysia, but with substantially poorer educational outcomes

Figure 5. Improvement proportion of students attaining each grade level, 1995 and 2001

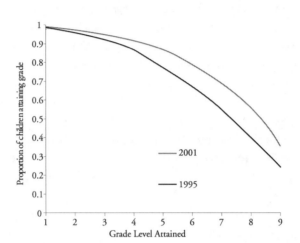

EFFICIENCY OF SPENDING IS LOW BECAUSE OF EXCESSIVE REPETITION AND DROPOUT. Because so many students repeat grades before advancing to the subsequent grade level, or drop out of school before completing their education, much of the money spent in education is wasted. For example, at the extreme, if there were no repetition or dropout from the compulsory grades, Brazil would have 45 percent more to spend on first through fourth grade education and 70 percent more resources for fifth through eighth grade schooling. This level of funding would make educational expenditures in Brazil equivalent to the educational expenditure levels seen in countries with substantially better educational outcomes, such as Hungary and Malaysia.

GAINS IN QUALITY ARE MORE DIFFICULT TO ACHIEVE. The key education issue in Brazil today is delivering educational services at a level of quality that is high enough to encourage children to attend school regularly, progress through the system, and graduate with adequate levels of learning achievement and skills. Brazil has begun to make some progress on this objective. For example, since 1995, repetition rates have declined by nearly 30 percent on average, with the greatest gains found in the poorest regions of the country. Nonetheless, Brazil needs to make a much greater effort to improve the effectiveness of its schools and consequent learning outcomes of its students. Brazil scored the worst among the 38 countries that participated in the Organization for Economic

Cooperation and Development's Program for International Student Assessment (PISA 2000). This outcome was recently confirmed by the results from Brazil's own national assessment system (SAEB). The 2001 SAEB assessment of fourth grade mathematics performance shows that only 47 percent of students exceeded level 3 out of the10 levels on the SAEB proficiency scale. Children who performed at level 3 or lower are unable to solve simple problems using units of money and time, cannot use data portrayed in graphs, and are not capable of recognizing the principle of place value in a decimal number system. For Portuguese language and reading performance in 2001, only 41 percent of fourth grade children surpassed level 2 on the 8 level proficiency scale. This means that 59 percent of fourth grade children cannot adequately infer the meaning of a word from the context in a written text, identify the main idea of an informative text, such as from a magazine or newspaper, and are unable to specify the main conflict in a plot from a narrative text.

Figure 6: Stagnation or decline in student achievement 1995 - 2001

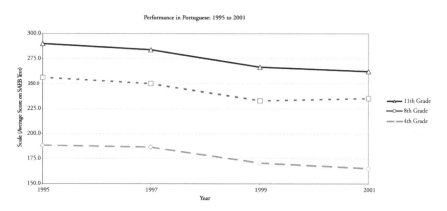

CAUSES OF DECLINING PERFORMANCE. Declining performance may have been the cost of increased enrollment and promotion. Figure 6 shows that since the SAEB tests were first implemented in 1995, test scores have steadily, although gradually declined. The cause of this decline is still not fully understood by researchers in Brazil. The government's explanation for this is that this same period saw an increase in enrollment and a reduction in repetition rates that were described above. Enrolling the last 10 percent of children who had been excluded from the system in earlier years, coupled with policies that may have encouraged teachers to promote students before they had acquired the necessary skills and knowledge, have contributed to stagnation or may have brought down average achievement. These results should generate an even stronger call to action to take measures that will dramatically improve learning achievement for all children.

Considerations for Policy Formulation

There are models of effective schooling and efficient school system management under implementation across the states and municipalities of Brazil, as well as elsewhere, that have been show to produce substantial gains in system efficiency and school outcomes. These models and practices need to be extended nationwide through the use of such policy instruments as incentives, accountability, institutional capacity building, public information and dissemination programs, and inter-jurisdictional collaboration.

Expand implementation of flow correction initiatives to raise efficiency. Given that persistent repetition and high numbers of over-age students at each grade have come to be well recognized in Brazil as the key determinants of the low efficiency that characterizes education systems in Brazil, an increasing number of initiatives have been designed and supported by creative educators and organizations in the last few years. These innovations include Accelerated Instruction (Classes de Aceleração), remedial summer school programs, learning cycle approaches (such as Ciclo Básico or Escola Candanga) that allow students to study in a more modular way and advance at their own pace within cycles, and academic credit mechanisms that allow students to advance to the next grade without successfully completing every subject. Because of the powerful impact these models have on improving the internal efficiency of school systems, there are built-in incentives for sub-national governments to deploy them. Nevertheless, federal and state governments should undertake a massive effort to disseminate the cost-effective benefits of these models and promote their use by every jurisdiction in the country until age-grade distortion is virtually eliminated. An added benefit of these types of flow correction initiatives is that they are pro-poor since lower income children, who are disproportionately more likely to repeat or drop out, will benefit most from such programs.

Develop and use performance information to drive up quality through public accountability. Brazil has seen tremendous progress on the development of educational assessment programs and statistics systems by the federal level, by quite a few state governments, and even by a number of municipal systems. Nonetheless, the potential power of information to create incentives for quality improvement has barely been tapped. For example, despite the availability of up-to-date and reliable data, the public does not know which states and municipalities are investing more astutely in education, which are more successful in raising school quality standards, and which have most improved student learning achievement levels and graduation rates. At sub-national levels, citizens are not accurately informed about which schools are being more successful with their students. Federal, state, and municipal governments alike have a civic responsibility to openly and routinely provide their citizens with readily digestible information on investment, expenditures, and performance at every institutional level. They should also inform their public on what policies, programs, and actions they are developing or implementing to improving student performance and school results. These actions will improve the schools' and governments' accountability to their citizenry.

INTRODUCE TEACHER CERTIFICATION AND ENHANCE PROFESSIONAL DEVELOPMENT. The teacher is the single most important player in the education system, but research in Brazil shows that large numbers of them lack the core competencies and subject-matter knowledge to be effective in the classroom. State governments, and even the federal government can help improve teacher performance by: (a) defining teacher quality standards with respect to content knowledge and classroom know-how; (b) establishing mechanisms, such as certification systems, incentive programs, and formal career plans to motivate teacher improvement on these standards; and (c) promoting the development of professional development programs with sub-national governments to provide the skills and abilities teachers need to attain the new standards.

DEVELOP AND DISSEMINATE MODELS THAT HELP SCHOOLS DEVELOP THEIR OWN COHERENT STRATEGY TO BEST SERVE THEIR PRINCIPAL CLIENT, THE LEARNER. When schools' own instructional efforts are not aligned on the objective of raising student learning, resources are wasted and results are jeopardized. Although the staff in most schools may complain about limited financial and human resources, many spend their scarce resources in fragmentary and ineffective ways, often with they belief that they are acting in the best interests of their students. Research in Brazil finds that disorganized schools are more likely to have staff who blame parents and students for low levels of learning, rather than accept their responsibility for assuring children's educational success. School teachers and other professional staff need both stimulus and assistance from their education secretariats to help them recognize the need for positive change, as well as to reevaluate and restructure their own management processes and instructional strategies around the objective of student learning. A program to support school restructuring of this sort is the School Development Plan initiative, which has been supported by the Ministry of Education's Fundescola Program, and by numerous state and local governments, and has been subjected to high quality external evaluation and validation. The School Development Plan provides a model for helping schools undertake this kind of self-diagnostic and strategic restructuring process. More than this even, many schools may need further assistance in the pedagogical arena. Such schools could benefit from packaged teaching/learning models that integrate curriculum standards, student learning diagnostic tests, instructional materials, and quality assurance processes, along with professional development for teachers. Escola Ativa, and Gestar are examples of such models that have been implemented with the support of the Ministry of Education and many sub-national governments. Although nearly all schools need the support of their local education authorities to build their capacity for continuous improvement, not all need a packaged teaching/learning model to achieve improved outcomes.

CONDUCT APPLIED RESEARCH TO IDENTIFY AND DISSEMINATE BEST PRACTICE. The Federal government, along with the academic community, has a responsibility to evaluate education improvement initiatives developed by municipal or state governments, universities, NGOs, or private groups, draw lessons from that research, and disseminate the findings to sub-national governments, and not just those who are making the efforts and taking the risk in developing and implementing new initiatives. The quality of this evaluation is critically important since so much of the research in Brazil uses traditional approaches comparing averages of different cohorts of students over time, or use case study models that cannot be generalized. Value-added models and randomized assignment experimentation methods, for example, would make it possible to examine the impact of programs or initiatives independent of family background or other exogenous factors.

Message 4. Strengthening municipal governance and accountability

Although FUNDEF provides a strong incentive for municipal governments to increase student enrollment, many municipal governments, especially the thousands of small to medium-sized municipalities, are not effectively using their administrative and financial capacity to improve the effectiveness of their schools, address the equity disparities that define their systems, or expand preschool services. Their accountability to their clients is constrained by an ambiguous division of responsibility for education with state governments. Many municipal school systems are characterized by a proliferation of programs and governing bodies operating with little communication and coordination, and weak managerial and technical systems.

Municipalities should recognize their constitutional mandate to provide adequate quality educational services equitably, but also understand that in the short run they will need to prioritize their support to schools serving children from the most vulnerable families first. The fact that some municipalities perform better than others with similar characteristics means that there are benefits to be gained if municipalities were to form partnerships to share information, policies, programs, and practices, working collectively to improve student results. The federal government also has an important role to play in setting standards and providing models of effective education secretariats; developing and disseminating tools to assist local secretariats with strategic planning, quality management, and accountability systems; and providing instruments that municipalities can adapt to structure their management and control systems. The federal government and state governments can also play a role in promoting the sharing of best practices across municipalities.

Context

On the grounds that municipal governments are closer to the point of educational service delivery and can therefore better manage educational resources and be more accountable to their clients, Brazil's legislative and policy reforms have promoted the municipalization of basic education. The FUNDEF amendment and law accelerated this process by providing financial incentives to jurisdictions for each student enrolled in their system. In 1996, just prior to implementation of Fund for Development and Maintenance of Elementary Teaching and Teacher Development (FUNDEF), about 42 percent of students in grades 1 through 4 were enrolled in municipal-run schools; by 2001, 63 percent were.

The allocation of municipal education expenditures and the consequent results point to the benefits of decentralization in the municipal management of resources. Municipal education systems have more students and more resources at their disposal. The transfer of resources to a local level have led to expenditure allocation decisions that appear to respond more closely to educational needs. In the area of capital expenditures, municipalities have invested judiciously in classroom construction to accommodate additional students – and World Bank research finds that there is a positive correlation between class size in 1996 and subsequent construction that reduced the problem of overcrowded classrooms. Municipalities have lower expenditures on personnel as compared to states (55% vs. 63%) and are able to spend more on non-personnel recurrent expenditures such as transportation. Municipalities historically paid lower salaries to teachers as compared to most states, but these salary differences have narrowed. One of the clearest advantages of municipalities occurs in the area of administrative personnel -whereas state system typically have a large bureaucracy of administrative personnel that do not necessarily provide for close support to schools, the administrative staff of municipal education secretariats have closer contact with the schools, because they are able to visit the schools more frequently and are otherwise better connected. Evidence on this comes from qualitative fieldwork carried out by the Ministry of Education and World Bank supervision visits of in the Northeast. The finding is further corroborated by quantitative analysis that compare state and municipal administrative spending.

FUNDEF HAS LED MUNICIPALITIES TO SUCCESSFULLY RAISE ENROLLMENTS. In the decade prior to the introduction of FUNDEF, municipal government were doing very little to increase enrollments. The impact of FUNDEF, with its clear economic stakes, is dramatic. Between 1996 and 2001, the overall net enrollment rate increased from 89 to 96 percent, with most of the gains coming from municipal school systems, which now represent 54 percent of total primary enrollment (compared with 34 percent in 1996.

BUT FUNDEF'S INCENTIVES ARE NOT SUFFICIENT TO ENSURE QUALITY OUTCOMES. It is difficult for many municipalities except perhaps the largest ones such as the state capitals, to be able to put together a team of qualified professionals to perform the activities needed to run a school system effectively. For example, a certain amount of technical expertise is required to make a multi-year plan of investments in maintenance or improvement of the physical infrastructure, which just one of the responsibilities of a municipal education system. In addition, training programs for municipal secretaries of education, while they may be important, may also be insufficient to overcome the constraints of institutional capacity. Institutional weaknesses found in many municipal secretariats include inexperienced leadership, fragile organizational structures, a low level of competency among administrative and technical staff, and a proliferation of programs and governing bodies operating with little communication and coordination. These limitations constrain not only the capacity to deliver routine services, but also the capacity to take corrective action, and thus achieve the objectives of equity and quality.

THE DIVISION OF LABOR IS NOT CONDUCIVE TO IMPROVED FUNCTIONING. The ambiguous division of labor and responsibility in the education sector, particularly between state and municipal systems, has introduced many complexities and inefficiencies into the system. Moreover, a municipality's accountability to its clients--schools, parents, and students--is constrained by the persistent and ambiguous division of responsibility for fundamental-level education between states and municipalities. This unbalanced dual structure weakens the capacity of the system as a whole to deliver effective education services and to achieve equity.

MUNICIPALITIES TEND TO FOCUS ON ADMINISTRATIVE ISSUES RATHER THAN SCHOOL SUPPORT. Many secretariats have bureaucratic structures that are designed to facilitate administrative functions rather than to maximize pedagogical support to the schools and address school improvement. Municipal secretariats frequently do not have enough people to specialize in separate functions, so financial management and materials acquisition and management of human resources, for example, may be carried out by the municipality's accountant and personnel manager rather than by secretariat staff. In addition, integrated functions are rare, such as pedagogically related school support and supervision aimed at enhancing learning in the classrooms. The result is that key functions do not get the policy or strategic attention they require for establishing norms and standards or allocating resources.

STRONGER LEADERSHIP AND DIRECTION IS ALSO NEEDED. The fragmentation of the education system into a large number of state and municipal systems has made it difficult to develop a shared, unifying vision. But many municipal secretariats lack a well-formulated vision and strategy because of the difficulty of attracting strong leaders. Seeing fund raising for the system as their major role, they bring in a large number of programs, activities, or projects from wherever they can get them. But since these interventions do not add up to a clear and unified plan, they pull the system and the schools in different directions.

MANAGEMENT PRACTICES NEED TO REFORM. Further impeding the ability of secretariats of education to deliver services effectively are weak management, excessive and divided control, and political interference. Lack of systems, skills, and incentives weakens the key management functions of leadership, planning, communication, and coordination. Political interference is pervasive as well. Political factors influence not only the choice of higher level goals for the education system, which may be appropriate, but the choice of lower level objectives, strategies, and actions, where technical and professional considerations ought to dominate. One of the most common results of political intervention in the education system is high staff turnover, which interferes with continuity.

THE EXPECTED GAINS FROM SOCIAL CONTROL MECHANISMS ARE NOT BEING ACHIEVED. Under FUNDEF legislation and regulation, FUNDEF councils were established in municipalities and states as an explicit measure to improve accountability. In fact, there is a proliferation of social control bodies to which schools and municipalities are supposed to report. Small municipal secretariats, and schools in those systems, have to work with at least five councils: the Municipal Education Council, the School Education Council, the FUNDEF Council, the School Lunch Council, and the Bolsa-Escola Council. Some municipalities have set up councils that are genuinely representative, with elected members from the municipal secretariats, teachers unions and parents associations. Councils in other municipalities are representative merely in name, with members nominally representing specific groups such as parents, but in truth being hand picked nominees of the mayor – quantitative data is lacking about the respective proportion of functioning and non-functioning councils. One of the initiatives of the Ministry of Education's Fundescola program has been the training of members of social councils about their rights and responsibilities. The training has been useful, but true empowerment of the councils requires additional steps, possibly combining the accountability to the local community with accountability to other branches of government such as municipal and state auditors, justice secretariats, and the federal government.

Considerations for Policy Formulation

While it is true that some state governments are providing support to strengthen municipal education systems, the majority are unable or in many cases, unwilling to do so[2]. Consequently, the federal government has an important role to play in: (a) setting standards; (b) providing models of effective education secretariat management and administration; (c) developing and disseminating tools to assist municipal secretariats of education implement strategic planning, quality management, and accountability systems; and (d) providing instruments that municipalities can use to structure their school and staff management and control systems. The federal government can also play a part in providing training around these objectives and tools, and promote cross-municipality sharing of best practices.

BUILD ON THE PREVIOUS EXPERIENCE OF SUCCESSFUL MUNICIPALITIES. Some municipalities and states have done much better than others on measures of efficiency and effectiveness through more judicious use of their own resources. The better performing municipalities have invested more adequately in upgrading and rationalizing the school infrastructure, instituted services of transportation for children, improved the quality of teachers and provided them with greater administrative and pedagogical support. The report, "Brazil Municipal Education: Resources, Incentives, and Results" (2002) provides evidence that such measures have led to an improvement in the learning and well being of the children. At the same time, there are numerous municipalities that lack a coherent educational policy, where the educational system remains highly politicized and clientelistic, and in which learning outcomes remain low. It is a policy imperative in Brazil today to bring up the lagging municipalities to par with the municipalities that have successfully overcome the same constraints to improvement. A model based on identifying the behavior of "positive deviants" (or "high outliers") that has been used internationally in a wide range of cases could be applied to municipal and even state education systems. In fact, there is well-documented evidence of the success in Brazil itself of an approach that takes a more dynamic view of decentralization. Such a view puts a high value on the importance of establishing feedback loops for the flow of information across and within sub-national entities and community organizations. The examples include the activities of the "priority action zones" (ZAPs) that form part of the federal Fundescola program, and a range of programs in the health and education sectors in Ceará.

---

[2] Issues related to the expansion of preschool services by municipalities are treated in Message 2, above.

HELP MUNICIPAL GOVERNMENTS RECOGNIZE THE SCHOOL AS THEIR MAIN CLIENT. Municipal governments' main responsibility is to strengthen schools and support school improvement processes to make all of their schools successful at raising student learning outcomes. To do this effectively, they have to realign all of their activities and practices around this objective. Municipal governments need to recognize that, while their ultimate beneficiaries are children, their immediate client is the school. Therefore, education secretariats should organize themselves to provide technical assistance and support to their schools and the teachers in those schools, at particularly to those schools which are most in need. Furthermore, with increasing demands for improving educational outcomes, states and municipalities need to resist the tendency to adopt multiple programs, untested initiatives, or policies that are not centered directly on student achievement through school improvement. Many sub-national governments need incentives and external support in the area of institutional development and capacity building to properly and openly examine their strategies and organizational processes, and make the kinds of structural changes that would assure a coherent program. Moreover, since school system reform is inherently political, external support for sustainable change in sub-national education systems needs to be coupled with broad-based public support for school improvement. A policy transformation that depends on a visionary or charismatic Secretary of Education, mayor or governor is not sustainable. External assistance and support, such as from the Federal government or, in the case of municipalities, from state governments as well, is needed here as well to stimulate public understanding of, and demand for, dynamic school reform.

FEDERAL AND STATE GOVERNMENTS CAN HELP MUNICIPAL RESOURCES GO FURTHER There are a number of ways in which the federal government assist municipalities improve the effectiveness of their educational services. Federal programs such as the Ministry of Education's Fundescola Program, and state programs such as Bahia's series of education projects serve as excellent examples of how these levels of government can help build the capacity of municipal governments' secretariats of education.

EVALUATION. First, the Federal government and state governments can provide assistance to municipalities to help them establish or deploy student, school, and teacher assessment and evaluation systems, or to assess the performance at state and municipal schools. With a few exceptions, most states do not have the technical capacity to provide municipalities with technical advice and support for these activities. The Federal government could develop, and at little marginal cost, provide municipalities (as well as states) with test packages that have equalization linkages with SAEB. With these kits, municipalities could routinely test student achievement to diagnose gaps in teaching and learning and to report results to parents and teachers. This would transform evaluation into a pedagogical instrument and provide for greater accountability and quality of instructional services. Alternatively, the Federal government could offer incentives to the private sector to develop such instruments for municipalities and states.

SUPPORTING STRATEGIC PLANNING, INSTITUTIONAL DEVELOPMENT, AND CROSS-MUNICIPAL COLLABORATION. A second area for the federal government is to help municipalities improve their strategic focus, management, supervision, and statistical systems. Again, this requires the development of training and mobilization programs and the design and dissemination of instruments to help municipalities improve their management and administrative systems. Municipalities need technical assistance to help them integrate annual strategic planning into their business planning processes and to introduce systematic and routine supervision programs designed assist their schools and professional staff improve performance and focus more effectively on student learning and success. In addition, the federal government can provide opportunities for municipalities collaborate with one another to share best practices and to cross-monitor one another's implementation of change and performance improvement.

CAREER PLANS FOR TEACHERS. A third area where the Federal government can help is in assisting Municipal government legislate motivating and cost-effective teacher career plans. These career plans can be used to reinforce national programs to improve teacher quality through standards setting and certification. The Ministry of Education has some experience with help in the area of teacher career plans thanks to Fundescola's development of comprehensive training packages for municipal career plans, including customized state-of-the-art software to help municipalities prepare the documentation to support the introduction of these teacher career plans in their legislation. Among the elements needed in career plans are: a) the inclusion of all educational professionals, not just classroom teachers; b) recruitment of teachers based on open competition; c) inclusion of a points-based system of horizontal and vertical differentiation in remuneration; d) incorporation of teacher qualification upgrading; e) incentives qualifications only from accredited institutions and would include a periodic assessment of teacher competencies; defined to include teaching and learning practices used in the classroom as well as enhanced co-operation of the parents and the community; and f) benefits would be explicitly defined on the basis of educational objectives.

CLEARING HOUSE OF EFFECTIVE TEACHING/LEARNING MODELS. Fourth, the Federal government can also help Municipalities by recommending technical guidelines and strategies for school improvement and reduction of educational disparities. This could include the development and dissemination of manuals, training materials, and technical assistance programs to help municipalities establish and support school improvement processes and equity improvement programs. This would include mechanisms to support funded school development projects and teaching-learning improvement programs and strategies. The Ministry also has a role in evaluating best practices across municipal governments and disseminating findings to municipal governments.

Message 5. Accelerating the provision of secondary schooling (grades 5-11)
At 40 percent, Brazil's secondary school net enrollment ratio is about that of the United States after World War I and behind the Latin American average of 50 percent. Yet evidence from cross-country data suggest that improvements in secondary school access and quality would yield the greatest payoff for Brazil. Moreover, a policy of increasing investments in secondary education is pro-poor (compared with increasing public funding for higher education). Improvements in promotion rates for primary school students would mean that much of the increased demand for secondary schooling could be accommodated through a reallocation of resources from the primary to secondary school level, but additional investments from state governments will surely be necessary.

Expanding investments in education to ensure substantial increases in secondary school coverage and quality could improve access to better quality schooling in grades 5–8, particularly for students from rural areas or very poor families, and provide more classes in grades 9 through 11 in urban areas. Mechanisms for expanding coverage and quality could include improving nighttime secondary schooling, expanding distance education, collaborating with private school systems, and leveraging traditional secondary school provision to far more students.

Context
Year after year, Brazil's labor market, like labor markets the world over, demands ever higher levels of schooling from its entering workers (see Policy Note on innovation). Rates of return to secondary education surpass those of primary schooling, and returns to higher education are rising even faster. But the average worker in Brazil has only about six years of schooling, whereas it is more than 11 years for OECD workers and 8 years in Asia. That not only undermines life options for Brazilian workers, but the nation's competi-

tiveness as well. This gap in educational attainment, which continues to widen as many of the more industrialized countries invest heavily in raising the quality of their work force, will be translated into an increasingly powerful demand by Brazilian youth for access to good quality secondary education.

SECONDARY EDUCATION COULD ALSO ADAPT TO THE KNOWLEDGE ECONOMY. In increasing access to secondary education, Brazil could also design the system to prepare youth for the move to a more knowledge-based economy. A knowledge economy is one which relies more on the use of ideas rather than physical abilities, and more on the application of technology rather than the transformation of raw materials or the exploitation of labor. Preparing youth to succeed in the knowledge economy requires an secondary education model based on the framework of lifelong learning, which supports learning and skill development throughout the life cycle. This is because continuous and rapid market changes in a knowledge economy mean that skills and abilities depreciate more quickly than before and could be constantly updated. Consequently, to compete under these conditions means that Brazil increasingly needs to provide its population with the kind of secondary schooling that gives graduates the flexibility to upgrade their skills and abilities throughout their life. This means that the secondary education can no longer emphasize content acquisition and task-specific skills but should focus instead on developing learners' decision-making and problem-solving skills, and the ability to learn on their own. Brazil has clearly moved in the direction of preparing youth for lifelong learning through two main policy actions. First, the government chose to completely separate technical education from secondary schools, making a clear choice for secondary education as the last stage of basic education, and dealing with technical education at the post-secondary level. Second, the Ministry of Education, in consultation with sub-national governments and other entities, developed a modern curriculum for secondary education (with the publication of the Parâmetros Curriculares de Ensino Médio) that emphasizes the development of core skills and problem-solving competencies.

Nonetheless, there is still a long road ahead for Brazil to meet these demands. The costs of expanding and transforming secondary schooling are substantial, and there are serious structural challenges facing the country to achieve this change. The good news is that the gradual decline in the number of students enrolling in fundamental levels will make it possible to finance all of the expansion in lower secondary education and almost half of the expansion in upper secondary education by gradually shifting resources between grade levels and making modest improvements within the fundamental cycle. The bad news is that these reductions will not be enough and additional resources may be necessary, particularly to adapt today's infrastructure and professional staff profile to tomorrow's demographic demands. The federal government could also provide incentives for state and municipal education secretariats to create a clearer division of responsibility for the different levels of government. Serious capacity issues may constrain this type of initiative, however, as mentioned above.

REPETITION IN LOWER GRADES IS A MAIN BARRIER TO EXPANDING SECONDARY EDUCATION. Repetition, rather than physical access, is the principal impediment to the expansion of secondary education. Repetition, which is widely used as a quality control and classroom management tool by teachers, results in the fact that only two out of three children who enter first grade in 1998 expect to complete lower secondary education (8th grade), spending 10 years on average to do so, while only one out of three first graders will eventually finish upper secondary education (11th grade), taking an average of 14 years to do so. Beyond the serious educational problems behind these indicators, such a system wastes resources, both human and financial. Drop-out tends to be particularly high in the "transition" grades of 5th and 8th, when students are moving between levels of the system and frequently between schools. If repetition were eliminated, there would be more than enough room in principle to accommodate all of the target population group at the primary and lower secondary level, with the possibility of using extra space to accommodate upper secondary enrollment.

MANY SECONDARY STUDENTS ARE YOUNG WORKING ADULTS. The legacy of repetition also shapes the profile of the secondary school population. Most students who enter upper secondary are already two or more years above their ideal age for grade (only 3% of 14 year olds have completed the 8th grade, compared to 44% for 18 year olds). In fact, 55% of the students enrolled in upper secondary are older than the target age group. Over one third have more than three years of lag. The fact that the survivors of lower secondary education (the clientele for upper secondary) are largely young working adults has deep implications for the identity of secondary schools and poses difficult tradeoffs and pedagogical challenges. Given the current profile of students in secondary education, a major challenge for reducing dropout and improving coverage in the short and even medium term is to provide more relevant and effective means of teaching young working adults.

Figure 7: Proportion of children enrolled in day/night shifts, by age.

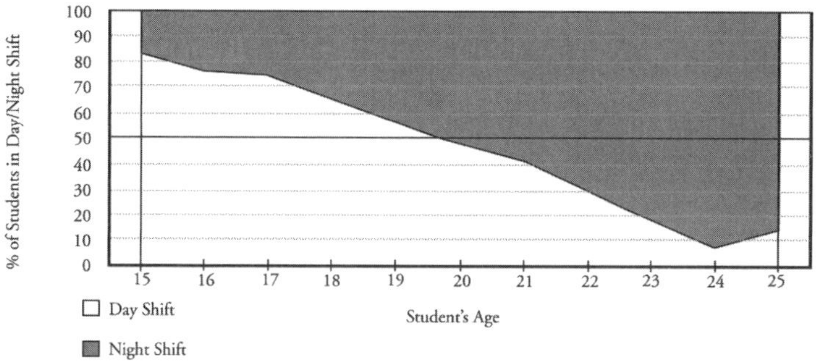

Source: IPEA, based on PPV 1996/97

To some extent, the expected tradeoff between work and school is diminished in Brazil due to the prevalence of night school. Around 60% of students enrolled in upper secondary education (9th – 11th grades) are enrolled in night schools, because a majority of them must work full time. Data from the survey of living conditions (PPV) show that the proportion of night shift students employed or looking for work is 57% versus only 23% for daytime students. This is a consequence of the fact that many students are forced to attend school at night in order to work during the day. The predominance of night schools is a central feature of secondary education in Brazil and one that is not likely to go away, at least in the short run. Figure 7 illustrates how the decision to study at night is largely determined by the age of the student; as he/she gets older and his/her age-grade gap increases, the student faces rising opportunity costs and strong incentives to study at night, as the last resort before dropping out altogether.

THE GROWING CHALLENGE OF TEACHER SHORTAGES. One additional constraint to the expansion of secondary education is the number of qualified professionals available to the system. Brazil today already faces an unprecedented shortage of secondary school (5th through 11th grade) teachers, especially in specialized subject areas. An INEP study of data from 2002 reports a gap of 250,000 teachers altogether, with shortages of 55,000 physics teachers and about the same number of chemistry teachers.

STATE RESPONSIBILITY FOR FINANCING THE EXPANSION OF SECONDARY EDUCATION. Under the Constitution, states are responsible for upper secondary education, while the responsibility for fundamental level education (which includes the lower secondary grades 5-8) is shared with municipalities. In fact, states are the overwhelming providers of both lower and upper secondary education, accounting for over two-thirds of total enrollments. Municipalities account for about 15 percent of enrollments, private providers for another 15 percent, and the federal government for 1 percent. Private participation is higher in upper secondary education, accounting for about 20 percent of enrollments and more than a third of all upper secondary education establishments.

Therefore, expanding and improving secondary education, particularly upper secondary (grades 9 – 11) have enormous fiscal implications for state governments, especially in the absence of earmarked funds for this purpose. Moreover, there is little flexibility to convert savings from gains in efficiency at lower levels of education into investment for increased supply of secondary education.

Considerations for Policy Formulation

Expanding investments in education to ensure substantial increases in secondary school coverage and quality could improve access to better quality schooling in grades 5–8, particularly for students from rural areas or very poor families, and provide more classes in grades 9 through 11 in urban areas. While in the major cities limited construction of new schools may be a priority, in smaller towns as well as in remote rural areas it may be impossible to achieve a minimum scale for operating a secondary school or to find the necessary teachers in all the disciplines. This means that the menu of options for expanding access should be broadened, not to substitute for daytime secondary schools, but rather to create viable alternatives to expand quality secondary education opportunities in those cases where it is not feasible to have a traditional daytime school.

EXPANSION BY REINVESTING SAVINGS FROM INCREASED EFFICIENCIES. A promising source of financing for upper secondary education expansion in Brazil will come with the correction of student flows at lower levels of education. As this flow correction continues to takes place, new students will be reaching secondary education, releasing classroom places, other educational resources such as teachers and support services, and the overall financial burden on the state and federal governments in their input to FUNDEF. The World Bank estimates that this opportunity will become increasingly viable as Brazil's student population in grades 1 through 8 begins to decline during this decade. Increasing system efficiency through reduction of repetition will have a direct impact on both the enrollments in and financing of upper secondary schooling. Based on current per-pupil expenditures, a yearly improvement of one percent in the efficiency of first through eighth grade schooling over the next ten years (that is, a yearly reduction of one percentage point in the repetition rate in each grade, which is by all accounts a conservative estimate), would yield sufficient savings to cover the cost of enrolling three million students in upper secondary education, that is, 47 percent of the expected increase in enrollments over the coming ten years. Nevertheless, it is important to point out that, while possible, the allocation of savings from primary education and lower secondary education to upper secondary education will not be politically easy, especially if much of the savings are obtained at the municipal level. Institutional and political barriers will also likely make the reallocation of resources difficult, especially if the savings are generated in municipal-administered systems. Collaboration agreements between states and municipalities may help overcome this institutional barrier. Alternatives to reliance on savings are widely discussed in the Bank's Secondary Education in Brazil study (2000).

EXPANSION BY REALLOCATION OF STATES' OWN RESOURCES. According to the 1996 education law, states have the responsibility of financing upper secondary education with the remaining resources left after their FUNDEF contribution, which is earmarked for primary and lower secondary, is discounted. If states were to allocate over the next ten years an average of 6.7% of their revenues and transfers (equivalent to 67% of the education minimum investment level mandated by the law, after contributing to FUNDEF) to upper secondary education, they could cover the cost of meeting expected demand and still have a third of those resources leftover for investment into other education sub-sectors. While this is an aggregate calculation that may vary from state to state, Brazil's aggregate demonstrates that a reallocation of current spending would suffice to attend the demand. Moreover, it is important to keep in mind that 25% of revenues is the minimum level of aggregate education spending established by the legislation: states could choose to devote higher percentages of their revenues to education, thus boosting per student allocations at each level to increase quality. Because these internal reallocations within state's fiscal policies may not occur spontaneously, the federal Government may want to explore offering incentives to promote this.

EXPANSION THROUGH PRIVATE-PUBLIC SCHOOL DELIVERY PARTNERSHIPS. Private schools account for about 15% of the enrollments in secondary education. This significant level of participation suggests that the private sector has contributed and can continue to do so in the expansion of the secondary system. It is clear that as the system expands to lower socioeconomic quintiles of the population, families will likely be less able to pay for secondary schooling and, as such, private provision of education may not be viable. However, government supply subsidies and charter school alternatives should be explored as opportunities for the government to use existing infrastructure and know-how in the private sector. These partnerships have some history in Brazil and should be further considered in order to determine the best design for their most effective implementation.

IMPROVE EFFICIENCY VIA 5TH - 11TH GRADE SCHOOLS (ESCOLA DE JOVENS). State governments should introduce, or in the case of several states, accelerate the creation of full program secondary schools. Referred to in Brazil as Escola de Jovens, these new schools integrate the last cycle of the fundamental cycle (5th –8th grades) with upper secondary, to cover all grades from 5th through 11th grades. The benefits of this model are both pedagogical and managerial. The Escola de Jovens builds its own identity around the characteristics of youngsters and avoids mixing children and young adults in a single space. This makes it easier to work pedagogically on the transitions from lower to upper secondary. From a managerial standpoint, the "shared responsibility" between states and municipalities for ensino fundamental is facilitated by setting some clear guidelines. This type of school would be more efficient in allowing the discipline specialists, for example in math and the various sciences, to work across all of the grades. Finally, it makes sense from an institutional point of view as responsibility for provision of primary education (grades 1-4) is increasingly being devolved at an accelerating rate to municipalities, while states remain the primary providers of both lower and upper secondary education.

INCREASING ACCESS AND COMPLETION THROUGH AN ACADEMIC CREDIT SYSTEM. One means of minimizing the wasted resources associated with repetition would be to introduce a credit system at the secondary level. In a credit system, certain minimum academic standards are built into required courses, and a certain number of these courses are required for graduation. Currently, a Brazilian secondary student who passes classes in three subjects but fails the other two may be forced to repeat the entire year, including those classes in which he/she did well enough to pass. Under a credit system, such a student would be required to repeat only those classes for which he/she did not obtain a passing grade, and would be able to move ahead with his/her peers in other subjects. Under this system, a student's failures would not outweigh achievements, thus helping to avoid some measure of the stigma attached to repetition. Credit systems are the norm in higher education around the world, but there are good examples of their use at the secondary level. They are attractive in that they help ensure that all students master a body of knowledge and demonstrate certain capabilities before graduation, but allow students to progress more at their own pace.

INCREASING COMPLETION THROUGH THE EXPANSION OF EQUIVALENCY EXAMINATIONS. Equivalency exams provide an important door between formal and non-formal education. These exams test content and skills knowledge equivalent to that which is expected for a particular grade level in the formal education system, but are open to anybody, including school dropouts, at any age. Although participation in an equivalency-exam preparation course is not required for test takers, most equivalency systems offer such a course on an informal basis (i.e. flexible hours and materials, and through a range of organizations). Most people taking an equivalency exam do so for one of two reasons: (a) they wish to continue their studies in the formal education system after having dropped out; or (b) they seek more formal recognition of their knowledge and skills levels in order to advance in the workplace. A large scale enhancement of equivalency exams in Brazil could help accelerate students' flow through the system while guaranteeing a minimum level of academic mastery among the students that are promoted based on the results of the exam. An excellent exam, called Exame Nacional de Certificação de Competências de Jovens e Adultos, already exists, but is relatively new, not yet widely disseminated, and tests only completion of secondary education. Additional exams could be offered to certify achievement of objectives for any grade level. The exams could be offered in flexible schedules, and in some cases where technology is available, they could be offered immediately on demand. Rules and regulations (such as number of times that a given test can be taken, length in time for which a given result is valid, and others) should be developed carefully. Past experiences in Brazil as well as international experiences can be very helpful in this effort.

EXPANDING ACCESS THROUGH DISTANCE EDUCATION. Distance education in Brazil and elsewhere in the world have a long and, under certain circumstances, successful history of providing education that is comparable to or better than that provided in traditional institutional settings in the same country, and many of these programs may be more cost-effective than formal schooling as well. Brazil has enjoyed a long tradition in the integration of distance learning and technology. The 1990's, however, marked a turning point in Brazilian distance education as a result of the dramatic increase in computer use and the widespread implementation of social marketing techniques for educational and social change, with Telecurso 2000, introduced in 1995, being an excellent example. Brazil should also examine the very successful Telesecondary program in Mexico, which provides distance secondary education to millions of students via packaged lessons that are delivered by means of videotape or satellite television broadcasts and facilitated by general instructors rather than cadres of discipline specialists.

Message 6. Improving the quality and efficiency of public higher education and facilitating expansion of quality private higher education

The Brazilian higher education system, like the education system overall, needs to get more value for the large amount of resources devoted to it. Brazil has fostered a technologically well-developed industry that in an era of globalization and rapid technological change increasingly demands highly skilled labor. The public sector, too, requires vital inputs in the form of teachers, doctors, nurses, and administrators to improve public service delivery for social development. The higher education system, however, has been unable to meet the increasing demand. The lack of adequate human capital has fueled high and rising returns to higher education over the last decade. Needed are better coverage and greater relevance of programs to meet the high demand for graduates, greater equity, higher efficiency, and more funding of science and technology.

Higher education can be improved to meet the needs of Brazil's youth, society, and the public and private sectors by improving the efficiency and coverage of public higher education and strengthen the market for private provision of higher education. The gains from reforming higher education could be enormous, because a better functioning system of higher education could help meet the large demand for advanced human capital, thus accelerating technological advances, competitiveness, and economic growth in Brazil. Realizing the gains is more a question of modernizing the regulatory framework than of spending additional resources. Policy tools could include development of a performance-based funding mechanism to encourage efficiency, targeted student loans, cross-subsidization, and increased focus on quality and relevance. For strengthening science and technology, steady funding, competitive funding of strategic sectors, strengthening of intellectual property rights, and consolidation of centers of excellence could have a large impact. A detailed account of Brazil's challenges and options in area of higher education quality and efficiency can be found in the report, "Brazil: Higher Education Sector Study (2000).

Context

THE CURRENT FUNCTIONING OF THE SYSTEM RESULTS IN UNDESIRABLE OUTCOMES. The higher education system has not yet risen fully to the challenge of the increasing demand for well-trained graduates. That shortfall has fueled high and rising returns to higher education over the last decade. The higher education system enrolls 15 percent of the college age cohort, which is less than half the coverage in Uruguay (30 percent), Chile (32 percent), and Argentina (36 percent). Among the key weaknesses:

- DISPARITIES IN EQUITY. Education at the high-quality public institutions is free and attracts a large pool of qualified youth. Only one of every nine applicants is accepted. Parental guidance and a good private secondary education give children from better off families an advantage in admission. Qualified, but disadvantaged students—most often from middle income and poor backgrounds—often lose out and end up attending private fee-charging institutions, often of lesser quality than public institutions.

- LOW EFFICIENCY IN STATE INSTITUTIONS. The government spends 24 percent of a large education budget on public higher education, but inefficiencies inflate per student costs. At 347 percent of GDP per capita in 1998, per student costs in public universities are by far the highest in the world. Costs per student in OECD countries are all below 100 percent of GDP per capita.

- INADEQUATE FUNDING OF SCIENCE AND TECHNOLOGY. Research suffers from a general lack of qualified personnel, especially at the doctoral level, and from not enough attention to the needs of the productive private sector needs. Weak protection of property rights reduces incentives for research and investment.

Considerations for Policy Formulation

The gains from reforming higher education in Brazil could be enormous, by helping to meet the large demand for advanced human capital, thus accelerating technological advances, competitiveness, and economic growth. But realizing the gains is more a question of modernizing the regulatory framework than of spending additional resources.

Policy tools could include development of a performance-based funding mechanism to encourage efficiency, targeted student loans, cross-subsidization, and increased focus on quality and relevance. For strengthening science and technology, steady funding, competitive funding of strategic sectors, strengthening of intellectual property rights, and consolidation of centers of excellence could have a large impact.

POLICY QUESTIONS FOR HIGHER EDUCATION. Several policy questions need to be answered before decisions can be made about how to improve higher education.

HOW CAN HIGHER EDUCATION BE EXPANDED WITHOUT JEOPARDIZING FISCAL STABILITY? Simply raising spending on higher education would either hurt basic education spending or result in fiscal instability. Instead, attention could focus on improving the quality of public higher education and strengthening the market for private higher education, primarily by addressing the inability of students to get loans to finance their studies. A revenue-neutral targeted student loan scheme could help to remedy the market failure. The government could also continue to improve quality assurance and monitoring systems for higher education, to provide better guidance on quality for students.

HOW CAN ACCESS TO LOW- AND MIDDLE-INCOME STUDENTS BE IMPROVED? Greater access for low- and middle-income students could be fostered through cross-subsidization. Public universities could begin to charge tuition fees, and a proportion of the receipts could be used to fund scholarships for poor students. The government could also consider emphasizing short-term higher education in technical skills, especially in provincial cities lacking a university. Such initiatives could enhance educational relevance and regional development.

HOW CAN RESOURCE USE IN PUBLIC UNIVERSITIES BE MADE MORE EFFICIENT WITHOUT COMPROMISING INSTITUTIONAL AUTONOMY? International experience shows the value of introducing incentives in the funding of higher education institutions through performance-based funding (output-related formula). This would shift resources from poorly performing institutions to the best managed ones, thereby encouraging improvements in efficiency through increased coverage, equity, and relevance within the current budget envelop.

HOW CAN PUBLIC RESEARCH BE MADE MORE RELEVANT TO PRIVATE SECTOR NEEDS? Public research could be made more relevant through a greater reliance on competitive funding mechanisms favoring sectors in which Brazil has a competitive advantage. Furthermore, the value of the science and technology sector could be enhanced through the provision of steady funding as opposed to the current irregular funding.

References

World Bank projects

- Fundescola III (Terceiro Projeto Fundo de Fortalecimento Escolar). US$ 160. Approved on June 13, 2002.
- Bahia Basic Education Project Phase I (Projeto de Educação do Estado da Bahia). US$ 90 million. Approved on December 20, 2000.
- Ceara Basic Education (Projeto de Qualificação da Educação Básica do Estado do Ceará). US$ 69.6 million. Approved on December 20, 2000.
- Fundescola II (Segundo Projeto Fundo de Fortalecimento Escolar). US$ 202 million. Approved on June 8, 1999.
- Science and Technology III - PADCT III (Terceiro Projeto de Reforma da Ciência e Tecnologia). US$ 155 million. Approved on December 18, 1997.

World Bank reports

This chapter summarizes the content of the following World Bank reports. Those, in turn, draw heavily from a wide range of literature on the subject from experts in Brazil and beyond, which are referenced in the mentioned Bank reports.

Ferrer-Andreu, Vicente. 2002. Capacity and Learning Enhancement and the Knowledge Economy, Background paper for the Brazil Policy Notes.

IPEA (Instituto de Pesquisa Económica Aplicada). 1999. Uma Avaliasão dos Custos e dos Beneficios da Educação Pre-escolar. Rio de Janeiro.

Levison, Deborah. 1990. Child Care in Metropolitan Brazil. World Bank Internal Discussion Paper. Report No. IDP-079 (revised April 22). Washington, D.C.: World Bank.

Paci, Pierella. 1999. Where Do The Poor Fare Best? A Distributional Analysis of Regional Differences in Enrollment in Education of Brazilian Children under 6. Background paper prepared for the report Boosting Poor Children's Chances: Early Childhood Development Services for Poor Children in Brazil. World Bank, Washington, D.C.

World Bank, 2002. Brazil Municipal Education Resources, Incentives, and results. Report No. 24413-BR. Washington, D.C.: World Bank.

World Bank, 2001e. ICR: Brazil: School Improvement Project - FUNDESCOLA I. Report No. 23296-BR. Washington, D.C.: World Bank.

World Bank, 2001d. Brazil: Early Child Development. Report No. 22841-BR. Washington, D.C.: World Bank.

World Bank, 2001c. Brazil: Eradicating Child Labor in Brazil. Report No. 21858-BR. Washington, D.C.: World Bank.

World Bank, 2001b. Brazil: Broadening the Base for Growth: A Report on the State of Bahia. Report No. 21377-BR. Washington, D.C.: World Bank.

World Bank. 2001a. "Brazil - Teachers Development and Incentives: A Strategic Framework" Report 20408 BR. Washington, D.C.

World Bank. 2001. "Brazil - An Assessment of the Bolsa Escola Programs" Report 20208-BR. Washington, D.C.

World Bank, 2000c. ICR: Brazil Third Northeast Basic Education Project. Report No. 20239-BR. Washington, D.C.: World Bank.

World Bank, 2000b. ICR: Brazil Second Northeast Basic Education Project. Report No. 20238-BR. Washington, D.C.: World Bank.

World Bank, 2000a. Brazil: Secondary Education in Brazil. Report No. 19409-BR. Washington, D.C.: World Bank.

World Bank, 2000. Brazil: Higher Education Sector Study. Report No. 19392-BR. Washington, D.C.: World Bank.

World Bank, 1998. PAD: Brazil: School Improvement Project - FUNDESCOLA I. Report No. 17402-BR. Washington, D.C.: World Bank.

World Bank, 1997. Brazil: A Call to Action. Report No. 18358-BR. Washington, D.C.: World Bank.

Other reference:

Ministério da Educação, 2001. Fatos sobre a Educação no Brasil - 1994/2001. Brasília, DF: MEC

2

Health

2

Health

Introduction

In the mid-1980s, Brazil embarked on far-reaching reforms that changed the structure, organization, and financing of the health sector, resulting in the Unified Health System (SUS, Sistema Único de Saúde). The first wave of reform (1984–89) focused on institutional restructuring, decentralization to the state level, and establishment of mechanisms for social participation, with a universal right to health care as the emerging system's core value. The second wave (1990–95) emphasized consolidation of a unified system, "municipalization" of service delivery, and implementation of financial mechanisms for allocating federal funds. The third wave (1996–2001) aimed to reorient the health care model for basic care, separate institutional roles, enact legal and regulatory changes, and introduce alternative payment mechanisms to support basic care.

The reform has tackled a number of systemic problems, but other problems remained unsolved and new challenges have come to the fore. The government is poised to launch the fourth wave of reforms, building on the lessons of previous phases.

Achievements of health sector reforms

Some of the key achievements of the reform:

- THE REFORM HAS DECENTRALIZED SERVICE PROVISION FROM THE FEDERAL GOVERNMENT TO MUNICIPALITIES, AND TO A LESSER EXTENT, STATE GOVERNMENTS. This process has been mostly successful. A majority of municipalities currently manage some, or all, public facilities and are responsible for the provision of basic health services in their territories. An indirect and praiseworthy consequence of

The draft of this chapter was completed by Jerry La Forgia in November 2002. The analyses and suggestions contained in this chapter are based on the international technical experience of the World Bank and are presented as a contribution to the debate and formulation of public policies.

this process has been the steady increase in municipalities' contribution to health finance (increasing from 7% of public spending in 1980 to over 15% in 2000[1]).

- INEQUALITIES IN RESOURCE ALLOCATION ACROSS STATES HAVE BEEN REDUCED. Poor states and municipalities currently receive a greater share of federal resources than before the reform. For example, between 1997 and 2001 total per capita public spending in the Northern and Northeastern regions increased by 113 and 133 percent respectively, while spending in the South and Southeastern regions increased by 60 and 70 percent. The introduction of per capita payments to finance basic care and an array of programs has directed comparatively more funding to poorer regions.

- THE EFFECTIVENESS OF THE PUBLIC HEALTH SYSTEM HAS IMPROVED IN PART BECAUSE OF REFORMS IN BASIC CARE FINANCING AND REORIENTATION OF THE SERVICE PROVISION MODEL. The introduction of the outreach-oriented Family Health Program together with an innovative financing model for basic care has resulted in increased spending and significant coverage extension for basic care.

- MODIFICATIONS TO THE LEGAL AND REGULATORY FRAMEWORK IMPROVED THE PRIVATE HEALTH INSURANCE AND DRUG MARKETS. Overall these laws constitute an important step toward improved market performance: establishing standards for: (i) licensure of private plans including solvency and reporting requirements, grievance procedures, benefits definition, and (ii) approving, marketing and selling of pharmaceuticals.

- POLICIES AND MANAGEMENT TOOLS HAVE BEEN ADOPTED TO IMPROVE THE EFFICIENCY OF SERVICE ORGANIZATION AND PROVISION. One such policy was the change in the relative reimbursement values of normal deliveries and cesarean sections, which resulted in a significant reduction in the number of c-sections. Another innovation was the price database (*Banco de Preços*), which has helped state and municipal managers to purchase inputs at better prices.

- AS SERVICE PROVISION WAS DECENTRALIZED, THE MINISTRY OF HEALTH STRENGTHENED ITS STEWARDSHIP FUNCTIONS. These include through policymaking, regulation, information gathering and analysis, priority setting, and development of mechanisms to set targets and goals. States and municipalities are expected to track indicators identified for monitoring targeted improvements in health.

These as well as other achievements have contributed to significant improvements in

---

[1] Medici, 2001.

health. Over the last 10 years, infant mortality has decreased by 38 percent, mortality from vaccine-preventable diseases in children is now negligible, diarrheal diseases are the cause of only 7 percent of deaths among children under 5, overall mortality from infectious diseases and parasites has decreased substantially, the number of new cases of HIV/AIDS has leveled off, the total fertility rate has declined to 2.2, and life expectancy has risen.

Despite these specific successes, the health system still faces structural and organizational challenges.

A new wave of health reforms

Brazil has chosen an incremental path to reform. Two recent measures, Constitutional Amendment 29 and Norma Operacional de Assistência à Saúde (NOAS/01), together with the Family Health Program, set the stage for the gradual implementation of a new wave of health reforms. These measures were approved after considerable discussion within government and consultation with civil society. Approved by Congress in 2000, Amendment 29 seeks to address the traditionally low levels of financing for SUS, mandating an increase in federal, state, and municipal contributions to health care. Regulation is pending.

Building on the *Norma Operacional Básica* from 1996, NOAS/01 regulations aim to systematically address several health sector concerns by reorienting resource allocation, institutional roles, and service organization and delivery. NOAS/01 defines a regionalization strategy that groups municipalities into microregions for pooling and optimizing resources, especially for referral services of medium complexity. The rules also set needs-based criteria for transfers across microregions, expand the package of basic services (Piso Assistencial Básico–Ampliado; PAB-A), increase the capitation rates for this package, and establish management tools (such as improved budget planning or *programação pactuada integrada*, the investment plan, and the Basic Health Agreement or *Pacto de Atenção Básica*) to improve planning and performance. Finally, NOAS/01 assigns a greater role to the states in monitoring and evaluating municipalities' performance.

Launched in 1994, the Family Health Program is the platform on which the government seeks to restructure the organization and provisions of publicly financed health care. The government plans to convert the passive-provider, facility-based delivery system to an active-provider, outreach model in which family health care providers deliver quality basic heath care to households and communities. The model aims to create a more efficient delivery system by focusing on prevention and early treatment, and using the Family Health Program as the gateway to higher level services.

Implementing these changes will be a daunting task. The current fiscal crisis may delay implementation of Amendment 29 and the Family Health Program. Whether the NOAS-mandated regionalization strategy will realign incentives, establish clear lines of accountability, and rationalize the patchwork of organizational arrangements, programs and payment mechanisms is an open question.

During the past two decades Brazil has identified problems in the health system and forged reforms to solve them. However, inattention to implementation strategies, lack of institutional capacity, especially at the state and municipal levels, lapses in policy oversight, and the emergence of new problems have resulted in an unfinished reform agenda. Within the framework provided by Amendment 29, NOAS/01, and the Family Health Program, the following policy recommendations focus on these gaps and present alternatives for meeting the challenges ahead.

Message 1. Raising equity through improved resource allocation and targeting of health subsidies
Health sector reforms have reduced inequalities in resource allocation across states and lowered mortality rates among children and adults. To reduce the remaining disparities in health status, health financing, and service utilization across regions, states, and municipalities; across income groups; and between urban and rural areas, solutions could include applying an equity-enhancing resource allocation formula derived from the implementation of Amendment 29 of the Constitution, reducing hidden subsidies to the well-off and incorporating incentives for states and municipalities to increase financing for basic and family health care.

Context
Health sector reforms have reduced inequalities in resource allocation across states and lowered mortality rates among children and adults. But substantial disparities remain in health status, health financing, and service utilization across regions, states, and municipalities; across income groups; and between urban and rural areas. Infant mortality still varies considerably across states and municipalities, per capita public expenditure on health varies from R$53 to R$297 across states, and private expenditure is even more concentrated in the richer states (tables 1 and 2). Utilization rates in the highest quintile are almost double those in the lowest quintile (table 3).

Table 1: Geographic inequalities in health status, 2000
Source: Datasus and IDB 2001.

Region and State	Infant mortality	Life expectancy
Brazil	**31.79**	**68.55**
North	**33.88**	**68.47**
Rondônia	33.06	68.26
Acre	44.18	68.29
Amazonas	30.98	68.85
Roraima	38.27	67.52
Pará	34.64	68.74
Amapá	31.64	69.02
Tocantins	32.95	68.41
Northeast	**52.36**	**65.78**
Maranhão	54.16	64.83
Piauí	45.29	65.65
Ceará	52.37	66.36
Rio Grande do Norte	48.66	66.42
Paraíba	60.25	64.44
Pernambuco	58.18	63.68
Alagoas	66.13	63.16
Sergipe	45.45	67.23
Bahia	45.38	67.67
Southeast	**20.61**	**69.58**
Minas Gerais	26.26	70.39
Espírito Santo	17.68	70.25
Rio de Janeiro	21.28	67.63
São Paulo	17.91	70.03
South	**17.17**	**71.03**
Paraná	19.67	70.28
Santa Catarina	16.35	71.34
Rio Grande do Sul	15.1	71.6
Mid-West	**25.08**	**69.42**
Mato Grosso do Sul	24.87	70.37
Mato Grosso	27.46	69.17
Goiás	25.02	69.58
Distrito Federal	22..63	68.98
10 best municipalities	**8.05**	–
10 worst municipalities	**117.14**	–

Table 2: Regional distribution of public expenditure on health, 1995

Region and State	Total public expenditure	Public expenditure per capita	Share of coverage by private plans (percent)
North	**1,062,222**	**95.46**	–
Rondônia	146,553	120.26	25.09
Acre	32,896	69.07	14.05
Amazonas	246,511	104.99	15.95
Roraima	67,491	277.17	6.68
Pará	361,448	66.48	22.65
Amapá	109,598	296.61	17.96
Tocantins	54,734	52.88	11.7
Northeast	**3,817,374**	**85.91**	–
Maranhão	377,933	73.07	5.9
Piauí	271,068	101.9	9.16
Ceará	562,818	83.37	15.53
Rio Grande do Norte	346,502	136.45	11.01
Paraíba	294,815	89.61	16.05
Pernambuco	613,504	83.45	21.74
Alagoas	213,955	81.81	12
Sergipe	124,831	77.69	15.54
Bahia	884,345	71.04	18
Southeast	**10,174,402**	**153.09**	–
Minas Gerais	2,087,985	126.07	25.98
Espírito Santo	287,177	103.22	22.78
Rio de Janeiro	2,098,125	157.6	31.75
São Paulo	5,701,115	168.67	39.18
South	**2,623,157**	**112.31**	–
Paraná	1,012,278	113.2	25.23
Santa Catarina	408,906	84.53	23.79
Rio Grande do Sul	1,201,973	125.5	32.08
Mid-West	**1,434,166**	**138.13**	–
Mato Grosso do Sul	155,216	81.26	24.76
Mato Grosso	175,609	79.47	13.46
Goiás	296,407	66.41	21.75
Distrito Federal	806,935	448.45	32.95
Unallocated	**2,626,203**	**16.86**	–
Brazil	**21,737,522**	**139.56**	**24.19**

Source: Fernandes (Coord) 1998; 1998 National Household Survey (IBGE 2000b). Public Expenditure in R$ 1.000,00. Expenditure per capita in reais.

Table 3: Utilization of health services in last two months, 1998 (percent)

	Brazil	1º Quintile	2º Quintile	3º Quintile	4º Quintile	5º Quintile
% Utilization (general)	13.19	9.92	11.75	13.18	13.98	17.15
By gender						
Male	10.27	7.9	9.36	10.26	10.5	13.33
Female	15.97	11.81	14.04	15.95	17.33	20.76
By age group						
<5 years	17.64	13.76	17.67	18.08	21.15	23.79
5 - 14 years	8.57	6.23	7.6	8.51	10.78	13.09
15 - 29 years	10.72	8.67	9.54	10.61	10.81	13.9
30 - 59 years	14.72	12.52	13.34	14.15	14.55	17.52
60+ years	21.55	15.36	18.56	20.94	22.02	25.34
By area of residence						
Metropolitan areas	14.91	11.42	12.65	13.32	14.85	18.83
Urban areas	13.22	11.26	12.32	13.51	13.54	15.33
Dense Rural areas	10.62	8.94	9.1	14.29	12.49	12.75
Sparse Rural areas	9.39	7.5	9.57	11.33	11.93	14.7

Source 1998 National Household Survey - PNAD (IBGE 2000b)

Not all inequities are within the purview of the health sector.[2] Evidence suggests that inequity is more pressing in health financing and health status than in service supply and physical access.[3] Physical access in rural and remote areas is difficult, but these areas represent a low proportion of the country's population and the Ministry of Health is gradually improving access by extending basic care/family health services. Important inequalities remain, however, for specific types of services that respond to how resources are allocated and services are paid for rather than the overall supply.

[2] Geographical and socioeconomic inequalities related to income, education, and access to water and sanitation also affect health.

[3] Couttolenc (2002).

Indirect public subsidies to well-off Brazilians also contribute to inequity. Private pre-payment plans have an incentive to provide less than comprehensive coverage to their enrollees, sending them to SUS-financed services for uncovered (and usually high-cost) care. At least 15 percent of SUS spending goes to the well-off (top three income deciles), mostly for expensive treatments,[4] reducing resources for less well-off. Government efforts to recuperate these costs from private plans have been frustrated by a lack of reliable data on actual costs of services provided. Another significant subsidy to the well-off is provided through income tax breaks to compensate for private expenses on health care, making public expenditure on health significantly higher and private expenditure lower than generally reported.

Referral services and complex care are generally concentrated in the Southeast and in large metropolitan areas, and hospital-based, high-technology procedures consume a large proportion of SUS expenditures.[5] SUS has had less success improving the equity of financing for medium- and high-complexity services than for basic care.[6] This situation results from a combination of payment and budgetary mechanisms within SUS that favor the delivery of complex care in states and municipalities with historically high levels of hospital capacity. Powerful states and municipalities that could finance a larger share of health spending are also more able to influence federal resource allocation, while the price structure favors the production of complex care to which the relatively well-off have greater access. In effect, the way care is financed and paid for helps to maintain an over-supply of secondary and tertiary care in some regions and an undersupply in others.[7]

A disproportionate financial burden falls on the poor, especially for drugs. In princi-ple, drugs are supplied free to those who use SUS-financed services. In practice, most drug consumption is purchased out of pocket. The burden of drug financing falls heavily on poor households, representing nearly 10 percent of income in families earning less than

---

[4] REFORSUS (2002). The real subsidy is probably significantly higher. Data limitations impeded estimation of the cost of hospital stays by income deciles.

[5] Hospital care accounted for 36 percent of Ministry of Health spending in 1997, and curative ambulatory care another 36 percent, while public health services represent 13 percent (IPEA, in Médici 2002).

[6] Negri (2002).

[7] NOAS/2001 defines a regionalization strategy for rationalizing the supply and improving access to medium- and high-complexity services (see discussion under Message 3).

two times the minimum wage per month.[8] Out-of-pocket payments for medical care (such as physician and hospital services) are generally low, except for dental care. This is a result of coverage expansion by SUS and private plans over the last two decades.

While the recently approved constitutional amendment (Amendment 29) is expected to significantly increase funding for the sector, it will not necessarily reduce inequalities. Because most of the increase in financial resources triggered by Amendment 29 will occur at the state and municipal levels, the health systems in wealthier and more fiscally sound states and municipalities may be the main beneficiaries. Nevertheless, this may also be an opportunity for the federal government to reduce the proportion of its funds allocated to these states, redirecting more resources to poorer states and municipalities.

Options

Improving equity will require continuing reforms already under implementation and introducing other changes in health care financing and organization. Reforms to improve equity cannot be separated from reforms to improve efficiency and quality. For example, the proposed policy to improve equity through adapting alternative resource allocation mechanisms fits well with the proposal for performance-based financing that links payments to results.

INTRODUCE RESOURCE ALLOCATION AND PROVIDER PAYMENT MECHANISMS TO IMPROVE EQUITY ACROSS STATES AND MUNICIPALITIES. There was considerable discussion in the early 1990s on the need to reallocate federal transfers more equitably across states, including the development of a formula for doing so. However, no consensus was reached. Passage of Amendment 29 presents an opportunity to implement measures aimed at improving the equity of financing. Strategies could include:

- Expanding capitation payments to include other types of care beyond the NOAS/01-mandated PAB-A and introducing adjusted capitation rates according to some indicator of need (epidemiological, demographic, socioeconomic) and costs. This measure has the additional advantage of consolidating and simplifying payment mechanisms (see Message 3).

---

[8] 1998 National Household Survey (IBGE 2000b) and Couttolenc, 2002.

- Implementing a model for equitable distribution of financing (across states) derived from implementation of Amendment 29, which would include relatively simple needs-based criteria based on one or two simple to measure indicators (such as infant mortality).[9]
- Developing an instrument for resource allocation among municipalities or microregions within states based on improved budget planning agreements (*programação pactuada integrada* or PPI). This measure would also improve efficiency by stimulating the regionalization of services of medium complexity.

REDUCE HIDDEN SUBSIDIES TO THE WELL-OFF: The government can reduce or eliminate subsidies that benefit mainly the rich, and strengthen targeting to the poor. This can be accomplished by modifying current regulation to:

- Require private insurers to pay the full cost of services provided to enrollees treated in public clinics and hospital. This measure implies developing and implementing a standardized cost accounting system to estimate the actual cost of services rendered.
- Reduce or eliminate income tax breaks for private (individual and family) health expenditures; this would require a focused analysis of the beneficiaries of these tax breaks.

STRENGTHEN AND EXPAND DRUG SUPPLY PROGRAMS FOR THE POOR: A recent Ministry of Health policy to increase the supply of generic drugs and make them financially more accessible to low-income populations may suffer from uncertain financing, difficulties in securing adequate supplies, and leakage to the non-poor. Measures to improve sustainability and targeting could include:

- Defining a partial rather than full subsidy, varying by groups of drugs (essential and nonessential, generic and proprietary).
- Expanding local production of generic drugs by public laboratories and private pharmaceutical companies.
- Improving the distribution of generic drugs by providing pharmacies more incentives to sell them (such as allowing higher margins).
- Launching social communication campaigns to inform the public of the option of generics, and to encourage physicians to prescribe them.

---

[9] Musgrove (1998) provides three examples of formulas for redistributive financing. A REFORSUS-financed study is modeling the application of formula drawing on the British experience.

Message 2. Increase the efficiency, effectiveness, and quality of service provision through improved resource allocation and aligned incentives

INCREASE PERFORMANCE ORIENTATION. The Ministry of Health has generally relied on norms, administrative procedures, and informational requirements for executing grant transfers and certifying municipalities and states for decentralized management of transfers and corresponding programs and services. These were useful first steps in health sector reform. The emphasis on inputs, information systems, and bureaucratic procedures could now usefully give way to a system based on stronger incentives for service managers to use resources well and provide quality care. Important next steps would be to set performance benchmarks for efficiency, effectiveness, and quality; provide financial incentives to achieve them; and monitor and evaluate the results. Implementation could include management tools such as contracts and performance agreements to stimulate the accountability of municipal managers and providers in terms of results, while linking financing to performance.

REDUCE FRAGMENTATION: While the reform improved intergovernmental coordination, it also contributed to other types of fragmentation that make it difficult for many states and municipalities to comply with their new institutional roles. Also, many lack the financial, managerial, and technical capacity to discharge the responsibilities vested in them. Less complex and more uniform payment mechanisms would help to integrate programs (70+) and levels of care. It would help to consolidate service- and program-specific payment mechanisms and rules into a smaller number of grants to states and municipalities and to align the financial incentives faced by municipal mangers.

Context

Despite great strides in improving the organization and provision of health care, the system is still hampered by low efficiency, effectiveness, and quality. Traditionally, insufficient financing was blamed for the problems of the health sector, but it is becoming increasing apparent that low performance also reflects inefficient allocation and use of resources and low priority to issues of quality. These problems are associated with several factors, some already mentioned for their effect on equity.

Patient satisfaction, quality, and effectiveness: While there are some centers of excellence in health care, SUS-financed services—whether provided in public or private facilities—are widely perceived to be of lower quality and effectiveness than other services.[10]

Although the extent of poor quality remains unknown, the capability of Brazilian hospitals, especially those affiliated with SUS, to deliver high quality services is in serious doubt. This is evidenced by: (i) well-publicized lapses in quality, prompting doubts in peoples' minds about the overall standards of care; and (ii) analytic studies on low quality care in hospitals contributes to infant and maternal mortality;[11] occurrence of avoidable deaths;[12] high hospital-acquired infection rates;[13] and unacceptably large variations in mortality rates by type of procedure, hospital size and volume of interventions.[14]

While the Ministry of Health, the private sector, and individual facilities have initiated small-scale efforts to promote a culture of quality improvement, this has not been a central tenet of health reforms. The private sector has established three accreditation programs, but application, which is voluntary, is limited, and each program applies different assessment criteria.[15] The Ministry of Health launched an accreditation program in the late 1990s, establishing the National Organization of Accreditation (ONA) and publishing an accreditation manual. By 2002 seven "accreditation institutions" had been certified, but only 14 hospitals have been accredited. Some observers believe facilities have little incentive to seek accreditation (which is voluntary) in part because the costs of accreditation are too high. Moreover, it is generally acknowledged that only a minority of hospitals would meet the minimum quality standards of a vigorous accreditation assessment.

---

[10] Couttolenc (2002).

[11] World Bank, 2002

[12] De gouvea et al, 1997; Bastos, et al 1996 ; Silva, et al 1999.

[13] Oliveira, 1997

[14] Carvalho and Pereira, 1998.

[15] Associação Paulista de Medicina's Programa de Qualidade do Atendimento Médico-Hospitalar (CQH) in the state of São Paulo, the Programa de Avaliação e Certificação de Qualidade em Saúde (PACQS) in the state of Rio de Janeiro, or the National Institute for Health Accreditation in Rio Grande do Sul.

The Ministry of Health has also established programs to promote quality of care in the nation's hospitals.[16] Several facilities have developed quality assurance programs, established medical audits, and adopted clinical protocols.[17] A 1997 survey conducted by the Health Ministry showed that only 82 hospitals in 13 states had implemented some form of quality improvement program. Although it is acknowledged that many others have initiated localized programs, no general accounting of these initiatives exists (including Health Ministry programs) in terms of results, sustainability and enabling (or disabling) conditions. An undetermined number of these initiatives have been discontinued as medical directors changed. Although the number of rigorous studies analyzing the quality of clinical care has increased in recent years, quality is not systematically assessed in most facilities.

Dysfunctional referral systems and lack of integration between curative and preventive care contribute to poor case management and discontinuity of care.[18] A recent World Bank study attributed stagnant levels of maternal mortality over the last decade to poorly coordinated and low quality prenatal, neonatal, and postpartum care.[19] Quality appears to be especially low in rural and remote areas, where it has been difficult to find health professionals (especially physicians) to staff the facilities.

Over 60 percent of all publicly-financed hospitals have less than 40 beds. These facilities generally do not possess the equipment or personnel to handle much more than primary care.[20] Even rudimentary clinical management is often lacking.

EFFICIENCY AND PERFORMANCE INCENTIVES: SUS financing and payment mechanisms are based mainly on the production of services and are unrelated to results or health outcomes. Instruments with incentives to promote efficiency, quality, and better health outcomes are lacking. Organization and management—especially the budget and planning system—focus on financial control and provision of inputs rather than performance and efficiency. Facility and local managers are encumbered by a multitude of financial con-

---

[16] These include the "Prize for Hospital Quality," National Program for Evaluation of Hospital Services, and the National Program for "Humanization" of Hospital Care.

[17] Ministry of Health (2002a); World Bank (1994).

[18] Mendes, 2002, Jain, 2001, MS, 2001.

[19] World Bank (2001).

[20] BNDES, 2002; Mendes, 2002

trols, data requirements, and mandated reporting, while having little autonomy to reallocate resources or define priorities.

Decentralization and financing reforms reflect policies that separate purchasing from provision. However, decentralization has not resulted in improving overall system effectiveness or raising the performance of hospital care. In nearly all cases the transfer of federal hospitals to state and municipal ownership and management has resulted in little or no change in how facilities are administered and managed. The vast majority are run as budgetary arms of municipal and state governments in which facility managers have little decision-making power over staffing, remuneration, financing, service supply and use of technology. Increasingly, this organizational model is considered a driver of low quality, patient dissatisfaction, fraud, low productivity and overall suboptimal use of available resources.[21] Still needed are reforms and instruments to stimulate greater accountability between payers and providers. Granting service and facility managers greater managerial autonomy while making them accountable to payers and patients for facility performance could improve performance. A recent study found that increased managerial autonomy at public hospitals results in lower mortality and reduced lengths of stay.[22]

Federal funds are transferred to municipalities through 78 mechanisms or programs, many linked to specific administrative requirements, planning, and control instruments. Reforms were designed to correct this fragmentation (and did consolidate a number of programs), but the payment mechanisms perpetuate it. Some mechanisms pay for production, others for coverage, and still others on a per capita basis. The transaction costs associated with this fragmentation are likely to be high, especially given the weak planning and monitoring capacity of most municipalities. The fragmentation of resources and payment mechanisms by program and type of care (hospitalization, diagnostic services, basic care) also interferes with achieving a comprehensive approach to health care. The PAB-A program, stipulated in the NOAS/01, expands the basic service package to include diagnostic, dental and other primary care services, and to pay for it through a single capitation payment. This is a major step in the right direction, though more consolidation is possible.

---

[21] IPEA, 2001; Silva et al, 1999; Marinho, 1998, 2001; Lima & Barbosa, 2001; Costa et al, 2000, 2001; Cecílio, 2000.

[22] Ribeiro (2002).

RESOURCE ALLOCATION AND USE: Although the proportion of health care spending, both public and private, that goes to curative and hospital care has been declining steadily in response to the strong focus on basic care and family health, it remains high. In addition, a significant proportion of SUS expenditures on hospitalization cover conditions that are preventable or treatable at lower cost in an ambulatory setting. Payment mechanisms tend to encourage hospital and complex care. Health authorities are encouraging the transfer of some hospital procedures to ambulatory settings (eye and other small surgeries, for example), but much more could be done.

Several other inefficiencies remain as well, as evidenced by variations in spending, quality, and practice patterns across the delivery system, especially in hospitals.[23] Nationally, there is an overcapacity in hospital services (average occupation rate below 48 percent[24]) and an oversupply of complex diagnostic services, while emergency rooms are often used as entry points to the health system and referral hospitals are crowded with patients with simple conditions. SUS reimbursement levels for hospital care are unrelated to actual costs, which frequently are unknown, and tend to overcompensate complex procedures (such as transplants) and undercompensate simple ones.[25] This mismatch encourages both public and private providers under SUS to specialize in better-paid procedures and may even encourage fraud.[26] The hospital prospective payment system (AIH) is not inadequate in itself, but low and distorted reimbursement levels may induce distortions (such as fraud and oversupply of specialized care).[27]

---

[23] Matos (2002).

[24] Ministério da Saúde (2000).

[25] Matos (2002).

[26] Private providers under SUS are not treated in the same way as public providers, since budget resources cover personnel expenditures for most public providers (representing around 2/3 of total expenditure), while private providers resort to treating private patients to cover part of the gap—or to fraud.

[27] Between 1995 and 1999 SUS increased general payments increased by 59 percent, and several services and procedures received additional increases in 2001, but the gap is still significant for many procedures. (MS/SAS, 2002).

Options

ESTABLISH A SYSTEMWIDE ORIENTATION FOCUSING ON IMPROVED QUALITY AND HEALTH OUTCOMES. The basic incentive structure created by the payment mechanisms needs to be redesigned to promote quality and effectiveness of care. This could be achieved by:

- Developing and implementing performance-based management systems and instruments (such as performance agreements and contracts) between payers and providers. This will involve setting specific goals (such as quality improvement) and priorities (ideally based on indicators of disease burden and costs) that are specified in performance agreements and contracts. The experiences of social organizations (*organizações sociais*) as contract managers in São Paulo and health foundations elsewhere offer possible models.

- Building on the experience of successfully implemented (and rigorously evaluated), alternative organizational arrangements (such as Public Social Organizations and Foundations) could introduce autonomous management and governance structures (with social participation) in public and SUS-financed private hospitals in combination with global budgets and performance agreements and contracts.

- Developing strategies and analytical tools to strengthen municipal and microregional managers' capacity to purchase services (from both public and private providers), including the crafting of standardized performance data for monitoring providers.

- Evaluating quality improvement programs implemented in Brazilian hospitals. Based on this evaluation, viable models and operational approaches for introducing these programs in other facilities, could be developed.

- Linking PAB and other transfers to performance indicators. The PABcon model, established for implementation of the World Bank Family Health Project, is an example of a performance-based payment mechanism.[28]

CONSOLIDATE ACCREDITATION PROGRAMS INTO A SINGLE SYSTEM.: To be effective, an accreditation system needs to be uniform, with strong buy-in from both public and private health care providers. This can be accomplished by:

- Evaluating the Health Ministry's recently implemented hospital accreditation program, comparing it to those applied in the private sector.

---

[28] PABcon will finance the transitional costs of converting primary care delivery from the existing model to the family health-based approach. Participating municipalities sign a contract with the Ministry of Health specifying performance targets at two-year intervals. Compliance with these benchmarks will trigger continued receipt of the transfer.

- Making provider participation mandatory or providing strong incentives for participation, for example, by publicizing the name of participating hospitals.

IMPROVE EFFICIENCY IN SERVICE PROVISION BY MODIFYING RESOURCE ALLOCATION PATTERNS AND PROMOTING INCREASED PRODUCTIVITY. Strategies could include:
- Rationalizing the supply of ambulatory and hospital-based care taking into consideration demand and supply, economies of scale, epidemiological profiles, and implementation of functional referral systems. This may involve converting a number of small hospitals (that are underutilized, economically unviable, or fail accreditation) to urgent care centers and family health units.
- Prioritizing resource allocations to improve the cost-effectiveness of interventions, by systematically evaluating and comparing interventions, and adjusting payment mechanisms to send clear signals to managers about service priorities.
- Developing guidelines and regulations on technological assessment, while incorporating systematic technology assessment methods in investment planning.[29]

REVISE THE HOSPITAL REIMBURSEMENT SYSTEM (AIH) TO REFLECT THE ACTUAL COSTS OF SERVICES. Despite adjustments to the SUS reimbursement schedule, payments remain unrelated to costs. Nor does the reimbursement schedule reflect system priorities. Getting the price structure right is critical to reorienting the current incentive system and correcting distortions. Strategies could include:
- Designing, testing, and implementing a standardized cost accounting system in SUS-financed public and private hospitals. Since a number of cost accounting systems already exist (but use different methodologies that prevent easy comparison), a good place to start is an assessment to determine best practices in cost accounting.
- Making payments reflect actual service costs while also functioning as incentives for more efficient use of facilities and levels of care by introducing retension funds and discounts around the measured average cost. For example, expensive procedures can be reimbursed below cost, while cheaper, but effective, alternatives could have higher reimbursement levels.

---

[29] The Ministry of Health is currently setting up an independent agency for technology assessment; the key issue here is to train staff personnel and/or potential consultants in economic evaluation applied to technology assessment.

- Implementing global budgets to fund a defined volume and set of hospital services. A global budget could be a better payment instrument for improving allocative efficiency and enforcing priorities.

Message 3. Rationalizing the organization and functioning of SUS

CLARIFYING INSTITUTIONAL ROLES. States are the logical entities for overseeing health care organization and delivery by municipalities. To fill that role, states need to develop the technical and managerial capacity for planning, coordinating, monitoring, and evaluating the implementation of national policies and the delivery of municipal-managed services. Still needed are feasible organizational and financial arrangements for implementing the regionalization proposal of NOAS/01, including strengthening the oversight functions of states; pooling municipal resources; sharing facilities; and piloting models for integrated delivery systems managed by microregional entities.

IMPROVING COORDINATION BETWEEN PUBLIC AND PRIVATE SECTOR PROVISIONS. Reform has centered on the public sector and, to a lesser extent, on private ambulatory and hospital facilities receiving SUS financing. Yet the non-SUS-financed private sector accounts for more than half of national spending on health and almost half of service utilization.[30] By taking the private sector more fully into account when developing programs and sector policies, SUS policymakers could contribute to sector-wide gains in efficiency by reducing redundancies in coverage, technology, and service supply. Clearly defining the roles of public and private providers would help reduce overlapping infrastructure, equipment, and service supply.

SUPPORTING SYSTEMIC EVALUATION. Various innovations have been introduced in the organization, management, and provision of health services by municipalities, states, or individual facilities, but little is known about their relative effectiveness.[31] Systematic evaluation, including evidence of impact, could allow successful initiatives to be replicated.

---

[30] According to the 1998 National Household Survey (IBGE 2000b) and recent estimates on health expenditure.

[31] A number have been supported by the World Bank-financed REFORSUS Project.

Context

As health authorities prepare to move forward with the next round of reforms, they face a set of systemic issues that could jeopardize implementation and sustainability unless further steps are taken to rationalize the system and create an incentive structure that fosters accountability of providers as well as payers. States, as the logical entities for overseeing health care organization and delivery by municipalities, are potentially key players in the system, but their role remains ambiguous. Traditionally, they have focused on direct service provision and, more recently, on monitoring and control of federal financial transfers. Under decentralization many hospital facilities and all basic care services were turned over to municipal management, and most federal transfers bypass the state level. States now need to develop the technical and managerial capacity to fulfill their functions in SUS: planning, coordinating, monitoring, and evaluating the implementation of national policies and the delivery of municipal-managed services.

CHALLENGES TO EXPANSION OF BASIC CARE: Two major Ministry of Health strategies for improving access to quality basic health services have been adoption of the per capita transfer for basic care (Piso Assistencial Básico, PAB) and implementation and expansion of the Family Health Program. Through the Family Health Program the government plans to restructure the way publicly financed primary health care is organized and provided. The merging of the Family Health Program with other transfers to create a single grant is under consideration in the Ministry of Health, but execution of that plan depends on the success and pace of expansion of the Family Health Program as well as implementation of the expanded care package (PAB-A)

Several threats have arisen to the long-term financial sustainability of the expanded Family Health Program. First, although Amendment 29 will increase financing for health, it is unclear what types of health services will benefit from the additional financing. In theory, financing could be directed to hospital-based care, which could wipe out the equity and allocative efficiency gains of recent years. Federal grant subsidies do not cover the full costs of provision (nor are they meant to) and must rely on complementary financing from municipalities and states, which may not channel all Family Health Program transfers to the program's activities (the Ministry of Health suspects some leakage to other types of care, but estimates are unavailable). The costs of expanding the Family Health Program vary considerably and relate in part to the degree of urbanization, the specific package of services, and municipal organizational and managerial capacity. These variations are not reflected in Family Health Program transfers. Finally, converting the current basic care model to the outreach-based Family Health Program may be costlier than anticipated.

Actual costs tend to be significantly higher for the Family Health Program than for the traditional model because of the higher salaries paid to health professionals, the broader set of services offered, and the human resource-intensive outreach activities.[32]

Gate-keeping roles and referral mechanisms: Any organizational arrangement involving formation of a service network will have to deal with three related but undesirable aspects of the health delivery system in Brazil: ease of access to emergency rooms and specialty services, weak referral and counter-referral systems, and absence of coordinated care or case management. In 2001, an estimated R$1.0 billion was spent on hospitalizations that could have been treated on an ambulatory basis, suggesting flaws in the referral system between hospitals and primary care providers.[33] The Family Health Program aims to introduce family physicians in a gatekeeper role, as case managers to guide patients through the delivery system. But there has been little contact between Family Health Program teams (lead by family doctors) and specialists and upstream referral facilities. An excess supply of specialists, a tight supply of primary care physicians, and the difficulty attracting qualified personnel (especially physicians) to poorer and remote areas are contributing factors. Establishing an orderly delivery network will require a role reversal in which primary care physicians, supported by non-physician providers, play a dominant role in guiding patients through the system (and consequently orienting the allocation of resources). Once implemented, the SUS smart card (Cartão SUS) initiative may contribute to effective referrals, but improving interaction among service levels and providers requires serious attention.

THE LIMITS OF DECENTRALIZATION: Many municipalities were ill-prepared for the large transfer of responsibilities that came with decentralization. Together with the multiple payment system, full-fledged "municipalization" is increasingly seen as a main cause of system fragmentation, as manifested in service duplication, overbuilt capacity, and the loss of economies of scale and resulting in higher operating costs. Many municipalities lack the capacity to effectively manage basic care. Most will be unable to manage the expanded (PAB-A) package of services. The NOAS/01 represents a mid-course correction aimed at reducing this fragmentation and can be seen as a step back from municipalization. The

---

[32] The most successful experiences of traditional-to-PSF conversion involve the substitution (rather than integration) of personnel by newly-hired PSF personnel, and in some cases were helped by exceptional political support that will be hard to replicate.

[33] Mendes, 2002.

success of the micro-regional proposal will depend on municipal buy-in, sharing and specialization of facilities, reorientation of financial flows, and clear role definition and differentiation (state, micro-regional, and municipal).[34] It is clear that some type of inter-municipal organizational arrangement, probably at the microregional level, will be needed to manage (or purchase) service delivery in shared and specialized facilities. A testing period may be warranted as each state attempts to find the proper balance between autonomy at the municipal level and coordination and enforcement of national policies. State leadership, as mandated by NOAS/01, will be fundamental to the successful design and implementation of regionalization models.

EVALUATIVE RESEARCH: SUS managers and policymakers tend to focus on planning rather than evaluation. Local and facility managers favor experimentation. Many potentially interesting experiences are designed, implemented, and sometimes abandoned (for various reasons) without proper evaluation. In particular, there is little systematic information about the costs, efficiency, and quality of health care provision. Referred to as the "silent reform"[35], these experiences represent a great source for best practices in improving efficiency and quality. Systematic evaluation, including evidence of impact, could allow successful initiatives to be replicated. (A few examples of initiatives deserving evaluation are listed in box 1.)

---

[34] There is evidence from the nascent implementation process that some states have interpreted regionalization as adding an administrative (micro-regional) layer between the states and municipalities. This will certainly raise costs but provide little value added in improving performance.

[35] Ribeiro, Costa and Silva (2001).

Box 1. Innovations in health service provision

Pilot activities can be a rich source of information on what works in Brazil, especially for improving the quality and efficiency of health services. The following are among those that would benefit from evaluation of their impact on sustainability, replicability, and effect on efficiency, quality, and equity of care.

- Some public hospitals have experimented with innovative forms of organization and management, such as social organizations (*organizações sociais*) and cooperatives (such as the PAS experience in São Paulo).

- Some municipalities have opted for ensuring complete autonomy for their local health system by establishing a health foundation independent of direct municipal administration (for example, Londrina in the state of Paraná).

- Accreditation, quality assurance programs, and quality promotion initiatives have multiplied in recent years, in both the public and private sector, but little is known about their impact on quality of care.

- Many public hospitals are contracting out services such as nutrition, laundry, and some diagnostic services, but the relative costs and benefits of contracting out vs. in-house services have not been evaluated systematically.

- In an attempt to increase and diversify their sources of revenue, a growing number of public hospitals, especially tertiary and university hospitals, have opened rooms or wards for treating private patients or patients covered by private plans. (A pioneering experience is INCOR in São Paulo). The effect of this strategy on efficiency, quality of care, and equity is unknown, as is its potential for ensuring sustainable funding for SUS patients.

- A few hospitals (such as Hospital das Clínicas in São Paulo and Projeto MORAR in Rio Grande do Sul) have established a home-care program for pre- and post-surgical care and care of chronic illness. The relative merits and costs of such programs require in-depth assessment.

- Preventive programs such as those promoting regular exercise, blood pressure monitoring, psychiatric ambulatory care, and the like have been adopted by a number of facilities or municipalities, often without a clear process of evaluation.

- More generally, some municipalities or states have been more successful in implementing specific programs and policies than others. Identifying the key factors for the success of these experiences would be important to improve the performance of other municipalities or states.

COORDINATION WITH THE PRIVATE SECTOR: The health system in Brazil can still be described as a collection of isolated, uncoordinated systems. SUS legislation usually assumes that SUS encompasses the entire health sector. However, the purely private sector (non-SUS financed) has only a marginal role despite its importance in financing and providing services (table 4). The absence of coordination with the private sector results in the duplication of coverage and services, while the benefits of innovation in one sector to financiers and providers in another, and to overall sector performance, are often missed.

Table 4. Distribution of service utilization by source of funding (1998)

	Brazil	1º Quintile	2º Quintile	3º Quintile	4º Quintile	5º Quintile
SUS services	49.80	78.30	74.00	62.50	43.60	15.00
Private Insurance/Plans	26.93	3.00	6.70	15.10	32.00	57.70
Out-of-pocket	15.88	4.80	8.30	13.40	17.70	27.30

Source: 1998 National Household Survey (IBGE 2000b).

Options

ENSURE FINANCIAL SUSTAINABILITY AND EQUITY OF PRIMARY CARE EXPANSION. The feasibility of expanding the Family Health Program and making it the central pillar of a reformed SUS health care model as well as improving quality and equity depends on ensuring financial sustainability. Possible strategies for achieving this include:

- Increasing the supply of medium complexity services in municipalities lacking installed capacity, based on criteria related to disease burden;
- Crafting regulations for Amendment 29 that direct more federal revenues to basic care, and establish incentives for the states and municipalities to do the same.
- Avoiding parallel delivery systems once the Family Health Program is expanded in areas with existing basic care facilities.

Rationalize facility networks and improve organizational efficiency. To strengthen management capacity and rationalize facility network and referral systems, the government could develop a three-tiered strategy for reorganizing service provision by:

- Consolidating financial flows and payment mechanisms, reducing their number to a minimum. These can include a needs-adjusted per capita amount for basic and medium complexity care. The NOASs have already proposed a broadening of the services paid on a per capita basis (PAB-A).

- Developing implementation strategies and operational models for crafting microregions, including the pooling of financial and technical resources and creation of governance structures to oversee service organization and delivery. One model could be based on the successful experience of municipal consortia (*consórcios municipais*). This measure can be used in conjunction with the formation of integrated delivery systems (see below).

- Testing strategies for integrated delivery systems, an organized system of providers capable of delivering a full range of primary, preventive, diagnostic, hospital, and health promotion services. The microregion strategy specified in the NOAS/01 can be interpreted as an attempt to form an integrated delivery system by combining physical, human, and financial resources for a group of municipalities. Integrated delivery systems attempt to align the incentives of providers at each level of care (primary, secondary, and tertiary) within a single governance and management structure. Usually through a contract with a purchasing entity (public or private), the organization is responsible for providing a comprehensive service package to its enrolled or "covered" population through its affiliated providers. There are many organizational models of integrated delivery systems. In Brazil, there are at least three: *organizações sociais* with a broadened scope of services, private pre-paid group practices (*medicinas de grupo*), and health foundations. The United States has several integrated delivery system models, some more than 50 years old. Contracting an integrated delivery system organization to deliver an integrated set of services could replace paying an array of providers (with an array of payment mechanisms) for individual services and programs. Drawing on national and international experience with integrated delivery systems and investing in pilot experiences could yield benefits for the entire health sector. It is best to start simply, by configuring an integrated delivery system for basic and medium-complexity care and applying a single, capitated payment.

- Systematically reviewing the main reasons for hospitalization, identifying illnesses that can be treated at a lower level, and developing interventions to prevent them.

INCREASE COLLABORATION AND COORDINATION WITH THE PRIVATE SECTOR: The public and private sectors face a common set of problems, from low quality of services to rising costs and precarious financial sustainability. Several opportunities for increasing coordination and collaboration have arisen in recent years, including:

- Clarifying the roles of the public and private sectors, exploring alternatives for reducing and avoiding duplication of infrastructure and services.
- Promoting appropriate health policies and programs in the private sector (disease prevention, care of the elderly, health promotion) exchange of information (costs, management tools), and joint ventures on research and evaluation.

SUPPORT SYSTEMATIC AND RIGOROUS ANALYSIS AND EVALUATION. Evaluation should contribute to decisionmaking at each level of government, as well as to consultations with social councils. There is an urgent need for systematic and comparative analysis of:

- Recent experiences in innovative models of health service organization (*organizações sociais,* health foundations) and finance.
- Data collected by IBGE (1998 National Household Survey, PNAD) and other organizations.
- Use of innovative management tools and alternative forms of contracting.
- Analysis of the sources of inequity in health (see Message 1).
- Comparative analysis of the different accreditation programs and quality assurance initatives (see Message 2).
- Managerial, financial, and technical practices prevalent in the private sector.

Message 4. Preventing and controling noncommunicable diseases and injuries through health promotion and social interventions
As communicable diseases are being brought under control, the costs of health services will increasingly be related to noncommunicable diseases, which are more expensive to treat. Public health programs to promote health and prevent and manage noncommunicable diseases are just beginning to take shape. A national health promotion strategy, including guidelines for implementing and monitoring specific interventions through cross-sectoral arrangements, coordinated care management, and linkages to the Family Health Program, would help Brazil reduce the human and financial costs of noncommunicable disease. The capacity of municipalities to set health priorities and disease prevention strategies will require strengthening.

Context
Brazilians are living longer and are much less likely to die from communicable diseases. Noncommunicable diseases are now the leading causes of death, with cardiovascular diseases, injuries, and cancer the top three causes, accounting for 62 percent of all deaths.[36] Noncommunicable diseases represent 75 percent of the years of productive life lost in Brazil.[37] Growing urbanization (80 percent of Brazilians live in cities) has contributed to changes in lifestyle (sedentary behavior, diet high in fats, cigarette smoking, substance abuse) that increase the risk of developing noncommunicable diseases at an earlier age.

Many noncommunicable diseases and injuries are completely preventable. Experience from other countries suggests that this requires a reorientation of the health system toward the promotion of healthy behaviors and away from an emphasis primarily on the treatment of diseases. Healthy behaviors that are associated with the prevention of noncommunicable diseases include smoking cessation, moderate physical activity (such as walking), a diet low in fats, normal body weight, and use of diagnostic tools such as PAP smears for cancer screening.

It is widely recognized that achieving major changes in health behaviors requires coordinated action across a range of sectors (IUHPE 2000) in addition to the health sector. In Europe, schools have been shown to be cost effective sites for health promotion interventions since healthy behaviors begin early in life and benefit from reinforcement during

---

[36] FUNASA 1998 data from the 2002 Ministry of Health Web site: www.saude.gov.br
[37] FUNASA Proposta nacional de monitoramento de agravos a saúde e doenças não transmissíveis (rascunho). Brasília, 2001.

adolescence. Comprehensive health promotion strategies also include legislation and activities in the workplace, in the community, and in other sectors like urban planning, social services, communication and media, and the private sector.

The North Karelia project in Finland shows how a community-based heart health project contributed to a 73 percent decline in cardiovascular mortality and a 49 percent decline in mortality from all causes.[38] Aggressive tobacco regulation in the state of California contributed to a 14 percent decline in lung cancer compared with 2.7 percent in the rest of the United States.[39] Likewise, there is considerable evidence on specific behaviors that reduce the incidence of injuries, such as moderate use of alcohol (and none before driving) and use of safety devices such as seat belts and helmets.

Measurement of the prevalence of behavioral risk factors for noncommunicable diseases has been sporadic. However, data suggest alarming levels of smoking (40 percent among men and 25 percent among women) and obesity (approximately 10 percent overall, but especially prevalent among poor people, who have the double risk of obesity and malnutrition).[40] The first national survey of behavioral risk factors is under way and will provide baseline information for monitoring the impact of future health promotion actions. Brazil also has had sporadic regulatory and population-based health promotion activities. Examples include legislation restricting cigarette advertising and banning smoking in public places; a national anti-smoking media campaign; work by an internationally recognized NGO in São Paulo *(Agita São Paulo)* on the ways to increase physical activity;[41] and plans to replicate the international "Healthy Municipalities" model in many Brazilian cities and to promote health through schools.

Noncommunicable diseases like hypertension and diabetes can cause death and major disabilities at a young, productive age. When prevention is not possible, the goal is to control the disease and reduce these health consequences with cost-effective, low-tech management. Management of noncommunicable disease requires a shift from acute care models toward a comprehensive model that screens effectively and assures continuity of care and adherence to treatment.[42] Ideally, a well-functioning referral network between primary and secondary and tertiary care would be available to support primary health care providers.

---

[38] Puska, Vartiainen, Pallonen, and others (1998).

[39] Fichtenberg and Glantz (2000).

[40] PAHO (1998a, 1998b); Peña (2002).

[41] Matsuda, Matsuda, and Andrade (2002)

[42] WHO (2000).

The stage is set for a more cohesive and comprehensive population health promotion strategy. Nevertheless, the Ministry of Health has yet to complete the consensus-building process on priorities in health promotion that could serve as the basis for a national heath promotion plan. Nor is there a national committee or other entity that could serve as a coordinating body among the various sectors and organizations involved in health promotion activities.

The Ministry of Health recently completed a process of identifying six major national health objectives. One of the objectives is "control of priority diseases". Hypertension and diabetes are 2 of the 11 priority diseases for which national indicators are included. Both are important precursors of cardiovascular disease, stroke, and other illnesses. Their prevalence in Brazil is high, estimated at 9 percent for diabetes and 10-20 percent for hypertension. Treatment requires long-term care, patient education, and self-management. Guidelines for management are available, but it is unclear how well these guidelines are being applied in primary care settings.

The Family Health Program, as the Ministry of Health's principle strategy for meeting the health care needs of the population, will address the prevention and control of noncommunicable diseases through individual and community-based health promotion, improved disease control activities, and by providing the education and support patients need to be informed, involved in, and able to manage their chronic conditions. There is great potential for working through community health agents, who have close links to the communities and families they serve, to promote healthy behaviors. Family Health Program physicians and nurses could also play a role by providing counseling on smoking, physical activity, nutrition, safety devices, and preventive health services such as PAP smears. Nevertheless, guidelines for Family Health Program teams on their roles and responsibilities in health promotion have not yet been developed.

Options

STRENGTHEN HEALTH PROMOTION STRATEGIES AND PROGRAMS TO REDUCE THE HEALTH BURDEN OF NONCOMMUNICABLE DISEASES. Health promotion activities are still at an early stage of development. The Disease Surveillance and Control Project (VIGISUS) is strengthening surveillance of noncommunicable diseases and has set up surveillance and information systems for behavioral risk factors. It has also contributed to the development of centers of excellence related to aging, cancer, and injuries. The Family Health Program is taking the lead on health promotion activities in health care settings. Efforts are beginning to define the roles and responsibilities of Family Health Program teams in health promotion. Nevertheless, these are nascent efforts and require continuing investment. Strategic actions to sustain this process could include:

- Elaborating a national population health promotion strategy with input from involved sectors and well-defined priorities, and defining clear goals and indicators for monitoring the impact of health promotion activities (little work on community or population based health promotion is currently being done at the state and municipal levels.

- Developing guidelines and capacity for supervising and monitoring health promotion actions by Family Health Program teams. While community health agents are expected to be part of the Family Health Program team, they will need training to prepare them since community-based work is different from individual and family-based activities.

SHIFT HEALTH CARE SERVICES TO A COMPREHENSIVE, COORDINATED MODEL BETTER EQUIPPED TO ADDRESS THE NEEDS OF PEOPLE WITH CHRONIC ILLNESSES (and away from the acute care model). The most successful models include those with linkages to community programs, health systems geared to continuity of care, an emphasis on self-management, and involvement of the entire health team including health educators and community health workers. While the Family Health Program includes diabetes and hypertension as two of its priorities, information on the effectiveness of its control programs is lacking. Strategies could include:

- Developing a coordinated and comprehensive system of primary health care to manage noncommunicable disease, including access to basic medications, preparation of long-term treatment plans focusing on patient education and adherence to treatment, and better coordination between primary and other levels of care.

- Evaluating the effectiveness of diabetes and hypertension control activities, provided through family health programs.

DEVELOP CROSS-SECTORAL APPROACHES AND COMMUNITY PARTNERSHIPS TO PROMOTE HEALTHY LIFESTYLES (active community environments, smoke-free spaces). Changing lifestyles and individual behaviors depends on coordinated activities across many sectors. Lifestyle decisions are often made during childhood and adolescence, making collaboration with the education system crucial.[43] Peer groups have been successful in changing some behaviors. Involvement of mass media and the communications sector is clearly important. In some countries, regulations have successfully reduced smoking, urban planning has helped make the environment conducive to a less sedentary lifestyle, and NGOs have worked at the community level to bring about changes in behavior.

Conclusion

Brazil is ready to start a new phase of reforms which could consolidate and deepen policies to improve equity of financing and access, improve the efficiency of resource allocation and use, increase the quality of care, and address new challenges related to the prevention and control of noncommunicable diseases. Meeting these objectives would also involve adjusting for the unforeseen but systemic problems emerging from decentralization and other reforms, including low management capacity, multiple payment systems, fragmented delivery of care, absence of performance-based management tools and financing mechanisms, and inattention to systematic evaluation. Together, these deficiencies contribute to an unaligned incentive structure for municipal managers and providers that contributes to inefficient resource allocation, high costs, and low quality.

The recent economic crisis may threaten the sustainability of some reforms, jeopardize implementation of others (such as Amendment 29), and increase the pressure on decision makers to further rationalize the organization and delivery of health care. It is becoming increasing clear that quality and efficiency issues are major impediments to improved system performance. Addressing these issues is a key challenge for the next reform phase.

---

[43] School health programs in the United States have resulted in a 37 percent reduction in the onset of smoking among 7th grade students, decrease in the prevalence of obesity, lower use of alcohol and marijuana (U.S. CDC, 2001).

References

World Bank projects:

- Health sector reform – REFORSUS *(Projeto de Reforma do Setor Saúde Rec. Cap. Assistencial—SUS)* US$ 300 million. Approved on June 20, 1996.
- Disease surveillance first phase – VIGISUS *(Projeto do Sistema Nacional de Vigilância Sanitária primeira fase)* US$ 100 million. Approved on September 17, 1998.
- AIDS & STD control II *(Segundo Projeto de Controle das DST/AIDS)* US$ 161.5 million. Approved on September 15, 1998.
- Family health extension project *(Projeto Programa Saúde da Família)* US$ 68 million. Approved on March 14, 2002.

World Bank reports:

This chapter summarizes the content of the following World Bank reports. Those, in turn, draw heavily from a wide range of literature on the subject from experts in Brazil and beyond, which are referenced in the mentioned Bank reports.

World Bank. 1999. Brazil – The World Bank Assistance Strategy for the Health Sector. Washington, D.C.

World Bank. 2002. "Decentralization of Health Care in Brazil – A Case Study of Bahia." Washington, D.C.

World Bank. 1994. "The Organization, Delivery and Financing of Health Care in Brazil: Agenda for the 90s." Report No. 12655-BR. World Bank, Human Resources Division, Washington, D.C.

World Bank. 2002. "Brazil: Mother and Child Health." Report No. 20693. Latin America and the Caribbean Region, Human Development Sector Management Unit, Brazil Country Management Unit, Washington, D.C.

Other references:

(IBGE) Brazilian Institute for Geography and Statistics. 2000a. *Estatísticas da Saúde – Assistência Médico-Sanitária* 1999. Rio de Janeiro.

(IBGE) Brazilian Institute for Geography and Statistics. 2000b. *Pesquisa Nacional por Amostra de Domicílios 1998 – Acesso e Utilização de Serviços de Saúde.* Rio de Janeiro.

Bastos, P.G.; Knaus, W.A.; Zimmerman, J.E. et al. 1996. The importance of Technology for Achieving Superior Outcomes from Intensive Care. APACHE III Study Group. Intensive Care Med., 22, 664-669.

BNDES. 2002. Hospitais Filantrópicos no Brasil. Volume I, II, III. BNDES, Rio de Janeiro.

Carvalho G.C.M. 2002. *O Financiamento Público Federal do Sistema Único de Saúde,*1988-2001. Doctoral dissertation, University of São Paulo.

Carvalho, J. and Pereira, T.R., 1998. Health Care Reform and Quality Initiatives in Brazil. Journal on Quality Improvement. 24 (3) 251-261.

Cecílio, L.C.O. 1999. *O Estado como Prestador Direto da Assistência Hospitalar: sim ou não?* Rev. Adm. Pública. 33(2): 23-37.

Cecílio, L.C.O. 2000. *Trabalhando a Missão de um Hospital como Facilitador da Mudança Organizacional: Limites e Possibilidades.* Caderno de Saúde Pública, 16(4): 973-983.

Costa, N.R.; Ribeiro, J.M.; Silva, P.L.B. 2000. *A Experiência Internacional de Reforma do Setor Saúde: Inovações Organizacionais e de Financiamento.* Revista Brasileira de Adm. Pública, 34 (1).

Costa, N.R.; Ribeiro, J.M.; Silva, P.L.B. 2001. *Inovações Organizacionais e de Financiamento: Experiências a partir do Cenário Institucional.* Campinas, SP.

Couttolenc, B. 2002. *"Estudo Empírico sobre a Exclusão Social em Saúde na Argentina, Brasil e Chile – Relatório Final Brasil."* Study for the ILO. Santiago.

De Gouvea, C.S.; Travassos, C.; Fernandes, C. 1997. Service Delivery and Quality of Hospital Care in the State of Rio de Janeiro. Revista de Saúde Pública, 31, 601-617.

Fichtenberg, C.M., and S.A. Glantz. 2000. Association of the California Tobacco Control Program with Declines in Cigarette Consumption and Mortality from Heart Disease. NEJM 343: 1772–77.

Gesaworld do Brasil: *Relatório Final do Projeto de Introdução da Função de Compra de Serviços na Secretaria de Saúde do Ceará.* 2000.

Gesaworld do Brasil: *Relatório Final do Projeto de Introdução da Função de Compra de Serviços na Secretaria de Saúde do Ceará.* 2002

IPEA. 2001. *Tendências do Sistema de Saúde Brasileiro. Estudo Delphi. Instituto de Pesquisa Econômica Aplicada,* Brasília.

IUHPE (International Union for Health Promotion and Education). 2000. The Evidence of Health Promotion Effectiveness: Shaping Public Health in a New Europe. Part 1. 2nd edition. Paris: International Union for Health Promotion and Education.

Jain, S. 2002. *Análise de Reestruturação dos Modelos Assistenciais de Saúde em Grandes Cidades: Padrões de Custos e Formas de Financiamento.* Brasília. Ministério da Saúde.

Lima, S.M.L. and Barbosa, P.R. 2001. *Planejamento e inovação gerencial em um hospital público: o caso do Hospital Municipal Salgado Filho.* Rev. De Adm.Pub. 35(3):37-76.

Kisil, M. 2003. *Revisão Analítica da Literatura: Qualidade e Performance Hospitalar no Brasil. Versão Preliminar.*

Marinho, A. 2001. *Estudo de Eficiência em Alguns Hospitais Públicos e Privados com a Geração de "Rankings".* IPEA *Texto para discussão no.* 794, May.

Marinho, A. 1998. *Estudo e eficiencia em hospitais públicos e privados com a geração de rankings.* Rev. De Adm. Pub. 32(6): 145-58.

Matos, A. J., and others. 2002. *Apuração dos custos de procedimentos hospitalares: Alta e média complexidade.* Ministério de Saúde, for REFORSUS, Brasilia.

Matsuda V, Matsuda S, Andrade D., and others. 2002. "Promotion of Physical Activity in a Developing Country: The Agita Sao Paulo Experience. Public Health Nutrition 5(1A): 253–61.

Médici, A. 2001. Brasil – *Financiamiento y Gasto Público en Salud en los Años Noventa.* Washington, D.C.: Banco Interamericano de Desarrollo.

Mendes, E.V. 2002. *A Atenção Primária à Saúde no SUS.* Escola de Saúde Pública do Ceará. Fortaleza.

Ministry of Health. 2000. *Assistência Hospitalar no SUS –* 1995-1999. Brasília: Ministério da Saúde.

Ministry of Health. 2001a. *Assistência à Saúde no SUS – Média e Alta Complexidade –* 1995-2000. MS/SAS. Brasília: Ministério da Saúde.

Ministry of Health. 2001b. *Estimativas de Impacto da Vinculação Constitucional de Recursos para a Saúde (Emenda Constitucional no. 29/2000). Cadernos de Economia da Saúde 1, Série J,* No. 4. Brasília: Ministério da Saúde.

Ministry of Health. 2001c. SIOPS – *Relatório de Atividades 2000.* MS/SAS. Brasília: Ministério da Saúde.

Ministry of Health. 2002. *Avaliação da Implementação do Programa de Saúde da Família em Dez Grandes Centros Urbanos: Síntese dos Principais Resultados.* Brasília. Ministério da Saúde.

Ministry of Health. 2002a. *Experiências Inovadoras, No.* 1, August. Brasília: Ministério da Saúde.

Ministry of Health. 2002b. Secretaria de Assistência à Saúde: *Relatório de Gestão* 1998-2001. Brasília: Ministério da Saúde.

Montonya Diaz, M.D. 2001. *Desigualdades Socioeconômicas na Saúde no Brasil.* IPE/USP, Texto para Discussão No. 14/2001. São Paulo.

Musgrove, P. 1998. "Compensatory Finance in Health: In Search of Geographic Equity in a Federal System." Paper presented to the Third International Seminar on Fiscal Federalism and Federal Finance, Faculty of Economic Science, National University of La Plata, Argentina, 24 April 1998.

Negri, B. 2002. *"A política de saúde no Brasil nos anos 90: Avanços e limitações."* Ministério da Saúde, Brasília.

Neri, M.C., ed. 2000. *Gasto Público En Servicios Sociales Básicos En América Latina Y El Caribe* – Brasil. Santiago: Economic Commission for Latina America and the Caribbean.

Noronha, J.C.; Pereira, T.R.S.P. 1998. Health Care Reform and Quality Initiatives in Brazil. Journal on Quality Improvement, 24 (5).

Nunes A., J.R.S. Santos, R.B. Barata, and S.M. Vianna. 2001. *Medindo as Desigualdades em Saúde no Brasil – Uma Proposta de Monitoramento.* OPAS/OMS/IPEA.

Oliveira, T.C. 1997. *Controle de infecção hospitalar como indicador de qualidade dos hospitais do municipio de Campinas e região.* Thesis presented at the State University of Campinas.

PAHO (Pan American Health Organization). 1998. "Diseases or Health Impairments." In: Health in the Americas. Scientific publication 569. Washington D.C.

PAHO (Pan American Health Organization). 1998. A saude no Brasil. Brasilia.

Pena, F.P.M. 2000. *Implantação do Modelo ISO 9002 na Área da Saúde: A Visão do Gestor da Qualidade em Quatro Unidades de um Hospital do Município de São Paulo.* Masters Dissertation, Escola de Administração de Empresas de São Paulo. São Paulo.

Peña, M., ed. 1998. The Faces of Poverty: Malnourished, Hungry and Obese? Washington D.C.: Pan American Health Organization.

Pessoa, L.R. 1996. *Terceirização nos hospitais públicos: mais um problema ou uma possível solução.* Masters Dissertation, National School of Public Health. Rio de Janeiro.

Puska P, E. Vartiainen, U. Pallonen, and others. 1998. Changes in Premature Deaths in Finland: Successful Long-Term Prevention of Cardiovascular Diseases. Bull. WHO 76.

REFORSUS. 2002. *"Aspectos distribuitivos do gasto público na saúde."* Estudo preliminar. Ministerio da Saude, Brasília.

Rehem de Souza, R. 2002. *O Sistema Público de Saúde Brasileiro. Seminário Internacional Tendências e Desafios dos Sistemas de Saúde nas Américas,* São Paulo.

Ribeiro J. M., and N. do R. Costa. 1999. *Consórcios Municipais no SUS. Texto Para Discussão No 669.* IPEA, Brasília.

Ribeiro, J., and others. 2002. *Estudo de novos modelos de gerencia de unidades hospitares.* ENSP; FIOCRUZ, for REFORSUS.

Ribeiro, J., N. Costa, and P.L. Silva. 2001. *"Inovações na gestão descentralizada e organizações hospitalares: os casos das Regiões Metropolitana do Rio de Janeiro e São Paulo."* In B. Negri and D. Di Giovanni, eds. Brazil: Radiografia da Saúde. São Paulo:UNICAMP.

Silva, L.K.; Russomano, F.B. 1996. Underreporting of Maternal Mortality in Rio de Janeiro. Bol. Oficina Sanit Panama. 22, 664-669.

Silva, P.L.B.; Costa, N.R.; Melo, M.A.C. & Ribeiro, J.M. 1999. *Reforma do Estado e Setor Saúde.* Brasília: CAPES/FINEP/CNPQ.

Teixeira P, M. Vitoria, D. Barreira, C. Dhalia, and E. Castilho. 2001. "AIDS Epidemic in BRAZIL: Present Situation, National Response and Future Trends." Actualizaciones en SIDA 9 (supplement 1).

U.S. Centers for Disease Control (US CDC). 2001. School Health Programs: An Investment in our Nation's Future. At-a-glance series. Atlanta, Ga.: DHHS/Center for Disease Control.

Victora, C. 2000. "Potential Interventions to Improve the Health of Mothers and Children in Brazil." Paper commissioned by the World Bank. Washington, D.C.

WHO (World Health Organization). 2001. "Innovative Care for Chronic Conditions." Meeting report 30-31 May, 2001. MNC/CCH/01.01. Geneva.

Xavier, A.C.R.; Batista, F.F.; Marra, F.; Longo, R.M.J. 1997. *Implantando a Gestão da Qualidade em Hospitais: A Experiência da Santa Casa de Misericórdia de Porto Alegre,* RS. Brasília, IPEA.

3

Social Protection

3

Social Protection

Introduction

For most people the best social protection is a job. Improving the functioning of the labor market and reducing labor taxation in Brazil would help create jobs, providing social protection for millions of people. Good macroeconomic management and employment-creating growth are thus key aspects of social protection.

In addition to facilitating employment-generating growth, governments need to provide social protection programs. These programs currently play a small role in Brazil's poverty alleviation strategy. Expanding well-designed programs for the poor could help reduce poverty and spur more rapid economic growth.

The possibilities for making social protection a more important tool for poverty reduction are limited in Brazil because of the excessive insurance provided to a few groups, particularly through the social security system. There is a pressing need to better balance social protection by providing more insurance to groups that are virtually uncovered while reducing the high levels of insurance provided to others, such as civil servants.

Possibilities for improving social protection in Brazil are presented below and discussed in this note.

The role of social protection in reducing poverty

Social protection includes public interventions that help individuals, households, and communities manage risk or that provide support to the very poor. The design and strategy of public social protection programs are key components in an integrated approach to poverty reduction. The emphasis and funding given to different programs should be flexible in order to allow programs to respond to macroeconomic trends and emergencies.

The draft of this chapter was completed by Polly Jones, with contributions from Asta Zviniene in November 2002. The analyses and suggestions contained in this chapter are based on the international technical experience of the World Bank and are presented as a contribution to the debate and formulation of public policies.

Over the past decade Brazil has reduced poverty and improved the health status and educational attainment of the poor. Economic stabilization and growth since 1994 have permitted earlier gains in poverty reduction to be sustained. This improvement in macro-economic management has mitigated the risk associated with previous stop-and-go economic policies and high inflation, which hurt the poor during the 1980s.

Despite these gains, poverty is unacceptably high for a country of Brazil's wealth. About 20 percent of the population—35 million people—have incomes below the poverty line. The high level of poverty increases the need for social protection programs, which fall into three main categories: labor market interventions (primarily unemployment benefits), social security (pensions), and social assistance.

High levels of inequality and poverty act as a drag on economic growth and productive capacity. Providing a social safety net to the poor can help improve economic growth. Analysis shows that during the 1990s, households in the bottom 10–15 percent of the income distribution benefited much less than other groups from better economic opportunities. This core of poor people needs to be supported.

Mechanisms to manage risk are more important for the poor than for the better-off, because the poor usually have less diversified sources of income and less access to credit markets or formal insurance. Gaps in social protection are critical for the poor, because their coping strategies may involve behavior that reduces social or human capital formation (for example, not sending children to school or not seeking necessary health care). Despite the greater need for social protection of the poor, coverage of the middle class is far greater than coverage of the poor in Brazil.

Characteristics of the poor in Brazil

Large regional disparities in poverty exist in Brazil, with a growing concentration of poverty in the Northeast and in rural areas. Because the localities most in need of social protection programs can least afford them, there is a strong rationale for federal social policies and financing. State and municipal governments also have important roles to play in social protection—by co-financing programs, for example, implementing programs, or organizing the participation of government agencies and civil society.

Most of the poor work, but most social protection programs are linked to the formal labor market, where relatively few poor people are employed. As a result, the poor must depend on informal mechanisms, some of which are associated with a decrease in future levels of social and human capital. High wage volatility seems to be a greater problem than the likelihood of unemployment. To the extent that this is due to the high level of informality (where incomes are more variable than employment), it points to the need for income security programs in the informal sector.

Public spending on social protection

Essential for adequate social protection for the poor in Brazil is good macroeconomic management and employment-creating growth. For most people, even the best-designed social protection program is a second-best solution compared with a job. Ensuring that the economy generates adequate employment and that labor markets facilitate employment creation is an important aspect of social protection.

That said, strong social safety nets are needed for potential crisis situations. Brazil appears to have fewer instruments and programs to draw on in emergencies than many other countries.

If social protection programs work effectively they protect people from declines in consumption during adverse situations, such as economic recession. It appears that social protection programs play a relatively small role in Brazil because the volatility of consumption is higher than the volatility of GDP. This implies that individuals don't have any "cushion" from a social protection program to shield them from macroeconomic changes. (It is the reverse in high-income countries, where social protection accounts for a larger share of spending). Public social spending in Brazil, including estimated expenditures by all levels of government, amounts to about 20 percent of GDP. Assuming perfect targeting of resources, it would take a relatively small additional amount—just 1.6 percent of GDP—to raise every poor person in Brazil above the poverty line.

Expenditures on social security represent nearly 60 percent of the total, or slightly more than 10 percent of GDP. Brazil spends more on pensions than most countries. In Mexico, for example, spending on pensions represents slightly less than 40 percent of total public social spending; in the United States the share is even lower, at about a third.

Social security spending in Brazil is heavily subsidized by general tax revenues, which augment the financing provided from contributions by beneficiaries. With the exception of the old age program, these programs do not benefit the poor to a great extent: less than 1 percent of social security spending reaches the poorest 10 percent of Brazilians, while 50 percent goes to the richest 1 percent.

In most countries, public social spending, particularly for social protection, compensates for the conditions and low income of the poor and thus tends to have an equalizing effect on income distribution. This is not the case in Brazil. Instead, because social security accounts for such a high share of public social spending and is so regressive, public social spending exacerbates Brazil's high levels of inequality. Because this effect is large, changes in social spending could have an immediate impact on reducing inequality. In contrast, investments in education, which are critical to alleviating poverty, will take longer to show results.

Social public expenditure in Brazil represents 17 percent of average household income. The best-targeted programs are childcare and kindergarten (2 percent), together with maternal nutrition (0.1 percent) and basic education (9.6 percent). The worst-targeted programs are pensions (56 percent) and college education (4.2 percent). Brazil, a relatively youthful country, spends more on its 21 million retirees than on the 48 million students enrolled in its preschools, schools, colleges, and universities.

Message 1. Increasing the potential of the economy to create jobs
Creating enough jobs to meet demand and increasing labor productivity to levels of other countries at Brazil's income level would provide millions of Brazilians with social protection. Possible reforms include moving negotiations over wages and benefits from the courts to the workplace, modifying the design of the Severance Fund (FGTS), and gradually reducing and introducing more flexibility into the mandated minimum benefits package for formal sector workers.

Context
At first glance, the labor market in Brazil would appear to function fairly well, with historically low recorded unemployment rates despite macroeconomic shocks. There is cause for concern, however, for several reasons.

JOB GROWTH IS INSUFFICIENT. Over the past 10 years employment has not grown as rapidly as the working-age population, despite a decline in labor force participation rates. This trend is worrisome, because it means that the Brazilian economy is losing out on the enormous potential benefits from steady increases in the labor force and employment. In Ireland and the Netherlands, for example, national income rose more than 1 percent of GDP a year as a result of higher labor force participation during the past 10 years.

Employment growth dropped off markedly in 1996, partly as a result of the financial crisis. But a structural shift also seems to have taken place. Despite the resumption of job creation in the past two years, the unemployment rate remains 2 percentage points higher than it was before 1998.

Job creation is important not only from an economic point of view but also from a social and ethical point of view. Being without a job can undermine the self-esteem of workers and the well-being of their families, even if they receive financial support from other sources.

LABOR PRODUCTIVITY IS TOO LOW. Labor productivity is 33–50 percent lower than in Malaysia and Mexico, two countries with income levels similar to Brazil's. Value-added per worker in Brazil was actually lower in 2000 than it was in 1980. In contrast, Chile's value-added rose almost 50 percent and the Republic of Korea's almost tripled over the same period.

THE POOR ARE NOT RECEIVING UNEMPLOYMENT OR SEVERANCE BENEFITS. Most of the poor work in the growing informal sector. They are therefore not eligible for the abono salarial, unemployment insurance, or severance payments, which benefit mostly the middle class. In 1980, 66 percent of the labor force worked in the formal market; by the late 1990s this share had dropped to just 40 percent. Both unemployment insurance and FGTS payments are regressive, with an estimated 13 percent of benefits going to the poorest quintile. Compared with formal sector workers, informal sector workers are also responsible for the needs of a slightly higher number of dependents, particularly elderly dependents. The excessive insecurity these workers face is a prominent feature of the Brazilian labor market.

LABOR MARKET REGULATION RESTRAINS JOB GROWTH. Labor market regulations in Brazil neither promote employment and productivity nor guarantee income security. The large size of the informal sector, the preference by many for self-employment, and low productivity and employment growth in regulated labor markets reflect the unsustainable nature of labor regulations. Brazil has not yet arrived at a mix of regulations and interventions that balances the objectives of employment, productivity, and security well. A survey of Latin American firms revealed that labor institutions, regulations, and interventions are viewed as especially onerous in Brazil.

LITIGATION IS WIDESPREAD. Widespread litigation discourages firms from hiring workers and serves as an inefficient means of negotiating wages and benefits ex post. The number of lawsuits in Brazil increased 60 percent over the last decade. More than 2 million lawsuits were filed in 2000 alone, implying that more than 6 percent of all salaried workers went to court. Labor courts exist in most countries, but nowhere does labor justice play as significant a role as in Brazil. Firms bear the direct costs associated with this litigation. Perhaps more important, frequent litigation means that the cost of labor in terms of future pay, fines, and legal costs is uncertain. Faced with this uncertainty, employers are cautious about hiring new workers. It is likely that the high level of litigation has reduced employment generation.

TURNOVER IS EXCESSIVE. Excessive turnover in the labor market tends to lower productivity, because workers do not stay long enough in one firm to receive training and accumulate experience. In Brazil 36 percent of workers have short tenure in their place of employment, a much higher proportion than in the United States, where 27 percent of workers have held their current job less than 2 years. Only 43 percent of workers in Brazil have long tenure, far fewer than in the United States, where 53 percent of workers have held their current job at least 2 years. One out of three workers changes jobs every year.

Labor turnover increased 60 percent between 1992 and 2001. In part, the change reflects the operations of the severance fund (FGTS), which inadvertently subsidizes turnover. Because of the lower than market rate of return on workers' balances in the fund, there is a perverse incentive to precipitate firing in order to be able to access the FGTS balance. The penalty for "unjust dismissal" (40 percent of accumulated balance) goes to the worker.

MANDATED BENEFITS FOR FORMAL SECTOR WORKERS ARE HIGH. Mandated nonwage benefits add 85 percent to wage costs. In part, the large and growing size of the informal labor market reflects the fact that mandated benefits price workers with low productivity out of the formal labor market. Minimum mandated nonwage benefits are more binding for unskilled workers: the lower the productivity level of the worker, the more onerous the burden of legislation on the employer. Under these circumstances, it is not surprising that low productivity workers are being pushed into the informal sector.

A UNIFORM MINIMUM WAGE COULD REDUCE FORMAL SECTOR EMPLOYMENT. Uniform national minimum wage setting hurt employment creation in the poorer Northeast region. Since April 2000 different minimum wages have been in effect in different parts of the country, with a minimum set by the federal government.

Evidence on the effect of minimum wages on poverty reduction remains inconclusive. Increases in the minimum wage can reduce employment (especially in industrial countries) and increase the size of the informal sector (especially in developing countries). But the impact depends on initial labor market conditions and the level of the minimum wage relative to other wages in the economy. In Brazil the role of the minimum wage in determining the level of other salaries and transfers also has to be considered. This makes the necessary empirical analysis even more complicated than in other countries.

Options

Even in well-functioning labor markets some interventions by the government are needed. Markets may fail to provide unemployment insurance because of asymmetric information. Job search information may be inadequate. Training programs can help compensate for low education levels. Micro-credit schemes can counter poorly functioning capital markets.

What policy priorities might promote employment creation and strengthen the social safety net? Specific options include:

- Moving negotiations over wages and benefits from the courts to the workplace. Policymakers could legalize renegotiations on the job and help make unions more representative.
- Eliminating the current subsidization of labor turnover by modifying the design of the FGTS. Workers in Brazil have an incentive to induce dismissals after accumulating severance rights.

More competition in the management of FGTS accounts could be encouraged, so that workers are paid market rates of return. Reducing the role of state banks is also consistent with the need to reduce the role of directed credit in Brazil. Doing so would decrease the tax component and reduce turnover. Alternatively, contributions to FGTS could be capped, so that the incentive to trigger a dismissal does not grow too large. A third option would be to, in effect, make the FGTS a "no-fault" insurance scheme. Eliminating the fine would reduce turnover and lead to greater investments in firm-specific skills. Yet another option would be to link reform of the FGTS with needed social security reform. FGTS accounts could be converted into private retirement accounts for workers, strengthening the role of what is now a very weak part of the social security system, facilitating other reforms, and addressing the undesirable duplication of unemployment insurance for formal sector workers.

- Gradually introducing more flexibility in some contracts. Mandated benefit legislation prices low-skilled workers out of jobs in the formal sector, creating significant inequities in access to formal safety net mechanisms. Reducing these mandates could increase productivity, employment, and earnings security for the poor.
- Eliminating the current overlaps in income support programs. Eliminating the overlap between unemployment insurance and FGTS could provide room to reduce payroll taxes or redirect unemployment insurance to poorer workers in the informal labor market.

Message 2. Achieving better balance within the system of social protection
The government has begun reallocating resources from generous programs benefiting the relatively higher income groups toward programs benefiting lower income groups, who receive inadequate social protection. Continuing this process and correcting the imbalance between coverage of older people, who are well protected, and the very young, who receive little protection, would do much to improve social protection in Brazil. Reducing the substantial subsidies paid for government workers' pensions and special pension schemes would allow funds to be reallocated to programs that are more likely to reach the poor. Lowering the heavy level of labor taxation needed to finance the social security system would increase the efficiency of the labor market and prevent the crowding out of private, voluntary savings alternatives to securing adequate retirement income.

Context
Brazil's social security system is made up of three main regimes. Half the labor force (formal sector workers), or about 30 million people, contribute to the general Social Security System for private sector workers (RGPS), which currently has 18 million beneficiaries. Another 3 million people contribute to and benefit from the pension regime for government workers (RPPS)[1]. Another 3 million contributors (about 5 percent of the work force) and 1.5 million beneficiaries participate in a system of supplementary pensions, which is dominated by the pen-

---

[1] Civil servants, which are hired according to RJU rules, have special pension regimes (RPPS). While private sector workers, which are hired according to the CLT, have the general pension regime (RGPS).

sion funds of public enterprises. Several state governments are introducing funded plans for civil servants to supplement RPPS benefits. The current system over insures a small group, leaving many people completely uncovered. A more balanced system would have a lower level of insurance but provide wider coverage.

Around the world policymakers have been paying increasing attention to social security policies in recent years. Populations are aging, and the generous promises of public pensions systems—established long ago with little regard to changes in life expectancy—are coming due. Governments around the world are dealing with the problem of preventing the swelling of social security deficits while still providing households with adequate protection. The measures taken have been diverse, but most have increased retirement ages, cut benefit levels, raised contribution rates, and even introduced privately managed individual retirement accounts. Brazil's dilemma is particularly difficult. Generous public pensions guaranteed by the 1988 Constitution, the end of inflation in 1994, and a shrinking contribution base as more workers migrate to the informal sector have caused public pension deficits to balloon. Significant reforms have been implemented over the past few years, including an amendment to the Constitution, but additional reforms are needed. Progress in this area will not only determine the extent to which Brazil can develop an adequate social protection system that is better balanced toward the poor and the young but will also determine whether the country will be able to sustain recent improvements in fiscal performance and create more jobs.

Social security is the single most important fiscal issue facing the federal government and subnational governments in Brazil today. Direct expenditures for public pensions and the cost of servicing the debt incurred on its behalf represent almost 10 percent of GDP. Despite reforms and high rates of labor and other taxes, the pension system is not fiscally sustainable. Without additional reforms, the situation will get worse. Despite a relatively favorable demographic situation—a large number of working-age people relative to the number of elderly—Brazil's pay-as-you-go pension deficits are expected to rise from 5 percent of GDP today to 10 percent of GDP in 30 years (see fiscal adjustment policy note).

The effects on the economy are pervasive. High labor taxation is part of the reason why the share of formal workers in the labor force has decreased to just 40 percent. Other high taxes increase the cost of doing business in Brazil. Social security spending crowds out spending on other programs, including social protection, which are better targeted to the poor. It also crowds out a role for fully funded private pension plans. High levels of public debt—caused in large part by the social security system—keep interest rates relatively high and crowd out private investment. These effects act as a drag on growth and the employment creation potential of the economy.

Options

What steps could be taken to make the system financially sustainable and better balanced? Further reforms are needed to reduce fiscal deficits, lower actuarial imbalances, increase equity and redistribution, reduce collateral inefficiencies, and facilitate growth of funded pension schemes. Measures also need to be taken to reduce the generosity of both the general and the government worker pension schemes.

The Government could reform social security by offering a smaller package of benefits to a large number of people. A basic nationwide system would leave space for additional insurance that people could buy through mandatory or voluntary fully funded defined-contribution schemes. Trimming the existing system and expanding coverage could ideally be done at the same time, so that the transition could be partially financed by additional contributions from an expanded contributor base.

Both the RPPS and the RGPS are riddled with subsidies paid for by the general population through implicit and explicit taxes. Subsidies could be gradually eliminated by increasing the retirement age. Compensating measures could be offered.

REFORMING THE PENSION REGIME FOR CIVIL SERVANTS (RPPS). Since the source of the immediate problem in social security is the civil servant pension scheme, these reforms have the highest priority. Although the system covers only 15 percent of Brazil's social security beneficiaries, it accounts for half of all pension expenditures. The deficits of all federal, state, and municipal pension schemes account for three-quarters of pension deficits in Brazil and represent 4 percent of GDP. These pensions benefit a relatively higher-income group. Since the deficit is financed through general tax revenues, it increases the burden of taxation on the entire economy and implies sizable transfers from the average Brazilian taxpayer. Horizontal inequities are also embedded in the system, especially at the federal level.

Several possible reforms have been proposed to help reduce the RPPS deficits. Not all of these reforms are feasible or would have significant effects. They include levying a contribution rate on retirees' benefits to expand the contributor base. Imposing such a levy would both improve financing and eliminate the anomaly that civil servants receive an increase in net income at retirement.

A second measure would be to raise the contribution rate for current federal civil servants as a temporary measure and not applied to new hires. This measure would improve finances only marginally. A third consideration is to increase the retirement age and establish the same age for men and women. Even after the 1998 reforms that raised the retirement age to 60 for men and 55 for women, the minimum retirement age for Brazilians does not reflect the higher life expectancy in the country, and there is a seven-year difference in the retirement age of current employees and new hires.

Fourth, concerning pensions, they could be adjusted based on the inflation index rather than the wage index because this is a more appropriate way to adjust for cost of living increases after retirement and is subject to fewer possible distortions. Fifth, changing the reference period for calculating benefits to cover the retiree's entire career would lower the replacement rate. This provision would affect both current workers and new hires.

A sixth step would be to change the RPPS formula to include the same *fator previdenciario* that has linked benefits to workers' contributions in the RGPS system since the 1998 reforms. This change would improve the current balance of the system, reduce labor market distortions, encourage later retirement, and adjust benefits by the worker's life expectancy. Finally, instead of protecting all current civil servants and applying the 1998 reforms only to new hires, reforms in the statutory public employment regime (RJU) system could be applied to younger civil servants (for example, anyone more than five years away from retirement). This reform would shorten the transition to a more sustainable regime and eliminate the abrupt change in retirement benefits between current workers and new hires – as used for state employees in Paraná and Pernambuco.

Figure 1 presents the projected financial situation of RPPS as well as the estimated cumulative outcome of possible reforms. The curve labeled "current laws" shows the financial consequences of the 1998 reforms. The vertical scale of the graph shows the percentage of the wage bill the government must contribute each year to be able to pay benefits. The reforms, especially the imposition of a ceiling on benefits equal to the ceiling in the regime for private sector workers, clearly have a substantial effect, reducing the government contribution from 120 percent to 55 percent of wages in 70 years. But the government contribution still remains high and the transition long.

The line labeled "Reforms 1–6" shows the total effect of the first six proposals presented above. The line "Reforms 1–7" applies the reforms to younger current workers. Both reform lines eventually take the system to the level at which the government has to contribute about 15 percent of insured wage to the pension system.

Figure 1. Projected deficits of the pension system for federal civil servants as a percentage of the covered wage bill

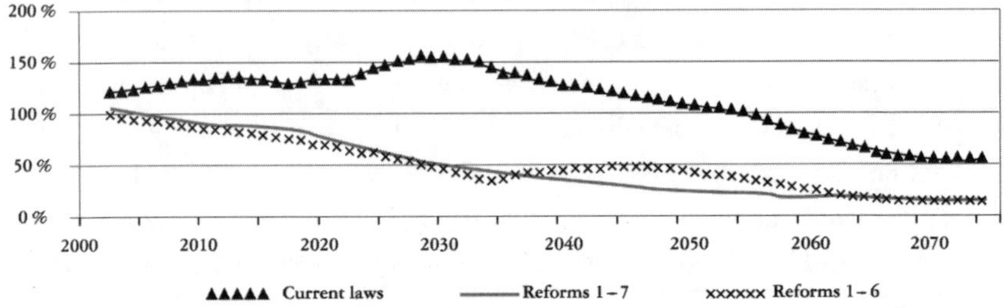

▲▲▲▲▲ Current laws   ——— Reforms 1–7   xxxxxx Reforms 1–6

Source: World Bank estimates based on MPAS data.

Governments at the state level are also affected by the burden of social security costs. In Ceara these costs accounted for 11 percent of total expenditures and 28 percent of total state personnel expenditures; the state financed about 85 percent of the benefits out of general tax revenues. The system thus implies costly subsidies financed from general tax revenues that are by and large not directed to the poor. Raising the fiscal sustainability of this program would release federal and state funds for reallocation to activities with a direct impact on poverty reduction.

Reforming public pensions for workers in the private sector (RGPS). Brazil has two parallel retirement benefit programs for private sector workers, the length of service and the old age program. In principle, workers can receive only one of the two retirement benefits.

The 1998–99 reforms stabilized the length of service program for another decade, but beginning in about 2009 fiscal balances will deteriorate rapidly (figure 2).

Figure 2. RGPS financial imbalances as a percentage of GDP

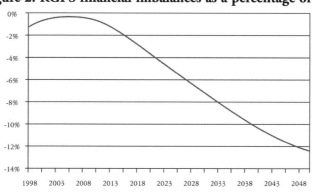

During the next few years it would be beneficial for the government to evaluate and introduce additional measures that address the medium- and long-term financial imbalance in this part of the system.

Government policymakers could consider five main reform options. One would be to increase the retirement age and establish a single age for men and women. Brazil's private sector retirement program does not have a minimum retirement age. That leaves the regime vulnerable to abuse and increases the probability of persistent future deficits. This reform alone would yield savings of more than 4 percent of GDP per annum once fully implemented.

Another would be to adjust the accrual rate of the fator previdenciário to reflect only that portion of the contribution rate meant to finance retirement benefits. Additional studies and discussions are needed to determine which portion of the contribution rate is meant to fund the length of service program. Once the determination is made, the formula could be adjusted accordingly. The formula could also be adjusted to reflect workers' entire wage histories, indexed not only to inflation but also to past wage growth in the economy.

One could also consider privatizing workers compensation insurance (for job related accidents). In many industrial countries, worker compensation insurance is left to well-regulated private insurance markets. Recent proposals to privatize this part of the National Institute of Social Security (INSS) are in line with international best practice. A detailed examination of the ability of the market to respond will be needed before adequate regulation can be devised.

Another idea is to curtail the incentives to switch from length of service to the old age program in order to prevent individuals from reducing their contribution levels. Finally, there could also be a limit to the number of benefits an individual can receive from the RGPS. Survivor benefits are currently paid to all eligible survivors, regardless of whether they receive their own retirement pension. In most industrial countries, beneficiaries must choose between the survivor benefit and their own retirement pension. The fiscal savings from this proposal could be substantial.

At the same time, the government could consider holding off on reforming the old age program, one of the most important poverty alleviation programs in Brazil. Although the program could be reformed, the fiscal savings would be negligible and changes could have deleterious effects on the poor and on other poverty programs. It therefore makes sense to put off any changes in this part of the pension system before more critical reforms with much higher payoffs are implemented and additional analysis of the appropriate role of the old age program in the context of Brazil's overall strategy to reduce poverty is conducted.

The old age program has been reformed less than other parts of the social security system. The contribution rule is not fully enforced in rural areas. As a result, collections in rural areas cover only 13 percent of the benefits paid to the rural sector. There is no link between contributions and retirement benefits.

The program has a positive impact on the incomes of poor rural households. About 80 percent of the beneficiaries of the old age pension program are women, and two-thirds of all rural pensions are in the old age pension program. The program has a substantial impact on poverty, keeping many people out of the bottom income groups, particularly in the rural Northeast.

Although it reduces poverty, the old age program is inefficient and could be improved. It transfers money to older people who are still able to work, rather than making smaller payments to the most needy across the age spectrum. It boosts income, but it does so only after people reach retirement age.

Several possible areas of the program could be reformed—the age between men and women could be equalized, for example, or the replacement rate reduced—but any reform needs to be evaluated in the context of other income transfers to the poor in Brazil. Many reforms could have undesirable effects on equity. Since the cost savings from reforms to the old age program would be minimal at best, reforms to this program should be considered with extreme caution and should be last on the list of policies implemented to put the social security system on sounder financial footing.

Policymakers should also keep in mind that over the longer term, if some of the reforms mentioned above are carried out, the need for the old age program is likely to diminish.

Message 3. Increasing the effectiveness of social assistance by expanding conditional income transfers, integrating services, and modernizing delivery mechanisms
Conditional transfer programs, including Bolsa-Escola and the Program for the Eradication of Child Labor (PETI), both tied to school attendance, seem well suited to conditions in Brazil and could probably be expanded effectively. Improving the monitoring of compliance with program conditions, strengthening the links with supply-side interventions, and increasing the size of the transfer would increase the effectiveness of both programs. Expanding programs targeting young children from poor households, who are currently underserved, would increase opportunities for better integrating services for poor families.

Context
Although spending on social assistance as a share of GDP doubled (from 0.3 percent to 0.6 percent) during the past three years as new programs were introduced or expanded, the role of social protection for the poor remains small in Brazil. Spending is relatively low compared with both Latin America, which spends 1.2 percent of GDP on social assistance, and the OECD, which spends 3.1 percent of GDP. (Abt Associates, Overview of Social Assistance, processed).

The main social assistance programs include pure cash transfers for poor people who are old or disabled and two conditional transfer programs, the Bolsa-Escola and the Program for the Eradication of Child Labor (PETI), both of which are tied to school attendance (table 1). In addition, smaller programs target young children and young adults and provide nutritional assistance.

Almost half of all social assistance spending in Brazil goes to the disabled and elderly. Another 40 percent is targeted to school-age children. Just 10 percent of social assistance is targeted to young children, and very little is aimed at young adults or low-income workers.

Options
A promising area for expansion are programs that yield more than one benefit—combining improvements in educational attainment with financial support to poor families, for

example. Programs that achieve both of these goals include conditional transfer programs and early childhood development activities, which have very low coverage. There are opportunities to better integrate services for poor families in most of these programs. Organizing services in ways that make it easier for households to know about and access the variety of interventions available is one reform that could help poor people. Better integrating these services would move the focus from a sector-based approach to one that addresses the household as a unit.

DISABILITY AND OLD AGE PROGRAMS. In 1993 the Social Assistance Organic Law established the *benefício de prestação continuada*, a pension of one minimum salary paid to the disabled and the elderly in households with per capita family income less than one-fourth the minimum salary. This program, the largest spending category within social assistance, accounted for 45 percent of social assistance spending in 2002.

Table 1. Spending on main social assistance programs in Brazil, 2000–02

Program	Expenditures (R$ million, deflated)			Coverage (thousands of people)			Cash transfer (R$ per person, current)		
	2000	2001	2002	2000	2001	2002	2000	2001	2002
Social services for the disabled	61.99	71.52	65.82	141	147	193	n.a.	n.a.	n.a.
Social services for the elderly	33.00	34.00	56.00	-	301	-	n.a	n.a	n.a
Lei Orgânica da Assistência (LOAS): Disabled beneficiaries	1,340.82	1,650.03	1,935.47	807	870	930	1,362 (151)	151 (180)	180 (200)
Lei Orgânica da Assistência (LOAS): Elderly beneficiaries	620.03	870.92	1,065.73	403	469	495	136 (151)	151 (180)	180 (200)
Bolsa-Escola	-	474.22	1,955.23	-	8,300	10,200	-	15	15
Eradication of child labor	178.81	288.80	427.82	395	750	866	25-45	25-45	25-45
Early childhood development services	249.98	233.07	227.97	1,500	1,601	1,610	n.a.	n.a.	n.a.

Note: Prices are deflated according to the IPCA per FGV Fundacao Getúlio Vargas as follows: 2000 = 5.97 percent, 2001 = 7.67 percent, 2002 = 2.29 percent (through April 2002). The minimum wage in Brazil is established every May, thus the two reference values for the LOAS. Figures for 2002 are estimated. – Not available n.a. Not applicable Source: , Ministry of Planning, Bolsa-Escola Secretariat, and SEAS /MPAS. Secretariat of Social Assistance/Ministry of Social Security and Social Assistance..

The number of people covered by these two programs expanded from slightly less than 400,000 in 1996 to 1.4 million in 2001.. About 500,000 elderly people are currently receiving benefits under the program. The number of disabled beneficiaries rose from 800,000 in 2000 to a projected 930,000 in 2002.

In part, this increase has come about because the minimum age required to receive assistance was reduced from 70 to 67. A possible improvement to the program covering the disabled would be strengthening controls designed to ensure that recipients are truly disabled. Better information and monitoring is needed for both programs to ensure that there is no duplication with other pensions. Monitoring reports suggest that targeting is adequate.

Conditional transfer programs. Two central tenets of Brazil's social safety net include devoting a significant share of social assistance spending on school-age children and making such assistance conditional on school attendance. In recent years governments at different levels in Brazil have expanded conditional cash transfers to poor families.

The Bolsa-Escola Program was started in two municipalities in Brazil in 1995. In 2001 the federal program covered 8.3 million children; by June 2002 coverage had reached 9.4 million children, or nearly a third of all school-age children in Brazil. The plan had been to scale up the program in order to cover the poorest municipalities by 2002, but the government has not yet done so.

This program has two objectives that fit Brazilian conditions well. The first is to promote better school enrollment and attendance among children, thereby improving educational attainment and their chances of earning an income above the poverty line. To participate in the Bolsa-Escola program, children must be between 6 and 15, they must attend school at least 85 percent of the time, and their families must pass a means test (per capita incomes must be less than half the minimum wage). The program pays beneficiaries R$15 per month per child up to a maximum of three children (R$45) per family.

An ex ante evaluation (Bourguignon) Ferreira, and Leite, 2002) suggests that Bolsa-Escola's impact on education has been substantial. The simulation suggests that the program could increase the school enrollment rate among the poor by about 4.4 percentage points, reducing the proportion of poor children not in school by 50 percent. The same analysis indicates that the conditionality attached to the transfer is key to its effectiveness. The program also provides poor families with a cash stipend that serves as a safety net. Although a rigorous evaluation has not been done, targeting of the program to poor households seems to have been reasonably effective.

How could Bolsa-Escola be improved? The main problem with the program is that it has not been scaled up sufficiently, in large part because the poorest municipalities—where need for the program is greatest—cannot afford to pay for it and cost-sharing from the federal government has not been sufficient. Expanding the program to cover secondary students in areas in which enrollment gaps between lower- and higher-income groups are significant could also be considered.

The size of the transfer also needs to be reconsidered. A higher level of transfer may be needed to ensure that the program is effective and plays a more important role in social protection. According to Bourguignon, Ferreira, and Leite, larger transfers would improve both the education and the poverty impact, which is currently quite minor. In similar programs in other countries the level of transfer is higher. Mexico's Progresa program transfers US$8–US$25 per month per child, with lower payments for primary students and higher payments for secondary students, plus an additional US$14 per household per month to pay for medical care. Colombia transfers $US6 per child per month for primary students, $12 per child per month for secondary students, and an additional US$20 per household per month for health care. In Brazil the federal program pays only R$15 per child up to a maximum of three children per family. In state and municipal programs, the level of benefit ranges from R$32 to R$65 per month per child.

Administrative improvements may also be called for. Work toward the development of a consistent, single, means-tested roster of households needs to be continued in order to improve efficiency, targeting, and cross-program coordination (with PETI, for example). In some municipalities, local governments are not adequately fulfilling their roles under the program, failing to list eligible families, create a Social Control Council, implement complementary activities, or monitor school attendance. Monitoring attendance is critical to implementing the program, but doing so has been weak and reliable information on the basis of which payments are made is not always available. In other countries (Colombia and Mexico, for example), the design of similar programs has been closely coordinated and complemented with supply-side investments. Such an option would be worth considering in Brazil.

Finally, although initial results seem positive, the program's impact has not been rigorously evaluated. Conducting an evaluation similar to that conducted on the Progresa program in Mexico could provide information that could help policymakers improve the effectiveness of the program

A related but separate program, begun by the federal government on a pilot basis in 1996 in the state of Mato Grosso do Sul, is PETI. Coverage had expanded to 750,000 children in 2001, and the target for 2002 is 866,000. Between 2003 and 2006 the plan is to consolidate and phase out the program, assuming that child labor rates would have declined.

PETI was initiated in order to eradicate the worst forms of child labor in urban and rural areas. It focuses on activities most harmful to child development, in areas in which the incidence of child labor is high, Social Development Indexes are below the national average, local groups are sufficiently organized to carry out their responsibilities under the program, and social mobilization is sufficient. The program currently operates in all states and in more than 1,000 municipalities.

PETI provides cash grants to families with school-age children (7–14) who are currently working and whose families' per capita income is less than half the minimum salary. Cash transfers are of R$40 per child per month in urban areas and R$25 per child per month in rural areas. In return for the payments, children must attend school at least 80 percent of the required number of hours, and they must attend the *jornada ampliada*, a program of after-school activities. Participation is limited to four years. Resources are transferred from the National Fund for Social Assistance to local governments to support implementation of the after-school activities. The cash transfer represents 55 percent of the costs of the program, while transfers for funding after-school activities account for 40 percent of program costs. The federal government finances the cash transfers. Local governments have responsibility for implementing the program, through state and municipal commissions on the eradication of child labor; in some cases they also supplement funding for school activities. Assessments indicate that in some parts of Brazil PETI has had considerable positive impact on community life by mobilizing parents, school administrators and teachers, the municipal and state governments, local worker unions, and NGOs.

PETI is needed because of the continuing problem of child labor in Brazil. Although the proportion of working children fell from 20 percent in 1992 to 15 percent in 1999, the incidence of child labor remains relatively high. Evidence shows that early entry into the labor market has a significant negative impact on future earnings and educational outcomes. Child labor reduces lifetime earnings by 13–17 percent overall and increases the probability of being poor as an adult almost 8 percent. Children who work tend to enter school later, and on average their educational attainment lags 0.5 years behind children who do not work. Working also reduces completed years of education by almost three years.

Eliminating child labor does not simply entail forcing the removal of children from their place of work. Many poor families depend on the earnings of their children, and many of these children have not been adequately served by the education system. PETI is well designed because it combines actions to promote education with a cash transfer to families and it involves the participation of federal and local governments as well as organizations of civil society.

The design of the program reflects several strengths. There are also areas in which improvement may be possible:

- The schooling requirement may need to focus on completion of basic education and entry into secondary school. An increase in the maximum age of children to, say, 16, could also be considered. Raising the maximum age would imply an easing of the duration limits to eliminate the four-year limit so as to permit children to complete their schooling.

- Now that the program has been extended into urban areas, the effectiveness of the targeting mechanisms (geographical, worst forms of work, family income) needs to be reviewed. Policymakers need to develop ways to ensure that some families are not left out. Assessments of the program have shown that targeting errors of exclusion are significant.
- The content of the after-school activities could be strengthened and linked more closely with regular schooling and remedial actions.
- Program monitoring needs to be improved to strengthen links with education services.
- The strategy and implementation of the program needs to be integrated with the complementary Bolsa-Escola program.
- The beneficiaries of PETI need to benefit from better integration of services provided by PETI and other social assistance programs, such as those providing vocational training to children exiting the program or literacy programs for adults.
- A formal impact evaluation of the program needs to be conducted to help assess targeting performance and the efficiency of the interventions.

NUTRITION AND EARLY CHILDHOOD PROGRAMS. The federal government administers several nutrition programs, the effectiveness of which could be improved by integrating nutrition and other services, such as primary health or, especially, early childhood education, which tends to increase effectiveness. The government has already initiated these reforms in some programs. *Bolsa Alimentação*, for example, started in mid-2001, moved from an in-kind benefit to cash transfers. The program hopes to reach 3.5 million pregnant and lactating mothers and young children in 2002. Administered by the Ministry of Health, the R$300 million program pays a monthly benefit of R$15 per beneficiary, up to three beneficiaries per household.

Real spending on nutrition for young children has stagnated at about R$250 million a year. The program aims to improve the living standards of needy children and their families by providing food, pedagogic activities, family and community counseling, and educational activities delivered by day care centers and preschools. Recently, responsibility for selecting the institutions that will receive funding and managing the contracts with them was decentralized to states and municipalities.

International evidence indicates that the returns to public investment in early childhood development and preschool services are high. Early childhood development programs can be particularly effective for the poor. Coverage of these programs in Brazil is relatively low, with less than 20 percent of all children younger than three years old covered by federal programs. These programs not only reduce risk, they also promote higher educational achievement. Children who attend early childhood activities complete primary school in a shorter time and attain higher levels of education than children who do not. In Brazil the estimated annual increase in income is about 10 percent a year for people who attended early childhood activities and 17 percent for people who attended preschool. The complementarities between these two levels of education are reinforcing, particularly for poor children (Barros and Mendonca, 1999).

There is evidence to suggest that there is room to improve the quality of these programs, specially because teachers lack sufficient training, standards, and materials.

Message 4. Addressing crime and violence by expanding community-based programs working with at–risk youth, victims of domestic violence, and others
In recent years the incidence of violent death in some Brazilian cities has reached levels comparable to those in Northern Ireland and Colombia. Possible measures to deal with the problem include compiling and making public more information on the nature of crime and violence; reforming the police, judicial, and penal systems, drawing on successful experience in other countries; and identifying people most at risk and integrating them into society. Successful programs are already functioning in Brazil, but they are under funded and reach too few people.

Context

The increasing prevalence of crime and violence in Brazil has become an issue of national concern. Unlike in other developing countries, violence in Brazil is not generally associated with political, sectarian, or religious factors.

Both the middle class and the poor reveal that security is one of their major concerns, as the recent "Voices of the Poor" exercise in Brazil revealed. Most people perceive street violence as the greatest threat, primarily because it appears to be random and to affect people whose behavior and social situation do not seem to invite it. In response to crime, government, companies, and private citizens have allocated significant resources to security, diverting those resources from productive uses.

The public has become more radical and demanding of political leaders for a solution to the rising tide of violence. Most of the public outcry has focused on reforming and strengthening the police and more effectively suppressing crime. While such solutions could lead to short-term results, they do not address the causes of different kinds of violence. Such efforts focus on the kinds of crime that provoke most fear in the public mind, but they neglect or even exacerbate other forms of violence, which may contribute to other forms of crime. They also do not address the issue of widespread corruption in the police forces and possibly in the judicial system.

Options

Investments are clearly called for, but first it is important to conduct further analysis to identify the most effective areas for intervention, beginning with establishing more securely the incidence and nature of crime and violence. There are indications that crime, particularly petty street crime, is significantly underreported by both citizens and the police. There is a need to conduct studies on the nature of crime and violence—where it occurs, the social status of both perpetrators and victims, and how people perceive crimes in which they are involved, as perpetrators or victims. The results of these studies must be made available to the general public. The public also needs to have access to data that indicate the effectiveness of different measures designed to combat crime, such as reorganization of the police, prosecutors' offices, and the courts. Transparency is difficult to achieve in criminal matters, but is essential if decision makers are to make credible decisions regarding how to prevent crime.

REFORMING THE POLICE FORCE. The division of police forces into separate civil and military entities with separate but overlapping responsibilities has been identified as a problem, but in most states little action has been taken on the issue, largely because entrenched interests are involved. The fact that the police are generally underpaid, poorly equipped, and inadequately trained has also been noted. Reorganizing and strengthening police forces is a necessary, but not sufficient, condition for reducing crime.

In recent years violent acts such as extra-judicial killings and kidnapping have been committed by current or former members of the police. Shakedowns and extortion are also practiced by on-duty police. It is necessary to reestablish the accountability of law enforcement in order to remove one of the greatest constraints to crime reduction. Brazilian authorities could learn much from successful reform of police departments in other countries. The involvement of the public and the rise of an informed constituency for police reform in the general public are probably the most basic conditions for police reform.

REFORMING THE JUDICIAL SYSTEM. Reform of the judicial system represents a major challenge. Judicial processes in Brazil are notoriously slow and inefficient. Court calendars are often clogged, and judges seem free to make decisions capriciously, without fear of judicial review. The costs of the judicial system are extremely high, as a result of salaries and generous benefits, set by magistrates themselves. These salaries and benefits are considerably higher than those of other public sector officials.

The system could be improved by administering more efficiently court schedules, and having seasoned judges supervise less experienced ones. In the long term a public constituency supporting judicial reform needs to be formed by a responsible press, legal scholars, the law schools, and politicians. Study of best practices in Brazil and other countries could be useful.

REFORMING THE PENAL SYSTEM. Brazilian prisons do not currently meet minimum international standards for safety and security. Investments are needed to improve both physical facilities and prison programs. Policymakers could benefit from studying other countries' prison-work programs, open jail programs for nonviolent prisoners, educational programs, and drug and alcohol treatment programs for prisoners.

UNDERSTANDING THE CAUSES OF CRIME AND WORKING WITH AT-RISK YOUTH. Reforming the police, and judicial and penal reform are necessary, but they are not sufficient conditions for reducing crime in Brazil because they merely repress crime rather than addressing its underlying causes. While more diagnostic studies are needed, there is widespread agreement that crime prevention requires reintegrating key segments of the population into a system of social control. Reintegration is particularly important for poor and middle-class men between 15 and 24, the age cohort most likely to commit violent crimes.

Some evidence suggests that violence is beginning to reduce the level of young men's educational attainment in Brazil, which lags behind that of young women. Lack of employment, lack of leisure and educational opportunities, and strong peer pressure to behave in what is perceived as a manly way may be factors in motivating young men to commit violent crimes. The premise of this "epidemiological" approach to crime and violence is that the enabling conditions for crime must be reduced, primarily by reintegrating people, especially young people, into social units in which non-state social controls are functioning. If the hypothesis about the social nature of criminal behavior in Brazil is correct, it is necessary to identify people most at risk and find ways of giving them a sense of belonging to a significant social unit.

Brazil is rich in programs that have worked with young people at risk for criminal behavior or addiction. These programs are woefully under-funded, however, and reach only a small percentage of those at risk . NGOs could contribute a great deal to new models of crime prevention. The success of neighborhood-based NGOs in reducing exposure to HIV in Brazil may convince policymakers skeptical about NGO involvement that a similar approach involving neighborhood organizations could also reduce criminal behavior.

References

World Bank projects

- Technical Assistance for Pension System Reform: PROAST *(Programa de Assistência Técnica para Reforma da Previdência Social)* US$ 5.05 million. Approved February 7, 2000.
- State Pension System Reform: PARSEP *(Programa de Apoio a Reforma do Sistemas Estaduais de Previdencia)* US$ 5 million. Approved June 30, 1998.

World Bank reports

This chapter summarizes the content of the following World Bank reports. Those, in turn, draw heavily from a wide range of literature on the subject from experts in Brazil and beyond, which are referenced in the mentioned Bank reports.

World Bank. Reform options for social security in Brazil. Washington D.C., August 2002.

World Bank. Brazil: selected issues in social protection. Washington D.C., July 25, 2002.

World Bank. Inequality and economic development in Brazil. Report No. 244-87-BR. Washington D.C., June 2002.

World Bank. Brazil Jobs Report. Report No. 24408 – BR. Washington D.C., May 31, 2002.

World Bank. Brazil: eradicating child labor in Brazil. Report No. 21858-BR. Washington D.C., December 6, 2001.

World Bank. Public expenditures for poverty alleviation in Northeast Brazil: promoting growth and improving services. Report No. 22425-BR. Washington D.C., June 11, 2001.

World Bank. Brazil: critical issues in social security. Report No. 22513-BR Washington D.C., May 2001.

World Bank. Attacking Brazil's poverty. Report 20475-BR. Washington D.C., March 31, 2001.

World Bank. Brazil: an assessment of the Bolsa Escola programs. Report No. 20208-BR. Washington D.C., March 15, 2001.

Other references

"Ex-Ante Evaluation of Conditional Cash Transfer Programs: the Case of Bolsa Escola" by Francois Bourguignon, Francisco H.G. Ferreira and Philippe G. Leite. (September 2002)

Paes de Barros, Ricardo and Rosane Mendonça, November, 1999, *Uma Avaliação dos Custos e dos Benefícios da Educação Pré-escolar.* IPEA

Update on Major Federal-Level Social Assistance Programs in Brazil by Thereza Lobo, et al. July 2002.

PART II

4

Financial Sector

4

Financial Sector

Introduction

Fundamental changes in Brazil's financial system in the 1990s have transformed its structure and increased its stability and transparency. Restructuring following the banking crisis of 1995-96 led to closure or privatization of state-owned banks and hence significant consolidation in the number of private domestic financial institutions, and the entry of private foreign banks.

Brazil's financial sector is sophisticated and financially stable. Yet structural impediments still constrain the financial system from fulfilling its overarching objectives of deep, efficient, and safe financial intermediation. Less pressure on the system from government finance, less financial taxation, resolution of the issues pending in the federal banks, further improvements in regulation and supervision, and improvement in the legal and institutional framework related to information and collateral execution would deepen the system, further reduce its vulnerability, and improve access.

Changes in the structure and operating environment of the financial system have been profound. The banking system lost its inflationary float income with the macroeconomic stability introduced with the Real plan. The resulting banking crisis of 1995-96 and subsequent bank restructuring programs led to significant consolidation and reduction in the number of private domestic financial institutions and a marked decline in state-owned financial institutions. Private foreign banks began to enter the sector.

In response to the external crisis of late 1998 and early 1999 further changes were introduced to improve the financial system's resilience, transparency, and governance. These included a more rigorous structure for regulation and supervision of the banking system, and notably, the introduction of consolidated global inspections. Stricter supervisory standards for federal banks led to their recapitalization in 2001 and to greater trans-

The draft of this chapter was completed by Anjali Kumar in November 2002. The analyses and suggestions contained in this chapter are based on the international technical experience of the World Bank and are presented as a contribution to the debate and formulation of public policies.

parency. Capital markets, especially corporate governance, have been strengthened in parallel with revisions to the Corporate Law and the law for the CVM. Comprehensive reform of the payments system has reduced systemic risk. As recognized, several areas still need to be addressed to further reduce risk and improve the efficiency of financial intermediation.

Message 1. Increase the depth, reduce the cost, and improve the composition of financial intermediation

Although Brazil's financial system is large, public sector debt absorbs most of the resources it mobilizes and much of the credit remains directed by the public institutions. Moreover, real interest rates have been among the highest in the world. A large part of financial institutions' assets consist of government paper. These institutions are consequently less inclined to hold more risky assets, such as loans, thus reducing available private sector credit. As recognized, less government borrowing, together with less directed credit would also help to reduce the high cost of financial intermediation (both interest rates and spreads) and the crowding out of private credit. Less financial sector taxation, including lower reserve requirements, would also reduce bank spreads, though it is recognized that the loss in fiscal revenue would have to be offset, and also that lower reserve requirements presuppose other mechanisms for monetary contraction, which will also have associated costs. An improved legal framework for the resolution of credit default and bankruptcy, better creditor information, greater ease or contestability of entry, and lower overheads would further reduce intermediation costs.

Context

Among the world's major emerging markets, Brazil appears to be in the middle of the pack in financial depth (table 1). Although East Asian economies such as China, the Republic of Korea, and Malaysia have deeper financial systems, Brazil fares better than other major Latin American countries and India and some other large countries.

Table 1. Depth of financial markets, Brazil and other emerging economies, 1999/2000 (percent, unless otherwise indicated)

Country	Private credit/ GDP	Equity market capitali- zation/ GDP	Equities value traded/ GDP	Domestic publics bonds on issue/ GDP	Domestic private bonds on issue/ GDP	Total financial assets[b]/ GDP	GDP per capita 1999[a] (Current US dollars)	Total financial assets[b] (millions of US dollars)
Brazil	40.5	39.0	17.0	40.9	8.9	139.7	4,350	780,739
Argentina	23.4	44.0	2.1	11.8	1.0	81.0	7,550	231,166
Mexico	28.5	24.7	7.9	9.2	2.1	68.3	4,440	386,366
India	36.4	34.2	104.7	21.8	0.4	92.8	440	437,293
China	128.9	42.5	66.8	19.5	8.5	199.4	780	2,153,717
Malaysia	103.8	146.5	65.5	29.6	50.0	370.9	3,390	331,302

a. Computed using the World Bank Atlas method. b. Simplified definition based on aggregate of assets described in this table. Source: World Bank (World Development Indicators); IFS, IFC (Emerging Makets Database); BIS

On a narrower definition of private credit limited to bank loans, bank credit is just 27.4 percent of GDP in Brazil, half as high as in Chile and lower than in OECD countries in 1999 (figure 1). Data for 2002 suggest no change in bank loans as a percentage of GDP and a possible increase in the share of debt securities (table 2).

Table 2. Domestic financial claims as a percentage of GDP, 2002

	Claims on		
Type of claim	Public sector	Private sector	Total
Bank loans	1	26	27
Debt securities	53	3	56
Equity securities[a]	6	18	24
Total	60	47	107

a.Assuming that equity cross-holdings are a third of total market capitalization.   Source: World Bank staff estimates

Figure 1. Bank credit as a share of GDP in Brazil and selected other countries, 1999

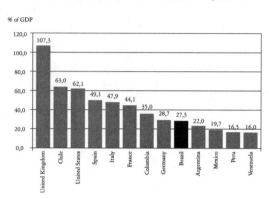

Government borrowing affects intermediation depth, costs, and soundness. Reducing public borrowing is important not only for fiscal reasons but also to increase the depth and soundness of the financial system. High public sector borrowing, most of it in the form of federal government securities, considerably elevates aggregate figures on financial assets. Despite Brazil's improved recent record on fiscal management, with an average primary fiscal surplus of 3.5 percent of GDP since 1999, the ratio of federal government debt to GDP rose from 43.4 percent of GDP in 1998 to 54.5 percent by the end of April 2002.

Most of the federal government's domestic debt is held by Brazil's financial institutions. The five largest banks in Brazil account for over a fifth of public debt on issue (21 percent), and the four largest pension and mutual funds hold 25 percent. Public debt holdings account for about a quarter of the banking sector's assets, three-quarters of mutual fund holdings, and 30 percent of the assets of pension and insurance companies.

This government borrowing has a crowding out effect on financial intermediation. Financial institutions prefer to hold safe and well-remunerated government assets rather than riskier assets such as loans. As a result financial entities in Brazil have less diversified assets, exposing them to more risk. Although the structure of the public debt (mostly indexed to the overnight interest rate or the exchange rate) implies that private holders of these assets are relatively protected against market risk (interest and exchange rate), in the event of major macroeconomic imbalances, these "safe" assets could become riskier, with adverse consequences for the financial institutions that hold them. Recent requirements (June 2002) to mark to market the value of all securities held by financial institutions has alerted these institutions to the potential impacts of changes in market valuation of securities.

GOVERNMENT BORROWING ALSO DRIVES UP THE COST OF FINANCIALINTERMEDIATION AND INTEREST RATES. Real interest rates in Brazil are among the highest in the world. Though at around 11–14 percent, not as high as at the end of 1999, Brazil's real interest rates are higher than in comparator countries, where they range from –2.5 percent to 11 percent (figure 2).

Figure 2. Nominal and real interest rates in Brazil and comparator countries, 1999

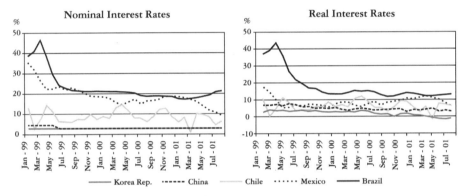

Source: Constructed from data from IMF, International Financial Statistics.

Spreads between borrowing and lending rates are also very high. Despite some decline in recent years, bank spreads began to rise again in early 2001 and remained at 30–50 percentage points, among the highest in the world. Although macroeconomic factors have been largely responsible for the recent deterioration in spreads, there are also significant underlying structural reasons for high spreads: high reserve requirements and forced investments, taxes on financial transactions, inefficient public banks, high loan loss provisions and costly contract enforcement. The Central Bank estimated the composition of bank spreads at the end of 2001 as 36 percent bank net margins, 29 percent taxes, 19 percent administrative costs, and 16 percent costs associated with defaults. This accounting decomposition may not adequately reflect the behavioral factors affecting spreads, however. Thus, for example, credit screening for selectively allocated credit could be poor, leading to higher defaults and thus greater spreads. An inefficient segment within the banking system, such as public banks charged with responsibility for channeling directed credit, could also boost average spreads (figure 3).

Figure 3. Spreads in bank intermediation in Brazil
(Percentage per month and total)

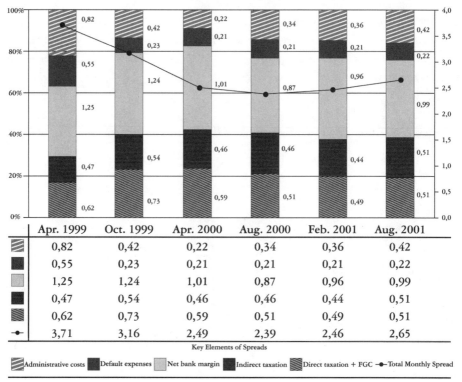

	Apr. 1999	Oct. 1999	Apr. 2000	Aug. 2000	Feb. 2001	Aug. 2001
	0,82	0,42	0,22	0,34	0,36	0,42
	0,55	0,23	0,21	0,21	0,21	0,22
	1,25	1,24	1,01	0,87	0,96	0,99
	0,47	0,54	0,46	0,46	0,44	0,51
	0,62	0,73	0,59	0,51	0,49	0,51
	3,71	3,16	2,49	2,39	2,46	2,65

Key Elements of Spreads

Administrative costs   Default expenses   Net bank margin   Indirect taxation   Direct taxation + FGC   —●—Total Monthly Spread

Source: Banco Central do Brasil, author's estimates .(1999, 2000, 2001a)

TAXATION ALSO CONTRIBUTES TO THE HIGH COSTS OF INTERMEDIATION. High direct and indirect taxation of financial institutions and financial transactions also increases spreads. Two social security taxes (the 3 percent COFINS and 0.65 percent PIS) are calculated on the basis of total revenue, adjusted for funding costs, rather than profits (see box 1 for a description of the major financial sector taxes). Until mid-2002 the CPMF tax was collected on virtually all financial transactions, but there are now exemptions for some types of institutions and for stock market transactions. The IOF, another tax on financial transactions, is collected on loans and short-term foreign exchange operations. Although less significant than the CPMF (rates were reduced in 1999), its discretionary character leaves the door open for distortionary effects. Tax rates are not uniform across financial instruments, creating opportunities for arbitrage across instruments.

The response to the taxes has been a reduction in financial intermediation and also, regulatory arbitrage. The impact of the CPMF on the stock market, whose strength depends on turnover and trading, was particularly severe, since the higher the turnover—and thus the liquidity—in the market, the higher the fiscal burden. A result was a shift in Brazil's capital markets to offshore locations and a reduction in domestic market liquidity. In banking, the CPMF resulted in a reduction in the number of checks being issued and the number of financial transactions (thus shrinking its own base) and an increase in interest rate spreads and interest rates on government bonds (thus partly offsetting the revenue gain from the CPMF). And because mutual fund transactions have been exempt from the CPMF, it has resulted in a shift from time deposits to mutual funds. Exemptions for consumer credit companies and some other financial institutions have introduced additional distortions.

Exempting stock market transactions from the CPMF in mid-2002 is a good start toward reducing distortions in the financial sector. But nearly all other financial transactions are still subject to the CPMF, which could lead to new possibilities of arbitrage. The fiscal importance of the CPMF could still be protected by changes that distribute the tax burden in a non-distortionary way across financial instruments and between financial transactions and real sector transactions.

Box 1. Financial sector taxes in Brazil

Direct taxation

Income tax: 25 percent for financial institutions and 20 percent for equity and fixed income mutual funds.

CSLL (social contribution on profits): 9 percent for financial institutions and 10 percent for equity and fixed income mutual funds.

COFINS/PIS (social security taxes): 3 percent for COFIN and 0.65 percent for PIS. For financial institutions the base for these taxes is total revenues minus interest rate costs.

Municipal tax on services (ISS): The rate varies across municipalities but in general is around 5 percent. The basis for this tax is also total revenue.

CPMF (Contribuição Provisória sobre Movimentacão Financeira): 0.38 percent of the transaction amount, applied to all financial transactions. Certain institutions and mutual fund investments are exempted (pension funds are not). Mutual fund contributions by individual investors are not exempt.

IOF (Imposto de Operações Financeiros): this tax on foreign exchange transaction, fixed and variable rate securities, and credit operations varies between 0.96 percent of the return for one-day investments on fixed-income securities to 0 percent for investments over 29 days; 0.0041 percent a day on loans, up to a maximum of 1.5 percent of the total loan amount (so that loans with a maturity of one year or more have a rate of 1.5 percent). The Central Bank can raise the daily rate up to 1.5 percent. The IOF also applies to insurance premium payments. Inter-bank transactions are exempt.

Indirect taxation

Reserve requirements and directed credit are the major forms of indirect taxation of the financial sector.

Demand deposits: 45 percent reserve requirement; 25 percent directed credit to agricultural sector.

Time deposits: 10 percent; 65 percent directed to housing loans.

Source: Central Bank of Brazil.

Other financial sector taxes, though less important fiscally, can also create distortions. The IOF, with rates regulated by the Central Bank, contributes less than 2 percent to total revenue. It has received less attention than some other taxes, but the variance in its rate by loan maturity and its discretionary character are potentially distortive. With the possibility of charging different rates for different credit operations (as was the case until 1999) comes the risk of segmenting credit markets. In April 2002 the government announced its intention to phase out the PIS and COFINS in a two-stage reform that would transform the PIS into a value-added tax within 90 days and the COFINS within 14 months. Since the taxes would no longer be levied on total revenues, and therefore no longer cascading, the proposed new structure would be more efficient for financial sector and other transactions.

REVERSE REQUIREMENTS ARE AN IMPLICIT TAX ON FINANCIAL INTERMEDIATION. Reserve requirements have been reduced since 1994, although macroeconomic conditions have sometimes led to temporary reversals, as toward the end of 2001 (table 3). Reserve requirements are down from 100 percent of average daily balances in 1994 (and 80–90 percent as late as 1999) to 45 percent on both sight and term deposits, and from 30 percent to 10 percent on time deposits. Still, the underlying structural issue of the high base levels remains. A gradual increase of remuneration rates for reserve requirements, which vary considerably by category, could be examined and alternative contractionary monetary policy instruments might be considered.

Table 3. Evolution of reserve requirements for financial institutions in Brazil, 1994–2001 (percent)

Date	Reserve requirement ratio on — Average balance	Reserve requirement ratio on — Marginal increase in balance	Reserve requirement ratio on — Average balance	Reserve requirement ratio on — Marginal increase in balance	Applications to deposits by category* — Demand deposits	Deposits at previous notice	Third party funds in trust	Receipts and taxes	Banker's drafts	Resources from executed guarantees	Liability transfer agreements, domestic transactions	Liabilities on payment services and funds from guarantees executed	Time deposits	Exchange rate acceptance notes	Debenture backed securities	Securities issued by the institution	Debt assumption agreements linked to operations overseas
Jun-30-1994	100	100	20	–	x	x	x	–	x	x	–	–	–	x	x	x	–
Jul-13-1994	100	–	20	–	–	–	–	–	–	–	–	–	x	x	x	x	–
Aug-24-1994	100	100	–	–	x	x	x	x	x	x	–	–	–	–	–	x	–
Aug-31-1994	100	–	30	–	–	x	–	x	x	–	–	–	–	–	–	x	–
Dec-19-1994	90	100	30	–	x	x	x	x	x	x	–	–	–	x	x	x	–
Dec-29-1994	90	–	27	–	–	–	–	–	–	–	–	–	x	x	x	x	–
Apr-20-1995	90	–	30	60	–	–	–	–	–	–	–	–	x	x	x	x	–
Jun-07-1995	90	–	30	–	–	–	–	–	–	–	–	–	x	x	x	x	–
Jul-20-1995	83	–	30	–	x	x	x	x	x	x	–	–	x	x	x	x	–
Aug-17-1995	83	–	20	–	x	x	x	x	x	x	–	–	x	x	x	x	–
Sep-04-1995	83	–	20	-50	–	–	–	–	–	–	–	–	x	x	x	x	–
Dec-20-1995	82 to 75	–	20	-50	x	x	x	x	x	x	–	–	x	x	x	x	–
Jun-28-1996	83 to 75	–	20	-50	x	x	–	–	–	–	–	–	–	–	–	–	–
Aug-07-1996	84 to 75	–	20	varying reduction	–	–	–	–	–	–	–	–	x	x	x	x	x
Jun-04-1997	85 to 75	–	30	–	–	–	–	–	–	–	–	–	x	x	x	x	–
Mar-02-1999	86 to 75	–	30	–	–	–	–	–	–	–	–	–	x	x	x	x	x
Apr-10-1999	87 to 75	–	25	–	x	x	x	x	–	–	–	–	x	x	x	–	x
May-06-1999	88 to 75	–	20	–	x	x	x	x	–	–	–	–	x	x	x	x	x
Jul-07-1999	89 to 75	–	20	–	–	–	–	–	–	–	–	–	x	x	x	x	–
Aug-24-1999	90 to 75	–	10	–	–	–	–	–	–	–	–	–	x	x	x	x	x
Sep-02-1999	90 to 75	–	10	–	–	–	–	–	–	–	–	–	x	x	x	x	x
Sep-08-1999	65	–	0	–	x	x	x	x	x	x	–	–	x	–	x	x	x
Oct-14-1999	65	–	0	–	x	x	x	x	x	x	–	–	x	x	x	x	–
Mar-14-2000	55	–	0	–	x	x	x	x	x	x	–	–	x	–	–	–	–
Jun-07-2000	45	–	0	–	x	x	x	x	x	x	–	–	–	–	–	–	–
Jun-23-2000	45	–	10	–	x	x	x	x	x	x	x	x	x	x	x	x	x
Sep-21-2001	45	–	10	–	–	–	–	–	–	–	x	–	x	x	x	x	x
Sep-26-2001	45	–	10	–	x	x	x	x	x	x	x	x	–	–	–	–	–

Source: Banco Central do Brazil

AN INTEGRATED REVIEW OF ALL FINANCIAL SECTOR TAXATION, EXPLICIT AND IMPLICIT, COULD GUIDE THE FORMULATION OF REFORMS IN TAX DESIGN WHICH ARE NONDISTORTIVE. As the government's fiscal position permits, a reduction in levels of financial sector taxation would be desirable to increase the depth of intermediation.

BANKING SECTOR PRACTICES ALSO CONTRIBUTE TO HIGH SPREADS. High operating costs in public sector banks may be creating an umbrella under which private banks can charge higher rates. Bank dominance of networks for the distribution of financial services has contributed to limited contestability in the sector, enabling banks to maintain high transaction costs and higher lending rates and to pass the high cost structures on to their clients higher lending rates and lower interest rates on deposits. Bank network dominance and the costs of maintaining networks are in turn affected by minimum capital requirements per branch and minimum branch standards, which raise the costs of opening branches. NON-PERFORMING LOANS CONTRIBUTE TO SPREADS. Since requirements to adequately classify loans and to provision for nonperforming loans were introduced in 1999, provisioning for bad loans has varied between 6.6 percent and 6.8 percent of total loans over the past two years.

NON-PERFORMING LOANS, AND THE COSTS ASSOCIATED WITH COLLECTION OF NON-SERVICED DEBT REFLECT WEAK CREDITOR RIGHTS AND PROTRACTED COURT PROCESSES, WHICH ALSO ADD TO THE COSTS OF INTERMEDIATION. Protracted judicial processes for collateral repossession and corporate reorganization and bankruptcy raise the cost of credit contract enforcement, boosting overhead costs and perceived risks. While creditor rights are reasonably well specified in the law, enforcement is weak. In São Paulo, for example, the congestion rate (ratio of cases pending to cases resolved per judge) is 277 percent; in Peru the rate is 164 percent. Remedies could include establishing specialized commercial courts to strengthen understanding of financial sector transactions and move cases more quickly through the court system, plus legal measures to strengthen creditor rights and improve collateral repossession.

Options

Several policy options could be considered to increase the lending and reduce spreads:

- REDUCING GOVERNMENT BORROWING LEVELS. While far-reaching and fundamental in the effect on the financial sector, this option would depend on macroeconomic and fiscal developments.

- REDUCING FINANCIAL SUSTEM TAXATION. While reducing overall levels of taxation would be difficult in view of the need for a strong fiscal position, reducing the distortionary impact of some taxes would be a valuable first step. Selective elimination of taxes (as with the CPMF on stock transactions) would be a later option, as the fiscal situation improves.

- CONSIDERING SIMPLIFICATION AND A PHASED REDUCTION IN REVERSE REQUIREMENTS. Simplification of the structure of reserve requirements for various deposit categories could be monetarily neutral and could be implemented in the short term. A reduction in reserve requirements would have a negative impact on the Central Bank's balance sheet and affect government financing and international reserve holdings; it would need to be phased in gradually while strengthening other mechanisms for monetary policy, such as the interbank rate or rediscount rate.

- REDUCING BANKING SYSTEM INEFFICIENCIES BY REDUCING THE ROLE OF DIRECTED CREDIT, rationalizing the role of public banks (as discussed in message 3) and increasing contestability. Simplifying entry requirements for opening new branches as well as new banks would boost competition. Examine possibilities for consolidation and competition in distribution networks.

- CONSIDERING OPTIONS FOR IMPROVING CREDITOR RIGHTS, EXECUTION OF COLLATERAL, AND COURT PROCESSES, such as greater judicial training in financial sector issues and in the need to base decisions on legal rather than social grounds. This is an important issue in bringing down the spread in lending, but also in increasing access to those who are willing to make an effort to pay and in developing a well functioning mortgage market.

- FURTHERING IMPROVE CREDIT INFORMATION AND STRENGTHEN CREDIT PRACTICES to reduce non-performing loans and improve access.

Message 2. Improving access to financial services

Access to financial services- deposits, payments and credit – has improved, but scope remains for further improvement. Financial services could be more evenly distributed geographically, with coverage increased in the poorer North and Northeast. Small entrepreneurs, who presently rely heavily on retained earnings, need better access to financial services. New technologies may help to expand services to small firms and firms in remote areas. Although Internet banking is relatively advanced in Brazil, there is scope for improving connectivity and telephone charge structures. Expansion of microfinance and nonbank financial services could also improve access to financial services, as could attention to the infrastructure for financial services, especially creditor information systems for small borrowers and the legal framework for collateral.

Context

Access to financial services is unevenly distributed geographically, with sparse services in the poorer parts of the country. Compared with developed economies, banks in Brazil serve a much higher number of inhabitants per branch.[1] But compared with other major countries in the region, Brazil's population is reasonably well served. Nonetheless, some 30 percent of municipalities and 6 percent of the population in Brazil have no access to formal financial services. Banking facilities are concentrated in Brazil's large southeastern states, while some 57 percent of municipalities and nearly 20 percent of the population in the North and Northeast have no access to formal financial services (table 4). In seven states, mostly in the North, more than 70 percent of municipalities lack a bank branch—nationwide, some 1,680 poorer and generally less populated municipalities (of 5,500 overall) lack access to banks. And when poorer regions are served by bank branches, services are more limited. Bank branches in the North and Northeast have to serve nearly three times as many clients as in the South, reflecting both constrained services and lower overall levels of economic activity in these regions. GDP per bank branch in the North, despite serving almost three times as many clients, is less than twice as high as in the South. The implication is that Brazil could focus first on improving the geographic distribution of services and only then on expanding the overall network of financial services.

---

[1] While an average bank branch serves 1,479 people in Germany and 3,568 people in the United States, it serves 9,331 people in Brazil.

Table 4. Regional distribution of bank branches in Brazil, 1996

Region	GDP per capita	Branches	Population per bank branch per capita	GDP per bank branch	Area per branch
North	3,836	645	17,501	67.1	5,974
Northeast	2,538	2,546	17,459	44.3	605
Southeast	8,170	8,281	8,090	66.1	112
South	6,174	3,440	6,835	42.2	164
Mid West	6,118	1,301	8,071	49.4	1,235

Source: World bank staff estimates on data from Banco Central do Brasil, Instituto de Pesquisa Econômica Aplicada, and Instituto Brasileiro de Geografia e Estatística.

FINANCIAL SERVICES ARE ALSO UNEVENLY DISTRIBUTED AMONG ENTERPRISES. Studies on growth constraints find that more than half of small and medium-size enterprises view lack of financing as the main impediment to their expansion. This is a particularly important issue in Brazil, where microenterprises and small and medium-size enterprises accounted for an estimated 99 percent of enterprises in 1994, employed around 59 percent of the labor force, and produced 41 percent of manufacturing industry income. Microenterprises alone account for as much as 90 percent of firms in Brazil, 24 percent of employment, and 13 percent of GDP. In addition, there are an estimated 14 million informal microenterprises and small enterprises in Brazil.

It is estimated that only about 10 percent of microenterprises and 20 percent of small enterprises have access to external sources of financing and that the bulk of bank financing to medium-size and small enterprises comes from public banks or microfinance institutions indirectly supported by public banks at subsidized rates. Despite this extremely low lending, default rates are as high as 15 percent. (Figure 4)

Figure 4. Population served per bank branch in Brazil and selected countries, 2000

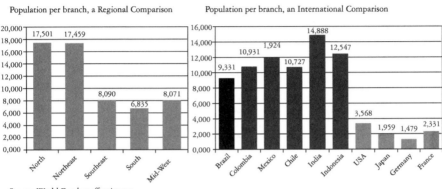

Population per branch, a Regional Comparison   Population per branch, an International Comparison

Source: World Bank staff estimates.

Even in larger corporations, commercial bank lending is low by international standards. Private commercial bank lending is typically short term and for commercial transactions such as trade finance, exports, or working capital. Medium and longer term bank finance comes from BNDES and other development banks, at below-market rates. Domestic capital markets have a very limited role in enterprise finance (figure 5). Only in the largest corporations is access to capital eased, by tapping into external markets.

Figure 5. Firm size and sources of investment finance, 2000

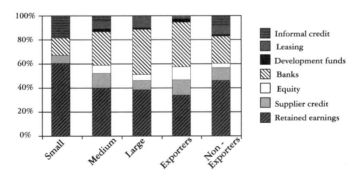

Note: Sample size: 200 firms.

Source: World Bank Business Environment Survey (2001).

NEW TECHNOLOGIES ARE INCREASING ACCESS. Expanded use of new technologies may help Brazil improve access to financial services in less served regions and segments of the economy. Developments in information collection, storage processing, and transmission technologies are strongly influencing all aspects of financial sector activity. Technology can reduce costs by substituting computers for paper-based and labor-intensive methods of accounting for customer deposits, withdrawals, and other transactions and for many internal operations. It can also reduce costs by providing services through such delivery channels as automated teller machines (ATMs), telephone banking, and online banking, enabling institutions to reach a wider geographic base.

Access to automatic teller machines has increased substantially in Brazil. ATMs have increased from about 5,000 in 1996 to more than 16,000 in 2001 (figure 6). Though in number of machines the southeastern region is better served than the rest of the country, with 59 percent of ATMs to the North's 4 percent, on a GDP per capita basis density is quite high in the Northeast. Still, the Southeast clearly remains the best served region, even adjusting for income differentials, and the North the worst served.

New technologies can also be used to expand financial services to smaller entities. For small loans financial institutions can increase efficiency by using credit scoring models—automated statistical methods for assessing default risk, which can reduce the need for human evaluation and allow underwriting of smaller loans—and by expanding and strengthening credit registries. Public services provided by the Central de Riscos at the Central Bank as well as private services, notably by SERASA, have been very valuable. Greater use could be made of positive credit information, though this would require modifications to laws on secrecy and information sharing. And the use of receivables-based finance could be strengthened through electronic linkages of small entrepreneurs and exporters with non-bank financiers, such as factoring or trade finance companies.

The Central Bank of Brazil has estimated that the Internet is the cheapest channel for delivering financial services, followed by ATMs, telephones, and branches. Estimated costs in 2001 for an average banking transaction ranged from R$0.24 (US$0.10) on the Internet to R$0.33 (US$0.13) for telephone dial-in banking services and R$2 (US$0.80) for transactions at a branch. Recognizing the cost effectiveness of the new technologies, Brazil's largest banks have developed extensive Internet-based service delivery, but most smaller Brazilian banks have not. Internet-based services are used by only about 4 percent of individual bank clients and 10 percent of corporate clients (some 90 percent of the 8 million Internet banking users are in higher income classes). Low connectivity, especially in rural areas, is another impediment, although connections are rising rapidly (figure 6).

Figure 6. Regional distribution of automatic teller machines in Brazil relative to population and income, 2001

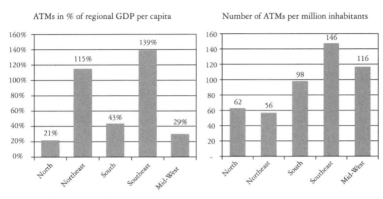

Source: World Bank staff estimates.

Telephones may be a better way for banks to reach lower income segments of the population and remote areas. Surveys indicate that cell phones, which are much cheaper in Brazil than in many other countries, are owned by many more low- and middle-income households than are computers (figure 7), though cell phone calls cost much more than fixed-line calls. Telephone availability, costs, and connectivity could be explored for increased access to financial services.

Figure 7. Costs of bank transactions and cellular phones in Brazil and selected countries

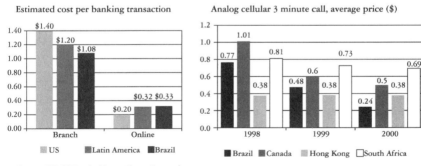

Source: World Bank, Tower Group Research

FOR VERY SMALL ENTERPRISES MICROFINANCE INSTITUTIONS AND OTHER NONBLANK FINANCIAL INSTITUTIONS ARE A PROMISING WAY TO INCREASE ACCESS TO FINANCIAL SERVICES. The policy environment for microfinance institutions has been considerably liberalized since 1999, but expansion has been slow, suggesting that impediments remain. Working groups established under the Communidade Solidária have recommended measures based on consultations with a wide spectrum of civil society, that could be further explored.

Solutions for increasing lending to medium-size and larger scale enterprises will be more difficult, as they involve issues such as the large role of public banks in intermediation and the crowding out of private lending by directed credit, as well as the development of capital markets. These issues are discussed further in the following sections.

Options

Several options can be considered for expanding access to financial services:

- Address the regional distribution of services before the expansion of services.
- Consider ways to use new information technologies to expand services to underserved regions and groups, for example, though tariff rationalization to improve phone connecticity or through multiple-person service points to ease access to phones and the Internet.
- Motivate private banks to increase service provision to lower income and remote households through measures that reduce the costs of such provision (better credit information, improved security interests, modifications to the secrecy law to allow reasonable consolidated credit information sharing).
- Encourage expansion of microfinance and cooperative services for small borrowers.

Message 3. Redirecting directed credit and rationalize federal banks

Directed credit has been greatly reduced, but a large proportion of credit in the financial system (40 percent), especially for the housing and rural sectors, is funded by implicit and explicit taxes, goes through the public banks, and is subject to administered interest rates. In discharging their selective credit mandates federal banks have accumulated large problem portfolios that have proved costly to the government. Much of this credit goes to clients who could borrow at market rates rather than to targeted clients. Limiting cross subsidization, focusing subsidies on consumers rather than sectors (see, for example, the Policy Note on Housing and Urban Issues), and improving collections would reduce costs to other borrowers and taxpayers while improving credit allocation and income distribution.

Federal banks have been largely recapitalized but still face issues to improve strategy and operational efficiency, reflected in high operating and overhead costs and large staffs. The need for recapitalization reflects losses on directed credit; renewed growth of their lending raises issues of how collection will be improved. Moreover, much of the public banks' credit is funded by earmarked taxes, in many cases payroll taxes for unemployment and workers' assistance, which raises distributional and governance issues, and may discourage formal sector employment (see Policy Note on Social Protection). Moreover, the federal banks low interest rates and collections have driven out private sector lending in some areas. Direct transfers linked clearly to government mandates would improve transparency, and could encourage private sector participation in these areas, but will need to be carefully done to avoid increased operational inefficiencies and non-performing loans and could be politically unsustainable. Solutions will differ for each institution, based on particular circumstances, but the key issues will be completion of the financial and operational restructuring with reforms in the governance framework and definition of a sustainable strategy and clear mandates for each of the federal banks, within the context of the pressures they face.

Context

Directed credit has been greatly reduced, but mainly by restructuring and the recapitalization by the government of non-performing loans, particularly mortgage loans. Directed credit shrank from about 54 percent of total credit in mid-2000 to about 38 percent in March 2002, following the government-financed restructuring of the federal banks that removed a substantial volume of directed credit (figure 8) from their books in exchange for government debt. Directed credit policies remain, and they make other loans relatively

more risky and costly. Most selective or directed credit is channeled through public financial entities, either directly or through onlending arrangements with other public or private financial entities. Some 57 percent of total directed credit is now channeled through
Banco Nacional de Desenvolvimento Econômico e Social (BNDES), with onlending
through other entities, mainly public, accounting for more than half that amount. There
are also mandated private sector programs: 25 percent of unremunerated demand deposits
must be devoted to rural finance, and 65 percent of passbook savings deposits are earmarked for housing loans.

Figure 8. Trends and composition of directed credit, 2000–02

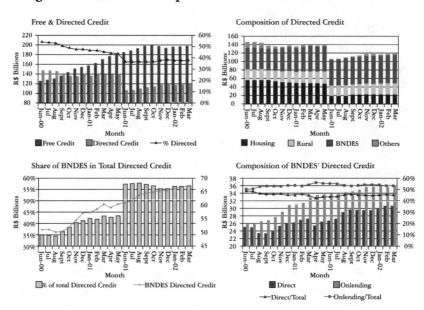

Source: World Bank Staff based on data from the Central Bank of Brazil

DIRECTED CREDITS ARE MADE USING LOW-COST, TAX-LIKE PUBLIC SECTOR FUNDS THAT ARE
SUBSIDIZED BY THE BELOW MARKET RATES PAID BY THE FUNDS TO THEIR CONTRIBUTORS.
The most important funds are the Employees Severance and Indemnity Fund (Fundo de
Garantia por Tempo de Serviço, FGTS); the Workers' Assistance Fund (Fundo de
Amparo ao Trabalhador, FAT); the joint Social Integration Program/Public Servant
Capital Formation Program (Programa de Integração Social/Programa de Formação do
Patrimônio do Servidor Público, PIS/PASEP); and Constitutional Funds. All five federal

banks manage such funds, but the extent to which these funds finance their operations or are used for onlending varies.

The FGTS has been a substantial source of external funding for Caixa Econômica Federal, which is its legal operating agent and to which it pays a management fee. FGTS accounts earn a return of the reference interest rate (TR) + 3 percent, well below market rates. The FGTS provides unemployment and other emergency payments (severance, death, retirement) to workers in the formal sector (see Policy Note on Private Sector Development). It is funded by an 8 percent employer contribution on salaries, established in individual accounts. Caixa uses these funds for investments in infrastructure, basic services and low-cost mortgages.

The FAT provides BNDES with about half its funding. The FAT is financed by a 0.65 percent tax on revenues of private firms, a 1 percent tax on revenues of public firms, and a 1 percent levy on the costs of nonprofit firms. Some 60 percent of its proceeds go to a supplementary unemployment insurance (including indemnifications for dismissal without just cause), annual salary bonuses (the "14th wage"), and a fiscal stabilization fund; the rest goes to BNDES, along with special deposits (money entrusted to BNDES by the Ministry of Labor from part of the remaining 60 percent of FAT funds). Constraints on FAT payments were relaxed and eligibility criteria were expanded up to the mid-1990s. BNDES is required to make annual cash payments to FAT at 6 percent interest on outstanding FAT funding, with the excess yield capitalized and added to the outstanding balance of FAT funding but callable by FAT only if BNDES is willing to pay.

PIS-PASEP funds make up 20 percent of BNDES's funding. PIS-PASEP, the precursor of FAT, was financed in a manner similar to FAT, which has taken its place. Since 1988 PIS-PASEP has received no new members or contributions, but it continues to earn income. Actuarial calculations forecast that the funds will be depleted over the next 21 years. BNDES has been in charge of investing PIS-PASEP resources since 1974 and guarantees a minimum yield equal to the TJLP, the long-term interest rate. BNDES assumes the credit risk on loans made with PIS-PASEP funds and in return charges PIS-PASEP an annual management fee of 0.5 percent on funds loaned and a credit fee of 1.5 percent of the outstanding amount of PIS-PASEP loans.

DIRECTED CREDIT AND ITS PRIMARY TARGETS. Most directed credit is provided at below market, but positive real interest rates, based on either long-term interest rates (TJLP) or reference rates (TR) calculated by the Central Bank, plus margins that vary by end-use and risk. A large part of directed credit fails to meet intended targets, however, with better-off farmers and middleclass homebuyers, for example, capturing much of the subsidies, rather than the poorer groups for whom the subsidies are intended. In agriculture the largest 2 percent of the borrowers receive 57 percent of the loans, while the smallest 75 percent of borrowers receive only 6 percent of credit. Moreover, Banco do Brasil, the main lender is now mainly concentrating on creditworthy borrowers. In housing, earmarked credit from private banks is invested in eligible housing securities issued by Caixa Econômica Federal, thus avoiding the risks associated with lending to small homeowners. Caixa mortgage loans, financed by these funds and FGTS, as well as its own mobilization of passbook deposits, have been directed more toward middle-income than low-income homeowners.

DIRECTED CREDIT POLICIES TAX BENEFICIARIES OF FGTS, FAT AND PIS/PASEP, AN IMPLICIT TAX ON FINANCIAL INTERMEDIATION, AND ENDED UP AS COSTLY TO THE GOVERNMENT BECAUSE OF NON-PERFORMING LOANS.. Directed credit has paid FGTS, FAT, and PIS/PASEP, and thus their beneficiaries, much less than market rates. Directed credit has acted as an implicit tax on other lending, because the low mandated returns on the forced investments in agriculture and housing have to be offset by higher rates on other loans. Finally, directed credit has resulted in costs to the government, when it recapitalized the federal banks and the FGTS to cover the losses on non-performing directed credit loans.

DIRECTED CREDIT AND THE PROBLEMS CONFRONTING FEDERAL BANKS. Federal government ownership in the financial sector is concentrated in five institutions: Banco do Brasil, Caixa Econômica Federal, Banco Nacional de Desenvolvimento Econômico e Social, Banco do Nordeste, and Banco da Amazonia. The first three dominate Brazil's banking system. Banco do Brasil, with assets of some R$170 billion (US$70 billion) is the largest bank in Latin America, with BNDES and Caixa in second and third places. The role of public financial institutions has been considerably reduced, but these five federal banks hold 40 percent of banking system assets, have an extensive branch network often reaching into remote areas, and play a major role in channeling credit funded by taxes or other forms of compulsory saving to specific agents and sectors. BNDES is effectively the sole provider of medium- and long-term capital for corporate investment, Banco do Brasil dominates agricultural sector lending, and Caixa Economica Federal has dominated mortgage lending. Their dominance has largely restricted private lending in these areas.

Federal bank portfolios have deteriorated over the years, reflecting their special mandates and programs, limited supervision and inspection, different norms for keeping accounts of targeted lending to specific sectors of the economy, and problems of internal efficiency and unclear accountability compared to private banks. By 2001 financial conditions in four of the federal banks (all but BNDES) had deteriorated and to restore their solvency, the government, as owner, had to recognize and absorb past losses, much of them attributable to credit operations the banks perform on behalf of the government. Going forward, the federal government assumed the risks and costs of the federal credit programs managed by these institutions, and subsidies provided through the banks are now to be recorded in the government budget.

Despite extensive financial restructuring and recapitalization in 2001, the federal banks still face challenges, which need to be addressed if the gains are to be sustained and consolidated.

Federal bank restructuring was large, yet did not appear to have completely restored these banks' capital. At Banco do Brasil financial strengthening included debt forgiveness, netting of obligations and swaps and an injection in new security issues at market rates. Together, these measures allowed Banco do Brasil to boost its capital adequacy ratio from 8 percent to 12 percent, the minimum standard, prior to restructuring.

The overall cost to the government of Caixa's restructuring is large. Financial strengthening measures included transfers of nonperforming loans to an asset recovery agency, debt cancellation, assumption by the government of Caixa's liabilities to the Central Bank, and transfers of bad assets to the government in exchange for new Treasury issues. These measures reduced Caixa's estimated bad debts and increased its equity, raising its capital adequacy ratio to almost 15 percent, meeting regulatory requirements.

Major pending issues relate to bonds to be received by Caixa as compensation for losses due to the inadequate indexing in real estate loans financed with earmarked (FGTS) funds, as these loans mature. The bills yield Selic-indexed interest, and their proposed swaps (which have already begun) will reduce the need for provisions and improve Caixa's liquidity and profitability significantly.

Banco do Nordeste and Banco da Amazônia (19th and 39th among Brazil's top 50 banks) appear to have negative net capital. Losses at both banks have been large and the challenges of capital strengthening programs such as those adopted for Banco do Brasil and Caixa are greater.

Restructuring so far has been largely financial. Operational reforms to improve governance and internal efficiency and avoid the buildup of new problem loans are crucial to the sustainability of the cleanup. Federal financial institutions face special problems of governance. Further reform of the federal banks depends on strategic decisions about their future roles. Contracts with the government, as owner, have been proposed to increase transparency. The proposed contracts would show the full cost of subsidized lending, including the operational costs and provisioning.

Proposals have been made to increase private equity participation in Banco do Brasil. However the proposed listing on the Novo Mercado may not significantly improve governance since minority private shareholders may not have a seat on the board of directors. International evidence suggests that they are unlikely to have an impact on a public bank's performance. Private participation would have to be greater to have a real impact on governance. Banco do Brasil does have a well-established banking franchise, but its sustainability depends on reducing its high-cost and nonperforming loans.

For Caixa Econômica Federal, its past losses and its multiple and important roles mean that a decision regarding its new directions is crucial. A new housing finance strategy would be needed if Caixa were to reduce its involvement in housing loans. Caixa is already branching into new areas such as credit cards and ATMs, where it faces strong competition from other institutions. The final costs of its recent restructuring package could be among the world's largest, reflecting past credit decisions and loan nonrecovery. As recognized, transforming Caixa into a successful bank requires reform. Important steps have been taken during and after the 2001 restructuring. By successfully turning around its credit and collection practices through reforms, Caixa could avoid the consideration of other, more radical options, for example, to convert it into a more specialized bank, make it a government agency, or other options.

BNDES is the most successful and efficient of the public banks, but it too faces future problems. BNDES is the major provider of longer term credit to small and medium enterprises, as well as large firms. However, much of its lending is on-lending to other banks, and the risk premia it allows may be insufficient. Like the other public banks, it too depends on subsidized funds. Moreover, BNDES depends on PIS/PASEP which is will gradually decline as employees covered by PIS/PASEP retire and become eligible for payouts. Hence, BNDES too will gradually need to rely more on market-based funding, which will mean higher lending rates. BNDES also plays a major role in the stock market and in venture capital, both of which raise governance issues. BNDES has begun to change from a lender to a cofinancier and market developer. It is already taking initiatives in cofinancing, project finance, and underwriting, where it acts as an important catalyst. It is discussing buying corporate bonds rather than making loans. Such a role could help standardize private bond contracts and accelerate the development of a secondary bond market. BNDES could also play a role in improving credit information, if it were to disseminate information on its own loans and on subborrower loans.

Banco do Brasil relies more on deposits than do Caixa and BNDES, but these include deposits from special funds. Almost half of Banco do Brasil funds consisted of deposits in 2001, including some 15 percent from judicial and other special deposits. About 7 percent of Banco do Brasil's funds in 2001 came from constitutional funds (Banco do Brasil is the Treasury agent for the Center-West Constitutional Fund, FCO) and onlending from BNDES, FINAME, Caixa Econômica Federal, and other financial institutions. Banco do Brasil also administers agricultural funds such as PRONAF and FUNCAFÉ, funded by earmarked taxes, and has an important role in financing the agricultural sector.

The two regional banks, Banco da Amazônia and Banco do Nordeste, in their role as managers of constitutional funds for regional development and onlenders of BNDES funds, may not have an adequate source of funds to sustain operations. Banco da Amazônia, in addition to administering the Constitutional Fund for Development of the North (FNO), provides loans under the National Family Farming Program (Programa Nacional de Fortalecimento da Agricultura Familiar, PRONAF) and the Rural Assistance Program (Programa de Assistência Rural, PRORURAL). Banco da Amazônia has accumulated pension liabilities that were not accounted for in its recent recapitalization. Banco do Nordeste operates the Constitutional Fund for Development of the Northeast (FNE) and the Northeast Development Fund (FINOR). It derives much of its income from managing FNE, prorated to its asset value.

It would be desirable to consider the social, economic, and governance implications of using off-budget taxes, such as FGTS and FAT (see Policy Notes on Social Protection and on Private Sector Development), and earmarked constitutional funds to finance below-market lending. Many of these subsidized loans go not to intended beneficiaries such as small, low income borrowers, but to large farmers, middle-class home purchasers, and state enterprises. And the funds such as FAT and FGTS earn returns well below market rates, implying a transfer from the contributors and beneficiaries to those receiving directed credit.

Options

- Measures to strengthen governance at federal banks and the funds they draw upon, through increased independence and accountability of managers and directors could help to consolidate recent gains from restructuring and avoid a new buildup of problem portfolios.
- Measures for improved internal efficiency could include bringing labor costs in public banks in line with those in private banks, reducing overhead costs associated with problem portfolios, and improving the transparency of cost allocation.

- New funding mechanisms would be desirable for federal banks, to make the banks sustainable, reduce potential future costs to the government, and to improve the efficiency of resource allocation in the financial system. More effective targeting of subsidies, especially in housing, rural, and municipal finance, would also improve the efficiency of resource allocation and the soundness of federal banks. The Federal Banks could gradually accustom themselves to paying higher interest on the funds they receive, which in turn would reduce the cross subsidization paid through high interest rates by other borrowers and low interest rates paid to the funds and their beneficiaries.

- Decisions as to directions for the public banks could have a greater emphasis on loan recovery, market development, and access to financial services, not just credit. This in turn would require decisions in other areas, such as improvements in the legal and judicial framework for loan recovery, access (as discussed above) and a housing strategy.

Message 4. Strengthening financial markets and nonbank financial institutions

Brazil's capital markets have had a gradual decline over the last four to five years. Reducing transaction costs could help to bring back larger companies, which now seek financing abroad. Other options could be explored for smaller companies, which have been unable to tap into these markets. A reinvigorated securities market would also enable Brazil's large pension funds to diversity their assets and reduce their problems of institutional risk, governance, and supervision.

Brazil has taken bold steps to strengthen the governance of listed companies and to extend the mandate of the securities commission (CVM). A larger budget and properly trained staff could help the CVM carry out its responsibilities. Its supervisory role could also be strengthened by greater information sharing with the Central Bank and by reform of appeals procedures that weaken its enforcement capacity. Updating minimum capital requirements for brokers and dealers and establishing criteria for greater transparency in order-flow and order-execution in secondary markets would also strengthen the regulatory and supervisory environment. Better techniques of asset and risk management and reduced concentration of government securities in the portfolios of institutional investors could improve the climate for capital markets. In addition, rules governing pension fund investment could gradually move towards a "prudent professional" rule, and the institutional framework for pension fund regulation and supervision could be simplified, merging the multiple regulatory agencies and regimes for closed- and open-end funds.

Context

Stronger nonbank financial institutions could provide an alternative source of financing to enterprises in Brazil, which rely very little on bank credit. The factoring industry and the leasing industry are relatively well developed, but the venture capital market is small and the securities market has contracted in recent years. The factoring industry financed R$27 billion, or 2.3 percent of GDP, in 2001, and leasing companies financed R$13 billion in purchases, or 1.1 percent of GDP. However, 70 percent of leasing is for vehicles and only 17 percent is used to finance machinery and equipment. Among the reasons are poor collateral registries for machinery and equipment, easier repossession for cars, and tax accounting rules for leasing that may be too complex for smaller firms. And enforcing claims on collateral is difficult given the seniority of debt to public authorities and employees and strong borrower protection laws. BNDES has several venture capital funds, such as BNDESPAR, but there is virtually no private venture capital market. Weak credit risk assessment institutions, disclosure standards, and auditing seem to be the primary reasons for the underdeveloped private market.

The performance of Brazil's capital markets is mixed. Institutional investors' assets have been expanding and derivatives markets are flourishing, but securities markets have shrunk in the past few years in number of listed firms, market capitalization, and amount of finance raised (tables 5 and 6).

Table 5. Brazilian stock market indicators, 1994-2002

Year	Number of listed companies	Market capitalization		Mutual funds, net assets	Foreign portfolio net news
		Amount (US$ millions)	Percent of GDP		
1994	544	189	34.8	50.5	
1996	550	217	28.0	99.5	3.59
1998	527	161	20.4	108.0	(2.46)
2000	459	226	37.8	147.1	(1.83)
2001	428	185	31.1	148.0	(0.73)
2002(Jan)	424	173	29.2		

Source: Comissão de Valores Mobiliários (www.cvm.gov.br)

Table 6. New issues in primary capital markets in Brazil, 1996-2002

	1996		1997		1998		1999		2000		2001		2002(Jan)	
Item	No.	Value (R$ million)	No.	Value (R$ million)	No.	Value (R$ million)	No.	Value (R$ million)	No.	Value (R$ million)	No.	Value (R$ million)	No.	Value (R$ million)
Shares	24	1,178	23	3,965	20	4,112	10	2,749	6	1,410	6	1,353	1	351
Corporate bonds [a]	83	7,211	40	6,041	41	6,297	29	5,084	38	7,313	37	14,575	1	100
Commercial paper	13	499	28	5,147	69	12,903	65	8,044	44	7,591	31	5,266	2	7
Other [b]	187	2,056	294	2,218	241	4,223	138	2,001	132	2,132	140	1,493	4	25
Total	307	10,945	385	17,371	371	27,536	242	17,879	220	18,445	214	22,687	8	484

a. Nonconvertible. b. Convertible corporate bonds, real estate funds, motion picture production certificates, subscription bonuses and livestock investiment schemes. Source: Comissão de Valores Mobiliários (www.cvm.gov.br)

Several factors have contributed to the stock market contraction. The CPMF transaction tax on securities market transactions, lifted in mid-2002, reduced liquidity in secondary markets for cash securities. Larger firms, able to access international markets, tended to increase their presence in overseas exchanges through American depository receipts (ADRs), and some even delisted themselves from the Brazilian exchange. Limited voting shares, inadequate board representation of minority shareholders, and no tag-along rights for minority shareholders also played a part.

Recent moves offer the promise of a renewal of Brazil's stock market—if further steps are taken. In 2001 amendments to the Corporate Law substantially restored tag-along rights for minority shareholders, introduced obligatory tender offer provisions, and restricted the issuance of new nonvoting shares. The authority and independence of the securities market regulator, CVM, were strengthened. Its mandate was expanded in a number of areas, including supervision of the futures exchange and of debt mutual funds. And in mid-2002 the CPMF transactions tax on stock market transactions was repealed.

These are a very good beginning, but developing the market will not be easy. With the largest companies going abroad to raise capital, Brazil's equity market will increasingly have to serve medium-size and small firms. These are largely family controlled, with a small public float. Changes in the law have clarified many aspects of mergers and acquisitions, but important grey areas remain, as in indirect transfers or control. Continuing improvements are needed in corporate governance, enforcement of new codes, and disclosure requirements, including improvements in information quality.

Brazil's securities commission also faces a number of challenges. It remains underfunded and continues to shoulder responsibilities that most securities regulators do not have. The CVM has limited authority to hire staff, to deploy them as needed, or to pay them a competitive salary, affecting staff quality and retention. The problem is compounded by a weak certification process for securities regulators. Thus the CVM has limited capacity for market surveillance and onsite inspection of market participants or for participating in self-regulatory organizations including the São Paulo Stock Exchange (BOVESPA) and the Brazilian Clearing and Depository Corporation. (CBLC), which is responsible for clearing and settlement in the Brazilian equities market. And while the CVM's jurisdictional mandate over the futures market and mutual funds has recently been enhanced and clarified, it lacks the capacity to discharge its responsibilities adequately.

The CVM also lacks adequate access to information. The Banking Secrecy Act blocks access to information made available to the Central Bank as regulator or to tax authorities from being made available to the CVM. This limits CVM's ability to track or prosecute offenders detected in the course of its surveillance activities. And the CVM's enforcement capacity and credibility are further circumscribed by an elaborate and often prolonged appeals procedure through the CRSFN, a multiagency appeals commission.

Derivatives markets in Brazil developed as an effective substitute for the overregulated and heavily taxed cash securities market, encouraged by tax incentives and by the trade guarantees and leverage available to participants in BMF, the commodities and futures exchange. Going forward, however, highly liquid derivatives markets combined with illiquid cash securities markets can give rise to price indeterminacy and complicate valuation and settlement of derivatives, increasing the volatility of prices and returns. The repeal of the CPMF on cash securities transactions should ease the return to a more appropriate balance of stocks and derivates trade.

Strengthening prudential regulation of securities markets and surveillance of secondary markets is also desirable. An updating of minimum capital requirements for participating brokers and dealers would exclude criteria unrelated to risk (such as location or number of agencies) and increase attention to asset-liability composition and liquidity. Net capital rules could provide early warning of needed capital injections and asset sales. Secondary market supervision could be enhanced by establishing criteria for order flow and execution and increasing order transparency.

Brazil's institutional investor funds have accumulated rapidly in recent years and now constitute 20 percent of GDP. Closed-end pension funds dominate, but open-end funds are growing rapidly. Insurance penetration, despite remarkably rapid recent growth, remains low. Brazil's institutional investors could become important components of its financial markets, once structural issues affecting the funds and their operating environment are addressed.

Investment funds in Brazil have the same high exposure to government assets as do banks. Asset diversification is difficult, however, with the contraction in equities markets and lack of safe investment opportunities. In the medium term investment regulations could allow pension funds to invest overseas and to apply the "prudent expert" rule, to provide greater flexibility in asset allocation decisions, together with a gradual move to asset liability management techniques in place of the value-at-risk approach.

Brazil's pension funds may be underfunded. The effects of high unpaid contributions, conservative mortality estimates, and high discount rates applied to calculations for provisions need to be assessed and addressed. The valuation of pension fund assets remains opaque. Mark to market rules introduced in June 2002 initially caused market turmoil, partly due to the lack of uniform asset valuation standards and known price vectors to serve as benchmarks for valuation. The early development of uniform benchmarks is important. In the medium term new performance benchmarks for different asset classes could be considered.

Also, in the medium term, competition and entry issues could be examined, in view of the high concentration levels in a small number of very large funds, the high fees charged to retail investors, and the dominance of bank distribution networks.

Options

For nonbank financial institutions,

- For leasing companies, better collateral registry for machinery and equipment, easier repossession rules, and simplified tax accounting for leasing for small firms could encourage greater use of equipment leasing.
- Venture capital markets could be expanded by encouraging BNDES to take on a more development-oriented role and by improving accounting and disclosure standards.

For Brazil's stock markets, consider:

- Monitoring implementation of corporate law and further clarifying grey areas, such as indirect transfers of control in mergers and acquistions

- Addressing the obstacles the CVM faces in funding, hiring and remuneration, and enformcement power.
- Strengthening the CVM's capacity for surveillance and inspection, in coordination with participating self-regulatory organizations including BOVESPA and CBLC.
- Introducing modifications to the Secrecy Act to permit the CVM to share information available to the Central Bank as regulator or to tax authorities, to expand its ability to track or prosecute offenders detected in the course of its surveillance activities.
- Monitoring the impact of repeal of the CPMF on the growth of cash securities and derivatives markets with a view to restoring a more appropriate balance.
- Updating minimum capital requirements and adopting net capital requirements for participating brokers and dealers to exclude criteria unrelated to risk (such as location or number of agencies) and enhance attention to asset-liability composition and liquidity.
- Establishing criteria for increasing transparency in order flow and execution in secondary markets.

In the pension fund industry,

- Encourage asset diversification in investment funds and introduce the "prudent expert"' rule to allow fund managers greater flexibility in asset allocation decisions.
- Encourage a gradual move toward asset liability management techniques in place of the widely used value-at-risk approach.
- Assess and address shortfalls in pension funds.
- Introduce uniform asset valuation standards and known price vectors as benchmarks for valuation for pension funds. In the medium term the development of new performance benchmarks for different asset classes could be considered.
- Competition and entry issues could also be examined in view of the high concentration levels in a small number of very large pension funds, the high fees charged to retail investors, and the dominance of bank distribution networks.

Message 5. Reinforcing the regulatory foundations of the financial system

Beyond the basic laws, attention is needed to the regulatory framework for the financial system. Standards that may be best practice in advanced countries may need adaptation in the context of Brazil's macroeconomic and financial environment, for example, to further strengthen capital adequacy. Stronger supervision standards could include a focus on reducing currency and maturity mismatches in Brazil's financial institutions.

Context

Several overarching issues affect all financial institutions in Brazil. Key among them is increasing the independence of the Central Bank and reducing the vulnerability of its top personnel to political processes. Institutionalizing the independence of monetary policy and financial supervision would parallel the independence conferred on fiscal policy by the Fiscal Responsibility Law. Legal protection for supervisors is also vital. Accelerated resolution of these and other issues related to the legal framework awaits the passage of a proposed amendment to Article 192 of the 1988 Constitution that would allow regulation of the system by multiple specialized laws.

Article 192 leaves a large number of complex but basic financial sector issues (Central Bank independence, foreign bank entry, deposit insurance, interest rate ceilings and regulatory and supervisory arrangements) to be regulated by a single enabling law (Lei Complementar) at a later date. Passage of the amendment to enable a series of pending reforms in financial sector regulation is fundamental to systemic financial system reform. The amendment came close to passage at the end of 2001, with approval by the Senate and by a specialized subcommittees of the House, but passage has not yet been completed.

Crucial to strengthening the institutional foundations of the financial system is ensuring monetary policy autonomy and accountability for the Central Bank through a proposed new Central Bank law or amendment of the Financial Institutions Law (4595/64). This could be supported by spelling out the objectives of the Central Bank, protecting its operational autonomy for a fixed period in pursuing these objectives, and establishing qualifications for its president and directors and setting terms that do not coincide with the terms of the Brazilian president. Independent external auditing and suitability standards for board member would help to maintain accountability and ensure professionalism.

The proposed new Central Bank law or a specific new law could provide legal protection for Central Bank senior supervisors by insulating them from costly and time consuming lawsuits or providing protective indemnification or insurance. Most countries now protect bank supervisors, through either general provisions protecting civil servants in the discharge of their duties (as in the United States) or through specific laws for bank supervisors. The laws would spell out the responsibilities and obligations of banking supervisors and establish codes of conduct to prevent abuse of office. Provisions of the Banking Law relating to licensing, governance, the duties of directors and managers, external auditing, and enforcement could also be reviewed. Reducing differences in provisions for private and public financial institutions and ensuring that governance conditions apply equally to both would improve efficiency. In terms of regulatory standards for financial institutions, it should be recognized that best practice in advanced countries may need adaptation in the context of Brazil's macroeconomic and financial environment, for example, to further strengthen capital adequacy. Reducing currency and maturity mismatches in Brazil's financial institutions, through the enforcement of stricter supervision practices, could also be helpful.

There are also overlaps to be resolved in the institutional arrangements for supervision of institutional investors. The Secretaria de Previdência Complementar, which falls under the Ministry of Social Welfare, is responsible for oversight of closed-end pension funds, currently the largest market segment, while the Superintendência de Seguros Privados oversees open-end funds and also regulates the insurance industry. A merger of these agencies has long been contemplated and could be facilitated by amending Article 192, although change through executive order could also be explored. Standardizing regulations would be a further important step.

Some of the greatest institutional challenges to Brazil's financial system, such as the form and function of the federal banks and the successful operation of Brazil's pension fund, depend on clear regulatory direction. And that depends on strong supervisory agencies, with clear operating mandates.

References

World Bank projects

- Central Bank Technical Assistance Loan – PROAT I (Projeto de Aperfeiçoamento dos Instrumentos de Atuação do Banco Central) US$ 20 million. Approved on November 18, 1997.
- Bank of the Northeast Microfinance Development – CREDIAMIGO (Programa de Crédito Produtivo Popular para o Nordeste) US$ 50 million. Approved on May 30, 2000
- Technical Assistance for the Financial Sector – PROAT II (Projeto de Assistência Técnica ao Setor Financeiro) US$ 14.5 million. Approved on September 4, 2001.

World Bank reports

This chapter summarizes the content of the following World Bank reports. Those, in turn, draw heavily from a wide range of literature on the subject from experts in Brazil and beyond, which are referenced in the mentioned Bank reports.

Beck, Thorsten, Ross Levine, and Norman Loayza. 1999. "Finance and the Sources of Growth." Policy Research Working Paper 2057, World Bank, Washington, D.C.

Caprio, Gerard, and Patrick Honohan,. 2001. Finance for Growth: Policy Choices in a Volatile World. Policy Research Report Series. Washington, D.C.: Wolrd Bank.

Caprio, Gerard, and Daniela Klingebiel, 1996. "Bank Insolvencies: Cross Country Experience." Policy Research Working Paper 1620. World Bank, Washington, D.C.

de Ferranti, David, Guillermo E. Perry , Indermit S. Gill, and Luis Serven. 2000. Securing our Future in a Global Economy. Washington, D.C.: World Bank.

Dollar, David, and Aart Kraay,. 2001. "Growth is Good for the Poor." Policy Research Working Paper 2587. World Bank, Washington, D.C.

Honohan, Patrick, and Daniela Klingebiel. 2000. "Controlling the Fiscal Costs of Banking Crises." Policy Research Working Paper 2441. World Bank, Washington, D.C.

King, Robert G., and Ross Levine. 1993. "Finance and Growth : Schumpeter Might be Right." Policy Research Working Paper 1083. World Bank, Washington, D.C.

World Bank. 1997. "Brazil - Central Bank Modernization Technical Assistance Project." Project Appraisal Document 16867. Washington, D.C.

World Bank. 2000a. "Brazil—Northeast Microfinance Development Project." Project Appraisal Document 20330. Washington, D.C.

World Bank. 2000b. "Brazil—Selected Issues in Social Protection." Volumes 1 & 2. Report 20054. Washington, D.C.

World Bank. 2001a. "Attacking Brazil's Poverty: A Poverty Report with a Focus on Urban Poverty Reduction Policies." Volumes 1 & 2. Sector Report 20475. Washington, D.C.

World Bank. 2001b. "Brazil - Financial Sector Technical Assistance Loan Project." Project Appraisal Document 22603. Washington, D.C.

World Bank. 2001c. "Brazil—Financing Municipal Investment : Issues and Options." Economic Report 20313. Washington, D.C.

World Bank. 2001d. "Brazil—Programmatic Financial Sector Adjustment Loan Project." President ' s Report P7448. Washington, D.C.

World Bank. 2001e. "Business Environment Survey." Washington, D.C.

World Bank. 2002a. "Brazil—Jobs Report." Volumes 1 & 2, Report 24408. Washington, D.C.

World Bank. 2002b. "Brazil—Second Programmatic Financial Sector Adjustment Loan Project." Program Document 24067. Washington, D.C.

World Bank. World Development Indicators database.

Other references

Afanasieff, Tarsila Segalla, Priscilla Maria Villa Lhacer, and Márcio I. Nakane. 2002. "The Determinants of Bank Interest Spread in Brazil." Central Bank of Brazil Working Paper 46. Brasília.
(www.bcb.gov.br/mPag.asp?codP=769&cod=316&perfil=1&idioma=P).

Albuquerque, Pedro H. 2001 "Impactos Econômicos da CPMF: Teoria e Evidência.Central Bank of Brazil Working Paper 21. Brasília.
(www.bcb.gov.br/htms/public/wps/wps21.pdf).

Bank for International Settlements. Web site databases. (www.bis.org).

Central Bank of Brazil. 2000 and 2001. "Juros e Spread Bancário no Brasil." Brasília.

Central Bank of Brazil. 2001. "Interest Rates and Banking Spreads." Focus Report. Brasília.

Central Bank of Brazil. Various years. "Boletim do Banco Central do Brasil – Annual Report." Brasília.

Central Bank of Brazil. FOCUS reports, various issues. Brasília.

Comissão de Valores Mobiliários. Web site databases. (www.cvm.gov.br).

Holden, Paul, and Vassili Prokopenko. 2001. "Financial Development and Poverty Alleviation: Issues and Policy Implications for Developing and Transition Countries." Working Paper WP/01/160. International Monetary Fund, Washington, D.C.

Instituto Brasileiro de Geografia e Estatística. Web site databases. (www.ibge.gov.br).

Instituto de Pesquisa Económica Aplicada. Web site databases. (www.ipea.gov.br).

International Finance Corporation. Emerging Markets database. (www.ifc.org).

International Monetary Fund. International Financial Statistics database. (www.imf.org).

Koyama, Sergio Mikio, and Marcio I. Nakane. 2001. "Os Efeitos da CPMF Sobre a Intermediação Financeira." Central Bank of Brazil Working Paper 23. Brasília.
(www.bcb.gov.br/mPag.asp?codP=769&cod=316&perfil=1&idioma=P).

Roemer, Michael, and Mary Kay Gugerty. 1997. "Does Economic Growth Reduce Poverty?" Harvard Institute for International Development, Cambridge, Mass.

Westley, Glenn D. 2001. "Can Financial Market Policies Reduce Income Inequality?" Inter-American Development Bank, Washington DC.

5

Infrastructure

5

Infrastructure

Introduction

The quality of a country's infrastructure, and of its infrastructure regulation, plays a big part in determining its productivity and competitiveness. Much of this has to do with logistics—the handling of materials from the procurement of inputs to the delivery of the final product. Logistics now account for the biggest share of the cost of doing business in Brazil, the so-called Custo Brasil. Estimated at about 20 percent of GDP, about twice the level in OECD countries, logistics costs represent a third of firms' operating costs on average and up to half in some industries. With globalization and the reorganization of production and distribution chains, logistics and related infrastructure services have taken on even greater importance in determining productivity and competitiveness and thus in guiding firms' location decisions. The cost and reliability of energy supply are also important determinants of productivity. And local infrastructure is a key determinant of productivity and the quality of life in local communities.

This chapter examines the main public policy issues and options in Brazil's infrastructure sectors and suggests government actions to strengthen infrastructure services and thus reduce logistics costs, increase productivity, and promote the resumption of sustainable income growth.

The high costs of logistics

Logistics costs are now the biggest component of the cost of doing business in Brazil—the so-called Custo Brasil. With globalization and the reorganization of production and distribution chains, logistics and related infrastructure services are becoming a key determinant of the investment climate and of firms' location decisions.

The draft of this chapter was completed by Jacques Cellier, with contributions from Jayme Porto-Carreiro, Jose Luis Guasch, Jose Luis Irigoyen, and Aymeric-Albin Meyer in November 2002. The analyses and suggestions contained in this chapter are based on the international technical experience of the World Bank and are presented as a contribution to the debate and formulation of public policies.

Many interacting factors contribute to the ongoing reorganization of the production and distribution chains and to globalization. Consumer demand for customized products contributes to the expansion of to-order and just-in-time production and direct-delivery distribution technologies. The liberalization of trade and capital flows and the rising education levels in low-income countries contribute to the relocation of production processes, leading to complex global manufacturing chains. Facilitating and promoting these changes are improvements in information technology and the greater speed and reliability of freight transport services, which allow much lower inventory levels.

Globalization is leading to increased world trade, which has doubled over the past 15 years while global output has risen by only about 50 percent. More important, international trade flows are changing rapidly. Many developing countries like Brazil, which used to supply mostly raw materials to industrial countries, are now exporting rapidly growing volumes of manufactured products or components. But these new trade flows are also more volatile, since production processes can be quickly moved to more competitive locations. In deciding on the location of production units, firms increasingly consider trade-offs between the costs of production and the costs of stockholding, transport, and distribution—that is, logistics costs.

A recent study estimates logistics costs in Brazil at about 20 percent of GDP, almost twice the level in OECD countries (figure 1).[1] The same study estimates that logistics costs account for an average 35 percent of industry operating costs in Latin America, ranging from 11 percent for textiles to 60 percent in some food industries. By contrast, logistics costs account for only 20 percent of manufacturing costs in OECD countries, varying from less than 15 percent in the automotive industry to about 30 percent in food industries. Thus there seems to be ample scope for reducing the costs and improving the reliability of logistics systems in the region, particularly in Brazil.

Inventory and warehousing costs are the largest component of logistics costs, accounting for almost 40 percent in the region. Inventory costs are obviously proportional to interest rates, which have remained high in the region, particularly in Brazil. But a study shows that inventory levels in Brazil and many other developing countries are typically twice as high for final products and three times as high for raw materials as in the United States, where inventories are estimated at about 15 percent of GDP (figure 2).[2] The cost to the Brazilian economy of the additional inventory holdings is huge, exceeding 4 per-

---

[1] J. Luis Guasch, ongoing work on logistics in Latin America.

[2] Guasch and Kogan 2000.

cent of GDP at a 15 percent interest rate.[3] The study concludes that the low quality of infrastructure services, particularly transport, is the main cause of the high inventory levels in developing countries.

Figure 1. Logistics costs as a share of GDP

Figure 2. Ratio of inventory levels to U.S. inventory levels

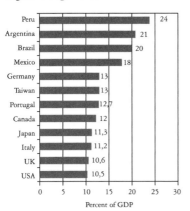

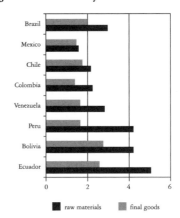

Transport and transshipment costs represent about a third of logistics costs in Latin America. Brazil's domestic freight transport market has in recent decades been dominated by the trucking industry, which is essentially unregulated. There are many informal businesses offering low-quality services, a high incidence of cargo theft, and evidence of overcapacity, with a large share of empty return trips and truckers unable to cover their fixed costs. Moreover, the poor condition of road networks reduces the efficiency and reliability of trucking services, increasing operating costs by 10–30 percent and affecting delivery schedules. A World Bank report estimates the additional cost to the economy at about 2 percent of GDP.[4]

Following their recent restructuring and privatization, railways have been increasing their share of traditional markets (particularly the grain market), boosting productivity, and improving service quality.[5] But with a few exceptions, railways have been unable to compete with truckers in the more lucrative general cargo business or in the long-distance segment. Shipping lines too are increasing their participation in the bulk market along the

---

[3] Newton de Castro 2001.

[4] World Bank, "Brazil: Federal Highway Rehabilitation and Decentralization Project."1997.

[5] World Bank, "Brazil: Federal Railways Restructuring and Privatization Project," 1996.

coast, following the deregulation of the industry and the reform of the ports. But their participation in the general cargo market remains marginal.

The ongoing reform of the ports system has already led to significant reductions in port costs and tariffs. Between 1997 and 2000 port tariffs were reduced by about 50–70 percent in U.S. dollar terms (including the effect of the Real devaluation).[6] And private operators have improved their performance. But labor costs in many Brazilian ports remain substantially higher than those in other ports in the region and elsewhere, and administrative processes and documentation requirements remain cumbersome.

Resolving these issues in the transport system would do much to remove the impediments to providing efficient, reliable multimodal transport services, substantially reducing logistics costs for Brazilian firms. But following the recent waves of privatization in the transport sector, the main issues now relate to government policies and the regulatory framework, which could do more to encourage private operations and investment in transport. There are also some issues specific to multimodal transport, and these too relate to inadequate regulation as well as to a lack of effective arbitration mechanisms. A conservative estimate puts the avoidable logistics costs related to multimodal transport issues in Brazil at more than US$3.2 billion a year.[7]

Administrative costs—including customs, losses, and insurance—account for the remaining 30 percent of firms' logistics costs in the region (figure 3). In OECD countries there is a clear trend toward contracting out logistics to third parties and even entering into long-term strategic alliances with logistics service providers, reducing firms' administrative costs and allowing them to focus on their core business. But in Brazil regulatory issues hamper such a strategy. For firms involved in foreign trade, customs represent a major cost, more than 10 percent of operating costs on average. Brazil's cumbersome customs procedures and practices hamper international trade and regional integration. Little progress has been made in implementing the decisions of the MERCOSUL Council to facilitate regional trade, including agreements to harmonize procedures, standardize forms, and ultimately develop joint customs operations.

Although not part of logistics costs, energy costs also account for an important share of manufacturing costs. And the reliability of power supply is a critical factor in firms' location decisions. This is a particular concern in Brazil, where the power shortage from

---

[6] Geipot and World Bank, A Reforma Portuaria Brasileira", 2001.

[7] World Bank, "Brazil: Multimodal Freight Transport: Selected Regulatory Issues", 1997.

Figure 3. Structure of logistics costs in Latin America

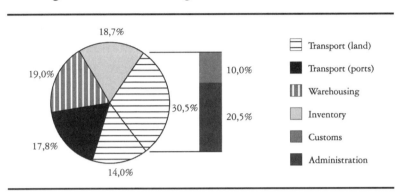

18,7%

19,0%

30,5%

10,0%

20,5%

17,8%

14,0%

Transport (land)

Transport (ports)

Warehousing

Inventory

Customs

Administration

June 2001 to March 2002 led to costs to the economy estimated at almost 1 percent of GDP. The power sector reform initiated in the mid-1990s led to the privatization of about a quarter of the country's generating capacity and two-thirds of its distribution assets, but the vertically integrated Eletrobras system continued to dominate the market. Moreover, while public sector investment was cut drastically, the regulatory framework did not encourage private investment in generation or transmission capacity. As a result energy supply grew by an average of only 3.8 percent a year in 1995–2000, while demand rose by 4.5 percent. And the newly created sector institutions—the regulatory agency, national system operator, and wholesale market—failed to respond effectively to the worsening situation, resulting in the crisis.

Clearly, there is ample scope for improving the efficiency and reliability of logistics and energy supply systems in Brazil. Such improvements could boost competitiveness substantially, since even a relatively small reduction in a product's final price and more reliable delivery schedules can lead to substantial gains in a firm's market share. A modest reduction in logistics costs of, say, 15 percent could reduce firms' costs by about 5 percent on average, which could have a substantial impact on Brazil's economic growth. Because of the large inefficiencies at ports and border crossings, the impact on external trade and regional integration could be even greater. Finally, improvements in the logistics systems and rural infrastructure services in the country's more remote and less developed regions, particularly the North and the Northeast, could substantially increase investment and growth opportunities in these regions and thus help reduce poverty and regional disparities.

Message 1. Building a stable regulatory framework for efficient and equitable provision of infrastructure services

Strengthening the legal and regulatory framework for infrastructure would encourage private investment. Key measures would be to clarify or revise important legal concepts and regulations across infrastructure sectors and to build independent regulatory institutions capable of developing and enforcing effective regulations, designing and supervising concession contracts, ensuring the accessibility and affordability of services for the poor, and increasing regulatory transparency and credibility so as to reduce investors' risks.

Context

Brazil has made rapid progress in bringing the private sector into the provision of infrastructure services. But much remains to be accomplished. The main challenges lie in deepening and sustaining reforms, resolving financing issues for the less attractive concessions, building a sound regulatory framework and effective regulatory agencies, and implementing a consistent, sustainable strategy for improving poor people's access to infrastructure services. The last two have been the major weak links in Brazil's infrastructure reform program.

The legal and regulatory framework for infrastructure has major weaknesses. In general, the law gives disproportionate power and discretion to public authorities. The interpretation of several key legal concepts remains ambiguous, prolonging contract negotiations and increasing transaction costs. Regulatory arrangements are neither transparent nor consistent across sectors and are vulnerable to political interference, leading to numerous disputes and contract renegotiations and wasteful rent seeking. And there is little scope for resolving disputes other than through slow, cumbersome, and unpredictable judicial processes. These weaknesses raise concerns about the stability and credibility of regulations and contracts, substantially reduce private sector interest, and jeopardize the feasibility of many projects.

Regulations can be effective if implemented and enforced by effective institutions. Effective, independent regulatory institutions can reduce actual and perceived investor risks by increasing the transparency, credibility, and predictability of regulations and by helping to settle disputes. They can reduce the likelihood of capture by operators or politicians. They can foster technical, allocative, and dynamic efficiency by safeguarding against monopolistic practices. And they can ensure the sustainability of tariff regimes and concession contracts.

REGULATORY INSTRUMENTS. Most regulatory agencies in Brazil lack adequate regulatory instruments for carrying out their regulatory oversight functions. Several agencies are preparing to reset tariffs in the five-year review, yet they lack cost and financial models for the concessions. Moreover, they have only poor-quality information on the operations of the concessionaires. Regulators need good information on concessionaires' operations, financial transactions, and service activities to carry out their regulatory tasks—not only adjusting tariffs but also performing periodic reviews, establishing detailed quality and technical standards, monitoring compliance with regulatory requirements, imposing penalties for noncompliance, benchmarking performance, resolving disputes between operators and between operators and consumers, and advising the government on policy issues, licensing decisions, and concession design.

Regulatory agencies still need to develop essential instruments for effective regulatory oversight, including:

- TECHNICAL SUPPORT—direct or shared access to a technical unit capable of undertaking the in-depth technical studies required for effective tariff reviews and adjustments
- REGULATORY ACCOUNTING AND INFORMATIONAL STANDARDS—to facilitate the processing of information from operators and the evaluation of concessionaires' performance
- COST AND FINANCIAL MODELS—essential for regulatory oversight, tariff adjustments, evaluation of productivity factors, and the like
- EFFICIENCY AND PRODUCTIVITY MEASUREMENTS—for setting and adjusting tariffs
- BENCHMARKING EXERCISES—with comparable indicators on performance from other operators within and outside Brazil, for the purpose of benchmarking.

CONCESSION DESIGN. Existing concessions are often fragile, particularly in the water, roads, and energy sectors. The fragility results from serious weaknesses in the process for awarding concessions and from key features of the concession contracts—weaknesses stemming largely from the role played by potential concessionaires as advocates for privatization combined with the inexperience and limited resources of those granting concessions, particularly municipal administrations in the water sector. Many concessions are renegotiated within three years of award, often at the expense of consumers. The high incidence of early renegotiation reflects poor concession design, lack of credibility, and weak regulation. Significant improvements are needed in the design of concessions.

Concession contracts could specify the role of the regulatory agency in setting tariffs, establishing and revising standards for service quality and customer care, and monitoring compliance with these standards. They could also clearly specify the agency's powers to demand information and to apply sanctions for noncompliance, including contract termination.

Well-designed concession contracts and bidding procedures can help reduce risks. The usual approach of awarding concessions on the basis of some combination of technical criteria and lowest tariff creates poor incentives and encourages future renegotiation of contracts. A better option is to establish appropriate tariff levels and structures, together with clear rules for adjusting and revising tariffs, before awarding the concession. The concession could then be awarded to the qualified bidder willing to make the highest up-front payment for a prespecified annual concession fee, or on the basis of the highest concession fee for a fixed up-front payment. Qualification criteria should generally relate to bidders' financial capacity, experience, and technical capability. For roads, the minimum present value of revenues is a salient criterion.

Regulators and the concession authority should generally resist the temptation to renegotiate contracts except under clearly defined circumstances. Instead, they should use the regular process of revising tariffs, usually at five-year intervals, to address any issues created by very high or very low rates of return, changes in contractual obligations, and a need to provide better performance incentives.

Appropriate service and performance targets are crucial to good concession design. Concession contracts need to specify targets that are consistent with incentives provided by tariffs. They also need to ensure that the cash flow is not negative for more than two or three consecutive years and to give new operators of large concessions at least two or three years to achieve targets. Concessionaires should not be required to take over existing contracts and programs and should be free to decide how best to achieve the targets.

TARIFF STRUCTURES AND ADJUSTMENTS. Most infrastructure services in Brazil would benefit from a revision of their tariff structure. A good tariff structure creates incentives for users to make efficient decisions about service consumption and for operators to make appropriate decisions on investments. But the tariffs for infrastructure services in Brazil often deviate from an efficient pricing structure. Moreover, these deviations do not appear to be aimed at raising varying amounts of revenue or explicitly linked to equity objectives.

Relying on a two-part tariff and simple block pricing could improve Brazil's tariff structures. The variable part of the tariff could be set close to the marginal cost of producing services, while the fixed part could be set to ensure financial viability, based on appropriate benchmarking. To meet equity objectives, the fixed part could vary according to ability to pay. But the differences should not be so large as to induce customers to leave the system or to discourage potentially desirable customers from locating within the service area.

Tariff adjustments and revisions are often ad hoc and negotiated, with mayors, governors, or ministers having to approve each price increase. As a result prices often drift out of line with costs. The uncertainty causes operators to limit their investments to activities with immediate returns and discourages potential investors. To address this problem, concession contracts could specify clear pricing principles (such as efficiency, equity, simplicity, and financial viability), tariff structures, and procedures for setting and changing prices—and make them public and subject to independent regulation. Critical in implementing such pricing principles and procedures is the use of benchmarking and comparative efficiency analyses. Thus concession contracts should require companies to supply data on such efficiency measures as unit costs, staffing levels, and collection rates.

Brazil's concession law includes a clause guaranteeing the financial equilibrium of concessions under conditions that are not clearly defined. Although applied inconsistently across sectors, the clause has often provided an across-the-board rate of return guarantee, creating a disincentive to increase productivity. The clause has often enabled concessionaires to pass on to consumers almost any cost increase—including those due to their own inefficiency. It would therefore be important to regulate the application of this clause across sectors, possibly restricting it to events that are not under the control of the operator and could not be foreseen at the time of bidding and to scheduled revisions of tariffs. The regulation should also provide clear guidance on the criteria and methodology to be used. The United Kingdom's experience with price cap regulation offers lessons here (box 1).

Box 1. The United Kingdom's experience with price cap regulation

The United Kingdom introduced price cap regulation with the privatization of British Telecom (BT) in 1984 as a temporary scheme. The scheme was to be revised every four years, until competition provided effective consumer protection. It called for adjusting charges annually by the retail price index (to account for inflation) minus a percentage x (to account for expected productivity increases) according to a formula (rpi − x), which was applied to a basket of charges to give the operator some freedom in its price structure. Another formula (rpi − x + y) was used in the privatization of British Gas in 1986, but it was applied to average revenues from sales to small consumers and included an element (y) to pass variation in the costs of gas purchases on to consumers. A third formula was later introduced for water: rpi − x + q, with q equal to the cost of investment needed to meet quality targets.

At the four-year review of BT charges in 1988, the factor x, determining the real annual price reduction, was increased from 3 percent to 4.5 percent to eliminate a potential excess return predicted by the financial model that the regulator had developed in consultation with BT. In other cases, such as regional electricity utilities and the National Grid Company, the scope for reducing costs (and thus the x factors) proved to be substantially underestimated, requiring one-time cuts at the scheduled reviews.

Utilities remain unpopular in the United Kingdom, largely as a result of the high profits made in the early 1990s. But with the lessons of that country's experience and with better information, most experts agree that price cap regulation gives companies an incentive for increasing efficiency while also returning productivity gains to consumers after a short time.

Source: Green 1997.

SERVICES FOR THE POOR. Improving infrastructure services for poor people requires urgent attention. Given the importance of this need, a sectoral approach may be warranted, to ensure a coherent strategy for addressing the issues of subsidies, cost recovery, rural coverage, access, willingness to pay, service delivery mechanisms, regulation, and, most important, sustainability. Options to be explored include introducing subsidies (cross-subsidies or targeted subsidies), using competition based on the lowest required subsidy in allocating rights and obligations to provide new coverage, segmenting services by quality and type, and allowing exclusivity rights in unserved areas.

SECTOR STRUCTURE. Sector structure affects performance through its influence on competitiveness and scale economies. Most affected is telecommunications, where recent merger initiatives are raising concerns about the potential effects on sector performance. Recent mergers and acquisitions may affect performance in the rail and roads sectors as well, and there are also competition issues in the port and shipping subsectors. In the water sector selective agglomeration of municipalities is essential, to allow scale economies and cross-subsidies and thus ensure financial viability. By contrast, in the energy sector, restricting horizontal and vertical integration is more the issue. Across infrastructure sectors there is a need to develop the sector structure most conducive to effective performance and a minimal regulatory burden.

QUALIFIED REGULATORY PROFESSIONALS. The success of a regulatory undertaking depends largely on the competence and experience of the regulatory staff. To develop a corps of highly qualified professionals in all infrastructure sectors, Brazil's regulatory agencies and sector ministries need to formulate or improve policies on staff recruitment, compensation, and development and prepare staff development plans clearly identifying training needs. This is particularly important in the transport sector, where the regulatory agencies have just been established.

To improve the supply of training, the regulatory agencies and sector ministries need to encourage universities, institutes, and training centers to develop and offer appropriate training programs in infrastructure regulation. Some courses have been offered with the World Bank Institute's assistance or as part of sector projects. But permanent programs are essential to ensure the sustainability and effectiveness of regulatory institutions. With distance learning technology, such programs can now more easily bring in international experience. Although each sector ministry should promote sector programs with specialized institutes or centers, coordination across sectors will also be needed, a task that could be assumed by the Secretariat of Planning and Strategic Investment, SPI (MPOG).

Options

1. The federal government could clarify several unclear legal concepts that are applicable across sectors (such as the financial equilibrium clause of the concession law), the regulatory agencies' powers and their relationships with the antitrust agency (CADE) and state regulatory agencies, and the requirements for justifying their decisions.

2. The federal and state regulatory agencies could develop effective regulatory instruments, including cost and financial models and methodologies for measuring and assessing efficiency and productivity (benchmarking), and clearly specify regulatory accounting and informational requirements.

3. Most regulatory agencies could revise tariff structures and more clearly specify pricing principles and rules for adjusting and revising tariffs in concession contracts, including conditions and criteria for applying the financial equilibrium clause.

4. Regulatory agencies could address access and affordability issues for the poor by defining appropriate principles for public service obligations, cross-subsidies or direct and targeted subsidies, alternative technologies, and service delivery mechanisms, including small-scale providers (see message 5).

5. Regulatory agencies could review the design of concessions on the basis of such clearly defined principles and mechanisms, incorporating appropriate clauses in contracts and revising bidding procedures and evaluation criteria accordingly.

6. Regulatory agencies could more closely monitor the structure and performance of their industries, assessing the effects of recent mergers and acquisitions (particularly in energy and transport) and referring competition issues to CADE.

7. Regulatory agencies could mobilize universities and training institutes and use long-distance training technology to develop a corps of well-qualified regulatory professionals.

Message 2. Implementing coordinated strategies for infrastructure and capital market development

Developing the domestic capital market would increase the supply of finance for infrastructure projects—yet the very lack of "bankable" infrastructure projects is delaying the market's development. Brazil could address this dilemma through coordinated strategies for infrastructure and capital market development. The infrastructure strategy could focus on strengthening planning and project finance capacities, to equip sector administrations to prepare pipelines of projects that can be financed by capital markets with little public support. And the capital market strategy could introduce incentives and innovative financial instruments to attract or leverage private funding for infrastructure until the domestic capital market is sufficiently developed.

Context

The government of Brazil estimated that sustaining economic growth of about 4 percent a year would require investment in infrastructure (mostly transport, energy, and telecommunications) of about US$100 billion in 2000–07.[8] In the past Brazil has financed its infrastructure needs primarily through government and official donor support. Facing fiscal constraints and recognizing the inefficiencies associated with state-owned enterprises, Brazil launched a broad infrastructure privatization program in the early 1990s. It started with telecommunications, followed by energy and transport and then water and sanitation.

Private investment in infrastructure increased substantially throughout the 1990s. In particular, foreign direct investment in infrastructure increased from nearly nothing in 1995 to almost US$14 billion in 2000 (figure 4). But much of this was the result of divestitures, with only about US$4 billion going to new investments. With public investment declining sharply, total investment in infrastructure remained fairly constant, at about 2 percent of GDP. Moreover, the Asian crisis brought to light the risk of relying on foreign debt as a major source of funding for infrastructure. Currency devaluations required government and donor bailouts of infrastructure project creditors in most Asian countries. In Brazil most projects were less affected, but many planned projects had to be put on hold. The crisis also highlighted the need for project sponsors to mitigate foreign exchange risk by raising more of their debt financing from domestic capital markets. But the domestic capital market in Brazil, like those in most other developing countries, is characterized by short-term debt financing and high and volatile interest rates—and thus poorly suited for the long-term financing needs of private infrastructure projects.

Figure 4. Net foreign direct investment in Brazil, by sector

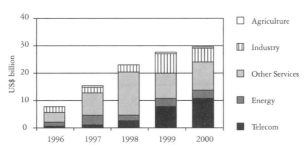

[8] Government of Brazil, Multi-Year Plan (PPA) 2000-2003, and The National Integration and Development Axes Study (the Eixos study).

But one of the most significant obstacles to further development of the domestic capital market is the lack of a pipeline of "bankable" infrastructure projects that would create a consistent demand for domestic financing. The long time needed for project development is inconsistent with the level of detail that the debt markets require to commit capital to a project. Moreover, government-related risks (contract compliance, dispute resolution, tariff and pricing regulation) are generally not sufficiently addressed in the legal and regulatory framework, leading to long negotiations and significant project and financing risks for investors.

STRATEGIC PLANNING. The strategic planning exercise initiated with the Study of National Integration and Development Axes (the Eixos study), which was carried out in 1999 under the coordination of MPOG and BNDES, aimed at formulating a new, spatial development strategy through an innovative "holistic and geo-economic" approach emphasizing environmental sustainability and private participation. The study identified a set of public and private investment opportunities in strategic sectors, focusing on investments that could produce significant synergistic and spillover benefits for the rest of the economy. But a preliminary review of the study by the World Bank identified a number of shortcomings that could be addressed to support effective strategic investment decisions, particularly in infrastructure.[9]

Further work could address the complexity of spatial and sectoral interactions, particularly with respect to the competitive advantages of regions (and countries) and sectors. This would require constructing a consistent analytical framework of relationships for each development axis, to allow reliable assessments of projects' spatial and sectoral impacts. In addition, project cost-benefit analyses should include financial analyses to help promote private participation.

The planning process also needs to address regional integration issues. As noted, the high logistics costs in the region are an important obstacle to the development of regional trade. Beyond coordinating national infrastructure programs, governments need to harmonize infrastructure policies, particularly those relating to regulation and public support for private investment but also customs procedures and transport equipment standards. The Mercosul Council and the recent Initiative for the Integration of the Regional Infrastructure of South America are effective forums for addressing these issues.

---

[9] Castro and Cellier, "The National Axes of Integration and Development Study: A Preliminary Review." 2000.

INFRASTRUCTURE PLANNING AND PROJECT FINANCE CAPACITIES. Sectoral and state planning capacities essentially disappeared during the period of high inflation. Moreover, because of the lack of cost-benefit analysis and project finance experience, there is little incentive for involving the private sector and many obstacles to doing so. And poor project concept or design and inefficient administrative processes extend the project development period, leading to commercial and noncommercial project risks and often making projects unviable for private financing.

To increase private sector participation in financing infrastructure programs, international experience shows, governments need to build effective infrastructure planning units with good project finance experience (box 2). These units could be responsible for developing pipelines of infrastructure projects aimed at maximizing private sector participation by optimizing risk allocation.

Box 2. The United Kingdom's model for developing public-private partnerships

Partnerships UK was established as a private company with a public interest mission: to develop projects in partnership with public entities. Most board members are from the private sector; two are appointed by the Treasury. The wider public interest is represented by an advisory council of key public sector stakeholders. The company's financial targets are set to fulfill its public sector mission while permitting a fair return on capital.

Partnerships UK helps public agencies develop and procure well-structured projects that optimize the allocation of risks among the partners. These projects maximize private funding and build stable relationships between the public and private sectors while saving on development costs. The development costs are generally shared between the public agency and Partnership UK, whose returns are tied to the success of the transaction.

The United Kingdom's experience has inspired similar initiatives in other European countries—such as the PPP Knowledge Center in the Netherlands and the Project Finance Technical Unit of the Economics and Finance Ministry of Italy—as well as in Canada and Japan.

Source: Partnerships UK, 2001

Brazil has taken a first step in this direction with the design of a public-private partnership unit in the Secretariat of Planning and Strategic Investments of MPOG.[10] Some next steps could be:

- Formally establishing the public-private partnership unit in MPOG and promoting the creation of counterpart units in the sector ministries and in the states' planning secretariats
- Preparing several pilot demonstration projects
- Developing pipelines of bankable infrastructure projects.

Given the lack of project finance experience in Brazil, these next steps may require specialized technical assistance and continuous efforts to train a corps of infrastructure planners and project finance specialists.

Once infrastructure projects are prepared, they will need to be effectively promoted among potential investors and financiers. Brazil has already taken steps to do so, beyond the traditional road shows and other conferences. It has created a public-private Internet-based network for promoting investments, *Investe Brasil*, as well as the government site *Infra-estrutura Brasil*. Other possibilities include seeking independent evaluation, rating, or certification of project proposals from recognized independent experts, credit rating agencies.

INNOVATIVE FINANCING INSTRUMENTS TO LEVERAGE PRIVATE FUNDING. The National Economic and Social Development Bank (BNDES) is the primary lender for infrastructure investments in Brazil, providing about US$5–7 billion in loans annually. BNDES has been financing at least part of the project debt on very favorable terms, making it difficult for project sponsors to attract private bank financing. In some cases cofinancing with the International Finance Corporation or Inter-American Development Bank has helped bring syndicate private bank loans (B loans) to close the transactions. Such direct financing has been necessary given the volatile macroeconomic conditions, the government's still small experience in structuring projects for private financing, and the nascent legal and regulatory framework.

---

[10] MPOG, Secretariat of Planning and Strategic Investments, "Brazil PPP Unit, Public Private Partnerships."

With the recent progress in addressing these constraints, however, the government could develop a strategy to gradually move from direct financing to indirect financing and to promote the development of the domestic capital market and private investment in infrastructure. The main domestic source for long-term investment funds is pension fund reserves, which increased from less than R$47 billion in 1994 to almost R$140 billion in mid-2001. Almost half was invested in short-term, fixed income public securities.[11] With interest rates falling, a large share of these resources could gradually move to variable income and private securities, especially if the rules governing pension fund investment were phased out and replaced by a more general "prudent professional" rule. And if there were a significant reduction in the perceived country risk, some of the enormous pension fund reserves abroad could be shifted to profitable long-term investments in Brazil, including in infrastructure.

Different countries have tested a number of instruments and financing facilities for promoting private investment in infrastructure.[12] These instruments include the full range of government guarantees covering political risks (such as government noncompliance with contractual obligations) or commercial risks (tariff rates) or helping to extend debt maturities (credit support). After being tested in pilot projects and implemented case by case, such instruments could be mainstreamed through special-purpose financing facilities offering both credit-enhancing guarantees and direct loans, where needed, to close a transaction. But these instruments and facilities, which would be gradually phased out as domestic capital markets become stronger, would require contingency planning and budgeting. India provides an interesting example of such a strategy (box 3).

---

[11] MPOG, Secretariat of Planning and Strategic Investments, "Long-Term Funding in Brazil: The Infrastructure Case."

[12] Dailami and Klein 1998; Darche 2000.

Box 3. India's Infrastructure Development Finance Company

After providing direct financing for a number of infrastructure projects, the government of India sponsored the establishment of the Infrastructure Development Finance Company (IDFC), a nonbank financing institution to stimulate private investment in infrastructure. Owned mainly by the public sector, IDFC aims to enhance the terms and conditions of funding for infrastructure projects through a broad range of financial instruments and project structures while also seeking market returns on its investments. It also advises the government on effective regulatory reform.

IDFC is managed by a board of three professional and eight part-time directors representing its shareholders. Its main sources of funding are equity provided by the government and multilateral and private entities, subordinated loans from the government and the Reserve Bank of India, and debt, mainly from the domestic market. The government modified regulations governing banks, insurance companies, and pension funds to allow them—and to create incentives for them—to invest in IDFC instruments. Initially targeting its equity investments and direct loans to the more profitable power and telecommunications sectors, IDFC has gradually moved into the riskier transport, water and sanitation, and municipal sectors with indirect instruments (take-out financing, contingent refinancing commitments, put options, bond insurance).

IDFC has faced a number of challenges. Among other things, it had to reconcile its developmental and commercial objectives, and deal with pressures from project sponsors to provide financial guarantees to compensate for the inadequate regulatory framework.

Source: Dailami and Klein, 1998

Options

1.   The federal government could build on the Axes study to effectively assess synergies and tradeoffs between investments in different regions and sectors, and opportunities for and obstacles to private investment. And the federal and state governments could strengthen the Multi-Year Plan (PPA) participatory processes to improve the quality of public spending.

2.   The federal government could establish the proposed public-private partnership unit in MPOG and counterpart units in infrastructure sector ministries, with trained professionals and expert assistance to develop pipelines of bankable infrastructure projects. State governments could establish similar units in their planning secretariats.

3. The federal government could review the obstacles to private investment in infrastructure. In particular, it could review the risks that the private sector is unwilling to take and the regulations governing pension fund investments, and identify appropriate financial instruments and regulations to mitigate those risks and facilitate private funding.

4. The federal government and BNDES could identify several priority infrastructure projects from the PPA strategic programs, assess the risks involved, design the projects and implementation structures, and test appropriate financial instruments to mitigate such risks and maximize private funding.

5. On the basis of the experience with the pilot projects, the federal government and BNDES could eventually mainstream such financial instruments through a temporary program or facility to be phased out once the domestic capital market is well developed.

Message 3. Promoting the development of an integrated multimodal transport system
Policies promoting the development of an integrated multimodal transport system would allow competition among different transport modes (railways, trucking, shipping), increase the efficiency and reliability of logistics services, and help expand interregional trade. Key policies would include further decentralizing the ports and highways sectors, reforming customs, improving regulation of railways and multimodal transport, and promoting investments to build connectivity between transport networks.

Context

HIGHWAY MAINTENANCE. Brazil's federal highway network, totaling about 65,000 kilometers (km), was built from the 1950s to the 1970s and represents a total asset of nearly US$10 billion. It carries most of the country's long-distance traffic. Maintenance has been inadequate for many years, with about 25–30 percent of the network rated in poor condition. The network's poor condition means that road users annually spend an amount equivalent to about three times its replacement value for operating their vehicles.

The fiscal reform of 1988 and the elimination of the road fund substantially reduced the funding for maintenance. And the national highway agency (DNER) proved unable to effectively implement a strategy for network rehabilitation and maintenance in line with the available funding. Moreover, its maintenance policy—contracting out the engineering designs, rehabilitation and other works, and maintenance and supervision services through traditional, input-based contracts—proved ineffective, with procurement and implementation delays leading to numerous design changes, cost increases, and contract modifications. As the agency's management has consisted increasingly of political appointees with little relevant experience, and subject to rapid turnover and to political influence in every operational decision, DNER has seen its execution capacity deteriorate and has been unable to implement the changes needed.

Broad policy and institutional reform was initiated to address these funding, policy, and management issues. The reform had several aims:

- To reclassify the highway network with a view to maintaining under federal jurisdiction only the main interregional and interstate highways of national interest, transferring to state jurisdictions highways of mainly local interest (about 20,000 km)
- To transfer highway sections with sufficient traffic to private concessionaires, who would recover all costs of operation, maintenance, and upgrading directly from road users through tolls (about 10,000 km)
- To contract out rehabilitation works and maintenance services combined on entire routes of the remaining network through long-term (five-year) output-based Rehabilitation and Maintenance Contracts (CREMA), with the contractors responsible for achieving specified levels of service
- To restructure the transport sector administration, terminating DNER and establishing a new national department of transport infrastructure (DNIT) responsible for executing public sector programs, a national agency for land transport (ANTT) responsible for regulating and supervising highway and railway concessions and land transport services, and a national agency for water transport (ANTAQ) responsible for regulating private infrastructure services in that subsector.

The decentralization program has not yet achieved its objective. The proposed law for reclassifying the highway networks, the so-called National Transport Infrastructure System (SNV) law, has stalled in congress on issues that are unrelated to the reclassification and have been resolved with the law for restructuring the sector administration. It is thus important to revise the proposed SNV law and to seek its approval, and, on this basis, to restart negotiations with the states to proceed with the decentralization program. With the SNV law approved, the initial target of transferring about 20,000 km to the states could be achieved in three to four years.

The concession program has made some initial progress. Federal highways totaling about 5,000 km and São Paulo state highways totaling about 2,500 km have been under concession for several years, and road users have generally been satisfied. But optimistic

traffic demand forecasts (and related investment obligations) and generous contract renegotiation rules have led to many contract modifications that may transfer commercial
risks to users. A comprehensive review of the concession bidding and contract documents,
in the light of the Brazilian and international experience, would help correct the main
shortcomings before proceeding with a new phase of the program. Depending on Brazil's
investment rating, a total of 10,000–15,000 km of federal highways could be under concession in the next three to four years.

The new highway rehabilitation and maintenance strategy is being implemented: the first
five CREMA contracts, covering more than 2,000 km, are under way, and about 6,000 km
are expected to be under such contracts by the end of 2002. The government recently
launched a maintenance program (CONSERVAR) based on similar concepts but limited to
emergency maintenance and initial repairs on about 10,000 km under two-year contracts.
Depending on initial results, one option would be to extend the CREMA program to the
entire nonconcessioned, nontransferable federal network (about 30,000 km), feasible over the
next three to four years. The service levels required from the contractors would be determined
on the basis of the resources made available to the sector. An amount of US$300 million a
year over four years would make it possible to nearly eliminate the severe maintenance back-
log accumulated during the previous decades and to maintain this 30,000 km network in
good condition, reducing vehicle operating costs by more than US$500 million annually.

PORT REFORM. The reform of the port sector was initiated in 1990 with the termination of the Portobras holding, which controlled all public port companies. The Port Law
of 1993 defined a new institutional framework emphasizing privatization of operations,
competition, and decentralization. Substantial progress has been made, particularly in privatizing port operations, which has reduced port costs. But some aspects of the reform
remain incomplete, and fully realizing the expected benefits will require resolving a few
important issues: labor redundancy in the ports; issues of decentralization, competition,
regulation, and supervision; and the customs issue.

The operation and maintenance of the major public port terminals have been transferred to private operators, and many private (own account) terminals have been authorized to operate for public use. These changes have substantially reduced port costs. For
example, in Santos, which was the costliest port in Latin America, container handling
costs have dropped from about US$400 to US$180. But the costs remain much higher
than those in European ports like Rotterdam (US$100) and even Buenos Aires (US$120).
Part of the problem is that port labor has not yet been adjusted to account for the mech-
anization of the ports (a significant number of the total workforce of about 35,000 may
be redundant).

Moreover, workers retain excessive advantages in work conditions and compensation (about 65–70 estivadores are paid on a full-container ship at Santos, compared with 15–20 at Buenos Aires and 7–8 at Antwerp). The impact on Brazil's competitiveness and trade is enormous—far greater than the cost of retrenching, retraining, and redeploying the redundant stevedores. But with little competition among terminals, private port operators and labor lack the incentive to resolve the labor issue. Thus an important priority for the government could be to facilitate negotiations between operators and labor unions and possibly to set up a program for retraining and redeploying excess port labor, as the Chilean government recently did (box 4).

Box 4. Chilean port reform

The government of Chile reformed that country's port sector by breaking up the state port company into 10 new state companies, one for each main public port. It offered single operators exclusive concessions for operation, maintenance, and improvement of the main container terminals, replacing the ineffective multioperator system. It designed the bidding process and concession contracts to enhance competition.

The employees of the stevedore companies demanded a return to the old labor licensing system and compensation for any workers laid off by the new concessionaires. The government first argued that this matter had to be settled between the private operators and the labor unions. But after several strikes the government agreed to set up a safety net for workers who would be laid off, including early retirement benefits. The cost of the safety net, equal to about 10 percent of the concession revenues, was negligible compared with the savings on port costs and their effect on external trade and growth. Clearly, the government's intervention in settling the private conflict was well justified by the national interest.

Source: Foxley and Mardones 2000.

The public dock companies have essentially withdrawn from port operations. They have leased terminals to private operators under various bidding procedures and types of contracts and established technical and economic regulations, mainly on an ad hoc basis, with little consistency across ports. But they have not yet reorganized to carry out the port authority functions jointly with the port authority councils, as required by the law. And through their administrative councils, several dock companies remain directly controlled by the Ministry of Transport. To complete the reform as mandated by the law and to promote competition among ports where feasible, the remaining federal dock companies could be transferred to the appropriate state or municipality and all the dock companies could be reorganized and strengthened to effectively carry out their port authority functions. In addition, the regulatory agency (ANTAQ) could establish a set of norms and performance standards for the port authorities and supervise their performance.

CUSTOMS REFORM. Brazil's customs procedures and practices emphasize collecting revenues, intercepting contraband, and producing trade statistics rather than facilitating trade. Some progress has been made with the establishment of a computer-based clearance system (SISCOMEX), initially only for exports, and a number of inland bonded warehouses, and in implementing MERCOSUL agreements for joint customs operations and standardized declaration forms. But customs remain a strong barrier to foreign trade and investment. The progress with SISCOMEX and the MERCOSUL agreements represents a good opportunity for broader reform, which could emphasize the trade facilitation objective, a complete reengineering of clearance procedures, and retraining and redeployment of staff. Also essential would be opening clearance services at major terminals in the interior and at private ports. Mexico provides an example of successful customs reform (box 5).

Box 5. Mexico's customs reform

Following reforms to open the economy and facilitate trade, the government of Mexico undertook broad reform of customs in 1989. The reform gave the Ministry of Finance's Directorate General of Customs the sole mandate for facilitating physical clearance and preventing smuggling. It decentralized customs administration and required tariffs to be paid to commercial banks rather than customs officials. The reform also introduced bonuses for customs staff for meeting productivity targets. And it deregulated the customs broker industry while making irregularities subject to stiff fines.

The reformers streamlined the enormous body of laws and regulations, and publicized the rights and obligations of traders and customs officials to enhance transparency. They simplified customs procedures, reducing the number of steps from 12 to 4. Ports and customs operations are now controlled through interconnected computerized information systems, and shipments are selected for inspection by computer, removing the element of discretion. New inland inspection sites facilitate container transit at ports.

The reform led to savings estimated at 5 percent of the value of trade in the first year—nearly 1 percent of GDP—mainly by reducing transit time (to three days on average) and related inventory and warehousing costs, reducing brokerage fees, and eliminating "undocumented" expenses. Moreover, the collection of customs duties increased by about 15 percent.

Source: The World Bank, Report No. 16361-BR

Regulation of transport services. Although railway and port operations have been privatized for some time, and major highways concessioned to private operators, the regulatory agencies for land and for water transport were established only in February 2002. As a result the regulatory agencies are not yet fully operational, and many regulatory issues, some long anticipated, have not yet been resolved. The main issues include technical regulations for captive user rates, interrailroad traffic and related access pricing, and reversible assets at the end of the concession; supervision of port terminal concessions; gaps and excesses in information requirements; unclear rules for contract renegotiation and other issues relating to concession models; and anticompetitive behavior, ownership concentration, and vertical integration.

Progress has been made in removing restrictions on entry into coastal shipping and multimodal transport and on inland circulation of containers. But many regulations remain that restrict competition, including restrictions on foreign capital in road transport and coastal shipping, the cargo reservation agreement with Argentina, and restrictions on international transit by trucks.

Because of the lack of regulatory experience in Brazil, building up the regulatory agencies will require extensive support in training staff, refining organizational structures, formulating regulatory and supervision strategies, developing regulatory instruments and procedures and information systems, and the like. But there has been much analysis of the technical regulatory issues,[13] and after joint review and discussion of the proposals, the regulatory agencies could proceed rapidly with implementation.

The problems relating to the concession models—such as the geographic structure of the railway network and the economic and financial equilibrium clause of the concession law—suggest that the new agencies should reassess these models before proceeding with new projects or with the planned renegotiation of existing contracts. In addition, initial work on the ownership concentration issues in railway and highway concessions needs to be reviewed and completed by the regulatory agencies to assess the need for involving the antitrust agency (CADE).

Fostered by regional trade bloc initiatives (Mercosul, the North American Free Trade Area, the Latin American Integration Association) and by agricultural and industrial growth in the interior of Brazil, trade within and among regions has expanded rapidly, requiring important changes in transport systems. To provide efficient, comprehensive

---

[13] World Bank, "Brazil: Public-Private Partnerships in Transport Infrastructure—Progress and Challenges."

logistics services to agricultural, industrial, and commercial shippers, freight carriers will have to find innovative multimodal transport solutions that maximize productivity and service quality. That will require much better integration of the transport systems.

Some progress has been made in integrating the privatized railroads and port terminals. But there is still a need to define and enforce rules for effective multimodal transport operations. Such rules would clearly define the responsibilities of the multimodal transport operator (OTM) with respect to individual carriers, establish effective conflict resolution mechanisms, promote the standardization of equipment and of electronic data systems, and encourage the establishment of Internet-based freight marketplaces.

ELIMINATION OF TRANSPORT BOTTLENECKS TO IMPROVE CONNECTIVITY. A pipeline of transport infrastructure projects was identified under the PPA planning process supported by the Axes study and some public consultations. Despite its shortcomings, the Axes study, whose assessment of investment opportunities focused particularly on bottlenecks and missing links between development axes, could be usefully updated and built on to provide a basis for prioritizing sector investment programs and projects.

A particularly important priority could be improving the connectivity of the freight railway networks. A recent economic analysis of the freight railroad industry shows that physical and regulatory constraints to their connectivity are key obstacles to increasing their competitiveness and market shares in the long-distance segment, which in turn is critical for ensuring their long-term viability and for developing efficient multimodal transport and logistics services.[14] Resolving the critical bottlenecks, particularly in the São Paulo metropolitan region, and building some important missing links and intermodal terminals, will require effective partnerships between governments (federal, state, municipal), operators, and major shippers.

The Ministry of Transport and its agencies could develop the capacity to prepare a pipeline of such public-private transport infrastructure projects, in line with the priorities defined under the Axes study and with a government strategy for supporting public-private partnerships in infrastructure. Projects could include appropriate risk mitigation instruments where necessary to promote private sector management and financing (see the previous section). It is expected that priority would be given to critical transport infrastructure projects in major interregional corridors, particularly to ensure connectivity. But

---

[14] Newton de Castro 2002.

the many tradeoffs—such as between investing in the highly congested corridors in the Southeast and investing in the corridors leading to the poorest regions in the North and the Northeast—could be analyzed under the Axes study, with the government support strategy adjusted accordingly.

Options

1. The federal government could complete the restructuring of the transport sector administration by supporting appropriate staffing, operation, and funding of DNIT, ANTT, and ANTAQ; reorganizing the Ministry of Transport and strengthening its policy formulation and strategic planning functions; and liquidating the Federal Railway Company (RFFSA), the North-South Railway Company (VALEC), and the Brazilian Urban Train Company (CBTU).

2. ANTT could revise the concession design and bidding process, taking into account domestic and international experience, and complete appropriate feasibility studies, the federal government could consider concessioning major federal highway corridors to private operators.

3. The federal government could seek the approval of congress for a revised SNV law and then restart negotiations with state governments for decentralizing federal highways of mainly local interest.

4. DNIT could proceed with contracting the operation and maintenance of the remaining federal highways through performance-based contracts, improving the contract design and bidding process on the basis of the experience with the pilot contracts. And it could strengthen its network planning, management, supervision, and audit functions.

5. State governments and highway agencies could experiment with performance-based contracts for the maintenance of their networks and, drawing on the experience in Rio Grande do Sul and Goias, decentralize the maintenance of rural roads to municipalities or intermunicipal consortia.

6. The federal government could facilitate negotiations between port operators and labor unions and, if necessary, provide financing for the retrenchment, retraining, and redeployment of excess labor in the ports.

7. The federal government could delegate the remaining federally controlled public ports to states and municipalities under clearly defined conditions.

8. ANTAQ could develop norms and performance standards for the port authorities, provide assistance for their reorganization and strengthening, and supervise their performance.

9. ANTAQ could assess the costs and benefits of opening the coastal shipping market to foreign firms and of renegotiating the cargo reservation agreement with Argentina.

10. The federal government could reform customs, reengineering clearance procedures and opening clearance services at major inland sites and private ports to facilitate trade.

11. ANTT could clarify and enforce railway regulations, particularly those relating to captive user rates, interrailroad traffic, reversible assets, and line abandonment. It could also review ownership concentration issues and seek solutions to connectivity and access issues in the upcoming contract renegotiations.

12. ANTT could clarify and enforce rules for multimodal transport operations, including those relating to conflict resolution and standardization of equipment, and promote measures to facilitate the border transit of trucks and railcars.

13. ANTT and ANTAQ could clarify and enforce information requirements and contract renegotiation rules for all concessions, leases, and permits for service provision, and develop appropriate regulatory instruments and supervision and performance monitoring capabilities, including effective staff training programs.

14. ANTT, ANTAQ, and the Ministry of Transport could jointly establish a transport planning and project finance group or network with expertise in developing and structuring transport infrastructure projects for implementation and financing by the private sector with minimum public support.

15. The federal government's funding priorities in the sector could be:
    - A program for the rehabilitation and maintenance of the nonconcessioned federal highway network through performance contracts
    - Transport infrastructure projects that would resolve critical infrastructure bottlenecks and improve connectivity within and between transport modes—and thus improve the competitiveness of railroads and inland or coastal shipping in long-distance freight and allow efficient multimodal alternatives to trucking
    - Among these projects, those for which public funds or guarantees could leverage substantial private financing.

Message 4. Completing the reform of the energy sector
Completing the reform of the energy sector, revising regulations to restore incentives, and strengthening energy regulatory agencies would all help ensure an efficient and reliable energy supply. These policies would involve correcting the power pricing system and contracting structure, normalizing the functioning of the wholesale electricity market, introducing competition in gas supply, and mainstreaming successful demand management and energy conservation initiatives.

Context

Brazil's power sector is unique in that hydroelectric power accounts for 90 percent of the generation portfolio. Historically, generation and transmission were the responsibility of the federal company Eletrobras, while distribution was handled largely by state utilities. In 1995 Brazil initiated reform aimed at the vertical unbundling and privatization of the sector. Because of political resistance, the unbundling was never completed, and 58 percent of national generating capacity remains in the hands of vertically integrated Eletrobras subsidiaries. Still, 23 percent of generation assets and 64 percent of distribution assets were successfully privatized. The government also introduced an independent system operator (ONS) to dispatch generating plants on the basis of cost, and a new regulatory agency (ANEEL) to supervise the sector. Parallel reforms in the upstream gas market ended the legal monopoly of Petrobras, though in the absence of any structural reforms competition has been slow to develop.

Failures in implementing the new sector model ultimately led to the recent energy crisis. While the drought undoubtedly played an important part, the fundamental causes can be traced to regulatory deficiencies and pricing distortions created during the transition to the new power sector model. They also reflect a wider failure to implement the complete package of sector reforms as originally conceived. That has left the power industry in an awkward position between a centralized state-controlled sector and a privatized competitive market.

An analysis of the energy crisis reveals two important underlying causes of the current situation. Addressing these is critical for restoring the normal functioning of the system.

First, the pricing system has made financing new generating capacity, particularly thermal plants, extremely unattractive. There are several important problems: Natural gas can be obtained only through restrictive, dollarized take-or-pay contracts offered by Petrobras, the sole importer of gas from Bolivia. The regulated price cap allowing distributors to pass energy purchase costs through to customers is said to be significantly lower than the true long-run marginal cost of developing new plants and compensates only partially for exchange rate movements. Because of the low short-run marginal cost of operating hydroelectric plants, thermal energy is dispatched only occasionally and the resulting income stream is too erratic to cover capital costs or the gas supply contracts.

Second, the contracting structure provides inadequate incentives for generators and distributors to ensure a reliable supply of energy to end users. Although both were aware of the impending supply crisis, neither chose to respond by trying to develop additional sources of power. Distributors had 100 percent of their load covered and no way to cover the costs of contracting additional energy supply margins. Moreover, because of the pricing problems, merchant plants had no incentive to enter the market.

Once the normal functioning of the sector is restored, the next step would be to correct remaining structural problems. Resolving the pricing and incentive problems is a fundamental prerequisite for moving toward the long-term vision for the sector and will also help restore the sector's normal functioning. But realizing the full potential of the power sector reform will require completing the original package of institutional and structural reforms. Two key concerns persist.

First, the modest progress in unbundling the power sector has left the generation sector dominated by publicly owned Eletrobras subsidiaries. Together, these control 58 percent of capacity, preventing the development of effective competition. Moreover, although no longer a legal monopoly, Petrobras continues to dominate the upstream market for gas supply.

Second, the new regulatory and oversight institutions created by the reforms are not yet functioning adequately. There are important issues relating to the coordination of efforts and clarification of jurisdictions between policymakers and regulators, on both the economic and the environmental side. Concerns also remain about the governance structure of the independent system operator. In addition, during the reforms the sector has lost a critical mass of technical experts needed to support the development and implementation of energy policy.

Completing the energy sector reform could require focusing on the following priorities (figure 5).

Figure 5. The next steps in power sector reform

Power crisis *Dysfunctional sector* (December 2001)	Short term *Functional sector* (2002)	Medium term *Optimal sector* (2003 — 04)	Long-term vision
Major energy supply crisis with 20 % rationing	Resolve immediate crisis and related disputes	Reform functioning of wholesale power market	Universal access to reliable electricity service
Major financial disputes over compensation for crisis	Restore normal functioning of wholesale power market	Resolve problems with policy and regulatory bodies	Efficient and competitive market for generation
Complete paralysis of new wholesale power market	Correct distortions in electricity tariffs	Complete unbundling of vertically integrated utilities	Private sector operation and financing of new capacity
Electricity tariffs that do not reflect economic costs	Raise electricity tariffs toward cost-covering levels	Take measures to reduce market power in generation	Impartial administration of transmission network
Private sector unwilling to invest in new generation	Introduce incentives for reliable energy supply	Privatize remaining public generation assets	Transparent, consistent, and accountable regulation
Needs of rural and urban poor not fully integrated	Take measure to protect urban and rural poor	Expand coverage of electricity in rural areas	Well-resourced, effective policymaking body

REGULATORY REFORM. At the core of the reform program are a series of tariff reforms designed to remove the distortions that now discourage private investment. In particular, generation and distribution tariffs need to be overhauled to move them toward cost-covering levels and remove distortions affecting the behavior of power utilities. Equally important is to introduce an effective system of incentives to ensure that distributors provide reliable energy supply to their customers. Finally, there is a need to address shortcomings in the framework for environmental regulation that are preventing the timely and consistent application of environmental licensing procedures.

MARKET REFORM. The success of the new power sector model will depend on efficient wholesale markets for both electricity and gas (the critical input for thermal generation). A crucial first step will be to normalize the functioning of the electricity wholesale market, which has been unable to settle any transactions since its inception in September 2000. Complementary measures would be to improve the governance of the independent system operator and to correct significant biases that have crept into the dispatch model. Another would be to introduce greater competition in gas supply and to diversify the contractual options for gas purchase. Scandinavia provides an interesting example of a competitive wholesale power market (box 6).

Box 6. The Eltermin market: hedging risk in the spot market for power

Opponents of power sector reform in Scandinavia claimed that excessive price volatility made it impossible to implement a competitive wholesale power market in the Nordic area. The competition would lead to excessive concern with profit margins, which in a power system that is 60 percent hydro (and, in Norway, nearly 100 percent hydro) would lead to unmanageable price fluctuations. The opponents of reform were proved wrong. The creation of Eltermin, a financial market, provided effective instruments for hedging price risks.

The power sector reform led to Nord Pool, the world's first multinational commodity exchange for electricity. Established in 1993, Nord Pool is owned by the two national grid companies, Statnett SF in Norway (50 percent) and Svenska Kraftnät in Sweden (50 percent). The four countries served by Nord Pool have generating capacity totaling almost 400 terawatt-hours. Transactions can be conducted through Nord Pool's electronic trading system or by telephone bidding. Settlement and delivery are carried out as financial price-hedging settlements with no physical delivery of electricity.

Market participants trade financial contracts for base-load electricity covering periods from one day to three years. All contracts are settled against the reference price (system price) provided by Elspot, the Nord Pool physical market. The contracts listed on the financial market are futures, forwards, and options.

Futures are listed for shorter delivery periods (days, weeks, and blocks), and forwards for longer delivery periods (seasons and years). Futures contracts have daily cash settlement, while with forward contracts the profit (or loss) accumulates until the delivery period.

Since the financial contracts have the system price as their underlying price, and market participants take physical delivery at the price in their area, which differs from the system price because of transmission constraints, demand arose for an instrument allowing a perfect hedge. Nord Pool responded by listing the contract for difference, a forward on the difference between the system price and the different area prices.

Options contracts can be used to insure a power portfolio against price declines or increases. Combining options and forward contracts offers greater opportunities for dealing with the risks associated with power trading.

The annual turnover of contracts traded at Nord Pool represents 200 percent of the spot market turnover. But financial contracts are not traded only at Nord Pool; independent brokers also intermediate financial instruments.

Source: Nord Pool

INSTITUTIONAL REFORM. The incomplete reforms left structural problems both within the sector and among the government institutions that oversee it. Correcting the institutional framework will require completing essential groundwork, including an independent assessment of the performance of regulatory agencies and the design of a mechanism for appealing regulatory decisions. Also needed are interim measures to prevent the abuse of market power arising from vertical integration.

ENVIRONMENTAL SUSTAINABILITY. Although Brazil has a sound framework for environmental regulation, shortcomings in the institutional framework prevent its timely and consistent application, obstructing private investment in the sector. Remedying these problems will require designing a series of interventions. In addition, efforts to maintain the balance between energy demand and supply should focus not only on expanding supply but also on managing demand.

UNIVERSAL ACCESS. Among the shortcomings of the sector reform is that it gave distribution concessionaires complete discretion in determining tariff discounts for low-income urban consumers and formulating rural electrification plans. Introducing a sound, consistent set of principles and eligibility rules for low-income tariff discounts would protect poor urban consumers. And defining a coherent strategy for rural electrification, with clear targets for each operator, would ensure that service reaches the rural poor within 2–10 years, depending on the region.

Options

1. The federal government and ANEEL could proceed with economic regulatory reforms—in particular, revising the generation and distribution tariffs to ensure appropriate cost-recovery and restore incentives for reliable energy supply.
2. The federal government and ANEEL could establish efficient wholesale energy markets by normalizing the functioning of the electricity market, improving the governance of the independent system operator, and introducing competition and diversified contractual options for gas supply.
3. The federal government could correct the sector's institutional framework once essential groundwork is completed, including an independent assessment of the performance of the regulatory agencies and the design of a mechanism for appealing regulatory decisions.

4. ANEEL and the antitrust agency (CADE) could review recent mergers and acquisitions and address the potential for abuse of market power arising from vertical integration.
5. The federal government and ANEEL could promote energy conservation and demand management by mainstreaming successful initiatives.
6. The federal and state governments and ANEEL could formulate coherent strategies for rural electrification and introduce appropriate regulations to ensure the accessibility and affordability of electricity for the poor.

Message 5. Improve access to local infrastructure services for the poor
A renewed focus on local infrastructure can help restore sustainable growth, reduce poverty, and promote social inclusion. Well-targeted, decentralized, output-based programs and pro-poor regulation of privately provided services could improve access to local infrastructure services for the poor and increase the effectiveness and sustainability of public infrastructure programs.

Context
The recent national census shows that only 19 percent of Brazilians—32 million—live in rural areas. But that is only because a 1938 law decreed that all municipal centers would be considered urban areas. Under the OECD definition of rural areas as those with less than 150 inhabitants per square kilometer, 43 percent of Brazilians—about 74 million—live in rural areas. A large share of these, an estimated 20–25 million, do not live near all-weather roads and therefore have only limited access to markets, off-farm jobs, and social services. An estimated 2–4 million rural households lack access to electricity and are thus unable to conserve perishable food or irrigate their fields. And most rural households lack access to safe, potable water and to sewerage or septic tanks, making them vulnerable to disease (see the Water Supply, Sanitation, and Pollution Note). If Brazil is to achieve its poverty reduction objective, the rural poor must gain greater access to water, transport, electricity, and telecommunications.[15]

Government and World Bank surveys and reports on rural poverty show that the rural poor consider the lack of adequate infrastructure services a major cause of the poor qual-

---

[15] For a discussion of irrigation issues, see the Water Resource Management Note, and for a discussion of water and sanitation issues, the Water Supply, Sanitation, and Pollution Management Note.

ity of their livelyhoods and an important factor in the decision of young adults to migrate to cities. They tend to identify rural transport, electricity, and irrigation as the most critical services, since the lack of, or poor quality of, these services leads to low productivity on their small farms, undermines the competitiveness of their products, and limits their access to education, health care, markets, and other services (see the Rural Development Note). The lack of reliable rural transport reduces children's school attendance and undermines the efficiency and quality of education (since it requires establishing many small schools in isolated rural communities, often with unqualified teachers, rather than one good school). It also restricts the access of adults, particularly women, to jobs in urban centers and the access of rural landless workers *(boias-frias)* to farm jobs.

DECENTRALIZED AND PARTICIPATORY PLANNING AND MANAGEMENT OF PUBLIC PROGRAMS. The design and implementation of public infrastructure programs have traditionally been highly centralized in Brazil. Federal and state programs are generally prepared sector by sector and managed by federal ministries or state secretariats, with little or no involvement of or consultation with municipal governments, the business community, or local beneficiaries. As a result there is a multiplicity of public programs with little coordination among the three levels of government and even among the sector programs of the same government. And a lack of spatial coordination among public sector programs has led to poor results on the ground and inefficient use of public resources.

Recent analytical work in Brazil and elsewhere[16] emphasize the need to address these issues through:

- An integrated, multisectoral strategy to improve the delivery of basic infrastructure services while also strengthening ecosystem and water resources management, improving education, establishing effective social safety nets, and reforming land, labor, and capital markets
- Greater spatial focus and coordination of programs, concentrating infrastructure investments in areas with clear potential for environmentally sustainable development and building on rural-urban and public-private synergies
- Decentralization coupled with institutional strengthening at the local level and appropriate mechanisms for community participation, all aimed at ensuring effective delivery of public infrastructure services

---

[16] World Bank, World Development Report, Rural Poverty Strategy, and "LAC Region Action Plan for Rural Development."

- Output-based rather than input-based funding of local infrastructure programs, to provide incentives for efficiency and results on the ground.

In particular, there is a need to decentralize the planning and management of public programs, increasing public consultation and private sector participation and strengthening the capacity of municipalities and communities to participate in the process. Many experiments offer lessons in this area, most notably the participatory budget process in Rio Grande do Sul and the associations of municipalities created in Parana. There are also interesting experiments in the North and the Northeast. In Tocantins' southeastern and northern regions, for example, pilot projects set up and train municipal and regional development forums to promote public-private partnerships and effective community participation in elaborating local and regional agendas for sustainable integrated development. State governments could base their decentralization strategies on such experiments and implement them along with monitoring and evaluation systems. The federal government could provide appropriate incentives through such federal programs as the Projeto Alvorada by increasingly linking funding to results rather than to inputs.

INFRASTRUCTURE AND SUSTAINABLE DEVELOPMENT STRATEGIES. Infrastructure investments can have big impacts on local and regional development, but these impacts are not always positive. Building or upgrading roads in isolated, undeveloped areas can increase migration and settlement, and using land and other natural resources in ways that may not be sustainable can lead to irreversible degradation of the resources, upsetting sensitive ecosystems and the lives and cultures of indigenous peoples (see the Natural Resource Management and Rural Development Notes). The Polonoroeste Program, which paved the BR-364 highway and constructed feeder road networks in the states of Mato Grosso and Rondonia in the early 1980s, provides an unfortunate example of such impacts. But it also offers interesting lessons for the formulation of regional development policy.

To promote sustainable development, infrastructure programs must be designed and implemented as part of a clear strategy for local and regional development. And they must be complemented by effective policies, programs, incentives, and regulations to promote the sustainable use of land and natural resources, the protection of indigenous and other vulnerable peoples, and the conservation of fragile ecosystems and biodiversity. Progress has recently been made in some states, particularly Tocantins and Mato Grosso, in formulating such sustainable development policies *(políticas de gestão e ordenamento territorial)* and in designing the key instruments for implementing them.

An important public policy instrument is economic-ecological zoning (ZEE). By integrating a broad range of variables and the views of local populations through a participatory process, ZEE identifies possible uses of land and other natural resources that are economically, ecologically, and socially sustainable or acceptable. It also identifies areas that should be protected for purposes of conserving the environment or biodiversity or promoting development for indigenous peoples. Together with socioeconomic maps, ZEE constitutes an essential framework for planning and designing local and regional public infrastructure programs. But infrastructure programs, particularly those in less developed regions, should be complemented by economic instruments (such as taxes and incentives) to guide private sector actors away from unsustainable activities and toward sustainable ones, effectively enforced regulations that restrict certain activities or uses of land and natural resources, and campaigns to inform and mobilize local communities.

RURAL ROAD MAINTENANCE. Most rural municipalities lack any capacity to maintain their roads. State governments provide some assistance, allocating road maintenance crews and equipment to the maintenance of municipal roads while the municipalities contribute fuel and crew per diems. But these arrangements, decided centrally case by case and on the basis of political considerations, are inefficient: they affect the work of the state road agencies on the state networks and generally have limited results.

More permanent solutions are needed for municipal roads. Several states are testing alternative policies and programs, including strengthening municipalities' road maintenance capacity by training engineers and road crews (Rio Grande do Sul), establishing intermunicipal road consortia (Parana) or a municipal road maintenance division in the state road agency (Bahia), contracting out maintenance activities on the state network and transferring state road staff, equipment, and know-how to intermunicipal associations (Goias), and establishing a dedicated road fund through higher road user taxes (Mato Grosso, Goias). The lessons from these experiments should be systematically disseminated, perhaps through the Association of State Road Agencies or the state associations of municipalities.

Efficient municipal road strategies would upgrade the most important municipal roads, identified through participatory mechanisms, to all-weather condition by having local contractors build (standardized) bridges and culverts and maintain a network of roads to minimum levels of service permitting all-weather access to municipal centers.

The effects of such rural road programs on economic growth and on the quality of life of the rural poor have been well documented.[17]

RURAL ELECTRIFICATION. Power utilities, whether public or private, generally have poorly defined service obligations. By law, they are responsible for expanding the grid in their territory and for bearing the costs. But in practice, they do not have explicit targets for reaching households without access, and customers pay most of the connection costs. Utilities lack incentives to invest in rural electrification and to make efficient choices between alternative technologies. Some states, such as Tocantins, fund part of the investment in rural electrification. But the inability of poor people in remote areas to pay their share of the connection costs has impeded grid expansion. A special federal program, *Luz no Campo* (Light in the Country) is helping to bridge some of the financial gaps, but funding under such programs has been a recurrent problem.

To resolve this situation, ANEEL is seeking agreements with concessionaires on universal access plans with explicit targets and timetables. But concessionaires, which have a right to maintain a financial balance and often have little interest in serving poor consumers, are trying to recover more than their already high costs of new connections. Another option might be to work with small-scale providers—entrepreneurs, cooperatives, or nongovernmental or community-based organizations—which are generally more responsive to the needs of poor consumers.[18] They could improve affordability by using cheaper technologies, including mini-grids or even household solar panels. A recent law allowing the government to grant subconcessions in areas where the existing concessionaire fails to achieve its service obligations might facilitate this option.

Options

1. Through the Multi-Year Plan (PPA) process, the federal and state governments could consolidate and integrate their many programs for local and regional development, harmonizing objectives, criteria, and incentives; emphasizing output-based funding and private provision of local infrastructure services; and improving the targeting of programs to the poor and to areas with proven potential for sustainable development.

---

[17] World Bank, Operations Evaluation Department 1998.
[18] Baker and Trémolet 2000.

2. The federal and state governments could decentralize the planning and management of public programs, promoting effective community participation and public-private partnerships in elaborating and implementing local and regional agendas for sustainable development.

3. The state governments could effectively integrate their regional development, environmental management, and public infrastructure strategies through economic-ecological zoning and appropriate economic incentives and regulatory instruments for sustainable development.

4. Using appropriate incentives, the federal and state governments could strengthen the capacity of municipal governments or promote associations of municipalities (or both), enabling them to gradually assume responsibility for contracting, regulating, and supervising the delivery of public infrastructure services.

5. The state governments could assist municipalities or associations of municipalities in building the capacity for upgrading essential rural roads to all-weather conditions and maintaining adequate levels of service, increasingly through performance-based contracts with local contractors.

6. The federal and state regulatory agencies could clarify the public service obligations and tariff setting rules in concession contracts with utilities, particularly as they relate to universal access and affordability of service for the poor, and strengthen their supervision of utilities' compliance.

7. The state governments or regulatory agencies could experiment with small-scale service providers, which tend to be more responsive to the needs of the poor and more likely to provide affordable services by using alternative technologies.

References

World Bank projects under implementation

- Energy Efficiency Project *(Projeto de Conservação de Energia Elétrica – PROCEL)*. US$ 43.4 million. Approved on October 5, 1999.
- Energy Sector Reform Project *(Projeto de Reforma do Setor de Energia)*. US$400 million. Approved on June 23, 2002.
- Federal Highway Rehabilitation and Decentralization *(Projeto de Reabilitação e Descentralização das Rodovias Federais)*. US$ 300 million. Approved on June 12, 1997.

- Goias State Highway Management Program (Programa de Gerenciamento da Malha Rodoviaria do Estado de Goias), First Phase. US65 million. Approved on August 23, 2001.
- Rio Grande do Sul State Highway Management Project *(Projeto de Gerenciamento da Mallha Rodoviaria do Estado do Rio Grande do Sul)*. US$70 million. Approved on May 15, 1997

World Bank reports

This chapter summarizes the content of the following World Bank reports. Those, in turn, draw heavily from a wide range of literature on the subject from experts in Brazil and beyond, which are referenced in the mentioned Bank reports.

World Bank. 2000. "Brazil: Public-Private Partnerships in Transport Infrastructure—Progress and Challenges." Report No. 20702-BR. 2 vols. Washington, D.C.

World Bank. 2002. World Development Report. New York: Oxford University Press.

World Bank. 1996. "Brazil: Federal Railways Restructuring and Privatization Project." SAR No. 15580-BR. Washington, D.C.

World Bank. 1997. "Brazil Multimodal Freight Transport: Selected Regulatory Issues" Report No. 16361-BR. Washington, D.C.

World Bank. 2000. "LAC Region Action Plan for Rural Development." Washington, D.C.

World Bank. 1997. "Brazil: Federal Highway Rehabilitation and Decentralization Project." SAR No.16425-BR Washington, D.C.

World Bank. 2001. Rural Poverty Strategy. Washington, D.C.

World Bank, Operations Evaluation Department. 1998. "Feeder Roads in Brazil." OED Precis No. 160. Washington, D.C.

Other references

Baker, Bill, and Sophie Trémolet. 2000. *"Micro Infrastructure."* Viewpoint 220. World Bank, Private Sector and Infrastructure Network, Washington, D.C.

Castro, Newton de. 2001. "Freight Transportation and Logistics in Brazil: An Overview." UFRJ, Rio de Janeiro

Castro, Newton. de. 2002. *"Estrutura, Desempenho e Perspectivas do Transporte Ferroviario de Carga."* UFRJ, Rio de Janeiro

Dailami, Mansoor, and Michael Klein. 1998. "Government Support to Private Infrastructure Projects in Emerging Markets." Policy Research Working Paper 1868. World Bank, Washington, D.C.

Darche, Benjamin. 2000. "Local Capital Markets and Private Infrastructure Development: Global Best Practice Review." Public-Private Infrastructure Advisory Facility (PPIAF), Washington, D.C.

Foxley, Juan, and Jose Luis Mardones. 2000. "Port Concessions in Chile." Viewpoint 223. World Bank, Private Sector and Infrastructure Network, Washington, D.C.

Geipot and World Bank. 2001. *"A Reforma Portuaria Brasileira."* Washington, D.C.

Green, Richard. 1997. "Has Price Cap Regulation of UK Utilities Been a Success?" Viewpoint 132. World Bank, Private Sector and Infrastructure Network, Washington, D.C.

Guasch, J. Luis, and Joseph Kogan. 2000. "Inventories in Developing Countries: Levels and Determinants—A Red Flag for Competitiveness and Growth." Policy Research Working Paper 2552. World Bank, Washington, D.C.

MPOG, Secretariat of Planning and Strategic Investments. "Brazil PPP Unit, Public Private Partnerships." Position paper. Brasilia

MPOG, Secretariat of Planning and Strategic Investments. "Long-Term Funding in Brazil: The Infrastructure Case." Brasilia

6

Private Sector Development

6

Private Sector Development

Introduction

With an especially entrepreneurial population, the private sector holds the key to Brazil's transformation as an advanced, and vibrant economy over the next 25 years. In great measure the private sector produces the economy's goods and services, undertakes the investments, generates the employment, and is accordingly the driving force behind the economy's growth and poverty reduction. Indeed, a central objective in encouraging the development of the private sector is to spur the country's socio-economic development. Other institutions, including government, are complementary in efficiently supporting broad-based progress.

Certain contributors to a vibrant private sector are treated in other chapters. Most important among these is macroeconomic stability. Reforms to the tax system and within the financial sector complement macro stability to form what is taken here to be the overall enabling environment for the private sector. Against this background the present chapter discusses public-sector administrative requirements of companies, cross-sector regulatory issues, labor market regulations and institutions as they pertain to companies, property rights, trade policy, industrial policy, and regional policy. These areas interact strongly with macroeconomic, tax, and financial policies, and without the appropriate conditions in these three areas the private sector cannot be expected to flourish.

The draft of this chapter was completed by Bill Tyler in November 2002. The analyses and suggestions contained in this chapter are based on the international technical experience of the World Bank and are presented as a contribution to the debate and formulation of public policies.

Options for improving the environment for private sector development are presented below and discussed in this note.

The public sector sets the rules and ideally provides a conducive environment for investment. Therefore, the public sector plays a crucial supporting role through public governance and economic policies. An unsupportive policy environment can stifle private sector development and with it the growth of the economy. There are limits on what the government can do in a modern economy. But there are also lessons on what it might not do.

Over the past 30 years many countries have struggled to redefine the role of the government in the economy. Brazil has been one of those countries. In this redefinition the government would provide:

- Public goods (which the private sector cannot, or has little incentive, to provide, such as national and personal security, property rights, public health)
- Market interventions to remedy clearly demonstrated market failures (such as environmental degradation or preservation and abuse of monopoly)
- Macroeconomic stability
- Distributional equity (which, depending upon social norms, is unlikely to be guaranteed through the functioning of market forces).

The policy environment for the private sector has been vastly improved in recent years. Some lingering problems remain. Some of these are discussed in other Policy notes (macroeconomic vulnerability, distortions and complexities in tax policies, and distortions in the financial sector). Others are discussed here, drawing on international experience on how to strengthen public governance in areas pertinent to the private sector, such as contract enforceability (figure 1).

Figure 1. International comparison of governance measurements

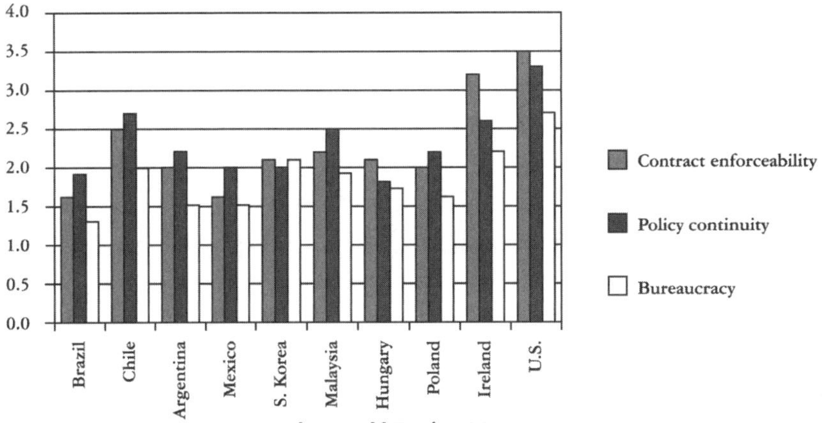

Source: BERI Survey, as reported in World Bank, 2001.

Message 1. Reducing barriers to market entry for new firms

Fewer constraints on market entry could enhance investment, encourage competition, and promote productivity growth in the potentially vibrant Brazilian society. A reduction in administrative barriers can make it easier for new firms to get started by reducing the time and cost involved. The government might simplify and unify administrative procedures for firm registration (commercial and tax), land acquisition, site development, and environmental approvals.

Context

Brazil could shorten the time required to establish a new business. While ensuring an adequate regulatory framework. It takes some 82 days for an average new firm to complete the process (figure 2). One reason it takes so long is that there are so many separate official procedures (15, compared with only 3 in Ireland, an example of good practice in this area).

To register as a partnership (limitada) or corporation (sociedade anônima), a company must obtain licenses and permits from federal and state environmental, health, and labor authorities. It must register for taxes at three levels of government—federal, state, and municipal. And it has to present documentation at every step, including attesting to membership in the relevant trade association.

Figure 2. Number of days to complete procedures for new businesses

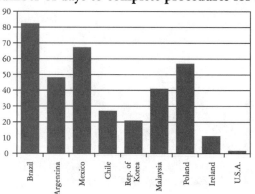

Source: Djankov and others (2000), as reported in
World Bank (2001).

To register as a Brazilian corporation the company must have at least one director who is a Brazilian resident. Steps include opening a bank account, legalizing firm documents, getting INPI approval of any contract involving technology transfer, registering the foreign investment at the Central Bank, transferring funds to Brazil, compiling documents, and getting the state commercial council (junta comercial) to approve the registration. This process takes some 60 days in Brazil but less than 30 in such economies as Chile; Hong Kong, China; Malaysia; and Singapore.[1]

A firm locating in Brazil needs to obtain temporary workers' permits to help with the start-up or to train local employees. Approvals are needed from the Ministry which issues visas, the Ministry which examines the need to bring in workers from abroad, and the institute which approves the skills being imported. Among the considerations to grant such permits seems to be whether imported workers are seen as displacing local labor rather than bringing skills.

A manufacturing facility acquiring land needs to identify, purchase, obtain installation licenses and register the property. The first three steps require important and essential zoning and environmental permits and municipal and state approvals for the intended land use. At the same time, registration can take between 3 and 12 months, depending on location and activity.[2] The same process in Hong Kong, China, Malaysia, or Singapore takes less than a month.

---

[1] FIAS, Vol. II, 2001, p. 54.

[2] FIAS (2001).

Once land title is secured and registered, site development needs to be approved. Location and building permits are required before construction can begin, and an operation permit is required before a building can be occupied. Pre-construction permits include approvals on design, health, environment, and utility connections from municipal, state, and federal entities. These are crucial elements of a good regulatory framework. But yet the process takes at least 30 weeks in São Paulo and 28 weeks in Rio de Janeiro,[3] increasing start-up costs for new business and investment.

Options

There are three general options for dealing with these problems:

- MINIMAL CHANGES TO THE PRESENT SYSTEM OF APPROVALS. The system of approvals, permits, clearances, and authorizations has evolved gradually. Its role in meeting environmental and urban concerns is important and needs to be maintained. But it can also distorts the market, protecting existing market participants from competition from new firms contesting their markets. And it confers discretionary powers on government officials. Small changes could be sought without confronting the interests of the currently protected.

- MAJOR STREAMLINING AND REVAMPING OF THE REGISTRATION AND APPROVAL PROCESS. Fundamental change would not be financially burdensome, but it would require a new approach and difficult institutional changes. The basic approach would be to unify approvals.

  Reforming the administrative procedures for new investment and new businesses could include the following:

  - Introducing greater flexbiity for firms to get temporary work permits would facilitate the flow of new technology and information to Brazil.
  - Considering the role of INPI in the work permit approval process.
  - Reducing the number of documents required for business registration and instituting a centralized system, most likely at the state level, with one identification number for the company nationwide.

---

[3] FIAS (2001).

- Unifying tax registration, with one tax identification number for the federal, state, and municipal levels, and eliminating the duplication of documents required for tax registration at different government levels.
- Strengthening the capacity and staff capabilities of the environmental regulatory and control institutions and clarifying the roles and responsibilities of the federal, state, and municipal authorities.
- Supporting municipal plans to strengthen land-use zoning.
- Reevaluating the system for transferring and registering real property and real estate.

These suggestions could be implemented in the short to medium term. Consistent with this approach would be establishing a "one-stop shop" for registering firms and obtaining the necessary approvals for beginning operations.

- FACILITATING AND ENCOURAGING ESTABLISHMENT OF INDUSTRIAL PARKS. Industrial parks facilitate the establishment of new businesses and investment. In Ireland an estimated 65 percent of foreign direct investment in recent years has been physically established in industrial parks. The administrative costs for new market entrants are reduced, especially if the new firm rents space and facilities in the park. Even if it elects to buy property within the park and build to its own specifications, the process is considerably simplified. Industrial parks have been especially useful in attracting foreign investment because they commonly provide (at a price) administrative support and advice. An export processing zone—a form of industrial park with a special free trading regime—can also attract new business and investment, both domestic and foreign. Industrial parks also offer opportunities for public-private partnerships, when public land is leased to a private industrial park developer.

Message 2. Improving the regulatory framework

To improve the potential impact of the sector regulatory agencies, increase consistency and clarity in antitrust and competition policies, and limit the opportunities for discretionary behavior and abuse, government could improve the regulatory framework by developing a consistent set of antitrust and competition policies; considering the role and functioning of the antitrust agency (CADE), the National Institute for Industrial Property (INPI), and the sector regulatory agencies; eliminating approval requirements for technology transfer, franchise, and licensing agreements; and initiating a national deregulation program to revoke efficiency-reducing regulatory decrees, cut out inconsistencies, and otherwise deregulate the economy.

Context

The costs of excessive regulation can be substantial for businesses and for the economy, creating a general drag on all businesses. Regulations may favor some activities over others by design, by unintended consequences, or by the implicit structure of costs. More than adding to the cost of doing business, poor regulation also increases uncertainty about the returns from investments and individual transactions.

Uncertainties about the future supply and adequacy of infrastructure (especially for electricity, transportation, telecommunications, and ports) also impede private investment—uncertainties caused in part by the regulatory environment. In many infrastructure areas nascent regulatory agencies are still defining their roles in the aftermath of privatization, and private investors are concerned about the impact of future regulation on infrastructure supply. As illustrated by the 2001 energy shortages, the adequacy and pricing of electricity, strongly shaped by the evolving regulatory environment, is critical for many industrial investments.

Regulation in Brazil touches all areas of private sector activity and all economic agents. It can be general, topic specific (tax, financial, trade, foreign exchange transactions), or sector specific (public utilities, energy). In recent years, spurred by privatization, sector-specific regulatory agencies have been established at the federal and state levels.[4] At the federal level new regulatory agencies have been established for petroleum (ANP), electric

---

[4] The regulatory frameworks and issues associated with individual sectors are being dealt with in the sector-specific Policy Notes.

power (ANEEL), telecommunications (ANATEL), road transport (ANT), civil aviation (ANAC), water (ANA), and sanitary surveillance (ANVISA). They have been staffed for the most part by former employees in the line ministries, where policymaking functions still rest. Only time and good performance will strengthen public and investor confidence in the regulatory processes.

Common issues on the regulatory framework in Brazil are on the tax burden and tax administration, labor, licensing, customs and trade, foreign exchange, and the environment (figure 3). The costs of regulatory compliance are seen to be high[5] and to undermine the international competitiveness of Brazilian firms. Brazilian corporate income taxes are the highest in Latin America, and many other taxes are highly distortionary. Compliance costs are high as well, since there are nearly 60 indirect, income, payroll, and property taxes, plus additional minor levies that firms must pay at the federal, state, or municipal level.

The transfer of technology, important for the country's competitiveness, is impeded by regulations for limiting foreign exchange expenditures and repatriations. The patent office (INPI) is charged with approving transfers of unpatented industrial technology to Brazil. INPI must approve all agreements for technology transfer through licensing, franchising, or leasing arrangements before the Central Bank can authorize payment (in foreign exchange) for remitting royalties abroad. INPI commonly questions the type and conditions of technology transfer, pricing arrangements and terms, royalty rates, and other details. Brazil also has a 15 percent withholding tax on remittances of royalties on imported technology. Chile and Costa Rica have no regulations or taxes related to technology transfers.

Foreign exchange restrictions were rendered obsolete by the move to a floating exchange rate system. Yet export transactions must be accompanied by a foreign exchange contract with a Central Bank-approved bank to prevent exporters from having access to the foreign exchange proceeds of the sale. Such requirements complicate exports.

There are also questions about antitrust legislation and competition policies. Under Law 8,884 of June 1995 three government agencies are charged with enforcing the country's antitrust regime: CADE *(Conselho Administrativo de Defesa Econômica)*, SEAE

---

[5] A study in 1992 (Stone, Levy, and Paredes, 1992) included a survey of regulatory compliance for Brazilian and Chilean garment manufacturers. For small Brazilian firms it was estimated that on average firm management spent 15 percent of its time in meeting compliance with government regulations. For Chile the comparable figure was 6 percent. Many procedures from 1992 remain in place.

(*Secretaria Especial de Acompanhamento Econômico*, of the Ministry of Finance), and SDE (*Secretaria de Direito Econômico*, of the Ministry of Justice). While there are some over-lapping functions among the three agencies, CADE has primary responsibility for pro-tecting competition and consumers.

Figure 3. Dimensions of the regulatory burden in Brazil

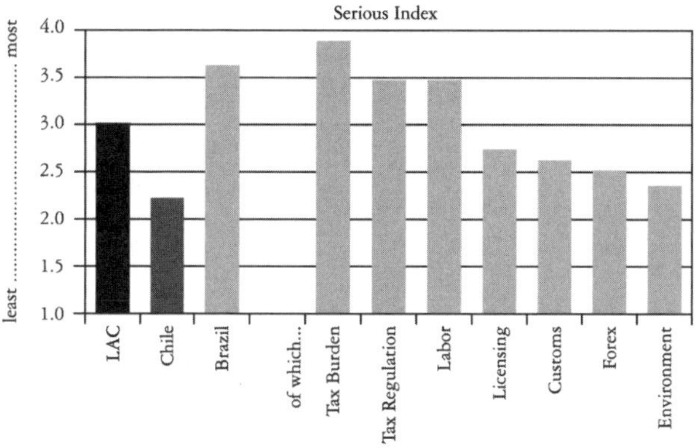

Source: *World Business Environment Survey, reported in World Bank, Brazil: New Growth. Agenda, 2001.*

Antitrust regulations (and policies) focus largely on approvals of mergers and acquisitions and rulings on complaints of anticompetitive behavior. In practice, however, there has been little action against anticompetitive behavior, and complaints are routinely shelved for "lack of evidence." Excessive legalism appears to be a problem. By law CADE must rule on all mergers and acquisitions of firms over a certain size (including the multinational parent firms of Brazilian subsidiaries). Some observers believe that CADE approvals are almost automatic;[6] others claim that, the high approval rate notwithstanding, decisions are unpredictable and could benefit from economic analysis. Although CADE's powers are broad and its responsibilities extensive, its capacity remains limited, in part because of inadequate resources.

---

[6] In 1996–97, a full 78 percent of the requested mergers were approved as submitted, with another 17 percent approved on the satisfaction of CADE-mandated conditions (Ollaik 1999).

Options

While there are regulatory problems, doing little or nothing to change the regulatory environment would have a high cost for the country. If the goal is economic modernization and development, there are problems over a wide range of topics and sectors affecting economic efficiency and competitiveness and requiring attention at the federal, state, and municipal government levels. An additional difficulty is that there is no easy consensus in Brazil on what a proper regulatory environment entails. Economic efficiency and social welfare are good points of departure. Some general options for proceeding:

- REDUCE RESTRICTIONS ON TECHNOLOGY TRANSFERS. Firms and individuals could be left to handle agreements and contracts on the transfer of technology to Brazil. A free flow of information is needed for economic development, unimpeded by government. This could mean relieving INPI from participating in the process.

- REFORM FOREIGN EXCHANGE TRANSACTIONS, ECONOMIC SAFEGUARDS RESPECTED. Restrictions on the ability of Brazilian citizens and firms to deal in foreign exchange need to be evaluated and reduced. Prudential regulation of the banking system would be the regulatory role of the Central Bank.

- DEVELOP A CONSISTENT POLICY FRAMEWORK AND GOVERNMENT PROGRAM FOR ANTITRUST AND COMPETITION POLICIES. There is currently little agreement on what such a policy framework should entail. That framework would serve as the benchmark for guiding future government actions and reforming present legislation, rules, and practices.

- REEVALUATE THE ROLES AND FUNCTIONING OF CADE, SEAE, SDE, INPI, AND THE SECTORAL REGULATORY AGENCIES, TAKING THE POLICY FRAMEWORK MENTIONED ABOVE AS A POINT OF REFERENCE. The assessment criterion would be the public interest—that is, social welfare maximization. For the organizations enforcing antitrust regulations, linking the SEAE and SDE functions with CADE has merit.

- INITIATE A NATIONAL REGULATORY REFORM PROGRAM. A high-level interministerial council could be charged with reassessing regulations and refoming them.[7] This
  would involve impact studies of existing regulations and, in future, impact studies of
  any proposed new federal regulation—to assess its benefits and costs to Brazilian society before implementation. In the interests of transparency and public debate, the
  results of these studies and other analyses could be published on the program's Website.

Message 3. Increasing efficiency in the labor market
The labor market can benefit by relying more on collective bargaining them on the legislative code than on collective bargaining. By shifting that balance, Brazil could reduce
labor turnover, increase productivity, decrease payroll costs, shrink the informal labor
market, and lessen the reliance on litigation. Possible measures would entail realigning
incentives for hiring, retaining, and firing workers; relaxing rules, including on mandated
minimum nonwage benefits, to leave more to decentralized collective bargaining; increasing the use of labor arbitration for dispute settlement at the workplace; modernizing the
labor courts and reducing their role in employee–employer negotiations; reducing reliance
on payroll taxes through tax reform; and redesigning the severance pay indemnity fund
(FGTS) to reduce incentives for labor turnover.

Context
The labor market has three problematic elements: widespread informality, high turnover,
and extensive labor litigation. Less than half the work force is now in the formal market,
down from more than 60 percent in 1990. The informal labor market share is greatest for
low-skilled workers. High and growing informality reflects workers in the formal market
enjoying mandatory benefits that price many workers (self-employed or informal wage

---

[7] A precedent for such an initiative can be found during the Collor administration. Between May
1990 and May 1992 it was responsible for revoking some 112,000 decrees dating back to the beginning of the Republic. Among its accomplishments were allowing retail establishments to function
on Sundays, easing controls on credit card use, deregulating some downstream activities in the
petroleum industry, eliminating a domestic wheat distribution monopoly, liberalizing the civil air
transport regime, deregulating investment in chemicals, and deregulating coal production. See
World Bank (1994).

earners) out of formal labor markets. Salaries in the informal labor market are about 60 percent of those in the formal market, controlling for occupational category and economic sector.

What contributes to the high labor market informality in Brazil? High payroll taxes, other costs of formal employment for employers, a high index of production informality and small firms, and the importance of the rural economy are all factors. This informality has the damaging consequence of low coverage for the safety nets of FGTS and unemployment insurance, contributing to low earnings security for those working in the informal labor market.

High labor turnover is another characteristic of the Brazilian labor market. One worker in three changes jobs every year, and the rate has been increasing, rising 60 percent between 1992 and 2001. High turnover rates mean less incentive for employers to train workers. And less on-the-job training and investment in the labor force mean lower productivity and slower productivity growth, undermining competitiveness.

A third characteristic is frequent litigation. More than 2 million cases are currently before the labor courts. The system is slow and costly. It also adds uncertainty to employee-employer relations, since judicial decisions can go beyond the expected. The added costs and uncertainty discourage employment expansion, especially in the formal market.

These characteristics are a reflection of the legal, regulatory, and institutional environment of Brazil's labor markets. Three dimensions of that environment deserve particular attention: the labor courts, which enforce the Labor Code; the collective bargaining laws and institutions; and the severance and unemployment arrangements, as represented by the FGTS.

LABOR COURTS. The Labor Code (or CLT, *Consolidação das Leis do Trabalho*) dates from 1943 and represents a consolidation of the corporatist labor laws implemented during the 1930s. The core principle of the code is a benevolent, paternalistic state that regulates almost all aspects of the relation between employers and employees. The state determines the specific terms of employment with minimal negotiations between workers and employers. In addition, the constitution has numerous articles that accord workers rights that cannot be negotiated—even by mutual consent.

The CLT is enforced by an elaborate system of labor courts. In addition to enforcing legislation, the labor courts have the legal authority to make new rules (*poder normativo*) and to negotiate disputes between employers and employees. Incentives favor the use of labor courts to resolve disputes. There are no administrative costs to workers for filing a grievance, and cases can be filed up to five years after severance. The burden of proof is on the employer to demonstrate that the employee's claims are imaginary or exaggerated. With nothing to lose, workers have an incentive to file claims.

For employers there is little incentive to fully obey the rules and laws, since a common outcome, failing a negotiated settlement, is a ruling to split the contested amount. Cases commonly take two years. About two-thirds of litigated grievances deal with nonwage benefits, enshrined in law but frequently disregarded in the market, even for formal employment. The average court settlement results in about 40 percent of the contested amount being paid to the worker.

The consequences of relying heavily on the labor courts to negotiate settlements include congested labor courts, adversarial employee-employer relations, informal labor contracts, high costs for firms, uncertainty about decisions, reluctance to hire, and low productivity.

COLLECTIVE BARGAINING. Under the CLT unions are established on an occupational basis, while employer associations are organized by sector. Only one union for each occupation is allowed in a given municipality. Collective bargaining is weak, and various impediments hinder effective job negotiations at the workplace:

- The labor court system discourages workers and employers from negotiating directly.
- The CLT mandates an established floor for benefits for any collective bargaining agreement.
- A union levy is collected from all (formal) workers regardless of union membership (60 percent is transferred to the designated union), undermining union incentives to represent the workers or to improve their working conditions
- Monopoly union representation also weakens the incentives of the unions to act on behalf of workers. There is no competition between unions for members (and dues), providing little incentive to the unions to represent workers well.

SEVERANCE FUND (FGTS). When it was established, the FGTS was an important step in providing all covered formal sector employees with some income security. Under the FGTS employers contribute 8 percent of a worker's salary to an individual FGTS account, which earns a government guaranteed real return of 3 percent annually. The worker has full access to the account balance in the case of severance or retirement and partial access for home purchases and certain medical expenses.

As it has evolved, however, the FGTS has unintentionally created a powerful incentive for labor turnover. Departure from a job means getting access to the otherwise illiquid resources in a worker's FGTS account. If the dismissal is judged to be without just cause (most are so judged), the employer must pay the worker a fine amounting to 40 percent of the accumulated FGTS balance. And because the rate of return on the FGTS account is less than the market interest rate, it is rational for workers to try to get the money as early as possible and invest it elsewhere at a market rate.

Options

Possible reforms would include realigning hiring and firing incentives for greater economic efficiency, reforming the labor code by making it more flexible and bringing it more in line with best practice elsewhere, encouraging more negotiations in the workplace, and increasing earnings security by widening the safety net for workers. These changes would reduce litigation and labor turnover, helping to boost productivity and encourage job creation. In keeping with these general objectives, some options for reform could include:

- THE MANDATED MINIMUM BENEFITS UNDER THE CLT. The mandated nonwage benefits accorded to employees under the CLT distort the labor market and have deleterious consequences for the economy. Mandated nonwage benefits total some 85 percent of the wage paid to the worker. Reducing the minimum mandate, through legislation, would lower informality in the labor market, and thus increase productivity, employment, and earnings security.

- COLLECTIVE BARGAINING PRACTICES. Other measures to strengthen collective bargaining and help redirect employee–employer negotiations to the workplace include eliminating the mandatory union levy and monopoly union representation. Both measures would allow unions greater freedom of action and create more competition among unions, stimulating greater responsiveness to worker interests. They would also lower labor turnover, and increase employment and productivity.

- THE FUNCTIONING OF THE LABOR COURTS. A major objective in any redefinition of the role and function of the labor courts is to curtail their role in negotiations between employers and employees, leaving such negotiations to the workplace. Three options arise: changing current legislation to reduce the floor on benefits and allow collective or individual bargaining on more issues in employer-employee relations; increasing the costs of using the labor court system; and allowing greater use of arbitration to settle disputes under collective bargaining arrangements or individual contracts. These measures would promote less adversarial workplace relations, and foster more employment.

- REDESIGN THE FGTS. The FGTS plays an important role in the economy. Redesigning it to eliminate the incentive for labor turnover would increase labor market efficiency. Options would include:
  - COMPETITION IN THE MANAGEMENT OF FGTS ACCOUNTS. Greater competition to manage individual FGTS accounts could result in higher rates for

return, decreasing the incentives for workers to leave their jobs to get better returns on the money in their FGTS accounts.

- CAPPING CONTRIBUTIONS TO THE FGTS. This would reduce workers' incentive to bring a case to the labor courts in order to trigger FGTS-raising fine.
- ELIMINATING THE FINE FOR DISMISSAL WITHOUT JUST CAUSE. This would make the FGTS a "no-fault" insurance system, encouraging greater investments in firm-specific skills, and leading to higher productivity.

MAKING THE FINE FOR UNJUST DISMISSAL PAYABLE TO THE GOVERNMENT INSTEAD OF THE WORKER. With fines paid directly to the government—possibly to an earmarked fund to provide assistance or retraining to unemployed worker—workers' incentives to trigger a fine would be reduced, with less labor turnover and litigation.

Many of the suggested reforms would require legislative action, including in some cases constitutional amendments. Political realities probably mandate proceeding on a phased basis, but even such change could bring lasting benefits to the economy and its private sector agents—employers and employees alike.

Message 4. Strengthening property rights and contract enforcement

Stronger and more consistent enforcement of property rights could foster investment and financial intermediation and improve private perceptions of the judicial system. Strengthening property rights would involve judicial system reform—using more binding precedents, limiting appeals, expanding judicial enforcement, and making greater use of arbitration in contract disputes. Property rights could be strengthened through bankruptcy reform, expanded protection of intellectual property, greater scope for the private sector to enter freely into enforceable contracts, and improved corporate governance to better protect the rights of minority stockholders.

Context

The judicial system is central to the enforcement of property rights and contracts. But the judicial system in Brazil is seen as slow and sometimes unpredictable, and many judges are young, inexperienced, and poorly paid. Court cases can last for years (multiple appeals are not only possible but standard), increasing costs and uncertainty.

Larger firms, especially foreign firms, try to avoid the unpredictability of the Brazilian judicial system by writing contracts in which the parties agree to adjudicate disagreements in a foreign jurisdiction. Brazilian courts do not always accept the handling of such disputes in foreign jurisdictions for contracts performed in Brazil.

Another means of short-circuiting the Brazilian judicial system is to include an arbitration clause in contracts. In 1996 Brazil adopted a modern arbitration law envisaging such dispute resolution. But there are questions about its constitutionality, and the Supreme Court has yet to rule on it.

Government regulation frequently restricts the freedom of contracting parties to enter agreements, constraining their economic choices and increasing transaction costs. INPI has not approved technology licensing agreements in which the parties have agreed to a contractual designation of a foreign jurisdiction for the settlement of contractual disputes. Local governments have frequently voided contracts between landlords and tenants that do not conform to government-determined norms, even those adopted after the contract was signed.

The new Industrial Property Code of 1997 gave a major boost to the protection of intellectual property in Brazil, but obtaining a patent is still a long process, reportedly taking five to eight years (compared with an average of two years in the United States). The code adopted a position for Brazil more consistent with international practice and conforming with World Trade Organization agreements on Trade-Related Aspects of Intellectual Property Rights (TRIPs). In a recent study by the Inter-American Development Bank measuring protection of intellectual property Brazil performed slightly better than Argentina, India, and Panama, but weaker than Chile, Costa Rica, South Korea, Mexico, and Peru. [8] Areas of weakness are patents, enforcement, administration, industrial secrets, and biotechnology.

Options

While sweeping reform may seem to be the answer, there are reasons for a more gradual approach. Despite widespread dissatisfaction with the judicial system, there is still debate even among legal scholars and experts about what sweeping judicial reform should include. The judicial system is broad-ranging and complex, involving far more than enforcement of property rights and economic legislation. Reform of other aspects of the system, such as the criminal justice system, might not harmonize well with stronger enforcement of property rights and contracts. And reform of the judicial system may be

---

[8] This work is reported on in FIAS, Volume I, 2001, p. 38–39.

politically difficult. More gradual changes might avoid some of the resistance sure to be mounted against radical reform and result in appreciable improvement.

Suggestions for policy action, centering on the strengthening the enforcement of property rights and contracts through the judicial system, would include:

- GRADUALLY REFORM SPECIFIC FEATURES OF THE JUDICIAL SYSTEM. Property right enforcement would be improved through greater use of binding precedent, less recourse to appeals (including, perhaps, more use of "final judgment" rules to block interlocutory appeals), stronger judicial security once court decisions are rendered, wider use of judicial enforcement to ensure compliance with court rulings, greater use of arbitration in contract disputes,[9] and a clear ruling on the legality of appealing to foreign jurisdictions to settle disputes if specified by contract.

- PERMIT CONTRACTING PARTIES GREATER FREEDOM IN ENTERING INTO CONTRACTS. Parties to a contract should be allowed to agree on its terms, and contracts could be enforceable in Brazilian courts or some other specified jurisdiction.

- REEXAMINE THE BANKRUPTCY LAWS. An overhaul seems necessary to facilitate enforcement of financial contracts. Provisions would be directed to fostering economically efficient debt workouts, with procedures that can be effectively administered in a timely manner.

- UPGRADE THE PROTECTION OF INTELLECTUAL PROPERTY RIGHTS. INPI could reprioritize its activities to focus on patents and patent protection, where work is now slow. To free INPI staff to work on patent cases, INPI could be relieved of other responsibilities, particularly for the issuance of temporary work permits for foreign workers and licensing agreements for technology transfer. INPI staff, once freed from those unnecessary functions, could be retrained and reassigned to patent work—the core function. The Industrial Property Code could be amended (in Article 68) so that a patent holder that is abusing its market power would be best dealt with as a case of market abuse rather than opening up the possibility of removing protection under patent law.

---

[9] Greater use of arbitration may require a ruling on the constitutionality of the Arbitration Code (Law 9307) by the Supreme Court.

Message 5. Focusing industrial policy on horizontal evenness across economic activities, a more open trade policy regime, and higher productivity growth
Uniform incentives across sectors can diminish distortions, improve social welfare, and enhance economic performance. Less domestic protection can boost export performance and increase competitiveness. Ways to achieve these goals would be to promote competitiveness and investment more actively, liberalize trade policy (through unilateral, regional, and multilateral initiatives), and stimulate exports (simplifying procedures, eliminating cascading tax effects, and allowing export processing zones).

Context

Policy interventions that create distortions in the price system generate incentives (and disincentives) for various economic activities. Activities receiving what appear to be incentives may actually be discriminated against by the overall constellation of economic policies including import taxes, export taxes, and other trade restrictions. For example, Brazilian agricultural production received generous credit subsidies in the early 1980s (resulting in macroeconomic imbalances and high taxpayer costs). But agriculture was still discriminated against on a net basis because of the greater incentives to industrial activities—mostly through trade policies.

Brazil has a large and diversified industrial sector, nurtured from the 1960s to the 1980s by heavy domestic market protection, frequently at the expense of less protected activities. But the result was many uncompetitive manufacturing activities that could survive only behind protective barriers against competing imports. Productivity growth in this period was slow for the most part, with economic growth coming mainly from physical investment. Some Brazilian manufactured products began to compete in world markets, but only through a costly system of export subsidies. The legacy was a reasonably well-developed industrial sector and a private sector that believed that the government should protect and subsidize its growth

Trade policy reform began in earnest in 1990. CACEX (the foreign trade control agency) was closed. Most nontariff barriers were lifted, and tariffs were reduced from an average of 32 percent in 1989 to 11 percent in 1994. Since then there has been some retrogression, with tariffs edging up to an average of 14 percent in 2000. Brazil's trade policy regime is more closed than those of some of its competitors, many of which continued with trade reforms in the late 1990s.

The effects of the trade policy reforms and related measures have been considerable, with one disappointment: the weak export response. Part of the explanation lies in exchange rate policy. The Plano Real was based in part, at least initially, on using the exchange rate as a nominal anchor for macroeconomic stabilization. The result was an overvalued currency that until 1999 blocked the export expansion expected from trade policy reforms. Other factors that explain export performance since 1999 are declining terms of trade, infrastructure bottlenecks (for example the 2001 energy crisis), the collapse of Argentine demand for Brazilian exports, and a slowdown in the world economy. However, trade liberalization seems to have gone far toward ending Brazil's economic isolation from the rest of the world. Productivity gains have accelerated thanks to greater openness and so competitiveness has increased. Brazil is now better positioned than ever before to take advantage of economic opportunities in the world economy.

A study in the early 1980s found that Brazil's trade policies favored the capital goods and heavy industry of the more industrialized Center-South and penalized the labor-intensive manufacturing and agriculture of the poorer regions, notably the Northeast.[10] Although effective and nominal protection rates have been reduced since then, the overall structure remains little changed, suggesting that Brazil's poorer regions are still discriminated against (although less so) by overall trade and industrial policies. The Northeast's mediocre export performance supports this evidence.

Options

How can industrial policies take advantage of the benefits available through greater economic interaction with the rest of the world? One way is to pursue industrial policies that encourage productivity increases and achieve a more level playing field across sectors. This would allow the private sector to develop in an economic environment relatively free of government-imposed price distortions. A more open trade regime, without anti-export biases in economic policies, would be consistent with such an approach and should result in greater productivity growth, better economic performance overall, faster export growth, and higher wages for unskilled labor. The three parts of this strategy:

- HORIZONTAL INDUSTRIAL POLICY AND INVESTMENT PROMOTION. The primary objective of industrial policy would be to systematically increase the competitiveness of the economy and, in so doing, to enhance economic efficiency. Achieving international competitiveness and even treatment of sectors requires an open trade and invest-

---

[10] See Tyler 1984.

ment regime. Such openness would enhance competitiveness, reduce the scope for market abuse and monopolistic practices by domestic firms, and promote greater economic growth and welfare. In addition to trade policy initiatives (discussed below), some options for possible improvement include the following:

- EMPHASIZE TECHNOLOGY ACQUISITION AND INNOVATION.[11] Rationalizing public spending on technological innovation could enhance its effectiveness. More effective public-private partnerships could increase the flow of technological knowledge to the private sector. Applying international best practice to income tax treatment of enterprise research and development (R&D) activities and eliminating licenses and government approval for technology transfer would increase Brazil's access to internationally developed technology.
- EMPHASIZE EDUCATIONAL SYSTEM IMPROVEMENTS IN BOTH COVERAGE AND QUALITY AT FEDERAL, STATE, AND MUNICIPAL LEVELS. Productivity and competitiveness rise with a better prepared work force.
- REDUCE THE ELEMENTS OF THE "CUSTO BRASIL" (the additional expenses imposed on businesses by inefficient or unproductive practices). Areas where speedy action might be possible include reducing the indirect tax burden on tradable goods production; improving transportation facilities and regulatory framework (coastal shipping, ports administration), and easing burdensome customs procedures.
- DO MORE TO ATTRACT FOREIGN DIRECT INVESTMENT. An important dimension of investment promotion is to actively encourage foreign direct investment, especially in competitive, technology-intensive areas likely to result in export activity and backward linkages. Greater reliance on industrial parks and export processing zones might be helpful.
- PROACTIVE TRADE POLICY REFORM. Actions to reduce trade barriers—both those imposed on Brazilian goods and services in international markets, and those that Brazil imposes on its citizens could be pursued on several fronts:
  - UNILATERAL ACTIONS. All nontariff barriers for imports, especially license requirement, could be eliminated other than those to protect national security, public health, or the environment. The government could also eliminate all remaining export taxes.

---

[11] Policy Note on Innovation and Technology, July 2002.

- ACTIONS WITHIN Mercosul. Further reductions could be sought in the common external tariff, and implementation of a uniform tariff could be agreed.[12] Through Mercosul Brazil could pursue negotiations to enter free trade arrangements with the European Union and the Free Trade Association for the Americas (FTAA).[13] Achieving both would result in greater welfare gains for Brazil than the sum of each separately. An important objective would be to secure maximum access to those markets without restrictions—being allowed to export agricultural products and without being subject to antidumping actions.
- MULTILATERAL TRADE NEGOTIATIONS. In the context of the Doha trade round, access to the developed country markets becomes an option and is of vital importance in determining Brazil's gains from new trade agreements.

- EXPORT PROMOTION MEASURES. In addition to reducing antiexport biases by curtailing domestic market protection, incentives for export sales could be increased by reducing some of the costs of exporting (frequently associated with the "Custo Brasil"). Suggested for special attention are:
  - PURSUE TAX REFORM ALONG THE LINES INDICATED UNDER MESSAGE 2. Tax reform would eliminate credit accumulation under the ICMS and remove cascading taxes (PIS/PASEP, COFINS, CPMF), which penalize exports. Before enacting the tax reform—a medium-term priority—measures would be needed to allow reimbursing exporters for the accumulated cascading taxes paid in previous stages of production.
  - SIMPLIFY EXPORT PROCEDURES. The complex SISCOMEX, which requires numerous authorizations and forms, could be streamlined in the short run.

---

[12] A recent study by the World Bank shows that the implementation of a revenue neutral uniform tariff for Mercosul would bring substantial welfare gains to Brazil. See Tarr and others (2002). A revised version of that paper is a part of World Bank, Brazil: Trade Policies to Improve Efficiency, Increase Growth, and Reduce Poverty (2002).

[13] The Bank estimates show welfare gains, and poverty reduction, for Brazil resulting from both the FTAA and a free trade agreement with the EU. Tarr and others (2002).

- END THE GOVERNMENT FREEZE ON PERMITTING APPROVED EXPORT PROCESS-
  ING ZONES TO OPERATE. Several export processing zones, ready to begin operations, have been held up by high-level federal government decisions. The
  incoming government could grant permission immediately, an action that
  would yield beneficial results in a relatively short period. Over the longer term
  export processing zones would help expand exports, generate employment,
  and attract new investments (including foreign direct investment).
- CONTINUE TO PROMOTE EXPORTS, especially from small and medium-size
  enterprises, through the national Agency for the Promotion of Exports
  (APEX). International experience shows that trade promotion organizations,
  such as APEX, can foster exports.

**Message 6. Reformulating regional development policies to emphasize competitive-
ness, good governance, and social development**
A goal of government policy has long been to accelerate the convergence of regional per
capita incomes, especially for the North and Northeast, toward the national average. The
dissolution in 2001 of SUDAM and SUDENE—the two main government institutions
responsible for regional development—provides an opportunity for reexamining regional
development policy and its instruments and institutions. A new approach emphasizing
competitiveness, private sector development, good governance, and economic diversification away from traditional and subsistence agriculture offers promise in reducing persistent regional income disparities. In the near term, however, special efforts could be made
to continue to address the problems of the rural poor in the Northeast's semiarid areas.

Context
Although national growth has been accompanied by substantial reductions in poverty, the
Northeast continues to lag behind other regions by a large margin: per capita income in
the Northeast is still less than half the national average (table 1).[14] For the North and
Northeast, the case for some sort of regional development policy is compelling for eco-

---

[14] While per capita incomes for the Northeast as a whole have not converged on the national average, the performances of individual states are varied. See World Bank, Brazil: Poverty Reduction
Growth and Fiscal Stability in the State of Ceará (1999).

nomic and social reasons. Convergence can take generations, especially for less industrialized economies. Government intervention can prevent the perpetuation of large income disparities across regions. But the fact that incomes in the North and Northeast did not converge toward the national average over the past 40 years suggests that the elaborate regional development schemes designed to bring that about have not achieved expected results.[15]

Table 1. Gross domestic product per capita by region, selected years, 1960–99
(Index: Brazil = 100)

Region	1960	1965	1970	1975	1980	1985	1990	1995	1999
North	61	54	56	48	62	62	64	65	60
Northeast	46	49	39	38	41	46	44	45	46
Southeast	145	143	153	149	144	136	138	138	137
South	105	102	94	107	106	114	106	119	119
Mid-West	58	73	71	73	87	104	122	90	94
Brazil	100	100	100	100	100	100	100	100	100

Source: FGV and IBGE estimates as reportrd in Gomes (2002)

Income convergence has been greater for the Mid-West region. The rapid agriculture-led growth in Mato Grosso and Mato Grosso do Sul, based on competitive high-value market-led production, attests to the importance of an appropriate incentive and price environment and good governance.

For the Northeast, regional development programs have centered on constitutionally and other legally mandated transfers of federal public revenues. The Constitutional Loan Fund for the Northeast (FNE) transfers an earmarked portion of the federal income and industrial product taxes, amounting to nearly 1 percent of the Northeast's GDP, to the Banco do Nordeste Brasileiro (BNB) for lending in the region at highly concessional rates. Despite the low rates, arrears and loan repayments are a problem. BNB's emphasis is on agriculture, small producers, and the least economically promising semi-arid areas, so while the credit subsidies do increase investment, the activities are frequently not economically sustainable.

Until May 2001, when it was dissolved, the Investment Fund for the Northeast (FINOR, *Fundo de Investimentos do Nordeste*) also received earmarked federal tax transfers

---

[15] For an example, see Gomes (2002).

to promote investment in the Northeast. In 2000 FINOR transfers amounted to 0.29 percent of the Northeast's GDP. SUDENE financed approved projects with these resources in exchange for bonds issued by benefiting firms. Very few of these bonds have been repaid. Indeed, many approved projects were never completed, suggesting that they were not well chosen. As with other investment subsidies, there has been a bias toward capital-intensive activities and technology. Repeated problems led to the closure of FINOR and SUDENE.[16] A new institution, ADN (*Agência para o Desenvolvimento do Nordeste*), enabled by a Medida Provisória, is to replace SUDENE, and a new fund (FDN, *Fundo de Desenvolvimento do Nordeste*) is to replace FINOR. Implementation of both awaits the incoming government.

Discretionary federal government investments and capital transfers to the Northeast are also an important dimension of regional development. For 1999 IPEA estimated that direct federal investments and transfers to Northeastern states and municipal governments for capital expenditures amounted to 0.8 percent of the Northeast's GDP.[17] These investments, carried out by different agencies, are frequently uncoordinated and sometimes not economically founded. Better coordination, greater integration, and more exacting economic analysis for public investment projects seem to be required. The *Programa Plurianual* (PPA) might be a logical point of departure for the incoming government. A question to be posed is whether the "Eixos Strategy" in the PPA is sufficiently pro-Northeast.

FDN, FINOR, and direct federal investments and capital transfers to the Northeast, while significant, are overshadowed by other transfer programs, including social security payments and health and education programs. The largest net transfers are to the Northeast, amounting to 7.7 percent of the region's total income, with substantial net transfers also in favor of the North (table 2). Given the magnitude of these transfers, their overall impact in fostering development and reducing poverty has to be questioned.

Clearly, a fresh approach is needed, especially for the Northeast, and the, as yet, undefined instruments of the ADN and FDN provide an opportunity.

---

[16] A strict parallel can be drawn with SUDAM for the North, also shut down for similar reasons in May 2001.

[17] As reported in World Bank, Brazil: Maranhão State Economic Memorandum, Vol. 2, Annex 3, p. 21.

Table 2. Net federal government interregional resource transfers, 1999

Region	Percentage of regional / national income
North	3.8
Northeast	7.7
Southeast	-1.9
South	0.6
Mid-West	-5.3
Brazil	0.0

Source: IPEA estimates as reported in Gomes (2002).

Options

Regional development strategies everywhere are based on reducing regional income disparities by fostering faster economic growth in the poorer regions. For the Northeast a principal determinant of economic growth appears to be private investment.[18] Public investment is also important but does not appear to affect growth directly. Public investments should complement private investment by providing public goods or overcoming other market failures rather than substituting for private activities. An example is public infrastructure investments, such as in electric energy and water supply, that lower production costs and are associated with greater private investment.

A regional development strategy for the North and Northeast would stress competitiveness and productivity growth through market-based interventions to improve the functioning of product, labor, credit, and land markets and to stimulate private investment. Over the longer term, that would imply economic diversification away from traditional and subsistence agriculture.

SHORT-TERM IMPERATIVES. If the objective of regional policies is to reduce income disparities, the inescapable fact is that poverty in the Northeast is heavily concentrated in rural areas and agricultural activities, particularly in semiarid areas. A transition will

---

[18] See World Bank, Public Expenditure for Poverty Alleviation in the Brazilian Northeast (2001), for a discussion of analytical work and data supporting this conclusion and the complimentary role of public investment.

clearly take time, yet poverty needs to be addressed in the short run. Agriculture will remain prominent in the regional economy in the short term, and will continue to be a main source of livelihood for the poor, including many small landholders and landless rural workers. Some public investments in support of agriculture, even in semiarid areas, thus has economic merit, especially in education, extension, and feeder roads to improve marketing possibilities. For water development projects, economic analysis should be exacting. Market-based approaches to land reform, including the development of rural land markets (especially for land rentals), hold special promise. Social funds, relying on community support and participation, having proven effective in the Northeast, and could be continued. And income transfers, justified on equity grounds, can play an important role, as in the expanded rural pension system (*previdencia rural*).

LONGER TERM STRATEGIC INITIATIVES. The sertão and semiarid areas of the Northeast, with limited and irregular rainfall, are not well suited for competitive agricultural production. So diversification, over time, away from traditional and subsistence agriculture in those areas is essential. Easing that transition—including some migration out of the *sertão*—would be a central theme in regional development. Another would be vastly improved living standards, reflected in a wide range of better social indicators, including improvements in health, education, housing, access to opportunities, as well as increased incomes. Attaining this will require greater competitiveness in the Northeast's production and greater integration with the national and world economies.

A gradual reorientation of public investments toward activities providing infrastructure for off-farm employment opportunities and more orderly urban development would be part of the longer term framework. While some elements of a longer term strategy may take time to materialize, beginning early may enhance the benefits. For example, educational benefits may be especially important for the Northeast in increasing employment opportunities, widening horizons, and improving health.

Many elements and options for the design of regional policies have been treated elsewhere in this or other Policy Notes. Some of these elements however have a special relevance for regional development and are noted here:

• DEREGULATE LABOR MARKETS. Lowering mandated minimum wages and nonwage benefits would have major benefits for the North and Northeast by expanding formal labor markets, increasing income security, and expanding employment. Regionalizing the minimum wage, with lower minimums for the Northeast and North, would have similar effects.

- EXPAND THE COVERAGE AND QUALITY OF THE EDUCATION SYSTEM. Massive investments in education would be a cornerstone of any regional development strategy for the Northeast or North. While the emphasis would be on primary education, improvements in secondary and university education would not be neglected. The private sector role in education could also be enhanced. Overall, a more unified and comprehensive human resource development strategy would increase productivity and enhance competitiveness. And by increasing marketable job skills, it would facilitate the relocation of labor out of noncompetitive agriculture in the semi-arid areas.
- EMBARK ON TAX REFORM. Most recent proposals for tax reform include reform of indirect taxes. Replacing the ICMS and other indirect taxes with a nationwide value added tax would effectively end the "fiscal wars" (*guerras fiscais*) between states and enable state governments to focus on features other than ICMS-based incentives to attract new investments to the Northeast. In the end, spotlighting the economic advantages and the importance of good governance is likely to make the Northeast more attractive as an investment site.
- STIMULATE THE DEVELOPMENT OF EXPORT PROCESSING ZONES AND INDUSTRIAL PARKS. Likely to be especially important for the Northeast and North in attracting new private sector investments,[19] export processing zones and industrial parks offer ample opportunities for creative partnerships between the public and private sectors.
- SHIFT THE LENDING PRIORITIES OF THE FNE. Redirecting FNE resources to more efficient uses and de-emphasizing agriculture, small enterprises, and the economically unpromising (for agriculture) semi-arid areas, and changing the way the BNB on-lends those resources, might be beneficial but might require new legislation.

---

[19] In the Amazon region, converting the Zona Franca de Manaus—set up to produce for the domestic market—into a full-fledged export processing zone could bring substantial benefits to what has become a depressed area.

- PROVIDE SHAPE AND DIRECTION FOR THE NASCENT ADN AND FDN. The still-undefined ADN and FDN offer an important opportunity to implement new initiatives in regional development for the Northeast. Some criteria for shaping and directing the new institutional arrangements could include an emphasis on competitiveness, private sector development, cluster formation, and attraction of new investment, including foreign direct investment.[20] Some experiments might be attempted with employment subsidies, rather than investment subsidies.

References

World Bank reports related to private sector development

This chapter summarizes the content of the following World Bank reports. Those, in turn, draw heavily from a wide range of literature on the subject from experts in Brazil and beyond, which are referenced in the mentioned Bank reports.

FIAS (Foreign Investment Advisory Service). 2001. Brazil: Legal, Policy and Administrative Barriers to Investment in Brazil. Report by the Foreign Investment Advisory Service of the World Bank Group. Volume II of this report is available as *Barreiras Jurídicas, Políticas e Administrativas aos Investimentos no Brasil: Barreiras Administrativas aos Investimentos no Brasil – O Caso de São Paulo e Rio de Janeiro. Rio de Janeiro.*

World Bank. 1994. Brazil: An Assessment of the Private Sector. Two volumes, Report 11775-BR. Latin America and the Caribbean Regional Office. World Bank, Washington, D.C.

World Bank. 1995. Brazil: Structural Reform and Sector Policies. Report 13913-BR. World Bank, Latin America and the Caribbean Regional Office, Washington, D.C.

World Bank. 1998. Improving Brazil's Export Performance. Report 17768-BR. World Bank, Latin America and the Caribbean Regional Office, Washington, D.C.

World Bank. 1999. Brazil: Poverty Reduction, Growth, and Fiscal Stability in the State of Ceará. State Economic Memorandum, in two volumes, Report 19217-BR. World Bank, Latin America and the Caribbean Regional Office, Washington, D.C.

---

[20] Over the past 30 years, the period covering the Article 34-18 and FINOR incentives, there has been very little fresh foreign direct investment in the Northeast. The foreign firms that have undertaken manufacturing operations in the Northeast have almost invariably been established first in the Center-South.

World Bank. 2001a. Brazil: The New Growth Agenda. Two volumes, Report 22950-BR. World Bank, Latin America and the Caribbean Regional Office, Washington, D.C.

World Bank. 2001b. "Brazil: Trade Policies to Improve Efficiency, Increase Growth and Reduce Poverty." Four volumes, Report 24285-BR. World Bank, Latin America and the Caribbean Regional Office, Washington, D.C.

World Bank. 2001c. Building Institutions for Markets: World Development Report 2002. New York: Oxford University Press.

World Bank. 2001d. From Natural Resources to the Knowledge Economy: Trade and Job Quality. Washington, D.C.; World Bank.

World Bank. 2001e. "Public Expenditures for Poverty Alleviation in Northeast Brazil: Promoting Growth and Improving Services." Report 2225-BR. World Bank, Latin America and the Caribbean Regional Office, Washington, D.C.

World Bank. 2001f. "State Economic Memorandum: Micro, Small and Medium Enterprises in Northeast Brazil." World Bank, Latin America and the Caribbean Regional Office, Washington, D.C.

World Bank. 2002a. "Brazil: Jobs Report." Two volumes. Draft report. World Bank, Latin America and the Caribbean Regional Office, Washington, D.C.

World Bank. 2002b. "Brazil: Maranhão State Economic Memorandum." Two volumes. Draft report. World Bank, Latin America and the Caribbean Regional Office, Washington, D.C.

World Bank. 2002c. Promoting Growth and Development in Lagging Regions. Conference volume organized by the World Bank Subnational Regional Economics Thematic Group. Washington, D.C.

Other references

Banco Central do Brasil. Boletim Mensal. various issues. Rio de Janeiro

Castelar Pinheiro, Armando. 1996. "Judicial System Performance and Economic Development," BNDES Ensaios 2. Rio de Janeiro.

Castelar Pinheiro, Armando, and Célia Cabral. 1998. *"Mercado de Crédito no Brasil: O Papel do Judiciário e de Outras Instituições."* BNDES *Ensaios 9*. Rio de Janeiro.

Djankov, Simeon, Rafael La Porta, Florencio Lopez de Silanes and Andrei Shleifer. 2000. The Regulation of Entry. NBER Working Paper W7892. Cambridge, Mass.: National Bureau of Economic Research.

FIESP (*Federação de Indústria do Estado de São Paulo and Fundação Getúlio Vargas*). 2001. *Carga Tributaria e Competitividade da Industria Brasileira*. São Paulo.

Kaufmann, Daniel, Aart Kraay, and Pablo Zoido-Lobaton. 2002. "Governance Matters II." Policy Research Working Paper 2772. World Bank, Washington, D.C.

Maia Gomes, Gustavo. 2002. "Fifty Years of Development Policies for Brazil's Northeast: What Worked, What Didn't." Paper presented at World Bank Conference Promoting Growth and Development in Lagging Regions. Washington, D.C.

Mesquita Moreira, Maurício. 1999. *"Estrangeiros em uma Economia Aberta: Impactos Recentes sobre Produtividade, Concentração e Comércio Exterior."* BNDES Texto para Discussão 67. Rio de Janeiro.

Mesquita Moreira, Maurício, and Fernando Puga. 2000. *"Como a Indústria Financia o seu Crecimento: uma Análise do Brasil Pós-Plano Real."* BNDES Texto para Discussão 84. Rio de Janeiro.

Musgrave, Richard A. 1959. The Theory of Public Finance: A Study in Public Economy. New York: McGraw-Hill.

Ollaik, Leila. 1999. "Goals and Results in Public Policy: The Case of Brazilian Competition Policy." Master's thesis, St. Cross College, Oxford University, Oxford.

Rowat, Malcolm, Michele Lubrano, and Rafael Porrata. 1997. Competition Policy and MERCOSUR. Technical Paper 385. World Bank, Washington, D.C.

Stone, Andrew, Brian Levy, and Ricardo Paredes. 1992. "Public Institutions and Private Transactions: The Legal and Regulatory Environment for Business Transactions in Brazil and Chile." Policy Research Working Paper 891. World Bank, Washington, D.C.

Tarr, David G., Glenn Harrison, Thomas Rutherford, and Angelo Gurgel. 2002. "Regional, Multilateral and Unilateral Trade Policies for Growth and Poverty Reduction in Brazil." Unpublished Working Paper. World Bank, Washington, D.C.

Tyler, William. 1984. *"A Incidência Regional de Incentivos Não-Espaciais no Brasil."* Revista Brasileira de Economia 38 (3): 183–204.

Tyler, William. 2002. "Strengthening the Policy Environment for Export Growth in Brazil." Unpublished Working Paper. World Bank, Washington, D.C.

Wilmore, Larry. 1992. "Transnational and Foreign Trade: Evidence from Brazil." Journal of Development Studies 28 (2): 314–335.

7
Innovation and Knowledge

7

Innovation and Knowledge

Introduction

The ability to innovate in order to move closer to the technology frontier is key to bridging the gap between industrial and developing countries. Historically Brazil has shown strong support for technology and innovation which has allowed it to grow into the world class economy it is today.

Starting with Solow's neoclassical growth theory in the 1950s, economists have come up with various ways of modeling technology and innovation to explain differences in growth and productivity growth among countries. Nearly 50% of growth is associated not with factors of production accumulation but with the better use of those factors. To innovate, a country needs a knowledge-based economy, one able to create, absorb and capture, and diffuse knowledge. Knowledge is created through research and development (R&D), supported by a good incentive regime, competitive framework, and intellectual property rights regime. Absorbing and capturing foreign knowledge depends on trade and foreign direct investment (FDI)and associated R&D. Diffusing knowledge is achieved through information and communications technology and an efficient network structure.

The ability to develop technological capabilities and produce a knowledge-based economy depends, to a large extent, on the level of skills of the labor force, the number of scientists, the number of higher education graduates, and the science and technology framework.

Economic development and support for science and technology

During the 1960s and most of the 1970s, Brazil was one of the fastest-growing economies in the world. Growth slowed substantially in the 1980s, however, as a result of the slow-

This chapter summarizes a more comprehensive text entitled "Innovation and Technology in Brazil," written by José Luis Guasch in May 2002. The analyses and suggestions contained in this chapter are based on the international technical experience of the World Bank and are presented as a contribution to the debate and formulation of public policies.

down in manufacturing. During the 1990s annual GDP growth fell to 3 percent, and manufacturing output grew just 2.1 percent a year. By the end of the twentieth century, many East Asian economies that had been poorer than Brazil in the 1960s had pulled ahead (table 1).

Table 1. Selected economic indicators, 1999

Country	Gross national income per capita (US$)	Annual GDP growth (percent)		Annual growth of manufactured output (percent)		Share of manufactured exports (%) of total)
	1999	1980-90	1990-99	1980-90	1990-99	1999
Brazil	4,350	2.7	3.0	1.6	2.1	54
Chile	4,630	4.2	7.2	3.4	9.0	17
Korea (Rep. of)	8,490	9.4	5.7	13.0	7.1	91
Malaysia	3,390	5.3	7.3	9.3	9.7	80
Mexico	4,440	1.1	2.7	1.5	4.0	85

Source: World Bank 2001b.

Brazil emerged from World War II with a strong impetus for import substitution. The war resulted in strong unsatisfied demand for capital goods and consumer durables, which could not be imported for more than a decade. The 1940s and 1950s saw the development of policies that led to the establishment of many new firms, with the emphasis on infrastructure and heavy industry. These policies included protection of local markets and special treatment for foreign investors to induce them to set up manufacturing facilities in Brazil. Efforts to copy technology led many domestic firms to develop in-house engineering departments whose main job was to produce technological knowledge that could help adapt products to domestic demand.

By the 1970s the diminishing excess domestic demand for capital goods and consumer durables and the lack of competitiveness in international markets due to protectionist policies led to a slowdown of industrial growth. The 1980s and 1990s witnessed a diminishing of the relative importance of the Brazilian industrial sector in terms of value-added and employment: industrial GDP declined from 45 percent of total GDP in the early 1980s to 38 percent in 1990 and less than 30 percent in 1999, and industrial employment fell 26 percent between 1990 and 1999. The combination of a domestic slowdown and the rapid outward movement of the world's technological frontier accounted for the rapidly expanding gap between Brazilian and world productivity.

The government-led import substitution industrialization model that sheltered the industrial sector from foreign competition survived until the late 1980s, when Brazil implemented a series of reforms aimed at enhancing the role of market forces and building an export-oriented economy. In 1988 Brazil liberalized trade. In 1991 it signed the Mercosul trade agreement, and in the early 1990s it began its privatization program, which it accelerated in 1996. The drive toward reform, however, was hampered by persistent high inflation and macroeconomic instability during the late 1980s and much of the 1990s.

Support for science and technology since the 1950s

Brazil began supporting science and technology in the 1950s. In 1951 it established the National Research Council to promote research in all areas. Strengthening science and technology in this period was a matter of prestige, and much of it was driven by the military.

Support for science and technology increased during the 1960s. The 1968–69 development plan defined an explicit science and technology policy, at the federal level, for the first time. The plan proposed creation of a National System of Scientific and Technological Development (SNDCT), of Science and Technology Basic Plans that would spell out the actions envisioned in the national development plans, and of a National Fund for Scientific and Technological Development (FNDCT) to finance the SNDCT. In 1972 the *Secretaria de Tecnologia Industrial* (STI) was established under the Ministry of Industry and Commerce, which was in charge of fostering technological development in public and private enterprises. The 1970s and 1980s saw a strong emphasis on technology development and a large role for the state.

In the late 1990s a new series of more technology-oriented measures was put in place with the *Programa de Apoio ao Desenvolvimento Científico e Tecnológico* (PADCT). PADCT I and II, which invested US$470 million in 4,500 projects between 1986 and 1997, were schemes put in place by the government with the support of the World Bank. They focused on building research infrastructure and training scientific personnel. A reform and investment program was implemented with a total planned expenditure of some $360 million for 1997–2001. The program included a series of schemes to support R&D cooperative projects (between the government/university sector and the business sector), basic technological research, and various services (metrology and standards, intellectual property rights regime, evaluation and monitoring).

To spur the innovative capability of the economy, the Brazilian government has established ten sectoral funds using resources from a tax on services provided by recently privatized enterprises, and it plans to set up a public venture capital fund. It has established the National Council of Science and Technology Development (CNPq) and *Financiadora de Estudos e Projetos* (FINEP) to assist, finance, and facilitate R&D activities; created a Strategic Study Center within the Ministry of Science and Technology; passed an Innovation Law; drafted a white paper on science and technology post–*Livro verde*; created the *Serviço do Apoio às Micro e Pequenas Empresas* (SEBRAE), which promotes exports by small and medium-sized firms; and set up *Centros Nacionais de Tecnologia* (CENATECS). Together with the states, it has developed incubators and science and technology parks, and it has spread "cluster fever" across the country. Meanwhile, some states have implemented their own institutions, such as *Fundação de Apoio à Pesquisa do Estado de São Paulo* (FAPESP).

The current state of science and technology in Brazil

In many ways, Brazil is relatively well-positioned to create and reap the benefits of a knowledge economy. It has a highly entrepreneurial economy, makes significant public sector expenditures on R&D, provides significant institutional support to science and technology, enjoys significant FDI, and has excelled in certain innovation and technology programs. It has made cutting-edge contributions in information technology and automation, aerospace technology (satellites), nuclear technology, biotechnology, military technology, and agriculture. Within the region it has been a pioneer in implementing a science and technology program with structured institutions and incentive regimes.

This potential notwithstanding, Brazil currently ranks 49th among 75 countries rated in terms of the state of their technology (Sachs and Vial 2002). It ranks 38th on the information and communications technology index, which measures the extent of use of new technologies, perceived as a key factor in the ability to compete. In terms of ability to absorb new technologies, Brazil ranks 36th out of 48 noncore innovators. Despite this, Brazil is among the more innovative countries in Latin America, but it depends to a large extent on technology transfer.

The Knowledge Assessment Scorecard for Brazil, which rates countries on 15 dimensions of the knowledge economy, indicates much scope for improvement (figure 1). The scorecard is based on performance indicators and indicators of economic incentives, institutional regime, the innovation system, education and human resources, and the information infrastructure.

Figure 1. Knowledge Assessment Scorecard for Brazil

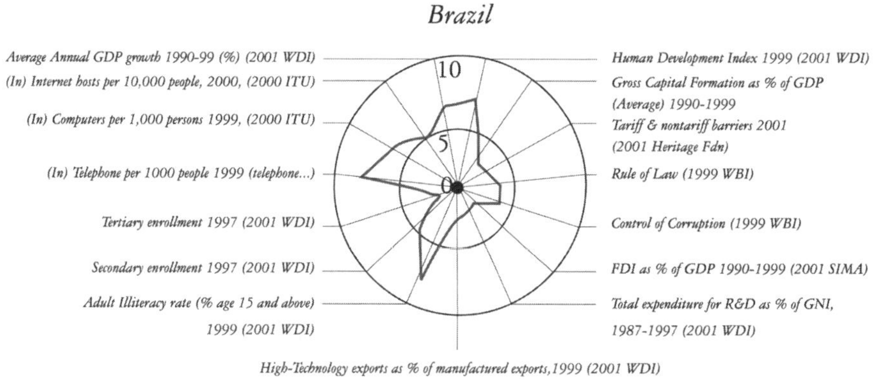

Brazil

Average Annual GDP growth 1990-99 (%) (2001 WDI)

(ln) Internet hosts per 10,000 people, 2000, (2000 ITU)

(ln) Computers per 1,000 persons 1999, (2000 ITU)

(ln) Telephone per 1000 people 1999 (telephone...)

Tertiary enrollment 1997 (2001 WDI)

Secondary enrollment 1997 (2001 WDI)

Adult Illiteracy rate (% age 15 and above) 1999 (2001 WDI)

High-Technology exports as % of manufactured exports,1999 (2001 WDI)

Human Development Index 1999 (2001 WDI)

Gross Capital Formation as % of GDP (Average) 1990-1999

Tariff & nontariff barriers 2001 (2001 Heritage Fdn)

Rule of Law (1999 WBI)

Control of Corruption (1999 WBI)

FDI as % of GDP 1990-1999 (2001 SIMA)

Total expenditure for R&D as % of GNI, 1987-1997 (2001 WDI)

Source: World Bank 2001a.

For Brazil to capture all the benefits associated with an innovative knowledge economy, it needs to address several issues. The government spends a significant amount on research, science, and technology, but its expenditures are unequal across regions, undermined by human capital considerations, and concentrated in the public sector. This policy note highlights challenges and suggests possible policy alternatives for financing knowledge creation, improving the regulatory environment to improve the absorption and capture of knowledge, using information and communications technologies to diffuse knowledge, and improving higher education to sustain development.

Message 1. Improving the impact of public funds for R&D.
Brazil, for LAC standards, spends a large amount of public funds in R&D, but with relatively little results. Strengthening the linkages between research institutions and industry is critical for leveraging scarce public funds, spurring private sector R&D, and for the creation of knowledge in Brazil. The government could achieve these goals by evaluating public programs for effectiveness and coherence, allocating public funds based on merit and competitive criteria, promoting private participation by transferring technology from the public sector to business. The incentive structure on appropriation of innovation rights could be modified, granting those rights to the university or researcher. Creating M.S. and Ph.D. programs run jointly by universities and the business sector could also increase the private sector's contribution to knowledge.

Context

Brazilian scientists and engineers have made important contributions in several areas. Brazilian scientists were the first to crack the genetic code of the Xylella bacteria, which attacks orange trees and grapevines; world-class technology programs have been developed in aeronautics (Embraer), satellites (CBERS), deep-water exploration (Petrobras), tropical agriculture (Embrapa), and biotechnology (Genoma). It illustrates the potential Brazil has to innovate if these efforts were systemic and created significant spillovers, rather than being highly focalized and spotty. All of these successful R&D investments have come from the public sector, however. Excluding state owned enterprises, less than 30 percent of Brazil's R&D is done by the private sector—much less than in Ireland (70% percent) Korea (73 percent), or the United States (70 percent) (figure 2). Brazil, along with Costa Rica, are the countries in the region that spend the most in terms of GDP, about 1.3%. Also Brazil is one of the few countries that has attempted to build a National Innovation System with a plethora of initiatives, with the Ministry of Science and Technology at the forefront. Given the fiscal constraints facing the public sector, a better and more leveraged use of those significant funds could bring improvements.

Figure 2. Public, private, and foreign R&D expenditure shares in Brazil and selected other countries, 1999

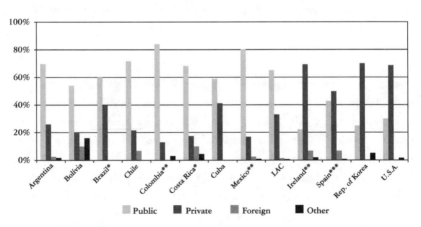

*1996, ** 1997, ***1998.
Note: For international comparison, public general university funds (R&D funds from the general grant received from the Ministry of Education or from the corresponding provincial or local authorities in support of overall research and teaching activities) are included under "public." Funds from the private nonprofit sector are considered "other."
Source: RICyT 2001; OECD 2001.

The efforts and programs set in place by the government to stimulate innovation are as follows. Since 1973, when it created FINEP, the Brazilian government has financed the development of domestic technology using four instruments:

- Subsidized loans, risk-sharing instruments, and venture capital investments from FINEP.
- Tax incentives for R&D by the Ministry of Science and Technology.
- Sector funds or research grants from the Ministry of Science and Technology.
- Support to technology-oriented companies through the Contec-Condiminum risk-sharing program of BNDESPAR, a subsidiary of the Brazilian National Development Bank (BNDES).

The Ministry of Science and Technology intended to revamp its innovation policy, but it has expanded programs instead of restructuring them based on evaluated effectiveness. In 2001 it introduced 10 sectoral funds, which provide R$1 billion in research grants. Despite that initiative federal support for R&D and funding provided by CNPq, charged with creating well-trained scientific and technological manpower, has declined.

Brazil offers five different types of tax incentives for R&D, some applicable to all industries and some applicable only to specific industries, such as the computer industry. The most prominent incentive applicable to all industries, Law 8661/93, includes the following financial incentives:

- Accelerated depreciation of machinery, equipment, devices and instruments, fittings, and tooling used in R&D.
- A 50 percent reduction in the industrial products tax payable on equipment or supplies purchased for use solely under the program.
- Accelerated amortization of outlays made for acquisition of intangible goods tied to R&D.
- Deduction of up to 4 percent of the income tax due on expenditures on technological and industrial R&D activities.
- Deduction as an operating expense of royalty, technical, and scientific assistance payments up to 5 percent of net income earned from the sale of goods produced with the technology for which such payments were made, provided that the pertinent transfer of technology agreement is ratified according to the terms of the Industrial Property Code.

Broadly, these five tax incentives boil down to loans for enterprises and grants for universities and research institutes. Currently, FINEP can finance up to 20 percent of the value of a project for variable repayment financing and up to 100 percent of the value of non-revenue yielding infrastructure projects, which are eligible for nonrefundable financial support. FINEP allocations have increased since 1990, but they have been volatile, more than doubling in 1991–95 and declining in 1995–2000. Not surprisingly, these allocations have followed the economic cycle, with significant reductions in slow growth years. While this volatility is understandable, it makes it difficult for firms and universities to invest in R&D, since investments tend to be long term and the reliability of the direct or indirect co-financing by the governments is critical.

Innovation surveys of the São Paulo area—the most dynamic region in Brazil—indicate that about 25 percent of firms introduced technologically modified products or processes between 1996 and 1998 (Quadros et al 2001). Although this figure is lower than the 50 percent typical in industrial countries, it is nevertheless substantial. Innovation is concentrated in intermediate goods, such as chemicals, and conventional engineering sectors. A large proportion of innovations is driven by demands and ideas from suppliers and clients rather than by science and research activities, a feature observable in industrialized economies, albeit in a lower proportion.

There are signs that a dynamic, small and medium-size, enterprise segment is emerging. More than 10,000 high-productivity firms with 20–500 employees have been identified, and the number of exporting companies has been increasing steadily in all size categories (although 450 firms were responsible for nearly three-quarters of manufactured exports in 2000.) These small and medium-size firms benefit from several export promotions and other programs, including SEBRAE, the well-funded service for support of small and medium-size firms, in conjunction with private actors and social organizations They also benefit from 45 industry-funded CENATECS and services provided by universities, such as "dial technology" offices-for quick assistance to the private sector, which have grown in recent years.

Incubators to support techno-entrepreneurs are also spreading. Some of these incubators are part of larger structures, such as technology parks. A first cluster of science and technology parks is beginning to consolidate around the city of Campinas in the State of São Paulo, where 13 research universities and research institutions are responsible for 16 percent of the country's scientific output, generating 9 percent of national GDP.

Despite some efforts and successes, linkages between research institutions and industry are weak. Brazilian scientists do not manifest the same entrepreneurial spirit as people in other segments of the economy, partly because the incentive regime does not allow them to reap the benefits of their innovations. Only 462 Ph.D.s were working in business incubators at the end of 2000—less than 1.7 percent of the 27,700 Ph.D.s working in university departments and research institutions.

Options

A comprehensive evaluation of the effectiveness of current programs and initiatives could help policymakers revamp Brazil's public science and technology effort, consolidating programs and eliminating or modifying those with little added-value. Funds from the Ministry of Science and Technology could be allocated based on clear tradeoffs and objectives (such as excellence versus relevance, basic versus industrial research).

Private participation could be promoted by transferring technology from the public sector to business, by changing the incentive systems of property rights to publicly financed innovations and by rewarding joint university-private sector projects-via competitive allocated grants, and by creating industrial R&D M.S. and Ph.D. programs run jointly by universities and the business sector.

Message 2. Increasing the level and share of private R&D expenditures through a better incentive framework: providing matching grants, strengthening intellectual property rights, improving patent registration, and simplifying the bureaucratic regulatory framework

Fiscal and subsidy incentives, intellectual property rights and patent registration create incentives for the private sector to invest in R&D. To strengthen these incentives, a stronger intellectual property rights law could allow private firms to appropriate rents from inventions and innovations. Fiscal incentives can be a trigger for increased private sector R&D. Given distortions in the tax system, subsidies such as matching grants appear more appropriate. The government could also simplify the bureaucratic steps required to register patents. A reduced number of government licenses would facilitate foreign investment and related technology transfers and put pressure on domestic firms. The government could also facilitate innovation ventures and improve technology norms, standards, and normalization.

Context

Intellectual property rights regimes affect the innovation climate. Laws governing inventions, industrial designs, trademarks, and software are adequate and comply with international standards, could be strengthened. However, the conditions governing their application are inadequate. The patent approval process takes five years on average. This needs to be shortened to less than a year. Enforcement of intellectual property laws is mediocre, because of judicial backlogs and the lack of judges adequately trained in intellectual property law (FIAS 2001).

Based on the index developed by Sherwood (2000), and Park (2002), Brazil's intellectual property rights environment is about average for Latin America and the Caribbean but well below OECD countries (figure 3). As for foreign patents, Brazilian law permits the issuance of compulsory licenses if the patent holder supplies the Brazilian market through imports rather than local production.

There are no incentives to stimulate invention based on R&D work performed in universities or in businesses funded by the federal government. Legislation such as the Bayh-Dole Act in the United States—which allows individuals to retain title to inventions developed under federally funded research programs and encourages their commercialization, notably through small and medium-sized firms—could help spur innovation in Brazil.

Figure 3. Protection of intellectual property rights in Brazil and selected other countries, 1997 and 2001

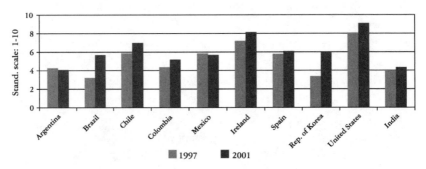

Note: Data for 1997 reflect whether "intellectual property is adequately protected in your country." Data for 2001 reflect the degree to which "patent and copyright protection is enforced in your country."

PATENT REGISTRATION. Although Brazil's inventive performance, measured by the number of patents deposited in international offices such as the U.S. Patent and Trademark Office (USPTO) and the World Intellectual Property Organization (WIPO), is improving, it remains mediocre and is not commensurate with the country's investments in science and technology (table 2). Countries such as India and Singapore, in which fewer patents were granted in 1987, had overtaken Brazil by a significant amount by 2000. Brazil grants more patents than other Latin America and Caribbean countries, but when adjusted by expenditures in R&D, its figures are below the regional average. Internationally, Brazil accounted for just 0.18 percent of total patent requests to the WIPO in 2000. In contrast, China accounted for 0.64 percent, the Republic of Korea 1.7 percent, and the United States 42 percent.

Table 2. Number of patents granted in Brazil and selected other countries, 1987–2000

Year	Brazil	Argentina	Mexico	India	South Africa	Singapore	Israel	Korea Rep. of	Taiwan (China)
1987	34	18	49	12	107	11	245	84	343
1988	29	16	44	14	103	6	238	97	457
1989	36	20	39	14	134	18	325	159	591
1990	41	17	32	23	114	12	299	225	732
1991	62	16	29	22	105	15	304	405	906
1992	40	20	39	24	97	32	335	538	1,001
1993	57	24	45	30	93	38	314	779	1,189
1994	60	32	44	27	101	51	350	943	1,443
1995	63	31	40	37	123	53	384	1,161	1,620
1996	63	30	39	35	111	88	484	1,493	1,897
1997	62	35	45	47	101	94	534	1,891	2,057
1998	74	43	57	85	115	120	754	3,259	3,100
1999	91	44	76	112	110	144	743	3,562	3,693
2000	98	54	76	131	111	218	783	3,314	4,667

Source: U.S. Patent and Trademark Office http://www.uspto.gov/.

Most Brazilian patents are granted to individuals and domestic companies (those receiving five or more patents). The share of domestic companies is increasing, but most patents are granted to companies such as state-owned Petrobrás. Multinational corporations have not received many patents, with just two companies receiving five or more patents.

Regulatory barriers to protecting intellectual property rights are hurting Brazil's ability to absorb and capture knowledge. These barriers include delays in processing patent applications; the requirement that the *Instituto Nacional de Propriedade Intelectual* (INPI), the national patent office, approve all royalty payments for technical assistance or technology transfer; and weak enforcement of property rights. Brazil's policy framework also provides insufficient protection for patent holders, and they have to take on a high cost burden. Plaintiffs, in patent infringement suits, for example, must establish precise monetary damage (FIAS 2001).

FOREIGN INVESTMENT. Brazil is still a relatively closed economy (figure 4). Its ratio of exports plus imports to GDP (22 percent in 1999) is one of the lowest in the world—less than half the 52 percent world average and much lower than the ratio in Germany (57 percent), the United Kingdom (53 percent), France (50 percent), China (41 percent), India (27 percent), and or the United States (24 percent). The only major country with a lower ratio than Brazil is Japan, with a ratio of just 19 percent. Brazil also has the highest non-tariff barriers in the Region. The lack of a large trade sector and the continuing high level of protection mean that Brazil is insufficiently integrated into the global knowledge economy.

Figure 4. Mean tariff barriers in Brazil and selected other countries, 1990 and 1999 (percent)

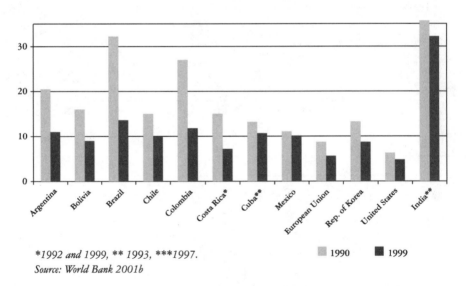

*1992 and 1999, ** 1993, ***1997.
Source: World Bank 2001b

■ 1990   ■ 1999

According to some qualitative indices, domestic competition in Brazil is adequate, suggesting that the main issue is low exposure to international competition. That is, Brazilian firms face less pressure than firms in other countries to improve their technology and productivity in order to keep up with the rapidly changing international environment.

Brazil's position in international trade has declined slightly over the past two decades. Brazil has shifted its export composition away from basic products toward industrial goods, a pattern that is consistent with trends in world trade. However, its comparative advantage has grown in resource-based sectors, while its competitiveness in technology-intensive sectors has declined. Market share has fallen in electronics, textiles, transport equipment, and processed agricultural products, and grown in steel, nonferrous metals, chemicals, and petrochemicals.

Traditionally, multinational corporations have been the main source of technological and managerial modernization in Brazil. Despite the growth in FDI flows and continuing investor confidence, however, the potential for FDI to operate as a knowledge precursor seems to be declining (Frischtak 2001). FDI is increasingly going to services and other nontradable goods, where competitive pressures are weaker, the knowledge gap is not as pronounced, and competitive advantage stems from the low cost of capital. Cumulative FDI flows in 1996–99 were 19.2 percent for industry and 79.2 percent for services. There are significant obstacles to high-quality FDI, including a restrictive regime on technology transfer (the systematic requirement for government licenses) and mediocre protection of property rights. A well-functioning intellectual property rights regime, fully in line with trade-related aspects of intellectual property rights agreements, would significantly increase foreign direct investment.

Despite a relatively unattractive policy framework, foreign investors have been active in Brazil, attracted by the size of the market and the country's natural resource base (figure 5), yet its FDI/GDP ratio is lower than in many other LAC countries. Restrictions on FDI have been beneficial to certain high-technology industries, such as aeronautics, but they have hurt other industries. Attempts to build a local computer industry through the state-owned enterprise COBRA were not very successful, for example, and the general feeling is that restrictions on FDI stultified the growth of a domestic industry.

Figure 5. Foreign direct investment in Brazil and selected other countries, 1989 and 1999

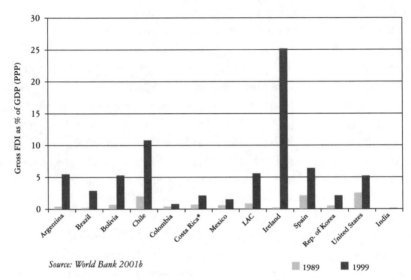

Source: World Bank 2001b

☐ 1989 ■ 1999

Options

Policy options for improving the capacity to absorb and capture knowledge include the following:

- Prepare a solid intellectual property rights law allowing private researchers to profit from inventions and innovations created using public funds.

- Review enforcement of property rights by the courts. The government has relatively little power to change institutional practices, but it could propose legislative changes.

- Strengthen INPI's institutional capacity to reduce the time it takes to process a patent application from the current five years to a period more consistent with international norms (most industrialized countries process patent applications in about 12 months).

- Increase pressure from foreign competition to raise firm productivity and spur domestic innovation, by lowering tariff and non-tariff barriers and eliminating restrictions on maximum share holdings by foreign companies operating in Brazil.

- Reduce government license requirements to facilitate the use of foreign investment and related technology transfers.

- Facilitate innovation ventures and improve technology norms, standards, and normalization.

• Abolish requirements for the approval of royalty payments. Such requirements are not part of the intellectual property frameworks of Chile and the United States, two countries Brazil could emulate in this area.

Message 3. Facilitating the diffusion of innovation and technology and improving the coherence of the national innovation system
Information and communication technology and an effective network system are critical for diffusing knowledge and information. It can improve education outcomes—a key requirement of the knowledge economy—and increase productivity at micro, small, and medium-size enterprises. Access to and use of information and communications technology could be increased by enhancing and passing e-commerce legislation, creating effective competition in the telecommunications industry, establishing credit programs or matching grants aimed at strengthening the technological capabilities of industries and firms, providing fiscal incentives for the emergence of "anchors" of diffusion of knowledge through the supply chain, optimizing cluster arrangements for the production and internal diffusion of knowledge, fostering technology transfer within the production chain, and promoting quality norms, metrology, normalization, and certification.

Context
Computer penetration is lower in Brazil than in Argentina, Chile, or Mexico (table 3). It ranks lower than Argentina and Mexico but slightly higher than Chile in terms of the percentage of companies conducting e-commerce. Developing the population's information and communications technology skills could increase Internet content.

Table 3. Information technology use in Brazil and selected other countries, 2000

Country	Internet hosts (per 10,000 people)	Mobile phones (per 1,000 people)	Personal computers [a] (per 1,000 people)	Telephone mainlines (per 1,000 people)
Developing countries				
Argentina	675.1	163.4	51.3	213.2
Brazil	293.9	136.3	44.1	181.8
Chile	1,657.7	222.2	82.3	221.3
China	173.7	65.8	15.9	111.8
Costa Rica	621.4	52.0	149.1	249.4
India	49.4	3.5	4.5	32.0
Korea, Rep. of	4,025.4	566.9	237.9	463.7
Malaysia	1,590.0	213.2	103.1	199.2
Mexico	274.3	142.4	50.5	124.7
Taiwan (China)	2,810.2	802.4	222.8	567.5
Industrialized countries				
Denmark	3,658.5	631.1	431.5	719.5
France	1,443.3	493.3	304.3	579.3
Germany	2,917.6	586.0	336.0	610.5
Portugal	2,494.1	664.9	299.3	430.3
Spain	1,327.0	609.3	142.9	421.2
United States	3,465.8	397.9	585.2	699.7
United Kingdom	3,011.8	727.0	337.8	588.6

[a] *Estimated. Source: ITU 2000*

Equipment costs have traditionally been one of the binding constraints to Internet connection. Recently, new producers (Compaq and Dell, among others) have entered the Brazilian market. With imports and competition from gray market producers, which together supply an estimated 50–60 percent of demand, these new entrants have caused prices to fall. Nonetheless, demand remains limited by Brazil's unequal income distribution, the high cost and limited availability of credit, and the 41 percent tax burden on information and communications technology products, which is considerably higher than in other countries.

Rapid technological changes have lowered the costs of information and communications technology. The cost of voice transmission circuits dropped by a factor of 10,000 over the past 20 years, and computing power per dollar rose by a factor of 10,000. The information and communications technology revolution, in turn, is increasing the power of electronic networks as research tools, permitting a larger set of new technologies to emerge. These changes are having a major impact on business and social interactions.

The privatization of Telebras and the liberalization strategy orchestrated by Anatel, the national telecommunications agency, have helped develop Brazil's information infrastructure in recent years. From July 1998, when 27 state-owned telephone companies were privatized, to December 1999, 7.6 million new telephone lines were installed, an expansion of more than 37 percent in a year and a half. During the same period the number of public telephones rose from 547,000 to 740,000. Local and long-distance phone rates fell (table 4), and quality improved, as measured by the network digitalization index, the average time to get a dial tone, and the number of orders placed for repair services per 100 public telephones. More than 271,000 phones purchased through expansion plans that had not been delivered in December of 1998 were installed by May of 1999.

Table 4. Telephone tariffs in selected countries in North, South, and Central America, 1998

(US$)	Residential		Business		Local	Monthly residential subscription costs as a fraction of
Country	Connection	Monthly subscription	Connection	Monthly subscription	call	GDP per capita
Argentina	150	12.8	150	36.4	0.10	1.9
Brazil	43	6.7	43	11.6	0.09	1.7
Canada	42	13.2	58	37.8	0.07	0.8
Chile	159	16.3	159	16.3	0.12	4.2
Peru	151	14.8	151	16.2	0.08	7.3
United States	44	19.9	70	41.3	0.09	0.8
Central America	121	6	159	9.9	0.06	4.4
South America	186	7	247	12.3	0.07	2.8
Caribbean	51	9.2	65	19.8	0.07	3.7
LAC average	107	8.3	145	16.4	0.07	3.3

Source: ITU 2000

Despite these improvements, "teledensity" in Brazil remains lower than in industrial economies. Brazil's fixed line teledensity is just 23.1 lines per 100 inhabitants, one third that of the United States and half that of Spain.

Considerable progress has been made in wireless phone service. In 1994 just 800,000 people in Brazil owned cell phones. That figure rose to 5.6 million by July 1998 and 15 million by December 1999. The launch of prepaid services increased demand and increased competition is driving down costs, allowing a growing proportion of the Brazilian population to benefit from access to telecommunications resources. Mobile service density is projected to grow from 14 to 32.6 accesses per 100 people between 2000 and 2005.

Less than 6 percent of Brazil's population has access to the Internet, because of lack of infrastructure, high prices, and low educational levels. Though estimates vary, partly due to definitional issues, about 9–10 million people, or 54–60 people per 1,000 population, can be considered "connected" to the Internet. This figures compares unfavorably with Mexico (95 per 1,000), Chile (156 per 1,000), and Argentina (174 per 1,000).

Despite the low penetration of the Internet, Brazil is Latin America's largest Internet market, representing more than 50 percent of all Internet users and nearly 80 percent of all e-commerce activities in the region. These statistics, combined with the fact that the Brazilian Internet market is growing at more than 50 percent a year, make Brazil an attractive market for international operators.

About 7–8 percent of the population 10 and older have access to broad informational resources, as of 2000. Ibope, a public opinion research institute that tracks Internet use in the country, concluded that 84 percent of users are upper or middle class and 14 percent are lower middle class. Just 4 percent of Internet users come from classes below the lower middle class, classes that make up most of Brazil's population. These data suggest that the Internet is still overwhelmingly an elite instrument in Brazil, where it is probably helping reinforce the already high inequality, when it should be a key productive instrument to access information and knowledge .

With few national Internet backbones, the cost of connecting to the network charged by the dominant provider (the privatized Embratel, which controls an estimated 70–80 percent of Internet traffic) is a multiple of equivalent services in other countries, where competition is more intense. On Brazil's current trajectory, low-income households and less developed regions will be left behind. It will take a great deal of government-supported funding to create affordable community Internet access centers and to provide basic education and training on how to use the Internet.

Finally Brazil has seen an avid interest for the development of networks, particularly clusters. While they come of all shapes and modes a better design and improved linkages with scientific institutions could add significant value. Many of the cluster have little to do with innovation, exceptions are the technology ones in Parana and

Pernambuco. Better information and commitment from the private sector on how to bring the innovation component would be highly desirable.

Options

One policy alternative for increasing diffusion of innovation and technology is to focus on access by small and medium-sized firms. Creating customer-based and demand-driven programs could foster the organization of technological information systems, technology targets, and technology services. Credit programs or matching grants aimed at strengthening the technological capabilities of firms and industries could be considered. Optimizing cluster arrangements of small and medium-sized firms could facilitate intelligent network development for the production and internal diffusion of tacit knowledge. To spur private sector–lead initiatives in developing innovation clusters, the government could seek commitments of substantial resources in order to achieve a critical supply chain mass and establish technological platforms involving subnational governments.

The government could also focus on information and communications technology, considering policy changes that would effect three types of changes:

- PROMOTE UNIVERSAL ACCESS TO TELECOMMUNICATIONS. Achieving the knowledge and innovation gains possible through high-speed communications depends on Brazil's low-income households and less developed regions not being left behind. In the North and Northeast regions of Brazil, the fiber optic infrastructure, fundamental for high-speed communications, increasingly depends on market potential and income levels. This vast area will continue to depend on geostationary or low orbiting satellite-based communication to meet its communication needs, including voice telephone. With an average tax of 28.6 percent, the cost of local calls in Brazil remains among the highest in Latin America, and dedicated connections are prohibitively expensive. Without alternative tariff plans (such as unlimited local calls or byte-based rates) for Internet usage, dial-up Internet access, which is currently the dominant mode of accessing the Internet, will remain too expensive for most consumers. Increasing access will require deregulation, more intense competition, and foreign investment. Public policies can create affordable community Internet access centers and provide basic training in the use of the Internet.

- ESTABLISH A TRANSPARENT POLICY AND REGULATORY ENVIRONMENT. Continued growth in e-commerce depends on several factors: user privacy, the legitimacy of electronic contracts, the provision of industry-specific insurance, and antitrust regulations (limiting mergers and acquisitions between telecommunications and Internet service providers). With the liberalization of various market segments and the change in the nature of services offered, there is a need for transparent policy and rules on these issues.
- INCREASE CONTENT IN PORTUGUESE: The volume of information available in networks is an indicator of a nation's knowledge capacity. In Brazil local content is emerging, but the Internet remains a predominantly English-speaking medium, restricting access by the vast majority of Brazilians.

Message 4. Increasing efficiency in public higher education, increasing enrollment and quality of private higher education, and particularly focusing on increasing coverage of secondary education

A good-quality higher education system is crucial if Brazil is to achieve the full benefits of technology transfer and the diffusion of knowledge that come with trade and FDI. Changing the funding formula in order to encourage competition among universities could help increase enrollment and improve the quality of higher education. Policymakers could improve the efficiency of public universities, increase access to public universities by lower-income students, and increase entry and participation of private universities by providing pecuniary and nonpecuniary incentives.

Context

The capabilities of a country's innovation system are determined by its human resource development system. Brazil compares unfavorably with other countries in terms of human resources.

About 48,000 scientists and engineers work in R&D in Brazil, but the full-time equivalent is just 21,500. As a percentage of the workforce, the figure is lower than in most other Latin America and Caribbean countries (figure 6).

Figure 6. Proportion of scientists and engineers employed in R&D in Brazil and selected other countries, 2000

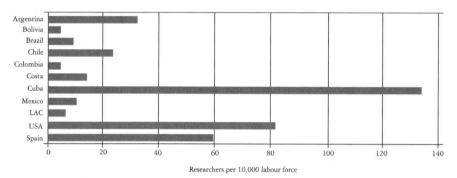

Researchers per 10,000 labour force

Source: RICyT 2001.

Educational attainment is low in Brazil (figure 7). For an economy at its per capita income level, Brazil has a low literacy rate (85 percent of the population older than 15). Its secondary enrollment rate (62 percent) compares poorly with that of China, a country in which per capita income is less than one-fifth of Brazil's but secondary enrollment is 70 percent. Progress has been made in recent years in Brazil, with a doubling of secondary school graduates—a trend that reflects both increased enrollments and reduced dropouts—but more needs to be done, particularly given the low priority that continues to be given to secondary education.

Figure 7. Highest level of education attained in Brazil and selected other countries, 2000

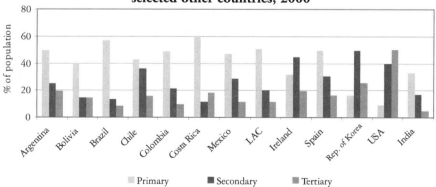

Note: Data include dropouts. Source: Barro and Lee 2000.

Brazilian enrollment rates in higher education lag behind the Latin American average (by 13 percent), and tertiary science enrollment is also lower than in other countries in the region, including Argentina, Bolivia, Chile, Colombia, Costa Rica, and Mexico (figure 8).

Figure 8. Tertiary science enrollment in Brazil and selected other countries

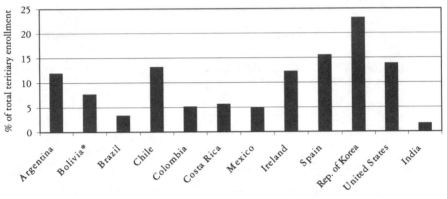

Note: Data are based on preliminary UNESCO estimations and refer to most recent year available during 1989–94. Source: UNDP 2001a.

Higher education enrollment in Brazil is higher than in China, although China may catch up with Brazil within five years. One reason China has been able to expand its higher education so rapidly is that it is has financed a third of the costs through student tuition. Brazil is not able to adopt a similar policy because its Constitution mandates free public higher education. As a result, it is left with a highly regressive system, since the children of the wealthier have access to free higher education that is of better quality than that provided by other institutions.

Options

To improve higher education in Brazil, policymakers could consider increasing the efficiency of public universities; shifting public funding to improve university access for lower-income students; facilitating increased entry and participation of private universities by providing pecuniary and non-pecuniary incentives ; and reconsidering the ban on charging tuition for public higher education.

To increase efficiency at public universities and enhance enrollment and quality in private higher education, Brazil could adopt performance-based funding of universities, establish standard of performance and disseminate information about quality of programs and success of graduates, remove barriers to foreign and private universities, and focus on better quality and relevance of private higher education, by adopting a demand-driven private-sector led approach. Adopting performance-based funding (output-related formulas) could shift resources from poorly performing institutions to the best managed institutions, thereby increasing coverage, equity, and relevance within the current budget envelop.

Policymakers could also consider introducing industrial R&D M.S. and Ph.D. programs at public universities. Denmark is an interesting case for study in this respect. Allowing scientists and engineers to profit from federally funded research could also improve the quality of public universities.

Finally the government could address the key weakness of the Brazilian education system: The low coverage of secondary education. Secondary education is the foundation and key base for the development of technological capabilities, and is in need of expansion if it is to guarantee equal opportunities for all.

References

World Bank reports

This chapter summarizes the content of the following World Bank reports. Those, in turn, draw heavily from a wide range of literature on the subject from experts in Brazil and beyond, which are referenced in the mentioned Bank reports.

FIAS (Foreign Investment Advisory Service). 2001. Brazil: Legal, Policy and Administrative Barriers to Investment in Brazil. (World Bank).

Park, Walter G. 2002. "Institutions and Incentives for R&D: Implications for LAC Economies." Background paper for Latin America and the Caribbean Region Flagship. World Bank, LAC Region, Washington, D.C.

World Bank. 2001a. Brazil: The New Growth Agenda. Vols. I and II. Latin America and the Caribbean Region, Brazil Country Management Unit, Washington, D.C.

World Bank 2001b. World Development Indicators. Washington, D.C.

Other references

Barro, Robert J. and Lee, Jong-Wha, 2000. International Data on Educational Attainment: Updates and Implications, "CID Working Paper No. 42", Center for International Development at Harvard University.

IMD & WEF, 1994. The World Competitiveness Report 1994, Joint publication by the International Institute for Management Development (Lausanne) and the World Economic Forum (Geneva).

IMD, 2001. World Competitiveness Yearbook, Lausanne: International Institute for Management Development.

ITU, 2000. World Telecommunication Indicators, Geneva: International Telecommunications Union.

Mani, Sunil. 2001. "Government, Innovation and Technology Policy: An Analysis of the Brazilian Experience During the 1990s." INTECH Discussion Paper Series 2001–11. Maastricht (NL): The United Nations University, Institute for New Technologies (INTECH).

OECD, 2001. Science, Technology and Industry Outlook, Drivers of Growth: Information Technology, Innovation and Entrepreneurship, Paris: Organisation for Economic Cooperation and Development.

Quadros, Ruy. 2001. "Technological Innovation in Brazilian Industry: An Assessment Based on the São Paulo Innovation Survey." International Journal of Technological Forecasting and Social Change 67 (2).

RICyT, 2001. S&T Indicators, available at http://www.unq.edu.ar/ricyt/indicolo.htm, Buenos Aires: Red Iberoamericana de Indicadores de Ciencia y Tecnologia), 2001.

Sherwood, R. M., "The TRIPS Agreement: benefits and costs for developing countrires," International Journal of Technology Management, Volume 19, No.1/ 2, 2000

UNDP 2001a. Human Development Report – Making New Technologies Work for Human Development, New York and Oxford: Oxford University Press.

UNDP 2001b. "Proposal for the preparation of an 'Investigation on Science, Technology and Human Development HDR Cuba 2002'", Aide Memoire, United Nations Development Program.

PART III

8
Development and Conservation of Forests

8

Development and Conservation of Forests

Introduction

Brazil is endowed with extraordinary natural wealth in its forests and savannahs. Development of these areas has traditionally meant "conversion": removing trees to use the soil for agriculture and cattle ranching. This happened first in the Atlantic Forest, of which very little is left; then in the Cerrado, where more than half the area is already occupied; and more recently in the Amazon, where most of the rain forest still remains.

The issue for the policy maker stems from the fact that private benefits of land are quite different from benefits to society: many of the benefits of keeping forest are not captured by those who own or use the forest, and conversely, many of the costs of cutting and clearing forest are not felt by those who do the cutting and clearing, but by present society and future generations. Such market failure calls for a role of government. A policy concerned with sustainability and equality needs to consider the use of natural resources, particularly the use of natural forests.

Brazil has already made extraordinary progress toward environmental protection and sustainable development: it has a highly advanced environmental legislation, including a rigid Forest Code, has set aside large areas for biodiversity protection, and has created other forms of conservation areas reconciling conservation, development and poverty reduction. More recently, the wide-ranging National Forest Program was created, concerned with sustainable use as well as conservation of this national asset.

The considerations of this chapter attempt to outline a strategy, based on the experiences and analyses of the World Bank, with five principal, linked messages summarized as follows

Brazil has extraordinarily large, rich and diverse forests. The Amazon is the world's largest remaining tropical forest. The Atlantic Forest and the Cerrado, the largest and

The draft of this chapter was completed by Chris Diewald in October 2002. The analyses and suggestions contained in this chapter are based on the international technical experience of the World Bank and are presented as a contribution to the debate and formulation of public policies.

most diverse savannah biome[1] on earth, are two among the world's 25 biodiversity "hotspots": extremely diverse, yet severely threatened.[2] The Atlantic Forest and much of the Cerrado have been converted to agricultural and urban use. The much larger Amazon Rain Forest has lost about one seventh of its original forest cover.

Clearing forests to produce sugar, beef, milk, fruit, coffee, grains and other crops has created wealth for the Brazilian people over the centuries. Even adverse conditions for agriculture, such as those of the Cerrado soils, have been overcome successfully by technology. But such production has not been sustainable everywhere. Unsustainable use has resulted in tracts of abandoned degraded land, soil erosion, changes in local climate, declining stream flows, and floods.

Brazil's native forests have served as seemingly inexhaustible sources of wood. Outside the Amazon, however, native timber has largely disappeared, replaced in part by pine and eucalyptus plantations, supported by large public subsidies or as captive supply for the pig iron and cellulose industries. Many of the plantations are being harvested for the last time and are not replaced (except for cellulose). The Amazon has become the prime source of tropical timber for Brazil (about 86 percent of Amazonian timber is consumed domestically). Logging thrives in the Amazon, moving from exhausted areas to new ones with abundant stocks.

Almost two-thirds of land reform and colonization occurred in the Amazon (in terms of area), which served as an escape valve, at low economic and political cost, for social problems arising in other regions. Migration has allowed many poor and not-so-poor people from other regions to attain a better livelihood.[3] But occupation of the Amazon created its own inequalities[4]—with highly concentrated land tenure, threats to traditional forest-dwelling families and communities, and the swelling of regional cities and towns with poor settlers abandoning their plots in the forest.

---

[1] A biome is major type of ecological community defined by its climate and vegetation, such as dry forests, rain forests, grasslands, savannas, etc.

[2] The Atlantic Forests primary vegetation covers just 0.07 percent of the earth's land mass, but harbors more than 2 percent of the earth's plants and vertebrates as endemic species, according to Myers, N. et al, Biodiversity hotspots for conservation priorities, Nature, Vol. 403 2000

[3] Schneider 1994

[4] One percent of all establishments, those with more than 2000 ha, occupy 47 percent of the total area of rural establishments. The 54 percent smallest holdings occupy just about 1.1 percent of the area (Chomitz and Thomas 2000).

Forests have been taken as a removable obstacle to agricultural development or as a source of timber. Yet even where agriculture and ranching appear to be sustainable, the loss of forest cover comes at a cost that needs to be weighed against the gains. The gains may not justify the losses in many cases. Brazilians are proud of the country's natural assets and increasingly value keeping Brazil's forests.[5] Other countries also express interest in the conservation of Brazil's forests for their importance for global climate and biodiversity. Brazil can benefit from this global interest, as it does already through the Pilot Program to Conserve the Brazilian Rain Forest and other externally funded programs.

The key forests

The ATLANTIC FOREST has lost some 92 percent of its original 1.1 million square kilometers of forest space to sugarcane and coffee plantations, cattle ranching, agriculture, and urban use. Some of today's most productive agriculture is located on former Atlantic forest land (though it is not without ecological problems) in the Southeast and South, but conversion elsewhere (Northeast) ended in widespread abandonment of pastures, or left sugarcane plantations maintained only by subsidies.

The CERRADO (2 million square kilometers), with its grassland, shrubs, and forest, has long been used for cattle grazing, but natural and planted pastures have increased rapidly in the last 40 years.[6] Today, it is an important new resource for Brazil's agricultural production, thanks to technological advances in adapting commercial crops to adverse soil conditions, but the increase in crop area is dwarfed by the increase in planted pastures. Including natural pastures, as much as half or even 70 percent of the Cerrado has been altered in some form.[7] The Brazilian Agricultural Research Corporation (EMBRAPA) considers 80 percent of pastures to be degraded.

The Cerrado is being occupied rapidly, with much less public attention than the Amazon. Yet science considers it the second richest biome in biodiversity in Brazil. Its ecosystems are endangered in two ways: through intensive agriculture and selective grazing (and overgrazing), which cause erosion, nutrient losses, soil compaction, pesticide pollution, and reduced stream flows from irrigation water use. The second risk is due to the

---

[5] WWF 2001 and MMA/ISER 2001.

[6] There is no legal definition of the "Cerrado" as there is for the "Legal Amazon." The Legal Amazon even contains some Cerrado lands, and thus there is some overlap between the two regions.

[7] Mueller 2002

removal of natural vegetation and to more frequent fires, with impacts not only on the bio-diversity and the general resilience of the ecosystems, but likely also on agriculture.

The government has promoted the penetration, occupation, and development of the AMAZON region (5.1 million square kilometers, 60% of Brazil's territory) since the 1960s. Economic growth, from a very low base and with subsidies, has been impressive over the last three decades. Rural GDP per capita in the Legal Amazon more than tripled between 1970 and 1995, mainly from expansion of pastures, but also from increasing productivity. While most direct subsidies have been removed, ranching and agriculture continue to grow. Social indicators in the Amazon have also improved, although they remain below the national average, and show extreme differences within the region. Improvements benefited largely the urban population.

Deforestation in the Amazon reached 15 percent of the original forest area in 2000, or 575,000 of 4 million square kilometers (figure 1).[8] Deforestation is concentrated in a belt along the southern and eastern edge of the Legal Amazon—80 percent of it in Pará, Mato Grosso, and Rondônia. Fire, a traditional, effective means of clearing forests and managing pastures, is often not controlled and escapes into adjacent forest or pastures, causing much larger fires than intended. The annual economic costs of property losses (fences, pastures and timber) and of respiratory diseases in the Amazon can be as high as US$ 120 million in drier years.[9]

Figure 1. Annual deforestation and the Amazon, 1989–2001

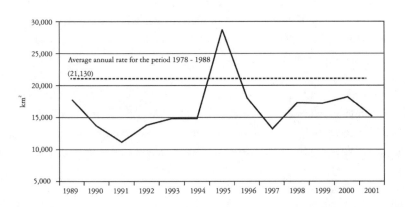

[8]   As   measured   and   published   by   INPE   from   satellite   images   INPE   2002: http://sputnik.dpi.inpe.br:1910/col/dpi.inpe.br/lise/2002/06.12.13.16/doc/Capa.htm

[9] Vera Diaz and others 2002

The causes of deforestation are under study, but in principle, clearing of forests occurs because it pays for people to do so, when and wherever forests are accessible, and not necessarily because of subsidies, ignorance or poverty.[10] Government infrastructure has provided such access to parts of the Amazon forest. Following that, a complex interaction among loggers, ranchers, land grabbers, speculators and small settlers, has developed its own dynamic. It is much less dependent on government intervention although the expectation of an expansion of public transport infrastructure and fear of (or hope for) expropriation for settlement schemes still plays an important role.[11]

Large cattle ranches occupy by far the largest part of the cleared forest (about 75 percent). Amazon cattle now represents a fifth of Brazil's herd. Ranches have often been formed from smaller lots cleared by small settlers on abundant land "ahead of the frontier," with government largely absent. Small pioneer settlers, gaining access to closed forests through private logging roads, farm their slash-and-burn plots for few years for subsistence crops. Cleared areas often change hands several times in a "race for property rights" and usually end up in the hands of those who are more capitalized, with better management skills and access to government services, including protection of property rights.[12] Lands have also been abandoned, for several reasons: excessive humidity, the cost of occupying the land for better-off owners speculating on land price increases with the advance of the frontier, or the high cost of securing property rights in the absence of government.[13]

But there is also evidence of stable, viable ranching and agriculture behind the frontier, of rising productivity and substantial private investment. Productivity and sustainability have improved over time from learning by doing. Many migrants have been able to do better than their peers in the regions where they came from, either from agriculture and ranching on land that increases in relative value or from sale of the land to others.[14]

---

[10] Nasi and others 2002

[11] The rate of deforestation has clearly not diminished with more stability of the currency since 1994. There are indications that deforestation is related to the rate of economic growth in Brazil, perhaps through growth in the demand for beef and timber. In as far as land prices have fallen since 1994, this would also suggest increased deforestation and less investment on cleared lands. Devaluation of the Real is likely also to have an impact on deforestation in as far as associated products (timber, beef and agricultural crops) are exportable.

[12] Schneider 1994.

[13] Schneider 1994.

[14] Schneider 1994.

At least 60% of the Federal Land Reform Agency's (INCRA) settlements are in the Amazon region. Rarely planned, these settlements usually regularized prior invasions of "unproductive" forest areas, followed immediately by clearing. Invaders had (or still have) reason to hope that land would be expropriated if cleared, and land owners had (or have) reason to fear expropriation if land was left under forest.[15] [16]Many settlers abandon or sell their plots later, and may stand in line for yet another settlement. Often, they do not receive property titles to their plots ("emancipação") for a long time, and government has been providing very little assistance to settlers in terms of extension, education, and health services, although this may be changing. Timber sales are an important source of settlers' early income.[17] The low level of skills, lack of off-farm employment, and a continuing stream of landless from the Northeast help to form a mobile pool of labor with low opportunity cost that accompanies the opening of new frontiers, tries to get formally settled, provides labor to logging and ranching concerns, or adds to the poor population of towns.

It is doubtful whether traditional rural settlements have helped to create a more equitable distribution of land,[18] to establish stable communities, or to reduce poverty in the Amazon, several promising examples of more sustainable settlements notwithstanding (e.g., Santa Carmem, Sinop, MT[19]). Federal policy changed in 1999, prohibiting land settlements in primary forest and refusing to expropriate land already invaded, but local practice remains largely the same.

Logging of native timber contributes importantly to the regional economy. Timber is obtained through selective logging or from clear-felling. Where timber is taken illegally from public land, the entire rent that could be collected by government is appropriated by loggers. "Unmanaged" selective logging causes substantial damage to remaining forests,

---

[15] Alston and others, 2001

[16] Medida Provisória de 2.183-56 of 2001 excludes expropriation of land for two years after an organized invasion, and excludes those who already benefited from settlement or participated in an invasion of public or private property from being candidates to receive a lot in a rural settlement.

[17] See IAG 2000, for a frank discussion of land reform in the Amazon.

[18] The distribution of land in the Amazon, with the exception of Rondônia, reflects that of the country as a whole: in 1995, 1 percent of all establishments, those larger than 2,000 hectares, controlled about 52 percent of all private land; the 54 percent smallest holdings had only about 1.5 percent of private land (Chomitz and Thomas 2000).

[19]IAG 2000.

and makes them more vulnerable to fire.[20] By law, selective logging must follow a management plan authorized by government. Few management plans are really implemented, and logs are often taken from unauthorized areas (including indigenous lands). The Brazilian Institute for the Environment and Renewable Natural Resources (IBAMA) has substantially reduced the number of active management plans, by suspension or cancellation, after critical reviews of their technical and legal adequacy and has clamped down on illegal logging, increasing the "cost of illegality" to loggers. Perhaps as a consequence, clear-felling has allegedly become a much larger, easier, and mainly legal source of logs in recent years, taken from rural settlements and other cleared areas, but this remains still to be proven.[21]

The challenges of sustainable development

Through the early 1990s policies favored the opening, occupation, and integration of forest regions, resulting in extensive forest removal. While active support to such traditional development has largely ceased, expansion of agricultural production in the Cerrado (and perhaps parts of the Amazon) remains a policy objective, and ambitious infrastructure plans may facilitate further access to Amazon forests. As knowledge has grown about the importance and complexity of ecosystems and the services they provide to the economy and the well-being of society, conservation concerns are beginning to play a larger role. With growing knowledge about the possible impacts of disturbing ecosystems and about the limits to transforming natural assets into other assets comes the unavoidable challenge to society and policymakers to make development sustainable.

Decisions need to take into account:

- PRIVATE VERSUS SOCIAL BENEFITS AND COSTS. What matters to settlers, farmers, ranchers, and loggers are the benefits and costs of converting forests that accrue to them, not the losses of environmental services and assets for which they do not pay, or the benefits from conserving natural resources for which they are not paid. These costs and benefits—"externalities"—are not being handled properly by the market. Rather, they are borne by the region, the nation, or the world.

---

[20] Moreira 1999.

[21] Smeraldi 2000, estimates the share of logs from clearfelling is 75 percent, from management plans as 10 percent, and from totally illegal operations (mogno) as 15 percent.

- Uncertainty. While private benefits, costs, and risks are usually well known, there is considerable uncertainty about the consequences of meddling with ecosystems, the magnitude of impacts, the value of assets and services lost, and thresholds (points of no return) that should not be crossed.
- Discounting the future. The benefits of conservation and the losses from consuming natural assets may be experienced only so far in the future that they have less weight in decisions of private agents and society. The impact of interventions may be recognized only after the damage has already been done. How do we take the needs and rights of our children and grandchildren into account?

Decisions become even more complex when the impact on the poor and on their chances of escaping poverty are considered. Many poor families living in and around the forests make a living from the forest or participate in forest conversion as migrant settlers. Reducing poverty will have to consider options for including these citizens in sustainable development and bettering their lives.

As more natural resources such as forests are converted to other uses, such as agriculture and ranching, the returns to these alternative uses diminish and the value of the remaining resource increases.[22] Between complete conservation and complete removal there must be some optimum degree of forest clearing at which cutting one more hectare has the same net benefit as keeping that hectare. That is the point at which deforestation should stop. Much of the debate on deforestation is really about this optimum. In practice, an optimum is difficult to determine because so little is known about future impacts and the value of what might be lost. Economics does not tell us reliably what is optimal, but it provides useful information for public discussion.

For the Atlantic Forest, optimum deforestation is not an issue since so little is left (less than 8 percent). In many places degraded and abandoned pastures demonstrate how little sustained value clearing has produced. The forest's environmental services are of growing importance for the large urban population of the region, for water supply, flood control, recreation, ecotourism, hydropower—even for agriculture and plantations.[23]

---

[22] The Black Forest in southern Germany had almost completely disappeared by the middle of the 19th century before the scarcity of trees was acutely felt and replanting on a large scale began. The fact that tree plantations appear and efforts are made to protect remaining natural stands as native resources dwindle has been observed in many countries (Hyde and others 1996)

[23] A large cellulose manufacturer in southern Bahia has carefully integrated native gallery forests with its eucalyptus plantations in recognition of the services provided by the natural forest.

Replanting is going on in the watersheds of São Paulo and other states, more owners are interested in creating private nature reserves, and IBAMA is recently taking a firmer stand on illegal logging and questionable hydropower schemes. Yet the Atlantic Forest remains under threat, suggesting that either society is not sure about the value of what remains or that powerful interests are prevailing against society.

In deciding whether to remove forests, to use them, or to protect them, the federal government will want to maximize the long-term benefits of land use (keeping or clearing forests) for Brazilian society as a whole, sometimes over the interest of private producers, states, and municipalities. The Forest Code (*Código Florestal*) and the creation and protection of indigenous lands, national parks, and reserves are examples where national interests already prevail. International concerns about forest loss enter federal policymaking where it is a party to international conventions, where it has entered into partnerships such as the Pilot Program to Conserve the Brazilian Rain Forest, or where Brazil could benefit from transfers from the rest of the world (carbon, biodiversity).

Keeping forests and other natural landscapes benefits many groups and people, while the cost (foregone opportunities) is borne by fewer stakeholders. It is much more difficult for the many to organize and speak out than it is for the few potential losers to make their voices heard. This calls for strong institutions that can mediate these conflicts and provide a level playing field for the parties involved. Such institutions currently don't exist related to use of land, although the National Water Agency and the river basin committees provide an example in the case of water.

Assuming that Brazilian policy is guided by some concept of sustainable development, options could be evaluated, keeping in mind the following long-term goals:

- Contributing to economic growth, income, and employment.
- Reducing poverty and providing a fairer distribution of assets.
- Maintaining the environmental services of forest ecosystems and conserving biodiversity.
- Minimizing the release of greenhouse gases.

Together, these four objectives are at the heart of sustainable development. Options for forest land use not only make different contributions to these four goals, and have different costs and benefits depending on the region, they also differ in how widely they can be applied.

Main options for land use are discussed in more detail in the Annex to this Chapter.

Message 1. Striving toward a shared Brazilian vision of the future of the biomes, and planning land use through a participatory process of political negotiation.
Since perceptions of the best land use in the Brazilian biomes are in conflict, consistent policies for the medium and long run should be guided by some common, widely shared vision of what Brazil's wants its major biomes to look like 20 – 50 years from now. Initiating a national dialogue on such visions requires some institution to lead it and to mediate necessarily arising conflicts.

Zoning has come to be considered in Brazil as an objective, scientific method to indicate best land use. Science contributes indeed to more rational thinking about land use, but zoning could gain from becoming more of a social, political process of negotiating land use and of mediating conflicts between potential winners and losers. Again, strong institutions are required to lead this process.

Zoning can provide the spatial dimension to planning in the public sector. As an intrinsic element of planning, zoning might best to be located in the Planning Ministry or state planning departments.

Context

A SHARED VISION FOR BRAZIL'S FORESTS. What should the Amazon, the Atlantic Forest, or the Cerrado regions look like 20 or 50 years from now? How much forest should remain, for what purpose, and where? What kind of development is desirable, with and without forests, and where? What kind of landscape does Brazil want to leave to coming generations?

There is no consensus on these questions—witness the debates on the Plurianual Plan "*Avança Brasil*" or the struggle in Congress about changes to the Forest Code—and likely there never will be full consensus. This does not mean that society could not strive toward such vision. Coherent national strategies and policies for a biome such as the Amazon or the Cerrado ought to be informed by a shared vision within society about the future of the biome. Getting close enough may not be possible any time soon, but a process to stimulate gradual convergence and reconciliation of disparate views and interests is nevertheless useful. A vision for a biome would contain some agreement on how much forest or natural vegetation should remain and would outline broad land uses in different subregions, resulting in a mosaic of uses and set-asides ("macro-zoning").

The "Integrated National Policy for the Amazon" (1995) mentions a new paradigm of occupation of the natural resources of the Amazon region. Its broad orientations have since led to some changes of legislation and rules, and to new programs. Maps and proposals exist for priority areas for biodiversity conservation and national forests. The

Amazon Region Protected Areas Program (ARPA) and the "*eixos de desenvolvimento*" contained in the PPA give further indications of broad land use proposed. A recent study commissioned by the World Bank compiles many of the views, plans, and proposals already present.[24] For the Atlantic Forest, rules and orientations are laid down in Presidential Decree 750 and in the National Environmental Council's (CONAMA) Guidelines for the Conservation and Sustainable Development of the Atlantic Forest (1998).

The Amazon and Atlantic Forests are declared a national patrimony in the Constitution; the Cerrado is not. Apart from the rules for *reserva legal* [25] in the Cerrado ecosystems of the Legal Amazon, there is no policy or guideline on how much of the 2 million square kilometers of the Cerrado should be used for production and how much should be left in a natural state. More than half the Cerrado has already been occupied, and occupation continues apace. Use of the Cerrado land for crops has an undisputed national benefit in terms of economic growth and exports, but it also reduces areas with native vegetation and displaces ranching into the Amazon.

The future of each of Brazil's major biomes is not only a matter for the state governments and inhabitants of these regions. The whole nation has an interest. A national discussion among representatives of a broad spectrum of Brazilian society could be set in motion to establish broad guides for the occupation and conservation of biomes. Within these guides, States and municipalities could then define their own visions and options for their territory. The discussion would be conducted openly and work with the best information, proposals, analyses, and scenarios available. Conflict will be inevitable and will require strategies for mediation and compromise.

Such discussion has so far occurred mainly at the state level. Representatives of a broad cross-section of Rondônia's society discussed scenarios for the future of the state in a comprehensive strategic planning exercise called UMIDAS. The Acre state government has conducted a discussion of land use options in this state, in the context of zoning. In the context of defining an "*Agenda Positiva*" for the Amazon, useful discussions were held among diverging interest groups in each state, even if they did not yet generate a shared vision in the region or in each state.

---

[24] Pasquis and others 2002.

[25] *Reserva Legal* is the portion of private properties that must be left under natural vegetation (forest) cover. It is generally 20%, but 80% in the Legal Amazon and 35% in the Cerrado ecosystems of the Legal Amazon.

It is not clear who could organize and lead a national discussion process, convene the stakeholders, provide the platform, share information, mediate conflicting views, and visualize the outcome of various stages of discussions. No ministry or agency has the necessary mandate, status, skills, and leadership, although the Ministries of Planning, National Integration, and Environment can all contribute.[26]

Visions for the biomes would also guide federal and state efforts at medium- and long-run planning in all ministries and agencies. Planning could increasingly incorporate environmental aspects of the long-term use of land. If medium and long-term planning in the framework of PPA is to become increasingly open, transparent and participatory, it could start with the discussion of visions for the major biomes and the mediation of necessarily conflicting views and interests.

USING ECONOMIC-ECOLOGICAL ZONING AND A PARTICIPATORY PROCESS OF NEGOTIATION. Economic-ecological zoning has raised high expectations for guiding land use at various levels in Brazil. Brazil is perhaps unique in making such effort for vast rural areas. But there are divergent views on what zoning can and should do. The recent national Decree 4297 on economic-ecological zoning (ZEE) does not foresee negotiating on a broad national guidance for each biome; it focuses more on detailed technical zoning. Indeed, zoning is still perceived widely as a technical exercise by teams of experts (geographers, geologists, agronomists, ecologists, economists, etc.) who compile, analyze, and map physical, economic, and social data and eventually produce scientific recommendations on land use for agriculture, pasture, forest, urban occupation, and other uses. Most of the comprehensive zoning work in the states of Mato Grosso and Rondônia, for example, consisted of technical studies and mapping.

While such studies are accumulating more and more knowledge about the land, this view of zoning puts too much faith in the power of science. Scientific information is important for understanding the consequences of various options of land use, but it cannot identify the natural "vocation" of the land, as some proponents still argue. Society has the freedom of choice, and choices are made through political negotiations. Society must

---

[26] The newly created Amazon Development Agency (ADA) could perhaps be a platform for leading the discussion on (and steering the implementation of) a future vision of the Amazon. This would, however, require that ADA be designed and structured as a national agency for the Amazon biome, representing the development and conservation interests of all of Brazil, not as a regional development agency representing mainly regional development interests.

somehow agree on how much land to dedicate to conservation, to managed forests, to pastures and crops; where; and for what long-term goals. Technical work should thus be guided by orientation and directives from the public; scientists themselves can suggest principles and rules. A regional or state vision for a biome would be an important input.

It is suggested that zoning be seen more as a political process of negotiation at various levels, well informed by scientific data, analyses and projections. The methodology of zoning so far has not included such political and social dimensions. Correcting this bias could also substantially reduce the cost of zoning. How much more information, at what additional cost, is necessary to come to zoning decisions that are "good enough"?

Methodologies on how to conduct public and participatory discussions and to mediate inevitable conflicts on land use at the state and municipal levels hardly exist, but would be of much help. Zoning in Acre, as well as zoning funded under the Pilot Program (PPG7) has experimented with such processes at the municipal level, mainly in Pará and Amazonas states. Discussions and negotiations should be preceded by an analysis of who the stakeholders are (they may be absent) and by "training for participation", to enable the participants to engage in a meaningful discussion. It should cover all stakeholder groups, potential winners and losers, and the State as mediator and advocate of nature and future generations.

Zoning as a result of political negotiations and conflict resolution requires strong institutions that lead the process. If zoning is to guide policies and planning for sustainable development, it is perhaps best managed by the federal and state level agencies responsible for planning. Mato Grosso, Rondônia and Tocantins are considering the integration of spatial and land use aspects (*"ordenamento territorial"*) into their planning departments. At the national level, it may be worth considering the creation of an agency with the responsibility for planning and managing land use (as the National Water Agency, ANA, does for water use), with high technical competence and the necessary political skills, needed to coordinate zoning and provide a platform for land use planning at the federal and state levels.

Once land use negotiations have achieved some consensus, that consensus could be made binding on public sector institutions for infrastructure planning, public credit, environmental and rural licensing, settlements, and related purposes. Private agents can be influenced to act in accordance with zoning through economic instruments.

Options

- Initiate a process of open discussion among a broad spectrum of representatives of Brazilian society, concerning a "vision" for the major biomes, making available all information on options for and limits to development.

- Integrate environmental and sustainability concerns into the mainstream of national planning, and assign zoning to planning agencies.

- Redefine zoning as a process of negotiation, intermediation of conflicts, and consensus-building, supported by science and technical studies. Develop methodologies for conducting this negotiation in states and municipalities. Strengthen institutions that lead the process and feed land use issues into government planning.

- Reduce zoning costs and limit technical work to that needed for decisions that are "good enough."

- Clarify and establish a hierarchy of zoning prerogatives: in principle, federal (macro) zoning should come first, then states, then municipalities (although in practice, this may, of course, not be rigorously carried through).

- Make zoning binding for planning and decision-making by all public agencies, and use economic instruments to induce producers and consumers to act in accordance with zoning.

- Establish capacity in state governments to maintain zoning and land use planning functions.

Message 2. Keeping options open and staying clear of the threshold of irreversibility

Forest ecosystems harbor biodiversity and provide environmental services with local, regional, national and global benefits. There are substantial uncertainties about the nature and extent of short and long-term impacts of forest clearing on the provision of these environmental goods and services lost, and of their value. The value of the benefits of complex ecosystems can only partly be estimated, and interfering with ecosystems may cause irreversible damages to the detriment of future generations, if it leads to loss of an entire ecosystem, diminishes its resilience, or leads to permanent changes in regional climate. It would be prudent to stay clear of uncertain thresholds or points of no return. Caution, ethics, and aesthetics may provide good arguments to conserve unique natural assets.

It may be wise for Brazil to keep its options open. Deforestation trades off uncertain or unknown future returns to functioning ecosystems (plus likely returns to sustainable forestry) against the more certain and immediate, but modest and not always sustainable returns from clearing land, which accrue to a very small number of people.

Context

IMPORTANCE OF ECOSYSTEM AND BIODIVERSITY FUNCTIONS. Among tropical countries Brazil is especially blessed with the unique natural wealth in its forests. It is a world champion in biodiversity, but conserving it has costs, including foregone opportunities, that not all groups may be willing to bear. Biodiversity exists only within ecosystems—such as upland rain forests, *várzeas*, dry forest, grass and shrub lands, coastal zones— and ecosystems depend on diversity (although they can adapt to changes in species composition).

What's so important about biodiversity and ecosystems? Biodiversity and ecosystems harbor genetic information that can yield benefits in agricultural, pharmaceutical, and other applications. They have been the source of important foods, beverages, and medicines, such as manioc, cocoa, palm oil, coffee, jaborandi, and guaraná, to name a few. Indigenous peoples have traditionally used more than two thousand plants for healing. Removing or severely altering ecosystems destroys as yet unknown but potentially valuable information, taking away the option of future use. Agriculture has thrived on reducing diversity, but it, too, relies critically on biodiversity for breeding, natural pest and disease management, and pollination.

Ecosystems provide other environmental services apart from biodiversity and such goods and services as timber, fiber, nuts, oils, fish, and tourist attractions. They retain soils, regulate the flow of ground and surface water, help clean air and water,[27] mitigate floods and the silting of rivers, and influence the local and regional climate. As stores for carbon, which may otherwise be released into the atmosphere, ecosystems are important for the global climate. Natural landscapes also provide enjoyment, esthetic value, and recreation to local inhabitants and visitors. Finally, people the world over value undisturbed nature simply for "being there," even if they have never seen the forests and know little about their biodiversity and services.[28]

---

[27] More recently, it has been discovered that plants emit volatile organic compounds that regulate crucial features of the atmosphere. These emissions depend on specific species present in an ecosystem and are particularly important for tropical ecosystems (Lerdau and Slobodkin 2002).

[28] Economists call this "existence value". Its value per unit of forest land lost is low when the remaining forest is still large, because the first parts lost make little difference to the perception of the biome's existence, but that value should rise as forest area is reduced (L. Anderson et. al. 2001)

For the Amazon forests the most significant role, apart from their enormous biodiversity and the value of timber and forest products, may be their contribution to the regional climate. The forest generates part of the region's abundant rain, as trees release much of the water back into the air. Reducing the forest cover could lead to serious alterations in climate and endanger the remaining rain forest. It could also affect other biomes, particularly the Cerrado and other areas in the Southeast, with their high-productivity agriculture so important for Brazilian exports. These impacts, as yet highly uncertain, are being studied under the Large-Scale Biosphere-Atmosphere Research Project (LBA). Scientific research has also shown that forest clearing can lead to the contamination of Amazonian rivers and fish with mercury, posing a risk to the riverine people who consume the fish.[29]

Conserving Cerrado ecosystems seems important for Brazil not only for its biodiversity and the apparently high potential genetic value of its species, but also for tourism and as an important complementary natural asset to its growing agriculture, particularly in terms of integrated pest management, erosion and hydrologic control.

What remains of the Atlantic forest is of the highest importance for biodiversity and as a provider of environmental services to the large urban populations of the region, for recreation and tourism.

WHAT IS THE ECONOMIC VALUE? Is there an economic value to biodiversity and ecosystem services? Several attempts have been made to estimate such value to society for the Amazon, but no firm results are available. Estimates vary dramatically, from negligible to very high, depending on concept and methodology.[30]

Table 1 shows figures from a recent study undertaken for the World Bank. Highly uncertain, the figures nevertheless illustrate that from the point of view of the owner, use of the standing forest for timber and other forest products pays him less than clearing and establishing pasture. Earnings from

Table 1

Standing Forest	US$/ha/year
Direct use value	37.7
- Timber	28.5
- Other forest products	0.2
- Eco - tourism	9.0
Indirect Use Value	
(Carbon stocking)	18.0
Option Value	
(Biosprospecting)	21.0
Existence Value	0.9
Total	77.6

Cattle Ranching	
(annual rent)	$33.4 - 49.5

Source: Seroa da Motta 2002.

---

[29] Veiga and others 1999, and Roulet/Lucotte 1999.

[30] Motta 2002.

ecotourism or receiving some remuneration for carbon kept in the standing forest could begin to make maintaining the forest more attractive. Adding the "option value" for the genetic information in biodiversity would swing the balance fully towards keeping forest cover.

Studies worldwide of the costs and benefits of converting forests and other "wild nature" areas to other uses generally find that the loss of non-marketed services to society outweighs the marketed benefits of conversion, often by a considerable amount.[31] It would certainly be worthwhile to deepen knowledge in Brazil about the environmental services of ecosystems and their value, as well as about the impact of agriculture and ranching on these functions, and use this knowledge to better inform public debate.

WHY WORRY ABOUT CONSERVATION? Given the uncertainties about the impacts of deforestation and the value of goods and services lost, a country might not want to base a decision solely on economic calculations. If the economic value of standing forests is so uncertain and not all the benefits are captured by Brazilian citizens, why worry about forest conservation? This may not be the right question to ask. The better question may be: if estimated economic values reflect only part of the social benefits of complex ecosystems, and if destroying the ecosystems may cause irreversible damages to the detriment of future generations, why risk it? There are valid reasons related to caution, ethics, and aesthetics for wanting to keep so unique an asset. The public's solid and growing support for forest conservation may be grounded precisely on these motives.

Converting forests to other uses, as all countries have done to varying degrees, need not be disastrous. It depends on the fragility of the ecosystems and the extent of conversion. Conversion may be irreversible if it leads to loss of ecosystems, loss of their resilience, or a permanent change in regional climate. It does not seem prudent to let deforestation move to an uncertain threshold or point of no return. Even where changes are reversible, it is generally much cheaper to prevent damage than try to restore forest cover later.

Of course, conservation has its costs. Use of forest land for agriculture and ranching contributes to economic growth and to exports. At the same time, deforestation trades off uncertain or unknown future returns to functioning ecosystems (plus likely returns to sustainable forestry) against the more certain and immediate, but modest and not always sustainable returns from clearing land, which accrue to a very small number of people. It may be wiser for Brazil to keep its options open.

---

[31] Balmford and others 2002.

State zoning integrates some biodiversity concerns but rarely considers the environmental functions of ecosystems, in part because not enough is known about them. Setting aside adequate amounts of land to secure environmental services from ecosystems and conserve biodiversity could be a key task of zoning.

EXPERIENCE WITH BIODIVERSITY CONSERVATION. Brazil has ratified the Biological Diversity Convention and enshrined the Amazon and the Atlantic Forest (among other biomes) as a national patrimony in the Constitution. Brazil has the largest area under protection in South America. More than a quarter of the Amazon is already protected in some way, although less than 4 percent is within areas defined as strictly protected. The ARPA program, funded by the Global Environment Facility (GEF), World Wildlife Fund, Germany, and Brazil, aims to expand strict conservation areas to more than 10 percent of Amazon forests (40 million hectares) and to support other conservation areas (extractive and sustainable development reserves). The creation of the largest national park in the tropics (Tumucumaque, with 38,000 square kilometers of forest) is a big step toward that goal and demonstrates Brazil's commitment to conservation in the Amazon.

The ARPA project has demonstrated the importance of consultation with stakeholders, including state and local governments, in the creation of parks and reserves, but without prejudice to the federal government's power to prevail over state and local interests, if necessary. Strictly protected parks and reserves and sustainable-use reserves can complement each other in a mosaic, even if sustainable use is not a substitute for strict protection.

Under the National Biodiversity Program (PRONABIO), with support from the GEF, Brazil has mapped priority areas for conservation for each of its large biomes in a scientific, but highly participatory way. The results of biome workshops are publicly accessible and represent extraordinary guidance for land use policies. The PPG7 Ecological Corridors Project, in the Amazon and Atlantic Forest, which aims at planning and managing biodiversity conservation for wider areas and to increase the connectivity among such units is the first attempt in Brazil to implement the corridor concept of biodiversity conservation.

Resources for creating and maintaining conservation units are scarce. A national strategy for biodiversity conservation (including federal and state governments) would have to identify priority actions among biomes and allocate adequate financing and staff to maintain a larger system of parks and reserves. Funding conservation requires creative new arrangements that involve the private sector and the international community.

Brazil cannot be expected to carry the burden of conserving its unique biodiversity alone, as conservation benefits not only Brazilians but the entire planet. International funding can and should be sought from official sources (such as the GEF), conservation

NGOs and the private sector to set up and maintain protected areas in the Atlantic Forest and the Cerrado. The ARPA project is going to do this already for the Amazon: it will establish the *Fundo de Áreas Protegidas* (FAP), an endowment fund that will receive contributions from GEF, official bilateral sources, and private sources. Investment income to be earned from FAP will be used to meet the costs of operating and maintaining conservation units in the Amazon. Eventually, FAP could cover these costs for conservation in all Brazilian biomes.

There is no mechanism in sight that would provide for larger global transfers to Brazil (and other megadiversity countries) in recognition of the global value of its forests. The emerging market on carbon offsets may one day provide a source of such transfers, but probably not in the short term. Without prejudice to its sovereignty, Brazil may want to initiate an international dialogue on the services it provides to the planet and a mechanism for compensation.

CONSERVATION ON PRIVATE LAND. Most remaining fragments of the Atlantic Forest are in private hands. Private interest in conservation there and elsewhere could be increased in several ways. The *Reserva Particular de Patrimônio Natural* (RPPN) is a suitable legal instrument to promote conservation, but it could be more attractive if the rural land tax (ITR) exemption were increased. In areas with growing ecotourism, private tourism businesses can be encouraged to subsidize communities in maintaining forest remnants, as a recent example in the Atlantic Rain Forest of Bahia demonstrates.

The requirement that all landowners of a region maintain the same percentage of their land as legal reserve is rigid. Without compromising environmental objectives, landowners could be permitted to trade legal reserve obligations among themselves. The opportunity cost of conservation areas varies with soil fertility and with distance from urban centers. In certain areas ecological needs would suggest that more land should be reserved, while in others less may be enough. Trading exploits this variation to achieve conservation goals at lower costs to owners than rigid per-property rules. In Paraná such trade has increased the willingness to conserve and the environmental value of the reserves.[32] World Bank studies concluded that (a) trading might not increase total forest cover but would reduce the opportunity costs of conservation; (b) trading is less efficient in forest-poor areas and (iii) there is more scope for trading if applied on a wider geographic scale; and (iv) transaction costs and the costs of monitoring and enforcement are greatly reduced if trading is limited to among larger properties.[33]

---

[32] Chomitz 1999.

[33] Chomitz, Thomas, and Salazar Brandão (forthcoming).

Because the opportunistic assembly of protected areas may result in conservation areas that are not large enough to ensure ecosystem viability (inadequate habitats, wildlife populations too small to maintain their genetic diversity), special incentives could be given to owners who designate their reserves according to environmental criteria and locate them contiguously with the reserves of their neighbors.[34]

The states of Mato Grosso, Minas Gerais, Paraná, São Paulo and Rondônia allocate a larger share of ICMS revenue to municipalities with a larger share of land under protection. It probably works best in states that are not "forest rich". This "ICMS ecológico" can also help traditional populations improve their livelihood, if their land is recognized as a conservation unit. In a similar vein, the federal allocation of the *Fundo de Participação dos Municípios* (FPM) *e dos Estados* (FPE) could also encourage local and state governments to promote reserves.

Paying owners for the environmental services that forests provide can encourage them to maintain forest cover. Costa Rica created in 1996 "a Payment for Environmental Services" program that pays forest owners who agree to manage or preserve areas under forest. Funds are collected by the National Fund for Forest Finance (FONAFIFO) from a tax on fossil fuels, international sales of carbon credits, and contributions by public and private beneficiaries of forest services (such as electricity companies). The program is also supported by a World Bank loan and a GEF grant. Payments vary from $200 a hectare (preservation) to over $500 a hectare (reforestation) per year over five years.[35] The principle could be tested also in Brazil, where the royalties paid by electricity companies for their reservoirs or the water charges in managed watersheds are a possible source of funding.

Monitoring the health of ecosystems. The health of ecosystems needs to be checked periodically, to stay clear of thresholds, to update knowledge about the environmental impacts of development and ecosystem responses, and to inform and educate the public. Monitoring and reporting should be by a largely autonomous agency on the basis of relatively few, but powerful indicators. Publication of results should not depend on approval of any particular ministry (as is currently the case with the data on deforestation rates published by the National Institute for Space Research, INPE).

---

[34] Furthermore, a model has been developed with support of the Bank and PPG7 that permits planners to find the lowest (opportunity) cost combination of lands that satisfies specific conservation requirements. Church, in preparation.

[35] Nasi and others 2002.

Options

Define the minimum desirable area to be set aside for biodiversity protection for each biome and each state, and use this as a directive for zoning.

- Prepare biome-wide plans for biodiversity conservation in the Cerrado, Atlantic Forest, and Caatinga, similar to ARPA. Expand the Protected Areas Fund (FAP) to cover eventually all biomes.

- Consider Costa Rica's experience with payment for environmental services.

- Reduce owners' costs of legal reserve by permitting trading of reserve obligations, and create incentives for landowners to locate reserve areas to maximize environmental impact and minimize fragmentation. (This requires, however, reasonably clear and secure property rights.)

- Promote "*ICMS Ecológico*" in less forest-rich states. Make the *Reserva Particular de Patrimônio Natural* (RPPN) more attractive to landowners, for example, through the ITR.

- Set up an autonomous system for monitoring the health of ecosystems and their functions, with a few indicators, and have results published regularly and independently.

Message 3. Getting ahead of the frontier and limiting open access

Where a natural resource such as forest is perceived as abundant, and where access to virgin forests is open to the seeking, settlers will "mine" abundant land and its nutrients for agriculture and ranching after burning the forest. Some likely climatic limitations not withstanding, clearing and use of forests will continue if unchecked.

Should government and society want to keep most of the remaining Amazon rain forest, government needs to get ahead of the moving frontier and establish an effective presence, to make land scarcer by reducing access to it. It should be aware of the rather predictable impact of roads that open entire new regions in the interior. The paving of existing primary highways, such as BR-163 in Pará, could have similar consequences, by easing access and reducing transport costs.

High priority should be given to setting aside public lands for maintenance of forest cover. While creating conservation units is easier in the less densely populated interior than near the agricultural frontier, it is essential that reserves be established where the frontier is currently heading and where infrastructure will soon open or facilitate access. The substantial expansion of National Forests (FLONAs) planned under the National Forest Program would be most important to this end. Where reserves are established, restrictions of access need to be enforced. Property rights, whether public, private or communal, need to be clarified and secured. In addition to traditional instruments of "command and control", several options are available to use economic instruments to increase and secure reserved areas.

Context

An abundantly available resource tends to be used liberally. In the Amazon, with 85 percent of the original forest still standing, forest land is abundant, while labor and capital are in short supply. Access to forests has been largely open to the seeking, made easy by the presence of trunk roads and the absence of protected areas, clear property rights, or state enforcement. Settlers will "mine" abundant land for agriculture and ranching after burning the forest.[36] In the *Cerrado*, however, at least half of the natural grass, shrub and woodlands have already converted to pastures and crops, mostly with established property rights. The Atlantic Forest is also a very scarce resource.

---

[36] Schneider 1992.

While land use in parts of the Amazon has become more intensive over time, particularly in areas where the frontier economy has consolidated as a function of new and growing urban centers, better transport infrastructure and connection to markets, more intensive land use does not seem to be reducing the pressure on the remaining forests. Theory also would not predict that.

However, there appear to be limitations. Agriculture and ranching in the Amazon may become apparently less attractive as they move into wetter regions north and westward. Increasingly smaller portions of land holdings are used productively as the climate gets wetter, and occupation virtually ceases where rainfall approaches 3,200 millimeters a year.[37] In the drier 40 percent of the Legal Amazon, almost half the land is in private establishments, but in the wettest 20 percent, even near roads, only one-tenth is. Stocking rates of pastures are lower in the wetter parts than in the drier ones.[38] The proportion of abandoned clearings increases sharply with annual rainfall.

Should government and society want to keep large parts of the remaining Amazon rain forest, government needs to get ahead of the moving frontier and make land scarcer by reducing access to it. This should raise the value (and price) of land and induce changes in behavior. Getting ahead also means knowing where the frontier is and where it is moving.

PRIMARY ROADS THAT OPEN UP THE INTERIOR LEAD TO DEFORESTATION. Building new trunk roads into previously inaccessible interior forest regions is the prime cause of deforestation.[39] If government wants to get ahead of the frontier and limit access, it could consider the rather predictable impact of roads that open entire new regions in the interior. The PPA foresees building few new roads, but the paving of existing ones, such as BR-163 in Pará, could have similar consequences, by easing access and reducing transport costs. Forests along BR-163 are already being cleared in the expectation of road paving, but government did not get ahead of that new frontier. Building or paving of local (tertiary) roads in the process of consolidation of the "old frontier" is a consequence rather than a cause of deforestation, and will be discussed in Message 5.

---

[37] Chomitz and Thomas 2000.

[38] Other reports point to higher productivity in transition and rain forests in comparison with drier Cerrado land. See Sant'Ana and others 2002.

[39] Alves 1999

PUBLIC RESERVES REDUCE ACCESS. Setting aside public lands as reserves, with varying access restrictions, is an effective means of maintaining forest cover. Forest lands with low market value but high environmental and social value are better kept in the public domain. To keep forests as functioning ecosystems, it matters less whether such reserves are for strict protection (*proteção integral*) or for "sustainable use" (national or state forests, extractive reserves, sustainable development reserves). The latter have a role not only for rural communities and the poor, but also as buffer zones around protected areas. Enforcing access control is difficult and costly in the Amazon, but evidence shows that simply demarcating public reserves, with a minimum of surveillance and enforcement, makes these areas less prone to invasion and degradation than other areas.[40]

Creating conservation units is easier and less costly (politically and economically) in less densely populated areas of the interior than near the agricultural frontier. Nevertheless, creating reserves where the frontier is currently heading and where transport infrastructure under the *Plano Plurianual* (PPA) will open or facilitate access deserves the highest priority (table 2). Thus the substantial expansion of national forests (FLONAs) planned under the National Forest Program for sustainable forestry (to 14 percent of the remaining forest area) deserves support. Priority should be given to creation of FLONAs on both sides of primary roads planned to be built or paved, to create a significant barrier to uncontrolled expansion of forest clearing, such as is occurring along the unpaved Cuiabá-Santarém highway in Pará.

Table 2

Potential Conservation Areas in the Amazon	
Strict protection areas	10%
Sustainable use reserves	5-10%
National forests	14%
Indigenous lands	27%
Private reserves	~20%

Demarcating indigenous lands, although not meant primarily for protection of the environment, has nevertheless proven to be also a quite effective barrier to forest clearing. Demarcated lands cover already more than 20 percent of the Amazon, and will eventually cover some 27 percent. Altogether, more than half of the Amazon forest could eventually be set aside as public land and at least a fifth on private land through reserva legal and *áreas de preservação permanente* (APP).

---

[40] Bruner and others 2001; Mahar and Ducrot 1998.

In the Cerrado, creation of additional parks and reserves should bring the share of areas under conservation to a level substantially higher than the current almost negligible one percent.

ENFORCING RESTRICTIONS ON ACCESS. Effective control of forest clearing on private or illegally occupied public land is feasible, given political will. The government of Mato Grosso has been enforcing federal and state law on the use of forest land with the help of remote sensing technology on larger land holdings (more than 500 hectares) and a sophisticated "rural licensing" scheme based on satellite images of properties to be provided by the owners. Deforestation has apparently dropped by a third since 1998 in Mato Grosso, and even more in the areas where the system has been applied.[41] Other states on the frontier (Pará, Rondônia, Acre) have apparently agreed to follow this example. There are, however, certain difficulties in transporting this system to other states: in Rondônia, for example, the average property is much smaller than in Mato Grosso, and in Pará, property rights are much less clear.

With political support at the highest level, the system could be expanded to the entire Cerrado. Coordination and clear assignment of responsibilities among federal (especially IBAMA) and state authorities are crucial. Settlement agencies such as INCRA would need to be involved as well. Settlements should not be planned or implemented in areas designated by zoning for maintaining forest cover. Environmental licensing of settlements –required but not practiced– is an important step in this direction.

CLARIFYING AND SECURING PROPERTY RIGHTS. Where property rights do not exist or cannot be enforced, intruders cannot be excluded. Owners with secure property rights are more inclined to plan and make investments for the longer term, and credit is more easily obtained to finance their investments. A study of small settlers on the Transamazônica showed that conservation and reforestation activities were more frequent and the selling of logs less frequent among owners with titles.[42] To ensure more sustainable land use by settlers, INCRA should award them definitive titles much earlier after resettlement.[43]

Particularly in the Amazon forest, property rights are often unclear or fraudulently established, with multiple claims on the same area. The Ministry of Agrarian

---

[41] MMA and World Bank 2002.

[42] Wood and Walker 1999.

[43] Schneider 1994.

Development is working to put order in this chaos. It revoked false titles on about 65 million hectares in the Amazon and released some 20 million hectares of repossessed land for conservation. The introduction of a unified rural land registry, to be used and updated by all involved agencies, has been a big step forward and needs to be fully implemented. The next step could include determining whether unoccupied land is public or private (*"discriminação"*) and legal limitations on the size of concessions and alienation of public land that state government can give to private individuals.

The practice of considering forest land as "unproductive" creates a fear of losing property through invasion and subsequent expropriation if the forest is not cleared. Although legislation has been adjusted, landholders still feel "safer" when they clear their land for (real or apparent) ranching.[44] Federal and state governments could seek to eliminate any remaining references to "unproductive forests" in legislation, rules, and practices of land agencies that may foster this attitude.

Given the weak results of settlements in the Amazon in providing more equitable access to land, and given the predictable reactions of landless and landowners to the practice of expropriation and settlement of encroachers, it may be time to review critically and objectively the entire strategy and practice of rural settlements in the Amazon and to consider alternatives that could still attain the intended objectives of agrarian reform. This may include expansion of the new model now being implemented in the Northeast (*"Programa Crédito Fundiário"*), financed by the World Bank, that allows settler communities to acquire the land they desire.

Property rights are also important for traditional rural communities that manage natural resources cooperatively. Brazil has recognized land rights of indigenous peoples, pioneered "extractive reserves" and introduced more recently "sustainable development reserves." Recognition of community use rights (*"concessão de uso"*) on public lands (with certain restrictions) and of common property rights outside public conservation units could further help to restrict uncontrolled access to natural resources and assist the poor in making sustainable use of resources. INCRA settlements, if continued, could contain provisions for sustainable use of "common land."

---

[44] It appears that the sudden rise in deforestation in 1995 may have been due, among other things, to fears at the time that a more rigorous implementation of land reform would make private forest land subject to expropriation.

USING ECONOMIC INSTRUMENTS TO INFLUENCE LAND USE DECISIONS. Apart from setting aside reserve areas and promoting secure property rights, there are other, "market-based" means of influencing land use decisions of settlers and owners. The "ICMS Ecológico" and a more flexible legal reserve were already discussed in message 2 above.

To compensate for the social losses from forest clearing, land clearing can be made more expensive. Substantial fees for deforestation licenses could be charged on a per hectare basis, with exemptions for smallholders. Fees in Mato Grosso are per license rather than per hectare cleared and are low on a per hectare basis for large owners. The level of the fee could be set to reduce expected gains from clearing substantially. Penalties for clearing forests without a permit—or for buying cleared land for which no fee or tax was paid—could be set higher than the fee, and the revenues could be used to strengthen surveillance and law enforcement. Alternatively, a special tax (in the sense of *"Contribuição de Intervenção no Domínio Econômico"*[45]) could be considered.

Economic instruments would likely do more to induce compliance and cost less to implement than punishment-based systems. But they will still require monitoring of actual land use. Law enforcement will be easier and more effective where decisions by the authorities and the behavior of economic agents are transparent and information is accessible. Systems for rural licensing, definition of legal reserves and authorizations of land clearing, logging plans, and log transport should enable any interested party to obtain information on what was approved, for whom and by whom, to diminish the potential for corruption.

Options

- Review the planning of major new roads and road paving projects within the context of a national vision for a biome and corresponding macro-zoning. Carry out assessments of regional environmental, economic and social impacts of major infrastructure projects.
- Give highest priority to zoning in the transition zone ahead of and behind the moving agricultural frontier.
- Create national or state forests and other conservation units along major roads, especially planned roads.

---

[45] Articles 149 and 177 of the Constitution. This is already being charged on imports and sales of petroleum and petroleum products, natural gas and natural gas products, and *'álcool etílico combustível'* (Law 10.336 2001)

- Expand the rural licensing system (wherever possible given property sizes and clarity of property rights) into threatened parts of the Amazon and into the entire Cerrado.
- Continue the clean-up of property rights in the Amazon, including distinguishing public and private land (*discriminação*) .
- Award definitive titles to INCRA settlers early, without loss of benefits from grants or credit.
- Facilitate secure community tenure rights.
- Make legal reserve obligations more flexible, including the trading of reserve obligations, to reduce the opportunity cost to owners and to reduce ecosystem fragmentation.
- Charge stiff per hectare fees (or taxes) for deforestation licenses.
- Remove any remaining incentives in the law that encourage clear-felling as a means of proving possession. Consider substituting the current model of land settlements after invasion and by expropriation with one that is based on *"crédito fundiário"*.
- Make information easily accessible to the public on licenses and monitoring results.

Message 4. Making standing forest more valuable by promoting its sustainable use, particularly by poor local communities

As a complement to a strategy of restricting access, the value of standing forests can be enhanced by promoting their productive use, through sustainable forestry, extractivism or agroforestry systems. All of these options are labor-intensive and can benefit particularly poor rural families and communities, who should receive priority in allocating land or public funds to these options.

The promotion of (private) certification of forestry and timber, the granting of logging concessions in national and state forests to qualified bidders, support to agroforestry in areas with reasonable access to markets, creation of sustainable rural settlements, and adjustments in public sector banks toward the needs of forest-based production, are all means to increase the value of standing forest.

Context

Market failures make natural resource conservation more difficult. Individuals usually take into account only their own financial gain from land use, not what society needs and cherishes. Policies can correct this market failure by making standing forest more valuable from the private point of view.

Such policies have important advantages for the livelihood of poor people. Many traditional forest dwellers in the Amazon – indigenous people, rubber tappers, nut gatherers, fishers – are defenders of forest conservation. The forest is often their only asset. Yet isolation and remoteness make their inclusion in society difficult. Sustainable forest use can help to improve the livelihood of the rural poor, but it may not be enough to lift them out of poverty.

Escaping poverty require access to other assets—through education and health services, and knowledge of technologies and markets. Assisting and empowering small farm families and communities must be part of a strategy to reverse destructive trends in the Amazon and the Atlantic Forest. But the number of smallholder families is probably too small (perhaps 700,000 families in the Amazon) for them to take over stewardship for more than some 15 percent of the remaining forest. And the rural population in the Amazon is decreasing. Better education will raise the opportunity cost of the young, who will want to leave the forest to pursue better opportunities. The behavior and impact of other, better endowed groups, such as ranchers, is much more dominant. The issue of sustainable development is certainly related to poverty reduction, but it goes beyond.

Options to raise the private economic value of the standing forest include sustainable (managed) forestry, including community forestry, extracting other forest products, fisheries, and ecotourism. All of these activities are more labor intensive than ranching or commercial agriculture.[46] Agroforestry may modify standing forest, but most often it affects "degraded" areas: abandoned pastures and secondary forest (*capoeira*).

MANAGED FORESTRY. Timber is currently by far the most valuable forest product. It can be obtained either in a "cut and run" way (*exploração predatória*) contributing to forest degradation or forest clearing, or in a sustainable way by careful long-term management of forests. The latter is now the subject of increasingly overbooked courses in the Amazon. It has been demonstrated that the efficiency of production is higher, and the cost of production is less, for a cubic meter of timber under "reduced-impact logging".

---

[46] Almeida and Uhl 1995.

PLANOS DE MANEJO required under Brazilian legislation are supposed to ensure sustainability, but few of these plans are actually implemented. Regulations are extensive, and government staff are scarce, and inadequately trained and motivated to analyze, approve, and audit these management plans.[47] Certification requires also sustainable management plans and more. To date, only about 290,000 hectares belonging to six firms have been certified in the Amazon (less than 1 percent of the regional extraction), and less than 50,000 hectares in the Atlantic Forest. Many more are in process. Demand for sustainably produced, certified wood is growing and may have already reached the equivalent of one-fifth of Amazon timber consumed.[48]

Exporters of tropical wood (particularly to Europe) are increasingly seeking certification, though they still represent only a small part of the market. A strong "buyers group" of Brazilian companies purchasing wood cannot yet satisfy its demand from certified Brazilian suppliers. A Brazilian investment bank hopes to invest millions of dollars in certified forest management. All these are hopeful signs.

There are also social advantages to sustainable logging. Predatory logging exhausts the stocks in one region and then moves on to new areas, such as along the Cuiabá-Santarém highway, where new sawmills set up shop every month. Logging centers (like Paragominas) go through a cycle of boom and bust. New communities can opt for a short-lived logging boom followed by a bust or for long-term forest resource management with sustained employment, at the sacrifice of higher initial returns. Sustainable forestry could create seven times more employment within the same area than ranching following unsustainable logging.[49] Poverty is more difficult to combat in unstable communities.

Sustainable forestry can be highly profitable, with rates of return up to 70 percent. Without promotion and support, however, and given the large domestic market with relatively low demand for certified wood, sustainable logging is less profitable than traditional, unsustainable logging.[50] Landowners still find ranching more attractive than giving a logger the right to exploit timber legally over a long cycle.[51]

---

[47] Barreto 2002.

[48] Viana and others 2002.

[49] Schneider and others 2001.

[50] Schneider and others 2001, and Pearce and others 2001

[51] Barreto 2002

SUSTAINABLE LOGGING ON PRIVATE LAND. One way to make sustainable logging more attractive is to increase the cost of producing timber unsustainably. Fines are already quite high, but loggers and landowners feel that there is a low probability of getting caught, so the expected cost of illegality is still low.[52] The policy focus could shift away from a dichotomy of "legal-illegal" towards one of "sustainable-unsustainable", where timber from clear-felling would not be illegal, but still unsustainable. In other words, rather than prohibiting certain forms of logging, unsustainable logging could be taxed rather than forbidden. "Predatory" logging would no longer be a crime, but it would be less profitable than sustainable logging.[53]

Whether illegal or unsustainable and taxed, more effective methods of controlling log origin and log traffic are required, with less opportunity for corruption. Identifying the origin of timber has always been difficult. Current technology allows looking for gaps in the tree cover from logging, and thus for comparing actual extraction against authorized or certified plans. But this has not been tried over large areas. An alternative system using satellite-based localizing technology for logging trucks, proposed by IMAZON under the G-7 Pilot Program, is currently being tested in the field. It allows the constant monitoring of a truck's position by satellite, similar to methods used by the US and New Zealand to control fishing.[54]

Certification would still require forest management plans, similar to those required by government. To boost compliance with officially authorized plans, auditing of management plans and operations could be carried out either by government staff who have not been involved in plan approval or, better even, by independent auditors. Given the current export ban on raw logs, exports could be permitted if logs were produced under certification.

Business leaders see insecure property rights as an important impediment to the adoption of long-term management plans on private lands. Cleaning out false titles and regularizing legitimate property titles is an important first step, starting with Pará, Mato Grosso, and Amazonas states. In addition, communities need secure tenure (property or use rights) if community forestry is to thrive.

---

[52] The cost of timber from illegal logging or illegal clearfelling is lower than the cost of legal operations for low probabilities of getting caught and punished (Barreto 2002).

[53] World Bank 1994, Vol. II.

[54] Barreto and Souza 2001.

Another obstacle to the expansion of managed forestry is the scarcity of labor skilled in the new methods and techniques. If managed forestry were to cover half of current timber production, some 9,200 additional trained technicians and operators and 700 forestry engineers would be needed.[55]

Sustainable forestry requires investments in inventory, equipment, pre-felling activities, certification, all of which must be financed. Credit should be available from official sources in Brazil and national and international investment funds and partnerships (all of which require certification). Equity capital of timber companies should also be available for reinvestment. Grant funds should be considered only for the startup of forestry operations in poorer communities.

There are also market-based means to make managed forestry more attractive. The Federal Government has already reduced the license fee for certified logging operations. The rural land tax (ITR) should exempt (consider as "productive") all forest areas, which would also make administration of ITR simpler. Products derived from unsustainably produced timber could be taxed differentially through the industrial products tax (IPI).[56] Where equipment needs to be imported for higher efficiency of sawmills, such equipment could be exempted from import duties if the sawmill is certified. Eventually, sustainable forest management might benefit from carbon credits, even if it is not among the most efficient mechanisms for reducing carbon emissions.[57]

SUSTAINABLE LOGGING ON PUBLIC LAND. The National Forest Program proposes to set aside some fourteen percent of Amazon forests (50 million hectares) by 2010 as FLONAs. Seventy million hectares of public forests would be suitable to meet domestic demand for timber.[58] Logging companies would bid for concessions to produce sustainably under public scrutiny. Government would be able to capture part of the "rent" from logging. Attracting companies to operate in national forests would depend on the characteristics of the concessions and on effective control of unsustainable logging outside the national forests. The absence of any land tenure problems for the companies in the FLONAs is an important factor.

---

[55] Barreto 2002.

[56] Haddad and Rezende 2002.

[57] Pierce and others 2001.

[58] Schneider and others 2001.

International experience with concessions has not been very encouraging. It suggests that concessions should be awarded competitively and transparently, and should encourage efficiency. Cameroon has had good experience with auctions of concessions through bids per-hectare from pre-qualified bidders. Management plans are required, and part of the concession revenue is allocated to local governments and communities. Independent observers are hired to help oversee concession award and monitor compliance. Overall, concession awards are today more transparent and management regulations simpler, short-term "rent-seekers" are gradually being replaced by long-term investors, communities have become stakeholders in forest management, and revenues have increased tenfold over five years.[59]

Sharing the revenue from taxes, concession fees, and other fees on logging with local governments and communities goes a long way toward gaining support for sustainable management and conservation of forest cover. Community involvement would help control unmanaged, unsustainable logging.

With all the requirements of know-how, equipment, certification costs and organization, are sustainable forestry and certification only accessible to large logging companies? There is no reason why communities should not undertake certification and sustainable forestry provided they get good technical and managerial assistance and credit and have secure tenure rights. One of the eight current certificates in native Amazon forest is held by a community of *seringueiros*.[60] However, the difficulties inherent in administration, management, market relations, decision-making and participation within a community should not be underestimated.[61] Partnerships with businesses and NGOs will be important. The Xicrin-Catetê indigenous community in the Carajás region was among the first in Brazil to seek certification, with support from Companhia Vale do Rio Doce (CVRD), and the assistance of a consulting firm and an NGO. If land distribution is not to be skewed further toward large holdings and logging companies, space should be allocated to community forestry on a priority basis in public reserves (national forests, extractive

---

[59] World Bank 20033.

[60] *Projeto Agroextrativista Chico Mendes (Seringal Cachoeira), Xapuri, Acre*

[61] Eba'a Atyi, and Simula 2002.

reserves sustainable development reserves,) community property rights should be recognized, and communities should receive preferential treatment on fees.

SUPPORTING "EXTRACTIVISM" AND AGROFORESTRY. Forests products other than timber have long been gathered from native forests: rubber, Brazil nuts, *pupunha, açai, palmito, babaçu* nuts, and even decorative fish. Recently, oils, fibers and medicinal plants have become important. While overall returns to extraction activities appear to be low[62], they are nevertheless important to the sustenance of traditional people in the forest and the Cerrado. Brazil pioneered the concept of extractive reserves after the murder of Chico Mendes in 1988, to protect rubber tappers and other gatherers from the aggressive expansion of ranching.

The Rain Forest Pilot Program (PPG7) has supported the establishment and consolidation of four extractive reserves in the Amazon, with more than 2 million hectares. It has demonstrated that conserving rain forests and improving the livelihood of traditional populations is possible. The cost of establishing and running the reserves compares favorably with that of operating protected parks,[63] even though they are somewhat less effective in conserving biodiversity. Without sustainable logging, extractive reserves will likely require some form of subsidy (preferably not by subsidizing the price of a commodity such as rubber) to make them financially sustainable, in recognition of the environmental services and protection provided by the reserves.

A particular success has been the matching of extractive production (oils, fibers) with demand from industrial partners in the cosmetics and automobile industries[64] through partnerships promoted under PPG7, the program Poverty and Environment in the Amazon (POEMA) and the *Bolsa Amazônica* project. But expectations of substantially raising the incomes of forest dwellers through extractive activities should be tempered with caution. The potential for marketing new and old Amazonian forest products is considerable, but so is the challenge, namely to guarantee steady supplies of high quality products. Extractive reserves can afford a more decent quality of life to those opting to stay in the forest. Lasting improvements will come from strengthening human capital through education, health and extension services, which are more difficult to provide to dispersed communities

---

[62] Wunder 2001.

[63] MMA and World Bank 2002.

[64] Natura, Cognis/Henkel, Daimler-Chrysler

AGROFORESTRY uses the standing forest by modifying or enriching its structure. More often, they restore some forest-like environment in now degraded areas. Many demonstration projects of this kind have been funded under the PPG7 in the Amazon and Atlantic Forest, with uneven success.

While agroforestry has come to be considered almost a panacea for saving rain forests and as a strategy for generating income and employment for family farmers, it is not without problems. Under proper conditions, agroforestry can indeed provide substantial incomes. Diversification over a range of species and products is desirable ecologically and commercially, but reduces the scale of production for each product. But agroforesty is highly demanding in many ways: production should be located close to markets, counting on good transport and communications infrastructure. Producers should count on effective technical assistance and extension for the sake of steady quantity and quality of products. Where communities organize for joint marketing or processing, they must have, or hire, professional management skills. Such favorable conditions are not available in many places in the Amazon or Atlantic forests.

Experience with the Pilot Program to Conserve the Brazilian Rain Forest shows that community projects have had an impact that goes far beyond improvements in material quality of life. They create "social capital." They foster inclusion, transparency, a new awareness of rights, opportunities, and powers, and often a stronger role for women. On the other hand, when traditional communities are led into the commercial world by well-meaning outside groups, care must be taken that they are not put under social strain, suffer from the unequal distribution of knowledge, influence, and bargaining power in the market, and fall into new dependencies. Ways have to be found in which communities can "meet the market on their own terms."[65]

NEED FOR SUPPORT. The Pilot Program to Conserve the Brazilian Rain Forest has been exploring and demonstrating extraction and agroforestry models in many ways. Some answers about what works and what doesn't and why are gradually emerging,[66] but systematic learning about criteria for success from the ongoing experiments should be much intensified. Otherwise, agroforestry remains a risky and possibly even unsustainable option that cannot be sold with confidence to banks or to family farmers and communi-

---

[65] Remarks by Prof. Marianne Schmink at the conclusion of the Conference on Working Forests in the Tropics, University of Florida, Gainesville 2002.

[66] MMA and World Bank 2002.

ties. Much more support should be given to research on agroforestry models, by EMBRAPA and other institutions. Other countries' experiences with rain forests could be brought to bear in a network of active knowledge sharing and research coordination.

Once reliable knowledge is available, it must be disseminated to those who could use it. Traditional agricultural extension services are in a precarious state in the Amazon and are not equipped to deal with "alternative" modes of production. In the Pilot Program and other initiatives, NGOs and research centers have been the main source of technical advice and extension to experimenting farmers. Such sources are limited in their reach. Innovative solutions are needed, involving the public and private sector as well as NGOs.

Funding for productive uses of the forest is available—it just has not been channeled toward such uses. The PROAMBIENTE program proposed by civil society organizations would change existing funding channels into environmental credit schemes to support forest enrichment, agroforestry, community forestry, extractivism, etc., and would use some of the funds for remuneration of environmental services. This aims in the right direction. Existing sources, such as FNO, ADA/FDA, and PRONAF, which, after all, amount to over R$ 3 billion a year, could be redirected to wards productive use of standing forests.[67]

World consumer demand increasingly seeks products with a "green" label. Extractive activities and agroforestry could gain much from the more systematic exploitation of an "Amazon" or "Brazilian Rain Forest" label. After "Coca Cola™", the word "Amazon" appears to have the second highest recognition by consumers worldwide.

Options

- Create a specialized agency concerned only with oversight over forestry production inside and outside national forests.
- Expand national forests (FLONAs) rapidly in the Amazon, especially along major roads planned for construction or scheduled for paving.
- Exempt certified timber operations from audits and simplify requirements for approval of management plans.
- Promote training of technical personnel, operators, and engineers in sustainable forest management.
- Train staff of the National Bank for Economic and Social Development (BNDES) and Banco da Amazônia (BASA) in technology and economics of sustainable forest management and agroforestry.

---

[67] IAG 2002.

- Adjust industrial products tax (IPI) to provide incentives for managed logging and certification. Exempt equipment imports for certified businesses from import duties.
- Create efficient and transparent forest concession systems, with concession fees on a per hectare basis, through auctions with qualified bidders. Involve local communities in revenue sharing and monitoring of logging operations.
- Give priority to community forestry in the allocation of lands in public conservation areas, and facilitate community property rights elsewhere.
- Stimulate agroforestry only in areas with reasonable access to urban markets (clusters). Continue stimulating *"pólos de desenvolvimento"*.
- Evaluate lessons learned from pilot projects systematically. Expand research on agroforestry and create effective technical assistance and extension services to transmit know-how to farmers.

Message 5. Promoting sustainable growth in the old consolidating frontier

Where the agricultural frontier has passed, land prices tend to increase relative to areas at the frontier, towns are developing, and infrastructure and services are increasing. Farmers tend to intensify their farming or ranching. This gradual consolidation of the "old frontier" could be supported by public investments, creating opportunities for poor, unskilled laborers to gradually enter into the non-rural labor market, and providing education and health services which help to stabilize formerly itinerant communities.

The apparent decline of plantation forests in the Southeast and South, due to non-renewal of plantations that have come to the end of their economic life, requires further analysis of the causes and possible instruments of intervention. The increased pressure that demand for timber may put on native (Amazon) forests is reason for concern. The use of public funds to assist small and medium scale farmers to establish plantations may be justified by its impact on poverty redution.

Context

INTENSIFICATION OF LAND USE AND GREATER OPPORTUNITIES FOR THE POOR. Large-scale conversion of forests has been going on since the 1960s in the Amazon and Atlantic Forests. In the areas first cleared, land has changed hands several times, new towns have grown up, and a sustained rural economy with tight links to urban centers and the national market has developed. Frequent turnover of farms has obeyed strong economic forces and has not necessarily led to degradation beyond the initial forest clearing.[68]

In the old frontier—in western Maranhão and eastern Pará, northern Tocantins and Mato Grosso, Rondônia along the BR 364, and eastern Acre—land prices have risen relative to the rest of the Amazon region (although they may have fallen in absolute terms after 1994). Land productivity in agriculture, particularly in cattle ranching, has increased, spurred by higher land prices and learning by doing. Ranches in eastern Pará, Mato Grosso, and central Rondônia are more productive than comparable ones in São Paulo State, supplying not just the region but all of Brazil. In Mato Grosso mechanized agriculture (soybean and cotton) has pushed cattle ranching northward.[69] In the process, requirements for legal reserves and permanent conservation areas were often ignored, leaving behind unviable fragments of forest or none at all. Some of this excess can be reversed, but not all.

While intensification is not likely, by itself, to reduce the pressure on forests, support for consolidation of the old frontier can complement the closing of the current frontier and do much to reduce poverty and increase community stability.

Investments in secondary and tertiary roads, rural electrification, telecommunication, research and extension, financial services, and education and health services will help to consolidate local economies and generate income and employment, activating a "virtuous employment multiplier" as the rural poor consume goods produced by others who are poor.[70] New opportunities for rural off-farm jobs and jobs in urban industries and services can attract small farmers and landless rural families in forest areas and help them break out of poverty. Better education and access to healthcare services can be provided to families in stable communities. The current program of stimulating "development poles" appears to support the notion of expanding the economy of the "consolidating frontier". Such investments could be funded from resources provided to FNO and FDA.

---

[68] Schneider 1994.

[69] Sant'Anna and others 2002.

[70] World Bank 2003, chapter 5.

Land titles in the old frontier are less of a concern since owners have a strong interest in securing clear property rights. Cost-effective methods for land regularization have been developed under the PRODEAGRO project in Mato Grosso, funded by the World Bank, which can serve as a model for other areas.

Zoning will be important for guaranteeing a minimum of environmental services and conserving biodiversity in the old frontier and in areas of transition from Cerrado to rain forests. Remaining forest fragments need to be joined to provide effective environmental services. No further land clearing should be allowed in the consolidating frontier. Degraded areas can be used for intensive agriculture. A combination of law enforcement and incentives should be applied to encourage forest restoration on already cleared land shown to be ecologically important.

IMPROVING FINANCIAL SERVICES. Sustainable use of forests and consolidation of the frontier economy would benefit from an efficient, client-oriented rural financial system. FNO, administered by BASA, receives large annual transfers from the federal budget, but appears to have difficulty lending to small farmers and regional businesses. FNO has accumulated large undisbursed funds and has high rates of arrears and default. A change in approach could redirect the current model of "directed" credit and create favorable conditions (i) for the access of rural producers to a system that considers them as clients, not as beneficiaries, and (ii) for discipline in the selection of clients and the supervision of credits (see Policy Note on financial sector).

ENCOURAGING PLANTATIONS, BUT LETTING THE PRIVATE SECTOR MANAGE THEM. Pine and eucalyptus plantations, established decades ago in the South and Southeast are reaching the end of their useful life and are not being renewed. The resulting severe supply deficit of timber will put heavy pressure on native forests in the Amazon and Atlantic Forest.

Why are tree plantations, which appear to be highly profitable investments in Brazil, not being renewed or expanded?[157] The answer to this question is not entirely clear. It probably has to do with the lack of financing terms compatible with the duration and growth cycles of plantations. Interest rates in Brazil are higher than the internal rate of return estimated for pine plantations, but this is true for many other products as well. The abundance of relatively cheap (but unsustainable) timber from the Amazon may be a further disincentive.

---

[71] Internal rate of return of 17 percent for pine, higher for eucalyptus, according to Rodigheri.

Public credit already finances tree plantations at more accessible interest rates. The subsidy implicit in lower rates can be justified with the reduction of the demand pressure on native forests. In the case of small producers, some form of subsidy may be considered on account of poverty reduction. The National Forest Program promotes rightly the family plantations of small and medium producers, and special subsidies should be restricted to these producers. At the same time, it appears imperative for an integrated forest policy, that unsustainable logging in the Amazon be tightly controlled.

The Forest Code distinguishes little between planted and native forests, and the intervention of the authorities in plantations can make investments more difficult. Tree plantations could simply be considered as "crops with a long growth period", and as such do not require much government intervention, except perhaps for an environmental license.

Reforestation of areas cleared before 1990 is recognized as carbon sequestration under the Clean Development Mechanism of the Kyoto Protocol. The market for carbon certificates from reforestation is uncertain and limited. The price for carbon offsets from reforestation is lower than that for "clean energy" projects, and the transaction costs for carbon credits in projects with many smallholders are high.[72] Nevertheless, Brazil can make good use of this option, as demonstrated by the PLANTAR project in Minas Gerais, which will benefit from future payments under the World Bank's Prototype Carbon Fund for carbon credits earned by planting eucalyptus trees, to substitute for imported coal.

Options
- In zoning, give priority to the old frontier and the transition areas from Cerrado to rain forests, with special attention to the need for environmental services in that region and for forest fragments of viable size.
- Admit no further forest clearing in the new frontier, and limit intensive agriculture to already degraded areas.
- In the consolidating frontier areas, support investments in local infrastructure, education and health, research and extension.
- Promote a new paradigm of client-oriented rural financial services, to substitute for supply-driven directed credit.
- Equip public sector banks to effectively apply the Green Protocol. Develop guidelines, train staff, and hire environmental specialists.

---

[72] Smith 2002, which estimates that the worldwide carbon market from reforestation may be in the order of 30 million tons a year, or 15 million hectares of plantations.

- Identify obstacles to the renewal of tree plantations, create suitable public sector credit facilities, and give small and medium-size farmers priority in incentives for planting.
- Treat tree plantations like crops, not like native forest, and let the private sector manage them without government interference.
- Explore carbon credit financing for plantations.

Annex: Options for Use of Forest Lands

Forest-Clearing Options

Options that require forest clearing are: cattle ranching, commercial agriculture, subsistence agriculture, and tree plantations (apart from mining and hydropower generation). Agroforestry does normally not require forest clearing; it may modify standing forests, but is most often used on already cleared areas. Tree plantations normally also use cleared land.

RANCHING is by far the most common option after forest clearing. It varies widely in its intensity: it has low productivity and profitability "at the frontier", after clearing, and without proper care becomes unproductive over time with weed and insect invasions and soil compaction. It can, however, become quite profitable over time as pasture land changes hands and as land prices increase: more resourceful final owners invest in renewal and improvement of pastures and cattle herds and manage their ranches more professionally. More recent establishments apply pasture rotation that avoids excessive, nonuniform grazing. Replenishment of soil nutrients is necessary in all cases (phosphates). Under those circumstances Amazonian ranches are sustainable, and have even higher indicators of productivity and greater profitability than comparable farms in the Southeast: annual net returns are around US$40/ha and internal rates of return range from 9% to almost 15%, excluding the value of land, but including the cost of forest clearing, although meat prices are about 20% less than in the Southeast. The higher productivity is attributed to the climate.

Cattle ranching has many advantages: low risk, low labor requirements, easy marketing of the product (live animals) and high liquidity of the investments. Pasture is still considered the most efficient way to demonstrate possession of forest areas. Social benefits are few: it concentrates landownership severely (less so in Rondônia) and offers few direct jobs. In some areas, it has led to violent conflicts over access to land. It does little for poverty reduction in the rural areas, except where small settlers sell their cleared land, and affects the poor adversely where it occupies forest that has been providing sustenance to poor extractivists. On the other hand, the development of an urban economy at the "old frontier", providing services to ranchers, creates indirect employment opportunities. Monoculture of commercial grasses over large continuous tracts favors the expansion of pests and diseases across pastures and animals, and reduces the humidity of the local climate[73]. By removing forest cover entirely, it has the greatest impact on environmental services, biodiversity and carbon stocks.

COMMERCIAL AGRICULTURE (rice, soybeans, beans, maize, cotton) produces high returns where rainfall is not excessive, land is flat, free of stumps and rocks, and where soil nutrients are replenished.[74] Soybean, however, is not (yet?) well adapted to high rainfall conditions. Mechanized commercial agriculture is incompatible with tree stumps and prefers older cleared areas (pastures, abandoned land) to newer ones. As such, it should not lead to much forest removal. Just as cattle ranching, it employs little labor, tends to concentrate land ownership and threatens to expel poor extractivists from their traditional lands (e.g., in southern Maranhão and northern Tocantins). More than ranching, commercial agriculture has environmental impacts through fertilizer and pesticide use, soil erosion and compaction, and on stream flows through irrigation.

SUBSISTENCE AGRICULTURE relies on nutrient mining and is only sustainable if land is left in fallow for a long period. Indigenous peoples have practiced a "slash-and-burn" shifting agriculture over centuries without major damage to the forest. In principle, it destroys forests just as ranching, but occurs on a much smaller scale, usually as a transition towards pasture use and often the later sale of land, even in INCRA colonies. It is obviously practiced by the poorer families, but by itself, is not likely to help them out of poverty. It may provide them with capital from the sale of logs and (later) of their plots.

AGROFORESTRY SYSTEMS combine annual, perennial and tree crops in a plant "consortium" with forest-like characteristics, mainly found in rain forests, but also in the Cerrado. Agroforestry types range from traditional (forest enrichment, managed "capoeira", home gardens) to commercial agroforestry systems[75]. They use mainly cleared land or second-

---

[73] Sant'Ana et al., 2002

[74] Sant'Ana et al., 2002

[75] Smith, N. and others 1998

ary forests (capoeira). They are adapted to the regional climate, have potentially high returns from a diverse mix of crops, high labor requirements and lesser impact on biodiversity than agriculture or ranching. They facilitate nutrient cycling, soil protection, natural control of plant pests and diseases, and they avoid fire and burnings. Many smallholder communities in the Amazon and Atlantic rain forests are trying out such systems, e.g., under the PPG7, but the full extent of lessons remains still to be learned. Where cash crops are involved, agroforestry is highly demanding in terms of on-farm and cooperative management, market information and marketing skills, research and extension services and transport infrastructure, but has the potential for high returns, income and employment generation where the conditions are right. (Shaded coffee plantations are a form of agroforestry, and are an interesting alternative for the plantations in the Atlantic forest and Cerrado that grow coffee without shade.)

TREE PLANTATIONS (for timber, coffee, cocoa, palm oil, etc.) have similar characteristics to agroforestry systems, but lack their diversity, and carry higher risks when they depend on one product only. They are an option for family farmers and large enterprises as a means to recover degraded pastures, but require secure property rights, good technical assistance/extension services and long-term credit. Both agroforestry and tree plantations may reap additional benefits from credits for absorbing carbon by adding biomass to degraded areas.

Options for the Use of Standing Forest

Options that make use of the standing forest are: use by indigenous populations, logging, extractivism, fisheries, ecotourism, bioprospecting and "carbon credits".

INDIGENOUS people have traditionally been using the forest sustainably for hunting, gathering, subsistence agriculture, and even agroforestry systems, although not without some impact on the ecosystem. With increasing contact with the "outside world" at the frontier, indigenous people may or may not continue sustainable use. The demarcation of indigenous lands and follow-on support to their populations has been important for the reduction of poverty, and a means to preserve environmental services, biodiversity and carbon stocks.

LOGGING: Much depends on how it is done: traditional "predatory" logging is a highly profitable operation, has destructive impact on the forest, leaves it susceptible to fire, and tends to lead eventually to total forest clearing. It does create employment in the forest and in the sawmills. It is not sustainable locally, as it relies on continuous opening of new areas. Managed (or certified) forestry does little damage to the forest, maintains forest environmental services, has little impact on biodiversity and carbon stocks, and employs more people than predatory logging. It is less (but still highly) profitable, and is constrained by several factors, such as secure land titles, credit and properly skilled manpower. Apart from export markets, there is a growing, but still small domestic demand for certified timber which is not met by domestic production. Managed forests represent a large opportunity for long-term exploration, and avoid the boom-and-bust cycle of traditional logging with its social disruptions, provide greater stability to communities, allowing the provision of better health and education services, and have thus potential for reducing poverty.

EXTRACTIVISM is the gathering of forest products such as rubber, nuts, oils, fibers and medicinal plants as practiced by the traditional forest communities for decades, even centuries. With restraint, extractivism has only small impacts on biodiversity, and preserves forest environmental services and carbon stock. Brazil's "extractive reserves" are a model for the conservation of biodiversity (although they conserve it less perfectly than strictly protected areas) by forest-dwelling populations drawing a livelihood from the forest. Extractivism is an obvious option for the rural poor in rain forests, but clearly produces only low incomes. Provision of health and education to dispersed communities is more difficult. The potential for lifting forest dwellers out of poverty through extractivism is likely to be limited, although there are promising recent experiences that match extractivists' supplies with industrial demand for oils and fibers. Fisheries by traditional communities are similar to extractivism, and help to conserve vulnerable floodplain ecosystems.

BIOPROSPECTING explores the economic potential of biodiversity of forests for genetic material for pharmaceutical and other purposes. It has raised high hopes for income and growth from standing forests (rain forests and Cerrado), including for the benefit of indigenous and other poorer communities, "owning" a certain genetic resource, through royalty payments. The value of, and earning potential from, bioprospecting is highly uncertain. Estimations of the per-hectare value of such benefits vary widely, but may be substantial.[76] Environmental impacts should be almost nil. Much depends on the degree

---

[76] Seroa da Motta 2002

to which the benefits from the development of pharmaceuticals and other products from genetic material can actually be captured by Brazil and its communities, as applicable laws and international agreements are well-intentioned but difficult to enforce.

ECOTOURISM has a much larger potential in the Amazon than so far realized. It relies on standing forests, and with appropriate safeguards, its environmental impact is minimal. While much of the income generated may not remain in the region, local employment and the share of income captured by the poor is still highly significant and favorable for forest conservation.[77]

CARBON CREDITS may be paid by foreign interested parties to forest owners or communities for capturing or stocking carbon in forest biomass. The Kyoto protocol does not allow for carbon credits related to standing forests, but it is expected that such credits may be forthcoming independently of the Kyoto protocol. Such credits would only require that forest be maintained; and would thus be compatible with extractivism and sustainable logging.

References

World Bank projects

- Amazon Region Protected Areas - ARPA. GEF - US$ 30 million. Approved on August 8, 2002.
- Paraná Biodiversity. GEF - US$ 8 million. Approved on May 21, 2002.
- Floodplain Natural Resources Management – Provárzea RFT - US$ 2 million. Approved on November 17, 2000.
- National Environment II – PNMA II. Loan - US$ 15 million. Approved on December 9, 1999.
- Support for Monitoring and Analysis – AMA. RFT - US$ 2 million. Approved on December 23, 1998.
- Emergency Fire Prevention and Control – PROARCO. Loan - US$ 15 million. Approved on September 10, 1998.

---

[77] Nasi and others 2002

- Fire Prevention Mobilization and Training– PROTEGER (*Projeto de Mobilização e Capacitação para a Prevenção de Incêndios Florestais na Amazônia*). USAID - US$ 1.1 million. Approved on August 20, 1998.
- Ecological Corridors (*Corredores Ecológicos*). RFT - US$ 5 million. Approved on December 28, 1997.
- Sustainable Forest Management – PROMANEJO.   RFT - US$ 2 million. Approved on April 16, 1997.
- Biodiversity Project – PROBIO. GEF - US$ 10 million. Approved on April 16, 1996.
- Indigenous Lands – PPTAL. RFT - US$ 2.1 million. Approved on July 6, 1995.
- Extrative Reserves – RESEX . RFT - US$ 4 million. Approved on November 16, 1994.
- Natural Resources Policy – SPRN. RFT - US$ 20 million. Approved on June 30, 1994.
- Demonstration Projects – PD/A. RFT - US$ 10.8 million. Approved on June 28, 1994.
- Mato Grosso Natural Resources Management– PRODEAGRO. Loan - US$ 190 million. Approved on June 18, 1992.
- Rondonia Natural Resources Management – PLANAFLORO.   Loan - US$ 157 million. Approved on March 17, 1992.

World Bank reports

This chapter summarizes the content of the following World Bank reports. Those, in turn, draw heavily from a wide range of literature on the subject from experts in Brazil and beyond, which are referenced in the mentioned Bank reports.

World Bank. The management of agriculture, rural development and natural resources. Report 11783-BR. Washington, D.C.: World Bank, 1994.

World Bank. Project appraisal document for the Costa Rica Ecomarkets Project. Washington, D.C.: World Bank, 2000.

World Bank. "Towards more sustainable coffee". In: Agricultural Technology Notes 30. Washington, D.C: World Bank, 2002.

World Bank. World Development Report 2003: Sustainable development in a dynamic world. New York: Oxford University, 2003.

Other references

Almeida, O. Sustainable settlement in the Brazilian Amazon. New York: Oxford University, 1996.

Almeida, O.; Uhl, C. *"Planejamento de uso do solo de um município na Amazônia Oriental utilizando dados econômicos e ecológicos"*, in Almeida, Oriana (Org.). *Evolução da fronteira Amazônica: oportunidades para o desenvolvimento sustentável*, Porto Alegre, Editora Caravelas, 1995

Altieri, M. "The Ecological Role of Biodiversity in Agroecosystems." Agriculture, Ecosystems, and Environment, Vol. 74, nr. 1-3:19-31, 1999.

Alves, D. "An analysis of the geographical patterns of deforestation in Brazilian Amazônia in the 1991-1996 period", paper prepared for the 48th Annual Conference on Patterns and Processes of Land Use and Forest Change in the Amazon, Center for Latin American Studies, University of Florida, Gainesville, 1999 (now in Wood C. and Porro, R. (Eds.) "Deforestation and Land Use in the Amazon", University Press of Florida, 2002)

Alston, L.; Libecap, G.; Mueller, B. Land reform policies, the sources of violent conflict and implications for deforestation in the Brazilian Amazon. Nota di Lavoro 70.2001. Milano: Fondazione Eni Enrico Matte, 2001

Andrae, S.; Pingel, K. Rain forest financial systems: the directed credit paradigm in the Brazilian Amazon and its alternatives. Berlin: Latin America Institute, 1999.

Balmford, A. et al.. "Economic reasons for conserving wild nature". Science, Vol. 297, Nr. 9 August 2002: 950-53, 2002.

Barreto, P. Sustainable forest management in Amazonia: incentives and disincentives. Washington, D.C.: World Bank, 2002.

Barreto, P.; Souza Jr., C. *Controle de desmatamento e da exploração de madeira na Amazônia: diagnóstico e sugestões. Relatório Técnico do IMAZON para o Projeto de Apoio ao Manejo Florestal do PPG7. Belém: 2001.*

Bruner, A.; Gullison, R.E.; Rice, R. E.; Fonseca, G.A.B. "Effectiveness of parks in protecting tropical biodiversity". Science, Vol. 291, Nr. 5 January:125-28, 2001.

Chomitz, K.; Gray, D. Roads, lands, markets, and deforestation: a spatial model of land use in Belize. Policy Research Working Paper 1444. Washington, D. C.: World Bank, 1995.

Chomitz, K.; Kumari, K. "The domestic benefits of tropical forests: a critical review". World Bank Research Observer, Vol. 13, Nr.1:13-35, 1998.

Chomitz, K.; Thomas, T. Geographic patterns of land use and land intensity in the Brazilian Amazon. Policy Research Working Paper 2687. Infrastructure and Environment and Development Research Group, Washington, D.C.: World Bank, 2000.

Chomitz, K.; Thomas, T.; Brandão, A. Salazar. All trees are the same, all trees are different: creating markets for habitat conservation when habitats are heterogeneous. Draft Policy Research Working Paper. Washington, D.C.:World Bank. [forthcoming]

Chomitz, K. Transferable development rights and forest protection: an exploratory analysis. Paper prepared for a workshop on Market-Based Instruments for Environmental Protection at Harvard University, Cambridge, Massachussets, 1999.

Church, F. et al.. Optimal biodiversity corridors. Santa Barbara: University of California.

Contreras-Hermosilla, A.; Vargas, M.T. Social, environmental, and economic dimensions of forest policy reform in Bolivia. Washington D. C.: Forest Trends; Bogor, Indonesia: Center for International Forestry Research, 2001.

Eba'a Atyi, R.; Simula, M. Forest certification: pending challenges for tropical timber. Background paper prepared for the International Tropical Timber Organization International Workshop on Comparability and Equivalence of Forest Certification Schemes, Kuala Lumpur, 2001.

Fearnside, P. "The potential of Brazil's forest sector for mitigating global warming under the Kyoto Protocol." Mitigation and Adaptation Strategies for Global Change, Vol..6, Nr. 3-4: 355-72, 2001.

Freris, N.; Laschefski, K. "Seeing the wood from the trees." The Ecologist, Vol. 31, Nr. 6, 2001.

WGBU (German Advisory Council on Global Change). Charging for the use of global commons. WBGU Policy Paper. Berlin: 2001.

Haddad, P.; Rezende, F. *O uso de instrumentos econômicos para o desenvolvimento sustentável: o ICMS Ecológico.* Paper for Brazil Ministry of the Environment and the World Bank, 2002a.

Haddad, P.; Rezende, F. *Proposta de medidas tributárias de estímulo ao uso sustentável da madeira.* Paper for Brazil Ministry of the Environment and the World Bank, 2002b.

Hyde, W.; Amacher, G.; Macgrath, W. "Deforestation and forest land use: theory, evidence, and policy implications". Word Bank Research Observer, Vol. 11, Nr. 2: 133-40, 1996.

IMAZON (Instituto do Homem e do Meio Ambiente da Amazônia). *Controle do desmatamento e da exploração de madeira na Amazônia: diagnóstico e sugestões.* Belém: 2000.

IAG (International Advisory Group of the PPG7). Land issues and the G7 Pilot Programme to Conserve the Brazilian Rain Forest. Special Report. Brasília: 2000.

IAG (International Advisory Group of the PPG7). Brazilian conservation policies and the Pilot Programme to Conserve the Brazilian Rain Forest. Special Report. Brasília: 2001.

Kaimowitz, D.; Angelsen, A. Will livestock intensification help save Latin America's tropical forests? Posted in LEAD—Livestock Environment and Development Discussion Forum, 2001.
(http://lead.virtualcentre.org/apps/cams/user/download.asp?idf_cams_forum=4&idf _cams_topic=241&idf_cams_documents=621)

Kaimowitz, D. Useful myths and intractable truths: the politics of the link between forests and water in Central America. CIFOR Working Paper. San José, Costa Rica: Center for International Forest Research, 2001.

Kishor, N.; Constantino, L. Forest management and competing land uses: an economic analysis for Costa Rica. LATEN Dissemination Note 7. Washington, D.C.: World Bank, 1993

Lele, U.; Viana, V.; Verissimo, A.; Vosti, S.; Perkins, K.; Husain, S. Forests in the balance: challenges of conservation with development: an evaluation of Brazil's forest development and World Bank assistance. Washington D.C.: World Bank Operations Evaluation Department, 2000.

Lerdau, M.; Slobodkin, L. "Trace gas emissions and species-dependent ecosystem services". Trends in Ecology & Evolution, Year 17, Nr. 7: 309-312, 2002.

Lugo, A. Working forests will be New Ecosystems. Paper presented at the Conference on Working Forests in the Tropics, University of Florida, Gainesville, 2002.

Mahar, D. Government policies and deforestation in the Brazilian Amazon. Washington, D.C.: World Bank, 1989.

Mahar, D.; Ducrot, C. Land-use zoning on tropical frontiers: emerging lessons from the Brazilian Amazon. Washington, D.C.: World Bank, 1998.

May, P.; Veiga Neto, F.; Denardin, V. ; Loureiro, W. 2002 "The Ecological Value-Added Tax: Municipal Responses in Paraná and Minas Gerais, Brazil" in Pagiola, Bishop e Landell-Mills (eds): Selling Forest Environmental Services: Market-based Mechanisms for Conservation. London, Earthscan, 2002.

MMA (Ministério do Meio Ambiente); World Bank. Lessons from the rain forest: experiences of the Pilot Program to Conserve the Amazon and Atlantic Forests of Brazil. Brasília: 2001

MMA (Ministério do Meio Ambiente); Instituto de Estudos da Religião (ISER). O que o brasileiro pensa do meio ambiente e do consumo sustentável: pesquisa nacional de opinião. Brasília: 2001

MMA (Ministério do Meio Ambiente). *Programa Nacional de Florestas.* Brasília: 2001.

Mueller, C. working paper prepared for the World Bank on Cerrado, 2002.

Nasi, R.; Wunder, S.; Campos, J. Forest ecosystem services: can they pay our way out of deforestation?. Discussion paper for Global Environment Facility Forestry Roundtable, Costa Rica, 2002.

Nepstad, D.; Moreira, A; Alencar, A. Flames in the rain forest: origins, impacts and alternatives to Amazonian fires. Pilot Program to Conserve the Brazilian Rain Forest, Brasília, Brasil, 1999.

Nepstad, D.; McGrath, D.; Alencar, A.; Barros, A. C.; Carvalho, G.; Santilli, M.; Diaz, Vera M. del C. "Frontier governance in Amazonia". Science, Vol. 295, Nr. 5555: 629-31, 2002.

Nitsch, M. The future of the Amazon: critical issues and scenarios. Lecture at the German-Brazilian Workshop on Neo-Tropical Ecosystems, Hamburg, 2002.

Pacheco, P. Deforestation in the Brazilian Amazon: a review of estimates at the municipal level. Washington, D.C.: World Bank, 2002.

Pasquis, R.; Machado, L.; Evangelista, C.; Fernandez, J.; Pontes, M. *As Amazônias: uma visão dos atores.* Preliminary draft, unpublished, Brasília, World Bank, 2002.

Pearce, D.; Putz, F.; Vanclay, J. "Sustainable forestry in the tropics: panacea or folly?" Forest Ecology and Management 5839 1–19, 2001.

Pfaff, A. What drives deforestation in the Brazilian Amazon?. Washington D.C.: World Bank, 1996.

Castro, E. Ramos; Monteiro, R.; Castro, C. Potiara. "Atores e relações sociais em novas fronteiras na Amazônia". Washington, D.C.: World Bank, 2002.

Redwood III, J. World Bank approaches to the environment in Brazil: a review of selected projects. Washington, D.C.: World Bank, 1993.

Rice, R.; Sugal, C.; Ratay, S.; Fonseca, G. "Sustainable forest management: a Review of Conventional Wisdom." Advances in Applied Biodiversity Science, Advances In Applied Biodiversity Science, No. 3, p. 1-29, 2001.

Rodigheri. H. R. "Indicadores ecológicos e socioeconômicos de plantios florestais na região Sul do Brasil". Embrapa - Florestas, Colombo, Paraná, 1998 (http://gipaf.cnptia.embrapa.br/itens/publ/sober/trab038.pdf)

Roulet, M.; Lucotte, M. The natural origin of mercury in central Amazonian ecosystems. Proceedings of the 5th International Conference on Mercury as a Global Pollutant, 23-28 May, Rio de Janeiro, 1999.

Barros, G. Sant'Ana de Camargo; Zen, S. de; Ichihara, S.; Osaki, M.; Ponchio, L. Economia da pecuária de corte e o processo de ocupação da Amazônia. Washington, D.C.: World Bank, 2002.

Schneider, R. Brazil: an analysis of environmental problems in the Amazon. Report 9104-BR. Washington, D.C.:World Bank, 1992.

Schneider, R. Government and the economy on the Amazon frontier. Latin America and the Caribbean Technical Department, Report 34. Washington, D.C.: World Bank, 1994.

Schneider, R.; Arima, E.; Verissimo, A.; Barreto, P.; Souza Junior, C. Amazônia sustentável: limitantes e oportunidades para o desenvolvimento rural. Brasília, Banco Mundial; Belém, Imazon, 2000. (Série Parcerias; Nr. 1)

Motta, R. Seroa. Estimativa do custo econômico do desmatamento na Amazônia. Washington, D.C: World Bank, 2002.

Smeraldi, R. et al. Legalidade predatória: o novo quadro da exploração madeireira na Amazônia. São Paulo: Amigos da Terra Amazônica Brasileira, 2002.

Smith, J. Making working forests a reality: how much can we expect from the Kyoto Protocol" Presentation (given by A. White) at the Conference on Working Forests in the Tropics, Universidade da Flórida, Gainesville, 2002.

Smith, N.; Dubois, J.; Current, D.; Lutz, E.; Clement, C. Agroforestry experiences in the Brazilian Amazon: constraints and opportunities. Programa Piloto para Conservação da Floresta Tropical Brasileira, Brasília, 1998.

Veiga, M; Hinton, J.; Lilly, C. Mercury in the Amazon: a comprehensive review with special emphasis on bioaccumulation and bioindicators. Proceedings of National Institute for Minamata Disease Forum '99. Minamata, Japan, 1999.

Vera Diaz, M. C. Vera; Nepstad, D.; Mendonça, M. J. Cardoso, Motta, R. Seroa, A.; Alencar, J.C.; Gomes, R.; Ortiz, R. Arigoni. O preço oculto do fogo na Amazônia: os custos econômicos associados às queimadas e incêndios florestais. 2002.

Veríssimo, A.; Cochrane, M. A.; Souza Jr., C.; Salomão, R.. "Priority areas for establishing national forests in the Brazilian Amazon." Conservation Ecology Vol. 6, Nr.1: 4, 2002.

Viana, V.; May, P.; Lago, L.; Dubois, O.; Grieg-Gran, M. Instrumentos para o manejo sustentável do setor florestal privado no Brasil. London: International Institute for Environment and Development (IIED), s.d.

von Amsberg, J. Economic parameters of deforestation. Policy Research Working Paper 1350. Washington. D.C.:World Bank, 1994

Wilson, T. Sustainable management: the business/economic side. Paper presented at the Conference on Working Forests in the Tropics. Gainsville: University of Florida, 2002.

Wood, C.; R. Walker. "Saving the trees by helping the poor: a look at small producers along Brazil's Transamazon Highway". Resources, Nr. 136: 14-17, 1999.

WWF (Worldwide Fund for Nature). Desenvolvimento e conservação do meio ambiente: pesquisa de opinião com lideranças e a população da Amazônia. Brasil, 2001

Wunder, S. From Dutch disease to deforestation: a macroeconomic link?. Copenhagen: Centre for Development Research, 1997.

Wunder, S. "Poverty alleviation and tropical forests: what scope for synergies?" World Development. Vol. 29, Nr.11, 2001.

9

Rural Development and Natural Resources

9

Rural Development and Natural Resources

Introduction

Brazil is a global player in the production and export of agricultural commodities, with a huge potential to expand agricultural area and increase market share in the coming decade. Agriculture and related sectors are critical to the Brazilian economy, accounting for about 27 percent of GDP when agro-industry is included. About 33 percent of Brazil's exports are agricultural, and some 23 percent of employment is tied to agriculture, with another 10–15 percent of the workforce employed in agro-industry.

The next generation of Brazilian policymakers faces the challenge of simultaneously addressing multiple issues across all sectors affecting rural development. They need to find ways to help rural people exploit opportunities in the non-farm economies of small towns and rural centers, while supporting commercial and small-scale agricultural growth as a central component in broad economic growth. Only coordinated, integrated policies and actions can capture the synergies that spell results in poverty reduction and natural resources management.

Consistent policies, equitable access, decentralized application and decision-making, and stronger institutions are key ingredients of the broad strategy for improving rural development and protecting natural resources in Brazil. Education and training are the sine qua non.

This chapter provides both the substance and the direction for policymaking in selected areas. It is supported by examples of successful, cost-effective models of community-based land reform and rural development, provision of basic infrastructure and services, and Integrated Natural Resources Management. These programs could be applied in flexible

The draft of this chapter was coordinated by Luiz Gabriel Azevedo and Luis Coirolo, and completed by Anna Roumani, Alvaro Soler, Luiz Gabriel Azevedo, Edward Bresnyan, Charles Mueller, and Alexandre Baltar in November 2002. The analyses and suggestions contained in this chapter are based on the international technical experience of the World Bank and are presented as a contribution to the debate and formulation of public policies.

ways in various parts of Brazil, as long as attention is paid to how they are scaled up and out. Suggestions for enhancing rural development and protecting the natural resource base are presented below and discussed in this note.

Alleviating rural poverty, particularly in the Northeast

Alongside this dynamic commercial sector exists another rural Brazil. Widespread poverty and deprivation affect millions of rural people in small-scale and subsistence farming households concentrated in remote, isolated, and sparsely populated areas with scant infrastructure, low productivity, and degraded lands. The modest cities and small centers of this region offer few opportunities.

While poverty is found in many parts of rural Brazil, including the Southeast, it is most severe in the Northeastern states, especially the vast, semi-arid Sertão region, which shows steady economic, social, and environmental decline despite decades of public programs intended to reverse it. The semi-arid region of the Northeast supports some 45 percent of the total population of the region and the largest concentration of rural poor in Latin America. Growth of the livestock and cotton sub-sectors in recent decades was the basis for significant agricultural expansion and diversification, but this growth has faded.

The obstacles to a better life in the Northeast—and thus the challenges for policymakers—are formidable. Millions of people are trapped in poverty by a weak and degraded natural resource base, drought, low labor productivity, highly skewed patterns of landholding, population pressures, and severe deficiencies in basic infrastructure and services, including financial services. High illiteracy and poor-quality education hinder successful migration or improved rural livelihood. Inadequate water supply, sanitation services, and water resources management, including drought mitigation efforts and pollution control, adversely affect the health and productivity of the rural poor, requiring coordinated efforts.

Reversing the degradation of the natural resource base

Accelerated expansion of the agricultural frontier for crops and pasture in the past 30 years combined with deficient land management policies and practices have caused Brazil to lose the equivalent of R$3.2 billion of topsoil a year to erosion and to suffer incalculable losses in biodiversity. While progressive farmers have increasingly adopted sustainable practices and environmental awareness and public intervention on behalf of the environment has grown, most croplands and grasslands continue to be managed using traditional or conventional methodologies, causing continued erosion and degradation.

Soil degradation by runoff erosion is universal and pervasive. Even in the semi-arid areas of the Northeast, heavy, erosive summer rains cause devastating losses to farmers' productive base, particularly in the small-farm sector. As both a cause and a consequence of rural impoverishment, soil degradation leads to diminishing yields and incomes, promotes further land clearing, and perpetuates negative effects on the water cycle and biodiversity. The tendency for public policy not to counteract the bias of market developments in favor of more technologically advanced and sophisticated producers means that small and semi-subsistence farmers face major obstacles to finding and adopting suitable practices to boost productivity and sustainability, and to arrest decline.

Reorienting social spending

Under the Millennium Development Goals, Brazil committed itself to cutting poverty in half by 2015. Doing so will require economic growth, social spending, and a major review and restructuring of a broad range of social programs to improve their cost-effectiveness, coverage, and efficiency. Between 1981 and 1999 annual social expenditures of about R$35–R$40 billion would have been required to eradicate poverty in Brazil. During this period federal, state, and local governments spent about R$100 billion a year, well in excess of those levels, but only 13 percent of those expenditures reached the neediest; most investments in education, health, and social security went—and continue to go—to the middle class and wealthy. Poor targeting and coverage of public expenditures is thus a crucial factor perpetuating poverty in Brazil.

Message 1. Focusing on all sectors affecting rural development, not just agriculture
Extreme poverty in Brazil is concentrated in rural areas and small towns. Reducing poverty in these areas requires sustained efforts in all sectors that effect rural development, not just in agriculture. Efforts must target the entire "rural space," made up of rural areas as well as secondary towns where 50 percent of the poor are employed in various forms of non-farm activity. Increasing incomes within this space is critical, but improvements in other areas are also needed. Changes include consolidating a more open and transparent rural society; increasing the accountability of rural institutions; implementing broad-based, pro-poor policies that foster rural growth by linking commercial agriculture and poverty reduction; increasing employment and enhancing competitiveness; increasing the poor's holdings of land, water, and natural resources and their capacity to manage them sustainably; and improving access to education, health, and finance.

Context

Brazil competes globally as a producer and exporter of agricultural products, including coffee, soybeans, maize, sugar, bananas, manioc, orange juice, and meat. Agriculture and related sectors and activities are critical to the Brazilian economy and to the rural sector. Agriculture accounts for about 11 percent of GDP (US$4.5 billion annually) and as much as 27 percent of GDP (US$15.2 billion annually) when agro-industry is included. About 33 percent of total exports are agricultural (US$16–US$17 billion annually) and some 23 percent of employment is tied to agriculture (33–47 percent including agro-industry). The employment creation potential of commercial agriculture is large and underexploited, especially in the Northeast region. With the world's largest remaining tracts of virgin land, much of which is readily convertible to agriculture, and vast pasture lands suitable for grain and oilseed production, Brazil is one of the few countries with an expanding agricultural area and real potential to increase its global market share.

This remarkable performance and potential stands in stark contrast to the "other" rural Brazil. Of the 23 percent of Brazil's population living in extreme poverty, the bias is strongly rural. Poverty is worse in both relative and absolute terms (that is, the poverty rate is higher and the number of poor greater in rural areas). Poverty and deprivation are widespread among small-scale, subsistence-sector farm households concentrated in remote, isolated, and sparsely populated areas with little infrastructure, low productivity, and degraded lands.

Poverty continues to disproportionately affect the Northeast, where about 17 million of Brazil's total poor and about 9.5 million of its rural poor live. Millions of people—45 percent of the total population in the Northeast—struggle to survive in the vast, heterogeneous, semi-arid region (the *sertão*), which is in steady economic, social and environmental decline (see Message 2). The obstacles to a better life in the rural Northeast are formidable: a weak and degraded natural resource base, frequent drought, low labor productivity, high illiteracy and poor quality and coverage of education, grossly inadequate access to basic infrastructure and services, highly concentrated landholding, and weak rural financial markets. Opportunity-based out-migration is continuous. Poor transportation links, under-developed roads, and inadequate communications infrastructure hinder market access. Lack of investment in human capital is trapping millions in poverty.

FOCUSING POLICYMAKING ON THE "RURAL SPACE". With extreme poverty in Brazil concentrated in rural areas and small towns and with 50 percent of the rural poor now employed in some form of non-farm activity, policymaking must address the "rural space." Reducing rural poverty and spurring economic growth require policymaking in a variety of sectors, including agriculture, agro-business, natural resource management, rural education, infrastructure in villages and secondary towns, and financial services and municipal development. Agriculture-based rural economies are increasingly tied to non-farm activities. According to Ferreira, Lanjouw, and Neri (2000), the incidence of rural poverty is typically higher in small urbanized centers whose economies are more likely to be linked with rural economies, than larger urban areas.

Linked, simultaneous actions are needed to reduce rural poverty. They include increasing the income and spending of the poor; improving access to productive and social assets, services, and facilities; empowering the poor to participate in political and social processes and to promote change; and reducing the vulnerability of the poor to risk. Success depends on sustained, consensus-based political commitment; the strong management and implementation capacity of state and local governments; and an understanding of the nature, causes, and dynamics of poverty to analytically underpin policy formulation and implementation.

SUPPORTING GROWTH IN AGRICULTURE. Rapid growth in the overall economy, with rapid urban job creation and expanded domestic demand for farm products, would significantly reduce rural poverty. But the type and structure of growth is as important as growth itself. Growth within agriculture—that is, growth of labor-intensive agricultural output and small-scale enterprises linked to the rural economy—not the shift of labor and capital out of agriculture into large-scale industry is what accelerates rural poverty reduction. Agricultural yields are also crucial: a 33 percent increase can decrease poverty by about 25 percent. Brazil therefore needs a pro-poor growth strategy, with agriculture as a prime vehicle. Growth that excludes the agricultural sector hurts the rural poor by reducing the overall growth rate and doing little or nothing to reduce poverty. Agricultural growth reduces poverty effectively because it both generates income for poor farmers and creates demand for the goods and services easily produced by the poor. The benefits of agricultural growth are shown in table 1.

Table 1. Benefits of agricultural growth

Farm economy	Rural economy	National economy
Higher incomes for farms, including smallholders	More jobs in agriculture and in the food chain upstream and downstream of the farm	Lower prices of food and raw materials, which raise real wages of the urban poor and reduce the wages costs of non-farm sectors
More on-farm jobs as labor demand rises per hectare, the area cultivated expands, or frequency of cropping increases	More jobs or higher incomes in non-farm economy as farmers and farm laborers spend additional incomes	Generation of savings and taxes from farming, which allows investment in non- farm sector, creating jobs and incomes in other sectors
Rise in farm wage rates	Increased rural jobs and incomes, which improve nutrition and health, and increased investment in education for rural population, leading to better welfare both directly and indirectly through higher labor productivity	Higher foreign exchange earnings, which allow import of capital goods and essential production
	More local tax revenues generated and demand for better infrastructure (roads, energy, communications) Second-round effects promoting rural economy	Release of farm labor, increasing production in other sectors
	Increased production chain links, generating trust, increasing information , building social capital, and facilitating non-farm investment	
	Lower prices of food for rural inhabitants, who are net purchasers of food	

Source: Irz and others 2001.

Market developments and government policies since the late 1980s (including trade openness, reduction of subsidized credit, vertical integration of processing and marketing, and deregulation of domestic marketing) have favored more advanced producers, with positive effects on commercial agriculture. These developments were necessary but insufficient to capture opportunities to link commercial agriculture to poverty reduction, and they had different effects on exported and imported products and on commercial agriculture and the poor. Indeed, existing policies have worked against low technology, small, and semi-subsistence farmers. The challenge is to find ways of assisting small farmers with the potential to survive in today's more competitive environment without providing permanent subsidies. It is particularly challenging for poor rural populations in the semi-arid regions of the Northeast, where agriculture and the physical environment are declining.

Supporting rural non-farm employment. Rural families living adjacent to the urban perimeters of municipal centers, where non-farm jobs are concentrated, tend to be less poor. But among the extremely poor, only 30 percent of rural income is from non-farm sources, because isolation exacts a price. Establishing forward linkages to agriculture (processing, storage, marketing facilities) can stimulate rural, non-farm activities. Under a rural livelihoods approach, households diversify across a range of assets, activities, and income sources that usually include aspects of the non-farm economy. Such diversification can lead to more predictable incomes and is an effective response to inherent rural volatility (drought, labor uncertainties) and the complementary nature of home-based activities (farm or non-farm).

Policymakers face a massive challenge in developing diversified opportunities for non-farm employment in the modest cities and small centers of the semi-arid region. These areas, described by Maia Gomes (2001) as "economies without production," are highly dependent on pension income, drought workfare programs, and income from family members in municipal employment. Industrial activity of any kind is scarce, the service sector is precarious, and natural resources are degraded. Rural, non-farm enterprises have economic advantage only in sectors that include natural resource–based extractive industries, traditional rural skills (artesanal), tourism, and any activity requiring proximity to the point of extraction, production, or cheap labor. These sectors act as rural exports, meeting urban rather than rural demand, and create rural growth. They can be the main engine of rural non-farm growth (table 2).

Providing poor households with productive assets. Poor families who remain in agriculture need more productive assets, especially land, which is particularly critical if labor demand does not grow substantially. But policymakers should recognize that the impact of land on farm productivity and income depends on simultaneous improvements in complementary productive factors (purchased inputs, machinery) and demographic factors (age of operator, education level). The Bank and its Brazilian counterparts have substantial experience in community-based land access (with complementary invest-ments) working through local land markets.

Almost all of the 16.5 million rural poor in Brazil belong to the 4.4 million households lacking enough land to subsist. Yet evidence strongly suggests that family farms can be more efficient and labor intensive than large farms, even in the Northeast. Skewed land-holding depresses agricultural productivity and employment. Economic distortions that fostered land concentration (agricultural subsidies, inflation, tax incentives) were lifted in the 1990s, reducing the incentives to hold land as a financial hedge. Land supply increased and prices fell, especially in the Northeast.

Table 2. Strategies to support rural non-farm employment

Strategy	Action needed
Remove general constraints to rural growth	Invest in transport, communication, education, and health
Facilitate urban-rural links	Facilitate the flow of migrants and remittances
	Increase the flow of market and price information to rural areas
	Establish regulations and standards that facilitate outsourcing and subcontracting
	Develop rural recreational amenities for the urban population
	Identify options for increasing access to social and business networks
Facilitate enterprise growth	Develop small towns
	Support producer associations for marketing and sourcing
	Remove regulatory or bureaucratic burden on small and medium-size enterprises
	Reform rural extension into business advisory services
Adopt sector or sub-sector specific interventions	Support industrial clusters
	Provide incentives for industry relocation
	Use planning gain in concession allocation to foster local economic linkages

Source: Ashley and Maxwell 2001.

Based on a successful pilot program in Ceará that rapidly settled 700 families on about 23,000 hectares, the federal government, in partnership with the Bank, developed the expanded *Cédula da Terra* project in five Northeastern states (box 1). When the program closes, at the end of December 2002, another 17,000 families will have been settled on 442,00 hectares, at an average cost of R$4,900 per family and R$190 per hectare. The successor to this project is the 14-state *Crédito Fundiário* program. This program, which targets lands not subject to expropriation and the poorest potential beneficiaries of the national land reform program, is financed 50/50 by the federal government (land acquisitions) and the Bank (on-farm investments). Community associations identify suitable lands and negotiate their purchase with willing sellers, receiving an investment grant for on-farm improvements. *Crédito Fundiário* is notable for the important role of rural workers' unions (CONTAG and FETAG) in implementation, technical assistance, and project evaluation.

Box 1. Lessons learned from market-based land access projects in Brazil

The community-based, market-oriented method for settling landless rural families is agile and effective. Communities take ownership of their land within 90 days, in most cases.

- Self-selection for participation is effective; the vast majority of beneficiaries have household incomes and characteristics consistent with the intended profile.

- The modestl size of community groups acquiring properties (about 15–30 families) appears to be an advantage. Groups with less than 15, or over 50 members, can face difficulties.

- Despite generally poor land quality in the Northeast, communities have consistently chosen good-quality land, at considerable savings compared with traditional methods and without increasing land prices.

- Land prices have been favorable, with costs per family significantly lower than the present value of initial expropriation prices in the Northeast.

- The success of community associations in mobilizing members, selecting land for purchase, designing a productive on-farm investment, and carrying it out has been impressive.

- The great majority of subprojects promise to be financially and economically viable. Financial returns are likely to exceed initial estimates in better agro-climatic areas; in the semi-arid *Sertão* water is the key determinant.

- Annual family incomes are expected to rise 200–400 percent from an initial R$1,400 (typical case) in three to six years, net of loan repayment amounts.

- Repayment of land loans is occurring in the original Ceará pilot properties, where families from 42 of 44 properties have paid without difficulty. Measures are needed to avert defaults.

- Strong management information systems and continuous evaluation are crucial to resolve problems promptly and monitor a project involving numerous community groups in multiple states.

Source: World Bank 2000b.

EXPANDING THE RURAL POVERTY REDUCTION PROJECTS. Recent successful experiences with community-driven rural poverty reduction mechanisms have reversed the pessimism associated with decades of failed rural development programs. The challenge is to expand coverage, deepen economic and social impact, and exploit the potential of these programs to integrate poverty-reducing activities, including productive and commercial activities, land reform, natural resource management, and education, across sectors.   Jointly financed by the Bank and state governments of the Northeast and several states of the South, a series of rural poverty reduction projects have successfully delivered funds directly to poor rural communities for cost-effective, sustainable investments in basic infrastructure, services, and productive activities. The core institutional feature of these projects is the project municipal council. In some cases, these institutions have evolved from purpose-specific commissions into project municipal councils with technical chambers to handle demands for specific projects, and finally into rural development municipal councils that coordinate demands for support from diverse programs and oversee the allocation of funding. In the case of the Northeast Rural Poverty Reduction projects, the councils (FUMAC) are representative bodies comprising 80 percent membership of beneficiary communities and civil society and 20 percent municipal authorities. Councils discuss and establish priorities working within an indicative annual budget, approve community proposals, and monitor and supervise subproject execution. An even more decentralized pilot variant of these councils (FUMAC-P) manages its own actual budget based on an annual operating plan, distributes funds to beneficiary associations for approved investments, and monitors execution. Beneficiaries contribute a minimum 10 percent in labor, materials, or cash under both models. Results of these projects are summarized in box 2.

Box 2. Impact of Northeast Rural Poverty Reduction projects

By 2000, about 50,000 subprojects in more than 1,400 municipalities were completed (77 percent infrastructure, 20 percent productive, and 3 percent social), benefiting about 1.7 million families with at least one investment (many received several), at a total cost of US$800 million.

Study of a sample of 8,123 subprojects funded in 1995 and 1997–98 revealed that at least 89 percent were fully operational, demonstrating the sustainability of investments chosen, executed, operated, and maintained by beneficiary communities.

Investments generated almost 100,000 additional permanent jobs, increased the area cultivated by more than 80,000 hectares, and generated sustainable annual income of US$200 million.

Implementation of productive subprojects and rural water supply works under these programs enabled families to take fuller advantage of available productive resources than families not participating.

Social capital rose markedly, with the impact depending on the levels of decentralization and participatory decision-making and communities' ability to control the allocation and management of budget resources for their investments.

The social capital created by the projects has been used by communities and municipal councils to access other sources of financing and programs previously not available to them.

Source: Van Zyl, Sonn, and Costa 2000.

Four crucial findings can be generalized to projects with similar institutional features:

- How, with minimal bureaucracy and greater transparency, the projects support decentralized resource allocation, employment generation and income enhancement, and social capital formation in poor communities.

- Councils' role as democratic vehicles for integrated, sustainable rural poverty reduction and development, with increasing capacity to influence broader local planning, and contribute to integrating policies and programs spanning the "rural space" while improving the targeting and impact of public resources.

- Superior outcomes when communities participate in selecting, financing, executing, operating, and maintaining investments themselves—real needs are met, costs are lower, and sustainability is better because of community ownership.

- Flexibility and adaptability of the mechanism for nationwide use under varying circumstances and across sectors.

Options

A suggested strategic framework for reducing rural poverty integrates policies supporting multiple paths to opportunity for a heterogeneous rural population with diverse needs. It could include the following strategies:

- Intensify agriculture in the economically viable small-farm sector. Policies to benefit small-scale, low-productivity farms are mainly poverty-reduction strategies, not agricultural growth programs. Successful "blueprints" for viable small-farm activities typically combine market and subsistence production and often irrigation, and include technical assistance–based intensification, community-based land access, and community-driven infrastructure investments (water supply, electricity and rural access roads). Credit, physical investments, and services for family farmers increase productivity and incomes, create jobs, and reduce out-migration. In areas where agriculture is declining, public programs might invest in adapted technologies for poor small-scale farmers with productive potential and improve transport infrastructure, technical assistance, access to credit, and farmer organizations to reduce agricultural transactions costs.

- Revitalize commercial agriculture to increase employment and reduce poverty directly by absorbing wage labor and indirectly by fostering growth of downstream processing. Efficient, market-driven expansion of irrigation in the Northeast can create new opportunities. Agricultural growth will be driven by commercial farmers, not the small-scale farm sector, in areas such as the semi-arid Northeast. Growth and increased employment depend on improved factor markets (markets for labor, water, land, and capital). Better education and labor code reform will improve employment opportunities for the poor in commercial agriculture. Since that sector produces most of Brazil's export crops, avoiding real exchange rate appreciations and sharp interest rate fluctuations and instituting trade policies that adopt relatively low tariffs on imported inputs and final products could markedly improve the sector's international competitiveness. Doing so would raise real wages and increase job opportunities on farms and in the processing and transport sectors.

- Stimulate the growth of rural nonfarm activities as a promising source of rural employment, especially in food processing and services. Evidence from Brazil and elsewhere strongly suggests that rural nonfarm opportunities are greater in areas better served by roads, electricity, and communications, in which factor and product markets work better and transactions costs are lower. In most cases, these are areas located close to urban centers. Women are highly represented in the rural nonfarm sector, particularly in education and domestic services. The critical ingredients for developing a thriving rural, nonfarm, opportunities-based economy are thus better education levels and good basic infrastructure. This strategy will not work for people living in more remote, low-density, and poorer rural areas.

• ACCEPT MIGRATION, ESPECIALLY OF THE YOUNG, INTO URBAN AREAS AND RURAL TOWNS AS INEVITABLE AND RATIONAL. Migration cannot solve the problem of rural poverty. But given the high incidence of rural poverty, the large number of very small farms, the large average family size in rural areas, and the low agricultural potential in the semi-arid Northeast, migration may be rational and even desirable. Rural-urban migration was a major factor in rural poverty reduction in Latin America in the 1990s, but also contributed to urban poverty, due to migrants' lack of education and skills for successful relocation. Data limitations hamper proper analysis of this complex subject, but findings in Brazil and experiences in other countries suggest directions for further research and policy.

• RAISE EDUCATIONAL LEVELS IN RURAL AREAS TO PREPARE MIGRANTS FOR SUCCESSFUL ABSORPTION IN BETTER-PAID URBAN AND RURAL NON-FARM EMPLOYMENT. Training and educational opportunities for the rural poor are crucial for easing their absorption into the general economy. Migration will also benefit family members who remain in their communities, through remittances. Providing young people with non sector-specific skills gives them access to opportunity-driven migration by equipping them to respond to better economic opportunities elsewhere.

• ENSURE A SAFETY NET FOR THE RURAL POOR WHO ARE UNABLE TO BENEFIT FROM OPPORTUNITIES IN COMMERCIAL AGRICULTURE, SMALL-SCALE INTENSIFICATION, OR MIGRATION. Older rural people, widows, and farm workers in poorly endowed areas who are marooned in extreme poverty with no viable future in agriculture are unlikely to benefit from new opportunities. A social safety net (for example, pensions) is crucial to providing them with basic, decent living standards. Safety net programs must be administratively accessible for people in remote, low-density areas with high illiteracy. The intergenerational aspect of rural poverty must also be acknowledged through parallel efforts to reach young people in the poorest households, educating them to escape the trap restraining their parents.

Message 2. Making bold changes to arrest agro-ecological decline and boost economic, social, and environmental sustainability in the semi-arid area of the Northeast
Almost half the population of the Northeast lives in the semi-arid region, which is in economic, social, and environmental decline as a result of frequent drought, the limited natural resource base, and rising demographic pressures on fragile lands. Many cities and towns lack viable productive activities, and dependence on pensions, drought workfare programs, and municipal employment is high. Policies to deal with the problem could include agro-ecological zoning for regional land planning and broad reform of the land tenure structure; productive reorganization through adaptive research, reform of regional technical assistance facilities, and credit and marketing services; and initiatives to reduce population pressures on the resource base.

Context

About 45 percent of the population of the Northeast lives in the semi-arid region, which covers large portions of all Northeast states except Maranhão. The region is in economic, social, and environmental decline or stagnation, exacerbated by its susceptibility to drought, its limited natural resource base, and increasing demographic pressures on fragile lands. Drought is unpredictable in severity, duration, and timing. The effects of drought are reduced in certain areas by dams and irrigation—irrigated agriculture is the only sub-sector that shows significant potential and expansion. Despite strong out-migration, the region's net population decline in the period from 1980 to 1996 was less than 1.0 million (10.1 million to 9.2 million). In many parts of the region, demographic pressure remains high and unsustainable, given the weak natural resource base.

Low-technology, dry-land agriculture is the economic mainstay of this region. Secondary and tertiary sectors are modest, given the fragile agricultural base on which they largely depend. Growth of the livestock and cotton sub-sectors underpinned significant agricultural expansion and diversification in recent decades, but that growth has faded and the sustainability of the region is declining.

Contraction of dry-land agriculture. Understanding the regressive processes affecting the region and the loss of capacity to support its populations requires a brief resumé of the evolution of dry-land agriculture.

The agriculture system of the *Sertão* includes all of Ceará, a large part of the states of Rio Grande do Norte and Paraíba, the center and west of Pernambuco, the central part of Bahia, and a small portion of western Alagoas. Between 1970 and 1985 the crop area in the *Sertão* increased from 7.7 million to 9.9 million hectares, and the planted pasture area rose from 3.6 million to 6.8 million hectares, with the natural pasture area remaining at 17 million hectares. In 1985 the farm area in the Sertão totaled 63.1 million hectares.[1]

In 1970 the farming sector of the *Sertão* was diversified, with seven basic production systems in place. The decline and virtual disappearance of tree cotton, a traditional mainstay of these diversified agricultural systems, and the expansion of cattle raising changed the landscape markedly.

The area and production of tree cotton (nearly all of it grown in the *Sertão*) peaked in 1977, with about 2.6 million hectares harvested and 438,000 tons—some 23 percent of total national cotton production—produced. Global price and marketing problems exacerbated by the entry and spread of the bicudo pest accelerated the decline in productivity. Harvested area declined to 656,600 hectares and production of only 47,100 tons (2.5 percent of national production) by 1989. Other commercial crops, such as the castor oil plant, sisal, tobacco, and corn, also declined.

The tree cotton crisis reduced rural activity and employment; changed production relations; caused an exodus of rural labor, with consequent growth in urbanization and slums in small cities; and intensified the concentration of landholdings. As a result, large-scale land ownership alongside small-scale subsistence became the prevailing pattern in the *Sertão.*

The tree cotton crisis contributed to a marked expansion of cattle raising and pasture area, filling the gap caused by the drop in cotton production and the decline of other commercial crops. The outcome was a predominantly extensive but relatively unproductive livestock system based mainly on natural pastures with limited support capacity, despite the increasing use of planted pastures. The surge in cattle raising significantly altered the pattern of diversified dry- land agriculture, leading to an agricultural economy based primarily on livestock multi-cropping, with localized variations based on climatic differences and soil suitability. Today two typical production "sectors" are evident: subsistence smallholdings with rudimentary farming activities, occasionally generating marketable surpluses, and large commercial farms with extensive livestock production and

---

[1] The 1995/96 agricultural census was not used because that census underwent a considerable change in methodology, which affected the comparability of its results with those of previous census exercises (1970 and 1985). The consistency of this last census is also questioned by many researchers in Brazil.

food crops as a secondary activity. There are some exceptions in more fertile zones and in irrigation projects.

The intense exploitation of land associated with subsistence farming is degrading soils and steadily expanding the area needed to maintain a given level of production. As a result, dry-land agriculture is contracting. The population of the semi-arid region— and indeed of the entire Northeast—depends increasingly on the Center-South for its food supply, even in normal years; during drought this dependence is even greater. The demographic intensity of this agricultural system, its land tenure structure, and the region's declining ability to absorb permanent workers and sharecroppers as a result of declining commercial crops means that at least in the short to medium term, subsistence survival cropping will continue to press on fragile natural resources.

Changes in rural employment. The declining sustainability of Sertão agriculture becomes even more evident when the evolution of rural employment is examined. From 1970 to 1985 the number of people employed in rural areas expanded from 3.0 million to 4.2 million, an average annual rate of about 2.2 percent. This rate is higher than the rate of expansion of cropped areas (1.5 percent per year) but lower than that of the area under cultivated pasture (5.7 percent per year), indicating growth of the livestock sector. The fact that the number of people employed grew faster than the cultivated area does not signify increased land productivity, since production did not rise; productivity is, in fact, stagnating in many areas for principal crops.

Labor retention results from the large size of the smallholder segment, where most workers are concentrated. The quest for survival by family members, not profit maximization, is the primary goal. In prosperous times, some family members may still relocate, but in an economic downturn, the flow is back to rural areas. This in-migration increases pressure on smallholdings, reduces productivity, and increases the number of people employed. This represents an unsustainable pattern of land occupation and use.

Since livestock raising is not labor intensive, there has been little increase in new permanent jobs to soak up this surplus labor. From 1970 to 1985 the number of temporary workers grew from about 299,000 to about 527,000. Part of this increase was associated with the building up of planted pastures and seasonal maintenance activities. In the same period the number of sharecroppers and assimilated laborers decreased from 218,500 to 174,200, as a result of both the tree cotton crisis and changes favoring temporary labor rather than permanent, salaried labor or sharecropping arrangements. Permanent labor linked to large-scale agricultural production has thus declined, while subsistence family labor has swelled. These workers are employed on a temporary and seasonal basis by commercial agriculture and in other intermittent activities, such as drought workfare programs. Again, comparability problems and methodological inconsistencies impede the use of the more recent data from the 1995/96 census.

PROSPECTS OF IRRIGATION IN THE SEMI-ARID REGION. Since most of the region's agriculture is rain-fed and therefore subject to the uncertainties imposed by droughts, irrigation could in principle reduce such uncertainties and allow the introduction of yield-increasing technologies. This would not only significantly expand agricultural output, but also absorb labor and generate income growth. While this makes wholesale expansion of irrigation a tempting solution for the social and environmental problems of the semi-arid region, it is important to note that the results of past investment in irrigation have not been consistently positive (see Policy Note on the water agenda).

Water is obviously a fundamental input, but the feasibility of irrigated agriculture also depends on topography, soil conditions, adequate infrastructure, institutional support, and market conditions for the products of irrigated activities. Considering all these restrictions, the availability of land with potential for irrigation declines markedly. Despite that, even the most conservative estimates confirm the possibility of doubling the current area under irrigation and the opportunity of increasing current productivity; this potential cannot be easily mobilized but should not be ignored.

LACK OF EDUCATION AND SKILLS. Social problems are an obstacle to any major attempt to rationalize, develop, and reorganize the region, economically or environmentally. The extremely low educational level of a large part of the population seriously limits the possibility of introducing conservation-oriented agricultural practices that would foster coexistence with droughts. Increased agricultural productivity will be difficult without such technologies, reinforcing the cycle of decline. Lack of the education and skills to either improve productivity or migrate successfully, combined with the mediocre performance in the past two decades of the Northeastern and Brazilian economies, virtually ensures continuation of this vicious cycle.

THE NEED FOR DECISIVE ACTION. Other sectors of the semi-arid regional economy offer no relief. Regional cities and towns are modest, with few industries, weak infrastructure, and poor social services, including healthcare and education. A poor person thus has little alternative but to survive in a rural area until retirement.

In recent years federal and state government interventions in the semi-arid region have increased. An impressive and often ambitious array of policies and programs to transform the region and improve its sustainability have been tried. With some striking exceptions, the results have been limited and the broad outlook remains depressed. Decisive action is essential to avoid a crisis of sustainability in the region and potential social unrest.

Options

There is no magic bullet for the region's recovery and growth; improvement in living conditions is likely to take place only over the long term. The following policy recommendations are not a blueprint for success, but they may indicate the principal actions necessary to reorganize the rural space.

The following actions are targeted mostly at the extensive hinterland, which is strongly dependent on agricultural activities:

- Conduct an agro-ecological zoning study for the entire region, which could serve as the basis for regional land planning. Actual zoning actions would take drought-induced uncertainties into account. Ecological-economic maps of the region could serve as the basis for preparing sustainable development master plans as well as defining the potential and limitations of the subregions of the semi-arid region. This in turn would allow for more efficient use of scarce financial resources.

- Reform the land tenure structure. Several million people are trying to survive on minute areas of land in a fragile, drought-prone ecosystem, while millions of hectares remain underutilized. Conventional restructuring—breaking up large land holdings to expand the number of smallholdings—is not adequate. Land tenure restructuring in the region requires the establishment of viable agricultural units that can survive even under drought and the adoption of innovative mechanisms and approaches (such as Crédito Fundiário). Another priority is strengthening property rights to land by formalizing informal titles so that the market can facilitate the formation of land holdings of more optimal size.

- Adapt agricultural activities to regional environmental conditions, taking into account the vulnerability imposed by drought. Agricultural activities need to be made minimally viable in drought years, which does not mean that these activities should be implemented only in areas where irrigation is feasible; because irrigated areas are limited, adopting such a policy would exclude most of the rural population. Instead, ways need to be found to accumulate and manage sufficient water to permit basic agricultural activities in drought years. Crops adapted to dry climates, such as castor bean and other oilseeds, as well as fibers such as sisal, drought-resistant grains, and adapted forage plants should also be developed or promoted. Reviving cotton in selected appropriate areas of the region could also be considered.

- REFORM THE REGION'S TECHNICAL ASSISTANCE FACILITIES AND SERVICES, AND PROVIDE ADEQUATE SUPPORT FOR CREDIT AND MARKETING. While emphasizing the dynamic competitiveness of enterprises, policymakers need to involve government in the initial stages of new activities, avoiding the paternalism and political interference that has marked such involvement in the past.

- RESETTLE SOME OF THE POPULATION CURRENTLY LIVING IN THE SEMI-ARID REGION. Even if reforms were successful, agriculture would not be capable of supporting the entire rural population at a minimum standard of living. Out-migration has been occurring for many decades, but it has taken place in a manner that does not guarantee an improved existence elsewhere. Recently, the nation's economic difficulties have made demographic resettlement even more difficult. Better economic performance is needed, along with actions to make the voluntary resettlement process less traumatic. Urban restructuring and measures to encourage diversification are needed, keeping in mind the productive vocations of the region's small and medium-size urban centers. Development of tourism and service sectors supporting diversified agriculture could also contribute in some areas. Investments in infrastructure and basic urban services are essential to create the minimum conditions required to raise regional urban centers to a position in which more dynamic economic activity is feasible.

- RECONSIDER IRRIGATION POLICY. The past problems and failures of "social" irrigation, in contrast with the successes of entrepreneurial irrigation, should not deter efforts to formulate a new policy for irrigation that would continue to support commercial irrigation, but would stress the development of a new model for small settlers. This would contribute to the absorption of the region's demographic surpluses, allowing the productive settlement of small farmers. This is a simple idea, but there are enormous difficulties in developing a real-world model that avoids the errors of the past and meets the pre-conditions for success, many of which—such as education and technical change—are addressed elsewhere in this section. In addition, priority should be given to rehabilitating and optimizing the returns of viable existing irrigation systems.

- IMPROVE EDUCATION. Education is key to reducing the region's human resource deficiencies and ultimately other major deficiencies. Without efforts to improve the quality of the educational system, the caliber of the work force, and human capital more generally, other development efforts, including the reorganization of agriculture's productive structure and the development of activities adapted to the region's characteristics, are unlikely to succeed. Specific actions needed include expanding and improving conventional educational networks in semi-arid areas and supporting programs to reduce adult illiteracy.

Message 3. Eliminating inefficiency, duplication, and waste in social expenditure programs, reallocating resources to proven, cost-effective, and well-targeted mechanisms

Public social expenditures in Brazil over the past 20 years have been more than sufficient to erase the poverty gap, yet extreme poverty persists. Both the skewed distribution and the inefficiency of social expenditures have contributed to the problem, particularly in rural areas. Emphasis should be shifted to programs generating the highest level of benefits for the poor per unit of public expenditure. Programs that demonstrate weak coverage and poor targeting should be retooled to improve their capacity to reach the poor.

Context

Poverty in Brazil is tied to an extremely unequal income distribution and the weak effectiveness of public expenditures. Social expenditures in Brazil represent about 20 percent of GDP, while per capita annual income is about R$5,000. Many countries with equal or lower levels of per capita income have lower levels of both poverty and inequality. Income inequality persists in Brazil not because of insufficient social expenditures but because of continued ineffective targeting of those expenditures.

The Government of Brazil has committed itself to reducing the incidence of extreme poverty (per capita income of less than US$1 per day) by 50 percent by 2015. Economic growth, social spending, and a quantum leap in the cost-effectiveness, efficiency, and coverage of a broad range of publicly funded programs will be needed to achieve this goal.

Between 1981 and 1999 the eradication of poverty in Brazil would have required estimated social expenditures of about R$35–R$40 billion year. Social expenditures by federal, state, and local authorities actually averaged about R$100 billion annually, well in excess of those levels, but only13 percent reached the neediest; most investments in education, health, and social security went—and continue to go—to the middle class and wealthy. Ineffective or non-existent targeting of resources is the major obstacle to serious poverty reduction, especially in rural areas.

Initial international comparisons indicate that Brazil's performance on such basic social indicators as infant mortality and youth literacy is not commensurate with its level of economic development. The problem is not caused by insufficient social expenditures: Brazil devotes some US$1,300 per capita to social expenditures, slightly more than other Latin American countries. Only Costa Rica, Panama, and Uruguay devote a greater share of GDP to public social expenditures. When both population and level of development are considered, Brazil's per capita public social expenditures are markedly higher—by as much as 50 percent—than would be expected for countries with similar characteristics. These figures suggest that poor performance on social indicators may reflect the manner in which public sector expenditures are allocated and targeted.

Indeed, public sector expenditures are strongly skewed toward social security and welfare. Social security expenditures in Brazil account for about 68 percent of public sector spending, a level exceeded only by Uruguay among the Mercosul countries. Among Latin American countries outside Mercosul, the share of social security and welfare expenditure is closer to 30 percent. In the newly industrializing countries of the Far East, social security and welfare make up as little as 20 percent of total public social expenditures. Brazil spends 116 percent more on social security than do other countries with similar GDPs.

Health and education expenditures in Brazil are being crowded out by social security spending. Health expenditure, at 11 percent of total social spending, is only slightly lower than the overall average of 15 percent for both Latin American and Far Eastern countries. Education expenditures, however, accounted for just 18 percent of total public social expenditures—markedly less than the average of 38 percent for Latin American countries outside MERCOSUL and the average of 52 percent for the newly industrializing countries of the Far East. Brazil spends 14 percent less on health and 21 percent less on education than countries with similar levels of GDP. World Bank (2002a) indicates that 43 percent of education expenditures in Brazil are allocated to tertiary education, a much higher proportion than the 19.5 percent for all Latin American and Caribbean countries. Given the tendency for tertiary education to disproportionately benefit higher-income classes, these findings suggest that Brazil's education expenditures may also be inequitably distributed.

The high level of resources devoted to social security is increasingly constraining more spending on education and health, and the situation is likely to worsen. World Bank (2002a) finds that the accounting deficit associated with the state pension system is set to double in the next five years and triple in the next decade, leading to substantial expenditures to finance the associated public debt. As a result, other already under-funded areas of public sector expenditure, such as health and education, could come under increasing budgetary pressure over time.

Despite the low overall effectiveness of public social expenditures, some rural social spending has been satisfactory in both coverage and targeting (table 3). The main elements of rural social expenditures include rural credit (R$10.3 billion lending, including debt rollover); rural pensions (R$10.8 billion); spending of the Ministry of Agriculture (R$3.7 billion), mostly related to programs to stimulate overall agricultural development; land reform (R$1.9 billion); education and health spending in rural areas (estimated at R$4.5 billion); infrastructure investments (including water resource investments accounting for R$0.7 billion); and drought relief programs (accounting for approximately R$1 billion in drought years). Total selected rural spending analyzed here (excluding credit programs that cannot be easily assigned to rural or urban areas and many subnational spending programs) amounts to approximately R$24 billion.

Table 3. Selected rural social spending in Brazil, 1998 (R$ billion)

Program	Expenditure
Rural pensions	10.800
Ministry of Agriculture	3.689
Ministry of Health	2.390
Education	2.170
Ministry of Agrarian Development (land reform)	1.950
Ministry of Environment	1.690
Drought relief	1.238
Subnational Rural Poverty Alleviation Projects (RPAP)	0.090
Total rural spending	24.017

Source: World Bank 2000 b.

COMMUNITY-BASED LAND REFORM. Evaluation studies reveal that the Cédula da Terra project is expediting land access for the rural poor. Self-selection into this demand-driven model has worked well, with about 85 percent of beneficiaries having an initial annual income below the poverty line. (Since no detailed assessment of overall land reform beneficiary income is available, the targeting rate of 85 percent is assumed to be applicable to the overall land reform program.) Based on the current rate of 100,000 land reform beneficiary families per year and a targeting rate of 85 percent, 85,000 poor rural families, or 3.8 percent of all poor rural families in Brazil, would benefit each year. The 372,000 land reform beneficiary families from 1995 to 1999 include 316,000 poor families, accounting for about 12 percent of Brazil's rural poor.

NORTHEAST RURAL POVERTY ALLEVIATION PROJECTS. Evaluations of the Northeast Rural Poverty Alleviation projects show that, depending on the state, 70–90 percent of beneficiary families have family income of less than two minimum salaries (about R$400 a month in 2002). Beneficiary income is probably under-estimated compared with the more detailed income calculation derived from the Living Standards Survey (*Pesquisa sobre Padrões de Vida*). Based on an average of five household members in the poor rural Northeast, about 70 percent of the benefits may be assumed to accrue to those considered poor for the purposes of this report (people with per capita income of less than R$72 per month). By 2000, about 50,000 subprojects were completed under the Northeast rural poverty projects at a cost of US$800 million (about 7,100 subprojects per year, costing about US$115 million), reaching 1.5 million rural families at a cost of about US$500 per family. With a targeting ratio of 70 percent, the projects would have reached 150,000 poor rural families in the Northeast each year, which, for the seven-year period, is about 40 percent of the 2.5 million poor rural families in this region.

DROUGHT RELIEF. The 1998–99 drought in Northeast Brazil affected more than 10 million people in eight states. The drought relief program focused on targeted food distribution, workfare, and a subsidized credit scheme to alleviate drought conditions. About 30 percent of all families affected received basic necessities and unprocessed or prepared meals under this scheme. The workfare component is estimated to have covered 1.2 million workers, or 60–70 percent of those in drought-affected areas who wanted to work at the offered wage rate. Three-fourths of program costs flowed out as wages to participants. In terms of overall efficiency, there is a strong case for relaxing current restrictions on eligibility and geographic targeting, to ensure wider coverage of the needy. About 100,000 families—about 1 percent of families affected by the drought—received subsidized credit totaling R$450 million. Both targeting and coverage of the credit were minimal, a critical issue.

Preparedness for and speed of response to drought need boosting. The federal funding response in 1998 was slow. In Pernambuco, for example, civic meetings to mobilize community members were held in August 1997 and the signals were clear beginning in early 1998, yet relief was not activated until May. Only in Ceará did relief programs begin in late 1997. Overall coverage of the 1998 drought relief effort was also inadequate. Higher aggregate funding and improved efficiency in reaching the worst-affected are needed, and the coordination of drought relief with anti-poverty policy in non-drought years must be tightened. Some attempts have been made to coordinate drought relief with other programs (for example, acceleration of Bank-supported rural poverty projects in drought-affected Northeast states), but such efforts have been mostly ad hoc and partial. Systematic coordination efforts must acknowledge that droughts are intimately connected to the general problems of rural development: high risk, credit and insurance market failures, under-investment in local public goods, and often weak local institutions.

PENSIONS. The government spends about R$11 billion a year on the rural pension scheme, but only 6 percent of the rural poor receive pensions, a much lower proportion than the 10–20 percent of higher-income groups who do so. About 13 percent of rural pension receipts accrue to the rural poor (10.5 percent in the rural Southeast, 14 percent in the rural Northeast). The rural poor receive about R$1.4 billion a year in pension receipts, representing one-quarter of their total aggregate income. In the rural Northeast about 4 percent of the rural population (occupying the top income quintile) receive 43 percent of the pension receipts; 25 percent of the rural population (occupying the bottom income quintile) receive about 14 percent of pension benefits.

WATER AND SANITATION. For the rural poor, coverage by water distribution systems remains minimal, as does access to trucked water (carro pipa). In the rural Northeast water trucking services largely serve the 25 percent of the local population who fall within the second income quintile nationally; the 50 percent of the rural population that is poor receive only 16 percent of these services. Less than 25 percent of the rural poor in the Northeast have access to any type of sanitation system; in the rural Southeast about a third of the population has at least some access to sanitation.

EDUCATION. Nationwide 32 percent of Brazil's rural population 15 and older is illiterate; in the Northeast, the rate of illiteracy is 46 percent. Targeting ratios in the Northeast are relatively high for day care (72 percent) and kindergarten (68 percent), but they decline steadily as education level increases. Primary school enrollment exceeds 85 percent in rural areas, but the Living Standards Survey suggests that 45 percent of rural children in the Northeast do not attend primary school. Less than 5 percent of the poor in the rural Northeast and Southeast attend secondary school.

HEALTH. The rural poor depend mainly on public health care, making very limited use of private health care services. Some 35 percent of public health care users in the rural Northeast are poor, compared with 22 percent in the rural Southeast.

AGRICULTURAL CREDIT. Like many other developing countries, Brazil provides directed loans and concessional credit to its agricultural sector. Only a small share of farm households have access to rural credit overall; the majority of the agricultural sector is thus not benefiting from subsidized directed credit. Forty percent of those receiving subsidized financing for agriculture are the rural poor, but only 2 percent of the rural poor have any access to subsidized agricultural credit.

COMPARISON OF RURAL SPENDING PROGRAMS. (figure 1). depicts selected rural social programs in three dimensions. The size of each sphere is proportional to annual spending per household (annualized in the case of investment programs), showing the relative importance of the program to beneficiaries. The horizontal position of the sphere shows the level of targeting of the program to the bottom income quintile. The vertical position of the sphere shows the reach (coverage) of the program among the bottom income quintile. For reference, the impact of distributionally neutral annual growth of 4 percent is shown in the top left-hand corner.

Programs shown in the lower left-hand corner are poorly targeted, with limited coverage of the poor. These programs include pensions, urban services, secondary education, and credit. Programs in the bottom right-hand corner are well-targeted but reach only a small share of the poor. They include market-based land reform, a relatively new program that is still expanding. Programs near the top left are universal. They include basic health care, education, and school lunches. The "ideal" social program, located in the top right-hand corner, is well-targeted and reaches a large share of the poor. Programs such as drought relief, workfare, and the Northeast rural poverty projects come close to these criteria for the Northeast.

The more complete the reach to the poor among these rural social spending activities, the more difficult is the control of leakage to the non-poor. In scaling-up small and well-targeted social development programs, policymakers need to reallocate funds from programs with inadequate coverage and targeting or redesign existing programs to improve their targeting and extend their reach. If the budget constraint is binding, there may be tradeoffs between benefit size and coverage.

Figure 1. Coverage and targeting ratios of selected social spending programs in Brazil, 2001

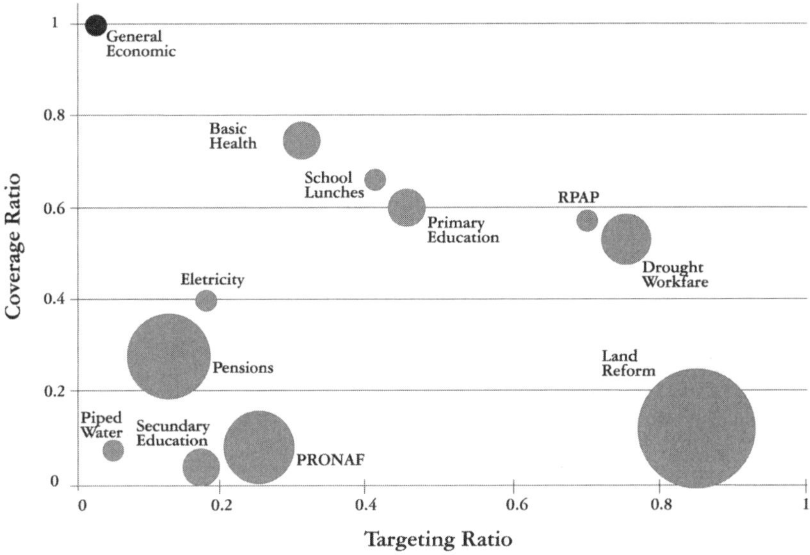

Source: World Bank 2001b.

Options

Many programs designed to target the rural sector in Brazil need to be reassessed in order to increase coverage and improve targeting. Given the binding resource constraint and the levels of rural need and demand, local, state, and federal governments need to invest in social programs with demonstrated ability to reach the maximum number of rural poor for a given level of funding. The following recommendations are intended to foster and facilitate a fresh analysis:

- Re-analyze the distribution of public social expenditures to more closely align it with Brazil's stated rural development priorities. While absolute per capita public social expenditures are high in Brazil compared with countries at similar levels of development, the structure and in some cases the low effectiveness of these expenditures, remain an obstacle for sustained rural development. Massive resources devoted to social security, for example, appear to constrain much-needed investments in health and particularly rural primary and secondary education. Increasing support to health and education would support the Government's stated resolve to reduce extreme poverty by 50 percent by 2015.

• SCALE UP PROGRAMS THAT TARGET THE RURAL POOR. Examples of such programs are market-based land reform, drought workfare, and the Rural Poverty Reduction Projects, in all of which at least 70 percent of beneficiaries are the rural poor. These three programs are demand-driven instruments for rural poverty reduction. Despite similar targeting capacity, benefit size varies across these projects: while an additional R$1 million would reach about 1,000 poor beneficiaries under drought workfare or the rural poverty projects, it would support about 34 poor families under land reform.

• RESTRUCTURE RURAL SOCIAL PROGRAMS WITH LIMITED COVERAGE AND POOR TARGETING TO INCREASE THEIR POVERTY REACH AND FOCUS. Subsidized directed agricultural credit currently reaches only a small fraction of the rural poor. Secondary education in rural areas is extremely limited, as is access to safe water and sanitation. Making greater use of the lessons learned from programs with better targeting and coverage—such as the importance of localized, participatory decision-making, decentralized administration of funds, and demand responsiveness—would increase the reach of rural social programs and reduce leakage to the non-poor.

Message 4. Adopting integrated natural resource management to reverse and prevent degradation, encourage preservation, and promote sustainable rural development
Every year Brazil loses more than a million hectares of topsoil to erosion, costing the country about R$3.2 billion annually. Expansion and consolidation of the watershed-based approach to integrated natural resource management can help reverse land and water degradation processes and promote a socially, economically, and environmentally stronger rural space. Farmers' use of sustainable modern methods of land management and soil and water conservation is a win-win situation in which adopters improve their profitability while reducing pressure on natural resources. Upstream land management activities benefit downstream ecosystems and populations, and they contribute to community and institutional development. The contribution of these activities thus extends well beyond their direct impact on soil and water conservation by leveraging the benefits of other integrated community-based poverty reduction activities.

Context

Brazil is a major exporter of coffee, soybeans, maize, sugar, banana, manioc, orange juice, and meat. Agriculture represents 15 percent of total GDP (27 percent if agro-industries are included) and employs about 18 million people, on about 3.7 million farms. Total cropped area is estimated at about 40 million hectares, pastures cover about 180 million hectares, and about 20 million hectares are cleared fallow land.

Most land currently producing was cleared in the last 30 years. Significant areas of unsuitable land were deforested and put under cultivation, with negative results for the environment; most of these areas have now been abandoned. Exposed to erosive rains, these vulnerable areas continue to degrade and to adversely affect downstream lands and rivers through silting of hydraulic infrastructure and natural waterways.

As a consequence of deficient land management, Brazil loses the equivalent of more than 1 million hectares of topsoil to erosion every year, representing annual losses of about R\$3.2 billion. Biodiversity has also been seriously affected by expansion of the agricultural frontier; losses caused by the use of mistaken natural resource management practices are incalculable.

Public intervention and a growing environmental awareness have helped reduce the incorporation of unsuitable land to production, while agricultural research has contributed to integrated management of resources and increased yields, thus reducing the need for area expansion. Progressive farmers have been adopting sustainable land management practices in recent years, diminishing negative environmental impacts. Most crop and grassland areas continue to be managed using conventional or traditional technologies, however, causing soil erosion and degrading natural resources.

Soil degradation by runoff erosion is a universal, pervasive phenomenon in Brazil. Even the semi-arid regions of the Northeast suffer heavy, erosive summer rains that cause irrecoverable losses to farmers' production base. Soil degradation is most destructive in the small-farm sector. In a perverse vicious cycle, soil degradation is both a cause and a consequence of rural impoverishment that leads to declining yields and revenues, promotes land clearing, harms the water cycle, and reduces biodiversity. This destructive cycle is perpetuated by market developments and government policies that have reinforced the bias toward technologically advanced producers and against low-technology, small, and semi-subsistence farmers, who find it difficult to find and adopt suitable, sustainable resource management practices that might reverse it.

The link between natural resources management and the poor is two-fold. First, many natural resources are commonly shared assets, and since the poor have fewer of their own assets, natural assets make up a larger share of the total wealth of the poor than of the non-poor. Second, limited financial capacity means that whatever access poor people have to ownership of natural assets will be mostly to fragile, lower value resources with lower intrinsic productivity and more prone to degradation due to improper management. That is, natural resources are an important part of the livelihood of many poor people.

INTEGRATED NATURAL RESOURCE MANAGEMENT. Integrated natural resource management refers to responsible and broad-based management of the land, water, forest, and biological resource base needed to sustain agricultural productivity and avert degradation of potential productivity. It involves the assessment of tradeoffs between productivity and environmental services, profitability, and cultural concerns, focusing on the impact of resource management on social, economic, and cultural concerns.

Integrated natural resources management is an efficient approach to achieving the highly interdependent goals of conserving the environment, eradicating poverty, and attaining food security. It is often characterized by its support of flexible, diverse, careful, and intensified management rather than of intensification of production in the simple sense.

Among the strategic tools used in integrated natural resources management are programs of integrated catchment management and integrated water resource management. Both programs are used in national planning for integrated management of land, water, and forest resources at river catchment scales of 5,000–500,000 square kilometers. The boundary ascribed is always the physical watershed. Integrated natural resources management is also being promoted with community groups and in some cases even with individual farmers, through community-based natural resource management of common property, open access, and privately owned resources in micro-catchments of 5–50 square kilometers. Integrated natural resource management is also central in current thinking on poverty alleviation.

Governments and development agencies have turned to integrated natural resources management to safeguard the natural resource base and improve agricultural productivity. While the experience in Brazil and elsewhere highlights the merits of this approach and the flexible use of the catchment as the planning unit for natural resource management, its scope is limited and the concept still faces challenges of scaling up and out. The scaling-out of successful experiences in some areas to others with similar characteristics will involve some adaptation and require supporting research and flexible implementation. Scaling-up the approach to reach more beneficiaries across larger areas within a reasonable time period will depend on creating the conditions for community participation. As demonstrated by the series of Bank-supported projects in southern Brazil, success in scaling up and out will depend on the effective adaptation and integration of lessons into new operations.

Contrary to the common view, the catchment may not always be the optimal unit for all activities, because neither catchments nor the groups who live among them, are homogeneous; their problems and the possible solutions are varied. Complex and prescriptive external solutions have little chance of fitting and may be inappropriate or unacceptable to the majority of farmers.

Integrated natural resources management activities need to fit into the increasingly decentralized context of targeted programs in Brazil. Greater participation of state and local governments and beneficiary communities in targeted expenditures is being promoted to achieve efficiency gains, greater commitment, and long-term sustainability. The experiences in Paraná, Santa Catarina, and Rio Grande do Sul show that success depends critically on adequate localized technical assistance and training. Special measures are needed to foster the involvement or evolution of technical assistance service providers in areas in which official extension is weak or non-existent. Sound operational strategies should include robust monitoring and evaluation systems. Bank experience proves that even highly decentralized projects can be operated efficiently and transparently when appropriate monitoring systems are used.

Beyond the institutional and operational complexities faced, expansion of the integrated natural resources management concept will require focused research to build knowledge to help people manage the natural resources on which they depend. Better understanding of the circumstances underlying patterns of natural resource use, and the needs for and implications of introducing natural resource management methods in different ecological, socioeconomic, and policy environments, is needed. Increasing the capacity of the rural environment to reduce poverty and foster food security and environmental sustainability also implies developing systems to address emerging issues that could further marginalize poor farmers. These include market-driven bio-technological developments, globalization of trade, climatic change, and changing patterns of land use.

IMPROVING LAND MANAGEMENT AND STOPPING SOIL DEGRADATION: OUTCOMES IN SOUTHERN BRAZIL. The agricultural "modernization" campaign promoted by the government in the 1970s to foster production and generate export surpluses produced some perverse effects in the southern states. Widespread deforestation, incorporation of unsuitable land to production, intensified tilling, and increased use of agro-chemicals caused severe erosion and increased water pollution. The states of Paraná and Santa Catarina invested heavily in developing a strategy to revert natural resources degradation back to environmentally superior, sustainable farming systems. With the help of external experts, researchers and technicians in both states established an effective technical strategy, initially tested in pilot areas and subsequently implemented statewide, through several successful World Bank–supported land management projects.

The technical strategy adopted to improve land management and stop soil degradation had three core objectives: maximizing soil cover to avoid the rain-splash effect, improving soil structure to maximize infiltration, and handling excess surface runoff. The strategy also included an important pollution control objective. The operational strategy sought adoption of the micro-catchment as the core geographical planning and implementation unit.

Municipal micro-catchment commissions were created in each participating municipality to select the micro-catchments and set annual investment priorities for their jurisdiction. A formal commission was set up in each micro-catchment. Local extension workers helped prepare a participatory survey, and a micro-catchment management plan was prepared and approved by each commission. Micro-catchments and municipal micro-catchment commissions received intensive leadership and management training. Technical training was provided to assisted farmers, addressing the main land management and agro-environmental problems and introducing relevant technologies.

The outcome was impressive: about 2,100 micro-catchments were assisted in Paraná and 530 in Santa Catarina, benefiting 300,000 small-farmer families (200,000 in Paraná and 100,000 in Santa Catarina), at an average cost of about US$700 per assisted family or US$80 per hectare. At completion, soil losses in assisted areas were down 50 percent. Runoff water in streams contained lower levels of suspended solids, coliform bacteria, and pesticide residues, reducing silting and water treatment costs in downstream areas and the incidence of waterborne diseases and pesticide poisoning. Maintenance costs for rural roads fell by as much as 80 percent, while better all-weather access stimulated both commercial and social activities. The new land management practices proved more profitable to farmers than the practices they replaced.

These Bank projects incorporated features common to successful community- based natural resource management experiences, including a reasonable initial degree of social organization to facilitate collective action, flexibility and focus on adaptation rather than adoption, provision of tangible benefits to participants in a short space of time, and subsidized investments with mandatory beneficiary contribution (in cash or kind) to increase commitment. The lessons are summarized in box 3.

Box 3. Lessons of micro-catchment programs in Southern Brazil

Catchments of 80–120 families enabled extension technicians to work efficiently and facilitated association and participatory planning.

A quality soil and water management implementation scheme, jointly executed by the farmers of a micro-catchment, had greater environmental impact than traditional, individually implemented soil conservation schemes.

The participatory experience developed by the micro-catchment strategy enabled small farmers to successfully shift from strictly agro-environmental activities to more comprehensive integrated rural development schemes . Use of micro-catchments—a proven, versatile strategy for multi-purpose, sustainable rural development—is already being replicated with local adaptations in Mato Grosso, Mato Grosso do Sul (improved land management in buffer areas of the Pantanal to protect against silting and pollution), and São Paulo (water resources management program). New projects are underway in Parana and Santa Catarina.

Rural extension was the pivotal component of micro-catchment projects. Extension technicians were responsible for key activities, motivating and mobilizing farmers, and helping them correctly define their problems and understand and adopt the technical strategy recommended.

The roads component and the incentive fund were important factors motivating farmers to meet and discuss their individual and collective technical and other problems.

Source: adapted from Marzall, 2002.

Options

Policymakers face a variety of options for dealing with the degradation of natural resources:

- REPLICATE THE LAND MANAGEMENT EXPERIENCE USING THE MICRO-CATCHMENT APPROACH, WITH APPROPRIATE ADAPTATIONS, IN ALL SMALL-FARM AREAS. Combining micro-catchment–based integration of natural resources management with poverty alleviation is the preferred strategy for sustainable rural development. While its adaptation for the semi-arid Northeast would focus on water saving, in the humid Amazon regions the focus would be on the sustainable management of native forest and the intensified use of already deforested areas. Land use would be adjusted according to soil type, topography, climate, and technological level adopted.

- IN THE LARGE-SCALE, ENTREPRENEURIAL FARMING SECTOR, WHERE THE MICRO-CATCHMENT APPROACH MAY NOT BE APPLICABLE, ADOPT DIFFERENT LAND MAN-AGEMENT STRATEGIES BASED MAINLY ON ENFORCING ENVIRONMENTAL LEGISLATION AND INSTITUTING SPECIFIC INCENTIVES. The government could provide grants to co-finance the protection or recomposition of gallery vegetation as well as of severely eroded areas that are generating downstream damage. It could also sponsor annual land management competitions in which integrated natural resources management practices adopted by competing farms are analyzed, with appealing prizes awarded to the winning farms.

- ADAPT TECHNICAL AND OPERATIONAL STRATEGIES TO TACKLE WEAK INSTITUTIONS, FARMERS' CAPACITY CONSTRAINTS, AND FINANCING CONSTRAINTS OF BENEFICIAR-IES AND STATE AND FEDERAL GOVERNMENTS. Whatever policy options are undertaken, planning flexibility will be needed to adapt the strategy to different local conditions across and within states.

- RETHINK THE OLD EXTENSION MODEL, AND DEVELOP AND SET UP NEW PARADIGMS BASED ON PARTNERSHIP SCHEMES. Lack of reliable, coordinated institutional structures, especially the lack of qualified state extension services, represents a big hurdle in most states. Small farmers in many states have traditional backgrounds, and extensive training of beneficiaries and technical assistance agents is required. Good farmer capacity was the basis for successful implementation of the Paraná and Santa Catarina projects. Beneficiary farmers generally had long experience with market-oriented production, associated forms of development, and extension-assisted technological development and were therefore responsive to the projects' proposals.

- SET UP CO-FINANCING SCHEMES TO LEVERAGE THE LIMITED FINANCIAL RESOURCES OF BENEFICIARIES AND STATE GOVERNMENTS.

References

World Bank projects

- Rio Grande de Norte second Rural Poverty Reduction Project *(Segundo Projeto de Combate à Pobreza Rural no Estado do Rio Grande do Norte)*. US$ 22.5 million. Approved on June 27, 2002.
- Santa Catarina Natural Resources & Poverty Project – PRAPEM *(Programa de Recuperação Ambiental e de Apoio ao Pequeno Produtor Rural no Estado de Santa Catarina)*. US$ 62.8 million. Approved on April 25, 2002.

- Sergipe second Rural Poverty Reduction Project *(Segundo Projeto de Combate à Pobreza no Estado de Sergipe)*. US$ 20.8 million. Approved on January 29, 2002.
- Bahia second Rural Poverty Reduction Project *(Segundo Projeto de Combate à Pobreza Rural no Estado da Bahia)*. US$ 54.4 million. Approved on June 26, 2001.
- Ceará second Rural Poverty Reduction Project *(Segundo Projeto de Combate à Pobreza Rural no Estado do Ceará)*. US$ 37.5 million. Approved on June 26, 2001.
- Pernambuco second Rural Poverty Reduction Project *(Segundo Projeto de Combate à Pobreza Rural no Estado de Pernambuco)* US$ 30.1 million. Approved on June 26, 2001.
- Piauí second Rural Poverty Reduction Project *(Segundo Projeto de Combate à Pobreza Rural no Estado do Piauí)*. US$ 22.5 million. Approved on June 26, 2001.
- Land-Based Poverty Alleviation I – SIM *(Programa de Crédito Fundiário e Combate à Pobreza Rural)*. US$ 202.1 million. Approved on November 30, 2000.
- Maranhão Rural Poverty Reduction Project *(Projeto de Combate à Pobreza Rural no Estado do Maranhão)*. US$ 80 million. Approved on November 20, 1997.
- Paraíba Rural Poverty Reduction Project *(Projeto de Combate à Pobreza Rural no Estado da Paraíba)*. US$ 60 million. Approved on November 20, 1997.
- São Paulo Land Management 3 Project *(Terceiro Projeto de Conservação e Manejo de Solos – Microbacias Hidrográficas de São Paulo)*. US$ 55 million. Approved on October 28, 1997.
- Agricultural Technology Development Project – PRODETAB *(Projeto de Apoio ao Desenvolvimento de Tecnologia Agropecuária para o Brasil)*. US$ 60 million. Approved on May 22, 1997.
- Rio Grande do Sul Land Management and Rural Poverty Reduction Project *(Projeto de Combate à Pobreza Rural do Rio Grande do Sul)*. US$ 100 million. Approved on April 22, 1997.
- Land Reform and Poverty Alleviation Pilot Project *(Cédula da Terra - Programa Piloto de Apoio à Reforma Agrária)*. US$ 90 million. Approved on April 22, 1997.
- Paraná Rural Poverty Reduction Project *(Projeto de Combate à Pobreza Rural do Paraná)*. US$ 175 million. Approved on June 27, 1996.

World Bank reports

This chapter summarizes the content of the following World Bank reports. Those, in turn, draw heavily from a wide range of literature on the subject from experts in Brazil and beyond, which are referenced in the mentioned Bank reports.

Datt, Gaurav. 1990. "Regional Disparities: Targeting and Poverty in India." World Bank. Washington, D.C.

Vélez, Carlos E., and Vivien Foster. 1999. "Public Social Expenditure in Brazil: An International Comparison." Washington, D.C.: World Bank.

World Bank. 1996. "Staff Appraisal Report, State of Paraná Rural Poverty Alleviation and Natural Resources Management Project." Report 15554-BR. Washington, D.C.

———. 1997. "Staff Appraisal Report, State of Rio Grande do Sul Natural Resources Management and Rural Poverty Alleviation Project." Report 16404-BR. Washington, D.C.

———. 1998. "Implementation Completion Report, Land Management I Project: Paraná (Loan 3018-BR)." Report 18164. Washington, D.C.

———. 2000a. "Implementation Completion Report, Land Management II Project: Santa Catarina Project (Loan 3160-BR)." Report 20482. Washington, D.C.

———. 2000b. "Project Appraisal Document, Land-Based Poverty Alleviation Project I." Washington, D.C.

———. 2001a. "Rural Poverty Alleviation in Brazil: Towards an Integrated Strategy." Latin America and the Caribbean Region, Brazil Country Management Unit, Poverty Reduction and Economic Management Sector Unit, Washington, D.C.

———. 2001b. "Rural Poverty Reduction in Brazil: Towards an Integrated Strategy." Report 21790. Washington, D.C.

———. 2002a. "Inequality and Economic Development in Brazil." Brazil Country Management Unit, Poverty Reduction and Economic Management Sector Unit, Latin America and the Caribbean Region, in collaboration with Instituto de Pesquisa Econômica Aplicada, Washington, D.C.

———. 2002b. "Reaching the Rural Poor in the Latin America and Caribbean Region: Rural Development Strategy." Washington, D.C.

———. 2002c. "Staff Appraisal Report, State of Santa Catarina Natural Resources Management and Rural Poverty Reduction Project." Report 23299-BR. Washington, D.C.

Other references

Araújo, Caetano, and Mauro Márcio Oliveira. 1994. *"Agricultura de Sequeiro, Pecuária e Pesca no Semi-Árido Nordestino."* SEPLAN-PR, ÁRIDAS Project. Brasília.

Ashley, Caroline, and Simon Maxwell. 2001. "Rethinking Rural Development." Development Policy Review 19 (4): 395–426.

Belcher, Brian, Carol Colfer, and Kenneth G. MacDicken. 2000. "Toward INRM: Three Paths through the Forest." Integrated Natural Resources Management in the CGIAR Approaches and Lessons Series. CGIAR, Washington, D.C.

CGIAR (Consultative Group on International Agriculture Research). 1999. "Integrated Natural Resources Management (INRM): The Bilderberg Consensus." Draft Summary Report of the Reducing Poverty through Cutting-Edge Science Workshop, International Centers Week, October 25–29, Washington, D.C.

Datt, Gaurav, and Martin Ravillion. 1998. "Why Have Some Indian States Done Better than Others in Reducing Rural Poverty?" Economica 65: 17–38.

De Barros, Ricardo, Ricardo Henriques, and Rosane Mendonça. 2001. *"A Estabilidade Inaceitável: Desigualdade e Pobreza no Brasil."* Discussion Paper 800. Brasília: National Institute for Applied Economic Research (IPEA).

DFID (Department for International Development), United Kingdom; Directorate-General for Development, European Commission; UNDP (United Nations Development Programme); and World Bank. 2002. "Linking Poverty Reduction and Environmental Management, Policy Changes and Opportunities: A Contribution to the World Summit on Sustainable Development." London.

Ferreira, Francisco H.G., Peter Lanjouw, Marcelo Neri. 2000. "A New Poverty Profile Using PPV, PNAD and Census Data." Discussion Paper 418. Department of Economics, PUC-RIO.

Gilling, Jim, Stephen Jones, and Alex Duncan. 2001. "Sector Approaches, Sustainable Livelihoods, and Rural Poverty Reduction." Development Policy Review 19 (3): 303–319.

Government of Brazil. 2000. *"Projeto Alvorada."* Brasilia.

Irz, Xavier, Lin Lin, Colin Thirtle, and Steve Wiggins. 2001. "Agricultural Productivity, Growth and Poverty Alleviation." Development Policy Review 19 (4): 449–466.

Ivo, Marzall. 2002. "Brazil: Proposal for a National Land Management Program Based on the Paraná and Santa Catarina Experience." Unpublished document, Brasília.

Kam, Suan Pheng, Jean Christophe Castella, and Chu Thai Hoanh. 2000. "Methodological Integration: Lessons from the Eco-Regional Initiative for the Humid and Subhumid Tropics of Asia." Integrated Natural Resources Management in the CGIAR Approaches and Lessons Series. CGIAR, Washington, DC.

Kerr, John, and Kimberly Chung. 2002. "Evaluating Watershed Management Projects." Water Policy 3: 537–554.

Landell-Mill, Natasha, and Ina T. Porras. 2000. "Silver Bullet or Fool's Gold? A Global Review of Markets for Forest Environmental Services and their Impact on the Poor." London: International Institute for Environment and Development.

Lovell, Christopher, Alois Mandondo, and Patrick Moriarty: 2000. "Scaling Issues in Integrated Natural Resource Management." Integrated Natural Resources Management in the CGIAR Approaches and Lessons Series. CGIAR, Washington, DC.

Magalhães, Antonio Rocha. 1992. "Understanding the Implications of Global Warming in Developing Regions: The Case of Northeast Brazil." In Jurgen Schmandt and Judith Clarkson, eds. The Regions and Global Warming: Impacts and Response Strategies. Oxford: Oxford University Press.

Maia Gomes, Gustavo. 2001. Velhas Secas em Novos Sertões. Brasília: IPEA.

Mellor, John. 2000. "Faster, More Equitable Growth: The Relationship between Growth in Agriculture and Poverty Reduction.." CAER II Discussion Paper 79. Cambridge, Mass.: ABT Associates.

Mikos, Philip. 2001. "The European Commission Perspective on Rural Development: Integrating New Trends into Multi-Sectoral Approaches." Development Policy Review 19 (4): 545–552.

Mueller, Charles C. 1995. "Organização e Ordenamento do Espaço Regional Nordestino." SEPLAN-Pr, ÁRIDAS Project. Brasília.

———. 1996. "Organização e Ordenamento do Espaço Regional do Nordeste." Planejamento e Política Públicas 13: 35–109.

Nobre, Paulo. 1994. "Clima e Mudanças Climáticas no Nordeste: Relatório Temático." SEPLAN-PR, ÁRIDAS Project. Brasília.

Projeto ÁRIDAS, Nordeste. 1995. "Uma Estratégia de Desenvolvimento Sustentável." Brasília: Ministry of Planning and Budget.

Schnepf, Randall D., Erik Dohlman, and Christine Bollin. 2001. "Agriculture in Brazil and Argentina: Developments and Prospects for Major Field Crops." U.S. Department of Agriculture, Market and Trade Economics Division, Economic Research Service, Washington, D.C.

Souza, Hermino Ramos de. 1994. *"Agricultura Irrigada e Desenvolvimento Sustentável no Nordeste do Brasil."* SEPLAN-PR, ÁRIDAS Project. Brasília.

Start, Daniel. 2001. "The Rise and Fall of the Rural Nonfarm Economy: Poverty Impacts and Policy Options." Development Policy Review 19 (4): 491–506.

UNESCO and the World Bank. 2000. Higher Education in Developing Countries: Peril and Promise. Task Force on Higher Education and Society. Washington, D.C.: World Bank.

USAID. 2002. Brazil Overview. Washington, D.C.

Van Zyl, Johan, Loretta Sonn, and Alberto Costa. 2000. "Decentralized Rural Development, Enhanced Community Participation and Local Government Performance: Evidence from Northeast Brazil (draft)." World Bank, Washington, D.C.

Wiggins, Steve, and Sharon Proctor. 2001. "How Special Are Rural Areas? The Economic Implications of Location for Rural Development." Development Policy Review 19 (4): 427–36.

10

Municipal Urban Services, Housing, and Land Markets

10

Municipal Urban Services, Housing, and Land Markets

Introduction

Access to shelter and to high quality public services are prerequisites for growth and poverty reduction. Brazil has a strong urban economy (80 percent of the population lives in urban centers and 90 percent of GDP is created in cities) that could come closer to reaching its full potential if several impediments were removed. The current system of fiscal federalism encourages the proliferation of small municipalities, which often lack economic viability. Local authorities with responsibility for urban transport, critical for ensuring access to employment for the poor and for shaping efficient and harmonious cities, need to coordinate their activities more effectively, with stronger support from the central government. Urban pollution remains a problem that often hurts the poor more than others. And housing is too expensive for poor families: 60 percent of new households are unable to afford even the cheapest types of market housing, in part because over-regulation and monopolistic practices boost the prices of land and formal housing. Municipalities, the main local public service providers, need stronger management and financial accountability capabilities and a greater willingness to rely on the private sector. Improvements in municipal management capacity, fiscal transfers, urban transport systems, and housing policies would do much to improve the quality of urban life and to meet the needs of the urban poor for services, access to assets, and growth potential.

The draft of this chapter was completed by Dean Cira in November 2002. The analyses and suggestions contained in this chapter are based on the international technical experience of the World Bank and are presented as a contribution to the debate and formulation of public policies.

461

An urbanized country

With some 80 percent of the population living in urban areas, Brazil is one of the most urbanized countries in the region and the world. Consider these facts:

- Ninety percent of the country's GDP is generated in cities.
- Poverty is increasingly urban (more than 50 percent).
- Urban environmental problems harm the urban poor more than any other environmental issue.
- Municipalities in Brazil's decentralized environment are on the front lines of delivering services to urban dwellers and manage a large share of public sector financial resources.

A key challenge for Brazil is to make cities more livable and more competitive by maximizing agglomeration economies (efficiency gains derived from market size and the efficient exchange of goods, services and information) and minimizing congestion costs (traffic, pollution, crowding, violence, loss of social capital and economic opportunity).

Urbanization trends

Large metropolitan areas account for about a third of Brazil's urban population: some 53 million people live in Brazil's 12 metropolitan regions. The highest urban concentrations are in the Southeast (about 60 million), followed by the Northeast (about 30 million). And despite the drop in urban population growth rates from 2.5 percent in 1991 to 1.4 percent in 1996, indicators still point to growth of the urban population. In addition, new households continue to form at the rate of 3.6 percent a year, with important housing and urban policy implications considering that some 60 percent of new households will not be able to obtain formal housing.

Urbanization is occurring at different speeds in different regions, with the fastest rates in the North, Center-West, and Northeast (figure 1). Small towns and medium-size cities are growing most rapidly. Population continues to grow faster in the periphery than in the urban core, where populations are even declining in many cities. For small and medium-size cities the challenge is to plan for increased population growth, while for metropolitan areas it is to contend with the impacts of congestion and growth at the periphery.

Figure 1. Annual urban population growth rate, 1991-96

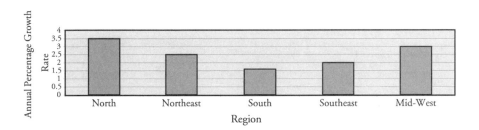

Urban poverty trends

There are methodological problems with estimating the incidence of urban poverty in Brazil. According to the national household survey (*Pesquisa Nacional por Amostra de Domicilios,* PNAD), there were 18.3 million urban poor in Brazil in 1996, or slightly more than half of Brazil's poor population. While the distribution of urban poor in small towns (less than 20,000 people) and metropolitan areas and large cities (more than 100,000 people) was roughly equal, it was highest (roughly 60 percent) in medium-size cities (20,000–100,000 people). Geographically, the highest concentration is in the Northeast, followed by the Southeast (table 1). Estimates by the National Institute for Applied Economic Research (IPEA) put the number of urban poor at twice that (38.5 million), however, with most of them in large metropolitan areas.

Table 1. Spatial distribution of urban poverty in selected metropolitan regions and annual population growth rates 1996

Metropolitan area	Distribution	Population	Poverty rate (percent)	Annual population growth rate, 1991-96
São Paulo	Metro Core	9,039,102	1.59	
	Periphery	7,392,054	4.03	
	Total	16,606,648	2.73	1.46
Rio de Janeiro	Metro Core	5,628,095	3.75	
	Periphery	4,547,560	8.52	
	Total	10,245,599	6.13	0.77
Belo Horizonte	Metro Core	2,001,355	4.91	
	Periphery	1,443,130	10.57	
	Total	3,751,727	8.56	2.09
Salvador	Metro Core	2,264,616	24.33	
	Periphery	441,217	34.78	
	Total	2,793,265	26.97	1.68
Recife	Metro Core	1,372,441	23.09	
	Periphery	1,557,369	28.78	
	Total	3,086,994	27.68	1.14
Fortaleza	Metro Core	1,948,334	20.06	
	Periphery	590,095	41.86	
	Total	2,598,690	26.26	2.32
Belém	Metro Core	854,196	16.69	
	Periphery	107,387	40.55	
	Total	961,583	19.35	2.23
Porto Alegre	Metro Core	1,321,845	5.10	
	Periphery	1,842,622	6.49	
	Total	3,306,749	6.43	1.43
Curitiba	Metro Core	1,261,993	2.00	
	Periphery	831,006	4.68	
	Total	2,211,392	3.69	3.40

Source: World Bank 2000 c, Statistical Annex.

Despite methodological problems in measuring urban poverty, several points are clear: there are more urban poor than rural poor; urban poverty is likely to increase with the continued population growth of urban areas, particularly medium-size cities; and the nature of poverty in large metropolitan areas is different from that in rural areas, considering the congestion effects of urban poverty. And the sprawling effects of urban poverty increase the costs of providing essential urban services (water supply and sanitation, transport), segregate the poor from the middle class, often separate the urban poor from jobs, and increase crime and violence.

According to a World Bank (2002f) study on urban poverty, crime and violence are most prevalent in areas of rapidly increasing population density and weak or nonexistent social and civic networks, such as the periphery of large cities and metropolitan regions. Crime and violence make it harder to escape urban poverty as they restrict residents' ability to leave their homes, often forcing the urban poor to forgo employment and education. Local business opportunities are also reduced by crime and violence, leading to further social exclusion and entrapment in poverty.

Congestion problems in large urban centers also disproportionately affect the poor. Distorted land policies force most of the urban poor to seek housing solutions outside the formal sector, where there is no clear land tenure and limited provision of essential urban services. At the same time, consolidated inner cities of metropolitan areas are losing population, so that infrastructure lies idle. The growth of informal settlements in large cities also contributes to environmental degradation of sensitive areas. The challenge in large urban areas is to correct the consequences of informal growth, while finding ways to revitalize decaying city centers. Building an inclusive society requires addressing the causes and consequences of urban poverty; facilitating access to economic opportunities and assets such as housing, land, and urban services; and building partnerships with the urban poor so that they are included in local decisionmaking.

Medium-size cities and towns have other problems, among them a lack of technical capacity. Of the more than 5,000 municipalities in Brazil, over 3,500 have populations of less than 20,000. These small centers have the costly trappings of big cities with elected mayors, councils, and management teams. But they lack the capacity to provide many essential urban services and the scale to deliver them efficiently. As the first point of entry for rural migrants, small towns and medium-size cities will continue to experience rapid growth in population and poverty. The challenge is to manage growth so as to avoid many of the congestion problems that the large urban centers now face.

Institutional framework

Brazil is one the most decentralized of developing countries. The 1988 Constitution established municipalities as the third level of government. It gave states and municipalities more revenue raising power and freedom to set tax rates, reduced the federal government's share of tax revenues, and increased automatic transfers from federal to state and municipal governments to more than half of public sector revenues. Municipalities claim around 19 percent of total public sector revenues, thus their ability to adequately manage revenues and expenditures is important to Brazil in maintaining fiscal stability (see Policy Note on the quality of fiscal adjustment). Reforms such as the Law of Fiscal Responsibility (*Lei de Responsibilidade Fiscal*) have introduced more stability for subnational fiscal matters. Still more could be done to assist local governments to increase their own-source revenues (large municipalities collect only about 14-24 percent of potential local revenues), manage expenditures, and provide incentives for greater private sector participation in subnational lending.

Responsibility for essential services is more ambiguous. Services such as water supply and sanitation, education, and health are the joint responsibility of the federal, state, and local levels of government. The result is often a lack of coordination among multiple initiatives. In metropolitan regions, where there is a need to cooperate across jurisdictions, there are few incentives and no permanent institutional arrangements for doing so. State governments could play a key coordinating role in facilitating inter-municipal cooperation in large metropolitan areas and in supporting the creation of municipal consortia to address issues of capacity and scale for service delivery in smaller municipalities.

The federal government is generally responsible for defining policies, programs, and guidelines on housing, water supply and sanitation, and transportation in urban areas; issuing norms on urban law; and determining national and regional territorial plans. The Secretariat of Urban Development *(Secretaria de Estado do Desenvolvimento Urbano, SEDU)*, while responsible for taking the lead in this area, has offered little policy direction. Another important player is Caixa Economica Federal, Brazil's second largest government-owned bank, which has financed urban infrastructure, housing, and services and has often shaped urban policy.

States have responsibility for functions not assigned to the federal government or to municipalities. They are responsible for planning and executing urban, regional, and sector policies and programs. While few states have assumed this responsibility, those that have include Paraná, which is active in financing urban investments, and Ceará, which recently began promoting regional development, focusing on urban centers and identifying strategic infrastructure investments to promote growth.

The following sections take a closer look at some of these issues, beginning with municipal management of the financing of municipal investments, urban transport, urban pollution management and then housing finance, policy and urban land markets.

Message 1. Encouraging stronger municipal management and fiscal discipline, to leverage recent progress

Municipalities account for more than half of public investment in Brazil. Delivering the services their constituencies demand requires a multipart strategy that continues to build municipal financial management capacity, develops market friendly mechanisms for financing municipal investments, promotes private sector participation in the delivery of urban services, encourages citizen participation and accountability in local management and decisionmaking, and avoids the proliferation of small municipalities. More efficient municipalities could be encouraged to deal directly with the private sector for financing or outsourcing. A system of market-based discipline for local borrowing could gradually be developed to reward the best run local units. Urban services could also benefit from better coordination of capacity building programs at state and federal levels and greater social inclusion and participation in local decisionmaking, notably through participatory budgeting at the municipal level.

Context

A SNAPSHOT OF THE SECTOR. Brazil's public sector is highly decentralized. Municipalities represent 19 percent of public revenues (5.4 percent of GDP), 13 percent of public spending, and 24 percent of gross investment. They finance a large part of social expenditures: 31 percent of primary and secondary education, 20 percent of health, and 82 percent of housing and urban infrastructure.

Brazil has some 5,500 municipalities of widely varying size, economic structure, and fiscal outlook. Most of the municipalities are small: 75 percent of them have fewer than 20,000 inhabitants. Most of the small municipalities are fiscally weak and almost completely dependent on transfers from federal and state governments. At the other extreme, two mega-cities, Rio de Janeiro and São Paulo, dominate the fiscal and economic landscape, accounting for almost 10 percent of Brazil's population and two-thirds of municipal debt.

The national Constitution defines municipal revenue authority and revenue sharing. Functional responsibilities, however, are defined in general terms that often result in an overlap of state and municipal responsibilities. Municipalities, for example, have responsibility for "household services" such as solid waste disposal, water and sanitation (often provided by states, however), and some public transport. They also share responsibility with the states for education and health and, in recent years have acquired increasing responsibility for infrastructure investments required for economic and social growth of communities. Government estimates put investment needs for municipal infrastructure (water supply, sanitation, and housing) for the next seven years at about R$50 billion. This is about three times what municipalities are currently investing annually in these sectors.

Municipalities have developed innovative approaches to dealing with city finances, service delivery, private sector investments, and governance, including strong public participation, accountability, and transparency. The model of participatory budgeting in Porto Alegre and Belo Horizonte has been replicated in over 100 municipalities. Increasingly, municipal governments are seeking small loans from the National Economic Development Bank (BNDES) to finance improvements in fiscal management and tax administration. These innovations tend to take place in larger cities and municipalities with larger numbers of good managers who are able to innovate and improve fiscal responsibility and municipal management.

Smaller municipalities are a greater challenge. They have high rates of poverty, but lack the size to benefit from economies of scale or the desire to form associations with other municipalities to improve the efficiency of urban service delivery, for fear of losing autonomy. They are also often reluctant to levy local taxes, as anti-tax platforms are often integral to their political campaigns and to strategies for creating new municipalities. In the past 10 years, nearly 1,700 municipalities have been created, 90 percent of them with fewer than 5,000 inhabitants. They survive almost exclusively on federal transfers, and controlling their creation could be a high priority, as could finding ways to improve the capacity of existing small municipalities to better deliver essential services.

The increased responsibility assigned to municipalities by the constitution has raised questions of fiscal management capacity. Within the fiscal program of the government, priority has been given to improving the financial outlook and responsibilities of municipalities through a coordinated effort to focus on the quality of municipal financial management, with an emphasis on tax collection and revenue generation, financial planning, investment decisionmaking (including private sector participation), and participatory budgeting. All this is to be done in the context of transparency and public integrity, to enhance accountability and address issues of corruption. Federal, regional, and state programs aimed at addressing these issues are well regarded and important. Better coordination and information sharing among these programs would improve their effectiveness.

AN IMPROVING PICTURE OF TAX COLLECTION, REVENUE GENERATION, AND EXPENDITURE MANAGEMENT. Own-source revenues account for an average of 35 percent of municipal revenues and federal and state transfers for the rest. Small municipalities, however, depend almost exclusively on transfers. Per capita revenues increase with the size of the municipality, so that municipalities with populations between 200,000 and 3.0 million have 45 percent higher per capita revenues than smaller municipalities.

The municipal share of tax revenues is 5.4 percent, which is low compared with Spain (8.7 percent), the United States (16.3 percent), or Japan (37.7 percent). Recent data suggest that overall municipal revenues are increasing (195 percent from 1989 to 1996), but transfers are increasing at a slower rate (88 percent). When municipal managers are committed to improving services and the public can sense the improvements, resistance to tax increases lessens. Natal increased its own-source revenues from 15 percent to 40 percent of total revenues in less than 10 years due to improved efforts at tax collection coupled with visible improvements in service.

The most important municipal taxes are the tax on personal and professional services (ISS), which accounts for 40 percent of tax revenue, and the tax on urban property (IPTU), which accounts for 32 percent. Making stronger efforts to collect the ISS would likely yield substantial revenue gains. Increasing property tax collections is largely a matter of more frequent valuations and better collections efforts. User fees for such services as trash collection are also important to municipalities, accounting for about 20 percent of revenue. Betterment fees to pay for certain capital investments are a little used tool in Brazil. When they have been used, such fees have often been successfully challenged administratively and in the courts, suggesting a need for a stronger legal framework to promote their use.

Municipalities have little scope for increasing transfer revenues, which depend mainly on macroeconomic performance. The current federal transfer system favors small municipalities over large ones and help promote the formation of new, small, economically nonviable municipalities. Offering opportunities for greater participation in municipal decisionmaking to people living outside the center, who often feel excluded from the political life of the municipality, could reduce the incentive to create new municipalities.

On the expenditure side, personnel is the largest single item of recurrent expenditures, taking an average of 45 percent of municipal budgets. This could be a target for reducing expenditures and increasing savings, but the 1988 Constitution makes this more difficult, with pension benefits fixed at 100 percent of exit salaries and indexed to salary increases, liberal eligibility for retirement, and prohibitions on reducing nominal wages. Recent amendments offer the promise or greater municipal discretion over personnel costs: the 19th Amendment grants municipalities temporary authority to dismiss civil servants, and the 20th Amendment toughens retirement criteria. The impact of these amendments on municipal expenditures will not be known for some time.

Because small municipalities depend heavily on transfers as a main source of revenue, there is not much potential for dramatic increases in overall municipal revenue. Small and medium-size municipalities do, however, have considerable potential to increase their own-source revenues and their investment capacity, given proper capacity building programs to improve their financial management capabilities.

BRAZIL HAS RECOGNIZED THE IMPORTANCE OF SOUND FINANCIAL MANAGEMENT AT THE LOCAL LEVEL. Despite high levels of tax evasion, a political reluctance to increase taxes, and lack of knowledge of how to do it, most municipalities collect some or all of the taxes under their control. A recent BNDES study indicates that 99 percent of the 4,622 municipalities surveyed in 1996 collected some taxes. Recent government efforts to improve municipal financial planning and management—the National Program to Support Administration and Fiscal Management in Brazilian Municipalities (PNFAM), the National Program to Modernize Tax Administration and Management and Management of the Basic Social Sectors (PMAT), the Banco do Nordeste Farol program, and various programs financed under state municipal development projects and programs—are encouraging, but all could benefit from increased integration and a clearer focus on regional coverage, and training methods of each program. The Fiscal Responsibility Law also improves incentives for municipalities to better manage their financial resources.

Good financial planning, budgeting, and management require transparency and accountability. Many Brazilian cities, most notably Porto Alegre and Belo Horizonte, have long traditions of participatory budgeting, bringing transparency and accountability into public expenditures. The efficiency and effectiveness of these programs needs to be studied in greater detail, but the trends are encouraging in bringing greater accountability to the public sector at the local level and combatting long-standing perceptions of corruption.

A GREATER ROLE FOR THE PRIVATE SECTOR. The future of municipal investment in Brazil will surely include a large role for the private sector. Private sector participation in the delivery of urban services in Brazil and elsewhere has led to improved service quality and reduced costs and can relieve the financing burden on local governments for needed investment.

Though private sources of credit for municipal infrastructure are likely to remain limited over the short term, the growing involvement of the private sector in municipal service delivery has created a need for a comprehensive policy dialogue aimed at establishing the proper incentives and institutional framework to ensure that initiatives currently under way can be sustained and replicated. While the long-term vision for increasing private sector participation is contingent on macroeconomic stability, legal and regulatory reform, and capital market development, medium-term efforts could aim to improve accountability and transparency, leverage government-supplied credit in a more effective manner, and explore options for new mechanisms based on international experience.

The types of projects that have the highest potential for private investment in municipal infrastructure and that serve the largest population are water and sanitation concessions, build-own-transfer (BOT) arrangements, and asset sales. Private sector participation in solid waste management—collection and disposal—is more limited, with large metropolitan areas the most likely to welcome private sector participation, although many medium-size municipalities have some type of third-party private contract for solid waste collection. For all services, small and medium-size municipalities represent significant challenges for private sector participation in large part, as indicated earlier, because of their small populations and political resistance to forming associations that could create larger service areas.

Private sector participation in infrastructure is only one of many options available to municipalities, and clarifying the role and rationale for public or private sector delivery or investment in infrastructure calls for an assessment of local market conditions, including regulatory and legal frameworks. Decisions would depend on whether the good or service is jointly or privately consumed (public or private good); conditions of production (extent of economies of scale that create natural monopolies, whether high sunk costs deter new suppliers from entering the market or whether the activity is contestable); the degree of coordination in production (technical standards, for example) needed for efficiency; externalities and social objectives (extent of benefits and costs associated with production that affect people other than those directly involved in the activity); and characteristics of user demand (such as degree of consumer access to information about supply alternatives, existence of substitutes).

Several policy guidelines flow from these conditions:

- For activities involving public or quasi-public goods, natural monopolies, or projects with high sunk costs, there is a case for public sector planning or financing, or for private sector ownership with regulation, as in the provision of network trunk-type infrastructure like pipelines for water supply and sanitation and port installations. Awards would be made through competitive bidding for the right to operate the monopoly. The public sector would ensure that consumers are protected from possible abuses of the monopoly and that other providers of services using the network facilities have fair conditions for access.
- For most activities involving capital with low sunk costs (such as road freight transport), entry by the private sector could be fully liberalized.
- Externalities, social service objectives, and certain features of user demand may provide justification for public intervention in infrastructure activities, through regulation or fiscal transfer and subsidies, but rarely justify outright public ownership.

The financing of municipal investments, whether they include private sector participation or not, depends on the ability of the domestic capital market to supply debt financing with maturities and terms that meet the financial requirements of infrastructure investments and the need for interest rate stability. In the absence of a domestic capital market with the financial depth needed to meet the demand for infrastructure investment, the current landscape is dominated by the two major public development banks and, at the margins, by internationally supported municipal development funds (see Policy Note on the financial sector). In the short and medium terms, options for expanding the role of municipal development funds in lending for private sector participation and developing mechanisms for financing infrastructure with private sector involvement could be examined (see box 1 for the story of a local development fund in France that was successfully privatized).

Box 1. Crédit Local de France: Privatizing a local public development fund

Crédit Local de France (CLF) evolved from a subnational public development fund into a fully private, profitable financial institution in the post World War II period. That experience shows how public finance institutions can naturally mature into private institutions. Today, CLF is a private joint stock company, classified as a specialized financial institution. The Ministry of Finance is represented on the CLF board and has veto power over its decisions. CLF cannot accept deposits, but funds itself by selling bonds on domestic and international capital markets. It has long been one of Europe's largest bond issuers, raising the equivalent of 8 billion euros in 1998.

CLF's mission is to be a reliable, permanent, and long-term partner to local governments, whatever their size. It seeks long-term partnerships with local governments that go beyond its lending activities. It advises clients throughout the decisionmaking process and works with them on a daily basis, especially on ways of improving transparency and management efficiency. In this, it contributes to national efforts to foster local development, environmental protection, and economic renewal.

Currently, municipal development funds provide loans for water, sewerage, street paving, solid waste management, public markets, and general economic development, among others. Where administrative restrictions (such as the Fiscal Responsibility Law) preclude borrowing by subnational governments, municipal development funds could consider loans to private providers of municipal infrastructure. This would require new credit analyses and loan administrative skills for municipal development fund staff. These skills could be developed with support from BNDES and other large public banks with experience in lending to the private sector for urban services. More immediate options might include privatizing municipal development funds; establishing new, private, for-profit municipal development funds; and cofinancing and providing advisory services for lending to private sector providers of municipal infrastructure and services, to assist in evaluating lending risk.

Options

- The Fiscal Responsibility Law should strengthen formerly weak municipal capacity building programs and thus Brazil could continue to consolidate capacity strengthening with reforms that might include:

  - A national government initiative to encourage the exchange of experiences in municipal capacity building programs in financial management.
  - A scaling-up of technical assistance efforts in municipal management by protecting and expanding successful experiences of state municipal development funds.
  - Better federal coordination of the related initiatives of PNFAM, PMAT, Banco de Nordeste, and the School of Fiscal Administration (ESAF) of the Ministry of Finance. The World Bank could assist in this process by bringing together the World Bank Institute and operational programs and partnerships with the Brazilian Institute for Municipal Administration (*Instituto Brasileiro de Adminstração Municipal*, IBAM), IPEA, and João Pinheiro Foundation (*Fundação João Pinheiro*, FJP), among others.
  - Dissemination of best practice on promoting transparency and accountability in municipal budgeting and management. In the short-term, the World Bank could assist in this effort through a partnership with its operational programs and the World Bank Institute.

- Gradually introduce market instruments in the municipal credit market by:

  - Facilitating knowledge sharing between municipalities and private lenders.
  - Encouraging private-public lending partnerships among municipal development funds or federal lending institutions and private lenders for loans to municipalities, municipal enterprises, or free-standing revenue generating projects.
  - Privatize state municipal development funds.
  - Establish new private sector municipal development funds.
  - Support a municipal finance program targeted to the Northeast in a partnership with the Banco de Nordeste do Brasil (BNB) to establish a legally autonomous entity with fully commercial lending practices within BNB.

- Improve and encourage greater options for private sector participation in urban services and infrastructure.
- Reduce the proliferation of small municipalities and improve the capacity of those that exist by:

  - Removing the incentives (fiscal transfers) for the creation of new small municipalities.
  - Creating incentives and the proper framework for the development of municipal associations to increase the capacity and scale of smaller municipalities for improved service delivery and for cooperation with the private sector and to reduce the costs of goods and services through cooperative purchase and service agreements. Arrangements could be modeled on councils of government, which provide services, advice, and technical assistance (such as on land use planning and budget planning) to small municipalities on a cooperative basis, spreading costs and allowing for higher levels of service.

Message 2. Integrating urban transport systems and taking advantage of the advances in decentralization
Urban transport systems should offer a wide menu of transport options that focus on serving the poor and integrating land use and transport planning. Brazil's urban transport systems suffer from a lack of coordination, particularly between the federal and state levels. As the number of medium-size cities grows in population and importance in Brazil, planning for their integrated land-use and transport needs and avoiding the more costly investments that result from lack of proper planning become increasingly vital. Not only will proper coordination and planning make cities more efficient, productive, and sustainable, but integrated planning, with balanced transport systems, will benefit the poor most directly, providing for a fairer transport system that works well for all income classes.

Context
SUSTAINABILITY IS FUNDAMENTAL. Sustainable transport focuses on increasing mobility and accessibility while reducing externalities such as bad air quality and congestion. Strategies that increase travel choices for all segments of society, provide incentives for alternative modes of travel, and increase the interconnectivity and efficiency of transport systems are the cornerstone of a sustainable urban transport program. The public sector

has an important facilitating role to play in planning and maintaining adequate urban transportation systems linked to integrated land use planning to avoid such negative externalities as:

- Traffic congestion and the resultant increased travel times, fuel consumption, and vehicular emissions and decreased economic productivity.
- Urban sprawl, resulting from a preference for low-density development and causing stress on urban transport systems and inducing environmental problems.
- Air quality deterioration, caused by excessive dependence on automobiles, which emit toxic pollutants and other hydrocarbons and particulate matter, which damage the environment and health.
- Noise associated with road transport, which causes stress and other health problems, lowers property values, and can harm natural habitats.
- Water quality, which can be negatively affected by impermeable road surfaces, increasing the risks of flooding and other problems.
- Social equity and mobility, which are compromised when urban transport systems place too much emphasis on individual modes of transportation and less on basic accessibility.
- Safety, which is compromised by poor traffic management, lack of alternative transportation modes (such as bicycle paths), and poorly maintained facilities.
- Energy use and climate change, which increase when motor vehicles predominate in urban transport.

Brazil has examples of best practice urban transport and land use planning in Curitiba, which is recognized worldwide as a forward thinking city that has planned well for growth (box 2).

Box 2. Curitiba plans for its future

Curitiba has shown the world what can be achieved in the automobile era through an integrated approach to urban and transport planning in a medium-size city. Curitiba uses 25 percent less fuel than cities of similar population size and socioeconomic characteristics following a 28 percent shift from automobile use to bus use, according to a 1992 study by the International Institute of Energy Conservation in Washington, D.C. Curitiba purportedly has the cleanest air of all Brazil's medium to large cities. Despite the second highest rate of motorization in Brazil (following Brasilia), the city has fewer congestion problems thanks to a high, 75 percent share for public transport modes (compared with 57 percent in Rio de Janeiro and 45 percent in São Paulo).

Curitiba prevented transport-related problems before they occurred. In the 1970s and 1980s, Curitiba was experiencing one of the highest rates of growth among Brazilian cities (about 4 percent a year) and set upon a path of acquiring rights-of-way to plan for the future growth of the city, including planning for future transport needs. Other cities in the region, such as Bogotá, Colombia, have borrowed from the Curitiba's planning book to address growing transport problems. The lessons learned from Curitiba suggest that:

- Integrated planning needs to be pragmatic, and development of the transport network has to be incremental.
- Political will is indispensable, as is an institutional and regulatory framework that insulates the long-term process from political interference.
- To ensure citizen acceptance, the development model has to demonstrate improvements in the quality of life and in accessibility to jobs and services for citizens of all socioeconomic status (in Curitiba the poor spend about 10 percent of their income on transport—the national average is 20 percent);
- Public-private partnerships are possible: in Curitiba Volvo invested in the bus service.

THE IMPORTANCE OF MEDIUM-SIZE CITIES. Under a broad definition of medium-size cities (populations of between 250,000 and 1.5 million, excluding state capitals), Brazil has more than 30 (table 2). These cities are often local growth poles, acting as hubs for agriculture or industrial activities, and other times are satellites of major cities. Among them are Campinas and Santos in São Paulo, Niterói and Campos in Rio de Janeiro, Juiz de Fora in Minas Gerais, and Petrolina in Pernambuco. Population growth rates of medium-size cities are among the most rapid in Brazil. And with that growth comes growth in demand for urban services such as housing, water supply and sanitation, solid waste management, and urban transport.

Table 2. Brazilian municipalities with more than 10,000 inhabitants, 2000

Number of inhabitants	Number of municipalities	Average annual population growth rate 1991/2000 percent [a]
10,000 to 19,999	1381	-0.03
20,000 to 49,999	964	1.2
50,000 to 99,999	301	1.8
100,000 to 249,999	140	3.1
250,000 to 499,999	53	3.7
500,000 to 999,999	18	3.5
1,000,000 and above	13	2.3

a. Author's calculations using IBGE census data.

Urban transport and land management will have a strong impact on the shape and performance of these cities. Federal and state governments need to decide their roles on this issue. Recently, federal interventions have focused on decentralization of the urban rail operator, the Brazilian Urban Transport Company (Companhia Brasileira de Trens Urbanos, CBTU), and have concentrated on the seven largest cities, to the neglect of urban transport in medium-size cities. The links between urban transport planning and land use planning also need more atention. Brazil's medium-size cities play an important role in the urban hierarchy. Timely investments in urban transport and integrated land use planning can easily avoid the need for more expensive retrofitting investments in the future that will require the restructuring of land use and travel patterns. The federal government can facilitate that future planning, along with local and state governments.

IMPROVING INSTITUTIONAL COORDINATION. The role of the federal government in planning for the growth of medium-size cities and in urban transport more generally is not clear. Federal government responsibility for urban transport was severely curtailed under the 1988 Constitution, which devolved greater responsibility for urban transport planning and policy to state and local levels. Since the 1988 Constitution, the federal government has focused on decentralizing suburban rail systems to the states, while retaining its role in promoting coordination and good practice at the subnational level. But the result has been the neglect of urban transport issues at both federal and local levels. Few cities have developed comprehensive urban transport plans, and those that exist (with the possible exception of the Pitu in São Paulo) are essentially rail-centered public transport plans.

By law, responsibility for urban transport lies with SEDU and is clearly outside the realm of the Ministry of Transport. SEDU has not had the capacity to fulfill its mandate, creating a serious institutional gap in policy formation and program development. More federal attention could help to ensure accountability for fiscal transfers to subnational governments; oversee and help manage the spillovers and synergies that are at the core of metropolitan governance; understand the relation between urban development and transport and the impacts that transport decisions have on city productivity, income growth opportunities, and public sector finances; disseminate best practice in urban transport; analyze the unintended effects of federal policies in other sectors on urban transport; and promote coordination between states and local governments.

FINDING BALANCE. The federal government could, for example, play a greater role in ensuring that urban transport systems are more efficient and equitable. Buses, not rail, are the major mode of transportation in Brazil, particularly for the poor. Bus companies are owned and managed by private operators, but bus service seems to be in crisis, with politically strong bus-owner cartels receiving 25-year concessions without competitive bidding. Greater efficiency could be achieved through competitive tendering of operational rights and use of infrastructure. Informal van service, for example, could be revamped to operate in association with bus operators, competing for franchises to prevent the cartelization of bus services and the undermining of competition.

Creating a more equitable system to provide greater access to the poor is essential. The poor are, after all, the main users of public urban transport. But urban transport costs are very high relative to household income for those who are not eligible for the "*vale transporte*" (an employer-provided public transportation subsidy unavailable to those working in the informal sector), and the number of walking trips has increased dramatically in the past several years, as recent analysis has shown for São Paulo and Fortaleza.

Not only the federal government but states and municipalities could define the weights they assign to three sometimes competing objectives: poverty reduction, elimination of subsidies, and financial sustainability of operators. The challenge is to balance these objectives to maximize social welfare. A sustainable urban transport strategy would, in that vein, incorporate a variety of policies, programs, and measures intended to preserve and improve mobility and accessibility while reducing negative externalities, such as congestion and air pollution. Strategies that increase travel choices, provide incentives to use alternative modes of travel, and increase the interconnectivity and efficiency of transport systems are the cornerstone of a sustainable urban transport program. The elements of such a program would include:

- PUBLIC TRANSPORT AS A CENTERPIECE. Public transport is the backbone of a sustainable urban transport strategy, and in rapidly growing areas it is the only means of adequately meeting mobility needs over the long term. By creating a viable alternative to private automobiles, efficient public transport systems can reduce congestion and air pollution and increase accessibility across all social strata to places of employment and services.

- TRAFFIC MANAGEMENT. Appropriate road and intersection design and efficient traffic management can eliminate bottlenecks, better accommodate public transport, integrate pedestrian and bicycle travel, and facilitate traffic flow. Smoother traffic flows decrease the rate at which vehicles consume fuel and produce emissions.

- EFFICIENT PARKING POLICIES. Efficient, balanced parking pricing and supply management can help to curb car use and promote the use of public transport, as well as support concentrated land development. Efficient parking charges can have a greater effect on traveler behavior than other costs, because parking charges are often incurred on a trip-by-trip basis, unlike fuel purchases and other operating costs that are incurred periodically.

- NON-MOTORIZED TRANSPORT. Non-motorized solutions, part of a balanced transport system, require government commitment, funding, and integrated transport and land use planning. Attention to land use is important since increasing density by providing a more compact mixture of residential, commercial, and employment centers is critical for successful use of bicycles and walking.

- INTEGRATED LAND USE MANAGEMENT. Urban form, which is influenced by land use policies, has a direct impact on motor vehicle travel. Trips are shorter where development patterns make locations more accessible to each other, thus promoting alternatives to automobile use. Well planned, integrated land management can reduce automobile use, increase use of public transport, and provide greater transport access to all segments of society, especially the poor.

- ENVIRONMENTAL MANAGEMENT. Advances in technology have made engines cleaner burning, reducing impacts on air quality. Stricter emissions regulations can reduce air pollution, as can inspection and maintenance programs to ensure that improvements are sustained.

Options

Short-term actions

Lack of capacity is one of the greatest impediments to functional coordination of the transport sector and enhanced effectiveness of functional decentralization. The federal government could pursue a program of institutional reform and capacity building that could include:

- Development of a strong advisory function in urban transport planning for states and municipalities. Specific actions could include improving the transport planning and investment appraisal capacity of SEDU and integrating the activities of SEDU and the Ministry of Transport.
- Development of a financial basis for supporting capacity building at state and municipal levels and promoting intermunicipal coordination. This could include not making financial support automatic, but subjecting it to appraisal criteria such as conventional cost-benefit analysis and linking financing to achievement of structural reforms to ensure well integrated and modally coordinated decision-making. International financing (such as World Bank loans and federal loan guarantees) could be made available on a competitive basis, with financing going to reform-minded municipalities.

Intermediate-term actions

- The federal government could consider launching a medium-size cities program, cofinancing with states and municipalities an investment program to meet urban transport needs for the next 10 years. The World Bank could assist technically and financially. To be effective, such a program would require that municipalities:

  - Establish regional transport coordination commissions.
  - Establish integrated urban transport, land use and air quality strategies with clear criteria for evaluating priority investments.
  - Include financing mechanisms that ensure financial sustainability.
  - Work toward the progressive participation of the private sector in operations and management.

• In larger cities, where the negative externalities of an inefficient urban transport system are very costly, the states and federal government could co-finance investments in mass transit solutions, such as dedicated busways, that decrease congestion and facilitate access for people with low incomes. To see that these objectives were met, the federal government would need to strengthen the ability of SEDU to provide technical assistance to localities and provide the proper financial framework so that localities have incentives to cooperate. These would include the same incentives for financing as indicated above.

Message 3. Strengthening the relatively well established and decentralized legal institutional framework for pollution management
There have been great advances in the management of urban pollution. Further advances could be achieved by focusing on two objectives: introducing more flexible economic pollution control instruments and integrating urban ("brown") environmental concerns into all urban sector policies and activities. Such mainstreaming would particularly benefit the urban poor, who suffer proportionately more from urban environmental problems than wealthier urban residents. The effort could be led by the federal government, using the PPA and fiscal reform efforts as springboards. The capacity of environmental agencies could be expanded at all levels. Giving them a greater variety of pollution management tools could help them do that, while also having a positive fiscal impact by introducing economic instruments for pollution abatement.

Context
URBAN ENVIRONMENTAL PROBLEMS AFFECT THE POOR MOST ACUTELY. Links between economic growth, poverty alleviation, and environmental conditions are not entirely clear, and many gaps in knowledge remain. What is clear, however, is that brown environmental issues, such as urban water supply and sanitation, solid waste management, and air quality, affect the urban poor more than others. Integrating environmental concerns into urban sectoral policies and activities remains a major challenge for the federal government. Equity concerns mean that policy tradeoffs are no longer two dimensional. Where in the past policy decisions yielded clear win-win or win-lose results, the emerging poverty-equity dimension in pollution management makes policy decisions more complex and win-win-win opportunities harder to find. A clear example is the elimination of subsidies: while increasing economic efficiency and potentially reducing environmental

impacts in various sectors, eliminating subsidies can make the poor net losers. Likewise, industrial development, which increases economic output and generates jobs, clearly increases pollution, even if the impacts can be mitigated.

Environment-poverty linkages depend on the ways in which poor people interact with the natural resources base. For obvious reasons, poor people are at greatest risk from air and water pollution, flood and hillside erosion, and other forms of urban congestion and pollution because they tend to live in more polluted and inhospitable environments. They are also more vulnerable because they cannot afford to pay to protect themselves from the impacts of pollution or to receive treatment once they have been harmed. The problem is made even more regressive because the poor typically consume and benefit less from the products, materials, and services that typically generate the greatest congestion and pollution.

Pollution abatement programs in Brazil would generally benefit the poor more than other groups. Some basic social indicators help to illustrate the point. A poor child in Brazil is six times more likely to die in the first year of life than a child born to a wealthy household. In the Philippines, a poor child has twice the chance of a wealthier child of dying in the first year. Even for air pollution, a relatively equal opportunity hazard, average air contaminant concentrations can be higher in poorer urban areas than in richer ones: they are twice as high in the poor northern part of Rio de Janeiro and Baixada Fluminense than in the wealthier areas along the coast. Still, a better understanding of the links between urban poverty and pollution in Brazil is required.

IDENTIFYING PRIORITY PROBLEMS. While extreme forms of pollution in large urban areas such as Rio de Janeiro and São Paulo are clear priorities on the pollution agenda in Brazil, assigning priority to moderate pollution problems in these very large urban areas and to more intense forms of pollution in medium-size cities remains a challenge. Considering both social costs and specific incidence among the poor, it is hard to predict which of these actions will have a higher return and which will benefit the largest share of the poor population. In any case, an effort by all levels of government to address problems based on more rational, cost-effective strategies is a must. Environmental action planning would be a step in that direction (box 3).

Box 3. Environmental action plans

Many countries have developed national environmental action plans, and subnational entities have followed suit with local environmental action plans. An environmental action plan is a dynamic document that can help set environmental targets and policies over time. It ensures that environmental policies are based on careful technical and economic analysis, public support, and political backing. An environmental action plan can be part of an active policy to build support among stakeholders for improved environmental management that includes building alliances with the legislative branch, municipalities, and NGOs.

International experience suggests that successful environmental action plans include three elements: identification of priority problems, identification of priority actions based on diagnosis of the causes of priority problems and analysis of cost-effective solutions, and effective implementation, including involvement of key stakeholders, and integration with broader development objectives. Successful environmental action plans require a skillful merging of sound technical and economic analysis and the active participation of stakeholders. An environmental action plan spells out targets and priorities for action. Based on these targets, performance targets can be prepared for the environmental agencies. Environmental agencies would periodically report back on improvements and resources required for these achievements.

Source: World Bank 1998.

Generally, the first priority of the brown environmental agenda is water supply and sanitation because the population not served is almost entirely poor, and the health implications are the most obvious (see the Policy Note on water management and water supply and sanitation). Solid waste management is among the top priorities of the brown environmental agenda, one that affects the poor most acutely: only 37 percent of the poorest urban dwellers receive adequate solid waste collection, compared with 88 percent of wealthier households. Up to 40 percent of solid waste generated in Brazil remains uncollected, and of that collected only 28 percent receives environmentally sound treatment or disposal. The consequences are obvious: the spread of vector-borne diseases, aggravated flooding, water pollution from open dumps, and health and other risks in informal settlements near dumps. The problems of solid waste collection and landfill maintenance speak to inadequate institutional arrangements.

In the Beberibe River Basin, one of the poorest areas of the Recife Metropolitan Region, municipal authorities collect only 423 tons of the 540 tons of solid waste generated each day. An estimated 50 tons a day is collected informally (recyclable materials), leaving about 66 tons of solid waste that is deposited in streams, canals, hills, and valleys. This problem of poor solid waste management practices and lack of institutional coordination repeats itself in many large and medium-size cities, though some have found solutions (box 4).

Another important urban environmental issue is particulate matter air pollution in São Paulo and Rio de Janeiro. While a lack of data makes it difficult to rank problems by overall costs and incidence among the poor, the problems would surely include severe localized pollution from industries, mining, and other production activities and moderate damage imposed by metropolitan water pollution. Local governments assess the severity of all these problems and decide accordingly on priorities.

Box 4. Solid waste management and the urban poor

There are examples of good solid waste management practices in Brazil. In Curitiba, the *Lixo Que Não é Lixo* municipal recycling program encourages recycling by exchanging "garbage" for bus tickets, surplus food, and school notebooks in favelas. Likewise, recycling/income generation programs in Belo Horizonte and UNICEF's *"Crianca no lixo, nunca mais!"* program are also examples of good waste reduction strategies in low-income areas. Common principles from these experiences seem to be:

- Work with, not against, the informal sector.
- Provide incentives for poor communities to participate in solid waste management.
- Emphasize conservation, recycling, and waste minimization.
- Focus on the most vulnerable groups.
- Invest in marketing and public relations.

Incorporating community-based, income generating solid waste management practices into integrated urban upgrading programs at the municipal level can be an effective way to minimize the impacts of solid waste pollution on the urban poor.

INCREASING POLLUTION MANAGEMENT INSTRUMENTS. Most of these problems are a consequence of policy and institutional failures. Pollution management is largely decentralized in Brazil, and legal and institutional frameworks are fairly well developed. Most states have good basic capacity. Municipalities, too, are taking on initiatives and improving local capacity. Nonetheless, capacity remains weak in the poorest states, and in richer states the environmental problems often exceed the capacity of local agencies to enforce legislation. Thus enforcement remains a major hurdle to good pollution management, despite a relatively consolidated institutional framework. The capacity issues must be addressed in the short term.

Related to the enforcement problem is the limited experience with pollution management instruments and a reliance mainly on licensing. Recent advances to make the system more agile are promising, but efforts still focus more on licensing than on other instruments. A system based entirely on command and control regulations tends to perpetuate an excessive reliance on government budgets to finance pollution prevention and abatement, while the universally accepted polluters-pay principle is neglected because of resistance by polluters and governments' inability to enforce all regulations.

Most developed countries and many developing countries have introduced some economic instruments in their pollution management systems (box 5). They complement command and control regulation with instruments based on the polluters-pay-principle and aim to reduce perverse incentives, charge for natural resource use, impose surcharges on energy inputs, and use tradable pollution permits. These instruments, in combination with command and control regulations, which remain the basis of effective pollution control strategies, have proven to be cost effective in most cases.

Box 5. Experience with economic instruments for environmental protection

Most practical experience with the use of economic instruments for environmental protection has been in OECD countries, primarily the use of changes in a number of European countries and tradable permits in the United States. The potential gains of economic instruments, however, are larger in developing countries where overall control levels are lower, and it matters more which sources are controlled. Examples of effective economic instruments include:

- A charge on emissions of nitrogen oxide by power and heat producers in Sweden is refunded based on energy production and thus is revenue neutral. The charge achieved emission reductions of 44 percent from 1990 to 1993.
- A system of tradable credits for leaded gasoline phase-out in the United States greatly aided the phase-out (1982-87) and reduced its costs.
- Sulfur dioxide allowance trading in the United States aimed at reducing emissions from 19 million tons in 1980 to 9 million tons in 2000. The system complements an elaborate system of command and control regulations.
- Wastewater discharge fees in the Philippines were introduced in 1997 and are the first of a series of environmental user fees that will ultimately cover all pollutants (of water, air, and land).

Source: World Bank 1998.

INTEGRATING ENVIRONMENTAL ACTIVITIES WITH ACTIVITIES IN OTHER SECTORS. Perhaps the most urgent change required in Brazil's environmental management system is integrating environmental activities with activities in other sectors, a difficulty faced by many other countries, developed and developing alike. Environmental agencies are forced to take a watchdog approach to environmental management and a confrontational position toward other sector ministries. Requiring wastewater treatment in projects that focus on connecting poor communities to sewerage networks is an example of a confrontational approach, when an integrated approach would suggest phasing such investments in over time (beginning with wastewater collection and gradually moving toward wastewater treatment in low-income communities as part of a comprehensive wastewater treatment strategy; see Policy Note on water management and water and sanitation). Integrating sector policies and environmental regulations may be the single most important short-term initiative that environmental agencies at all levels in Brazil could pursue. At the municipal level this could include, for example, integrated favela upgrading projects with land, transport, and urban services planning to reduce urban sprawl, congestion, and air pollution.

Such integration or mainstreaming requires that adequate information be available to all stakeholders, such as private agents who might willingly cooperate were they better informed of environmental regulations; vulnerable populations, such as the urban poor, who may benefit most from good environmental policy; and governmental agencies that can implement actions to make environmental policies more effective. Better and more inclusive decisionmaking also requires greater transparency and accountability in environmental decisionmaking.

Options

- The Federal Environmental Ministry could work to integrate environmental policies with other federal secretariats. The PPA and fiscal reform efforts represent the two best opportunities for the Environmental Ministry to work more closely with the Ministry of Finance and the Planning Ministry.

- The Federal Environmental Ministry could work more closely with states to coordinate the national system. A stronger federal presence could promote coordination between states, establish a federal regulatory framework and minimum national ambient standards, and prevent damaging competition between states and provide capacity assistance and information to weaker states.

- In the short term, environmental agencies at all levels could make a concerted effort to prioritize environmental problems, use environmental indicators to guide their policies and actions, and bring greater transparency and accountability to their agencies. Specifically, the national government, states, and municipalities could prepare environmental action plans using international best practice elements (box 3)

- States could review their licensing requirements and introduce more flexible pollution management instruments, including market-based instruments. Modernizing efforts could include reducing bureaucratic requirements, focusing more on aggregate environmental and ambient quality objectives, and decentralizing licensing of minor activities to municipalities. In addition, economic instruments, such as polluter pay principles, could be introduced to complement licensing processes and other command and control instruments. (box 5).

- State and municipal governments could also integrate their environmental policies and actions, particularly water supply and sanitation, urban planning, and transport. Integration is especially important for low-income communities that suffer most directly and broadly from problems of urban pollution.

Message 4. Reformulating a national housing policy using the public sector as an enabler of markets, targeting subsidies to the poor, and deepening housing finance

Housing and housing finance in Brazil are underdeveloped relative to most of Latin America. Housing has the potential to be an important economic sector, contributing to job creation, expansion of the finance system, and creation of household wealth. Housing can also be a powerful tool in redistributing income and wealth. Since 1995, however, federal investment in housing for households below the median income level has declined considerably relative to spending for households in the top 30 percent, increasing disparities in an already inequitable housing system. For poor families, the situation is very serious. In addition to 5.4 million underserved households (living in rudimentary shelter, cohabiting with other families, or homeless), 65 percent of new urban households (about 1.2 million a year) cannot afford the cheapest house produced in the market, which has led to the proliferation of informal settlements and clandestine land subdivisions. Overregulation, market inefficiencies, constrained resale markets, the rapid rate of urban population growth, and unequal income distribution all severely impede upward mobility of households. Reform could make housing finance and subsidies more efficient and fair, allowing the financial system to work for middle and higher income groups while redirecting and targeting subsidies to households "at the margin" of the formal housing market and the poor. To have meaningful impact, solutions—for housing finance, subsidies, and land management—would need to be integrated and extended to all levels of government.

Context

A SECTOR IN NEED OF DIRECTION. Since the collapse of the National Housing Bank (*Banco Nacional da Habitação*, BNH) Brazil's public sector has shied away from intervening in housing policies or promoting a consistent housing strategy. As a result, housing policy needs coordination across all levels of government, beginning at the federal level. There are few federal housing programs that benefit the poor. Most federal housing programs are targeted to middle-income households. Between 1995 and 2000, for example, governments in Brazil spent an estimated R$12 billion on housing programs. Only the 10 percent of these funds targeted to lower-income groups came from the central budget. The remaining 90 percent came from the severance fund (FGTS; for details, see the Policy Note on the private sector), in the form of subsidized credit for middle-income households (earning up to 12 minimum salaries) at below market rates of interest. Some 80 percent of the R$12 billion came from the municipalities directly, 12 percent from the states, and only 8 percent from the federal government. By comparison, expenditures in health accounted for 12 percent and education for 6 percent and social security for 40 percent.

In February 2001, Brazil's Congress passed a constitutional amendment that guarantees the right to adequate housing to all Brazilians. The challenge now is to accomplish this while maintaining fiscal and political discipline. There is clearly a role for the public sector to play in meeting the housing needs of Brazil's poor population, calling for a coordinated and revamped approach. But this can only be done in tandem with efforts to boost demand through resource mobilization and residential savings and an unshackling of mortgage markets and supply constraints in order to increase access to housing by all segments of the market. Brazil faces a triple challenge: addressing the accumulated housing deficit, improving the existing stock of housing, and serving the housing needs of an estimated 1.2 million new households each year, within the constraints of macroeconomic stability and public finance discipline.

According to official estimates, 5.4 million households live in less than adequate housing conditions—homeless, living in substandard housing, in housing with substandard urban services, or in overcrowded conditions. These are by and large poor households, with over 65 percent of them living on less than three minimum salaries. Nearly half of these households live in Brazil's northeast, and most of them in urban areas and many in "informal" settlements.

**Table 3. Informal housing units by metropolitan region, 1998
(thousands, unless otherwise indicated)**

Metropolitan area	Provisional or homeless	Substandard (favela or other)	Tenements	Other	Informal housing as a share of total housing (percent)
Recife	0.2	207.5	3.0	1.8	31.9
Belem	0	48.7	1.7	0.2	28.5
Fortaleza	0.41	77.8	1.7	5.8	21.2
Porto Alegre	0	36.1	3.2	9.2	17.3
Rio de Janeiro	0.58	333.3	29.0	29.0	14.1
Belo Horizonte	0.25	80.4	8.5	3.7	12.9
Salvador	0.84	25.7	7.8	1.5	12.8
Curitiba	0	23.3	1.8	5.5	10.8
Sao Paulo	2.6	227.3	19.1	30.4	9.4
Federal District	1.68	6.9	14.0	2.3	8.3
Total	6.56	1,066.9	89.8	89.3	13.8

Source: IPEA/ DIRUR based on PNAD/ IBGE 1998.

POVERTY AND REGRESSIVE POLICIES EXACERBATE THE PROBLEM. Every year more than a million new households enter the housing market. Only about a fifth of them will be able to purchase their homes through the private mortgage market. Another 20 percent will qualify for some kind of subsidized credit. The remaining 60 percent of households will neither be able to afford a downpayment on a new unit, nor have access to formal financial markets to finance a home. These families will either double-up with another family or seek housing through informal markets.

The principle obstacles to the acquisition of safe and adequate housing for the vast majority of Brazilians are a lack of purchasing power, the high cost of housing, and the high cost of housing finance. Assuming that households can spend approximately 30 percent of household income on housing, fewer than half of Brazilian households earn enough to find housing on the open market (and that includes FGTS). The average cost of a small, 35 square meter house in the formal market is around R$20,000. Assuming a down payment of R$2,000, less than half of all Brazilian households would be able to afford the financing on the remaining R$18,000.

The bar to access could be lowered if there were corrections in supply constraints (market and government failures) that inflate the cost of housing. While there is a lack of empirical data on impediments in land and housing markets, there is ample anecdotal evidence to identify several problems that impede their efficient and equitable functioning: constrained supply of vacant and developable land, a lack of adequate network infrastructure to serve vacant land, poorly executed urban master plans that are also too restrictive, excessive and inappropriate zoning and subdivision standards, inadequate financial mechanisms for infrastructure investment, limited access to housing finance. All of these problems lead to the continued growth of informal settlements.

Land use regulations and housing standards tend to be onerous for many would-be developers, who are often driven to illegally subdivide land for sale. Easing land use regulations and making building standards more flexible could reduce the cost of housing, perhaps by as much as half. But even if that were to happen, in many urban markets the supply of affordable housing would still be constrained by a high concentration of land ownership and an oligopolistic construction industry. While recent urban legislation intended to increase access to land markets by the poor is promising, time will tell whether the recently passed urban law *(Lei de Estatuto da Cidade)* will indeed increase access to land and housing assets for the urban poor. But there are several problems. The law does not tackle restrictive land subdivision or land use laws, regulations, and development standards at all levels of government, and there are major capacity constraints at the local government level in implementing the new legislation (see box 6).

Box 6. *Lei de Estatuto da Cidade*

After 12 years of debate, the first significant urban legislation was approved since adoption of the 1988 Constitution. The *Estatuto da Cidade* defines the powers and responsibilities of municipalities in execution of the constitutional provisions and has some innovative and perhaps controversial elements. The law identifies important urban policy instruments such as the *Plano Diretor*, or urban master plan, that allows for progressive property taxation on "underused land," opens the door to greater transparency and public participation in local governance, and allows for an acceleration of adverse possession rights on squatted or informally occupied land.

The new legislation, important as it is, may not have the impact its supporters hoped for in providing greater access to land assets by the urban poor unless parallel changes in laws and regulations affecting land subdivision and tenure regularization norms are also undertaken. For example, if under the new law an owner of "underused urban land" is forced to subdivide, there is no mechanism to ensure that land is subdivided in a way that will make it affordable to lower income households (if that is the intent). Barring local reform of the subdivision approval process, the land could still sit idle for years as the subdivision process lags. In addition, the legislation is sufficiently complex that only the most sophisticated municipalities will have the capacity to implement it, which means that much of the law could be ignored by most municipalities. In addition, the provisions of the law dealing with land do not include atention for land economics principles. Greater analysis of this law is needed.

DIVERSIFIED FINANCING IS NEEDED. FGTS-related interest rate subsidies through Caixa Economica Federal and tax benefits through the Brazilian Savings and Loan System (*Sistema Brasileiro de Poupanca Emprestimo*, SBPE) have alleviated some of the financing constraints for formal sector housing for households as low as the 70th income percentile (approximately R$1,000/month). But the limitations of Caixa housing finance programs are well known: funding cycles are uneven and cause interruptions in financed projects; there is a large degree of regressivity in the programs, which generally benefit relatively higher income households; regional distribution of funds is uneven, with richer regions benefiting over poorer ones; the subsidized finance schemes impose a high degree of risk on the government; and there is a lack of competition and participation in the federal programs, with Caixa having a virtual monopoly on these resources. Being the major source of housing finance in the country, the FGTS is focused solely on subsidizing finance, forgoing opportunities to leverage its capital, and ignoring other important limitations to the housing sector such as land and infrastructure constraints. There is an unwarranted focus on new, formal sector housing in most federal FGTS financed schemes, leaving nonauthorized housing out as a potential form of collateral for finance, whether subsidized or not.

INFORMAL SETTLEMENTS ARE SPREADING. At the local level, Brazilian policy has largely overlooked the expansion of its cities. Overcentralized urban regulations have focused on enforcement of zoning and construction permits and less on flexible planning that could help to equilibrate demand and supply in the developable land market. Less onerous land subdivision processes and more flexible housing standards could go a long way to increasing the availability of at least minimally serviced land, with public and private rights-of-way well demarcated and affordable to lower income families (box 7).

Box 7. Constraints to land supply for housing

The supply of land in Brazil is controlled in large measure by Federal Law 6766/1979, which regulates subdivision, and municipal *Planos Diretores*. Federal Law 9785/1999 replaced law 6766 to regulate illegal settlements, expropriation laws, land registration, and the parceling of urban land. Some basic elements that have important bearing on the poor include:

- Land subdivision for urban purposes is authorized only in urban zones, and no rural land can be parceled for urban purposes. This artificially limits the legal expansion of cities and increases the value of urban land.

- Development is prevented on steep hills and in flood plains. This inhibits urban upgrading programs that in some cases, with proper drainage work and geotechnical retention works, can provide safe places to live in already occupied informal settlements without socially disruptive and high cost resettlement;

- Up to 35 percent of land in any urban development must be reserved for urban equipment and infrastructure, including parking and other public spaces. This limits the ability to create special use districts, such as affordable housing districts, that could reduce some of these requirements that raise costs and price many poor out of the market.

- Urban lots cannot be smaller than 125 square meters, with at least 5 meters of street frontage. Again, this serves to price out the urban poor, who would benefit from smaller lot sizes.

- Subdivided land must be fully serviced before a developer can sell plots, precluding progressive infrastructure schemes that could benefit the urban poor.

- Land, subsidy, and housing finance issues cannot be treated separately. They require intersectoral and intergovernmental cooperation and coordination. Brazilian policymakers could focus on improving the efficiency and equity of housing and land markets, improve the transparency and targeting of housing programs and housing subsidies, transform the housing finance system to one that can mobilize capital market funds and private savings, and address the growing informality of Brazilian cities, by reducing regulatory and other government restriction on the availability of urban developable land.

Options

LAND AND HOUSING MARKETS. Corrections in supply constraints (market and government failures) could help to reduce the high cost of housing and stop the growth of informal settlements.

Short-term actions at the federal level

- Assess the current flows of formal and informal housing and subdivided land in urban areas with a view toward developing more appropriate and effective urban land and housing market policies. Lack of knowledge is a key impediment to better policy.
- Revise the legal and regulatory framework to allow progressive infrastructure development and create incentives for subdividing urban land for low- and moderate-income housing.

Intermediate-term actions at the federal level

- Create a training program in urban land economics and real estate for urban planning professionals and academics that will build capacity and proficiency and enable practitioners to apply land use tools effectively.
- Develop or consolidate existing federal housing programs into a matching grant scheme for states and municipalities, that would include support for nongovernmental organizations and community-based organizations tied to other reforms in the sector, especially liberalization of urban land markets, with the objective of increasing the supply of land and housing for low- and moderate-income populations (below median income levels).

Intermediate-term actions at the local level

- On the basis of studies of formal and informal market flows, liberalize urban land markets by reforming urban master planning, subdivision regulations and processes, local building codes, and zoning ordinances, making them tools to facilitate appropriate land use and development and increase, rather than decrease, the supply of land available for the production of low- and moderate-income housing.
- Design local urban upgrading programs that put more emphasis on land tenure regularization and registration and integration of social and economic opportuni-

ties, promote private sector participation, target subsidies to the poor, and promote cost recovery.

HOUSING FINANCE AND FINANCE-LINKED SUBSIDIES. Housing finance reform has already begun with the imminent transformation of the SBPE toward greater liberalization, transparency, and contract enforceability. If fully implemented, this will trigger other related housing reforms. But more needs to be done. Whereas local governments would be involved in much of the reform in land markets, the federal government plays the key role in reforming housing finance:

Short-term actions

*   Reform of FGTS, to end its credit market distorting propensity and the regressivity of embedded credit subsidies, might include:

    *   Opening access to the funds by other lenders (mostly banks), after an independent assessment of the counterpart risk, and using FGTS funds to attract more lenders into lower-income lending.
    *   Transfering some FGTS administrative functions (like the recourse guarantee) from Caixa Economica Federal and widening the intermediary margin.
    *   Not allowing lenders to repay FGTS with Mortgage Assistance Fund (FCVS) bonds at par value.
    *   Lowering the limit on eligible income but allowing interest rates to be raised to market levels (as market rates decline to more affordable levels) at least for the higher eligibility levels. One way to do that would be to auction funds across various lenders according to their returns paid to the FGTS.
    *   Offering a wider range of refinancing terms.
    *   Accepting trust deeds as collateral for credit *(alienacāo fiduciária)* and letting eligible lenders apply their own scoring tools.
    *   Allowing purchases of existing housing stock and rental construction to be eligible for housing finance, increasing affordable options.
    *   Allowing FGTS members to use their accrued contributions as safe collateral for housing credit (particularly if there is no pledged property title).
    *   Permitting FGTS members' wage contributions to automatically (and partially) cover the monthly amortization of a housing loan made by any lender.

Intermediate-term actions

- Make necessary legal and regulatory reforms to stimulate the primary mortgage market, including:
  - Expediting the out-of-court foreclosure process.
  - Explicitly authorizing capitalization of interest in certain cases, and setting the order of amortization repayment.
  - Adjusting consumer protection, standardizing contractual conditions, and selecting sound and transparent amortization schemes and floats or indexes.

- Improve the regulatory framework for International Mortgage Services LLC (*Serviços Financeiros Imobiliários Ltda.,* SFI), and encourage standardization and larger issues and elimination of the tax on financial transactions (*Contribuição Provisória sobre Movimentação ou Transmissão de Valores e de Créditos e Direitos de Natureza Financeira* (CPMF).
- After FGTS adjustments take effect, design new transparent and upfront subsidies to facilitate access to finance by moderate-income groups. These could be funded from budgetary allocations and other funds.

INSTITUTIONAL STRUCTURE. Recent moves toward greater housing policy coordination by the National Council on Housing should help to strengthen housing policy at the federal level. Since the collapse of the National Housing Bank (*Banco Nacional da Habitação,* BNC) the federal government has been reluctant to take a more proactive role in the housing sector by setting the direction of housing policy, establishing new housing programs, or coordinating activities in the sector. The federal government could move to reform the institutional structure of the sector, with both short- and long-term actions.

Short-term actions

- Activate the National Urban Development Council and consolidate its political and technical legitimacy. One of the council's immediate objectives could be to define the functions of each level of government in the sector.
- Redefine the function of Caixa, FGTS, and SEDU.
  - SEDU could conduct policy diagnosis, propose policy changes, and provide sectoral information and training.

- Caixa could be a competitive operator with other financial institutions in the market, with the same access to public funding, putting it on an equal footing with other financial institutions.
- FGTS's role might be analyzed in light of its function as a provident fund and severance payment mechanism. The forced savings scheme may be phased out over time or be restructured to be remunerated at market rates.

- Develop an institutional matrix that identifies the most critical institutional and regulatory problems in the sector and at each level of government, and prioritize actions for reform.
- Establish a Federal Housing Fund with its own administrative unit to manage housing assistance programs. The fund would have multiyear funding allocations from the budget and other sources and would coordinate international agency funds for the housing sector. It would focus on the low- and moderate-income end of the market, but should not be a second-tier lender.

References

World Bank projects

- São Paulo subway extension (*Programa de Integração de Transportes Urbanos— Projeto da Linha 4 do Metrô de São Paulo*). US$ 209 million. Approved on January 22, 2002.
- Fortaleza Metropolitan Transport Project (Projeto Trem Metropolitano de Fortaleza) US$ 85 million. Approved on December 4, 2001.
- Goiás management and improvement of roads (*Programa de Gerenciamento e Melhoria da Malha Rodoviária de Goiás*) US$ 70 million. Approved on August 23, 2001.
- Salvador train decentralization project (*Projeto de Descentralização do Sistema de Trem Metropolitano de Salvador*) US$ 150 million. Approved on June 17, 1999.
- São Paulo integration project Barra Funda-Roosevelt (*Projeto de Integração Centro-Ligação Barra Funda – Roosevelt, São Paulo*). US$ 45 million. Approved on April 7, 1998.
- Rio de Janeiro transport state program (*Programa Estadual de Transporte* – PET, Rio de Janeiro) US$ 168.8 million. Approved on March 5, 1998.

- Rio Grande do Sul Highway Management (*Programa de Rodovias Estaduais do Rio Grande do Sul*) US$ 65 million. Approved on May 15, 1997.
- Bahia regional and urban development – PRODUR/BA (*Programa de Desenvolvimento Urbano e Regional da Bahia*). US$ 100 million. Approved on March 4, 1997.
- Belo Horizonte transport decentralization project (*Projeto de Descentralização do Sistema de Transporte Urbano de Belo Horizonte*) US$ 99 million. Approved on June 29, 1995.
- Recife transport decentralization project (*Projeto de Descentralização do Sistema do Recife*) US$ 102 million. Approved on June 29, 1995.
- Ceara Urban Development and Water Resource—PROURB/CE (*Projeto de Desenvolvimento Urbano e Gestão dos Recursos Hídricos do Ceará*). US$ 140 million. Approved on September 6, 1994.

World Bank reports

This chapter summarizes the content of the following World Bank reports. Those, in turn, draw heavily from a wide range of literature on the subject from experts in Brazil and beyond, which are referenced in the mentioned Bank reports.

Rebelo, Jorge. 2001. "A Program for the Strategic Development of Brazilian Medium-Size Cities." World Bank, Washington, D.C.

World Bank. 1998. "Brazil: Managing Pollution Problems." Policy Report. Washington, D.C.

World Bank. 2001. "Brazil—Financing Municipal Investment: Issues and Options." Gray Cover Report No. 20313-BR. Washington, D.C.

World Bank. 2002a. "Back to Office Report. Housing Finance Reforms in Brazil." Washington, D.C.

World Bank. 2002b. "Back to Office Report: Subnational Housing Policy Dialogue Mission." Washington, D.C.

World Bank. 2002c. "Brazil—Managing the Challenges of the Urban Sector: Contributing to a National Urban Strategy." Washington, D.C.

World Bank. 2002d. "Brazil National Housing Policy: Maintaining Momentum for Reform." Policy Notes on Housing Finance, Subsidies, and Land Policies. Washington, D.C.

World Bank. 2002e. "Brazil—Progressive Low-Income Housing: Alternatives for the Poor." Washington, D.C.

World Bank. 2002f. "Brazil: Public Policies to Fight Urban Poverty." Washington, D.C.

Other references

Fernandes, Edésio. 2001. "A New Statute for Brazilian Cities." University College, London.

Fernandes, Edésio. 2001. "Combining Tenure Policies, Urban Planning, and City Management in Brazil." University College, London.

11

Water, Poverty Reduction, and Sustainable Development

11

Water, Poverty Reduction, and Sustainable Development

Introduction

Water is a key element of Brazil's strategy to promote sustainable growth and a more equitable and inclusive society. While Brazil's achievements over the past 50 years have been closely linked to the development of its water resources, new challenges that urgently require policy attention have emerged.

Brazil's recent accomplishments in developing its water resources are significant. For instance, access to electricity has increased from less than 500 kilowatt hours (KWh) per capita in 1970 to more than 2,000 KWh per capita in 2000 . These impressive results have been achieved in large part through the development of hydrogeneration, which currently accounts for 81 percent of Brazil's installed capacity (64 gigawatts of a total of 79). In water supply and sanitation, the results are no less impressive. Over the last 40 years Brazil has expanded water supply and sanitation services to an additional 100 million and 50 million Brazilians, respectively. Today, 77 percent of the population has access to potable water service and 47 percent to sewerage service. The area under irrigation has grown from 2.6 million hectares in 1995 to approximately 3.5 million hectares in 2002. Although the Amazon has been used for inland navigation for more than 80 years, river transportation has increased steadily in recent times and has been integrated into a multimodal transport system. Since 1991, 19 states and the Federal District have adopted legislation to modernize water resources management. A federal law governing the administration and management of water resources was passed in 1997. The National Water Agency (ANA) was created in 2000 with the mandate to implement the National Water Resources Policy. Indeed Brazil is recognized internationally as an innovator and an emerging leader in water resources management.

The draft of this chapter was completed by Abel Mejia and Luiz Gabriel Azevedo; with contributions from Martin Gambrill, Alexandre Baltar, and Thelma Triche in October 2002. The analyses and suggestions contained in this chapter are based on the international technical experience of the World Bank and are presented as a contribution to the debate and formulation of public policies.

Despite these remarkable achievements, serious challenges remain to be addressed by the next generation of policymakers. Brazil faces a dual crisis in the management of its water resources—droughts in the Northeast and water pollution near large urban centers. Almost all rivers crossing urban areas are highly polluted, causing serious health problems in poor populations, environmental damage, and higher water treatment costs for downstream users. Water supply and sanitation services are unevenly distributed—service coverage is particularly low in the North and Northeast—and the poor are less likely to have access to adequate service than are other consumers. Most irrigation, water supply, and sanitation services are inefficient and financially unviable. It is the poor who suffer most from scarce and poorly managed water resources, inadequate water supply services, and the unhealthy environment that exists in the absence of adequate water supply, sewerage, and wastewater treatment. Good management of water resources and access to basic water and sanitation services promote employment generation, improved health, and better environmental quality in human settlements, all of which are critical for the alleviation of poverty. Progress will require reform and innovation on several fronts: legal, institutional, financial, and technical.

This policy note focuses on water resources management and water supply and sanitation services. Although they are distinct activities that require different institutional management models and funding mechanisms and water supply and sanitation is only one of the water-using sectors, water resources management and water supply and sanitation are interdependent, have closely linked implications for poverty alleviation, and face many similar challenges. Because water issues and policies cut across numerous other sectors, occasional reference will be made to Policy Notes in this series that deal with municipal and urban management and housing, rural development and natural resources management, and environmental conservation.

In fact, a recurring theme in these notes is the need for mechanisms to promote coordination between the water sector and other related sectors such as urban planning and management, solid waste collection and disposal, health, land-use planning, and environmental protection. Inconsistent policies across sectors result in wasted resources and prevent the coordination of interventions and the consequent reaping of their cumulative benefits. Several sectors face the same constraints that are blocking progress in the water sector (for example, the weak institutional capacity of small towns and the lack of appropriate arrangements for the coordination of policies, planning, and management of operations in metropolitan regions). Coordinated interventions will have multiple benefits.

The financial challenge of expanding water services to the poor and increasing wastewater treatment and water pollution control in Brazil is considerable. The cost of developing new water resources is increasing due to the scarcity or contamination of nearby sources and the distant location of alternative sources. The cost of providing services to marginal areas, where access is problematic, or to small towns, where the population is more spread out, is higher than in the more densely populated center cities. Moreover, expansion of services to the poor (who have a limited ability to pay and lower consumption habits) could result in lower average revenue unless perverse tariff structures are reformed. As population increases and more water-using amenities are introduced, the volume of wastewater increases relative to the capacity of the environment to dispose of it naturally, necessitating the costly expansion and improvement of wastewater collection, transportation, and treatment capacity. Treatment costs could also rise with the adoption and enforcement of increasingly stringent drinking water quality and environmental standards.

A strategy for dealing with the financial challenges of the water supply and sanitation and water resources management sectors will require reforms to ensure that subsidies are carefully targeted to the poor, realistic environmental and engineering standards are adopted, tariff regime and bulk-water pricing reforms are implemented to promote water conservation practices, innovative financing programs are established to create incentives to improve operational efficiency, and a clear legal framework is set up to turn around the investment climate.

Recent performance of the sectors

Water resources management

The 1934 Water Code was the first relevant water resources management legislation in Brazil. However, not until the 1988 Constitution was a national water resources management system established. The Constitution divided the country's waters between the union and the states, and states began to implement their own water resources management systems. São Paulo pioneered this process and approved a water resources management act in 1991. Since then 18 other states and the Federal District have adopted water laws. After negotiating for six years, Congress adopted a national water policy (Federal Law 9433) in January 1997 that incorporates most modern water resources management principles and instruments.

The remarkable progress in the development of legal frameworks and policy instruments was not followed by widespread progress in effective implementation. One of the few exceptions was the introduction of bulk water charges in Ceará. In July 2000, Federal Law 9984 created the National Water Agency (ANA) with the mandate to implement the national water policy. The central role of ANA in finding solutions to the many challenges of water resources management cannot be overstated.

Among the many water resources management challenges in Brazil, two stand out for their enormous social impact and the pressure they exert on governments for the development of large investment programs: droughts in the Northeast and water pollution in and near large urban centers. About 2 million households in the Northeast, most in extreme poverty, lack adequate water supply. Almost all rivers crossing urban areas are highly polluted, compromising the health of poor populations, creating environmental damage, and increasing the cost of water treatment for downstream users. Finding effective solutions to these two challenges will require close coordination between water resources management and the provision of water supply and sanitation services.

As in many other countries, water resources management in Brazil has historically relied on heavy investments in basic infrastructure for irrigation, hydropower, water supply, flood control, and navigation. The contribution of many of these investments to the country's development cannot be questioned. Brazil has made impressive progress in hydropower production and the extension of water supply and sanitation services. However, the overall return on water infrastructure has not been consistently positive. Projects have been abandoned or have taken so long to complete that the original goals have been overtaken by new circumstances. Even where projects have stimulated regional economic growth or met the demands of growing cities, the lags between investment and downstream benefits have greatly reduced the present value of those benefits. Finally, a heavy emphasis on large investment projects has been accompanied by neglect of the administration, operation, and maintenance of water infrastructure.[1] As a result, efficiency is low and potential benefits have not always been realized.

The contribution of investments to improved water resources management has been mixed. Progress in addressing water pollution and meeting water demands in some areas must be balanced against evidence of increasing salinity of irrigated land, greater vulnerability to floods in urban areas and to intermittent droughts and water shortages, and little to no improvement in key indicators of water quality. All of these negative effects and conditions disproportionately affect the poor.

---

[1] This is widely acknowledged for irrigation projects, but it is equally a problem for large investment programs in water supply and sanitation, as in the River Tietê program in São Paulo and the Guanabara Bay program in Rio de Janeiro.

Water supply, sanitation services, and water pollution control

While overall access of Brazil's urban households to water supply service is high, at about 90 percent, coverage varies considerably from region to region and state to state, and quality differs dramatically from one part of a city to another. Some 56 percent of urban households are connected to a sewerage system and 16 percent have septic systems, but the unevenness of coverage is even more dramatic for sanitation than for water supply. Very little wastewater is treated. Coverage rates for water supply and sanitation are highest in the relatively affluent South and Southeast and lowest in the poorer states of the North and Northeast. A large part of the unserved population lives in peri-urban areas, favelas, and small towns, with mainly lower-income populations. Only 18 percent of rural households have piped water service, and 13 percent have either sewerage or septic tanks.

Growing urbanization is straining the capacity of the sector to expand. While there were large gains in the share of urban households with access to water supply and sanitation during the 1970s and 1980s, stagnation set in during the 1990s, as the number of new connections barely exceeded the number of new urban households. Growth in water supply coverage slowed from 14 percent in 1980–91 to 3.5 percent in 1991–2000.[2] The deceleration was associated with a marked decline in sector investment: average annual investment fell from 0.34 percent of GNP in the 1970s to 0.28 percent in the 1980s and 0.13 percent in the 1990s.

The sector's capacity to mobilize investment resources is weak. In 1999, combined receipts of all the state water companies and a representative number of municipal water and sanitation entities barely exceed combined costs. Performance varies substantially, but only 10 of the 27 state companies fully cover their costs (Bittencourt and Araújo 2002). The weak financial performance is due in part to inefficiency and the high cost of maintaining aged infrastructure. Perverse tariff structures also contribute. Low tariffs for the first block of consumption benefit many consumers who do not need subsidies, unnecessarily depressing revenues and limiting funds for services that could be more directly targeted to the poor.

---

[2] During 1980–91, an additional 32.4 million urban residents got access to water supply, bringing coverage to 86.3 percent. During the last decade of the century, 28.1 million more people got water, bringing coverage to 89.8 percent.

Selected reforms have already been undertaken by various sector actors, but clearer policy direction and innovative financing mechanisms would be needed to reverse the trend of deceleration in progress. Major changes in the institutional, regulatory, financial, and incentive structures in the sector, at all levels of government, would be needed to avoid further increases in the number of poor people who lack access to basic services and continuing environmental degradation.

Message 1. Creating a sound institutional and legal framework for water resources management to enhance poverty reduction and promote efficient water use and sustainable economic growth
The development of a sound water resources management framework to ensure the sustainable use of water requires further work on three critical policy issues. One is the establishment of a secure and enforceable water-use rights system, which is essential for creating incentives for improving water management and for reducing overexploitation. Establishment of a framework for allocating and transferring water rights would make it possible to take advantage of the full benefits of a system of water-use rights. A second is the application of water use charges, which would signal the economic value of water, generate resources for managing water infrastructure, encourage more efficient use of water resources, and promote the accountability of water users. A third is clarification of the roles and responsibilities of ANA, the National Water Resources Council, the Secretariat of Water Resources, the Secretariat of Hydraulic Infrastructure, state water agencies, and decentralized river basin institutions, which is essential for developing truly cooperative institutions within a framework for resolving conflict.

Context
The legal, regulatory, and institutional frameworks for water resources management (water agencies, decentralization, river basin entities, participation of stakeholders, regulatory reforms) and the instruments for improving management of water resources present important challenges.[3] Improved water resources management may enhance poverty

---

[3] There are many important instruments (river basin and state plans, information and decision support systems, water quality goals), but water rights and pricing are considered by many in the water sector as critical for the development of water resources management systems, including the introduction of all these other instruments.

reduction strategies in various ways. Social inclusion is promoted by adopting participatory and decentralized approaches. Environment-related risk and health issues are addressed, thus reducing the vulnerability of the poor. Equity of access to water resources can be promoted through appropriate legal and regulatory reforms. The burden on poor women and children, who often travel long distances to fetch water, can be relieved through facilitated access to water. The reliability and sustainability of water sources may be increased through appropriate pricing of bulk water. In addition, microcatchment approaches for jointly managing land and water resources have been successfully used with direct benefits for the poor (see Policy Note on rural development and natural resources management).

LEGAL AND INSTITUTIONAL FRAMEWORK. Many of the problems in the water sector are associated with poorly defined responsibilities within and across levels of government, unclear rules and regulations, uneven enforcement, and weak capacity for monitoring compliance. The passage of the National Water Law and the creation of ANA were important steps in improving water resources management. While further refinements to the institutional, legal, and regulatory frameworks are important, significant advances in water resources management can be accomplished by focusing now on a small number of key challenges, such as water rights and water pricing, and strengthening state and basin institutions.

ANA's mandate is to implement the national water policy by carrying out regulatory functions (water rights administration) and executive functions (such as development and operation of the national water resource information system). While ANA's regulatory function is important, it should not attempt to resolve every conflict in water resources management. Some conflicts will inevitably involve disputes requiring broader negotiation and judicial resolution. Following the general framework of Brazil's state reform, policymaking for water resources remains the responsibility of core government structures, in this case the Ministry of Environment through its Secretariat of Water Resources.

ANA has also undertaken initiatives to develop positive incentives and demonstrate good practice in water resources management. Such promotional activities should not dominate ANA's activities or distract it from its primary regulatory role. The *Compra de Esgoto* program, for example, which reimburses a portion of the investment cost of creating or expanding wastewater treatment plants in critical regions where river basin committees are up-to-date in paying abstraction fees, can be viewed as an important pilot initiative rather than a comprehensive solution to wastewater treatment. Once tested and refined, such programs would have to be taken over by water supply and sanitation institutions with the mandate and capacity to implement the programs on a large scale. This will require substantial reform and institutional strengthening of the water supply and sanitation sector.

The constitutional provision dividing the country's waters between the union and the states, and the continental dimensions of many river basins in Brazil, make water resources management inherently complex, requiring considerable coordination. The forging of strong partnerships with states and river basin agencies to carry out ANA's regulatory and executive functions and to decentralize functions, where possible, would be among ANA's priorities.

Decentralization is a core value of Brazil's national water policy. While attention may focus on the role of river basin committees in defining priorities and reconciling competing interests, the committees cannot function properly without substantial and costly technical support. Currently, the development of river basin management is trapped in a vicious circle. New institutions must demonstrate competence to rally support and establish credibility. To do that they need resources, both human and financial, to support sound technical work and fund new investments. Getting resources requires levying charges on water users, which users will find acceptable only once agencies have demonstrated their competence.

With a few exceptions, the performance of state water agencies is generally weak. In Brazil's water resources management system, river basin agencies are not a substitute for state agencies because state agencies have the unalienable authority to grant water rights. In addition, not every basin within a state's territory warrants the creation of an agency. Most state water agencies, however, lack appropriate human and financial resources. Overcoming these deficiencies will require strong political support to deal with vested interests and to identify opportunities for implementing the necessary reforms.

ANA could coordinate federal support to strengthen local capacity and help local institutions break the vicious circle described above. However, the continued reliance of much of the sector on investments financed by or through the federal government means that the effectiveness of decentralization is likely to be less than expected or desirable.

WATER RIGHTS. The complexity of formalizing rights for a fungible resource with deep cultural implications in an administratively weak environment should never be underestimated. Water rights and water pricing are interdependent instruments that can jointly improve the way water is managed by making explicit the mutual obligations and responsibilities of water resources management agencies and water users, preserving the interests of society as a whole, and taking environmental concerns into account. The application of the concept of transferable property rights to the use of water is controversial in Brazil, both legally and socially. Nevertheless, experience in other countries has shown that reforms which threaten the perceived rights of existing users are unlikely to succeed unless the perceived rights are both recognized and grand-fathered. Therefore, even if reliance on market arrangements for the disposal, transfer, or use of water resources proves undesirable or legally difficult, clear definition of water use rights is still required for effective water resources management.

Although surface water and groundwater should be managed in an integrated way, groundwater has distinguishing features that require special attention. Once an aquifer is contaminated, it becomes very difficult, and often economically unfeasible, to restore it to its previous quality. Important aquifers have been overexploited, with water tables already deep and dropping every year. In urban areas, the problem is closely associated with deficient water supply services (as in the metropolitan area of Recife). In the absence of reliable water supply service, households resort to wells to complement their water supply. In rural areas, expansion of irrigated agriculture is putting major pressure on groundwater (as in the western part of the state of Bahia).

BULK WATER PRICING. Reforming bulk water pricing gives rise to a series of fundamental and healthy changes by giving users an indication of the economic value of the resource, thus helping to promote its more efficient use; providing financial resources to guarantee adequate administration, operation, and maintenance of water infrastructure; and funding (at least partially) water resources management and development.

Although many studies have been carried out in various states and river basins to estimate the optimum price of water that captures the economic values of alternatives uses, the two most successful initiatives have adopted values decided through broad political negotiations with the main water users. These are in Ceará, the only state currently charging for bulk water, and the Paraíba do Sul River Basin, where the introduction of bulk water pricing was recently approved by the river basin committee. The general public, however, still views paying for bulk water as yet another government tax—a serious political constraint in a period of economic and political uncertainty. The challenge is to demonstrate to users that introducing bulk water charges, developing a system for allocating secure water rights, applying participatory and decentralized management at the basin level, and developing adequate regulatory and institutional frameworks will enhance the reliability of water resources systems.

Options

Several steps would help to create a sound institutional and legal framework for water resources management to enhance poverty reduction and promote efficient water use and sustainable economic growth:

- Clearly defining the roles of ANA, the National Water Resources Council, the National Secretariat of Water Resources, and state and river basin water agencies.
- Identifying ANA's priorities and immediately developing a strategic business plan.
- Concentrating state governments on creating properly staffed autonomous water agencies, initially with public funding.
- Basing federal support for state initiatives on demonstrated willingness to implement reforms, through a monitorable, time-bound action plan.
- Committing ANA's finance and technical resources to ensuring that at least two strategic river basin agencies are operating within the next two years.
- Identifying priority basins for ANA's direct intervention (for example, Paraíba do Sul, Piracicaba, Paraná, São Francisco) and establishing local partnerships for managing lower priority federal river basins.
- Strengthening the involvement of municipalities in water resources management.
- Continuing ANA's important and active work in the international arena, exchanging experience and consolidating Brazil's leadership position.
- Assigning high priority in ANA to promoting the adequate functioning of the national water rights system and establishing a sequenced action plan for advancing it.
- Establishing clear and simple procedures for water rights administration that can be refined as ANA matures, focusing initially on quantitative issues and progressively integrating quality concerns.
- Emphasizing selectivity and sequencing at the state level, with states concentrating on high priority basins and aquifers, adopting simple procedures initially and gradually improving them.
- Establishing a realistic transition period to give users time to comply with the new regulations and enable water agency personnel to gain the confidence of users as partners rather than police.
- Developing ways to permit the transfer of water rights among users so as to increase water use efficiency.
- Establishing clear pricing objectives in ANA and local agencies based on cost recovery first, then economic efficiency.

- Justifying and targeting subsidies, which would still be needed, mostly in irrigation; making them transparent; documenting existing levels; and not linking them to the amount of water used to avoid perverse incentives to waste water; and at a minimum, setting user fees to cover the costs of administration, operation, and maintenance.

- Creating incentives for water resources management reform at the federal level by linking funding for institutional and infrastructure development with progress in reforms, thereby strengthening local agencies that are conducting the reform and helping users see the benefits of paying bulk water charges.

- Involving stakeholders in the reform process, whatever approach to reform is taken.

- Committing politically and financially at the federal level to implement bulk water charges in at least two federal river basins within the next two years, to avoid a loss of confidence in the water resources management system.

Message 2. Clarifying the institutional, legal, and regulatory framework to modernize the water supply and sanitation sector and improve its effectiveness

The institutional, legal, and regulatory framework is now outdated and inhibits further progress. Inconsistent federal policies and a lack of clarity in the roles and responsibilities of state and local governments on the planning, ownership, delivery, and regulation of water supply and sanitation services prevent sector institutions from performing at their fullest potential. The lack of clarity on ownership of assets and rules governing the award of concessions has impeded efforts to attract private investment and other forms of private participation.

Coordinated federal interventions that consistently promote efficiency and the expansion and improvement of service for the poor are needed. So, too, are legal frameworks that minimize political interference in water utilities, and regulations that provide companies with incentives for efficiency. Training and capacity building programs could enable municipal authorities to develop policies for water supply and sanitation services, plan investments, mobilize funding, choose appropriate institutional models for service delivery (whether through public or private companies), and monitor or regulate services (once municipal roles are clarified). Better coordination of water supply and sanitation planning and development with other urban interventions would make it possible to take advantage of synergies and reduce costs. Information on, and examples of, institutional models that promote better management and efficiency need to be disseminated.

Context

Institutional arrangements at the federal level have resulted in distorted and inconsistent policies and have impaired sector performance. The controversy over the assignment of responsibilities between state and local governments for planning, ownership, delivery, and regulation of water supply and sanitation services, while intensely debated for years, has yet to be resolved. The resulting policy and regulatory vacuum means that consumers often have little or no voice, service providers are not consistently held accountable for the quality and efficiency of services, subsidies are poorly targeted, and potential investors are reluctant to enter the market.

ROLE OF THE FEDERAL GOVERNMENT. The federal government's role in the sector needs to be clarified and strengthened. The roles of the many federal institutions involved in the sector—*Secretaria Especial de Desenvolvimento Urbano* (SEDU), *Caixa Econômica Federal* (CEF), *Banco Nacional de Desenvolvimento Econômico e Social* (BNDES), ANA, *Ministério de Planejamento e Orçamento, Ministério da Fazenda, Fundação Nacional de Saúde* (FUNASA)—are not clearly defined and uncoordinated, so that interventions are fragmented and lack direction. Funding criteria neither consistently give priority to services for the poor nor promote efficiency. A key role for the federal government would be to coordinate basic policies on major issues, such as subsidies and tariffs. Even if its primary role is financing, it could still promote key objectives by linking funding decisions to performance criteria (such as financial viability of systems and of utilities, preference for the poor, service quality improvements, and pollution abatement) and by designing tariff policies that enhance performance on these criteria. There is little capacity for sector policymaking at the federal level. This function is currently being performed by the Water Sector Modernization Program (PMSS), an unsustainable arrangement since this capacity will disappear when the program ends. A central institutional arrangement is needed that embraces both the urban and rural contexts and that coordinates water supply and sanitation policies with policies for urban development and slum upgrading, water resources management, and pollution control.

INCENTIVES FOR EFFICIENCY. As natural monopolies and essential public services, water and sewerage networks are not subject to competition in the market. Thus incentives for efficiency must be provided in other ways, such as through competition for the market where feasible, dissemination of performance information, consumer awareness-raising and public pressure, benchmarking, linking of public funding to efficiency and financial performance, transparent tariff reviews, and financial rewards for exceptional staff performance. Current institutional arrangements and oversight practices tend to allow political pressure, rather than incentives for efficiency, to dominate.

Substantial progress has been made in collecting and analyzing performance indicators from service providers through the SNIS. This information could become a powerful tool for comparing the performance of service providers and identifying the conditions and innovations that promote efficiency.

LEGAL AND REGULATORY FRAMEWORK. The lack of clarity in the roles of state and local governments concerning conceding power, regulatory authority and asset ownership in the water supply and sanitation sector has created a regulatory vacuum. While in theory municipalities own assets and are responsible for providing and regulating services, the system of state water companies, a legacy of the National Water Supply and Sanitation Program (PLANASA), has resulted in misalignments in the sector's incentive, efficiency, and accountability framework. There are no clearly established institutional arrangements for enforcing service quality standards or for setting and approving tariffs that promote financial viability and efficiency. Subsidies do not benefit those most in need. Consumers do not always have channels for making inquiries or registering complaints and are often unaware of their rights and responsibilities. The applicability of the Federal Concession Law to the water and sanitation sector remains to be established. A clear and neutral law governing competition for concessions for water supply and sanitation services, whether by public or private providers, is needed. The legal framework has no provisions for meeting the institutional needs of large metropolitan areas consisting of multiple municipalities or for dealing with the environmental stress caused by growing demand for water resources and the discharge of large volumes of wastewater. Neither need was foreseen when the legal framework was established. The lack of a legally sanctioned institutional model under which a group of municipalities, whether in large metropolitan areas or in a region with several small towns, can join together to plan, finance, and operate services, limits progress in effective service provision.

In the absence of a stable regulatory framework, clarity regarding ownership of assets, and rules governing the award of concessions, it has been very difficult to attract private investment and other forms of private participation.[4] A federal complementary law on water supply and sanitation services that aimed to clarify the framework was proposed several years

---

[4] The challenge of establishing independent regulation in Brazil also covers publicly owned or managed water utilities.

ago. This law and several variants have been debated ever since, but none has been adopted. A number of alternatives, each with advantages and disadvantages, have also been proposed: a Constitutional Amendment, interpretation law, federal ordinary law, and state laws.

Municipal capacity. In 2000, only 45 of Brazil's 5,561 municipalities had a population of more than 100,000, almost 37 percent of the total population lived in towns of less than 50,000, and 49 percent lived in towns and cities of less than 100,000 (IBGE 2000). The capacity of towns and small cities to organize and manage water supply and sanitation services, coordinate them with other local actors, and cope with the multiple federal and state agencies involved (for example, river basin committees and environmental regulatory bodies) is limited. Rural areas that fall within the jurisdiction of small and medium-size towns pose a special set of problems. Viable financial and institutional arrangements to support the planning, development, and delivery of sustainable water supply and sanitation in small and medium-size towns and rural areas need to be identified and replicated. At the other end of the spectrum, practical and legally viable institutions for coordinating the planning and delivery of water supply and integrated sanitation services in large metropolitan areas also need to be developed.

The capacity of many municipal authorities to participate in planning water supply and sanitation services, mobilize investment financing, and supervise and regulate service delivery is also limited, as is their capacity to engage in urban planning and to coordinate and associate with nearby municipalities (in part, as mentioned, because there is no clear legal framework). When state companies provide services, municipal authorities are often not consulted and have little power to influence investment and service planning decisions. When municipal entities provide services, experience is mixed. Some municipal service providers enjoy adequate autonomy and are reasonably efficient. Others are impeded by institutional arrangements that do not promote efficiency and good financial administration and may encourage political intervention in day-to-day management. Municipal authorities need training and capacity building to make appropriate policies for water supply and sanitation services, participate effectively in planning and mobilizing funding, choose proper institutional models for service delivery (whether through public or private companies), and regulate services (once their regulatory role is clarified). Information on institutional models that promote better management and efficiency needs to be disseminated.

The Association of Independent Municipal Water and Sewerage Service Providers (ASSEMAE) has a relatively strong training program and the size and influence needed to be an important partner in strengthening municipal capacity. In addition, organizations and training approaches that address a broad range of municipal services and interventions could be used in training and capacity building. A multisector approach to capacity building and technical assistance could promote better integration and coordination across sectors.

Options
Several measures could help to clarify the institutional, legal, and regulatory framework and improve the effectiveness of the water supply and sanitation sector:

- Creating an appropriate institutional structure at the federal level to guide policy-making and interventions in water supply and sanitation. One possible model is a national water supply and sanitation council with representatives of states, municipalities, service providers, and users, that is coordinated by the federal government through an independent executive agency.

- Linking federal funding to improvements in performance (as proposed by the PMSS program managed by the federal government, BNDES, and CEF), and applying output-based aid and other approaches to federal transfers and credit programs that promote efficiency, particularly for discretionary financing through federal budget allocations.

- Reaching agreement in Congress on key sector legislation that clarifies the roles of different levels of government on the conceding power for concession award in metropolitan areas and the institutional framework for regulating water supply and sanitation.

- Establishing federal and state programs to develop the capacity of local governments to formulate water supply and sanitation policies, participate and develop incentives to foster cooperation in investment planning and financing, collaborate with nearby municipalities, and regulate services in accord with a clarified role for municipalities.

- Using federal and state matching grants and other technical and financial support to municipalities to provide incentives for multisector interventions and to develop integrated approaches for upgrading favelas and (where appropriate) regularizing and upgrading illegal settlements.

- Legislating federal rules and mechanisms to promote appropriate forms of municipal association.

- Disseminating information, at federal and state levels, on principles and institutional models that promote efficient public delivery of services and efficient regulatory structures.

- Disseminating information by federal, state, and municipal governments on the potential advantages, limitations, and challenges of private sector participation; the conditions necessary for success; and ways to avoid mistakes, as well as studying and disseminating best practice in regulating both public and private operators.

Message 3. Introducing appropriate and flexible tools to more effectively manage urban water pollution

Water pollution from inadequate urban wastewater collection and treatment has become a major problem that undermines quality of life, health and economic development, particularly in large metropolitan areas. It has a disproportionate impact on the poor in the slums surrounding Brazil's largest cities. Adoption of environmental standards from Europe and the United States has not led to improvements in environmental quality, because the cost, affordability, and the timing of the introduction of standards were not evaluated, nor were practical approaches developed for implementing them. It was assumed that the cost of investments in sewerage and wastewater treatment would be reflected in the consumer tariffs for sanitation services, but tariffs did not rise to cover these costs, nor did sufficient outside funding become available.

Realistic federal and state programs are needed that give a high priority to mobilizing the large investment resources that are required. The federal government could best promote effective pollution control by providing investment finance or guarantees for innovative and financially viable projects. Three issues need to be addressed. First, analysis of the health and environmental benefits, and of consumer willingness-to-pay, will help to justify the cost of investments and serve as a basis for establishing public funding levels and cost recovery objectives. Second, in the absence of adequate funding, more flexible standards or a phased approach to attaining standards may be needed to avoid blocking provision of basic sanitation services to the poor. Third, a more integrated approach to urban development and slum upgrading, including an aggressive program to regularize land ownership in slums, would promote more effective pollution control and increase residents' willingness to pay for services; a major effort is required to promote cooperation among agencies and levels of government in such integrated urban development approaches.

Context

Less than 10 percent of the wastewater produced in urban areas is treated, not only causing significant environmental degradation, but also immediately and seriously reducing the quality of life and harming the health of urban populations, particularly the poor. The adoption of ambitious environmental standards has not had much effect, because the cost and affordability of the standards were not evaluated, practical approaches to implementing them were not developed, and, in any case, the necessary finance is not available to meet them. Many factors contribute to water pollution: untreated wastewater, lack of adequate drainage, poor solid waste management, erosion due to run-off, and seepage of hazardous substances. Effective management of the brown environmental agenda requires coordination of interventions that are now divided among several sectors and tiers of government.

INTEGRATED WATER POLLUTION CONTROL AND URBAN UPGRADING. An integrated approach is likely to enhance the benefits of a wide range of interventions to improve the brown environmental agenda and upgrade slums. Poor households will be more willing to contribute to the cost of sewerage if they have some security of tenure. The health benefits of effective solid waste collection and disposal complement those of water supply and sanitation, and effective solid waste management is an essential component of water pollution control. Integrated approaches to tackling urban water pollution and urban upgrading depend on cooperation among a variety of sectoral and governmental actors and require a serious look at the role of effective metropolitan government in planning and implementing basic infrastructure services for the brown environmental agenda in Brazilian cities. Models for effective metropolitan governance and for other cooperative programs need to be developed, and state and municipal authorities need training and support to undertake such programs. This requires better definition of the roles and responsibilities of state and municipal governments, a subject treated in Message 2.

HEALTH AND ENVIRONMENTAL COSTS AND BENEFITS. Analyses of the health and other quantifiable benefits of sewerage and wastewater treatment generally demonstrate that the benefits justify the cost of basic services. Nevertheless, the cost, particularly of wastewater treatment, is high. Full cost recovery may double the water bill and require tariffs that are beyond the willingness and ability to pay of many poor households. Some cost recovery, even if only symbolic, is important because it establishes the concept that sanitation services are economic goods, but it should not be a barrier to access. Partial public funding is justified by the savings in public health costs and other externalities. Systematic analysis of the potential savings in public spending on health care, and of the willingness and ability of households to pay, is therefore useful for setting initial fees and subsidy levels. Examination of policies and mechanisms for subsidizing sewerage and wastewater treatment in the United States and the European Union might identify useful models.

APPROPRIATE STANDARDS. The cost of sewerage and wastewater services can vary substantially depending on the technical standards adopted for construction and the quality of the wastewater effluent. High standards may not be affordable and could even block provision of basic services to the poor if adequate public funding is not available. Lower cost options, such as condominial sewerage combined with decentralized primary and secondary wastewater treatment plants, may not meet existing standards everywhere in Brazil. For example, the requirement that treatment plants be placed at a minimum distance from dwellings is problematic in congested settlements. To make the introduction of basic sewerage and wastewater treatment feasible, standards may need to be made more flexible or phased in gradually.

Options

Appropriate and flexible tools for more effectively managing urban water pollution could include:

- Coordinating a program at the federal level for developing urban environment infrastructure for priority metropolitan areas that incorporates the lessons of the last 10 years for improving institutional and financial models.
- Establishing federal partnerships with state and municipal governments on integrated approaches to tackling urban water pollution, the brown environmental agenda, and urban upgrading through cooperation across sectors and tiers of government, promotion of effective metropolitan governance, capacity building and technical assistance to metropolitan stakeholders, development of effective policies and strategies, and dissemination of best practice approaches.
- Developing indicators and methodologies at the federal level for valuing the health and environmental benefits of wastewater treatment, and carrying out cost-benefit analysis, as feasible.
- Continuing the *Compra de Esgoto* program and refining it as needed to promote expanded implementation.
- Encouraging ANA, CEF and BNDES to pilot other innovative project financing and guarantee systems to leverage private financing for expanding environmental infrastructure.

- Prioritizing integrated and phased brown environment agenda programs with strong slum upgrading components, and identifying and disseminating best practice approaches, at federal, state and municipal levels.
- Having the National Environment Council (CONAMA) conduct cost-benefit analyses and evaluate the affordability of river water quality standards and environmental discharge standards to determine whether they are consistent with progress in water pollution abatement. If appropriate, CONAMA would adjust standards or issue guidelines for more flexible or phased compliance, particularly in cases where this will expedite investments in new wastewater collection, transportation, treatment, and discharge capacity.

Message 4. Introducing a consistent water policy that promotes equity of access to water and sanitation services as a means of reducing poverty and promoting economic development in less developed regions

Delivering adequate water supply and sanitation services to the poor would have significant health benefits and would promote Brazil's inclusive-development agenda. Development of water infrastructure and services in the underserved regions in the North and Northeast would contribute to a more equitable society, greater social cohesion, economic development, and job creation.

More coherent sector policies and interventions would help to achieve these objectives. The relatively large fiscal resources spent by the federal government through dozens of programs and discretionary budgetary allocations could be more effectively targeted to underserved populations and regions. Coordination of the interventions of key infrastructure and service sectors at both policy and program levels, and a more integrated approach to urban planning and slum upgrading, would result in greater synergies and less waste. A transparent framework of federal investment funding policies with well defined priorities and criteria could promote efficiency and target the poor. Tariff policies could be adjusted to reduce the large distortions created by cross-subsidies and eliminate disincentives to serve the poor. Transparent subsidies could guarantee access to service for poor customers only rather than subsidizing all residential users. Alternative technologies, realistic and affordable technical standards, and innovative institutional models that incorporate strong community participation could help to bring services to poor people within a reasonable time frame.

Context

Disparities in service coverage (between rich and poor, north and south, urban and peri-urban, and small and large municipalities) and quality (from satisfactory in the large city centers to intermittent, unreliable, and unsafe in peri-urban areas, small municipalities, and rural areas) constrain progress in reducing poverty and achieving broad based economic and social development. Municipalities, particularly the very small and those in the North and Northeast, are ill-equipped to address this problem alone. Recent federal interventions do not appear to be well-targeted, with spending based on considerations other than economic criteria. Even social programs with water supply and sanitation components, such as the Ministry of Health's *Programa Alvorada*, have not been used effectively to promote economic efficiency, improve health, reduce poverty, and improve service sustainability. Poorly designed regulatory regimes often disadvantage the poor. Regional data on children with fecal-oral illnesses in Brazil show a clear correlation between hospitalization and lack of adequate water supply and sanitation services (*Conselho Nacional dos Secretários Municipais de Saúde*, cited in Abicalil 2002, Table 6). Pan-American Health Organization/World Health Organization studies have shown that water supply and sanitation services reduce the incidence of typhoid fever by at least 80 percent, tracoma and schistosomiasis by 60–70 percent, and gastrointestinal infections and diarrhea by 40-50 percent (Heller 1997, cited in Abicalil 2002, p. 8).

An integrated approach to poverty reduction. A more consistent approach to poverty reduction would promote better cooperation among different service providers. The federal government could articulate poverty reduction policies, priorities, goals, funding criteria, and guidelines that would apply to all interventions aimed at reducing poverty (funding for basic services, institutional strengthening, and so on.). Thus, for example, if eligibility criteria for subsidies for several services were the same, applications could be combined and services could be developed and managed jointly. This could lighten the management burden for small towns and encourage an integrated approach to upgrading favelas. The challenge would be to get the representatives and promoters of various services to agree on common priorities and criteria.

In planning improvements in services to the poor and overall upgrading of *favelas* and other forms of informal urban settlements, there are tradeoffs and synergies to be considered among different types of infrastructure and services. For example, constructing straight roads is usually more costly and requires reconfiguring more households than constructing roads aligned with the existing physical environment. But straight roads reduce the cost of installing piped water and sewerage networks and collecting solid waste.

Integrated planning would consider such tradeoffs and synergies within and across sectors, as well as the perceived needs of the community, and select options accordingly, developing a desirable sequence for the gradual introduction of infrastructure and services.

Integrated planning is particularly important in light of the 2001 federal law establishing the *Estatuto da Cidade*, which provides a comprehensive framework for urban development, including legalization of land titling to address informal land use. While implementation of the law is expected to remove legal impediments to charging tariffs in the affected areas, legalization will impose additional financial strains on water utilities (and other service providers) for the enormous investments in infrastructure that the legalized settlements will require.

SECTOR FINANCING POLICIES. Brazil spends more than R\$ 2 billion a year on water supply and sanitation, but these allocations do not appear to be targeted consistently to improve services for the poor or to promote more efficient service delivery. Investments of about R\$44 billion will be needed over the period 1999–2010 to meet the universal service goals for water supply and sanitation proposed by the government. Generating the required funding is not the only challenge: a more important issue is how funding is allocated and used to promote improvements in efficiency and financial viability. There are a number of sources of funding for the sector—including the federal budget and the Severance Fund (FGTS, which is administered by CEF and BNDES), BNDES investments, *Programa Alvorada* (administered by FUNASA), ANA, international lenders, and bilateral aid—but their criteria for allocating funds are not consistent. As a general rule, water utilities with the greatest need to improve performance and expand services cannot access funding. In addition, political pressure has occasionally driven hasty preparation and implementation of funding programs. Finally, many utilities that need funding do not know how to access it, because of weak institutional capacity. As a result, federal funding initiatives are less effective than they might be.

To make funding criteria more consistent, the federal government could establish financing policies that better target the poorest regions and provide incentives for efficient and sustainable delivery of services to the poor. Where feasible, output-based aid could replace or complement input subsidies (output-based aid links funding to desirable and quantifiable outputs, such as a baseline volume of water actually delivered to poor consumers or the number of new sewerage connections in low-income areas). The challenges of a policy of targeted funding are both technical and political. The technical challenge is that while output-based aid is potentially very useful, it is not always easy to design and implement. Approaches would need to be pilot tested, evaluated, and if appropriate, refined before introducing them on a large scale. An example of an output-based aid pilot is ANA's *Compra de Esgoto* program, described above. The political challenge would be to minimize allocations based purely on political interests rather than poverty reduction and economic criteria. Strong leadership would be needed to consolidate political consensus on the importance of targeting aid to the poor and to create peer pressure to conform among decisionmakers.

To ensure that water supply and sanitation companies in the poorest regions can access funding, and as part of a more integrated approach to poverty reduction, the federal government could establish a central office to facilitate the channeling of funds for a variety of interventions that benefit the poor directly without creating perverse incentives for utilities. One potential source of funds for sewerage and water consumption subsidies might be the Federal Poverty Alleviation Fund.[5]

TARIFF POLICY. In most parts of Brazil a low tariff applies to the first block of consumption or a minimum consumption fee applies to all domestic connections—and sometimes to commercial and institutional connections—which benefits many who do not need subsidies and reduces funds available to assist the poor. This approach creates a disincentive to expand service to low-income areas where consumption is very low. A better alternative would be a true social tariff (normally covering at a minimum the cost of operations and maintenance) that would apply to poor consumers only. All other users would pay at least the full cost of service for all water consumed and some or all would pay more than full cost so as to cover the deficit created by the social tariff. A second-best alternative is to allow residential users with moderate levels of consumption (levels high enough to cover basic sanitation needs) to pay a tariff that does not reflect full cost but is higher than the social tariff.

Another way to assist the poor is to provide direct subsidies to eligible households or to service providers on behalf of eligible households. While this alternative is economically most desirable, it is administratively more complicated. Brasília's current scheme is an example of this type of subsidy and is worth detailed study. The government of the Federal District pays the water utility an amount equivalent to the water and sewerage bills of poor families consuming less than 10 cubic meters a month. To be financially feasible, direct subsidies would require an allocation from the federal budget or local gov-

---

[5] Other potential sources of funds are direct subsidy programs from the federal government, such as *Bolsa Escola* and other social protection network programs.

ernment budgets. However, even if federal and local governments provided funding for direct subsidies to cover part of the cost of poor households' water and sewerage bills and other consumption needs, ongoing administration of direct subsidies for monthly consumption would require greater institutional capacity than many municipalities have.

While consumption subsidies are likely to be necessary for some time, connection subsidies could substitute for or complement consumption subsidies. In some areas connection subsidies would be sufficient to ensure that the poor get water. Thus, targeted subsidies might have to be introduced over several years, and different strategies might be needed for different services and locations, depending on local administrative capacity, the ease of identifying the poor, and the ability of the poor to pay the cost of the local service. More gradual elimination of the low tariffs for the first consumption block might also be politically more palatable.[6]

APPROPRIATE TECHNOLOGIES, STANDARDS, AND INSTITUTIONAL MODELS. A variety of technologies, institutional arrangements, and payment schemes for delivering water and sewerage services and wastewater treatment have been used in small towns, illegal settlements, and favelas, some developing spontaneously, others in a more formal manner. While piped sewers are essential in crowded urban areas, properly designed septic tank systems can be appropriate solutions in less densely populated areas. In some cases, communities have organized themselves to install, deliver, and pay for services. Evaluation of experiences with a variety of options could identify the conditions that promote success, assess the tradeoffs, and determine whether low-cost technologies are appropriate. For example, the advantages of a lower cost investment may be outweighed by higher operation and maintenance or other costs over time, or the technology may be inconsistent with other urbanization and upgrading interventions.

Technologies that are otherwise appropriate may not be consistent with stringent drinking water and environmental standards. For example, in very crowded low-income settlements, it may not be possible to place small primary wastewater treatment installa-

---

[6] For example, since about 35 percent of the population in Brazil is poor and 40–60 percent of residential customers consume within the first block of consumption, the tariff applied to that first block could be replaced with a real social tariff. The challenge is to revise the current structure and introduce a real social tariff. In addition, a progressive tariff structure could provide an incentive for more efficient use of water resources and, in the case of a foreseeable scarcity, apply tariffs on higher blocks of consumption that reflect the long-term marginal cost of providing the services.

tions as far from housing units as required by law. Noncritical standards may need to be relaxed so that high standards do not prevent the introduction of basic services.

Finally, the poor may have difficulty dealing with large formal water and sanitation institutions because of low levels of literacy, problems budgeting income and expenses, lack of access to banking services, difficulty of transportation, and similar problems. Innovative, small local institutional arrangements and outreach facilities can help to overcome these barriers for low-income households and communities. This is an area where greater coordination among service sectors could produce important synergies.

Options

Several measures could promote greater equity in access to water supply and sanitation services as a means of reducing poverty and promoting economic development in less developed regions:

- Conducting federal and state public expenditure reviews of the water supply and sanitation sector to determine how well funding has been targeted toward improving services for the poor and for regions most in need, and reviewing the weighting of water supply and sanitation coverage and quality in formulas for allocating fiscal resources to states and municipalities.

- Examining at the federal level the need for and feasibility of funding targeted sewerage connection or consumption subsidies and, if appropriate, identifying a reliable source for the subsidy including the possibility of using the Federal Poverty Alleviation Fund.

- Evaluating, at the federal level, experience in Brazil and elsewhere and disseminating information on best practices to reach the poor, including appropriate technologies and levels of service, practical methods for phasing in drinking water quality and environmental standards, institutional arrangements for outreach, and demand management and other techniques for managing consumption.

- Providing technical assistance to states and local governments to develop the capacity to access funding and to design and deliver services to the poor.

- Developing national guidelines for targeted social tariffs or connection subsidies and, as much as possible, linking them to financing programs.

- Developing, through CONAMA, affordable, simplified, and phased standards for water supply sources and wastewater effluent discharge.

- Reviewing the costs and benefits and affordability of federal drinking water quality standards and the timeline for full compliance to ensure that the standards are not a barrier to improving service to the poor.

- At the local and utility levels, establishing project planning teams to analyze and compare options for providing service in favelas and other low-income areas (installation costs, operating and maintenance costs, useful life, financial viability, practicality in different settings, environmental impacts, effect on social integration, and efficiency); for collaborating with planners in other sectors to identify potential conflicts or synergies with other interventions and services; and for developing decentralized, user-friendly institutional arrangements that facilitate access to service by the poor.
- Targeting federal and state investment funding to less developed regions and towns for well-designed and sustainable programs that directly benefit the poor. Output-based aid approaches, aimed at promoting efficiency and service to the poor, could be pilot tested and, if effective, mainstreamed.
- Piloting at local and utility levels a variety of methods for directly subsidizing services (through both connection and targeted consumption subsidies) for poor households in selected communities.

Message 5. Increasing the provision and expansion of affordable, good quality services by improving the efficiency of water and sanitation companies

Although utility tariffs are at a level that could cover operation and maintenance costs and leverage substantial investments, half of all utilities in Brazil present operational deficits that require fiscal support to avoid bankruptcy. Reliable information about the performance of service providers, a powerful tool for promoting efficiency, can be used to educate consumers, benchmark best practices, and develop yardstick competition among service providers. Substantial progress in collecting and analyzing performance indicators has been made over the last seven years through the National Water Supply and Sanitation Information System (SNIS), which makes it possible to compare the performance of state, municipal, and private service providers throughout the country.

Analysis of key benchmark comparators confirms the need for a number of policy reforms and incentives to improve performance on several key indicators. Reducing excess staff to improve productivity while preventing political interference in hiring would be key elements of a reform policy since most public utilities are heavily overstaffed and remain captive to special interests. High unaccounted-for water losses—as much as 40 percent in many utilities—compromise financial performance and waste a scarce resource; abstraction charges, pollution fees to finance river basin investments, tariffs that reflect the full cost of service, and other financial incentives are essential to reduce unaccounted-for water losses and wastage by users. Revenue collection is a serious problem in many companies, but improving collections is difficult when service is poor. Innovative funding programs that provide up-front resources in poor states and reward sustained improvements could help. Private sector participation—if well designed—could improve efficiency, but it has been controversial in Brazil and has not always been used wisely. Efforts to promote private sector participation could focus on good preparation of transactions that promise to improve the efficiency of existing services and generate investment funding for high priority projects, such as improved service for the poor and for wastewater collection and treatment.

Context

Public water supply and sanitation utilities predominate in Brazil, and most investments are funded by public resources or publicly channeled resources. State and municipal authorities tend to politicize decisionmaking in water and sewerage utilities and thus to interfere in day-to-day management. Even privately operated utilities are sometimes subject to politically motivated terms and conditions. As a result, utility management frequently lacks the autonomy to operate efficiently and either cannot be or is not held accountable for outputs and costs.

Although utility tariffs are high enough to cover operation and maintenance costs and leverage substantial investments, half the utilities in Brazil present operational deficits that require fiscal support. Collection rates and staff productivity are too low in many utilities, and water losses are too high almost everywhere. Utility managers need the incentives, autonomy, and resources to improve the efficiency of investments, management, and operations, and the efficiency gains should be allocated to improve service coverage and quality and to maintain affordable tariffs. More efficient and autonomous utilities will be better able to mobilize the internal and external investment resources needed to pursue higher levels of service coverage and quality for the poor and to expand wastewater collection and treatment.

PRODUCTIVITY. The international standard for the ratio of utility staff to connections is about 2 per 1,000—although the ideal number depends on local conditions, such the density of connections. In 2000 in Brazil, the ratio in state utilities (including utility employees and those of contracted services) varied from a respectable 1.7 per 1,000 to a high of 9.0. The average was 3.7 for state utilities, 5.8 for municipal utilities, and 6.4 for privately operated utilities (SEDU and IPEA 2001, p. 11).[7] There are a number of strategies that can be used to improve productivity. Some are relatively painless. Since political interference and special interest pressure are at the root of excess staffing, political leadership needs to be committed to rationalizing staffing and to ending the political pressure to hire excess staff. To ensure the success of any plan to improve productivity, labor representatives could be involved in designing the strategies and presenting them to affected staff.

An important first step is to determine the desirable staffing profile and pursue it steadily over several years. If services are expanding, some of the excess staff can gradually become more productive. Most excess staff are unskilled and have few alternatives in the labor market. An intensive staff training program could eliminate the problem of idleness and improve employment options. If large numbers of unskilled staff are near retirement, they could be offered early retirement with appropriate compensation. For skilled staff, a generous severance package might be sufficient to generate voluntary departures. All these

---

[7] The unexpected high staffing levels in privately operated utilities may be due to the fact that SNIS classifies local utilities owned by the public sector but operated under corporative law as private utilities.

strategies involve costs, and many would have to be funded from fiscal sources or external assistance to avoid a financial drain on already stressed utilities. In the long run these strategies can be very cost-effective—but only if there is strong political commitment to avoid politically motivated hiring.

There are several choices to be made. A vigorous effort to reduce excess staff in a short time may be politically difficult. A more restrained approach using the least controversial strategies could yield moderate improvements and is less likely to encounter political and labor resistance.[8] Contracts with private operators guaranteeing employment for several years should be carefully reconsidered. It may be more productive to postpone private sector participation until staffing levels have been rationalized. Finally, the failure to recognize skills acquired by sector staff contributes to labor market rigidities. Recognition of skills through formal training and certification would increase workers' flexibility to move among utilities or to other sectors.

UNACCOUNTED-FOR WATER. One of the most egregious indicators of inefficiency is the high level of water losses, measured as the ratio of the volume of water billed to the volume placed in the distribution system. Although several service providers in Brazil have achieved important improvements, average losses are still very high. In 2000, 3 of the 26 state companies had losses of less than 30 percent, and 7 had losses greater than 50 percent; the average was 39.4 percent. For municipal utilities, losses ranged from less than 20 percent to more than 70 percent and averaged 40.3 percent overall and 30.2 percent for privately operated utilities (SEDU and IPEA, p. 12).[9]

These high water losses not only affect the companies' financial performance, but also waste a valuable and scarce resource. Faced with the rising cost of developing new water sources, sometimes at great distances, and the growing competition for water among various users, service providers cannot afford to waste water. While water resources management policies that favor allocations for human needs exist and may seem necessary, they should not encourage waste. Bulk water pricing is an excellent example of the type of mechanism that river basin committees could establish to promote efficient use of water.

---

[8] In Brazil, where some utilities with very good productivity indicators have more outsourced employees than direct employees, a review of outsourcing strategies and results is needed. Successful cases such as CAGECE (the Ceará state water company) should be assessed to determine the most effective approaches.

[9] SNIS data classify local utilities owned by the public sector that operate under corporative law as private utilities.

REVENUE COLLECTION. Overall revenue collection losses for state utilities are about 12 percent, but this masks large variation among utilities. Of the seven utilities with losses greater than 25 percent, five are in the North, one in the Northeast, and one in the Southeast. State utilities in the Mid-West and South have consistently good collection ratios. While the data for municipal utilities present some analytical problems, a number of municipal utilities appear to have serious collection problems. Improving collection is difficult where service is unreliable, but most surveys indicate that where service is good people are willing to pay. It is almost impossible to achieve big improvements in service quality without adequate resources. One strategy is to pursue improvements that do not require costly investments while resolving administrative problems of billing and collection. Innovative funding programs that reward sustained improvements in performance would be useful, but to get the process started, substantial up-front funding would be needed for utilities in the poorer states.

PRIVATE SECTOR PARTICIPATION. Private sector participation has been promoted as a means of improving efficiency and attracting investment finance. Experience in Brazil and elsewhere shows that private sector participation can result in better performance when contracts are well prepared and awarded on the basis of transparent criteria, incorporate incentives for the private operator to achieve clearly specified performance targets while obligating the public authorities to set reasonable tariffs, and are enforced fairly and effectively. These criteria are not easy to meet, and poorly prepared and implemented private sector participation can do more harm than good.

Much of the debate over private sector participation in Brazil has been motivated by ideology rather than more neutral financial and economic considerations. Concessioning water utilities to private operators and selling water company shares have both been promoted as a means of generating fiscal resources to pay off debt or to use for other public purposes. Such approaches do not necessarily serve the interests of the water supply and sanitation sector and its customers. In developing an approach to private sector participation, funding agencies and policymakers at federal, state, and municipal levels could focus on improving efficiency and generating investment funding for high priority projects (particularly expansion and improvement of service for the poor, and wastewater collection and treatment).

Options

Several measures could expand affordable, good quality services by improving the efficiency of water supply and sanitation companies:

- Developing mechanisms for river basin committees to promote efficient use of water and reduce unaccounted-for water. Educational campaigns on the value of water resources for water company staff and the general public would create public awareness and a better appreciation of the cost of water losses.
- Linking the funding and lending decisions of federal and state funding agencies to efficiency and financial performance criteria and giving priority to well-designed programs to serve the poor and underserved regions, including establishing federal policy to direct lending by CEF and BNDES. The criteria adopted by PMSS (which include targets for selected financial indicators, staff productivity, and metering) could be adapted as a framework for evaluating utility performance.
- Introducing further discipline to the sector through regular assessments by recognized credit risk rating agencies, based on detailed criteria for their introduction.
- Eliminating minimum consumption levels, which contribute to inefficiency and poor collection performance, from tariff structures.
- Using SNIS data as a benchmarking tool for federal and local funding agencies and policymakers, as well as for service providers generally.
- Encouraging research institutions and the media to use information from SNIS and other sources to analyze and compare the performance of utilities, and publishing the results in the media to promote public awareness and create pressure for improving efficiency.
- Using service providers and professional associations to provide courses to managers and staff on strategies and methods for improving efficiency.
- Authorizing and encouraging service providers to reward managers and staff who make exceptional contributions to improving efficiency.
- Conducting research and disseminating best practices and guidelines at the federal level on private sector participation, aimed specifically at avoiding costly mistakes, capturing potential efficiency gains for consumers, and generating investment resources.
- Conducting research and disseminating best practices and guidelines at the federal level on best practices in the efficient management of publicly owned utilities.
- Collecting and analyzing data at the federal level on the cost of service in small towns and rural areas, similar to SNIS data on urban areas.

Message 6. Identifying priority investments in water resources infrastructure and improving management of existing infrastructure, as prerequisites of further investments
In 1998 and 1999, governments in Brazil spent US$3.3 billion (US$875 million of it by the federal government) on emergency drought alleviation in the Northeast for an affected population of some 10 million. Natural cycles of drought could be addressed more effectively through better management of water resources, including sufficient storage and distribution capacity to carry the region through dry cycles. Irrigated agriculture is an intense, employment-generating activity, but Brazil exploits barely 15 percent of its irrigation potential. Expansion of water supply in many cities of Brazil faces increasing costs since nearby water sources have already been used by utilities or are polluted. Utilities tend to expand supply rather than make optimal use of existing capacity by reducing water system losses (which exceed 25 percent in most cities) and using metering and price signals to encourage users to reduce waste. The 2001 energy crisis reduced anticipated GDP by an estimated 2 percent; Brazil has developed only 42 percent of its hydropower potential.

Funding for two complementary types of investment could help to minimize the escalating cost of droughts and take fuller advantage of water resources: rehabilitating infrastructure and developing institutional and financial arrangements that promote sustainable operation and maintenance, and constructing new hydraulic infrastructure based on sound social, environmental, economic, financial, and institutional criteria. Community-managed infrastructure could be encouraged where feasible, but the large amount of funding needed and current government budgetary constraints suggest the need to foster public-private partnerships.

Context

A strategy to minimize the escalating cost of droughts and take fuller advantage of water resources must address two issues. One is weak administration, operation, and maintenance of water infrastructure and the associated deterioration and poor financial performance of existing systems. The other is a tendency to allocate funding to new hydraulic infrastructure on the basis of political criteria and short-term expediency rather than sound social, environmental, economic, financial, and institutional criteria. Community-managed infrastructure should be encouraged wherever feasible, but the amount of funding required and current government budgetary constraints suggest the need to foster public-private partnerships. In the semi-arid region of the country, infrastructure development should be contingent and part of a broader drought management strategy that includes other aspects such as watershed management, early alert systems, insurance mechanisms, contingency plans, and better use of economic instruments for managing water demand. Such a strategy could also encompass aspects related to the income and livelihood of the poor and vulnerable groups during periods of extreme drought.

Making better use of existing infrastructure. The tendency of federal and state governments to emphasize new investments rather than proper administration, operation, and maintenance of existing systems—common in water resources management around the world—has resulted in infrastructure degradation, poor service delivery, and stranded investments.

The framework and measures necessary to achieve better utilization of existing infrastructure are both widely agreed and familiar to policymakers in Brazil. A movement to create accountability by transferring management responsibility to local users has been under way since the 1990s. The river basin approach, the creation of irrigation districts under federally funded infrastructure programs, the transformation of water supply and sanitation service providers into more autonomous and financially viable companies, and the growing use of private sector participation are among the measures that have been used. But this effort remains incomplete.

The critical issues are autonomy, financial viability, and accountability of institutions and service providers. The cost of administration, operation, and maintenance is small relative to the initial investment in infrastructure, but failure to allocate adequate resources for this purpose can rapidly undermine the benefits of an investment. Service providers that depend entirely on revenues from user charges to cover the full cost of efficient service have a strong incentive to operate and maintain their infrastructure properly and ensure continuity of supply—otherwise users would not be willing to pay.

Collective infrastructure for irrigation, navigation, flood control, and related purposes presents a more complex problem. The beneficiaries are more diverse, and it is difficult to charge directly for the services. In addition, this infrastructure is often more redistributive than productive in character, and the promoters are often more interested in the profits and political benefits that accrue during construction than in the longer term rewards of mobilizing water as a factor of production. Projects that serve an identifiable group of commercial farmers or other users, with a clear interest in better services and the ability to exert pressure on the institutions responsible for administration, operation, and maintenance, are more likely to be operated efficiently.

In 2001 an estimated 100,000 hectares of land in public irrigation projects was not in production in the Northeast. The reasons extend well beyond water infrastructure and include issues of credit, insurance, guarantees, market development, strategic planning, extension support, and off-farm technical assistance for marketing, commercialization, financing, and business planning.

The most reliable way of ensuring better use of existing infrastructure is to require that the institution that builds the infrastructure share significantly in the risks associated with future operations. It is also important to ring-fence each system with its own accounts and to require periodic audits, so that financial performance is transparent and resources cannot be transferred to new investments at the expense of the performance of existing systems. However, practical experience with public services suggests that separating responsibility for investments from responsibility for operations (while a second-best solution) is often the only way to create incentives for adequate administration, operation, and maintenance—particularly when regulation is not well established and investments are influenced by political considerations.

Despite growing acceptance for the principle of charging water users, there is still strong resistance to implementing cost recovery, especially for small and medium-size farmers. Many users consider access to free water an established right, even though the services are unreliable or the quantity of water delivered is insufficient. Many studies demonstrate that current arrangements tend to benefit the large water users who are not required to pay for water but can exert more pressure on the operator and thus receive better service than smaller users. These large users would thus stand to gain relatively less from cost recovery and other arrangements that promote better management, although even they are likely to be better off. All users are understandably reluctant to support changes that introduce or increase charges unless they are confident that better services and higher incomes will result. Thus building confidence and credibility is essential.

DEFINING PRIORITIES FOR NEW INFRASTRUCTURE. The pressure to fund new investment projects is strong and often results in projects that are large and highly visible; are designed to meet too many needs and are thus highly complex and difficult to manage; include components that lack justification on their own; are based on unrealistically high estimated rates of return; do not take risks into account; do not incorporate recovery mechanisms to cover the full cost or even just the costs of administration, operation, and maintenance; and are based almost entirely on engineering and investment studies, with inadequate attention to sustainability.

The politically and institutionally contentious São Francisco interbasin water transfer project, as currently conceived, reflects many of these features and is aimed at meeting a multiplicity of needs. The value of urban water demand is critical to the claim that the project is economically viable, but a more comprehensive study of options for meeting these demands would probably identify lower cost options that rely either on local sources or on better management of water currently used for irrigation.

To address these issues, ANA has been asked to certify whether projects proposed for federal assistance contain reasonable provisions to ensure adequate funding and management capacity for administration, operation, and maintenance after completion. Recognizing the problem is a significant step forward, but it is not clear how effective this scrutiny can be, and it places a huge responsibility on ANA. Unfortunately, plans put forward by states or other project sponsors often have limited credibility.

Even so, difficulties familiar to any capital-intensive project remain. Since the effects of failure to operate and maintain infrastructure are not immediately visible, potential or actual water users may argue that zero or minimal charges will encourage rapid take-up of newly available resources. Public bodies responsible for the construction or regulation of the infrastructure will probably waive charges or set them at a level well below the long-run cost of administration, operation, and maintenance. This makes economic sense in the short term provided charges are increased as demand builds up. But it is common for low initial charges to be converted to quasi-property right: users believe they should never have to pay realistic charges for their water.

There are two, possibly irreconcilable, perspectives on the nature and design of water management projects: the need to meet many competing demands and objectives, and extensive evidence that clear and focused objectives are essential to effectiveness. The first perspective tends to result in overly complex projects, shelves of unused studies, or protracted delays as the basics are reexamined in an effort to improve the final outcome—a recipe for an unsatisfactory portfolio of investments. Serious choices have to be made among competing demands and objectives because both water and financial resources are limited.

Options

Several measures could help to identify priority investments in water resources infrastructure and improve management of existing infrastructure:

- Transferring water infrastructure to financially autonomous, accountable organizations once construction is complete.
- Appointing independent regulators to set water charges (whether covering full costs or only administration, operation, and maintenance costs), and resolving disputes over the coverage and quality of service.

- Recognizing the undeniable need for new water infrastructure to promote economic growth and poverty alleviation.
- Selecting and prioritizing public investments in water infrastructure on sound social, environmental, economic, financial and institutional criteria; targeting the poor; and incorporating wide social participation, especially by project beneficiaries and other affected people.
- Before implementing new irrigation infrastructure, developing a comprehensive irrigation strategy to rehabilitate and optimize the return on viable existing systems.
- Planning and implementing hydraulic infrastructure projects based on systematic assessments of the returns from existing systems.
- Using infrastructure funds with clearly defined criteria for project design, selection, and implementation to impose economic and financial discipline on investments.
- Encouraging private investment in the development and administration, operation, and maintenance of water infrastructure within a publicly established long-term development strategy supported by an adequate legal and regulatory framework, without crowding out community-managed infrastructure and beneficiary participation in design and management of water systems.
- Developing public sector initiatives to promote a more collaborative public-private partnership approach. These should include assessing options based on upstream hydrologic, economic, environmental, and social conditions; using public funding for components that produce public benefits (such as flood protection); assisting the private sector to manage foreign exchange risk (when long-term fixed rate local currency financing is not available, and when short-term financing does not match the economic life of the assets); blending public and private sector funding to lower the overall cost of capital; using more output-based aid, disbursing funds on the basis of actual services delivered; and creating adequate legal and regulatory frameworks at national, state, and local levels.

References

World Bank projects

- Ceara Integrated Water Resources Management Project - PROGERIRH *(Programa de Gerenciamento e Integração dos Recursos Hídricos do Estado do Ceará)*. US$ 136 million. Approved on January 6, 2000.
- PROSANEAR II Technical Assistance Project *(Projeto de Assistência Técnica em Saneamento para População de Baixa Renda)*. US$ 30.3 million. Approved on January 6, 2000.
- Federal Water Resources Management Project – PROÁGUA *(Programa de Desenvolvimento Sustentável de Recursos Hídricos para o Semi-Árido Brasileiro)*. US$ 198 million. Approved on April 2, 1998.
- Second Water Sector Modernization Project – PMSS II *(Projeto de Modernização do Setor Saneamento)*. US$ 150 million. Approved on March 5, 1998.
- Bahia Water Resources Management Project - PGRH *(Projeto de Gerenciamento dos Recursos Hídricos do Estado da Bahia)*. US$ 51 million. Approved on September 11, 1997.
- Ceará Urban Development and Water Resources Management Project – PROURB *(Projeto de Desenvolvimento Urbano e Gestão de Recursos Hídricos do Ceará)*. US$ 140 million. Approved on September 6, 1994.
- Espirito Santo Water and Coastal Pollution Management Project *(Projeto de Despoluição dos Ecossistemas Litorâneos do Espírito Santo)*. US$ 100 million. Approved on June 28, 1994.
- São Paulo, Paraná and Federal Water Quality and Pollution Control Project *(Projeto de Qualidade da Água e Controle da Poluição - PQA/São Paulo, PQA/Paraná and PQA/Federal)*. US$ 239.8 million. Approved on July 2, 1992.

World Bank reports

This chapter summarizes the content of the following World Bank reports. Those, in turn, draw heavily from a wide range of literature on the subject from experts in Brazil and beyond, which are referenced in the mentioned Bank reports.

Asad, M., L.G.T. Azevedo, K.E. Kemper, and L.D. Simpson. 1999. Management of Water Resources: Bulk Water Pricing in Brazil. Technical Paper 432. Washington, D.C.: World Bank.

Azevedo, L.G.T., and L. D. Simpson. 1995. Brazil – Management of Water Resources. LA1 Economic Notes 4. Washington, D.C.: World Bank.

Brook, P.J., and S.M. Smith, eds. 2001. Contracting for Public Services: Output-Based Aid and Its Applications. Washington, D.C.: World Bank.

World Bank.1999. "Brazil: Regulations for Better Water and Sewerage Services." Report No. 19568-BR. World Bank, Washington, D.C.

———. 2000. "Brazil: Private Participation in the Water Sector: Case Studies, Lessons, and Future Options." Report No. 19896-BR. World Bank, Washington, D.C.

———. 2001a. Bridging Troubled Waters – Assessing the Water Resources Strategy Since 1993. Washington, D.C.: World Bank, Operations Evaluation Department.

———. 2001b. "Implementation Completion Report for the Jaiba Irrigation Project (Loan 3013-BR)." World Bank, Washington, D.C.

———. 2002. "Water Resources Sector Strategy—Strategic Directions for World Bank Engagement." World Bank, Washington, D.C.

Other references

Abicalil, Marcos Thadeu. 2002. "A Atual Situação dos Serviços de Água e Esgotos no Brasil." Unpublished document, Brasília.

ANA (Agência Nacional de Águas). 2002. Programa Despoluição de Bacias Hidrográficas: PRODES, Manual de Operações. Brasília.

Banco do Nordeste. 2001. Políticas e Estratégias para um Novo Modelo de Irrigação. Banco do Nordeste, Fortaleza.

Bittencourt, A.G. and R.G. Araújo 2002. "A Agenda Ambiental Marrom e o Setor de Abastecimento de Água e Esgotamento Sanitário no Brasil: Os Problemas do Atendimento ás Populações Urbanas Pobres e do Controle da Poluição Hídrica." Unpublished document, Brasília.

Dinar, A. 2000. "Political Economy of Water Pricing Reforms." In A. Dinar, ed., The Political Economy of Water Pricing Reforms. Oxford University Press, New York.

IBGE. *(Instituto Brasileiro de Geografia e Estatistica)*. 2000. *Censos Demográfico.* Brasília.

Lobato, F. J. 2002. *"Elementos para uma Estratégia de Gerenciamento dos Recursos Hídricos no Brasil – Áreas de Cooperação com o Banco Mundial."* Unpublished document, Brasília.

OECD (Organization for Economic Cooperation and Development). 1998. Water Management: Performance and Challenges in OECD Countries. OECD, Paris.

Porto, M. 2002. "Water Resources, Water Supply, and Sanitation in Metropolitan São Paulo." Unpublished document, Brasília.

SEDU *(Secretaria Especial de Desenvolvimento Urbano da Presidência da República)* and IPEA *(Instituto de Pesquisa Econômica Aplicada).* 2001. *Diagnóstico dos Serviços de Água e Esgotos – 2000. Sistema Nacional de Informações sobre Saneamento.* SEDU/IPEA, Brasília.

PART IV

12
Macroeconomic Stability

12

Macroeconomic Stability

Introduction

It is widely recognized today in Brazil that macroeconomic stability is essential for equitable socio-economic progress. Policies for stability, while complex and tough, have increasing support and acceptance. This chapter considers the vital underpinning that macroeconomic stability provides to all other actions, and the striking progress to date. It also sets out main messages ahead.

Macroeconomic stabilization, 1994–98 and 1999–present

Brazil is a very different country today to what it was 10 years ago. There have been far-reaching and impressive achievements in terms of policy and institutional reform. Over the decade, Brazil gradually inserted itself more fully into the global economy, and achieved notable monetary stabilization.

In the first macroeconomic stabilization phase, during 1994–98, Brazil brought inflation under control, bringing it down from 2,500 percent a year in 1994, to less than 4 percent in 1998. A crawling exchange rate band served as the nominal anchor and price controls were lifted, establishing a more rational and efficient economic environment. Privatizations and banking reforms were carried out simultaneously. Trade policy reform stimulated productivity growth and reduced Brazil's economic isolation, improving the investment climate and attracting new foreign direct investment flows, which rose from less than US$1.5 billion in 1994 to almost US$30 billion in 1998.

The draft of this chapter was completed by Santiago Herrera, with contributions from Fernando Blanco, in November 2002. The analyses and suggestions presented here are based on the international technical experience of the World Bank and are presented as a contribution to the debate and formulation of public policies.

Price stabilization stimulated growth and favored poverty reduction. From 1994 to 1997, GDP growth exceeded 3 percent a year, after four years of near zero growth. Inflation had mainly hurt the poor. In 1993, one year before stabilization, the proportion of people below the poverty line was 43 percent, while in 1995, this proportion had fallen to less than 34 percent.

With inflation under control but without the structural changes still needed to keep fiscal accounts in check, public finances took an unsustainable path. Fiscal deficits coupled with tight monetary policy to sterilize capital inflows caused interest rates and interest payments to rise. Public debt soared from 29 percent to almost 42 percent of GDP. On the external front, the use of the exchange rate as a nominal anchor, together with abundant capital flows, led to the appreciation of the currency in real terms. With the currency appreciation and the availability of external credit, domestic savings fell and external debt rose from US$152.5 billions in 1994 to US$224 billion in 1998.

The international crisis of 1997–98, combined with Brazil's fiscal and external vulnerabilities, resulted in a sharp slowdown in GDP growth to less than 1 percent in 1998/99 interrupting the poverty reduction trend. In January 1999, Brazil abandoned the crawling exchange rate band, allowing the currency to float, and the real depreciated by more than 35 percent in real terms.

In the second phase of stabilization, from 1999 onward, Brazil altered three key policies. It adopted an inflation-targeting framework for monetary management, it allowed the exchange rate to float freely, and it established ambitious targets for the primary fiscal balance. This switch established a consistent, credible macroeconomic framework that provided the basis for maintaining stability and creating an appropriate environment for private investment.

Increasingly ambitious primary fiscal balance targets were achieved mainly through tax revenue increases. This stabilized the public debt ratio and improved the primary balance by about 4 percent of GDP. With the devaluation of January 1999, Brazil reduced its current account deficit from US$33.4 billion in 1998 to US$21.0 in 2001 and adopted an inflation targeting regime that kept inflation under control. Brazil's external debt declined from a peak of $224 billion in 1998 to $210 billion at the end of 2001. The trade balance registered a surplus, with most of the adjustment coming from a slowdown in imports following the exchange rate adjustment and weaker than anticipated growth. The 2002 $12 billion trade balance is the highest since 1993. If sustained, it would imply a stable future path for Brazil's external debt. The change in policies made the economy more resilient to shocks and enhanced growth prospects, differentiating Brazil from many other emerging economies. While capital was flowing out of the region after the 1998 international capital markets crisis, it continued to flow into Brazil after its adjustment. The bright performance of 2000 offered a glimpse of the hoped-for benefits from adjustment. With growth of 4.5 percent and falling unemployment and poverty, Brazil finally seemed to have moved to a sustainable path for public and external debt, and higher growth.

However, the shocks of 2001 and 2002 exposed Brazil's remaining vulnerabilities. The shocks included a domestic energy crisis, a slowing world economy, greater risk aversion in markets following the September 11 terrorist attacks in the United States, Argentina's debt default, and market jitters ahead of Brazil's presidential elections. These events led to reduced access to international capital, depreciation of the Real, higher inflation, interruption in the declining trend in domestic interest rates, and lower growth. Despite Brazil's fiscal adjustment, the shocks of 2001 and 2002 led to a sharp rise in the debt to GDP ratio, renewing fears about the sustainability of Brazil's public debt. And despite the reduction in external financing requirements, the sudden drying up of capital flows cast doubt on Brazil's external solvency.

Brazil has shown many times before that it is able to make the right policy choices. Today, it has a better institutional framework and a much more transparent public sector. And the experience of other countries with high public debt burdens shows that Brazil has been moving in the right direction since 1999. These examples and the lessons of Brazil's own history could guide the country in setting its policy agenda for the years ahead.

Several characteristics of the Brazilian economy in mid-2002 are especially relevant here:

- The ability to buffer shocks is by far one of the most important achievements of Brazilian policymaking in the last years. By creating a positive and predictable climate for investment, stability provides the basis for future growth and poverty reduction. The policy changes since 1999 have made the economy better able to absorb shocks and have enhanced growth prospects.

- To stabilize public debt, Brazil accumulated significant primary fiscal surpluses. New legislation has institutionalized fiscal responsibility at all levels of government, and this is likely to be sustained. Adjustment has been achieved primarily through increased tax revenues, now quite high by international standards at 34 percent of GDP. Since taxes are not well designed, they exert substantial drag on the economy. Expenditure cuts are made more difficult by earmarking and constitutionally mandated expenditures, which severely compress discretionary spending.

- Public debt, mostly domestic, has increased to more than 55 percent of GDP, despite the 1999–2002 fiscal effort. The currency depreciation and, to some extent, higher domestic interest rates, are the main reason. With a high share of public debt indexed to exchange rates or short-term interest rates, a currency depreciation or interest-rate increase has an immediate impact on public sector financial liabilities. And that leads to continuous revisions of public sector solvency calculations by private agents.

- The Brazilian Central Bank has skillfully managed the transition from the fixed to the flexible exchange rate regime through the introduction of an inflation targeting system. It is mostly thanks to that effort that inflation remained subdued following the currency devaluations of 1999, 2001, and 2002. Nonetheless, the credibility of monetary policy is limited by the composition of the public debt and the lack of institutional guarantees that create an appropriate environment for Central Bank action and accountability.

- Brazil's corporate and financial sectors are sound. The public sector has absorbed most recent economic shocks. Low financial leverage gives the aggregate corporate sector a robust balance sheet, though this is partly a consequence of crowding out by public debt and inefficiencies in the financial system. The high cost of capital exerts a major drag on investment.

- With a 10 percent share of exports in GDP, Brazil remains a relatively closed economy, even compared with other large countries. Exports have responded to the depreciation, but the response has been weakened by some deterioration of export prices and the collapse of exports to Argentina, which constituted 10 percent of Brazil's exports. Until very recently, the improvement in the current account balance has come from a substantial compression of imports.

- Over half of Brazil's external debt is owed by the private sector. While total external debt is modest, at 40 percent of GDP, the ratio of external debt service to exports is high because of Brazil's low trade. In absolute terms, external debt has been decreasing, while the ratio of external debt to GDP has increased owing to the depreciation of the currency. Brazil has little external short-term debt, and virtually all of it is owed by the private sector. External debt is sustainable under a range of reasonable assumptions but requires large rollovers (US$30 billion in 2002), which create exchange rate vulnerability in periods of low international liquidity.

- Foreign direct investment, which has financed more than 75 percent of the current account deficit since 1998, has been gradually declining, along with the current account deficit. It could decline even faster if global conditions deteriorate. Foreign direct investment has also been largely domestic market- rather than export-oriented, with big flows into privatized or deregulated services such as telecommunications and financial services.

A glance at macroeconomic policy options

Views differ about the relative policy emphasis given to fiscal performance, interest rates, growth policies, and the trade balance. Positive reinforcement between all four elements means that they form what can be either a virtuous circle of growth and stability or a vicious circle of stagnation and crisis. At the risk of oversimplification, different entry points in the circle lead to different prescriptions or emphases. The premises behind each prescription vary, and following one approach to the exclusion of the others has weaknesses.

A higher primary surplus increases investor confidence, reduces the domestic and external cost of capital, and increases investment and growth. Higher growth and revenues and lower interest payments make the arithmetic of debt sustainability easier to satisfy. The weakness of this strategy lies in the uncertainty of the growth response. In an institutional environment insufficiently supportive of private sector activity (high taxes, regulatory uncertainties, inefficient financial sector), the risk is of a recession-led low-growth trap that renders debt sustainability harder, not easier.

An easing of monetary policy by the Central Bank lowers lending rates, spurring both growth and fiscal performance. Such interest-rate cuts "in a vacuum" have been discussed widely in Brazil. But easing the policy rate (Selic) raises inflation, and at present there is little space for monetary easing without jeopardizing inflation targets and the credibility of the Central Bank. Furthermore, there is not a tight link between the overnight policy rate and longer term market rates, which are determined by investors' willingness to lend. The implicit assumption of multiple equilibria that drives proposals of rate cuts—with investors willing to lend at lower interest rates because of the lower perceived default risk accompanying these lower rates—is no more than an assumption. Taking it as the basis for policy would risk undermining the current framework of macroeconomic management, and credibility, that has taken time to build.

Direct policies to promote growth (improvements in the investment climate, increased directed credit and subsidies) may generate revenues that would relax fiscal constraints, allowing interest rates to fall and higher growth to continue. But the impact of such growth policies is variable and comes with a considerable time lag. Policies implying higher spending (such as directed credit) can backfire if worsening fiscal performance undermines investor confidence. Fiscally, neutral growth policies could aid stability provided they do not lead to inefficient resource allocation, but they cannot be relied on for revenue dividends in the short run.

Policies that target an improvement of the trade balance, such as export promotion and import substitution incentives, are often presumed to reduce the need for external finance and thus its cost (through the risk premium). Through the lower interest rates and possibly an appreciated exchange rate (assuming no capital outflows), fiscal balance may also improve under this assumption. However, restrictive trade policies may well cause higher spreads (risk premia), since the policies would signal to markets a regime shift toward protectionism. And while better export performance is clearly desirable in itself, the weak response of Brazilian exports to the recent depreciation of the real in the presence of a global downturn shows how heavily such improvements depend on accompanying external conditions. Moreover, restricting imports to improve the trade balance may be self-defeating if that damages productivity (and then exports) in the medium term, through reduced competition and higher input costs. There is also the risk of reciprocal restrictions on Brazilian exports.

Thus the appropriate response would address more than one entry point in this cycle, emphasizing the value of the primary fiscal surplus, the risk inherent in the debt composition, and the importance of productivity over active trade policy in building exports. Recognizing the interdependence of external and fiscal vulnerabilities and the influence of each on overall vulnerability, it is important to consider which variables have the greatest effect and which lie most within the government's control.

Continuing with current policy, Brazil has a chance at lasting stability, but it is not guaranteed. The mainstay of the status quo is assurance that the sound management and credible framework that have come together since 1999 will continue to apply. Even with such assurance, however, vulnerability can persist, given public and external debt levels. With further action, Brazil can avoid the unsettling episodes and low-growth scenarios of 2001 and 2002.

For this reason this note suggests six messages with suggestions that could help establish a virtuous circle of stability and growth.

Message 1. Maintaining macroeconomic stability as a prerequisite for sustainable long-run growth and poverty reduction

Growth is crucial for the sustainability of public debt and the external account and as an engine for poverty reduction. The long-run adverse effects of volatility in inflation, exchange rates, and asset prices in reducing investment and slowing growth are well documented. Macroeconomic policies and variables—such as inflation, government size, credit to the private sector and trade openness—affect growth directly. They also affect poverty levels. In Brazil, changes in growth have been the single most important factor explaining variations in poverty. Studies for Brazil and for large sets of countries have found a negative association between inflation and growth and between government size and growth and a positive association between credit to the private sector and growth and degree of trade openness and growth.

There is also evidence in the short run of a strong correlation between uncertainty and poverty indicators. High-frequency data (from the Monthly Employment Survey) reveal a high correlation between the poverty gap and sovereign spreads. This result derives from the close association between capital flows and economic activity.

Context

The macroeconomic volatility in Brazil during the 1980s and early 1990s and high inflation had a negative impact on growth and, thereby, on poverty indicators. Volatility affects growth mainly through its effect on investment. Research shows that volatility of inflation, the exchange rate, and asset prices negatively affect the rate of capital formation and hence future growth rates.

Another direct way in which macroeconomic volatility affects poverty is through the adverse effect on income distribution. People in higher income deciles, with more access to a variety of financial instruments, are better able to protect themselves from inflation than people in the lowest income deciles, who hold a higher proportion of their assets in money. In a study of the macroeconomic determinants of poverty in Brazil during 1981-96, Amadeo and Neri (2000) found that periods of accelerating inflation coincided with periods of lower levels of income and greater income inequality, effects that reinforce the negative impact of macroeconomic volatility on poverty.

There is evidence that volatility in financial markets affects poverty indicators even in the short run (figure 1), an association explained by the high correlation between capital flows and economic activity. Capital tends to flow in (and spreads to decrease) as economic activity accelerates, increasing wages and labor income and reducing poverty indicators.

While research has shown that macroeconomic policy affects poverty by influencing growth in the long run, it also affects poverty indicators directly. One of the most robust findings (Thomas 2002) is a short-run positive relationship between an increase in the interest rate and an increase in poverty. Inflation is also associated with rising poverty gaps, with an impact similar to that of interest rates. This would imply that, for reducing poverty, controlling inflation is as important as lowering real interest rates. Brazilian evidence (Thomas 2002) also shows that fiscal balances are an important explanatory variable, with poverty gaps rising as deficits increase, primarily due to the impact of this variable on output (negative) and interest rates (positive).

Since macroeconomic volatility adversely affects growth, stability is a precondition for sustainable growth and poverty reduction. Stability creates a predictable environment in which households and firms can make long-run plans. This boosts investment and improves its allocation, leading to more growth, employment, and poverty reduction. Since the poor are hurt most by inflation, poverty alleviation policies should be supported by a coherent price stabilization strategy.

Macroeconomic stabilization has been the most important economic achievement of recent years. Continuing with current sound macroeconomic policy, Brazil has a chance of lasting stability, but it is not guaranteed. Even so, vulnerability will persist for some time, given public and external debt levels.

Figure 1. Sovereign spreads and poverty gap in Brazil

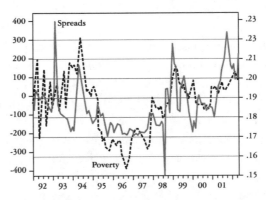

*Sovereign spreads are deviations from Latin average and
Poverty is P1 poverty gap indicator.
Source: Thomas (2002) and Herrera (2002)

On the domestic front persistently high real interest rates are a threat to sustainable fiscal policy and economic growth, while on the external side sluggish export growth and large external financing requirements are a potential source of instability. Though the currency may not be overvalued, large external financing requirements expose the economy to external capital market shocks, giving rise to a currency risk premium. This exposure affects domestic interest rates and exchange rate behavior, influencing perceptions of public sector solvency given the degree of indexation of government obligations to the dollar or to short run policy interest rates.

Hence, public debt sustainability and external sustainability are closely related, as domestic interest rates are linked to currency risk premia, country risk levels, and inflation expectations. These linkages create concerns about public debt and external sustainability, exacerbating volatility and uncertainty, dampening growth prospects, and increasing poverty.

Options
Preserving a stable macroeconomic environment is an essential condition for sustainable growth and poverty reduction. As stability is threatened by fiscal and external vulnerabilities, addressing them constitutes the most important challenge of macroeconomic policy over the next years.

On the fiscal front, Brazil would need to deepen its past efforts, and improve the quality of adjustment to permanently reduce fiscal vulnerability. Once this happens, external vulnerability and currency risk premia will decrease. On the external side, the long run answer to reducing external vulnerability is raising productivity to improve the international competitiveness of exports.

Message 2. Increasing the primary surplus above that achieved in recent years to provide insurance against future shocks and guarantee fiscal sustainability

Given that the primary balance is the main variable under direct government control among the variables affecting the path of debt ratios, the primary balance could act as insurance against future, unpredictable shocks. An adequate primary surplus would facilitate attaining a virtuous circle of debt reduction, lower interest rates, and higher growth

Brazil's real interest rates are unusually high. Examination of the determinants of real interest rates shows that short-term rates are explained by monetary policy that responds appropriately to inflation expectations and exchange rates, while the longer term rates depend on considerations of public sector solvency. That means that interest rates are influenced by the size and composition of public debt.

The main variables that affect public debt dynamics are the primary balance, growth, interest rates, and exchange rates. Simulations of public debt paths show that the debt to GDP ratio stabilizes and falls under current fiscal policies. In reality, however, growth, interest rates, and exchange rates are subject to unpredictable shocks. When scenarios incorporate this source of uncertainty, further action would be needed to guarantee a declining public debt path.

Uncertainty also stems from the imperfect information that agents have on the true commitment and ability of the sovereign to pay its debt obligations. To diminish the uncertainty, the primary balance is used as a signaling tool that creates a separating equilibrium that allows distinguishing dependable governments and ends up lowering the cost of debt for the dependable government. In the past, Brazil used its primary balance in the face of adverse external shocks to signal its commitment to honor debt obligations.

Context

In a strong fiscal adjustment effort over the past three years, the Brazilian government abandoned the unsustainable path that public accounts had followed in the early 1990s. The primary surplus rose from –0.2 percent of GDP in 1998 to 3.25 percent in 1999, 3.5 percent in 2000, 3.7 percent in 2001, and it is expected that it will reach 4% in 2002. Brazil's strong response to an adverse external environment differentiated it from other emerging economies, including Argentina (figure 2).

Figure 2. Public debt and primary balances in Argentina and Brazil

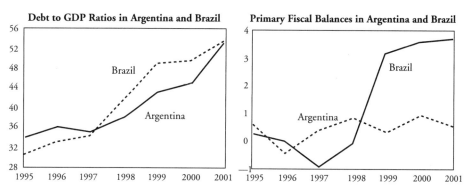

Nonetheless, with the shocks experienced from 1999 to 2002, some domestic and others external, public debt rose from 49 percent of GDP in 1998 to more than 55 percent in 2002. While at first sight Brazil's public debt sustainability problem lies more with the high real interest rate it faces than with the size of its debt (figure 3), the two are related. Although the short-term interest rate (empirically) reacts to inflation expectations and exchange rates, longer-term rates (empirically) depend on considerations of public sector solvency.

Figure 3. Net public debt and interest payments in a sample of countries

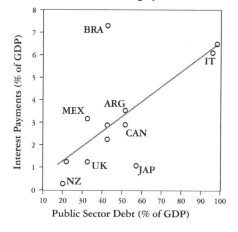

By raising the primary balance targets, Brazil could insure itself against unpredictable shocks. The main source of uncertainty arises from shocks to the variables that influence debt sustainability dynamics—exchange rates, interest rates, and growth in output. Assuming that these variables evolve under the most likely scenarios, Brazilian public debt is sustainable and will reverse its increasing trend in the near future. However, once uncertainty arising from shocks to any of the determinants is incorporated, a higher primary balance would be desirable to increase the likelihood of a declining debt ratio over time.

Uncertainty about the magnitudes of these shocks gives rise to a positive relationship between sovereign spreads and the debt ratio and a negative relationship between spreads and the primary balance: a higher debt ratio reduces the likelihood of debt sustainability for any given shock to exchange rates or interest rates. Similarly, a higher primary balance will increase the probability of debt sustainability, and hence lower the cost of external finance (sovereign spreads), for any given shock.

Another source of uncertainty that gives rise to a relationship between the cost of external finance and the public debt ratio and primary balances is agents' determination of the government's commitment to pay its debt obligations. This uncertainty allows weak governments to issue debt and pretend to be dependable governments. Two types of equilibria are generated in this setting. One is a pooling equilibrium, generally prevailing at low interest rates and small debt ratios, in which both governments (dependable and weak) initially run primary deficits, and weak governments default when debt matures. The other is a separating equilibrium, prevailing when debt ratios are large and the cost of borrowing is high, in which dependable governments generate a primary surplus to signal their true type while weak governments default because the costs of mimicking the actions of dependable governments are too high. The primary balance is used as a signaling tool that creates a separating equilibrium that ends up lowering the cost of debt for the dependable government.

Uncertainty, thus generates a positive relationship between primary balances and risk ratings and a negative association between debt stocks and risk ratings. This relationship implies that as debt increases, sovereign spreads will rise. Similarly, if the primary balance rises, spreads will fall. Brazilian historical data support this type of behavior, which is similar to that of European countries that were able to lower their public debt burden, but contrary to that of Argentina, which was unable to generate the required primary balances as its debt indicators rose

Based on this relationship, an improvement of the fiscal stance would imply falling spreads, and vice versa, given Brazil's historically high debt ratio. Also, based on the historical data on this relationship, this model can be used to estimate the long run primary balance consistent with a given level of spreads and a given debt ratio, for illustration purposes (table 1). These results confirm that for Brazil to attain investment grade spreads, there need to be adequate levels in the primary structural balance.

Table 1. Long-run primary balance: illustrations with target sovereign spreads at different debt to GDP ratios (basis points)

Debt ratio (Percent GDP)	Sovereign spreads				
	500	600	700	800	900
45	4.5	3.9	3.4	2.9	2.3
50	5.2	4.7	4.2	3.6	3.1
55	6.0	5.5	5.0	4.4	3.9
60	6.8	6.3	5.8	5.2	4.7

Source: Herrera (2002)

Options

As the sustainability of Brazil's public debt depends on the volatility of domestic interest rates, exchange rates, and domestic output, shocks such as were experienced in 2001/02 can push the economy off a sustainable path, resulting in higher spreads and making the situation worse. The primary surplus can act as an insurance against these random shocks that affect the debt to GDP ratio.

With the primary balance seen as a signaling mechanism and insurance against volatility, a higher surplus sets in motion a virtuous circle of debt reduction and growth. Brazil could opt for raising the primary fiscal surplus through structural reforms to increase the quality and flexibility of public spending (see Policy Note on fiscal sustainability). Such an increase in the primary surplus should be seen as an investment: tomorrow's returns in the form of stability and growth will repay today's sacrifice.

Taking the route of structural reform would seem to need constitutional fiscal reforms. Indeed, with underlying structural reforms for flexibility and efficiency, further cuts likely to compromise essential services can be avoided. These reforms, desirable in their own right on equity and efficiency grounds, would decisively increase the chances of stability, even under adverse circumstances.

Message 3. Achieving a more flexible spending structure and a simpler tax structure so that fiscal efforts can rely more on expenditure cuts than on tax increases to ensure long-term fiscal sustainability

Given expenditure rigidity, the adjustment on the federal fiscal accounts between 1999 and 2002 was based on revenue increases. But there is a limit for an adjustment based on revenue increases. International experience shows that fiscal adjustments that have permanent effects rely more on current expenditure cuts than on revenue-raising policies or capital spending cuts. As expenditures begin to follow the revenue increases, fiscal adjustment efforts are weakened, and the only effect is an increase in government size. Evidence also shows that most capital expenditure cuts sacrifice the delivery of public goods, which eventually generates public pressure to reverse the cut. Cuts in current expenditure, however, generally lead to better functioning labor markets, enhancing overall productivity. To diminish the rigid expenditure component, it is important to act on the main source of fiscal imbalance, the special social security regime for government employees. Other measures to reduce earmarking of revenues and reduce mandated spending are important to regain more flexibility for fiscal policy. One attractive option would be to change the basis for transfers to states and municipalities from a percentage of certain revenues to a percentage of total primary spending. This would lead to a systematic fiscal burden sharing across government levels and increase the federal government's control over total expenditures. Extension and strengthening of the Fiscal Stabilization Fund (DRU) would also be important.

Context

As Brazil enters its fifth year of rigorous fiscal effort, it confronts two fundamental issues: the continuity and the quality of the current fiscal adjustment. International evidence suggests that, to be lasting, fiscal adjustment needs to rely more on cuts in current spending than on revenue increases or cuts in capital spending. Revenue-based adjustments create pressures to spend, while capital spending cuts sacrifice public investments, and social pressure eventually tends to reverse them. Equally important, the quality of fiscal adjustment depends on its effects on economic efficiency and growth prospects, the current level of economic activity, and the welfare of different groups within society. The quality of adjustment is low when it reduces investments in public goods and services (because of a positive correlation between public investment and economic growth), relies on raising taxes that produce higher deadweight losses, fails to protect social expenditures that benefit mainly less advantaged groups, or accentuates economic cycles, particularly during recessions.

Because of rigidity, constitutionally mandated expenditure requirements, fiscal adjustment by the federal government has depended heavily on revenue increases and, to a lesser extent, cuts in capital expenditure, rather than on broader and more extensive current expenditure cuts, and non-financial expenditures rose (table 2). Patterns were similar at state and local levels. Total federal revenue grew by 19 percent or 3.6 percent of GDP, with tax revenue increases of 23 percent or 3 percent of GDP. There was no increase in revenue in the social security system, however. Brazil's tax burden has risen from about 25 percent of GDP in the early 1990s to 34 percent in 2001. These taxes, especially the increasing share of indirect cascading taxes and the high tax rates applied to a narrow base, generate distortions and hamper growth. Thus, further increases are undesirable because of the efficiency losses they promote.

Expenditure also grew, but only half as much as revenues, at 10 percent or 1.8 percent of GDP. As in 1995–98, capital expenditures remained stable while current expenditures accounted for most of the increase—largely social security benefits and intergovernmental transfers; personnel expenditures remained stable. Thus, the composition of expenditures continued to deteriorate, with the share of capital expenditures declining and that of current transfers increasing.

At the federal level, the high degree of expenditure rigidity stems from three factors: the job tenure stability rules for public servants, which make reductions in payroll expenditures very difficult; the increasing share of social security and social assistance benefits in non-financial expenditures; and the constitutional earmarking of an important part of federal tax revenues. An indicator of the increasing rigidity of non-financial federal expenditure since the 1988 Constitution is the rising share of personnel costs, social security and assistance transfers, and intergovernmental transfers, which rose from 55 percent of non-financial expenditures in 1986 to almost 80 percent in 2001. In 1986 the share of investment and other current expenditures was about 51 percent of total non-financial expenditures; today it is less than 20 percent (figure 4).

Figure 4. Brazil: non-financial expenditure composition

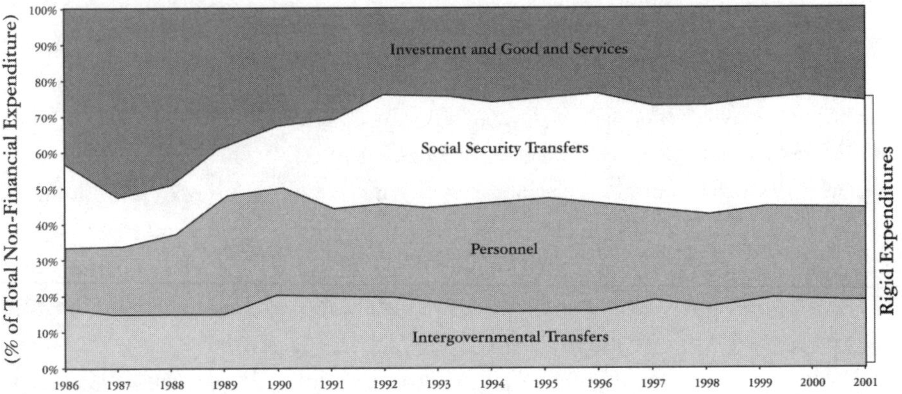

Source: STN and Blanco Herrera 2002

Table 2. Federal government primary surplus changes, 1995–2001

Categories			Variations 95/98 -			
	1995 - 1998	1999 - 2001	(B) - (C)	Percentual	Decomp. I	Decomp. II
	(A)	(B)		Variation		
I Total Revenue	18.6	22.2	3.6	19.2	206	100
Treasury Revenue	13.6	17.1	3.5	25.4	199	96
TaxRevenue	12.0	14.8	2.8	23.1	160	77
Other Treasury Revenues	1.6	2.3	0.7	42.8	39	19
Social Security Revenue	5.1	5.2	0.1	1.1	3	2
II Total Expenditure	18.4	20.2	1.8	10.0	-106	51
Personnel and Social Contributions	5.2	5.2	0.1	1.0	-3	1
Social Security Benefits	5.4	6.2	0.8	14.1	-44	21
Other Current and Capital Expenditures	4.8	5.0	0.3	6.0	-16	8
Subsidies	0.2	0.3	0.1	32.7	-4	2
FAT	0.6	0.5	0.0	-0.9	0	0
Other Goods and Services and Investment	4.0	4.2	0.2	5.6	-13	6
Intergovernmental Transfers	3.0	3.8	0.7	24.2	-42	21
Primary Balance (I - II)	0.3	2.0	1.7	595.4	100	

Source: Secretary of the Treasury

Similar rigidities constrain state and local governments. Since the benefits conferred by the 1988 Constitution apply to the overall public sector, the share of personnel and social security expenditures increased at state and local levels as well, reaching more than 70 percent of primary expenditures.

The social security system is the main source of imbalance and expenditure rigidity, generating deficits that have to be covered by the Treasury (rising from 3 percent of GDP in 1995 to 5.2 percent in 2001). The other main sources of expenditure rigidity are constitutional earmarkings, required minimum levels of spending in social areas, and mandatory transfers of fixed shares of the main federal taxes to states and municipalities, which are partly earmarked for education spending. The Health Amendment of 2000 requires that the government maintain a minimum ratio of health expenditures to GDP.

Brazilian fiscal policy is procyclical in nature: in the short run, output increases are associated with a decline in primary balances while output contractions are associated with rising primary balances. This pattern accentuates the troughs in the business cycle, particularly during recessions, generating surpluses following a financing crisis. During output expansions, fiscal policy tends to be less restrictive, increasing credibility problems in times of trouble. (Gavin et.al., 1996)

Brazil's fiscal policies are procyclical for a variety of reasons: a) Limited access to international credit markets force the government to abandon a tax-smoothing approach and to tighten fiscal policy in the face of shocks; b) Taxes are heavily dependent on cyclically sensitive income; c) Increased spending in good times prevents the generation of large primary surpluses (increase savings), to use (dis-save) during recessions .

Options

The Brazilian tax burden is already high, so continuing and strengthening fiscal adjustment requires cuts in spending. To increase the primary surplus, structural measures are needed that will eliminate spending rigidities. One place to start is with the structural imbalance of the social security system for public sector employees. Short-run measures could include taxing beneficiaries of the RJU employment regime and increasing contributions to the pension program.[1] A medium-term step would be to break the link

---

[1] Further reform of the social security system for public sector workers has already been attempted but was ruled unconstitutional by the Supreme Court. This implies that a Constitutional amendment would be needed in order to address structural imbalances.

between pension levels and wage increases of active workers, indexing pensions to inflation rather than to the minimum wage. Reducing earmarking is also important for recovering expenditure flexibility at the federal level.

Other measures to reduce earmarking of revenues and reduce mandated spending are critical to regain more flexibility for fiscal policy. One attractive option would be to change the basis for transfers to states and municipalities from a percentage of certain tax revenues to a percentage of total primary spending. This would lead to a systematic fiscal burden sharing across government levels and increase the federal government's control over total expenditures

For greater flexibility, extending DRU beyond 2003 would make it possible to exclude 20 percent of net tax revenues from earmarking. This is a second-best measure that would be needed until earmarking and mandated expenditures have been reduced to manageable levels. To indicate orders of magnitude, increasing the DRU to 30 percent could help raise government savings by 1.1 percent of GDP. Moreover, the DRU could be modified as to set this "retention rate" on the gross tax revenues, which would imply additional federal savings at the expense of transfers to states and municipalities. This modification could be justified given federal government's need to distribute the adjustment burden across different government levels. Many state and municipal expenditures are on vital social services, however, so care would be needed to assure that gains in efficiency and spending quality accompany such measures.

Improving the quality of fiscal adjustment means increasing the government's capacity to support growth of the economy through an adequate and efficient provision of public goods and services. The composition of public expenditure would need to be rebalanced by increasing capital expenditures and decreasing current expenditures. Social security system reform would again be a priority. On the revenue side, the quality of fiscal adjustment could be improved by simplifying the tax system, eliminating the distortionary cumulative taxes, and broadening the tax base.

As Brazil deals with pressing adjustment issues, it benefits from the Fiscal Responsibility Law that corrects a previous bias toward fiscal deficits and helps guarantee fiscal solvency, as well as other measures to effectively extend fiscal controls to the subnational level. The law is a product of broad political consensus. As Brazil progresses along the road of fiscal management, it could consider modifying the Fiscal Responsibility Law along the lines of the Chilean structural balance rule, which imposes an explicit commitment to keep a 1 percent structural surplus each year. In Brazil, the Fiscal Responsibility Law could be modified to define the structural balance in primary terms, thus excluding interest payments, which may be the most procyclical component of the fiscal balance.

Chile's case can serve as an indicative comparator. Chile's net debt is 15 percent of GDP. The implicit primary structural balance surplus oscillates around 2 percent of GDP. Since the fiscal rule should be adapted to consider differences in the debt level and for differences in the volatility of the variables that determine debt paths, an appropriate structural primary balance target for Brazil would likely be higher than the currently observed primary surplus. If considered appropriate, such a policy change should be implemented gradually and in a way that does not imply and cannot be interpreted as a relaxation of the fiscal stance.[2] To avoid such misinterpretation, the IMF methodology (Hagemann, 1999) could be adopted as it was in Chile to enhance credibility of fiscal policy management.

---

[2] To avoid the possibility of market sentiment reversals, the structural balance could be calibrated in such a way that the observed surplus is not below the 2002 level, even in a slowdown scenario.

Message 4. Managing public debt to moderate rollover risk and mitigate the fiscal dominance problem that arises from the short maturity and indexation of domestic public debt to the Selic rate or the exchange rate

Brazil has made significant progress in public debt management, particularly in extending debt maturity and duration. But much of the debt still remains of short duration and maturity. With the relatively short maturity of the debt, indexation to the Selic rate can constrain the role of monetary policy, since the public could believe that the Central Bank will not raise interest rates to adequate levels because of the effect on governments debt indicators. As a result, anti-inflationary policy can lose credibility, and agents could doubt the Central Bank's willingness to let the currency float freely when public debt is indexed to the dollar. The composition of public debt could be altered to enhance anti-inflationary policies by shifting away from dollar indexation. Debt management based on price-indexed debt could enhance the credibility of monetary policy. However, the maximum desirable share of this type of securities in the total portfolio is limited. The first-best solution for building credibility is an autonomous Central Bank, complemented by sound macroeconomic management. Without adequate credibility, the slope of the yield curve would make the cost of maturity extension prohibitive.

Context

There have been very positive fiscal outcomes in recent years. Yet, Brazil's net federal debt has tripled in the past eight years. Initially, the cause was loose fiscal policy (until 1998) and recognition of hidden liabilities, bail-out operations for states' bond debt, restructuring and privatization of state banks (PROES), the private financial system support program (PROER), and the restructuring of federal banks (Caixa Econômica Federal and Banco do Brasil), which account for nearly a third of the increase in federal debt since 1994. The floating of the real in 1999 and its substantial depreciation have led to further increases in public debt (about 20 percent). However, the main factor has been the extremely high real interest rate, which averaged 16 percent during this period, explaining over half the increase in public debt. By mid-2002, Brazil's net public debt reached more than 60 percent of GDP, and gross public debt (including contingent liabilities and net debt of public non-financial firms) is estimated at around 80 percent of GDP.

Brazilian public debt has three key features: First, it is mostly domestic, with the ratio of domestic debt to external debt at 4:1; second, and despite the above-mentioned progress, it has relatively short maturity and duration; and third, it is strongly biased towards indexed debt. These three features interact and induce significant vulnerability of the economy. In fact, market perceptions and debt structures influence each other in both directions. Perceived vulnerabilities and external shocks have made it more difficult to improve the debt structure, which in turn has contributed to the persistence of vulnerabilities.

A key feature of Brazil's domestic public debt is the recent evolution toward indexed instruments. Until 1997, when the debt to GDP ratio was relatively stable, fixed-rate securities accounted for more than 40 percent of domestic debt. After 1998, when the debt ratio increased significantly, the share of fixed-rate securities fell to single digits, except for 2000. This negative association between debt size and share of fixed-rate instruments in total debt has also been documented for other highly indebted countries such as Belgium, Ireland, and Italy during the 1970s and 1980s. As government debt rises, the temptation to devalue debt (through surprise inflation shocks, for example) increases and, as investors anticipate this government behavior, they demand higher returns. To keep financial costs under control, the issuer may reduce maturities to compensate for the increased cost. In Brazil, however, maturities have lengthened at the cost of biasing towards indexed securities. However, indexation reduces the effective duration, especially when instruments are indexed to overnight interest rates.

By increasing public debt, raising interest rates to control inflation increases the perceived risk of public sector insolvency. Higher interest rates may not be thought to be sustainable, therefore, and inflationary expectations may not adjust, reducing the effect of monetary policy. Both a lack of credibility and a weak link between short- and long-term rates render inflation less sensitive to monetary policy. The same principles reduce the credibility of exchange rate policy.

Nonetheless, it is important to distinguish short-term interest rate and exchange rate indexation from inflation indexation. Bonds indexed to short-term interest rates and exchange rates account for some 80 percent of domestic debt, while fixed instruments and bonds indexed to inflation account for 20 percent.

A country without enough credibility in its monetary institutions and policies may find it difficult to issue long-term debt at fixed nominal interest rates in domestic currency. Indexing to inflation is a good temporary solution for reducing currency, rollover, and interest rate risks. A major advantage of indexing to inflation is that it sharply reduces the government's incentive to create inflationary surprises, and thus enhances the credibility of monetary policies. Since the high premium for potential inflationary surprises is eliminated, lower nominal interest rates are possible.

Extending maturity, indexing more debt to prices, and issuing more fixed coupon instruments would all serve the objective of breaking the link between debt and monetary policy established by the short maturity and indexation to the policy interest rate (Selic), and thus free monetary policy from "fiscal dominance". These changes generally imply higher financing costs, initially at least, while the credibility of a declining future path of inflation and interest rates is built up (and validated by sound fiscal management).

Lengthening debt maturity (both the average life of debt and its duration) is important for two reasons: first, to reduce exposure to short-term interest rate fluctuations and second to reduce the rollover risk. Although related, the two risks are different. A long duration reduces the sensitivity of the cost of debt service to fluctuations in policy rates. It thus eliminates an important constraint on monetary policy. Long-dated debt allows the Treasury to spread out rollovers. It thus reduces the risk of a funding crisis (the risk of going to the market to roll over a large volume of bonds at a time when interest rates are particularly high and the market particularly thin).

In fact, the government has attempted to reduce debt indexation to the Selic and the exchange rate and expressed this in its annual borrowing plans. However, the macroeconomic situation of 2001 and 2002 turned the implementation of this strategy difficult.

Thus, it is with inflationary expectations under control and expected interest rates declining that the cost of extending the duration of domestic debt can be accomodated, given the slope of the yield curve on government obligations. Interest rate expectations depend on the government's capacity to convey to investors its commitment to service debt. The clearest such signal is, as mentioned, a sustained primary fiscal surplus.

Options

Lengthening the average duration of Brazilian debt will be a gradual process. One possibility, some suggest, is a bond with a put option, which gives the creditor the option of redeeming the bond before the maturity date. Borrowers offer put options as a means of lowering spreads in the belief that spreads will decline over time, or at least remain stable, so that the put would not be exercised. Bonds carrying a put option allow the government to lengthen the maturity of the debt without paying the premium that the market is asking. Such premiums often arise not so much from different assessments by the government and the market of the outlook for trend inflation, but rather from the incentive the government has—and that market participants anticipate—to raise the inflation rate ex-post in order to reduce the real cost of debt service. Put options eliminate the inflation incentive and thus the market's anticipation of such an incentive.

Lengthening the maturity and duration of public debt requires building a liquid market for securities at all maturities. Liquidity in the secondary market for government paper (for delivery) is much lower than in the repo and derivatives markets (table 3). These markets, which are not subject to reserve requirements or the tax on financial transactions (CPMF), have drained much of the liquidity from the cash securities markets (and from secondary markets for delivery). Additionally, repos, futures, and swaps were not considered fixed-income securities until very recently, and so were subject to income or capital gains taxes quarterly rather than monthly, as is the case for a cash fixed-income instrument. These factors inhibit the development of a secondary market for government debt.

Indexation is a substitute for credibility, albeit a very imperfect one. In Brazil, most indexation is to the Selic or the exchange rate. Indexation to the Selic rate can render monetary policy less effective, while indexation to the exchange rate can lead to concerns about floating.

The credibility of monetary policy can be enhanced by issuing price-indexed debt. However, there are practical limitations to the use of this type of securities. Most countries limit the share of this type of instrument to 20 percent of total debt. Thus the first-best solution for credibility is an operationally autonomous Central Bank complemented by sound macroeconomic management. With credibility, the slope of the yield curve will make the cost of extending maturity acceptable.

Table 3. Liquidity of Brazilian markets

AVERAGE TURNOVER BY TYPE OF MARKET	US$ Billions	Shared in Total
Selic: Government Security Turnover	75.17	68.6%
Repos	64.09	58.5%
Secondary Market (For Delivery)	10.31	9.4%
BMFb / (derivatives)	21.07	19.2%
BMF DI Futures * /	10.49	9.6%
BMF Swaps	0.40	0.4%
IBOVESPA futures	0.36	0.3%
CETIP: All privately issued Securities	11.00	10.0%
REPOs with Private Securities	4.80	4.4%
Swaps registered with CETIP	1.01	0.9%
CDIs	2.17	2.0%
CDBs	0.10	0.1%
Debentures over SND	0.07	0.1%
Clearing de Cambio and SISBacen: Dollars Spot * /	2.00	1.8%
BOVESPA for Equities	0.29	0.3%
Sisbex	0.08	0.1%
Grand Total	109.60	100.0%

Daily average turnover in December of 2001 unless indicated.

* / Daily average in May 2002, converted from Reais at an exchange rate of 2.4

Source: Glaessner (2002)

The switch to more long-term fixed rate instruments and price-indexed securities could entail higher financial costs that are worth considering in order to reduce rollover risk. This has to be a gradual process given the endogeneity involved, in particular in the size of the debt, real interest rates, the slope of the yield curve, and portfolio composition. The gradual de-indexation of debt can be attained by initially issuing nominal fixed-coupon debt of short maturity and price-indexed debt of longer maturities. The sequencing of actions would begin with the most exogenous variables, notably the primary fiscal balance.

Bonds with put options are useful when markets have different expectations (too pessimistic) compared to the fundamental outlook of the authorities. They should be considered as a step in the direction of lengthening maturity of public debt, as their primary role is to gradually make the investor more comfortable with longer maturities. This instrument would be used only during a transition, as the insurance provided by the put option would no longer be necessary once the authorities' program and objectives are fully credible. This instrument, however, has several disadvantages, namely the difficulty in pricing the option, which may lead to high market premiums (IMF, 2002), though empirical evidence on this topic is scant, and this limitation applies to any complex financial instrument. Additionally, bonds with put options have the disadvantage, that in volatile or adverse situations the puts will be exercised, implying a strong pro-cyclical nature of the payments implicit with this type of liability.

Alternative instruments, such as those currently used by the authorities, or a fixed rate bond with an interest rate swap, are examples of other instruments that could be used in the proactive debt management strategy to lengthen the maturity of public debt. The need for gradual de-indexation of public debt to short term policy rates and the exchange rate, and the need for lengthening maturity and duration are important. This process should be supported by structural reforms outlined in different sections of this report.

In addition to sound macroeconomic management (primary surplus, credibility in anti-inflationary policy), the desired change in portfolio composition will require a market development strategy. Brazil has begun this institution-building process of building capital markets by strengthening Treasury operations, formulating and disseminating annual borrowing plans, developing the auctions markets, and introducing limited repo markets.

Message 5. Enhancing the effectiveness and credibility of monetary policy to lower interest rates

Given the four to one ratio of domestic public debt to external debt, there are at least three clear linkages between monetary and financial policy and debt management. The first link is through the yield curve, which the Central Bank may alter in multiple ways. Unless inflation expectations are under control, however, the term spreads will be high and the maturity structure cannot be lengthened. A major policy achievement in Brazil in the past decade has been the eradication of inflation. Institutionalizing Central Bank autonomy and accountability and reducing reserve requirements and directed lending, would help to consolidate that course and lead, eventually, to lower interest rates. These measures would need to be supported by adequate fiscal policy.

The second link between financial sector policy and public debt management comes about because financial intermediaries are the main holders of public securities, and operations are concentrated in a few players. This concentration may give market power to buyers, who may collude to set prices. It amplifies rollover risk, as the agents are all from the same sector and are affected by the same shocks. And financial intermediaries have bargaining power as a result of the potential for the transmission of shocks to the rest of the economy, which may lead them to assume greater risks and call for support if they run into trouble.

A third link between public debt management and financial sector policy is established by public banks. The public sector absorbs the credit risk of public banks, including their capital requirements and occasional recapitalization requirements, which add to public sector debt. Support to public banks in the past has accounted for approximately 20 percent of domestic net public debt.

Context

With a ratio of domestic to foreign debt of four to one, there is an important link between public debt management and the functioning of domestic financial and capital markets. The market's efficiency, from a macroeconomic perspective, depends heavily on the Central Bank's actions and on private agents' expectations about these actions. The link between public debt management and monetary management is amplified by the indexation of short maturity securities to the policy interest rate. The efficiency in national resource mobilization will play a major role in determining the cost to the government and to society of the government's domestic financing requirements.

Since 1999 Brazil has established a consistent, credible macroeconomic framework. By any standard, Brazil negotiated its way through the 1999 and 2001 crisis with extraordinary ease and speed. What allowed this quick recovery was the triple regime switch to a floating exchange rate system, inflation targeting that provided a clear rule for monetary management, and strict fiscal policy.

The Central Bank has been extremely skilled in inflation targeting, keeping inflation and inflation expectations stable through two large devaluations in 1999 and 2001. However, the Central Bank does not enjoy the institutional guarantees that protect the independence of other central banks. This lack of institutional safeguards could be a factor explaining the high level of policy rates needed to hold inflation at the target rates.

While a consistent policymaking framework lowered average interest rates during 1999–2001, interest rates nonetheless remain high. Identifying the determinants of interest rates is thus important for a better understanding of the constraints of monetary policy. Two factors explain the level of interest rates in Brazil: monetary policy and the way it affects and reacts to inflation and exchange rate expectations and term premia. Short term rates are basically determined by the reaction to inflation and exchange rate expectations, while longer term rates are influenced by term premia.

Brazilian data show that, since 1999 the short-run policy rate has moved one for one with inflation expectations, providing a clear rule of central bank behavior well known to market participants. The longer term rates (one or two years) depend on the term premium, which reveals market concerns about the sustainability of public debt. This premium is highly correlated with sovereign spreads in international capital markets. Hence, from the stable relations among sovereign spreads, the primary fiscal balance, and the level of public debt described above, it may be inferred that the term premium is closely related to the public debt level and the primary balance. Empirical evidence shows that real interest rates are sensitive to all these variables.

In 2001, with short-term rates averaging 18 percent in nominal terms, lending rates in Brazil averaged 48 percent for business loans and 78 percent for personal loans. With the inflation rate (measured by the Consumer Price Index) below 8 percent, it is clear that most long-term lending is unsustainable at these rates. What explains spreads of almost 50 percentage points between short-term policy rates and lending rates?

The main causes are taxes and the net banking margin (table 4). Taxing financial intermediation is attractive because of the low administrative costs and difficulty of evasion. A
variety of tax and quasi-fiscal instruments affect financial institutions and financial intermediation in Brazil. Some are explicit taxes included in the tax code, such as the income
tax, social contribution on profits tax (CSLL), the tax on financial operations (IOF), taxes
on gross revenues (PIS and COFINS) and the tax on financial transactions (CPMF). The
chief quasi-fiscal instruments, not included as taxes in the budget, are high, unremunerated reserve requirements and directed credit at subsidized rates.

Table 4. Decomposition of the spread between lending and short-term rates

Item	Percentage points (nominal rates)
Term premium	5 - 8
Taxes	12 - 13
Credit risk provisioning	6 - 7
Administrative costs	7 - 8
Net banking margin	14 - 15
Total	40 - 50

*Source: World Bank. Brazil Country Economic Memorandum 2002. Calculations based on BCB (2001) and methodology
described in the text.*

The net banking margin is the result of several factors. One is the high level of reserve
requirements and forced investments (directed credit), which are an implicit tax on financial intermediation. The use of reserve requirements as a monetary policy tool to control
liquidity reduces the cost of debt financing for the government but increases bank lending spreads and hence lending rates for private sector firms, which are forced to seek foreign financing, increasing external vulnerability and impeding development of the financial sector. Another contributor to high margins could be operational performance of
public banks. The costs of nonperforming loans and the market concentration also contribute to high net banking margins.

As a result, credit as a percentage of GDP is low—and falling. Total credit went from
58 percent of GDP in 1993 to around 30 percent between 1994 and 2000, after the Real
Plan stopped inflation, in part through very high reserve requirements and interest rates.

In a comparative study of financial intermediation, Brazil's liquid liabilities as a share
of GDP, at 28 percent in 1997, were lower than the average for Latin America and well
below the average of 58 percent for upper middle-income countries and 76 percent for
OECD countries (Beck and others 1999). Private credit as a share of GDP, at 30 percent,

was equal to the average for Latin America but well below the 50 percent average for upper-middle-income countries and 89 percent for OECD countries. The study also found that Brazil has a low level of efficiency in financial intermediation with a high annual net interest margin (7.8 percent compared with averages of 5.5 percent in Latin America and 2.7 percent in OECD countries) and high overhead costs (7.3 percent compared to 5.8 in Latin America and 2.7 percent on OECD countries). Weak enforceability of creditor claims was found to be a major cause.

The risk diversification strategy of public debt is related to the financial sector for two reasons. First, because the holders of public debt are mostly financial intermediaries, whose operations are concentrated among very few players. Three banks and seven mutual funds hold well over half of government debt. This concentration may give market power to buyers who may collude to set prices. It amplifies rollover risk, as the agents are from the same sector and are affected by the same shocks. Financial intermediaries have a bargaining power derived from the potential for transmission of shocks to the rest of the economy that may lead them to assume greater risks and then seek support in times of trouble. Given that interest payments on domestic debt constitute a wealth redistribution from taxpayers to domestic bondholders, bond holding concentration implies a regressive expenditure structure.[3]

The government has attempted to enhance competitiveness in the financial sector and de-concentrate the public bond markets. An example of these efforts is the Treasury Direct Program, created in January 2002 to sell public bond over the internet, to small investors, facilitating broader access to this market.

The second link with financial structure comes when, through the actions of public banks, the public sector absorbs the credit risk of private sector economic agents. This leads to higher public debt, whether through repeated capital injections or direct subsidies. Improving the role of public banks and enhancing their risk monitoring effectiveness will reduce public exposure to private sector risk and in turn reduce spreads in the banking sector.

---

[3] Interest payments on domestic debt are about 6 percent of GDP, and if payments are proportional to bond holdings, then 10 institutions would be direct beneficiaries of 3 percent of GDP.

The interactions between Brazil's monetary policy, financial structure, and debt composition also increase external vulnerability. Countries with shallower financial systems relative to their public debt pay higher costs to finance this debt (figure 5). And the link from monetary policy to debt encourages the use of reserve requirements as a monetary tool, since this reduces government financing costs at the expense of higher banking spreads for the private sector. This interaction increases the gains from acting on all three fronts simultaneously: diversifying government debt issuance toward fixed coupons, reducing concentration in the banking sector, and limiting the role of public banks.

Figure 5. Ratio of public debt to private sector domestic credit and implicit cost of the public debt in a sample of countries - 2001

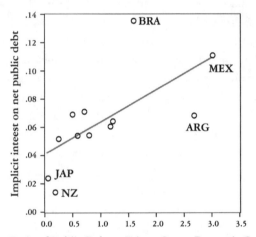

Ratio of Public Debt to Private Sector Domestic Credit

Source: own calculations BR_CEM

Options

A major policy achievement in the past decade has been the eradication of inflation. Two further steps would help to consolidate that course and reduce interest rates: institutionalizing the Central Bank mandate by law, making Central Bank autonomy and accountability clear, and reducing reserve requirements, and directed lending requirements. Both measures would also reduce bank margins and, together with further privatization of the banking sector, increase efficiency and help Brazil achieve the strong financial intermediation that is crucial for growth.

Also contributing to lending spreads are credit risk and bank provisioning. The government is working to reduce the conditions contributing to credit risk. The Central Bank has modernized the payment system and introduced a Credit Risk Data Center, making available on its Web site standardized information on credit operations—including interest rates for each type of operation, degree of arrears, and average operation term differentiated by financial institution.

Beyond these improvements, Brazil's banking system would benefit from more competition. Concentration of the banking sector continued to increase in 2001, and without enhancement of market contestability this could imply growing monopolistic rents and interest rates higher than would prevail in a competitive market.

Message 6. Keeping external sustainability, which requires a substantially positive trade balance, achievable with prudent fiscal and other policies to reduce anti-export bias and promote productivity gains

Recent export performance and trade balance adjustment provide grounds for optimism. With trade surpluses above US$ 12 billion, indicators of external indebtedness are expected to improve. Even with reduced estimated gross external financing requirements (current account plus medium-and long-term debt amortization) of more than US$ 35 billion for 2002 and 2003, Brazil remains exposed to risk of interruption in capital flows.

Export growth is the long-run mechanism for overcoming external vulnerability. The export response to the liberalization of the 1990s was lackluster, however, in part due to a decline in export prices. During the 1990s exports in nominal US dollars grew by only 5.8 percent annually while export volume indices have grown by 50 percent since 1996. Brazil's share of world exports today is less than half what it was 50 years ago. The low degree of openness is the major obstacle to an export-based reduction in external vulnerability. Import restrictions lead to losses in productivity growth, both through higher input costs and through reduced competition from abroad. Higher import penetration in Brazilian industries in the 1990s is statistically associated with significantly higher total factor productivity growth.

Reforms to improve the investment climate and boost productivity could encourage exports without incurring a fiscal cost. While uncontroversial in general terms, implementation requires the political willingness to confront entrenched interests. Policies would include tax reforms to reduce price distortions and anti-export bias, regulatory and administrative reforms to reduce the bureaucratic burden on the private sector, labor market reforms to reduce distortions, reforms to deepen financial markets and improve their efficiency, and judicial reforms to increase regulatory certainty and enforcement of private contracts.

Context

Despite the exchange rate devaluations of 1999 and 2001, Brazil's external adjustment was slower than its fiscal adjustment. The trade balance went from a deficit of US$6.7 billion to a surplus of US$2.7 billion, in 2001 and a projected US$ 12 billion surplus for 2002. With falls in the current account deficit and in medium- and long-term debt amortizations, external financing needs declined. The current account deficit fell to less than 2% of GDP in 2002, thanks to the currency depreciation and relatively low growth performance. The depreciation initially had only a modest effect on the value of exports, despite the low pass-through of the devaluation (30 percent) to inflation (8 percent), in part because export prices are so low—they are currently at their lowest level since the 1980s (figure 6). However, in 2002 the delayed effect of 1999-2001-depreciation jointly with further 2002-devaluation stimulated a growth in exports of 15%.

Figure 6. Brazilian Export Prices, 1980-2002
1996=100

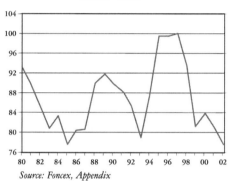

Source: Foncex, Appendix

The external debt burden, defined as the excess of the real interest rate over the growth rate applied to the external debt, is low relative to historical levels for Brazil (table 5). Yet, the implied trade surplus required is higher than that achieved until 2001. At 1.4 percent of GDP, the debt burden implies the need for an annual trade surplus of US$7 billion to stabilize external indebtedness. The 2001 trade surplus of US$2.7 billion was the first post-Real Plan surplus, and estimates for 2002 are for a surplus of about US$12 billion, enough to stabilize external indebtedness if permanently maintained. The evolution of the trade balance since the 1990s (figure 7) indicates that external adjustment is under way, especially since 1999. This fact creates room for optimism.

Table 5. External debt burden, 1970–2001

Percent of GDP	1970	1983	1991	2001[a]	2001[b]
Argentina	0.9	3.6	1.5	2.9	3.6
Brazil	0.0	3.0	1.6	1.4	1.4
Chile	1.9	3.4	0.9	2.3	0.0
Colombia	0.8	1.4	1.9	1.8	2.1
Ecuador	0.0	3.5	6.7	2.7	7.7
Mexico	0.3	3.5	1.8	1.0	0.0
Peru	1.9	5.0	3.2	2.9	2.5
Uruguay	0.8	4.9	2.3	2.5	0.7
Venezuela	0.5	3.3	3.8	1.4	2.1

a. Uniform 8 percent discount rate
b. Country-specific discount rates based on spreads.
Source: World Bank. Brazil Country Economic Memorandum 2002

Figure 7. Monthly trade balance in real terms
($US million deflated by U.S. CPI 1982-84=100)

Although large payments are due in 2003, the amortization profile of external debt is more favorable now than at the end of 1998, when almost half of external obligations matured within two years. By the end of 2001 the ratio had fallen to less than a third. Short-term debt to reserves also fell from 120 percent to 100 percent in the same period.

External vulnerability has been attenuated by the financing of most of public sector borrowing requirements domestically (table 6). This has boosted the cost of domestic financing and increased the propensity of large private sector firms to use external financing. Most amortizations due in the next four years are with the private sector. The predominance of private sector debt reduces external vulnerability and eases renegotiation in case of liquidity constraints (renegotiation may include debt rollovers or debt-equity swaps). Additionally, Brazilian external debt contains a relatively small proportion of financial sector obligations. This limits the propagation of international liquidity shocks to the rest of the economy and thus systemic risk (and with it the risk of the need for a generalized bailout, as happened in the Republic of Korean in 1997).

These developments in the external accounts are very favorable. Yet, gross external financing requirements (current account plus medium- and long-term debt amortization) remain high at US$ 38 billion for 2002 (table 6). An interruption in capital flows (as occurred in July–August 2002) can have a major impact on the exchange rate, with an adverse impact on long-term solvency. [4]

Table 6. Cross and net external financing requerements (billions of US dollars)

Item	1998	1999	2000	2001	2002	2003
1. Gross financing requirements	70.6	83.0	68.3	59.8	37.2	35.0
Current account deficit	33.4	25.4	24.6	23.2	8.0	7.0
Medium - and long-term amortization	37.2	57.6	43.6	36.5	29.2	28.0
2. Foreign direct investment	28.9	28.6	32.8	22.6	16.0	15.0
3. Net financing requirement (1-2)	41.7	54.4	35.5	37.2	21.2	20.0
4. International reserves (end of previous year)	52.1	34.4	23.9	31.5	27.8	14.0
5. Net financing requirement/GDP	0.05	0.10	0.06	0.07	0.05	0.05
6. Net financing requirement/international reserves	0.8	1.6	1.5	1.2	0.9	1.6

Source: World Bank. Brazil Conutry Economic Memorandum 2002

---

[4] The analysis considers a net financing requirement of 6 percent of GDP (table 6), with short-run elasticities of imports and exports to the real effective exchange rate of −.45 and .48, as estimated by Castro, Cavalcanti, Reis, and Giambagi (1998).

The long-run solution to external vulnerability is export growth. Many countries benefited from the sustained boom in world trade over the past 40 years (figure 8), but Brazil
(despite some spurts of rapid export growth) has not. Indeed, Brazil's share of total world
exports today is less than half what it was 50 years ago. The export response to the liberalization of the 1990s was also lackluster due to the decline in export prices. During the
1990s exports in nominal US dollars grew by only 5.8 percent annually, although export
volume indices have grown by 50 percent since 1996. Even after the devaluations of
1999–2001, exports grew only from U$48 billion in 1999 to U$58 billion in 2001, with
the response to the depreciation countered by a deterioration in export prices and the collapse of exports to Argentina, which accounted for 10 percent of Brazil's exports. The
international economic downturn and trade barriers imposed by industrial countries also
played a significant part in this disappointing performance.

A major obstacle to better export performance and further reduction in external vulnerability is Brazil's low degree of openness. Brazil's experience contrasts with that of the
Republic of Korea, whose exports reacted strongly to devaluation, leading to a quick
improvement in external indicators, because the country was already highly open. The
positive association between productivity growth and trade suggests that the low level of
aggregate imports is a key cause of the disappointing export response. Import restrictions
lead to losses in productivity growth, both through higher input costs (whether through
imported intermediate goods or through substitution of domestic intermediate goods)
and reduced competition from abroad. Higher import penetration in Brazilian industries
in the 1990s is statistically associated with significantly higher total factor productivity
growth. Thus, the long-run solution to reducing external vulnerability is a further opening of the economy.

**Figure 8. Imports in Brazil, China, and Mexico 1970–2001
(percent of GDP)**

Success in reducing external vulnerability also depends on foreign direct investment (FDI). Rising FDI as a share of trade flows is linked to economic efficiency, competitiveness, and productivity growth. Compared with other developing countries, Brazil has done well attracting FDI, with levels (as a percent of GDP) similar to China's and Mexico's (figure 9).

**Figure 9. Foreign direct investment in Brazil, China and Mexico 1970 – 2001
(percent of GDP)**

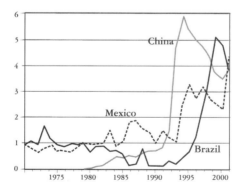

However, the composition and nature of FDI in Brazil are substantially different from that in China or Mexico. In the second part of the nineties, FDI destination shifted from manufacturing to services. The accumulated stock of FDI fell from 55 percent of the investment in manufacturing in 1995 to less than 29 percent in 2000. Offsetting this decline was growth in FDI in the services sector, whose share rose from 43 percent to 70 percent.

The shift from manufacturing to services could have two consequences. First, the change also reflects a shift away from investment in the production of tradable goods. With a few important exceptions (such as telephone equipment), little of the latest generation of FDI appears to be focused on producing for the export market. Second, the movement away from manufactures suggests that Brazil's investment climate may be less attractive than it once was. Services, such as telecommunications and banking (where FDI grew rapidly in the late 1990s), are largely nontradable activities and so are less likely to be sensitive to international competitiveness and the overall investment climate. The facts may partially explain why Brazilian exports did not surge after the FDI inflows, unlike the cases of China and Mexico (figure 10)

Figure 10. Exports in Brazil, China and Mexico 1970-2001 (% of GDP)

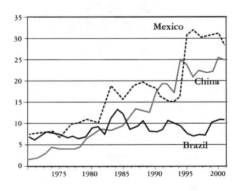

Source: World Bank. Brazil Country Economic Memorandum 2002

Options

Reforms to improve the investment climate and boost productivity are the key means of encouraging exports without incurring fiscal costs. While uncontroversial in general terms, these reforms require the political willingness to confront entrenched interests. They include tax reforms to reduce price distortions and anti-export bias, regulatory and administrative reforms to lighten the bureaucratic burden on the private sector, labor market reforms to reduce distortions, reforms to deepen financial markets and improve their efficiency, and judicial reforms to increase regulatory certainty and enhance the enforcement of private contracts. A fixed mandate for the Central Bank would also increase the perception of stable macroeconomic framework.

Given the scope for growth through productivity-oriented reforms, directed credit and import restrictions are best avoided. Directed credit comes at a fiscal cost, mainly subsidies to BNDES through the Workers Assistance Fund (FAT), and risks capture by vested industrial interests. About 40 percent of lending in the financial system passes through public sector financial institutions, which is high by international standards. The financing needs of the consolidated public sector crowd out private sector lending, further limiting the supply of market-allocated lending. Cutting these programs back too rapidly could damage the private sector, however. A better approach would be to gradually scale back the reach of directed credit, resulting in a corresponding deepening of market intermediation in the financial system.

Brazil could reduce anti-export bias by alleviating the tax burden on exports. While Brazil generally adheres to international best practice in exempting exports from indirect taxes, there are two problem areas. Individual state value-added taxes (ICMS) mean that exporters are sometimes unable to use their nontransferable accumulated tax credits. And several cascading taxes (PIS/PASEP, COFINS, and CPMF), while not directly levied on export sales, lack mechanisms for fully crediting producers for payments made at prior stages of production. Estimates of their cost range from 1 to 3 percent of f.o.b. prices (Tyler 2002).

The further reduction of trade barriers could yield important benefits for Brazil. A unified strategy could be pursued on several fronts, including eliminating remaining export taxes and the government's discretion to raise them; removing nontariff barriers other than those imposed for reasons of national security, public health, or environmental considerations; working within MERCOSUL to achieve further reductions in the common external tariff and establish a revenue-neutral uniform tariff and to reach free trade agreements with regional groupings, including access to the markets of the European Union and the Free Trade Association for the Americas; and engaging in multilateral trade negotiations under the 2001 agreements reached in Doha.

Finally, adequate primary surpluses, advisable for fiscal sustainability, would also improve the current account balance, at least in the short run, through the increase in public saving. In the medium term, private absorption should fill the gap left by the decline in public sector demand. Private sector expenditures can be more productive and can be accompanied by more stable financing sources, such as FDI, or more flexible contracts.

References

World Bank reports

This chapter summarizes the content of the following World Bank reports. Those, in turn, draw heavily from a wide range of literature on the subject from experts in Brazil and beyond, which are referenced in the mentioned Bank reports.

Blanco, Fernando, and Santiago Herrera. 2002. "The Quality of Fiscal Adjustment and Pro-cyclical Policies." Background Paper for World Bank Country Economic Memorandum, Brazil. Washington, D.C.

Cardoso, Eliana. 2002."Real Interest Rates, Bank Spreads and Financial Sector Issues." Background Paper for World Bank Country Economic Memorandum, Brazil. Washington, D.C.

Chuhan, Punam, and Gautam Datta. 2002. "How Heavy is the External Debt Burden?" Background Paper for World Bank Country Economic Memorandum, Brazil. Washington, D.C.

Del Valle, Clemente e Oliver Fratzscher. "Brazil's domestic debt management dilemma: can financial indexation dry the ice ?" Background paper for the Brazil Policy Notes. June 2002. World Bank. Washington, D.C.

Giavazzi, Francesco, and Carlo Favero. 2002. "Why Are Interest Rates so High?" Background Paper for World Bank Country Economic Memorandum, Brazil. Washington, D.C.

Herrera, Santiago. 2002. "Signaling Effect of the Primary Surplus." Background Paper for World Bank Country Economic Memorandum, Brazil. Washington, D.C.

Thomas, Mark Roland. 2002, "Macroeconomic Risk Factors and Poverty." Background Paper for World Bank Country Economic Memorandum, Brazil. Washington, D.C.

Tyler, William. 2002. "Foreign Direct Investment, Trade, and Productivity Growth." Background Paper for World Bank Country Economic Memorandum, Brazil. Washington, D.C.

Velloso, Raul. 2002. "Public Finance in Brazil: Policy Issues and Projections." Background Paper for World Bank Country Economic Memorandum, Brazil. Washington, D.C.

Other references

Amadeo, Edward, and Marcelo Neri. 2000. Macroeconomic Policy and Poverty in Brazil. UNDP Project on Macroeconomics and Poverty in Seven Latin American Countries. New York: United Nations Development Programme.

Beck, Thornsten, Asli Demirguç-Kunt, and Ross Levine. 1999. "A New Database on Financial Development and Structure." Policy Research Working Paper 2146. World Bank, Washington, D.C.

Castro, Alexandre, Marco Cavalcanti, Eustáquio Reis, and Fábio Giambagi. 1998. "A Sustentabilidade do Endividamento Externo Brasileiro." Texto de Discussão No 602. IPEA, Rio de Janeiro.

Central Bank of Brazil. 2001. Press Release on Monetary Policy and Financial Sector Credit Operations. Brasilia.

Figueiredo Luis Fernando, Pedro Fachada, and Sergio Goldstein, 2002. Monetary Policy in Brazil: Remarks on the Inflation Targeting Regime, Public Debt Management and Open Market Operations. Working Paper Series, Central Bank of Brazil. Brasilia.

Goldfajn, Ilan. 2002. "Indexation of Public Debt: Analytical Considerations and Applications to the Case of Brazil", Indexation, Inflation and Monetary Policy edited by Fernando Ieffort Klaus Schmidt Hebbel, Central Bank of Chile, Dantiago, Chile.

Guillermo Calvo, Alejandro Izquierdo and Ernesto Talvi (2002) Sudden Stops, the Real Exchange Rate and Fiscal Sustainability: Argentina's Lessons. Paper presented at IDB – II C 43 re Annual Meeting. Fortaleza – Brazil.

Gavin, Michael, Ricardo Hausmann, Roberto Perotti, and Ernesto Talvi. 1996. "Managing Fiscal Policy in Latin America and the Caribbean: Volatility, Procyclicality and Limited Creditworthiness." Inter-American Development Bank, Washington, D.C.

Thomas, Mark. 2002. Macroeconomic Management, Economic Growth, and Poverty Reduction: Time Series Evidence from Brazil, 1991-2002." World Bank, Washington, D.C.

13

Fiscal Sustainability

13

Fiscal Sustainability

Introduction

Brazil has been on a path of reform of its fiscal programs and policies and achieved impressive progress toward fiscal sustainability and effective fiscal institutions. Continued priority for fiscal sustainability remains important for efficiency and equity. This chapter builds on the far reaching recent progress and provides a few main messages.

In 1999 the Brazilian government initiated an ambitious fiscal adjustment program, turning away from the unsustainable path previously followed in terms of public accounts during the 1990s. The government has managed to raise the total primary surplus (federal, subnational, and state enterprises), from -0.2 percent of GDP in 1998 to 3.2 percent in 1999, 3.5 percent in 2000, and 3.7 percent in 2001 (figure 1). For 2002, the target level was increased to 3.9 percent of GDP.

Figure 1. Trends in primary balances

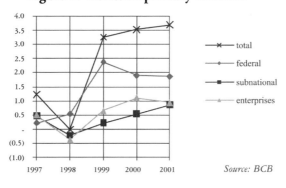

Source: BCB

The draft of this chapter was completed by Wiliam Dillinger, with contributions from Fernando Blanco, in November 2002. The analyses and suggestions presented here are based on the international technical experience of the World Bank and are presented as a contribution to the debate and formulation of public policies.

The Brazilian public sector will have to produce large primary surpluses over the next few years in order to stabilize debt to GDP ratio. Increased market confidence in the government's ability to service this debt should lead to lower interest rates and lower debt service costs, initiating a virtuous circle of economic growth and further falls in interest rates.

As Brazil enters its fourth year of adjustment, two fundamental issues are the sustainability and quality of adjustment. The public sector's ability to continue to produce the level of primary surpluses required to meet its interest obligations will determine the sustainability of the adjustment. Brazil's fiscal turnaround has been attained mainly from the revenue side and by means of short-term measures such as wage restraint and postponement of maintenance and capital expenditures. International experience has shown that adjustment based on cutting expenditure is more likely to succeed and is more sustainable than adjustment based on increasing revenue.

In 2001, the tax burden reached a historical peak of 34 percent of GDP. Further revenue increases seem both unlikely and undesirable. At the same time, the complexity of maintaining a strategy based on postponing rather than cutting expenditures has led to the perception that the current fiscal effort could be temporary, due to the importance of compressed expenditure categories.

The problem with this approach is the latent demand created for program and expenditure expansion.

Equally important is the quality of fiscal adjustment—its impact on economic efficiency and equity. While investment and maintenance expenditures have been reduced, social spending grew rapidly, especially for constitutionally protected programs, some of which benefit higher income groups (social security for government employees, higher education).

Structural fiscal reforms will be required over the next few years to increase flexibility in the spending structure, guaranteeing the continuity of the current fiscal effort and improving the quality of public spending. Emphasis will also be required to assure the continuity and expansion of recommended programs and to improve the quality of public goods and services. The following policy recommendations constitute elements such a possible agenda.

Message 1. Increasing flexibility in public expenditure

The rigidity of public expenditure is a major obstacle to improving the quality and targeting of public expenditures for poor and disadvantaged groups. Due to these rigidities, spending cuts that were necessary for fiscal adjustment have not necessarily focused on programs that should be cut but instead on programs that could be cut. Cuts in investment and maintenance spending would be expected to hurt efficiency. There have been significant improvements in targeting social policies. Yet, rising social spending continues to benefit in several cases the better off. Measures can be taken to alleviate expenditure rigidity and expand the options available to Brazil for maintaining fiscal stability. Given the magnitude of the financial imbalance in the social security system for public servants, its reduction represents the most pressing challenge. Reducing subsidies that benefit higher income groups, and earmarking, could reinforce fiscal stability maintenance and efficiency.

Context

Adjustment, to date, has focused on revenue increases since expenditures are largely inflexible. Social security and social assistance benefits are growing as a share of federal non-financial expenditures. Job security rules for public servants make payroll reductions difficult. A large proportion of federal tax revenues are constitutionally earmarked, including sharing with subnational governments. The 1988 Constitution increased this rigidity, by raising social security and civil service benefits, and expanding the intergovernmental transfer system.

Mandatory expenditures rose rapidly as a proportion of total non-financial expenditures, from 55 percent in 1986 to almost 80 percent in 2001 (figure 2). The main elements of these expenditures are personnel costs, social security and assistance transfers, and intergovernmental transfers to states and municipalities.

Brazilian civil servants have long enjoyed a wide range of benefits, including protection against dismissal (except for just cause) and pension benefits equal to 100 percent of exit salaries (the *sálario integral*). Before 1988, the public sector used a combination of multiple employment regimes and inflation to evade the rigidities of the statutory regime. Employees hired under the consolidated labor law (CLT) could be dismissed without cause. The CLT also capped pension benefits at the level of the RGPS, while inflation reduced salaries in real terms.

The 1988 Constitution established a single statutory employment regime for all staff, (the RJU), with all its associated benefits and rights, while the success of the Plano Real in curbing inflation eliminated inflation as a tool for holding down real personnel costs.

The federal government has nonetheless managed to hold annual growth in personnel costs to about 5 percent over the last five years, through wage and hiring freezes. However, at the state level, personnel costs have increased at an average annual rate of over 6 percent and now account for half of primary expenditures.

Recent federal legislation will, in time, give federal and subnational governments more control over their wage bills. The 19th Amendment abolished the requirement of a single employment regime, opening the door for an eventual return to a mix of statutory and CLT regimes. The amendment, however, applies only to new staff so it will be many years before it has a discernable impact—and implementation of this reform cannot start until further legislation is approved. Before hiring staff under the CLT, a federal law must define "careers of an exclusively public nature" that would remain subject to the RJU. It has yet to do so. States and municipalities are not so constrained and could adopt their own definitions of "careers of a public nature." Most, however, are waiting for federal legislation rather than proceeding on their own.

The biggest problem though for the public sector wage bill is the pension burden. In addition to the 100% replacement rate, staff have traditionally benefited from liberal eligibility criteria. The three levels of government transfer annually 4 percent of GDP, or 15 percent of federal tax revenue, to the public sector pension system.

Another source of rigidity is the General Social Security (RGPS) System for private workers. Here, the problem is not the social security benefit itself (since recipients contribute to the system during their working lives). Had the welfare (or pure transfer) payments to people making only the minimum wage been classified elsewhere in the budget as social assistance spending, the current RGPS social security deficit would be much lower—and might even have disappeared.

Three factors contribute to rigidity of social security spendings. First, social security payments under the RGPS are adjusted annually by at least the rate of inflation (minimum wage adjustments have exceeded inflation). Second, retirement benefits and pensions in the public sector are indexed to the wages of the active personnel. Third, the minimum wage has become the floor for any social security or welfare benefit.

Two other sources of rigidity are constitutional earmarking of minimum levels of spending in social areas. The 1988 Constitution introduced a new federal social budget concentrating on "social contributions": social contributions tax (COFINS), Social Integration Program/Program of Assistance to Civil Servants (PIS/PASEP), tax on financial transactions (CPMF), the social contribution on net profit (CSLL), and payroll contributions (such as contributions to social security INSS, contributions to the System and Educational Salary), all earmarked for the social sector. Under the 2000 health amendment to the 1988 Constitution the government is obliged to maintain a minimum ratio of health expenditures to GDP. The PIS/PASEP tax accounts for about 5 percent of federal tax revenues. Proceeds from the tax are earmarked for the workers assistance fund (FAT), which finances an unemployment insurance scheme for formal sector workers dismissed without just cause; the abono salarial, which supplements the wages of low wage formal sector employees; and the development programs operated by the National Bank for Economic and Social Development (BNDES) (figure 2).

Figure 2. Brazil: Federal non-financial expenditure composition

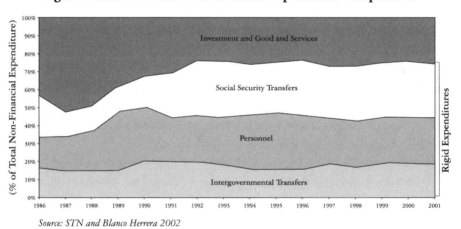

Source: STN and Blanco Herrera 2002

The 1988 Constitution also expanded the intergovernmental transfer system. Transfers to state and local governments accounted for 22 percent of federal primary expenditure in 2001. The largest transfers are the state and municipal revenue sharing funds, fundos de participação de estados e municípios (FPE and FPM, respectively). The 1988 Constitution mandated a gradual increase in these funds, which are financed from fixed shares of the federal income tax and the industrial products tax (IPI). From a base of 18 percent for states and 20 percent for municipalities, the proportions increased to 21.5 percent and 22.5 percent by 1993. The state governments also have to transfer funds to municipalities, part of which is earmarked for education.

State and local government expenditures are constrained by a high degree of rigidity. To meet the requirements of the 1988 Constitution, personnel and social security expenditures of subnational governments rose to more than 70 percent of primary expenditures. As with the federal government, the biggest threat to state fiscal stability comes from personnel expenditures and the inability to dismiss employees. A World Bank study (1998) found that state employees were poorly paid, on average, and that the continued freeze in wages would not be sustainable. However, because of the 100% replacement rate, any increase in the wages of active personnel automatically means increasing the cost of pension payments for future retirees, a strong disincentive to wage increases. This system places many states' finances on a collision course with the Law on Fiscal Responsibility (LRF). Further reforms of social security for state public employees and administrative state reforms are needed to meet personnel payments while continuing to comply with the LRF. With the already implemented measures and the implementation of reforms already proposed, the trend of rising personnel expenditure can be reverted.

Options
Several measures can be taken to alleviate expenditure rigidity and expand the options available to Brazil for maintaining fiscal stability. The discussion in the next three sections lays out the comprehensive justification for the reform proposals presented here.

- Given the magnitude of the financial imbalance in the social security system for public servants, reducing it is the most pressing challenge.
- For greater flexibility, extending the Fiscal Stabilization Fund.[1] The FSF, which expires in 2003, would permit 20 percent of the federal net tax revenues to be excluded from the earmarking system of resource allocation.
- Lately, there have been substantial improvements in social policy targeting, through programs such as Bolsa-Escola, Bolsa-Alimentação, Programa de Erradicação do Trabalho Infantil, among others. Still, reducing subsidies to relatively higher income groups could reduce expenditures and allow more spending to focus on relatively lower-income groups. One candidate is the system of tuition-free universities, another is the Unified Health System (SUS), both of which benefit relatively higher income groups. Requiring patients with private insurance to reimburse the costs of care in public facilities could reduce overall public health expenditures.

---

[1] In the early days of the Real Plan, a constitutional amendment led to the creation of the Fiscal Stabilization Fund (FEF) currently denominated DRU, which stands for "De-earmarking of Federal Funds", a budgetary mechanism through which about 20% of all earmarked resources are transferred to a resources fund which can be used freely in the budget. DRU has been renewed several times, and in its current version lasts until the end of 2003.

- Redirecting earmarked revenues from the PIS/PASEP (through FAT) and the Severance Fund (FGTS) to other purposes would increase flexibility. In 2000 only 32 percent of unemployment insurance beneficiaries and 34 percent of abono salarial beneficiaries were among the poorest groups. The overlap between FGTS and PIS/PASEP in coverage of unemployed formal sector workers could be reduced to free up resources that could be reallocated to other social areas.
- Reducing deductions on personal income taxes (IRPF) that benefit middle and high income groups could allow the resources to be redirected to efficiency-increasing incentives, through deductions in the corporate income tax (IRPJ), for such measures as hiring young workers.

Message 2. Reducing the imbalance in the social security system

The most important and persistent threat to fiscal stability is the public sector social security system RPPS, for staff subject to the RJU statutory public employment regime. Not only for the impact on fiscal accounts but also for equity reasons, reducing the overly generous benefits to retired public servants is essential for the sustainability of current fiscal efforts and improvements in the quality of public expenditure. The most direct means of reducing RPPS future benefits would be to introduce more realistic wage replacement rates for existing and new staff. The approval of the PL 09 and its regulation could offer staff a two-pillar option, with employee contributions based on wages. PL09 could significantly reduce retirement benefits of civil servants to more equitable levels if the two-pillar scheme were made mandatory for existing staff and if the reduction in benefits were extended to workers earning less than the RGPS maximum benefit (10 minimum salaries). Further reforms in the general Social Security System (RGPS), for the private sector workers, could include introducing a minimum retirement age and a graduated wage replacement schedule for benefits.

Context

Some recent measures have tightened eligibility criteria but, compared to other countries, retirement benefits for statutory public sector employees are still overly generous in Brazil, from the 100% replacement rate to liberal eligibility criteria. Until recent amendments, male non-teaching staff could retire after 35 years of service, regardless of age, and female non-teaching staff after 30 years. Teachers could retire five years earlier. "Service" meant employment in any position subject to RPPS or RGPS benefits. Thus a person could take a civil service position with a state government after spending most of his or her career in private employment and still expect a pension fully paid by the government.

The number of retirees eligible for RJU benefits is increasing with the aging of the labor force and the constitutionally mandated unification of employment regimes. Governments at all three tiers face the prospect not only of increased pension obligations to a growing number of statutory employees, but also a rapid increase in obligations to employees formerly under the CLT regime. In 2001, pensions consumed 11 percent of primary spending at the federal level and 16 percent at the state level.

These shares are expected to increase. A recent study commissioned by the Ministry of Social Security and Social Assistance estimates that federal spending on civilian retirees will increase by 40 percent by 2010, consuming two-thirds of the federal wage bill (Probus Suporte Empresarial 2001).[2] A recent World Bank (2000) study estimates that state pension payments will triple between 1998 and 2010. A study by the Fundação Getulio Vargas estimates the net present value of state pension liabilities to be R$288 billion, or about three times total net current revenues in 1999.[3]

The subsidy to the RJU pension system is particularly burdensome; a cash deficit of about 4 percent of GDP is projected to persist in the next years. This subsidy also reinforces inequality on the expenditure side: the RJU channels 43 percent of pension system benefits to just 9 percent of beneficiaries. (Table 1).

---

[2] Note that the projections assume a pension ceiling of Rs$12,720 applied to all future retirees and a sharp reduction in the number of active federal staff (from 457,000 in 2000 to 35,000 in 2035). Figures to be updated on the basis of PROST (Programa de Assistência Técnica para Reforma da Previdência Social)

[3] This includes liabilities to all existing staff—active and retired—but excludes liabilities to future staff who would replace existing staff as they retire. Of the total, R$169 billion are liabilities to existing retirees, R$86 billion to existing active staff, and R$ 32 billion to dependent survivors. Source: Schymura de Oliveira, Luiz, "Estimativa do Passivo Previdenciário dos Estados", unpublished report issued in connection with Convênio de Cooperação Técnica— Ministério da Fazenda/Fundação Getúlio Vargas.

Table 1. Contributions, benefits and deficit of the general Social Security System and public sector pension system, 1995-2001

	1995	1996	1997	1998	1999	2000	2001
I - GENERAL REGIME - INSS	(0.1)	(0.0)	(0.4)	(0.8)	(1.0)	(0.9)	(1.1)
Contributions (Net Revenue)	5.0	5.2	5.1	5.1	5.1	5.1	5.3
Benefits	5.0	5.2	5.4	5.9	6.1	6.0	6.3
II - PUBLIC SECTOR SERVANTS SYSTEM	(3.0)	(3.5)	(3.5)	(3.8)	(3.7)	(4.1)	(4.1)
Contributions	1.0	0.8	0.8	0.7	0.8	0.6	0.7
Inactives and pensionists	3.9	4.3	4.3	4.6	4.6	4.8	4.7
FEDERAL GOVERNMENT	(2.0)	(1.8)	(1.8)	(2.0)	(2.1)	(2.0)	(2.1)
Contributions	0.3	0.3	0.3	0.3	0.3	0.3	0.3
Inactives and pensionists	2.4	2.1	2.1	2.3	2.4	2.3	2.4
STATES	(0.8)	(1.4)	(1.4)	(1.5)	(1.4)	(1.8)	(1.8)
Contributions	0.6	0.4	0.4	0.4	0.5	0.3	0.3
Inactives and pensionists	1.3	1.9	1.8	2.0	1.9	2.2	2.1
MUNICIPALITIES*	(0.2)	(0.3)	(0.3)	(0.3)	(0.3)	(0.3)	(0.3)
Contributions	0.1	0.0	0.0	0.0	0.0	0.0	0.0
Inactives and pensionists	0.2	0.3	0.3	0.3	0.3	0.3	0.3
TOTAL	(3.0)	(3.5)	(3.9)	(4.6)	(4.7)	(5.1)	(5.2)
Contributions	5.9	6.0	5.8	5.9	6.0	5.7	5.9
Benefits	9.0	9.5	9.7	10.5	10.7	10.8	11.1

Source: MPAS, MF/SRF, MF/STM, MOG/Boletim Estatístico de Pessoal e INSS.
*Estimates

Recent reforms will reduce the scale of pension obligations to some extent (table 2). The 20th Amendment toughens the eligibility criteria for retirement, requiring 10 years of service, 5 years in the position from which the employee is retiring, a minimum retirement age (60 for men and 55 for women), and a years-of-contribution criterion (35 for men, 30 for women). The new criteria also apply to existing staff (though the minimum retirement age is lower, at 53 for men and 48 for women). In addition, the federal government and most states have instituted mandatory employee retirement contributions. Federal employees must now contribute 11 percent of their pay to the federal public employee pension system. State rates tend to follow suit. Some states have tried to impose retirement "contributions" on existing retirees, in effect reducing net benefits. The Supreme Court has ruled this unconstitutional.

While these measures will help, they will not be sufficient. The costs of financing the salário integral for the growing population of eligible retirees will require a level of employee contributions that is politically infeasible or a level of government contributions that is fiscally unsustainable. The most direct means of reducing benefits would be to remove the guarantee of the salário integral from the Constitution. But reducing the "acquired rights" of government employees has proved extremely difficult. More accomodative approaches have been used successfully in other countries. Reforms typically distinguish among three groups: existing retirees, whose benefits remain protected; newly hired staff, who are subject to a new, actuarially sound, package of contributions and benefits; and existing active employees, who are subject to a transition rule whereby the extent of benefit reduction is determined by how close staff are to retirement, with the reduction increasing with length of time to retirement.

In Brazil, Congress has been pursuing a more complex path, aimed at reducing benefits on the basis not of length of service but of wages. The most recent draft legislation (PL09) would offer staff a two-pillar option. Under the first pillar, benefits and contributions would be capped at the RGPS maximum, and the government would fully match employee contributions. Under the second pillar, a complementary pension would be set up on a defined-contribution basis, with no guarantee of benefits. Employee contributions would be based on wages, starting at the maximum level subject to RGPS. However, PL09 would only apply to public service entrants after its approval, thus having a negligible effect in the short term. (Table 2).

Table 2. Summary of recent and proposed pension reforms as of November 2002

Actions with immediate impact	Actions with delayed impact
Stricter criteria for pension eligibility introduced under 20th amendment	Amendment 19 allowing some categories of staff to be hired as CLTistas and thus subject to the RGPS benefit ceiling
Introduction of, and increases in, staff pension contributions	Proposed PL 09 complementary fund, which would cap benefits at RGPS maximum
Reductions in the base of the *salario integral*	

Advocates of the legislation argue that it would pass constitutional muster as long as the combination of the RGPS-based benefit and the likely yield of the complementary fund would reasonably approximate the beneficiary's exit salary. Even so, in its current form the legislation would have limited impact, for two reasons. First, existing staff would continue to have the option of retaining their current benefits package—the guaranteed salário integral. Given the uncertain returns on complementary funds, they would be likely to take that option. For new hires under the two-pillar option, there would be little impact on pension costs until a significant proportion of existing staff have retired. Second, the two-pillar option applies only to salaries above the maximum subject to the RGPS. Less than half of all federal workers, 15 percent of state workers, and 12 percent of municipal employees[4] fall into this category. The remainder would continue to receive the full salário integral.

Gross pension payments for retired private sector employees now consume nearly 30 percent of federal primary expenditures. This reflects the package of federally financed retirement benefits for private sector employees incorporated in the 1988 Constitution. Since 1988, the terms of the RGPS benefit package have been scaled back. In 1998, Congress removed the definition of pension benefits from the Constitution, making it legislatively easier to adopt lower benefits at a later time. It then shifted the definition of eligibility from years-of-service to years-of-contribution. The vesting period was increased from 5 years of contribution to 15 (to be fully phased in by 2011). It set a monthly benefit ceiling of R$1,200 a month (approximately 10 minimum wages at the time) indexed to inflation and introduced a fator previdenciário, which adjusts benefits to length of contribution and life expectancy at time of retirement. These measures are reducing the growth in RGPS benefits substantially. Additional measures have been implemented to fight evasion, to improve services, to improve incentives to enroll and to contribute to the system, to broaden the effort to credit recover and to increase revenues. But additional measures still bear consideration.

Options

There is a growing consensus as to the possible options to solve the social security problems. The most direct means of reducing RJU liabilities would be to introduce realistic replacement rates for existing and new staff. There is nevertheless a case for reintroducing PL09, if it is shorn of some of its limitations. If the two-pillar scheme were made mandatory for existing staff, it could have a significant near-term impact. Similarly, if the reduction in benefits were extended to workers earning less than the RGPS maximum, the law could significantly reduce RJU liabilities.

In the short run, as an example, taxing RJU beneficiaries at 15 percent could yield savings of between 0.2 and 0.7 percent of GDP, depending on the income threshold for exemptions and the extent to which states and municipalities followed the federal lead. Breaking the link between pensions and active workers' wages, indexing pensions to infla-

---

[4] The 12 percent estimate applies only to municipalities that are state capitals. PL09's impact on other municipalities would be more limited.

tion rather than the minimum wage, and raising contributions of active personnel to 15 percent could yield further savings.

For the RGPS system, two measures could reduce the growth of benefits. The first would be to introduce a minimum retirement age. Under the current eligibility criteria, male workers can retire after 35 years of contribution and female workers after 30 years, regardless of age. Although the fator previdenciário provides an incentive for workers to postpone retirement, nothing prohibits a worker from retiring at, say, 50 years of age and continuing to draw a pension for another, possibly, 30 years. The government could also reduce RGPS costs by introducing a graduated wage replacement schedule for benefits. Although benefits are capped at approximately 10 minimum wages, workers earning less than this amount receive benefits equal to 80 percent of their wage base, subject to the fator previdenciário. This replacement rate could be reduced for workers whose earnings are just below the level subject to the benefit cap, while remaining for workers at lower income levels.

Message 3. Reduced earmarking of revenues and mandated spending is critical for regaining flexibility for fiscal policy

Increasing the flexibility of public expenditure is an important condition for the continuity of fiscal adjustment and for the improvement of the quality of public expenditure. The large degree of earmarked revenues reduces the flexibility of expenditure allocations. Many measures could increase the flexibility of expenditures. The aggregation of existing program earmarkings into broad sectoral earmarking schemes would allow more flexibility. The revision and the definition of the period of validity of the earmarking rules would make them more compatible with the changing priorities of the government. In the short run, extending the Fiscal Stabilization Fund (DRU), which expires in 2003, would permit the exclusion of 20 percent of net tax revenues from earmarking. The re-inclusion of intergovernmental transfers to the base of the DRU retention would increase the federal government's primary surplus. Reductions in the transfers to states and municipalities could be regarded as a contribution to the overall fiscal adjustment. The reductions in intergovernmental transfers would also induce a greater tax collection effort, stimulate a more efficient allocation of resources, and inhibit the creation of small municipalities. Finally, changing the basis for transfers to states and municipalities from a percentage of tax revenues to a percentage of total primary spending would lead to a systematic fiscal burden sharing across government levels and increase the federal government's control over total expenditures.

Context

The large degree of earmarked revenues constitute an important source of low flexibility in expenditure allocation. In 2001, 80 percent of the fiscal revenue of the federal government was under some type of earmarking. Among earmarked revenues, the transfers to state and municipal governments accounted for 18 percent of federal primary expenditure in 2001. The largest such transfers are the fundos de participação, which are funded from fixed shares of the federal income and industrial product taxes. The 1988 Constitution mandated a gradual increase in the share of these taxes that go to the sub national governments. The transfers were to increase from a base of 18 percent for states and 20 percent for municipalities to 21.5 percent and 22.5 percent respectively by 1993. In 1994, Congress reviewed the legislation, enabling the federal government to reduce the base of the State Participation Fund (FPE) and the Municipal Participation Fund (FPM) by 20 percent through mid-1997 under the Fiscal Stabilization Fund. The expiration date of this fund was later extended through 1997 (under the rubric of the Fundo de Estabilização Fiscal), and again, through 2003 (under the rubric of Desvinculação de Receitas da União, DRU). However, the intergovernmental transfers were excluded from the DRU retention base in 1997, reducing the flexibility that federal spending had obtained through the Fiscal Stabilization Fund.

Using the FPE to force adjustment on state governments has some potentially adverse equity implications. The FPE is distributed among states on the basis of population and per capita income, with poorer states receiving a proportionately larger share. Therefore, broadening the DRU retention base with the inclusion of the intergovernmental transfers to states would harm poorer states more than richer ones. And because state governments play a prominent role in providing services to the poor (particularly in primary education and health), such cuts would fall particularly hard on lower income groups.

The equity implications of renewing the DRU are less clear for the FPM. The FPM is distributed on the basis of population alone, with very small municipalities receiving disproportionately large shares, regardless of the strength of their local tax bases. Changes in the FPM would therefore not necessarily fall on the poorest municipalities or disproportionately hurt poor households.

Options

Various measures could be taken to alleviate the rigidity of public expenditures. The aggregation of existing program earmarkings into broad sectoral earmarking schemes would allow more flexibility. The revision and the definition of the period of validity of the earmarking rules would make them more compatible with the changing priorities of the government. One attractive option would be to change the basis for transfers to states and municipalities from a percentage of certain tax revenues to a percentage of total primary spending. This would lead to a systematic fiscal burden sharing across government levels and increase the federal government's control over total expenditures.

For greater flexibility, extending DRU beyond 2003 would continue to exclude 20 percent of net tax revenues from earmarking. This is a second-best measure that would need to be retained until earmarking and mandated expenditures have been reduced to manageable levels. To indicate an order of magnitude, increasing the DRU to 30 percent would raise government savings by 1.1 percent of GDP. Moreover, the FPE and FPM could be re-included in the DRU base. The required delicate political balance could be justified by the need for the federal government to regain control over its budget and to distribute the burden of the adjustment across different government levels. Nevertheless, it would be necessary to assure that state and municipal expenditures in vital social services are preserved.

From a macroeconomic standpoint, the case for extending the Fiscal Stabilization Fund beyond the end of 2003 is compelling. The fiscal situation continues to be critical, and it is reasonable to expect states and municipalities to continue to shoulder part of the burden of adjustment. In theory, the federal government could find a more equitable solution. Rather than withholding 20 percent from the FPE, it could require richer states to contribute some of their own tax revenues to the federal government's fiscal effort. Revenues from the ICMS of richer states would offset relatively higher FPE transfers to poorer ones. But the constitutional and political obstacles would be substantial.

Message 4. Better targeting of social expenditures
Better targeting of social expenditures could improve the quality and sustainability of fiscal adjustment. Reducing benefits and increasing contributions for the overly generous part of the pension system would contribute to improving the quality of fiscal adjustment. Other steps include cost recovery from relatively high income users for health services and attendance at public universities. Since higher income individuals are the primary beneficiaries of personal income tax deductions, deductions could be reduced without hurting the poor. Additionally, overlaps between the Social Integration Program/Program of Assistance to Civil Servants (PIS/PASEP) and Severance Fund (FGTS) could be eliminated.

Context

Because many social expenditures in Brazil could be better targeted, the need to continue and even deepen fiscal adjustment could motivate a redirection of social spending to provide greater benefits to poor households.

While social spending grew rapidly between 1997 and 2001, little of the growth was directed toward low-income groups. Nearly half of federal social spending goes to pension payments to former employees in the private sector, whose incomes tend to be well above the median, and another 18 percent goes to pensions of former federal employees. Less than 1 percent of social security spending reaches the poorest 10 percent of Brazilians, while about 50 percent goes to the wealthiest 10 percent.

Education and health spending accounts for most of the remainder of social spending. Both categories of spending barely grew between 1997 and 2001. Education spending (including science and culture) rose at an average annual rate of 1.5 percent, and health (including sanitation) at a rate of 2.1 percent. While this slow rate of growth might have been expected to hurt the poor, the bias of some categories of health and education spending toward higher income groups alters the picture somewhat. Half of federal education spending (excluding the Fundef and Bolsa Escola programs, which are executed by local governments) goes to federal universities. This benefits largely relatively better-off families. Only one of every nine applicants to federal universities is accepted. Strong parental guidance and a good private secondary education give children from better-off families an advantage in admission. Qualified, but disadvantaged students—most often from middle income and poor backgrounds—often end up attending private fee-charging institutions, often of lesser quality.

Recent health sector reforms address some of the weaknesses of the system of national health insurance, SUS. The 1988 Constitution obligates the federal government to provide free health care to all Brazilians. Although private insurance continues to make an important contribution to health care financing, and states and municipalities finance much of the cost of public clinics and non-specialized hospitals, SUS expenditures constitute a major claim on the federal budget. In 2001, they constituted about 6 percent of total federal primary expenditure. Hospital care accounts for about 36 percent of MOH spending. However, an unknown proportion of spending for curative, ambulatory care, accounting for another 36 percent of federal spending, is provided in hospitals. Public health programs and services represent about 13 percent. Total spending on hospitals is unknown in part because of lack of information on municipal financing.

Important improvements have been attained by shifting SUS funding for basic care to a per-capita basis. Recent reforms reduced financing disparities. Still, a share of SUS funding continues to be consumed by high income groups. Since the mid 1990s funding for basic care and an array of MOH programs is allocated to populations, reducing inequalities in resource allocation across states. Nevertheless, allocations for medium and high complexity care are based on historical allocations which favor relatively regions where high complexity hospital infrastructure is concentrated. Also, because SUS funding is provided regardless of patient income or private insurance coverage, an estimated 15 percent of SUS benefits accrue to relatively higher-income segments of the population, mostly for treatments uncovered by private insurers. Regressive tax policies such as tax breaks for private medical expenses including insurance premia also contribute to inequalities.

Unlike the federal government, which is involved primarily in making transfers to individuals (such as social security) and to subnational governments, the states are directly involved in the delivery of public services. Thus, cutting state social expenditures could harm equity more than cutting federal expenditures. A large share of state sectoral spending (which excludes debt service, public employee pensions, and legally mandated transfers to municipalities) is allocated to education and health care (figure 3). In 2000, education accounted for about 19 percent and health care (including sanitation) for 8 percent. As most state education spending is allocated to primary education, and the majority of health care spending goes to subsidies to public sector hospitals, cuts in expenditures in these sectors are likely to disproportionately hurt the poor.

Figure 3. Trends in sectoral composition of state primary expenditure

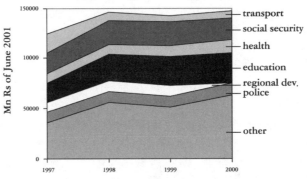

Source: STN.

Another area of government expenditure that warrants attention is the allocation of PIS/PASEP and FGTS resources. PIS/PASEP benefits only workers in the formal sector, excluding the majority of Brazil's (largely informal) labor force. The unemployment insurance and salary supplement programs do not reach the poorest. The unemployment insurance program duplicates some benefits offered under the FGTS. Although BNDES pays a fee for the use of PIS/PASEP funds, a substantial subsidy is involved.

FGTS, an unemployment insurance fund, is financed through a mandatory 8 percent payroll contribution paid into individual, interest bearing accounts, currently remunerated at a real interest rate of 3 percent, well below market rates. Workers (or their dependents) have access to their FTGS account if dismissed without just cause, upon retirement or death, or for the purchase of a private home or high health expenses. Over its history, the FGTS has maintained substantial positive balances (an excess of contributions over benefits). These are managed by Caixa Economic Federal and are earmarked to finance the bank's housing and urban development programs. The use of the funds is overseen by a council with representatives of workers, employers, and the federal government, which determines the spreads that may be charged by Caixa and its financial agents. The low rate paid on FGTS accounts enables Caixa to charge interest rates that are below market levels. This subsidy is paid not by the government, but by the workers who contribute to the FGTS.

Options

Expenditure reductions could be achieved by curtailing subsidy programs that benefit the relatively higher income groups:

- One candidate is the system of tuition-free universities, in those aspects that benefit the relatively higher income families.
- One option would be to strengthen legislation requiring insurers to reimburse the costs of ambulatory and hospital care for privately insured patients in publicly-funded facilities. This would reduce the government's obligation to provide free health care to a segment of the population with the capacity and willingness to pay for it.[5] There are drawbacks to this approach, however. It would probably raise the premiums of private health insurance plans, which in turn, might cause some people to drop their private insurance plans.
- Deductions on personal income tax could be reduced. In 2003 these deductions totaled 0.3 percent of GDP and benefited the relatively higher income taxpayers.

---

[5] The government did issue such a regulation in March 2000, but it remains tied up in litigation.

- Because state and municipality spending is directed more to public goods and services than is federal spending and because the proximity of subnational governments to their constituents can result in better targeted programs, greater decentralization of social expenditures and programs could improve the targeting of public sector expenditures and favor less advantaged groups.

- Redirecting PIS/PASEP revenues (which account for about 5 percent of federal tax revenues) could increase government revenue and improve the targeting of social expenditures. Currently, about 7 percent of the proceeds go to the abono salarial, about 40 percent to the unemployment scheme, and about 22 percent to BNDES, which is legally entitled to up to 40 percent. The rest is invested in other federal lending programs. The second possible target of revenue redirection is the FGTS.

Message 5. Shifting the tax structure toward less distortionary taxes

The Brazilian tax system has become increasingly distortionary, with a rising share of indirect, cumulative taxes and overexploitation of a reduced tax base and turnover taxes that increase labor costs. The distortions created by this system hurt the competitiveness of the Brazilian economy. One reform option would be to phase out the social contributions tax (COFINS) and PIS/PASEP and replace them with a federal value-added tax, and transform the federal turnover tax on industrial products (IPI) into an excise tax. Another option would be to replace turnover taxes with a broadened federal income tax. Reform of the state value added tax on goods and services (ICMS) could also be considered, from fully federalizing the tax to standardizing key parts of the tax that cause the greatest distortions.

Context

Brazil needs to maintain its relatively high level of taxation in order to generate the primary surpluses required to maintain debt sustainability. But the current tax structure (see table 3) imposes unnecessary costs on the economy. These could be reduced without harming tax yields.

The federal tax structure is dominated by two forms of distortionary taxes, turnover taxes and payroll taxes. Roughly 30 percent of tax revenues (including so-called contributions but excluding FGTS) fall into this category, including the PIS/PASEP, COFINS, and CPMF. As turnover taxes, their burden varies across sectors and across enterprises depending on the production structure and the number of stages in the production process. This can lead to significant distortions in relative prices, inefficient combinations of inputs, and industrial concentration and can discourage outsourcing to non-core business activities. The turnover taxes put national production at a competitive disadvantage in international trade.

Payroll taxes add to the cost of labor in the formal sector, creating an incentive to operate informally, with attendant losses of scale economies, access to credit markets, and other benefits that this implies. Payroll taxes, including Social Security contributions (RGPS), the salário educação, and various sector-specific taxes earmarked for apprenticeship programs and other worker benefits, account for slightly over 25 percent of federal revenue. The FGTS—although not considered a tax in federal accounting—also belongs in this group. Although workers can withdraw their FGTS funds under certain conditions, the rate of return on FGTS accounts is well below market rates. Employees would clearly be better off investing their FGTS contributions in private savings accounts. Because they cannot, the FGTS provides a similar incentive to operate informally as the officially recognized taxes on payroll.

At the state level, the ICMS—a form of value-added tax (VAT)—accounts for most (91 percent) of state tax revenues. Brazil is unique in having a VAT at the subnational level. With 27 different VAT regimes, rate structures, exemption policies, and administrative procedures vary widely, complicating the task of compliance for firms with sales in multiple states. In addition, the base of the tax has become heavily concentrated on relatively few goods and services—particularly fuel, power, and telecommunications—where tax yields are high because administration is relatively straightforward. This has introduced distortions in relative prices. By adding to the cost of doing business, the ICMS affects Brazil's international competitiveness. The state VAT also raises an equity issue. Because the tax is imposed on an origin basis, the richer states of the Southeast are able to shift part of the burden of their VAT onto the poorer states of the Northeast. To offset this, the Constitution provides for a complex system of federally mandated differentiated rates. This reduces the extent of interstate tax exporting but does not eliminate it.

Options

Proposals to reform Brazil's tax structure have been under discussion for several years. Much of the discussion has focused on federal turnover taxes. One option is to replace COFINS and PIS/PASEP with a federal VAT and transform the federal turnover tax on industrial products, the IPI, into an excise tax. This would provide a broad-based source of indirect tax revenues, while eliminating the distortions inherent in cascading taxes. Because the states already impose a VAT, there is some risk that a second, federal, VAT could raise the aggregate total VAT rate to excessive levels. This could be ameliorated by ensuring that the base of the federal VAT is as broad as possible and that it is supplemented by excise taxes on such products as tobacco and alcoholic beverages.

Recently, the Brazilian government amended the Medida Provisória 66 (MP-66). It transforms the turnover PIS/PASEP into a value-added tax base and exempts intermediate phases of exports from the IPI. As the MP-66 eliminates the cumulative nature of the PIS/PASEP, it improves the competitiveness of Brazilian industrial goods that compete with imports. The measure also establishes similar reforms of COFINS contributions for 2003.

As an alternative, turnover taxes could be replaced by a broadened federal income tax. At present, personal and corporate income taxes account for only 25 percent of federal revenue (figure 4). While major administrative reforms were implemented in 1995–96, there is substantial room to broaden the base of the income tax. One option would be to lower the threshold for tax liability. This is now roughly 1.3 times average income, thereby excluding the vast majority of Brazilian wage earners.[6] Deductions—many of which largely benefit relatively higher-income taxpayers—could also be reduced. Tax evasion can also be reduced. In 2001, individual filers accounted for less than 9 percent of personal income tax receipts. Recent Supreme Court decisions now allow banking data generated by the CPMF to be used to track tax compliance. The federal government is beginning to exploit this opportunity and should continue to do so.

Figure 4. Composition of federal tax revenues

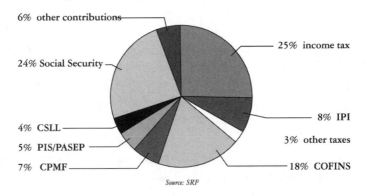

Source: SRF

---

[6] Although taxpayers earning less than this amount are subject to assessments based on presumptive income, these tend to greatly underestimate actual income.

Reform of the ICMS, another source of economic inefficiency, could also be considered (Table 3). In recent years, there have been several reform proposals. One option would be to federalize the ICMS. This would create a uniform system of rates and exemptions throughout Brazil, substantially reducing compliance costs for individual taxpayers. Proceeds of a centrally administered ICMS could be distributed among the states on a basis other than origin, substantially reducing the extent of interstate tax exporting. Another proposal is to leave the administration of the tax to the state (subject to national uniform rates and exemptions) while requiring states to impose a zero rate on interstate sales. While in theory this would reduce interstate tax exporting, in practice it would likely create a strong incentive for fraud. Proposals to address this flaw through an interim federal tax on interstate sales may be difficult to implement. (Table 3).

Table 3. Structure of federal taxation

Tax	Base	Earmarking
IR	Income, profit	FPE, FPM, and the regional funds FND, FNOR and FCO
IPI	Turnover	FPE, FPM, and the regional funds FND, FNOR and FCO
II	Imports	
CPMF	Financial transactions	
CSLL	Corporate profits	Social Security
IOF	Financial transactions	
ITR	Rural property	
COFINS	Turnover	Social Security
PIS/PASEP	Turnover / currently value added	BNDES, unemployment insurance.
INSS	Payroll	Social Security
FGTS	Payroll	Severance payments
Salário educação	Payroll	Education
"S" taxes	Payroll	Apprenticeships, small and medium-size enterprises,
ICMS	Value added	Shared with municipalities
IPVA	Vehicles	Shared with municipalities
ISS	Services	
IPTU	Urban property	

More modest reforms of the ICMS could be considered. A recently proposed constitutional amendment, rejected at the time, would have addressed the most egregious compliance problems while leaving the system of interstate tax rates and state tax administration intact. The proposal would have established nationally uniform rates for various classes of products, with a maximum of five rates; prohibited exemptions or reductions in the base of calculation by individual states; and authorized the Finance Policy Council (CONFAZ) to adopt a set of nationally uniform regulations for calculating the tax. The proposal bears reconsideration.

States could also reduce compliance costs by raising the threshold for ICMS tax liability. International experience shows that in most countries, 90 percent of VAT revenues are collected from the largest 10 percent of firms. This suggests that exempting small firms would not significantly reduce revenues. Critics have argued that exempting small firms would break the chain of tax credits and debits that is used to ensure compliance with the ICMS. International experience belies this claim. While the credit-and-debit system is a helpful adjunct to enforcement, international experience suggests that it is not essential.

Message 6. Continuing to enforce restrictions on subnational borrowing
In the past, excessive subnational government borrowing has contributed to fiscal instability in Brazil. To prevent a recurrence of excessive borrowing, the federal government enacted a series of controls on state fiscal behavior ranging from individual fiscal adjustment agreements with the states and caps on subnational borrowing to limits on bank exposure to the public sector. These controls are working and their continuation is important for fiscal stability. Continued implementation of the Fiscal Responsibility Law avoids the temptation to provide relief during periods of subnational economic crisis, sending a a clear signal to the private banks and the domestic bond market that the federal government no longer stands ready to come to the relief of states that threaten to reneg their obligations.

Context
In the past, excessive subnational borrowing has contributed to fiscal instability in Brazil. As recently as 1998, interest obligations of subnational governments totaled 1.59 percent of GDP. These have dropped because the federal government agreed to refinance the state debt on highly favorable terms.

To forestall excessive subnational borrowing, the federal government enacted a battery of controls on state fiscal behavior. These include individual state fiscal adjustment agreements (under Law 9496) and Senate caps on subnational borrowing (Resolutions 40 and 43), which impose fixed ceilings on new borrowing, debt service, and debt stock. In addition to these controls on the demand for credit, the federal government has also acted to restrict supply. Resolutions of the National Monetary Council limit bank exposure to the public sector to 45 percent of equity—a limitation that is particularly binding on Caixa Econômica Federal. This series of controls is capped by the Law on Fiscal Responsibility (LRF) and its companion enforcement legislation.

Options

These controls on subnational borrowing are working. According to data from the Secretariat of the National Treasury, net new borrowing by state governments (gross borrowing less amortization) declined from 22 percent of net current revenue in 1997 to 6 percent in 1999. While the stock itself continues to grow (figure 5), this growth is largely due to the recognition of off-budget liabilities to state-owned banks and the capitalization of interest under debt service caps, rather than new borrowing.

Figure 5. Stock of state debt

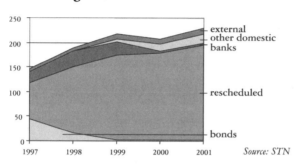

Source: STN

Federal attempts to control subnational fiscal performance had a mixed record in Brazil. Efforts to rein in state personnel spending and borrowing date back several decades, but have often succumbed to political pressure. International experience suggests that consistent enforcement, in the face of strong political pressure, will be essential to control subnational borrowing in the future. The LRF has so far been much more successful than previous attempts to establish subnational fiscal discipline. In order to consolidate the gains of the LRF, over the long term, the federal government will have to resist any temptation to provide financial relief during subnational economic crises. And it will have to continue to send clear signals to the private banks and the domestic bond market that it no longer stands ready to come to the relief of states that threaten to reneg their obligations.

References

World Bank projects

Municipal pension system reform – PREV MUN (Apoio a Reforma dos Sistemas Municipais de Previdências) US$ 5 million. Approved on July 25, 2002.

Strengthening Fiscal and Financial Management – PROGER (Projeto de Fortalecimento do Gerenciamento fiscal e Financeiro) US$ 8,8 million. Approved on May 24, 2001.

Technical Assistance for Pension System Reform – PROAST (Programa de Assistência Técnica para Reforma da Previdência Social) US$ 5.05 million. Approved on February 7, 2000.

State Pension System Reform – PARSEP (Programa de Apoio a Reforma do Sistemas Estaduais de Previdência) US$ 5 million. Approved on June 30, 1998.

World Bank reports

"Brazil: From Stability to Growth through Public Employment Reform," Report No. 16793-BR (February, 1998).

Herrera, Santiago. 2002. "Signaling Effect of the Primary Surplus." Background Paper for World Bank Country Economic Memorandum, Brazil. Washington, D.C.

Blanco, Fernando, and Santiago Herrera. 2002. "The Quality of Fiscal Adjustment and Pro-cyclical Policies." Background Paper for World Bank Country Economic Memorandum, Brazil. Washington, D.C.

Velloso, Raul. 2002. "Public Finance in Brazil: Policy Issues and Projections." Background Paper for World Bank Country Economic Memorandum, Brazil. Washington, D.C.

World Bank. 2000. "Brazil—Critical Issues in Social Security." Report 19641-BR. Washington, D.C.

Other references

Probus Suporte Empresarial. 2001. Avaliação dos Compromissos Previdenciais da União, Relativos a Benefícios Previdenciais Concedidos e a Conceder a Funcionários Públicos Atuais e Futuros. Governo Federal do Brasil, Ministério da Previdência e Assistência Social, Brasília.

14
Public Sector

14

Public Sector

Introduction

Over the past decade, Brazil has made important progress in achieving both social development and macroeconomic stability thanks to the consistent pursuit of sound macroeconomic, fiscal, and social policies. Sustaining these gains and continuing progress will require improved governance capacity to identify citizens' needs and demands and provide high quality public services while maintaining necessary fiscal adjustments over the medium term. Another key challenge concerns the country's rule of law institutions, both the perceived uncertainty and complexity of the country's legal and administrative environments and the growing concern with citizen security, with rising levels of crime and violence.

Five areas of reform priority merit attention. They were selected both for their intrinsic importance and for their cross-cutting effects on fiscal discipline, growth, and social inclusion. Some other important issues are discussed in other notes (for example, reforms of regulatory and property rights institutions in the Policy Note on Private Sector Development and specific institutional reform measures in sectoral notes).

The quality of governance—toward more effective government and rule of law

A growing literature on development identifies good governance and robust institutions as fundamental to economic growth and poverty reduction. Brazil has a mixed reputation for the quality of its governance. Its prudent macroeconomic management in recent years has inspired international confidence in the government's ability to maintain fiscal discipline, despite several difficult structural vulnerabilities (see Policy Notes on macroeco-

The draft of this chapter was completed by Yasuhiko Matsuda, Linn Hammergren and Leila Ollaik in September 2002. The analyses and suggestions contained in this chapter are based on the international technical experience of the World Bank and are presented as a contribution to the debate and formulation of public policies.

nomic and fiscal issues). Innovative public management practices include aggressive use of e-government, "one-stop shops," and participatory budgeting. Yet complaints persist about a slow and unpredictable judiciary, a difficult regulatory environment, and excessive bureaucracy. Unclear assignment of functions between states and municipalities, and generally weak institutional capacities at subnational levels also affect the quality of intergovernmental policy coordination and public service delivery. Allegations of corruption occasionally emerge.

In a survey of the perceived quality of governance (figure 1) Brazil scores well in comparison with the average for upper middle-income countries in "voice and accountability" (ability of citizens to participate in the selection of governments, media independence) and in "political stability/no violence" (perceptions of the likelihood that the government will be destabilized or overthrown by unconstitutional or violent means). These scores suggest that Brazil's democratic governance is seen to be well consolidated. But Brazil's governance is perceived to be significantly worse in "government effectiveness" (quality of public service provision, qualifications of civil servants, credibility of the government's commitment to policies), "regulatory quality" (market-friendly policies, burdens imposed by excessive regulation), and "rule of law" (incidence of crime, effectiveness and predictability of the judiciary, enforceability of contracts).

Figure 1. Quality of governance in Brazil, 2001

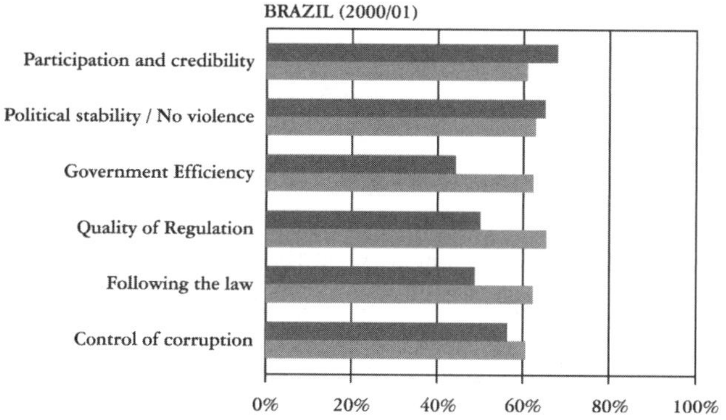

BRAZIL (2000/01)

Compared with the average income category (higher average income) (lower bar)
Percentage classsification of Country (0 to 100%)

Note: Data are based on aggregation of existing survey data (subjective perceptions of interviewees who range from experts to private investors). The data are presented with both point estimates and statistical margin of error (the thin line extending from each bar), showing, for example, that there is less divergence in perceptions about "voice and accountability" and "government effectiveness" than about "regulatory quality" and "political stability/no violence" scores.
Source: Kaufmann, Kraay, and Zoido-Lobaton 2002.

Brazil has made efforts to address these weaknesses. For example, the recent state reform agenda has transformed the discourse on public sector reform in Brazil. Increasingly, the vision of the state at the service of the citizens is seen as a basic tenet of public administration reform. Expanding access to public services, especially by the poor and the socially disadvantaged, is an important objective on its own. Brazil has made tremendous progress in universalizing some basic public services such as fundamental education and basic health care. Remaining are the more difficult challenges of improving quality and strengthening accountability in public service delivery. More can be done by stepping up the efforts to make administrative processes simpler and more transparent to citizens, thereby also reducing opportunities for administrative corruption, a pernicious form of inequality in access to good government.

As a result of the 1988 Constitution and subsequent reform efforts, Brazil now has an independent and relatively professional judiciary and public ministries. Still, there is discontent about judicial performance including limited access because of physical location and costs to the user, delays and court congestion, overly complex procedures, lack of predictable, uniform decisions, and excessive formalism.

Another high priority related to the rule of law and good governance is control of crime and violence. This is a complex social phenomenon that defies easy solutions. Solutions would inevitably be multidisciplinary and would include the role of the justice system and reform of the police institutions.

The key messages for governance and public sector reform in Brazil presented here emphasize government effectiveness and the rule of law, two areas of relative weakness identified in the comparative indicators of the quality of governance.[1] (Regulatory quality, another area in which Brazil is perceived to lag behind other countries, is dealt with in the Policy Note on private sector development).

Measures to increase government effectiveness

Context

The government's efforts to maintain high primary surpluses in order to protect the credibility of its macroeconomic management and debt sustainability has caused considerable strain in the budget execution system. Within that context, extensive use of revenue earmarking, which has increased dramatically since the late 1980s, and the high share of obligatory spending in the federal budget, which increased from 4.6 percent of GDP in 1999 to 7.9 percent in 2002,[2] have been accompanied by a dramatic decline in discretionary spending (figures 2 & 3). Although earmarking has its own logic in terms of protecting certain expenditures and programs from the uncertainty of funding availability in the annual budget processes, it has significant costs in terms of overall efficiency of public expenditure allocations. Several priority discretionary programs have suffered budgetary cuts, and their implementation has been

---

[1] Kaufmann, Kraay and Zoido-Lobaton (2002).

[2] Obligatory expenditures include those associated with constitutional transfers, subsidies, unemployment insurance, payments for judicial sentences, Fundef, Organic Law of Social Assistance (LOAS), Fundo de Combate à Pobreza, among others.

Message 1. Increasing flexibility in public expenditures and improving allocative efficiency through better policy planning and budget management
Efficient resource use and its institutional underpinnings are a key to delivering the government's policy objectives. Brazil collects a comparatively high level of revenues, but the burdens of fixed costs and debt payments and the country's continuing need for fiscal adjustments limit the resources available for discretionary public policy interventions, including the growing need to promote social development and contribute to poverty reduction. A two-track approach of reviewing earmarking to increase expenditure flexibility and strengthening policy planning and budgeting to improve expenditure efficiency would help the government achieve its policy objectives.

impaired by the lack of funding predictability. And the budget rigidity created by earmarking has led to at least two types of problems in efficiently delivering services to the poor and socially disadvantaged. Earmarked portions of the federal budget, such as social security payments and portions of federal education and health expenditures, tend to be regressive, and the government is unable to redirect these expenditures, at least in the short run. And while this overall rigidity is an overriding problem in public expenditure management, there is also evidence that constrained discretionary expenditures are not allocated and executed very efficiently.

REDUCING BUDGET RIGIDITY BY STRATEGIC MANAGEMENT OF BUDGET EARMARKING. In the medium term an important challenge is to increase the flexibility of the budget as an instrument for the strategic allocation of scarce public resources. Continuing structural fiscal reforms and a new approach to managing expenditure earmarking might be necessary. Removing constitutional and legal earmarking is not easy. Each earmarking decision represents a political settlement at a particular moment among various groups that legitimately seek to protect their interests within Brazil's complex fiscal arrangement. But a political agreement that may make sense in a particular context may no longer make sense as the context changes. Earmarking can also mask inefficiency since allocations are not tied to performance.

Figure 2. Composition of the budgetary revenue: 1870 to 2002

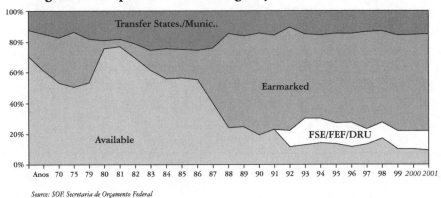

Source: SOF. Secretaria de Orçamento Federal

Figure 3. Evolution of primary expenditures

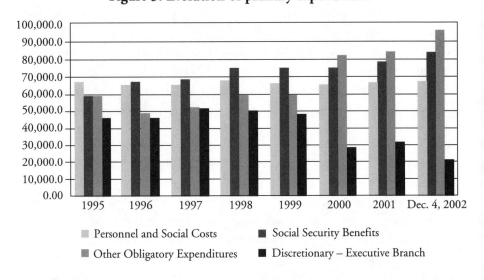

Earmarking tends to generate more earmarking. Earmarking reduces the total amount available for discretionary spending, and this lack of funding predictability then becomes a strong incentive for others to pursue legal protection of their spending priorities.

From an economic efficiency point of view, avoiding any constitutional or legal guarantees of expenditure categories is the preferred option, but it is probably unrealistic, perhaps even undesirable, given Brazil's political and institutional realities and the wish to protect at least those expenditures (certain social expenditures, for example) that a major-ity considers important.

A more flexible option would be to use ordinary law, rather than the Constitution, with a sunset clause so that costs and benefits could be reviewed periodically while some stability is ensured in the availability of funding for high priority areas. This process could be reserved for high priority expenditures and expenditures subject to high levels of fund-ing uncertainty if left to the still volatile annual budget process.

By separating considerations of specific legally earmarked expenditures from the rest of the budget, however, an important principle of good budgeting—contestability of com-peting claims for funding—is lost. One way to remedy this weakness is to use the Multiyear Plan (PPA) process as a framework for discussing expenditure protection beyond the annual budget cycle and defining broad policy and expenditure priorities of the government, debated and negotiated with Congress with inputs from society. The ear-marking decisions can be revisited every four years, when the PPA is renewed, within the broader framework of medium-term expenditure planning.

INVESTING IN SECTORAL MINISTRIES' MANAGEMENT CAPACITY FOR PLANNING AND BUDGETING. For greater expenditure flexibility to result in better use of available funds, a robust institution for guiding planning and budgeting is necessary. While Brazil's planning and budgeting systems have been strengthened considerably in recent years, especially in fiscal discipline and transparency and in reliability of financial management, which are important pre-requisites for effective expenditure management, the budget system remains highly com-plex and centralized.

Strong centralization combined with tight fiscal policy in a volatile macroeconomic environment accentuates funding unpredictability, which disproportionately affects dis-cretionary capital programs. Strong central control of aggregate spending limits does not necessarily mean that the government's central organs have good control over sectoral ministries' deliveries on stated policy objectives. Sectoral ministries enjoy considerable dis-cretion in allocating resources within the broad parameters set in the budget, and mech-anisms of intragovernment accountability for achieving stated policy objectives are weak. While some programs seem to be working well, there appears to be much scope for improving efficiency in resource allocation and execution through better management of the planning and budgeting process and stronger accountability in implementation.

A logical approach would be to build on the PPA initiative. One way to do that would be to continue with the centralized approach, in which the Planning Secretariat, in close coordination with the Budget Secretariat and interacting frequently with the PPA program managers, takes the lead in program definition, monitoring, and evaluation. Such centralization allows for tight fiscal control. But this approach imposes heavy transaction costs on the Ministry of Planning, which could jeopardize its institutional sustainability. Centralization is also likely to weaken sectoral ministries' incentives for adhering to the centrally defined policy priorities and accountability for managing their own policies and resources. The central planning organs may also face a contradiction between tight control for fiscal discipline and the funding of the government's expenditure priorities.

A more decentralized approach could allow each sectoral ministry a greater role in priority identification following general central guidance from the Ministry of Planning. This could combine greater sectoral ministry ownership of priority programs with the high priority policies and programs identified by the president and monitored by the Ministry of Planning. But before more planning and budgetary decisionmaking is decentralized to sectoral ministries, their institutional capacities for policy prioritization and expenditure execution need to be strengthened. One option would be to enhance the managerial autonomy of the PPA program managers and to integrate them fully into each ministry's organizational structure and management processes.

In a gradual approach to decentralization, sectoral ministries and other entities would have to demonstrate that they can present credible and coherent policy proposals and deliver on their stated objectives before being granted greater funding predictability and budget and managerial flexibility (including human resources as a budgetary item). This would also involve building up the institutional capacity of the Ministry of Planning to monitor agreed performance targets with each sectoral ministry. Proper ex-post accountability would require that the Ministry of Planning have the necessary political authority over the budget execution unit in question. Reforms to increase expenditure flexibility are prerequisites for this approach since without flexibility, the Ministries of Planning and Finance would not be able to assure greater funding predictability to sectoral ministries.

Enhancing the strategic orientation of the planning and budgeting system would also involve streamlining its procedures. The less the central organs (Ministry of Planning, in particular) have to worry about operational details of budget execution (for example, by managing the process of contingenciamento with control of budget flow), the more they can focus on broad policy and strategic issues.[3] In the absence of an updated public finance law (to replace the 1964 Law), the annual exercises under the Budgetary

---

[3] Schick (1997).

Guidelines Law (LDO) have had to shoulder much of the burden of specifying budgeting and financial management procedures, thus diluting its intended purpose of setting the strategic parameters for fiscal and expenditure policies. Strengthening the role of the LDO as strategic guidelines for both annual and medium-term fiscal and expenditure planning could greatly improve the integration of planning and budgeting. A new public finance law, if well-designed and fully implemented, could greatly increase the strategic content of budget and financial management decisions.

Some subnational jurisdictions (especially municipal) have had good results with the institutionalized use of participatory budgeting as a way of improving budget transparency and direct citizen voice in public policymaking. Where it has been successfully implemented, it has been lauded both nationally and internationally. But not all attempts at participatory budgeting have been a clear success. Exploring both successful and unsuccessful cases, and their impacts on the quality of public expenditure management and outcomes, would be beneficial.

BROADENING AND INSTITUTIONALIZING THE ANNUAL PPA EVALUATION. Systematic evaluation of government programs raises the level of public debate on policy choices and strengthens the accountability of government agencies for program implementation. Although evaluation is quite different from the audit/control instruments of fiduciary accountability, a good evaluation system could also help to detect misuse of public funds and thus reduce large-scale corruption.

The annual evaluations of PPA programs are a step in that direction. These efforts should be institutionalized and linked more systematically to the annual budget allocation decisions. Evaluations can be expanded to include in-depth program evaluations, performance monitoring and evaluation of government organizations, performance audits, and user satisfaction surveys.[4] Since not all of these can be managed by the Ministry of Planning as part of the PPA evaluation process, the government could develop a system of evaluation mechanisms that feed into each other for better program design and implementation, more efficient resource allocation, and enhanced accountability through continuous improvements in program performance indicators, monitoring of program implementation by the responsible ministries and program managers, and adjustments to the organizational arrangement for program implementation.

---

[4] The current annual PPA evaluations are limited to self-administered surveys of program managers and sectoral authorities about their subjective judgment of program design and implementation.

The evaluations could be centralized in the Ministry of Planning as is currently the case with the PPA annual evaluations or decentralized to the sectoral ministries, with the requirement that each ministry report evaluation results independently to the president and the Congress; Probably the most sensible choice would be to take a middle course, whereby a degree of centralized management continues while more and more responsibilities for detailed program evaluations are decentralized to the ministries/agencies responsible for delivering those programs. As the sectoral ministries and agencies take on a greater role, the Ministry of Planning could remain as central coordinator and focus on evaluating the government's strategic programs (the president's priorities), cross-sectoral programs (though these could also be evaluated by the sectoral ministries involved), and the overall planning framework (for example, the effectiveness of the existing implementation arrangement).

Application of these suggestions at the federal level could have a beneficial demonstration effect at the subnational level. The federal government might also consider institutionalizing a demand-based program of technical assistance for interested subnational governments to strengthen their planning and budgeting systems. With sufficiently streamlined procedures, the Ministry of Planning, with help from the National School of Public Administration (ENAP), might be able to respond systematically to such requests from subnational governments.

Options

Brazil could consider two sets of reforms to improve the efficiency and outcomes of policy planning and expenditure management.

Structural reforms could tackle the problem of expenditure rigidity by:

- Continuing to pursue structural fiscal reform measures including public sector pension reform, public sector pay and employment reform, and other measures discussed in the Policy Note on fiscal issues.
- Introducing mechanisms for periodic review of expenditure earmarking, such as:
  - Use of ordinary laws with sunset clauses, rather than Constitutional amendments, as a means of earmarking expenditures.
  - Use of PPAs for earmarking expenditures for the four-year plan period.

Procedural reforms and related capacity building efforts to strengthen policy planning and budget management capacities could build on such ongoing initiatives as the use of the Fiscal Responsibility Law (LRF) as a medium-term fiscal planning tool and the use of the PPA as a means to better integrate planning and budgeting. The government might consider the following alternatives to the current highly centralized approach to fiscal and expenditure planning:

- Helping sectoral ministries develop more rigorous policy and planning capacities before moving toward a more decentralized policy and expenditure management arrangement;

- Redefining the role of the Ministry of Planning and other central agencies in providing broad strategic guidelines and policy reviews.

- Proposing a new public finance law that codifies the recent modernizations of government fiscal and expenditure management and helps restore the LDO as a strategic guidance law.

Systematic use of program evaluations can be a powerful tool. Brazil could continue its efforts to improve the efficiency of expenditure allocations by providing better analytical bases for policy and budgetary decisions by developing an institutionalized system of program and performance evaluations either under the continued coordination of the Ministry of Planning (as an expanded form of the current PPA annual evaluations) or in a more decentralized system in which each ministry or agency is responsible for conducting program evaluations.

The federal government has the opportunity to continue to lead subnational governments by example in institutionalizing good policy and expenditure management. It could also consider developing a demand-driven program of technical assistance for willing state and municipal governments.

Message 2. Strengthening institutional incentives and capacities for efficient service delivery and fair access

Brazil has made considerable progress in social development over the past decade, expanding access to essential public services such as basic education and primary health through innovative policy interventions. But more needs to be done to improve the quality of public services and government responsiveness to citizens' needs. Improving quality is more difficult than expanding access and requires sustained efforts to augment the efficiency and accountability of the public sector. Measures to enhance service quality and the responsiveness of the state apparatus include better alignment of organizations to the government's policy objectives, more aggressive administrative simplification and debureaucratization, and fine-tuning of role assignments across levels of government, combined with incentives-based subnational capacity building programs.

Context

Governments at all three levels of the federation have begun to introduce a stronger service orientation and a sharper focus on results. These efforts are part of a long process of transition to a fairer, more inclusive, and more responsive state. While the view that the state should be at the service of citizens is now well accepted, the public sector's service orientation is still relatively new in Brazil. Citizens' perceptions of the quality of public services show a complex picture. A national survey of public service users conducted by the federal government revealed high levels (around 70 percent) (table 1) of satisfaction with various dimensions of public service quality. Universalizing access to basic public services such as primary education and preventive health care may have contributed to this reasonably positive assessments. But the survey also found significant divergence in satisfaction rates between richer and poorer regions. And a participatory poverty assessment carried out by the World Bank in 1999 documented very negative perceptions of access and quality in some public services, such as the police, and a resulting lack of trust in government.[5]

Policy alternatives to enhance service orientation and clarify responsibilities focus on organization of the government apparatus at each level of the federation, bureaucratic simplification and measures to enhance government efficiency and transparency, and greater clarity in assignment of functions across levels of government, especially between states and municipalities.

FOCUSING ON ADJUSTING INTERNAL ORGANIZATION OF THE GOVERNMENT AGENCIES. Organizational restructuring should proceed cautiously. It can create strong resistance, while its payoffs in terms of improved performance are uncertain. If implemented badly, large-scale organizational restructuring (especially if it increases the autonomy of line ministries and agencies) can create institutional incoherence, disrupt ongoing activities, and diminish the ability of the center to control line ministries and agencies.[190] The government's efforts and political capital, at least in the beginning, may be better expended on making sure existing structures work at their maximum potential rather than restructuring them.

---

[5] "Consultations with the Poor: Brazil – National Synthesis Report," May 1999. A background report for World Development Report 2000/2001: Attacking Poverty, as well as for the World Bank's Voices of the Poor project.

[6] These issues were discussed at a recent OECD conference on agencies. Distributed Public Governance: Agencies Authorities and Other Autonomous Bodies (Preliminary Draft), OECD.

Table 1. Public service user satisfaction rates (percent)

Dimension	North	North-East	Mid-West	South-east	South	National average
Guarantee of access/ process of service provision	68.2	65.5	66.0	72.2	77.7	71.2
Quality of assistance	68.0	67.6	66.2	75.0	83.0	74.1
Quality of service	70.0	68.9	68.9	76.1	80.5	74.7
Agility in assistance	67.3	63.5	61.6	64.8	73.7	65.9
Adequacy of physical facilities	72.2	65.9	66.6	74.0	81.1	73.0
General average	69.2	66.3	65.8	72.4	79.2	71.8

Source: Pesquisa Nacional de Avaliação da Satisfação dos Usuários, reported in Prates (2001).

A more moderate approach would seek to clarify external accountability arrangements by aligning internal structures, procedures, and management with the functions and objectives of each organization. The new program structure introduced with the PPA 2000-2003 could be a useful guide.

Another strategy to better align organizational performance with society's demands is to institute two-way communication between government service providers and citizens. Performance standards and expectations could be clarified through user surveys, scorecards, citizen charters, performance measurement and monitoring, and program evaluations. The new round of PPA implementation could incorporate a more explicit focus on organizational performance and government outputs, in addition to its emphasis on program outcomes.

CONTINUING WITH ADMINISTRATIVE SIMPLIFICATION AND MORE EXPLICIT EXTERNAL ACCOUNTABILITY. As one of the PPA programs for 2000-2003 the federal government has been trying to revamp a program of debureaucratization. The objective is to foster respect for public services and to protect people against bureaucratic abuse. Although the program has been in effect since 1979, there are no concrete indicators for evaluating its efficiency in integrating different ministries and government agencies, eliminating duplication, and reducing costs. More systematic external reporting and development of a set of measures for evaluating public sector efficiency and productivity and their impact on service delivery outcomes would be needed. For example, the PPA program manager could be required to report to the interministerial committee created to identify and simplify bureaucratic procedures in each area of public administration. The committee would produce systematic reports on estimated impact on bureaucratic efficiency and social outcomes. Debureaucratization could also be linked more explicitly to productivity growth in the public sector, improved transparency in service standards, and better mechanisms for citizen appeals of administrative abuse.

The most successful initiatives appear to to be related to the increasing use of internet E-government for tax collection, procurement, service registration, e-drawback for foreign trade, information on government procedures, monitoring of various processes, and even internal organization of government data by the extensive use of information technology tools which have helped the most in diminishing "paper work" and simplifying government procedures. Sometimes, political difficulties or coordination problems can impede efforts to eliminate duplication and simplify procedures across levels of government (such as firm registration, as discussed in the Policy Note on private sector development) or when actions are needed in more than one sector. An option for resolving such impasses is to create a forum in which the needs for intergovernmental coordination in debureaucratization are identified and actions by each tier of government monitored.

Another initiative for reducing bureaucracy and improving service provision is the "one-stop shop" that groups essential government services in one place and staffs them with client-oriented staff. Bahia SAC and Goiás Vapt-Vupt are examples of improved service delivery to citizens.

FINE-TUNING ROLE ASSIGNMENTS ACROSS LEVELS OF GOVERNMENT AND INTRODUCING INCENTIVE-BASED SUBNATIONAL CAPACITY BUILDING PROGRAMS. In Brazil, where most of the public services are delivered by subnational governments, intergovernmental relations are an important element of the broader institutional environment that affects quality of public service delivery. Some of the challenges associated with a decentralized state include how to balance decentralized authority with weak institutional capacity at lower tiers of government, how to finance subnational government operations without undermining their accountability, how to use the formal democratic processes, greater transparency, and citizen participation in governance to take advantage of the geographic proximity of the government to the population to enhance government accountability.

In Brazil's long established federal system, the rules of the game of political bargaining appear to be relatively stable, though most are informal and highly complex. The federal government's roles are fairly clearly established, but the division of responsibilities between states and municipalities remains ambiguous.[7] Functional ambiguity can lead to

---

[7] These issues are treated in more detail and more systematically in Brazil: Issues in Brazilian Fiscal Federalism, World Bank (2001), Report No. 22523-BR.

duplication and can weaken accountability to citizens. Intergovernmental fiscal relations are especially complicated and inefficient.[8]

There is an emerging consensus that hard budget constraints are essential for decentralization to work. A requirement for fiscal responsibility, such as that found in the LRF, by providing governments with a strong incentive to improve efficiency in financial operations, thereby also helps to improve service delivery.[9] The LRF provides an important and relatively easily verifiable benchmark against which Brazilian citizens can evaluate performance of their governments. Any move toward better electoral accountability and depoliticization of public administration is likely to improve the quality of democratic governance and public service delivery.

The LRF could also be a partial answer to the problem of weak management capacity, especially at the municipal level, a problem that often fails to respond to supply-driven capacity strengthening programs because of a lack of incentives to change. With its relatively severe sanctions, the LRF may help to create incentives for subnational governments to strengthen their capacity for fiscal and financial management. While it is too early to tell, the combination of strong incentives provided by the LRF and the availability of technical support through the federal government may prove to be more effective than traditional, supply-driven approaches.

Besides fiscal responsibility, strong institutional capacities and clear assignment of responsibilities and resources among different levels of government are essential for good public sector performance. In Brazil, most such ambiguities relate to the distribution of responsibilities between states and municipalities. While this is an issue for state governments to resolve, the federal government could help by encouraging clarification of role assignment, as is being attempted with the creation of the Unified Health System (SUS).

The PAB, in which the federal government certifies municipalities on the basis of their capacity to manage health services at different levels of complexity, appears to be a promising approach to encourage management strengthening using fiscal incentives. An evaluation of the capacity building impacts of the PAB and its "certification" process for full and partial management (gestão plena/semi-plena) are needed to determine its effectiveness, however. Without that there is no way to answer such questions as whether federally provided fiscal incentives are

---

[8] Not just the well-known problems of the inefficient revenue sharing arrangement but also the historical pattern of subnational fiscal indiscipline and federal bailouts.

[9] Beyond the Center: Decentralizing the State by Shrid Javed Burki, Guillermo E. Perry, and William R. Dillinger (World Bank, 1999).

being matched by local political accountability as a complementary incentive for municipal good governance. For example, even a relatively large municipality like Florianópolis lacks the human resources to qualify for full management certification, and that is unlikely to change as long as there is little incentive for the city government to try for certification and little citizen demand that the city rather than the state provide those services.

In addition to federal efforts to clarify accountability and provide incentives for better management at the municipal level through transfer-driven programs, some state governments are taking initiatives of their own. The government of Bahia has begun to define the responsibilities of the state and municipal governments in fundamental education and is experimenting with reforms to professionalize school management (including depoliticizing school director appointments) and school autonomy.[10] Other jurisdictions have used similar approaches to strengthening social service delivery. The federal and state governments can work together to further disseminate these experiences for the benefit of other states that have not yet tackled this issue.

Options

The ultimate objective of any public sector reform is to improve the ability of government to serve society. The quality and the efficiency of public service delivery in Brazil, where most service delivery functions are decentralized to state and municipal levels, could be improved by:

Measures related to organizational reform:

- Focus on making existing organizational structures work better in achieving identified results rather than undertaking major organizational restructuring as an entry point for performance-oriented public sector reform. To this end, the government might consider:
- Introducing explicit organizational performance targets as part of the next PPA.
- Realigning the internal structures of ministries and agencies to fit their objectives and outputs, clearly specifying expected performance standards for each.

---

[10] See for more detail Brazil Broadening the Base for Growth: A Report on the State of Bahia, World Bank Report No. 21377-BR, 2001.

Measures related to administrative simplification:

- Deepen the debureaucratization program by:
  - Establishing clear targets for program implementation and evaluating accomplishments and remaining challenges.
  - Linking it to enhanced transparency measures.
  - Providing citizens with simple mechanisms for recommending improvements and seeking redress for administrative abuse.

- Create mechanisms for better intergovernmental and intersectoral coordination in administrative simplification.
- Systematically disseminate innovative approaches to improving service delivery (such as "one-stop shops") and promote demonstration and learning effects among states and municipalities.

Measures related to municipal capacity building and adjustment to the intergovernmental relations

- Evaluate the capacity building impacts of ongoing initiatives including the LRF (and technical assistance on fiscal management available from ESAF, BNDES and other entities) and the federal certification of municipalities in the health sector, for application of similar methods in other sectors.
- Disseminate successful state efforts to clarify responsibilities between the state and municipalities and transfer functions to municipal governments.

Message 3. Professionalizing human resources throughout the public sector
Brazil's human resources management compares well with others, with its competitive recruitment system and strong professional career tracks. To professionalize human resources across the entire public sector, at all levels, governments could introduce more performance-oriented management practices in strategic nuclei that already benefit from relatively strong professional cores, build stronger technical and managerial capacities in weaker parts of the state, and depoliticize human resources management to reduce patronage and clientelism, especially at subnational levels.

Context

Creating a structural and organizational environment conducive to better performance is critical for improving the quality and efficiency of public services. But it is ultimately the availability of qualified human resources and the quality of their management that determine public sector performance.[11]

Brazil's comparative strength in its public sector human resources rests on merit-based recruitment *(concurso)* and a relatively strong labor market pool of professionals. But professionalization in the public sector is still incomplete. Many staff in the federal public sector entered public service before the introduction of the rigorous, competitive selection process, and many subnational governments have not fully institutionalized merit-based recruitment.

Staff in Brazil's federal public sector are recruited into distinct professional and occupational career tracks based on functions and qualifications. In the federal executive branch alone there are 63 career categories[12], and similar systems exist in the legislative and judicial branches and at subnational levels. This system has professionalized priority functions of the state on a selective basis, but it has also contributed to problems of institutional fragmentation. In Brazil, as elsewhere, personnel expenditures account for a large share of public sector spending. Pension benefits owed to public sector employees are a bigger concern to fiscal sustainability than salary payments (see Policy Note on fiscal policy). Cross-country data suggest that the aggregate staff wage bill in Brazil is not excessive, and its fiscal weight has declined, from 56 percent of net current revenues in 1995 to 35

---

[11] Brazil lies somewhere between the advanced OECD countries, where sophisticated management practices have been introduced to boost public sector performance, and the majority of developing countries, where politicization of the civil service continues to constrain governments' ability to develop the state's institutional capacity. Brazil counts on a strong core of professional civil servants, especially at the federal level and in certain areas (e.g., economic management, legal professions, diplomacy).

[12] As listed on table 3.4 of *Boletim Estatistico de Pessoal,* MP. Table 3, in this text, groups them for pay policy analysis.

percent in 2001[13] Although significant revenue increase in this period has a lot to do with this decline, the total number of civil servants also declined 10 percent between 1995 and 2001. Staffing levels fell 20 percent in the executive branch while rising 25 percent in the judicial branch and 14 percent in the legislative branch. The executive branch's share of total personnel expenditures military excluded fell from 67 percent to 58 percent, while that of the judiciary increased from 10 percent to 19 percent, a reflection of both the changing personnel numbers and differences in pay levels in these two branches..

Wage levels in the judicial and the legislative branches have been much higher than in the executive branch, according to a 1998 study.[14] The study also found the general wage level in the federal administration in the mid-1990s to be competitive with the private sector.[15] Since then, the federal government has implemented selective adjustments to salary levels in different career cataegories.

Many positions within the general career category (PCC) are not clearly public sector functions (CLT).[16] For positions dealing with what are more clearly public sector functions, the current employment structure, although complex, provides the government with the necessary tools for developing strong human resources. There are generalist and specialized careers, good training opportunities, and tools for motivating good performance. The challenge is to make better use of the tools already in place for improving personnel management by developing a longer term vision of human resources management in core areas of strategic government operations, from policy formulation to implementation.

---

[13] According to the data in the Public Sector and Employment database in the World Bank's Statistical Information Management and Analysis, Brazil's payroll for active civil servants as a share of the total public expenditure in 2000 (16%) is smaller than that in many middle-income countries included in the dataset (Colombia, Portugal, Mexico, Chile, Greece, Uruguay, Spain, Turkey, Panama, Paraguay, Venezuela, and Costa Rica). However, this result should be interpreted with caution as the complexity of classifications in each country and lack of methodological uniformity limit the direct comparability of these figures. National statistics, by the Ministry of Planning, show 16% in 1995, 12% in 2000, and 10% in 2001 (as share of budget, including debt service, prior to debt amortizations).

[14] "Brazil: From Stability to Growth through Public Employment Reform," Report No. 16793-BR (February, 1998).

[15] The study found that, on average, federal civil servants earned more than 20 percent more than their private sector counterparts. See, for more detail, "Brazil: From Stability to Growth through Public Employment Reform," Report No. 16793-BR (February, 1998).

[16] The number of new hires for PCC has been diminishing steadily since 1995.

In the parts of the federal government and subnational governments that have already achieved a degree of professionalism through competitive recruitment and strong professional career tracks, management of these personnel could be directed toward better organization for more effective government performance. This could involve the gradual introduction of greater flexibility in human resource management and cautious use of performance management instruments such as those used in some OECD countries.[17] In the parts of the public sector where human resource quality is weaker, efforts could be made to expand merit-based hiring and professionalism and to reduce patronage and clientelism, where they remain.

INTRODUCING STRONGER PERFORMANCE ORIENTATIONS IN THE STRATEGIC "CORE." The National Treasury Secretariat has been experimenting with a performance-based pay scheme with apparent success. Experimentation with other methods may also be warranted. All initiatives would need to be systematically evaluated before being fully institutionalized. But introducing OECD-style performance management techniques more broadly and systematically requires more flexible government personnel management. Making the 20th Amendment to the Constitution fully operational would be an important step, and reform of the public sector pension regime, to reduce the fiscal burden, would have the positive effect of allowing the government to use pay policy as a more flexible tool for performance management.

The federal government has a long tradition of using political appointees to inject managerial and technical skills into important government functions (Schneider 1991). This method has been institutionalized in the DAS *(Cargo em Comissão de Direção e Assessoramento Superior)* system, which places professional civil servants and technical and managerial experts from outside the public sector in mid- and high-level management positions. Thus the DAS system is both a performance incentive for civil servants and a means of bringing in qualified professionals from outside the public sector.

---

[17] For most countries in the region, advanced performance management techniques applied in a number of OECD countries may not be the most appropriate approach to strengthening institutional capacities for good public service delivery. However, Brazil, at least in some important areas of the public sector, appears to have developed minimum conditions to begin applying some of these techniques in a systematic way.

Determining the best mix of public and private sector talents in the DAS is a policy decision of the government based on its own policy preferences. But perhaps more important would be to institutionalize DAS qualifications and increase transparency in the selection process. The government might consider developing such a norm as part of a general personnel management law. The norm could specify minimum qualifications for DAS appointments, types of functions they can perform, conditions of their employment, and publication of certain information related to DAS appointments to improve transparency. Performance standards could be developed for each DAS position without denying the importance of political confidence as a criterion for their initial appointments and retention in the posts.

BUILDING STRONGER TECHNICAL AND MANAGERIAL CAPACITIES WHERE THESE ARE WEAK. The public sector career system has contributed greatly to capacity in key state functions including economics, fiscal and financial management, diplomacy, and the administration of justice. But most public sector jobs fall in the general PCC category, which account for nine-tenths of intermediate and auxiliary jobs and two-thirds of senior-level jobs. The PCC is a hodge-podge of occupations, mostly in public-service-providing ministries, and is less well paid (though not necessarily poorly paid). Ministries with staffs largely in PCC occupations have had substantial difficulty maintaining a qualified, permanent senior workforce. Applying the same financial incentives and professional opportunities to PCC staff as to those performing core state functions would be beyond the state's fiscal capacity.

PCC staff working in some ministries and agencies (such as social security administration and environmental regulation) have successfully pressed for creation of their own career paths. While this strategy may improve employment conditions for staff in specific positions, it may not notably improve performance. Good performance in core careers such as finance and planning goes back to a rigorous recruitment and selection process, so simply converting existing positions into careers with legally guaranteed privileges is likely to do little to improve the technical competence of staff in these positions, at least in the short term, pursued to its logical extreme, such a strategy is likely to become self-defeating as it will erode the relative pays and privileges of the original core careers and likely lead to a brain drain from those careers and possibly from the entire public sector.

Many ministries also hire consultants, often donor-financed, to circumvent the problems of a weak human resource base. There are currently around 7,000 donor-financed consultants in the federal government. While dwarfed by the total number of federal employees, consultants occupy a disproportionate share of senior-level posts in certain ministries such as the Ministry of Environment and tend to receive better pay than regular staff. Although the desire to have well-qualified and responsive staff in key posts out-side the core government functions is understandable, large-scale use of consultants is likely to create morale problems, undermine incentives to invest in long-term capacity building, and weaken the institutional memory and capacity of government agencies.

While the career system has strengthened the technical and managerial competence in strategic core functions, it may also have led to the so-called *corporativismo*, the overshad-owing of the general interests of the government and the public by the corporate interests of a bureaucratic career. In addition, the career system limits the government's flexibility in assigning capable staff across functions within the public sector: it is illegal for anyone in a specific career track to carry out a function belonging to another career track, except for political appointees *(cargos de comissão)*.

What is needed is the ability to distribute scarce managerial and technical skills across sectors as needed while avoiding the worsening of *corporativismo* and institutional frag-mentation of the public sector. One possible instrument is an expansion of the specialist in public policy and government management career (EPPGG, or gestores), taking advan-tage not only of the policy management skills of such staff but their greater mobility as well (this is not a sector-specific career). Managed properly, *gestores* can help reduce the gap in institutional capacities across sectors. Currently, *gestores* are assigned by the Ministry of Planning on the basis of requests from ministries, to ameliorate the uneven distribution of professional capacities within the public sector. The government could encourage sectoral ministries to develop their own medium-term human resource plans, detailing their requirements for mid-level and senior policy management skills. The gov-ernment-wide recruitment of gestores could then be based on these sectoral plans. If demand outweighs supply, the limited number of gestores could be assigned to meet over-all policy priorities, following transparent criteria, and future recruitment could be adjusted accordingly.

CONTROLLING PATRONAGE AND CLIENTELISM THROUGH TRANSPARENCY AND SOCIAL CON-TROL. Professionalization of government employment is still incomplete at the subna-tional level. Politically motivated appointments are not uncommon. Subnational govern-ments could follow the same suggestions on the establishment of transparent and objec-tive criteria for allocating appointed positions as at the Federal level, where many of the politically appointed managers (DAS) come from the ranks of the career civil service. Competent civil servants could also be given ample opportunity to apply for positions as an incentive for performance.

Another challenge at state and municipal levels is the management of front-line service delivery agents, such as teachers, health professionals, and police. These are highly unionized groups, and the work environment makes direct supervision of their work performance by supervisors difficult. Their vast numbers (especially teachers), makes even selective use of financial incentives to improve performance impractical.

One approach that has been used successfully in several countries including Brazil is social control, with service recipients monitoring performance. Social control mechanisms tend to work well when the top echelon of the bureaucracy or its political heads are strongly motivated to see that front-line bureaucrats perform well and when service recipients are well organized. But much still needs to be learned about the conditions that allow social control methods to work well. An evaluation of experience in Brazil could help to shed more light on various social control mechanisms.

A key to effective social control is transparency in government operations, including citizens' rights to know what services they are entitled to and how to access them. Citizens' Charters in the United Kingdom and Public Service Charters in the Republic of Korea are examples of the systematic introduction of transparency standards for government services. In Australia, the independent Productivity Commission publishes performance data on all state and territory governments. Another example of social control mechanisms is the public service scorecard used in India and elsewhere. An additional step, following the suggestion for the federal DAS, is to let an independent body serve as watchdog for subnational governments' personnel management, with particular attention to monitoring whether merit-based recruitments are fully implemented.

Options

Professionalizing public service at all levels of government would be a fundamental backbone of public sector reform. Although Brazil is well advanced in the quality of its civil service, challenges remain in correcting the imbalance in capacity between core careers and ministries and others at the federal level, and between the federal government and most subnational governments. Institutionalized rigidity, due to various legal provisions and informal and organizational characteristics, is also an obstacle to greater efficiency and better performance in human resource management. Two fundamental reforms that would have a positive impact on the quality and efficiency of government programs and service delivery and unlock possibilities for subsequent reforms are:

- Fully operationalizing the 20th Constitutional Amendment by enacting the necessary laws and regulations.
- Reforming public sector pensions, to permit more flexible and performance-oriented pay policy.

These reforms would facilitate the introduction of more performance-oriented public management reforms and improvements in the quality of fiscal adjustment by increasing the flexibility in government expenditures. Similar reforms could be pursued at the subnational level.

Measures to introduce a stronger performance orientation in strategic core government positions could include:

- Broadening experimentation with advanced performance management techniques with an explicit evaluation strategy.
- Developing more transparent criteria for managing DAS appointments at the federal level and equivalent political appointments at subnational levels.

To address the uneven distribution of professional competence in the public sector, the government could focus on:

- Expanding the public policy management career *(gestores)* as a means of strengthening strategic policy management capacities and of enabling more flexible management of senior managers across sectors and career boundaries.
- Experiment further with social control mechanisms to hold front-line service delivery agents accountable for their performance.

An obstacle to professionalization of public services, especially at subnational levels is the politicization of personnel management (clientelism, patronage). Possible ways to confront these problems are:

- Simplifying and increasing transparency in public service delivery and better informing citizens of their rights to public services.
- Making information on personnel, especially hiring, available to the public to facilitate social control.

Measures to Strengthen the Rule of Law

Message 4. Reorienting judicial reform to redress the supply and demand gap in judicial service provision

Brazil's judiciary is one of the most professionalized in the region. Brazil has been addressing remaining weaknesses, such as limited access, slow and complex procedures, and lack of predictable, uniform decisions, through conventional supply-enhancement measures such as computerization, alternative dispute resolution, and innovative use of small claims courts. Yet the gap between the supply of judicial services and the demand for them has not narrowed perceptibly. A new emphasis on more active management of demand merits consideration as a means of broadening access and reducing delay while containing the escalating costs of judicial services. Judicial governance reform could also enhance the judiciary's ability to develop and implement policies aimed at maximizing its value added within budgetary constraints.

Context

Brazil has overcome many traditional judicial system failings and now has one of the most professional judiciaries in the region, with minimum political interference in court decisions and operations. It is not entirely immune from problems such as judicial corruption and influence peddling. While federal law standardizes many organizational and operational details across the system, some state judiciaries are much stronger than others.

Common complaints about judicial performance as a whole (state and federal systems) include limited access (both physical location and cost), delays, court congestion, complex procedures, lack of uniform decisions, excessive formalism, and failure to discourage frivolous or bad faith litigation. Many complaints are related to the explosive growth in caseloads over the past 10 years, and the judiciary's inability to keep abreast of it.[18] Thus

---

[18] Between 1990 and 1998, caseloads more than doubled, from 3,617,064 to 7,467,189 filings (Sadek, 2001a, p. 14.) Post-1988 changes are still more dramatic; Rosenn (1998, p. 24) contends that total filings in 1988 were only 350,000. Currently, filings average about 700 per first instance judge, not an impossible workload, but one that requires attention to efficiency.Some judge receive many times this amount. The upper level courts, at both the state and federal level are especially affected in this regard.

Brazil's main challenge is to meet the growing demand for judicial services in the most socially beneficial way.

ENHANCING THE SUPPLY OF JUDICIAL SERVICES. Brazil has addressed the growing demand for judicial services through measures to increase service supply – reducing court delays, especially through the use of computer technology to accelerate case handling, and broadening access to ordinary citizens through small claims courts and alternative dispute resolution programs. Success in these efforts was aided by the consensus on the need for change, by the courts' lead in addressing it, and by the selection of appropriate remedies.

Most experts concur that automation can speed case processing and enhance workload management.[19] But complementary changes are also required – procedural simplification, improved courtroom practices, training, better monitoring, and so on.[20] It is not clear that such changes have always accompanied the introduction of information technology in Brazil. For example, while many courts now have computers, their use has not been maximized. Most courts have judicial statistics systems, but do not use them to monitor performance, track problems, and devise remedies. Many tribunals feature computer terminals for court visitors to check the status of their cases, but lawyers complain about inadequate provisions for filing or checking case status by Internet. Systematic efforts to evaluate impact and determine how to enhance it could help to guide further reform.

Small claim courts and alternative dispute resolution have been introduced to facilitate access to middle class and poorer citizens. While the success of these simplified proceedings could induce imitation by the ordinary courts, the small claims services seem to be suffering their own problems of congestion and, in some areas, a retreat to formalism. There is also some evidence that the main users are middle-class clients with small consumer complaints and that the poor have been relatively less benefited. Other criticisms include misapplication of alternative dispute resolution in certain cases (most notably

---

[19] There is considerable literature on this point, although most of it comes from advocates. See Malik, 2002 for a discussion of Latin America.

[20] See USAID, 2001 for a discussion of this point.

family violence) and a failure to calculate costs and benefits absolutely, in terms of the overall justice system, or against other uses of the funds to benefit poor clients.[21] Nonetheless, the experiment has been extremely popular, has improved the courts' image, and appears to be spreading rapidly. Even the federal courts have adopted the system for pension issues.

With some improvements, Brazil's current reform strategy of supply enhancement (increasing productivity and expanding targeted services) should go far toward addressing growing demand. Because reforms have emphasized improving access, remedies applied elsewhere were not attempted—for example, focusing only on automation and courtroom modernization (Mexico) or introducing judicial fees to curb demand (Peru) or monetary restrictions on appeals (Argentina). These measures pose barriers to the nontraditional users Brazil is trying to include.

MANAGING DEMAND TO PROVIDE COST-EFFECTIVE JUDICIAL SERVICES. While efforts to enhance supply could be improved, access, timeliness, and service quality cannot continue to increase indefinitely without absorbing far more resources than any society can afford.[22] Industrialized nations that have already introduced productivity and access enhancing reforms are having to consider more radical changes to keep delays, congestion, and costs under control.

Most of these changes add demand management to the standard supply enhancement measures. Greater predictability of judicial decisions and a shared interpretation of the rules (enhanced juridical security) and an emphasis on cases that advance them are part of the remedy. Other elements include proactive judging to eliminate delays and frivolous claims and motions, more effective enforcement mechanisms (including those against government), and a redirection of many complaints to alternative forums. What lies behind these measures is a belief that not all conflicts can be adjudicated and that those with a broader impact should be given priority. The judiciary's principal product is thus not conflict resolution (which can be handled in a variety of ways), but rather enforcement of the politically determined normative framework.

---

[21] All three are common criticisms of alternative dispute resolution and small claims courts – when they are provided to the poor as a subsidized service, they are usually well received. However, given a choice between courts and health posts or schools, one wonders what the result might be.

[22] This argument is nicely explored in the context of several countries in Zuckerman (1999). The authors are of various minds as to how or whether it can be resolved.

Brazil's situation also suggests a need for proactive demand management. Demand for judicial services is substantially increased by the judiciary's inability to set binding precedent and thus offer greater predictability in judicial decisions.[23] The judiciary provides citizens with access to their constitutionally and legally guaranteed rights, but on a case-by-case basis since individual rulings have no wider effect on judges or other actors. Ample opportunities for appeal and party-initiated delays worsen congestion. Government agencies' automatic appeal, as a matter of policy, of every ruling against them adds to the problem, as does their failure to execute judicial orders, especially when payments to private citizens are involved.

While recognizing the problems, Brazil has not been able to agree on solutions. A fundamental reason is that the current legal framework, especially rights and responsibilities set in the Constitution, is still under debate, with no consensus on how its multiple guarantees will be implemented. The judiciary has become the battleground for these political debates, and the lack of binding precedent contributes by preventing a definitive decision.

The underlying issues are constitutional and administrative as well as strictly judicial. Juridical security is more than a question of how the courts decide cases; it also affects how these decisions influence the broader actions of public and private parties, with implications ranging from the size and content of public budgets to what it means to enter into a contract. Any shift to a system where courts can more aggressively guarantee rights (through broadly binding decisions, enhanced enforcement capabilities, and the imposition of additional sanctions) requires reconsideration of the rights themselves. If decisions now delivered on a one-by-one basis are to be granted across the board, this would have radical implications for government budgets and private transactions and resources. By confining the impact of judicial decisions to individual cases, Brazil has avoided a more radical intrusion by the courts into public policy[24]—but at a greater cost to individual users and the public treasury. This is not a sustainable position over the long run.

---

[23] This formulation tends to pit lower and upper level judges against each other and to be linked to the notion that the former protect the interests of the poor, whereas the latter represent the elites and the politicians. This last argument merits empirical investigation, and even if found valid, still overlooks the way the appeals process undermines its impact.

[24] Where courts repeatedly favor the plaintiffs, certain policy decisions have indeed been crippled (see Ballard, 1999), but on the whole the current system appears to allow considerable executive abuses.

IMPROVING JUDICIAL GOVERNANCE. Whether it sticks with the supply-enhancement approach or introduces demand management, Brazil would benefit from improved judicial governance. Courts show a concern with addressing user needs and complaints, but lack the means to do so or to assess the success of their responses. International experience indicates that none of the three usual governance mechanisms – executive ministries, high courts (Brazil's current practice), or external councils – has any intrinsic advantage in tackling these challenges.[25] The underlying issue is not who governs, but how they interpret their role and how well prepared they are to implement it. Even the present system of decentralized control through state and federal high courts could be made to work better if court leadership understood its responsibilities differently and received assistance in meeting them. Without such changes, no alternative system can guarantee improvement.

In Brazil, however, the debate over new forms of governance, like that over binding precedent, is linked to interpretation of constitutional guarantees. Current arguments focus on the establishment of a judicial council with greatly enhanced oversight power and thus on the question of who (outsider or insider, upper level or lower level judges, state or federal courts) will control institutional policy. This question doubtless needs to be answered, but it is separable from the issues of the content of that policy and how consistently it should be enforced. As with juridical security, the current debate focuses on one dimension (who will exercise control), ignoring the others. This suggests that no matter who prevails, improvements in governance capabilities will still remain to be addressed.

Options

The future of judicial reform in Brazil depends less on what Brazilians decide about their judiciary than on how they evaluate their current constitutional and legal framework. Still, both aspects of the debate would benefit from a better empirical base—a better understanding of what Brazil's courts are doing, for whom, and with what impact. Current discussions are distinguished by the high content of unsupported opinion. Before

---

[25] See Hammergren (2002) for a review of regional experience. Ungar offers a more limited discussion of Venezuelan, Argentine, and Bolivian experience with councils. Brazil does have judicial councils, but their roles are limited to budgetary oversight for the courts under them. Unlike councils in other countries they do not manage the judicial career, which is controlled by committees internal to each jurisdiction.

assuming that lower level judges are more supportive of the interests of the poor, for example, it would be wise to review their decisions. Before arguing that larger budgets, more judges, and better salaries are required, it would be wise to review the composition and size of caseloads. Before adding more small claims courts to serve the poor, it would be wise to understand who uses them and for what purpose.

Brazil has many options for further reform. The major dimensions, each amenable to partial or incremental implementation, are as follows:

Continue with the current strategy based on increasing supply (or making the existing supply go further), but improve its impact by:

- Adding complementary training and reorganizing courtroom procedures to ensure that automation actually increases productivity.
- Upgrading statistical systems and statistical analysis to help judicial leaders track changes, identify problems, and rationalize the distribution of resources.
- Conducting studies of court use and case handling (especially in small claims courts) to determine whether they are serving the targeted population in the most satisfactory (and expedient) fashion;
- Further simplifying procedures for ordinary courts and cases along the lines used in small claims courts.
- Revising other laws to bring codes into compliance with modern practices.

If this is the dominant strategy followed, Brazil will have to pay more for judicial services or accept some decline in quality, timeliness, or access. If it wants to make those trade-offs explicitly and efficiently, it would do well to adopt a demand-management strategy in conjunction with or in place of supply enhancement. This approach would require far more political (and thus extrajudicial) involvement in setting priorities and enacting legal change. Elements, from least to most radical, are:

- Enhancing judicial statistics systems so that judicial leadership can understand and manage workloads and discuss the results with civil society to encourage public understanding of the problems.
- Revising the basic procedural codes to eliminate multiple opportunities for final and interlocutory motions and appeals; introducing training and incentive systems for judges to encourage more proactive case management.
- Expanding the use of binding precedent (súmula) to broaden the impact of judgments;

- Ensuring that binding precedents respond to and incorporate lower court decisions.[26]
- Applying binding precedents to government agents as well as judges. Because this will take more than a law, two more steps are recommended;
  - Enhancing judicial enforcement powers, especially for judgments against government.
  - Changing administrative law to redefine the civil and administrative responsibilities of government agencies and agents.

Unless political society wants to leave the question of which rights will be enforced entirely up to the judges, adoption of the more radical elements of this package will also require a review of constitutional and legal guarantees to reset priorities.

On a separate track, but essential to the implementation of either policy or any mix of the two, the following should also be considered:

- Upgrading judicial governance capabilities to enhance monitoring of performance, tracking of reform results (including user response), and forward planning (for anticipated new needs). These changes can be made independently of where governance powers are located.

These steps are not mutually exclusive, but they could be adopted selectively. If all are adopted, the judiciary's impact on enforcing societal norms should be greatly expanded. However, the content of the norms and the feasibility of increased enforcement depend on the quality of political choices. In both regards, Brazil could do far better and far worse than its current indeterminate system. The present arrangements are costly and not entirely rational, but with the addition of occasional quick fixes they more or less work. They neither bankrupt the government nor leave victims of abuse without recourse to legal remedies. Improving on the status quo is more than a question of changing how the judiciary operates; it also requires a far better understanding of social consequences, values, and possibilities.

---

[26] Much of the lower level (and attorney) opposition to the extension of the súmula might be overcome if it were made clear that they would be based on a thorough study of trial court decisions. In fact to do otherwise would invite arbitrary, non reality-centered guidelines.

Message 5. Responding to citizen concerns about crime and violence through a comprehensive review of the criminal justice system*

Citizen security may be one of the most important items on Brazil's current governance agenda. Rising (or apparently rising) levels of crime and violence affect all citizens, but the impact on the poor may be greatest because they have limited resources to protect themselves from crimes or to recover from them. The complex nature of crime and violence as a social problem calls for a comprehensive approach to criminal justice reform. The actions may start with reform of the state and federal police organizations, but should be followed by systematic improvements to the rest of the criminal justice system.

Context

In the current discussion of crime and violence in Brazil, three facts stand out:

- Violence and crime represent enormous and growing concerns on the part of all citizens
- Violent crime appears to be on an upswing, especially in large urban centers.[27]
- The criminal justice system does not seem adequate to the situation, and organizations like the police may even be contributing to the problem.[28]

These problems are not unique to Brazil, nor is the accompanying inability to speak with greater certainty about a variety of important details – ranging from the causes for these trends, the groups most affected either as victims or perpetrators,[29] temporal and geographic variations, social and economic costs, or the impact of recent remedial efforts.

---

* It should be noted that the World Bank is constrained as regards involvement in criminal justice reforms. Nonetheless, in recognition of Brazilian priorities, we have added this section, drawing on staff with experience in the area from work outside the Bank.

[27] Even in Rio de Janeiro and Sao Paulo levels of violent crime (as indicated by homicide rates) are still lower than elsewhere in Latin America. There also are indications (Da Silva and Gall 1999; Piquet Carneiro 2000) that violent crime may be leveling off. But police violence and a continuing rise in kidnappings (although only a small percentage of the serious felonies) have the public in an uproar.

[28] Aside from the periodic cases involving police, a frequently cited figure is that 10 percent of homicides are committed by the police. Many of these are "in the line of duty," but while police homicides totaled 8 for 2001 in New York, they were roughly 400 in Sao Paulo (Veja, 30/1/02, p. 71).

[29] See Piquet Carneiro (2000) for a first cut at this issue. However, the study is based largely on homicides and looks only at Rio and Sao Paulo.

Observers tend to agree that reliable statistics exist only from the mid-1980, they are still incomplete, and citizen perceptions are distorted by what is covered in the press and exaggerated or downplayed by opinion leaders. Because most studies have been conducted in urban areas, little is known about how the rest of Brazil has been affected.

Evidence is also being sought on the impact of crime on economic development and on the poor.[30] Both may be important in calling attention to the role of white collar and organized crime, which may be more costly than, if not as viscerally objectionable as, violent crime. Most public opinion polls tend to separate crime (or citizen security) and corruption. Even if the two dimensions have separate causes, they have empirical connections – as recent news items in Brazil suggest, violent crime may be one way for the corrupt to conceal their dealings. Where public authorities (especially the police) indulge in violence, the separation largely disappears. In any case, the most pressing reason for addressing crime and violence is arguably not economic but rather direct citizen demand for public security. This is a public service, one for which they pay, and one of the basic justifications for government.

Options

Demand is clear for policies that:
- Discourage crime.
- Protect citizens against what cannot be eliminated.
- Bring the guilty to justice.

These appear to be fairly consistent goals, involving no dramatic tradeoffs except in the amount of resources to be dedicated to each. Some remedies – putting more police on the street – could conceivably serve all three purposes. Proposals under discussion range from targeted quick fixes (more stringent laws, more police, more police equipment) to extremely long-term programs focusing on socioeconomic causes and cultural change.

---

[30] While Piquet Carneiro (2000) finds that socioeconomic status is not a determinant of victimization in general (although it does have implications for types of crimes), this is not the end of the story. Studies in other countries indicate that the poor may be more frequently victimized. Figures for Sao Paulo, where there is more segregation by socioeconomic level, suggest that poor neighborhoods suffer more violence. And even if victimization levels are comparable, the poor have fewer resources with which to counter the initial damage – they lack health and other kinds of insurance, savings and access to credit. A rich man who loses his car, buys another; a poor man walks.

While these longer term efforts may ultimately be the only remedy, efforts are also needed over the immediate to medium run.

Despite the appeal of short-term quick fixes, most experts in Brazil and elsewhere discount their efficacy. Policy recommendations focus on the criminal justice system, but as a whole, not in terms of isolated parts.

One of the first questions is whether to focus on the police or take on the entire criminal justice system simultaneously. The broader approach would mean changes to basic legislation, court reforms, and work with prosecution, defense, and prisons. Experience suggests that a police-only strategy has its drawbacks (as demonstrated most notably by U.S. experience). Improving police capacity without making other changes will, at the least, produce system gridlock (courts cannot process increased caseloads, prisons fill to overflowing, suspects ultimately found not guilty spend long periods in preventive detention) and, at worst, encourage greater police brutality and other abuses. If the police are believed to be the very weakest link in the criminal chain, this may be the place to start – just so long as the rest of the chain is not forgotten.

A second question is how to undertake police reform, a topic receiving considerable discussion in Brazil. Most experts agree that the ultimate need is a comprehensive reform to reengineer the entire organization; as one says, the solution is inevitably management (interpreted in the broadest sense).[31] This means changing the police mandate and mission and reorganization to match; vetting current employees to eliminate the worst; focusing training, recruitment, incentives, and procedures on both crime prevention and detection; improving contacts with the community; establishing effective internal investigation units; purchasing new equipment; and redistributing forces geographically and organizationally. The real options thus do not affect these overall goals, but rather secondary details and the sequencing of an implementation plan.

Among suggested options for reform:

- WHETHER TO UNIFY THE MILITARY AND CIVILIAN POLICE. While the two forces must coordinate their actions, how this can best be done remains a question. The answer could vary by location. Merging the two forces would require constitutional change. Something short of unification might be aided by common training programs, inter-force exchanges, and a clearer division of labor.

---

[31] Soares (2000).

- WHETHER TO FURTHER DECENTRALIZE CONTROL OF THE POLICE TO THE MUNICIPAL LEVEL. The emphasis on community policing makes this attractive, but it seems politically unrealistic. It has been suggested that for larger cities a separate municipal force might be created on an experimental basis. How this force would coordinate with the three existing ones (federal, military and civil) is unclear. Brazil clearly does not need more police forces. Thus a municipal force would probably have to replace at least the military and civilian police in the areas where it operates.

- WHETHER TO ADOPT A SINGLE NATIONAL POLICY OR ENCOURAGE INDIVIDUAL STATE RESPONSES – again, political feasibility and the many uncertainties argue against premature standardization. Rather than attempting a single national reform model, the federal government might encourage decentralized reform, set standards (for results), and facilitate funding (including loans) for implementation.

- WHO SHOULD MANAGE THE REFORM PROGRAM? How should police, other government officials, and citizens be represented? Leadership of the reform is extremely important. Ideally leaders would have police experience, but it is often difficult to find candidates with unblemished records. Civilian leaders are often ineffectual in combating corporate interests. One solution might be the New York model, with civilian commissioners overseeing a police chief recruited from within.

- WHAT STRATEGIES COULD BE USED TO PROTECT THE REFORM FROM DISLOYAL ALLIES AND OPPOSITION. Reform leaders need the full commitment of the highest political authorities. In Brazil, as virtually everywhere, those in opposition to police reform usually have good political contacts and the means to force others to their side (ranging from direct physical threats and blackmail to police strikes and unholy alliances with other political groups). One way to force commitment is the permanent, regularized participation of civil society representatives, backed by their own groups.

- Options for handling the renovation of personnel, especially as regards size, extent, and sequencing of transfers out; post-employment training (released police often make the best criminals);[32] programs for reorienting those who remain; and treatment and placement of newcomers (to minimize conflicts with remaining staff). There are no set formulas here; much depends on local assessments of the problem and on resources for dealing with it.

- Salaries and other incentives. No one doubts that a good police force is going to have to be paid better. Once an ideal salary level is determined (based on market studies), it may not be immediately attainable. Some reasonable increment combined with compensatory incentives (training, promotion systems) and a commitment to a gradual, across the board, increase is important.

- Within the basic reform unit (whether national, state, or municipal) whether to reform across the board or to concentrate on specialized units or pilots.

- How to integrate the prosecutors' office. Integrating other parts of the criminal chain can be postponed, but if prosecutorial services are not integrated and strengthened early, reformed police will find their investigations poorly represented in court.

- When and how to tackle the rest of the criminal chain. An early diagnosis of the most pressing problems here, both at present and as likely to be affected by improved policing, is critical. Reformers need to look ahead, even if the police are the most critical priority, so that they can be prepared.

Most of these questions have to be answered in the initial plan (although changes can be made later). Once police reform is underway, the rest of the criminal chain will have to be addressed. At this point the program to address crime and violence inevitably touches that of straightforward judicial reform, and any contradictions between the two will have to be addressed.

---

[32] So are displaced military. Recent newspaper reports in Sao Paulo indicated that drug gangs were being trained by former military. One major impediment to purging of personnel in many countries has been the fear that they would take to the streets as very adept criminals. In some cases (El Salvador following the civil war and the recreation of the police) this fear has been borne out.

References

World Bank projects

Municipal Pension Reform Project - PREV-MUN *(Apoio a Reforma dos Sistemas Municipais de Previdencias)* US$ 5 million. Approved on July 25, 2002.

Fiscal and Financial Management Technical Assistance Loan – PROGER *(Projeto de Fortalecimento do Gerenciamento fiscal e Financeiro)* US$ 8.8 million. Approved in May 24, 2001.

Technical assistance program for social security reform – PROAST *(Programa de Assistência Técnica para Reforma da Previdência Social)* US$ 5.05 million. Approved on February 7, 2000.

State Pension Systems Reform Technical Assistance Project - PARSEP *(Programa de Apoio às Reformas do Sistemas Estaduais de Previdencia)* US$ 5 million. Approved on June 30, 1998.

World Bank reports

This chapter summarizes the content of the following World Bank reports. Those, in turn, draw heavily from a wide range of literature on the subject from experts in Brazil and beyond, which are referenced in the mentioned Bank reports.

World Bank. 1997. World Development Report 1997: The State in a Changing World. New York: Oxford University Press.

World Bank. 2000. "Brazil: Structural Reform for Fiscal Sustainability" Report 19593-BR. World Bank, Washington, D.C.

World Bank. 2001b. "Brazil Planning for Performance in the Federal Government: Review of Pluriannual Planning." Report 22870-BR. World Bank, Washington, D.C.

World Bank. 2001c. World Development Report 2000/2001: Attacking Poverty. New York: Oxford University Press.

World Bank. 2001a. "Brazil: Issues in Brazilian Fiscal Federalism." Report 22523-BR. World Bank, Washington, D.C.

World Bank. 2002. World Development Report 2002: Building Institutions for Markets. New York: Oxford University Press.

Other references

Ballard, Megan J. 1999. "The Clash between Local Courts and Global Economics: The Politics of Judicial Reform in Brazil" Berkeley Journal of International Law 17(2): 230-77.

Burki, Shahid Javed, and Gulliermo E. Perry. 1998. Institutions Matter: Beyond the Washington Consensus. Washington, D.C.: World Bank.

Burki, Shahid Javed, Guillermo E. Perry, and Willima R. Dillinger. 1999. Beyond the Center: Decentralizing the State. Latin America and the Caribbean Studies. Viewpoints. Washington, D.C.: World Bank.

Da Silva, Jose Vicente, and Norman Gall. 1999. "The Police." Braudel Papers 21. Sao Paulo: Fernand Braudel Institute of World Economics.

Fajnzylber, Pablo, Daniel Lederman, and Norman Loayza, eds. 2001. *Crimen y Violencia en America Latina*. Bogota: Banco Mundial and Alfaomega.

Kaufmann, Daniel, Aart Kraay, and Pablo Zoido-Lobaton. 2002. "Governance Matters II: Updated Indicators for 2000-01." Policy Research Working Paper 2772. World Bank, Development Research Group and the Governance, Regulation, and Finance Division, World Bank Institute, Washington, D.C.

Hammergren, Linn. Forthcoming. "Judicial Councils: Trials and Tribulations of the Latin American Experience." Washington, D.C.: Carnegie Endowment for Peace.

Magaloni, Ana Laura, and Layda Negrete. No date. "El Poder Judicial Federal y su política de decidir sin resolver." Unpublished draft, Mexico, Centro de Investigación y Docencia Económicas (on file in World Bank).

OECD (Organization for Economic Cooperation and Development). 2002. "Distributed Public Governance: Agencies Authorities and Other Autonomous Bodies" (preliminary draft). http://www.oecd.org/pdf/M00021000/M00021217.pdf

Piquet Carneiro, Leandro, and Pablo Fajnzylber. 2001. *"La criminalidad en regiones metropolitanas de Rio de Janeiro y Sao Paulo: Factores determinantes de la Victimizacion y Política Publica."* In Pablo Fajnzylber, Daniel Lederman, and Norman Loayza, eds., Crimen y Violencia en America Latina. Bogtoa: Banco Mundia and Alfaomega.

Schick, Allen. 1997. The Changing Role of the Central Budget Office. Paris: Organisation for Economic Co-operation and Development.

Schneider, Ben Ross. 1991. Politics within the State: Elite Bureaucrats and Industrial Policy in Authoritarian Brazil. Pittsburgh: University of Pittsburgh Press.

Soares, Luiz Eduardo. 2000. *Meu Casaco de General: Quinientos Dias No Frente da Seguranca Publica Do Rio de Janeiro*. Rio de Janeiro: Companhia das Letras

Ungar, Mark. 2002. Elusive Reform: Democracy and the Rule of Law in Latin America. Boulder: Lynne Reinner.

Woolf, The Right Honourable Lord. 1996. Access to Justice. Final Report. London: HMSO.

Zuckerman, Adrian. 1999. ed. Civil Justice in Crisis: Comparative Perspectives of Civil Procedure. New York: Oxford University Press.